D0908975

Fleets of World War II

FLEETS
of
World War II

RICHARD WORTH

DA CAPO PRESS

This book is dedicated to
three men to whom I am very grateful—
Jim Young, Professor Clayton Halvorsen, and
Colonel Alexander P. Shine, USA (ret.)

Cataloging-in-Publication Data is available from the Library of Congress.

First Da Capo Press edition 2001
ISBN 0-306-81116-2

Published by Da Capo Press
A Member of the Perseus Books Group
http://www.dacapopress.com

Da Capo Press books are available at special discounts for bulk purchases in the U.S. by
corporations, institutions, and other organizations. For more information,
please contact the Special Markets Department at the Perseus Books Group,
11 Cambridge Center, Cambridge, MA 02142, or call (800) 255-1514 or (617) 252-5298,
or email j.mccrary@perseusbooks.com.

1 2 3 4 5 6 7 8 9—05 04 03 02 01

CONTENTS

ACKNOWLEDGMENTS

It was not all that long ago—at least in my estimation—that a search for data on the warships of World War II led inevitably to a well-thumbed copy of *Jane's*. Today, however, there exists a wealth of published sources, thanks to the diligence of such authors as Breyer, Friedman, Lenton, Whitley, Campbell, Raven and Roberts, Giorgerini and Nani, Lacroix and Wells, and many others—in fact, the trickle that began immediately after the war became a river with more tributaries than I have space to name. The "select" bibliography in this book pays tribute to a portion of the estimable research and analysis I've encountered over the years, even as my direct research for this work depended on less traditional bibliographic sources.

At this writing, after the turn of the millennium, I can also report having benefitted from a vast increase in the speed and efficiency of international communications, familiarizing me not only with a wealth of data previously difficult to access but with experts in World War II naval history I might not otherwise have worked with or even known.

In taking up this task, I have had the fortune to enjoy the company of generous friends eager to offer their help. First thanks go to the folks at the warships1.com website maintained by Guy Derdall and Tony DiGiulian. Other curators who have shared their resources include Guðmundur Helgason (www.uboat. net), Jan Visser (http://leden.tref.nl/~jviss000/ Default.htm), and Dr. Jari Aromaa (www.hut.fi/ ~jaromaa/Navygallery/index.htm).

As I set about gathering my materials, I had invaluable assistance from Nicholas Sumner, Lee Bacon, Joakim Wohlfeil, Lars Ahlberg, and the Boris Lemachko Collection (www. corbina.ru/~dlem/). Special mention goes to Neil Stirling, Stephen McLaughlin, Vladimir Yakubov, Peter Leinau, and Daniel W. Muir for their important assistance in my research. Nathan F. Okun and Stuart Slade have supplied me with information I could never have unearthed elsewhere.

My further appreciation goes to copyeditor Dean Vander Linde, whose own expertise in naval history proved valuable, and to Daryl Horrocks, editor at Sarpedon Publishers, whose unflagging acumen, energy and organizational skill are responsible for this work appearing in its present form.

And finally, I owe special thanks to Brian Viglietti and Dr. George H. Elder for all their help and encouragement.

In the currently rich context of naval literature I humbly submit *Fleets of World War II* as my contribution to this growing treasury. My aim has been to compose a volume that satisfies the curiosity about WWII navies that has long existed beyond pure statistics and fortune derived from the chaos of battle—in essence, a survey of practical combat potential. Before and during the greatest war in history, each nation attempted to create the best navy possible in accordance with its resources. In a real sense, the war on the seas was fought by the designers and planners of the great powers during a time of innovation and evolving technology. Today, fleets around the world continue to evolve, but during World War II they were suddenly put to the supreme test.

EXPLANATORY NOTES

This book catalogues all the major combat vessels of World War II: the battleships, destroyers, cruisers, carriers, and submarines, as well as the more important escorts, gunboats, and minecraft. As an examination of what "might have been," mention is made of significant units that failed to see war service. Certain vessels are excluded: landing ships, auxiliaries, various service and support craft—those whose primary function was not naval combat.

Each vessel has its statistics, but numbers alone can't adequately describe a ship, and more often than not, the numbers change throughout a ship's career; displacement rises, speed drops, guns are removed or replaced. In many cases, then, averages and estimates must suffice.

Displacement can be especially bewildering: full load displacement, light displacement, standard or normal or trial displacement measured in metric tonnes or long tons—things seemingly orchestrated for maximum confusion. This book uses standard displacement (measured in long tons—2,240 lbs) whenever possible, with the understanding that such values are inexact, varying with time and with each member of a class. As an exception, submarine listings show the normal displacement, both surfaced and submerged (eg., 1,321/1,571 tons); likewise, they have separate speeds on the surface and submerged.

For simplicity's sake, all guns are measured in inches; a notation such as "5/38" indicates a 5-inch, 38cal gun. The armament listings specify only those guns of at least 3-inch bore, including 12-pounders and 75mm guns; smaller weapons fall into the "light guns" category. The labeling of dual-purpose batteries is relative; any gun can shoot at an airplane, but it will be of little value in repelling an air attack unless it can elevate beyond 55°, and a truly effective weapon will elevate to 80–90° or more. Often, some members of a class will have DP mounts while others won't, and the specifics are lacking.

The ordnance tables list other available information, including the weight (in pounds) of the gun's heaviest shell, its maximum range with that shell (in yards), and the AA ceiling (in feet) for dual-purpose guns. Firing cycle denotes the theoretical number of seconds required to fire a gun and reload. But of course, a gun firing once every 30 seconds at 15° elevation may fire only once every 45 seconds at a higher angle, while a talented crew might manage accelerated performance for short periods. For example, some sources credit the *Bismarck* with achieving three rounds per minute in action against the British.

Torpedoes (also measured in inches, with the warhead weight in pounds) usually had two or more speed settings, which affected their range as well; "2200/43" means a range of 2,200 yards when running at 43 knots. The tables include the fastest and longest-range settings.

Aircraft complements and mines are noted in specific numbers whenever possible. As for depth charges and similar weaponry, almost every vessel smaller than a cruiser had some AS capability, and only exceptional cases receive a mention.

The date listed for each ship is its year of completion, sometimes estimated. The ship's speed usually refers to its designed speed in knots, but again, this is relative; actual speed varies according to a ship's load, its age, the fouling of its hull, and the conditions and temperature of the water.

ABBREVIATIONS

AA	antiaircraft
AC	aircraft complement (maximum)
AMC	armed merchant cruiser(s)
AS	anti-submarine
BB	battleship(s)
BC	battlecruiser(s)
CA	heavy cruiser(s)
cal	caliber
CAM	catapult-armed merchant(s)
CL	light cruiser(s)
CMB	coastal motor boat(s)
CV	aircraft carrier(s)
CVE	escort aircraft carrier(s)
DD	destroyer(s)
DE	destroyer escort(s)
DP	dual-purpose
FAA	Fleet Air Arm
FC	firing cycle
GB	gunboat(s)
grt	gross registered tons
IJN	Imperial Japanese Navy
MAC	merchant aircraft carrier(s)
mg	machine gun(s)
MGB	motor gunboat(s)
ML	minelayer(s)
mm	millimeter(s)
MMS	motor minesweeper(s)
mph	miles per hour
MS	minesweeper(s)
MTB	motor torpedo boat(s)
nt	normal displacement tonnage
PB	patrol boat(s)
RAF	Royal Air Force
RN	Royal Navy
rpm	rounds per minute
SC	submarine-chaser(s)
SS	submarine(s)
SW	shell weight
TB	torpedo boat(s)
TT	torpedo tubes or torpedo mounts
WW	warhead weight

THE WORLD NOT YET AT WAR

In 1918, the weary nations staggered into a world of relative peace, some still clinging to a "war to end all wars" optimism. But it was obvious, as these countries eyed each other's inflated navies, that military growth had become a habit impossible to sustain.

The Washington Treaty (1922)

The five great naval powers tried to prevent the sort of naval race that had preceded World War I. The 1922 treaty limited the improvement of naval assets and regulated ship tonnage and firepower, thus defining various warship types.

The "capital ship" was any gunship exceeding 10,000 tons or having guns larger than 8-inch. The treaty restricted these vessels to a maximum of 35,000 tons with guns of 16-inch bore; they would serve for twenty years before becoming eligible for replacement. (This clause created a "holiday" from battleship construction.) Each nation agreed to trim its fleet to a certain number and tonnage of capital ships.

Country	No.	Tonnage
Great Britain	15	525,000
United States	15	525,000
Japan	9	315,000
France	*	175,000
Italy	*	175,000

*All nations had to reach their number limits by 1935–1936 except France and Italy, who were likewise exempt from the construction holiday since the war had completely disrupted their dreadnought programs.

The Washington Treaty established the "standard" reckoning of displacement, which doesn't include a ship's full load of fuel or water—a boon for the United States. The large amounts of fuel necessitated by America's strategic position in the Pacific would have made the American ships much heavier than comparable foreign designs. Britain, which was developing the use of fluids in new underwater protection systems, also liked standard displacement.

The treaty restrictions at 10,000 and 35,000 tons utterly warped warship evolution; such absolute, arbitrary limits created a tightrope for design teams as they juggled specifications and tried to achieve some sort of balance—a stunt not often successful, as the various 10,000-ton "treaty" cruisers attest.

The treaty also limited the newest of naval weapons, the aircraft carrier, to 27,000 tons and 8-inch guns. The allotted tonnage did not include carriers of less than 10,000 tons, which went unregulated.

Country	Tonnage
Great Britain	135,000
United States	135,000
Japan	81,000
France	60,000
Italy	60,000

The Washington Treaty, which remained in effect through 1936, was the only inter-war naval accord to meet with success, largely because it came so soon after the war and all the signatories were either spent or sated. Also, it made special allowances to accommodate individual nations—America could have the overweight *Lexington* and *Saratoga*, Japan could finish the *Akagi* and *Kaga*, Britain could build its *Nelson* and *Rodney*. The international harmony, however, did not last long, and subsequent negotiations in Geneva in 1927 fizzled fruitlessly. Diplomats pressed on, convening in London with hopes for a new treaty.

FLEETS OF WORLD WAR II

The London Conference (1930)

France and Italy refused to sign. Britain proposed new restrictions for capital ships (25,000 tons and 12-inch guns), and no one listened. But some agreements emerged, allotting tonnage for light cruisers (with guns of 6.1-inch or less) and heavy cruisers (with guns exceeding 6.1-inch). Destroyer and submarine designs received displacement limits (1,500 and 2,000 tons respectively), allowing a few exceptions. These agreements also lasted through 1936.

	CL tng.	CA tng.	DD tng.	SS tng.
U.K.	192,200	146,800	150,000	52,700
U.S.	143,500	180,000	150,000	52,700
Japan	100,450	108,400	105,500	52,700

Second London Conference (1936)

As war approached, new proposals found their way onto paper, limiting individual ships: capital ships, 35,000 tons and 14-inch guns; aircraft carriers: 23,000 tons and 6.1-inch guns; cruisers: 8,000 tons and 6.1-inch guns.

Italy endorsed the agreement but would not sign. Japan walked out altogether, triggering a number of escape clauses, and the treaty became meaningless. Though Britain tried valiantly to establish the new restrictions, none of them took hold. And soon it didn't matter; war arrived.

FLEETS OF
WORLD WAR II

ALBANIA

After World War I, Italy guaranteed Albania's independence; in April 1939, Mussolini's troops invaded. The only noteworthy Albanian vessels were four Italian-built patrol boats (*Tirane, Durres, Saranda, Vlore*: 46 tons, 3-inch gun, 17 knots, 1926), which presumably fell into Italian hands.

ARGENTINA

Being so politically divided, Argentina maintained an international neutrality while struggling internally. In 1943, a coup overthrew the pro-Fascist government, but foreign policy remained without direction. Argentina finally declared war on Germany and Japan on March 27, 1945.

Ordnance

GUN	SW	RANGE	FC	NOTES
12/50	870	23,500	30	*Rivadavias*
9.4/40	500			*Belgranos*
10/35	353			*Independencias*
7.5/52	200	29,855		*Almirante Browns*
6/50	105		7.5	*Rivadavias*
	100	25,700		*La Argentina*
6/40	100			*Pueyrredón*
4.7/45	50		5	*Corrientes* class
	49			*Mendozas,*
				Cervantes class
4/50	31	19,900		*La Argentina**
	31			*Bouchards,*
				Córdobas, Catamarcas
4/40?	30			*Santa Fes, CA*

*Ceiling: 37,400

Heavy Units

INDEPENDENCIA, LIBERTAD (2,336 nt; two 9.4-inch, four 4.7-inch guns; 13 knots, 1893): British-built coast defense ships.

GENERAL BELGRANO, GENERAL PUEYRREDÓN (6,100 tons; two 10-inch, eight 4.7-inch guns; 18 knots, 1898–99): former Italian coast defense ships. *Pueyrredón* had eight 6-inch guns instead of the 4.7-inchers.

RIVADAVIA, MORENO (27,720 tons; twelve 12-inch, twelve 6-inch, four 3-inch DP guns, two 21-inch TT; 23 knots, 1914–15): American-built BB, a response to Brazil's dreadnought purchases. (Had Brazil taken possession of *Rio de Janeiro* or *Riachuelo*, Argentina might have countered with a third ship.) The design showed an international blend of features, as in its wing turrets, unique among American-built dreadnoughts. The guns resembled the standard American 12-inchers, and armor thickness neared that of contemporary American ships. Well-protected and handy when completed, the *Rivadavias* outclassed their Brazilian rivals, but time steadily drained away their value. By 1930, the navy sought viable methods of increasing the ships' firepower; proposals included a new model 12-inch gun, a heftier 12-inch round, and an upgrade to twelve 14-inch guns. Skimpy budgets had the final word.

ALMIRANTE BROWN, VEINTICINCO DE MAYO (6,800 tons; six 7.5-inch, twelve 4-inch DP guns, six 21-inch TT; 32 knots, 1931): Italian-built cruisers derived from the *Trento*, but much reduced and too compact, mounting even less armor than their Italian forebear. The main guns elevated to 45° in twin mounts, with their muzzles so close that their accuracy must have suffered. Despite such criticisms, the ships proved popular. Early plans included a third ship.

ARGENTINA

LA ARGENTINA (6,500 tons; nine 6-inch, four 4-inch DP guns, six 21-inch TT; AC 2, 30 knots, 1939): British-built training cruiser based on the *Arethusa*. She carried depth charges and usually one aircraft. Her 6-inch guns elevated to 45°.

Destroyers

In 1910, Argentina ordered 12 destroyers in Europe. Four from French yards (the *Mendoza* class: 940 tons trial displacement, four 4-inch guns, four 21-inch TT, 32 knots) ended up in the French navy as the *Aventuriers*. Four from Britain (the *San Luis* class) went instead to the Greeks as the *Aetos* class. Only German yards delivered their ships, so Argentina gave them four further orders (about 1,000 tons, four(?) 4-inch guns, four(?) 21-inch TT), but these were seized by the Germans.

CATAMARCA, JUJUY (1,010 tons, three 4-inch guns, four 21-inch TT, 27.2 knots, 1912): aging, German-built DD.

CÓRDOBA, LA PLATA (890 tons, three 4-inch guns, four 21-inch TT, 34 knots, 1912): German-built DD.

CERVANTES, JUAN DE GARRAY (1,522 tons; five 4.7-inch, one 3-inch DP gun, six 21-inch TT; 36 knots, 1927): ex-Spanish *Churruca* and *Alcalá Galiano*.

MENDOZA, TUCUMÁN, LA RIOJA (1,570 tons; five 4.7-inch, one 3-inch DP gun, six 21-inch TT; 36 knots, 1929): a successful British-built DD design based on the *Scott*. All three could make 38 knots.

CORRIENTES, ENTRE RIOS, BUENOS AIRES, MISIONES, SANTA CRUZ, SAN JUAN, SAN LUIS (1,375 tons, four 4.7-inch guns, eight 21-inch TT, 35 knots, 1938): British-built DD of a

The closely paired guns of the Argentine Veinticinco de Mayo *marked her as an Italian product.*

modified "G" class. *Corrientes* sank after a collision in October 1941.

Miscellaneous

PARANÁ, ROSARIO (1,055 tons, two 6-inch howitzers, six 3-inch guns, 15 knots, 1909): British-built river monitors.

BATHURST class (500 tons, three 3-inch guns, 16 knots, 1919): ex-German Type 1915 and 1916 MS. Argentina bought 10 units in 1922. One became the presidential yacht; two retired prewar; one became a museum in 1940; the other six lasted in a number of capacities until as late as 1951.

SANTA FE, SALTA, SANTIAGO DEL ESTERIO (775/920 tons, one 4-inch gun, eight 21-inch TT, 17.5/9 knots, 1932–33): Italian-built SS.

BOUCHARD class (450 tons, two 4-inch guns, 16 knots, 1936–39): eight modern MS built in domestic yards.

Argentina also built two gunboats (*Murature*, *King*: 900 tons, three 3.9-inch guns, 18 knots), but the war ended before their completion. *Uruguay* (550 tons, 1874) was an old sloop being preserved. A former training vessel (*Presidente Sarmiento*: 2,850 tons; three 4.7-inch, one 4-inch gun, three 21-inch TT; 15 knots, 1899) remained in service as a yacht.

AUSTRIA

Austria maintained a few small PB and MMS on the Danube; with the annexation in March 1938, they passed to German control. The largest vessel was the WWI veteran *Siofok* (50 tons, light guns, 13.8 knots), renamed *Birago* in German service.

BELGIUM

When Germany invaded on May 10, 1940, Belgium's few noteworthy vessels all became war prizes. *Zinnia* (1,200 nt, light guns, 17 knots, 1915), one of the old British "Flower"-class sloops, became *Barbara* in German service. A pair of disarmed ex-German TB, *Wielingen* (227 tons design displacement, 23 knots, 1916) and *West Diep* (109 tons design, 20 knots, 1915), returned to their former owners, who scrapped *Wielingen* but retained *West Diep* as the training vessel *Reiher*, later *Warendorp*. An incomplete ship (*Artevelde*: 1,640 tons, four 4.1-inch guns, 120 mines, 28.5 knots), intended as a royal yacht and patrol boat, underwent German modification and commissioned as *Lorelei*, later *K4*.

The Belgian government requisitioned a few trawlers (including two *Mersey*-class veterans of British WWI service) and received nine MMS transferred from the British.

BOLIVIA

Bolivia broke off relations with the Axis in early 1942 and declared war the following year. Landlocked and navy-less, the country made its primary contribution to the war effort via its natural resources.

BRAZIL

Of the South American ABC powers (Argentina, Brazil, and Chile), only Brazil made a firm commitment to the Allies, declaring war on Germany and Italy on August 22, 1942. Brazilian troops served with distinction in the Italian Campaign. The navy's most valuable contribution was its anti-submarine work in the South Atlantic.

Ordnance

GUN	SW	RANGE	FC	NOTES
15/45	1,951			*Riachuelo*
12/45	850		30	*Minas Gerais* class
6/50	100			*Parnaíba*
5/38	55	18,200	3	*Marcílio Dias* class*
4.7/50	45			BB, *Bahias*, *Paraguaçu*
4.7/40	45			*Pernambuco*
4/45	31			*Cariocas*
3.9/47	30	13,800		*Tamoios*

*Ceiling: 37,200

Battleships

MINAS GERAIS, SÃO PAULO (19,200 nt; twelve 12-inch, twelve 4.7-inch, two 3-inch DP guns; 21 knots, 1910): British-built BB. They ranked among the world's most potent dreadnoughts when completed, but fell quickly into disrepair. *São Paulo* remained inactive during the war. *Minas Gerais* was in suitable condition to warrant a refit in the 1930s, when she took on two more 4.7-inch guns.

RIO DE JANEIRO (27,500 nt; fourteen 12-inch, twenty 6-inch, ten 3-inch, two 3-inch DP guns, three 21-inch TT; 22 knots, 1913): the only dreadnought to mount seven centerline turrets, a magnificent if overloaded ship that never entered service with the Brazilian navy. Ordered from a British yard, she was sold incomplete to the Ottomans as *Sultan Osman I*, only to be confiscated by the British as *Agincourt*. Britain offered to sell her back to Brazil after World War I, but Brazil declined. If she had remained in service, she would have undergone alteration between the wars; such work often entailed the removal of torpedoes, a reduction in secondary armament, and an increase in AA weaponry. Her 12-inch guns resembled those in the *Minas Gerais*.

RIACHUELO (30,500 nt; eight 15-inch, fourteen 6-inch, ten 4-inch, four 3-inch DP guns, two 21-inch TT; 22.5 knots): replacement for the undelivered *Rio de Janeiro*. The Brazilians never settled on a specific plan before World War I ended the project. Possible displacements ranged up to 36,000 tons, with speed up to 25.5 knots. Armaments varied widely: twelve 14-inch, twelve 15-inch, ten 16-inch; up to twenty 6-inch; ten or twelve 3-inch instead of 4-inch; and four to six TT.

Other Vessels

IGUAPÉ, ITAJAHY (150 tons, light guns, 10 knots, 1908): German-built MS.

The Brazilian São Paulo *looks handsome here, but neglect left her a cripple.*

MATO GROSSO class (560 tons, two 4-inch guns, two 17.7-inch TT, 27 knots, 1908–10): the last six of ten British-built DD, re-rated as TB. Only one continued in service to the war's end.

BAHIA, RIO GRANDE DO SUL (3,100 nt; ten 4.7-inch, four 3-inch DP guns, four 21-inch TT; 27 knots, 1910): British-built cruisers. During the war, they shipped AS gear and served mostly in convoy duty.

JURUENA, JAGUARIBE, JAVARY, JAPURÁ, JURUÁ, JUTAHY (1,340 tons, four 4.7-inch guns, eight 21-inch TT, 36 knots): British "H" class DD ordered in 1938 but retained by the British.

Brazil built six destroyers, like the "H" class but fitted with American equipment, to replace the *Juruenas*. This *Acre* class (1,340 tons, four 5-inch DP guns, six 21-inch TT, 35.5 knots) reached completion postwar. Brazil had surpassed Chile and Argentina in the development of domestic shipbuilding.

HENRIQUE DIAS class (680 tons, one 3-inch DP gun, 12.5 knots, 1942): six British-built trawlers transferred to Brazil while being built in 1942.

MARCÍLIO DIAS, GREENHALGH, MARIZ E BARROS (1,500 tons, four 5-inch DP guns, four 21-inch TT, 36.5 knots, 1943–44): Brazilian-built version of the American *Mahan*-class DD. The reduced armament made these ships more stable than the originals.

Brazil received several escort vessels from the United States: eight *Cannon*-class DE, eight PC-craft, and eight SC-craft. The Brazilians had an additional SC-craft built especially for them.

PERNAMBUCO (470 tons, two 4.7-inch guns, 11 knots, 1910): Brazilian-built river monitor.

Brazil ordered three other monitors from British yards before World War I. The British bought them (*Javary*, *Madeira*, and *Solimões*: 1,260 tons full load, two 6-inch guns, two 4.7-inch howitzers, 11.5 knots) as *Humber*, *Mersey*, and *Severn* and used them extensively with success. Brazil failed to regain them postwar. Two went to the scrappers, but *Humber* became a crane ship and survived World War II in commercial use in France.

Brazil required many river gunboats; the largest were *Amapá* (290 tons, light guns, 15 knots, 1907) and *Oiapoque* (195 tons, light guns, 14 knots, 1907).

MARANHÃO (934 tons, three 4-inch guns, four 21-inch TT, 28 knots, 1913): ex-British DD.

HUMAITÁ (1,390/1,884 tons, one 4-inch gun, six 21-inch TT, 16 mines, 18.5/9.5 knots, 1927): Italian-built SS based on the *Balilla*.

TAMOIO, TUPI, TIMBIRA (680/844 tons, one 3.9-inch gun, six 21-inch TT, 14/7.5 knots, 1937): ex-Italian SS *Ascianghi*, *Neghelli*, and *Gondar* of the *Adua* class.

PARNAÍBA (620 tons, one 6-inch gun, two 3.4-inch howitzers, 12 knots, 1937): Brazilian-built river monitor.

PARAGUAÇU (430 tons, one 4.7-inch gun, 13 knots, 1939): Brazilian-built river monitor.

CARIOCA class (552 tons, two 4-inch guns, 50 mines, 14 knots, 1939): six Brazilian-built ML, also called the "C" class.

Some smaller vessels worked as minelayers, including *Itacuruça* (210 tons, 20 mines, 10 knots, 1901) and *Itapemirim* (340 tons, 30 mines).

RIO PARDO (132 tons, light guns, 20 knots, 1944): submarine-chaser designed and built in Brazil.

BULGARIA

Sentiments in Bulgaria tended toward Germany, as Nazi aggression presented a means to recover territories lost in World War I. This led Bulgaria to join the Axis in March 1941 and to cooperate in Hitler's Balkan operations. Tsar Boris refused to participate in Barbarossa, but followed the German lead in declaring war against the United States and Britain, a diplomatic formality that took on serious consequences by 1943 with the onset of strategic bombing by the Anglo-American air forces. An upsurge in guerilla fighting in newly recovered territories, the death of Tsar Boris, and the unrest of local communists set the government teetering. The situation verged on anarchy as the Soviet army approached from the east, and a new government made clear its animosity toward the Germans. A declaration of war followed in September 1944—no mere formality, as all-out warfare ensued. Most Bulgarian vessels transferred to Soviet control.

SMELY, DRSKI, STROGI, KHRABRY (97 tons, two 17.7-inch TT, 26 knots, 1908–9): TB fitted for minesweeping. Three of them went to the Soviets. Two additional sisterships had sunk prewar.

Germany offered Bulgaria its five *S1*-class MTB (48 tons, two 21-inch TT, 37 knots, 1939) but retained one or two. Several captured Dutch boats also went to Bulgaria, perhaps including two *TM51* type and four *TM54* type. Questions remain about this, a situation further confused by similarities between the *S1* and *TM54* designs. In any case, records mention transferred boats renamed *1–8* (at least), some of which—four to seven units—went to the Soviets.

The Bulgarians operated many small patrol craft, most notably two senile PB (*Belomorec, Chernomorec*: 77 nt, light guns, 17 knots, 1917), sisters of the old French Ch-craft.

CHILE

Insecure and politically divided, Chile responded sluggishly to the events of 1939–41. Operation Barbarossa succeeded in enraging the considerable number of Leninists, but even so, Chile turned a deaf ear to American requests for support after Pearl Harbor. On February 12, 1945, Chile finally declared a "state of belligerency" with Japan. The Chilean navy enjoyed an excellent reputation at home and internationally—hence, the American requests.

Heavy Units

GUN	SW	RANGE	FC	NOTES
		Ordnance		
14/45	1,586	24,400	30	BB
8/40	250			*O'Higgins*
	210			*Blanco Encalada, Huascar*
6/50	100			BB, *Chacabuco*
6/40	100		7.5	*O'Higgins, Blanco Encalada*
4.7/45	49		5	*Serranos, O'Briens*
4/45	31	16,430	3.5	BB*

*Ceiling: 31,000

HUASCAR (1,870 tons; two 8-inch, three 4.7-inch guns; 12 knots, 1865): built as an ironclad turret ship, by 1939 lying inert at anchor without boilers or perceptible value.

*Respect for the Chilean navy turned the old **Latorre** into an object of international envy.*

BLANCO ENCALADA (3,435 tons; two 8-inch, ten 6-inch, five 3-inch guns; 19 knots, 1894): like the following two cruisers, British-built. Original speed exceeded 22 knots, and the original battery of five 17.7-inch torpedoes had probably been removed prewar. The armor scheme, as skimpy as it was outdated, offered little protection.

O'HIGGINS (7,796 tons; four 8-inch, ten 6-inch, thirteen 3-inch guns, three 17.7-inch TT; 20 knots, 1898): more armor than in *Blanco Encalada*, but nonetheless obsolete.

CHACABUCO (4,500 tons, six 6-inch guns, 24 knots, 1902): armed with two 8-inch, ten 4.7-inch, and twelve 3-inch guns, plus five TT, until modified for training duty. The modernization concluded in 1941 and may have left five of her 3-inchers on board.

The lengthy careers of these vessels attest to the navy's conscientious upkeep. Though nothing could revive them as modern combatants, they remained valuable in coast defense and training.

ALMIRANTE LATORRE (28,500 tons; ten 14-inch, fourteen 6-inch, four 4-inch DP guns, four 21-inch TT; 22.75 knots, 1915): ex-British BB *Canada*. Chile ordered two ships from British builders, but the Royal Navy took them after the outbreak of World War I. *Latorre* reverted to Chile after the war, but her sistership *Eagle* (ex-*Almirante Cochrane*) remained with the British as an aircraft carrier.

The Chileans maintained *Latorre* in an exceptional state of repair throughout the war years but failed to fully modernize her. Thus her 14-inch guns, while respectable weapons, lacked range. Her armor, inadequate by 1915 standards, left her as vulnerable as a battle-cruiser.

The desperation after Pearl Harbor prompted an offer from the United States to purchase *Latorre* and some destroyers, but Chile declined.

Other Vessels

ALMIRANTE LYNCH, ALMIRANTE CONDELL (1,430 tons, six 4-inch guns, six 21-inch TT, 31 knots, 1913–14): British-built DD, good habitability. The original order included six ships, but Britain retained four, three of which survived to give Chilean service until 1933. Old age also pursued *Lynch* and *Condell*, and they barely outlasted the war.

GUACOLDA, TEGUALDA, RUCUMILLA, GUALA, QUIDORA, FRESIA (364/435 tons, four 17.7-inch TT, 12.75/10.25 knots, 1916–18): ex-*H13, 16–20*. American builders intended these subs for Britain—a combatant at the time—so the State Department ordered their construction removed to Canada. In the end, six transferred to Chile as partial compensation for Chilean vessels taken over in Britain (such as *Latorre*). The "H" class boats were wonderful, handy things, but rather dated by World War II. The *Guacolda*s began retiring in 1945.

ELICURA class (400 nt, two 3-inch guns, 14.5 knots, 1919): three coast guard craft built in Finland. Two sisters served in the Finnish navy.

SERRANO, ORELLA, HYATT, ALDEN, VIDELA, RIQUELME (1,090 tons; three 4.7-inch, one 3-inch DP gun, six 21-inch TT; 35 knots, 1928–29): DD ordered from Britain. Chile's coastline extends through the spectrum of climes, and this design required habitability in all areas. Unfortunately, they proved too lightly built for the harsh waters of the south.

The first three ships could serve as ML, and the last three as MS.

CAPITAN O'BRIEN, CAPITAN THOMPSON, ALMIRANTE SIMPSON (1,540/2,020 tons, one 4.7-inch gun, eight 21-inch TT, 15/9 knots, 1929): British-built SS based on the O-boats. Their large conning tower must have slowed their diving and caused underwater instability.

A few minor vessels served as coast guard craft. Proposals for two CL (3,000 tons) came to nothing. Chile went through this period with few modern vessels and little domestic construction.

CHINA

Like her army, China's navy fell victim to internal chaos and Japanese aggression. Chiang Kai-shek's inability to centralize authority doomed all prospects for a coordinated military build-up. Domestic builders completed some vessels, and

The Chilean submarine Capitan Thompson *resembled the British "O" types in design and appearance.*

others came from foreign yards, but the Chinese navy remained a miscellany of obsolete coast defenders and local gunboats without a chain of command. Another result of this disorder is an unreliable record of the vessels, some of which may have existed in name only while others have escaped the historian's eye. Name changes and the difficulty of rendering those names into phonetic characters have aggravated the confusion. The following lists attempt an accurate account of the most important vessels, including those active in the fight against Japan in the 1930s.

Cruisers

TUNG CHI (plus similar *Fu An* with light guns only: 1,900 tons; two 5.9-inch, five 4-inch guns; 11 knots, 1896); HAI YUNG, HAI CHOU, HAI CHEN (2,680 nt; three 5.9-inch, eight 4.1-inch guns, one 14-inch TT; 19.5 knots, 1898); and HAI CHI (4,300 tons; two 8-inch, ten 4.7-inch guns, five 17.7-inch TT; 24 knots, 1899): elderly, all used as blockships in 1937.

YING SWEI, CHAO HO (2,460-2,750 tons; two 6-inch, four 4-inch, two 3-inch guns, two 17.7-inch TT; 22 knots, 1911–12): British-built semi-sisterships for training duty, among the numerous victims of Japanese attack in 1937. The related *Helle* served in the Greek navy.

China ordered three small cruisers (1,860 tons, ten 4-inch guns, two 17.7-inch TT, 32 knots) and one more sizeable vessel (4,900 nt; four 8-inch, twelve 4.7-inch guns, two 17.7-inch TT; 28 knots) from a European yard in 1913, but the Great War prevented their completion.

NING HAI, PING HAI (2,200 tons; six 5.5-inch, six 3-inch DP guns, AC 2, 21-23 knots, 1932–36): a Japanese design with Japanese weaponry (standard CL guns with a 20,890-yard range; Type 6 torpedoes, removed prewar). The political situation delayed *Ping Hai's* con-

struction; in the meantime, the *Tomozuru* Incident revealed an instability hazard, and designers modified *Ping Hai* to reduce her top-weight. She commissioned with only three of her 3-inch guns, no aviation facilities, and a reduced power plant (for a 2-knot drop in speed). Though rated as cruisers, these ships better fit the definition of coast defense vessels, and they functioned as such.

In 1937, aircraft crippled both ships with 132-lb bombs (four hits on *Ning Hai*, eight on *Ping Hai*, plus near misses). Japan salvaged them and renamed them *Ioshima* and *Yasoshima*.

Destroyers and Torpedo Craft

HU PENG, HU NGO, HU YING, HU TSUIN (97 tons, three 17.7-inch TT, 23 knots, 1906–8): Japanese-built TB. By the 1930s, their best speed may have dropped to 13 knots. The Japanese captured *Hu Ngo* in 1937 and used her for a short time as *Kawasemi*.

At least four other TB (89–120 tons, 1895) and the DD *Fei Ying* (850 tons, two 4.1-inch guns, three 14-inch TT, 22 knots, 1896) lasted into the 1930s before their retirement.

CHIEN KANG, TUNG AN, YU CHANG (390 tons, two 3-inch guns, two 17.7-inch TT, 32 knots, 1913): German-built vessels generously rated as DD. Their speed fell as low as 20 knots. The Japanese sank *Chien Kang*, then raised her for service as the *Yamasemi*.

China placed several orders that World War I disrupted: six 985-ton DD from Germany; *Lung Tuan* from Austria (400 tons, two 3-inch guns, two 17.7-inch TT), intended as a prototype for 12 more ships, but taken by the Austrians; *Ching Po* from Italy (400 tons, two 3-inch guns, two 17.7-inch TT), taken by the Italians; and three more from Italy (500 tons, 30 knots).

America sent two *Evarts*-class DE to China in August 1945.

CHINA

KUAI 3, 4 (18 tons, two 17.7-inch TT, 40 knots, 1931): Italian MTB, plus four (?) in 1935.

KUAI 1, 2 (14 tons, two 17.7-inch TT, 40 knots, 1933): Thornycroft 55-foot MTB, taken over by the British at Hong Kong as *MTB26, 27*.

A previous *Kuai 1, 2* (ex-Italian *MAS218* class, sisters in the Finnish and Spanish navies: 13 tons, two 17.7-inch TT, 28 knots, 1918) retired around 1933. The Japanese captured two Chinese MTB, possibly this pair.

KUAI 5–8 (14 tons, two 17.7-inch TT, 45 knots, 1936): more 55-footers, plus 10 (?) similar by 1938. Names and fates of Chinese MTB remain a mystery.

KUAI 101–103 (49 tons, two 21-inch TT, 30-33 knots, 1937): German-built MTB.

China also attempted to buy *S2–5* and seven more German boats, but the international situation prevented it.

Gunboats and Patrol Vessels

Japan captured many of these vessels (those marked with an asterisk*). Most retained their names.

CHEN SHEN* (275 tons, one 3-inch gun, 10 knots, 1900): river GB.

TA TUNG, TSE CHIANG (900 tons; two 4.7-inch, one 3-inch gun; 20 knots, 1903): GB formerly named *Chien An* and *Chien Wei*.

LI CHIEH* (266 tons, light guns, 13 knots, 1909): GB renamed *Lisui* by the Japanese.

HOI FU (680 tons; one 4.7-inch, two 3-inch guns; nine knots, 1904): GB.

FU YU (630 tons, two 3-inch guns, 15 knots, 1904): ex-Portuguese gunboat.

KIANG CHEN*, KIANG YUAN, KIANG HENG*, KIANG LI* (550 tons; one 4.7-inch, one 3-inch gun; 13 knots, 1905–7): Japanese-built GB.

CHU CHIEN, CHU KUAN, CHU TUNG, CHU YU, CHU TAI, CHU YIU (740 tons; two 4.7-inch, two 3-inch guns; 11 knots, 1906–7): Japanese-built GB.

CHIANG KUNG, CHIANG TAI (250 tons, two 3-inch guns, 14 knots, 1909): plus two sisters (?) probably all sunk by 1938.

SHU SHEN (380 tons, two 3-inch guns, 10 knots, 1911?): GB with one 3-inch gun in a DP mount.

CHI JIH (500 tons, light guns, 13.5 knots, 1911): used as a yacht, survey vessel, and gunboat. Japanese destroyers sank her in 1937.

YI SHEN (350 tons, one 3-inch gun, 10 knots, 1911): gunboat.

KIANG HSI*, KIANG KUN* (140 tons, one 3.4-inch howitzer, 10 knots, 1911–12): GB.

YUNG FENG, YUNG HSIANG (780 nt; one 4.1-inch, one 3-inch gun; 13.5 knots, 1913): GB. China renamed the first vessel *Chung Shan*.

WU FENG (200 tons, light guns, 10 knots, 1913): yacht and GB scuttled in 1937.

YUNG CHIEN*, YUNG CHI* (860 tons; one 4-inch, one 3-inch gun; 14 knots, 1915): GB, renamed *Asuka* and *Hai Hsing* by the Japanese.

CHIEN CHUNG, YUNG AN, KUNG CHEN (90 tons, one 3.4-inch howitzer, 11 knots, 1916): river gunboats. *Kung Chen* sank in 1937.

HAI CHAO (1,250 tons, light guns?, 16 knots, 1916): ex-British sloop of the old "Flower" class.

HAI YEN (56 tons, light guns, 10 knots, 1917): sunk in 1937.

HAI FU, HAI OU (166 tons, light guns, 10.5 knots, 1917): gunboats.

HAI HUNG, HAI KU (190 tons, light guns, 11 knots, 1917): gunboats.

HAI HO, HAI PENG (211 tons, light guns, 12 knots, 1917–20): river gunboats.

WEI SHENG, TEH SHENG (932 tons; one 4.7-inch, one 3-inch DP gun; 15 knots, 1922): GB modified to carry two seaplanes. It's doubtful that they operated their aircraft before scuttling in 1937.

HSIEN NING (418 tons; one 4.7-inch, one 4-inch, one 3-inch DP gun; 17 knots, 1928): GB, basis of the *Ming Chuen* and *Yung Sui* designs.

YUNG SHEN (300 tons, one 3-inch gun, 10 knots, 1929): GB.

YUNG SUI (650 tons; two 4.7-inch, three 3-inch DP guns; 18.5 knots, 1929): river gunboat.

MING CHUEN, MING SEN* (465 tons; one 4.7-inch, one 4-inch, one 3-inch DP gun; 17.5-18 knots, 1930–31): GB. *Ming Sen* became a Japanese repair ship.

YAT SEN* (1,650 tons; one 6-inch, one 5.5-inch, four 3-inch DP guns; 16 knots, 1930): large gunboat, renamed *Atada* by the Japanese. China's haphazard armory, here pairing a Dutch 6-inch gun and a Japanese 5.5-inch gun, created pointless logistical complications.

JEN SHEN (300 tons, one 3-inch gun, 10 knots, 1932?): GB, plus possibly one other.

CHANG NING class (400 tons, light guns, 10 knots, 1932–34): 10 patrol vessels. The Japanese captured six, and these may be the ships renamed the *Bunsei* class.

TUNG HSIN*, TUNG TEH* (500 tons, one 3-inch gun, mines, 12 knots, completed ?): ML.

China had other minor GB (around 300 tons) and a couple dozen customs crafts (up to 500 tons) plus additional transfers from allies: from the Americans, the *Tutuila* (renamed *Mei Yuan*); from the British, the *Gannet*, *Sandpiper*, and *Falcon* (renamed *Ying Shan*, *Ying Hao*, and *Lung Huan*). The French discarded two gunboats which may then have served with the Chinese: *Balny*, renamed *San Min*, and *Francis Garnier*, possibly not renamed.

China ordered a pair of submarines from German yards, but the Germans confiscated them as *U120, 121*.

COLOMBIA

Colombia began severing diplomatic ties with the Axis powers shortly after Pearl Harbor, and then announced a "state of belligerency" against Germany on November 26, 1943. The size of the Colombian navy suited it only for local work, but *Caldas* apparently saw action against a U-boat.

MARISCAL SUCRE (125 tons, two 3-inch guns, 25 knots, 1910): ex-British GB.

1–4 (20 tons, light guns, 12 knots, 1913): British-built riverine motor boats.

A–D (12 tons, light guns, 28 knots, 1918): ex-

German motor boats serving on coastal and river patrol.

BOGOTÁ, CÓRDOBA (360 tons; one 3.5-inch, two 3-inch guns; 16 knots, 1919): ex-German Type 1916 MS used as gunboats.

PICHINCHA, JUNÍN, CARABOBO (120 tons, one 3-inch gun, 13 knots, 1926): French-built coast guard vessels.

CARTEGENA, SANTA MARTA, BARRANQUIL-LA (142 tons, one 3-inch gun, 15.5 knots, 1930): British-built GB of sound design.

ANTIOQUIA, CALDAS (1,219 tons, four 4.7-inch guns, eight 21-inch TT, 20 mines, 36 knots, 1934): ex-Portuguese DD *Douro* and *Tejo* purchased in 1933.

Colombia also received two American 83-foot Coast Guard cutters.

COSTA RICA

One of the few stable democracies in Latin America, Costa Rica joined the Allies in December 1941. In that same year, the government purchased a yacht to patrol one of its coasts.

CUBA

Cuba's navy, while larger than most in Central America, still lacked the resources for anything beyond local work. An expansion proposal—an ambitious program to include a 4,000-ton cruiser, two sloops of 2,000 tons each, and two of 1,000 tons—died young.

Cuba declared war on Japan, Germany, and Italy in December 1941.

BAIRE (500 tons, four 3-inch guns, 14 knots, 1906): elderly, German-built gunboat.

PATRIA (1,200 tons, two 3-inch guns, 16 knots, 1911): American-built gunboat used for training. Sources disagree on the gun size.

CUBA (2,055 tons; two 4-inch, six 3-inch guns; 18 knots, 1911): American-built GB.

DIEZ DE OCTUBRE, VEINTE Y CUATRO DE FEBRERO (218 tons, light guns, 12 knots, 1911): American-built GB.

CAPITAN QUEVEDO (115 tons, one 3-inch DP gun, 12 knots, 1932): Cuban-built coast guard craft.

Several small vessels mounted light guns for patrol duties. Cuba received twelve 83-foot Coast Guard cutters from the United States.

CZECHOSLOVAKIA

Partitioned into non-existence prior to World War II, Czechoslovakia found itself at the disposal of its German overlords, though an exiled military joined French and British forces in combat against the Germans by 1940 and a government-in-exile issued war declarations two days after Pearl Harbor.

Germany controlled the formerly Czech Danube flotilla. The largest vessel (*President Masaryk*: 230 tons full load, light guns, 10 mines, 16.5 knots, 1931) had the names *Bechalaren* and *GB1* with the Germans. About forty OM-boats and Mi-boats gave service; they ranged from eight tons up to the 60-ton

OMm35, 36 (light guns, 22 mines, 20 knots, 1939) which the Germans renamed *FM1, 2* and transferred to Romania. Hitler had intended to sell most of these vessels to Yugoslavia, but the Balkan ethno-political muddle prevented it. Ten MTB ordered from the United States never arrived.

DENMARK

Germany invaded Denmark on April 9, 1940. The Danes offered no resistance, so the Germans did not plunder the Royal Danish Navy. But tensions increased, and in 1943 Germany tried to seize all ships. The Danish responded with a mass scuttling, while a few vessels fled to internment in Sweden. The Germans repaired several scuttled units.

Coastal Defense

PEDER SKRAM (3,500 tons; two 9.4-inch, four 5.9-inch, eight 3-inch guns, four 17.7-inch TT; 16 knots, 1909): scuttled, then repaired and re-armed for German service as the *Adler*. The 9.4-inch shells weighed 353 lbs; the 5.9-inchers weighed 112 lbs. Two similar vessels retired prewar.

NIELS IUEL (3,800 tons, ten 5.9-inch guns, two 17.7-inch TT, 16 knots, 1923): designed to carry two 12-inch and eight 4.7-inch guns, which would have provided a much greater punch. Her 5.9-inch shells weighed 101 lbs. After scuttling, she became the German *Nordland*.

Two other coast defenders were proposed (7,000 tons; four 10-inch, eight 4-inch DP guns; 18 knots), but apathy hijacked Denmark's defense policies, killing this and other projects.

A pair of cruisers lingered as hulks: *Hekla* (1,322 tons, 1892) and *Fyen* (2,737 tons, 1883).

Torpedo Boats

HVALROSSEN (160 tons, one 3-inch gun, four 17.7-inch TT, 26 knots, 1913): the last of three Danish-built sisterships. (Almost the entire Danish navy emerged from Copenhagen Navy Yard.) The 3-inch shells weighed 14 lbs.

SPRINGEREN, SØRIDDEREN, STØREN, SØ-HUNDEN, NARHVALEN, HAVØRNEN, SÆLEN, HAVKATTEN, NORDKAPEREN, MAKRELEN (108 tons, two 17.7-inch TT, 24.6 knots, 1917–19): the first six converted to MS with one torpedo tube. *Søridderen* was renamed *Hajen* in 1943; she and *Springeren* operated as German MS.

DRAGEN, HVALEN, LAXEN (290 tons, two 3-inch guns, eight 17.7-inch TT, mines, 27.5 knots, 1931): forcibly leased in a disarmed state to Germany in 1941 as *TFA3, 5, 6*.

GLENTEN, HØGEN, ØRNEN (290 tons, two 3.4-inch guns, six 17.7-inch TT, mines, 27.5 knots, 1934–35): similar to the previous class and likewise "leased" as *TFA4, 1, 2*.

The Germans promised to provide materials for six new TB in compensation for the six they took. However, despite the delivery of some materials, the suspicious Danes put little effort into construction.

NAJADEN, NYMFEN (782 tons, two 4.1-inch guns, six 21-inch TT, 60 mines, 35 knots): laid down in 1942, completed to a modified design in 1947. The previous classes had included some modern features, but they lacked size and compared poorly with foreign counterparts. The *Najaden*s at least showed some advances.

DENMARK

The Danish Niels Iuel's *stunted weaponry proved no disadvantage in a fleet that attempted only scuttling and flight.*

Submarines

RAN, TRITON, GALATHEA (185/237 tons, three 17.7-inch TT, 13/6.5 knots, 1915–17): hull numbers B9, 10, 12—last of five *Ægir*-class boats, laid up prewar as too old for anything but battery charging. The Danes didn't bother to scuttle them, and the Germans ignored them as well.

ROTA, BELLONA, FLORA (301/369 tons, four 17.7-inch TT, 14.2/10.5 knots, 1920–22): also designated C1–3, the "C" class. *Rota* had an extra TT fitted externally. *Flora* may have retained some minelaying gear.

    All of Denmark's active subs went down in the 1943 scuttling. The Germans raised them but put none into service, due in part to the lack of suitable torpedoes.

DAPHNE, DRYADEN (308/381 tons, one 3-inch gun, six 17.7-inch TT, 13.4/6.9 knots, 1926–27): also numbered D1–2.

HAVMANDEN, HAVFRUEN, HAVKALEN, HAVHESTEN (335/407 tons, five 17.7-inch TT, 15.3/7.2 knots, 1938–42): also numbered H1–4. The German invasion led to H5's cancellation.

Minecraft

LOSSEN (628 tons, two 3-inch guns, 180 mines, 13 knots, 1911): minelayer that fell into German control.

KVINTUS, SIXTUS (186 tons, light guns, mines, eight knots, 1917–19): ML, both taken by Germany, *Kvintus* becoming *Fürstenburg*.

HENRIK GERNER (463 tons, two 3-inch guns, mines, 13.2 knots, 1928): a submarine tender also used for minelaying.

SØBJØRNEN class (270 tons, two 3-inch guns, mines, 18 knots, 1939–43): six MS later renamed *MA1–6*. The Germans put four into service, each with at least two name changes.

LINDORMEN (614 tons, two 3-inch guns, 150 mines, 14 knots, 1940): ML, initially renamed *Vs1401* by the Germans.

LAALAND, LOUGEN (350 tons, mines, 10 knots, 1941): minelayers, both taken by the Germans.

MS1–10 (70 tons, light guns, 10.5 knots, 1941): MMS. Six went to the Germans.

Patrol Boats

BESKYTTEREN (415 tons, light guns, 11 knots, 1900): used for fishery patrol.

ISLANDS FALK (760 tons, two 3-inch guns, 11.7 knots, 1906): used for fishery patrol.

HVIDBJØRNEN (1,050 tons, two 3.4-inch guns, 14.5 knots, 1929): given a Vs-number in German service.

MAAGEN (110 tons, light guns, eight knots, 1930): a fishery patrol vessel operating off Greenland.

DANNEBROG (1,130 tons, light guns, 14 knots, 1932): the Danish royal yacht.

INGOLF (1,180 tons, two 4.7-inch guns, AC 1, 16.5 knots, 1933): served Germany as *Sleipner* (?). Her 4.7-inch shells weighed 44 lbs.

HEJMDAL (705 tons, two 3-inch guns, 13 knots, 1935): renamed *Nerger* for German service.

TERNEN (100 tons, light guns, 8 knots, 1937): a surveying tender also used for patrol duties.

FREJA (322 tons, two 3-inch guns, 10.5 knots, 1939): the Germans took her, renamed her *Sudpol*, then decided to rename her *Freya*.

The Danes had many small patrol boats; *P1–38* all entered German service, as did nine K-boats (from *K1–18*, fitted for minelaying).

See also the section on **ICELAND**.

DOMINICAN REPUBLIC

Quarrels with Haiti occupied most Dominican attention, but the government did declare war on the Axis after Pearl Harbor. The only noteworthy naval vessels were three cutters purchased from the United States in 1938 (37 tons, light guns, 13 knots, 1924–25) and three 83-foot Coast Guard cutters transferred during the war.

ECUADOR

Having close ties with Chile, Ecuador remained neutral until declaring war on Japan in February 1945. Ecuador operated a few small craft, mostly for riverine action against Peru, and relied on Chile for major naval support. The United States supplied three yachts, including one that sank before its arrival.

EGYPT

Due in part to its limited self-defense forces, Egypt was a spectator through most of World War II but allowed the British war effort to proceed unhindered. Declarations of war against Germany and Japan came in February 1945.

The navy had a handful of motor boats, plus the more substantial *E1 Amir Farouq* (1,441 tons, light guns, 17 knots, 1926), the ex-British "Flower" class sloop *Sollum* (1,290 tons, light guns, 16 knots, 1917), and a trawler. The yacht *Mahroussa* (3,417 tons) and river gun-boats *Hafir* (74 tons) and *El Zafir* and *El Fateh* (128 tons) survived from the previous century. The Royal Egyptian Defense Council planned the construction of 36 new vessels, including one cruiser plus submarines and minecraft, but the war interfered. Plans to purchase four British MTB never went through.

EL SALVADOR

El Salvador declared war on the Axis in December 1941, a diplomatic nicety from a country without naval assets or internal stability.

ESTONIA

Circumstances developing in 1939–40 gradually forced Estonia into submission to the Soviet Union, and by August 1940, Estonia had disappeared. With the merging of the two navies, the Soviets began to retire units on Lake Peipus (part of the former border), then returned some to duty after the German invasion.

Estonia acquired a number of Russian T-type ML in 1918, and at least two (*Vaindlo* and *Keri*: 50 tons, light guns, mines?, 9 knots, 1918) lasted into the 1940s; the Soviets gave them new T-numbers, among other names. Several sisterships served the Finns as the *Paukku* class. A handful of other MMS and launches all displaced under 50 tons.

The subs represented the navy's only worthwhile offensive weapon. Estonia failed to complete a deal with Britain for the purchase of some MTB.

RISTNA, SUUROP (500 tons, one 3-inch gun, 175 mines, 12.5 knots, 1908): quaint side-wheelers; former Russian auxiliary minelayers also used for minesweeping.

LAINE (211 tons, one–two 3-inch guns, 12 knots, 1915): ex-Russian GB.

SULEV (228 nt, two 3-inch guns, two 17.7-inch TT, 10 mines, 24 knots, 1916): ex-German TB, renamed *Ametist* by the Soviets.

KALEV, LEMBIT (608/834 tons, four 21-inch TT, 20 mines, 13.5/8.5 knots, 1936): British-built submarines of modern design.

PIKKERI (500 tons, two 3-inch guns, 18 knots, 1939): gunboat and presidential yacht, in Soviet service as *Kiev* and *Luga*.

Minor units included the small gunboats *President* (Soviet *Issa*: 260 tons, light guns), *Mardus* (80 tons, two 3-inch guns, 11 knots), *Ahti* (Soviet *Embak*: 140 tons, two 3-inch guns, 1908), *Tartu* (Soviet *Narva*: 108 tons, two 3-inch guns), *Kou* (1939?), *Taara*, *Uku*, and *Ilmatar*. The Soviets converted at least three of their auxiliary ML from Estonian vessels.

ETHIOPIA

Having fled the country in the face of Italian conquest in 1936, Ethiopia's leadership had neither territory nor navy. British forces recovered the territory in 1941 but did not establish an Ethiopian navy. Ethiopia officially declared war against the Axis on December 1, 1942.

FINLAND

After refusing an exchange of lands with the Soviet Union, Finland found itself at war with its gargantuan neighbor. The Winter War began on November 30, 1939, and an inspired defense merely delayed the inevitable Soviet victory until March 12, 1940. With the advent of Operation Barbarossa, Finland joined forces with Germany. The outcome of the Russian campaign gradually became clear; by September 1944, the Finns had ceased fighting the Soviets and had begun fighting the Germans.

Coast Defense and Escort Vessels

AURA (400 tons, two 3-inch guns, 12 knots, 1907): coast guard vessel performing escort duty.

The similarly named presidential yacht, *Aura II* (563 tons, one 3-inch gun, 1884), also functioned as an escort.

*The Finnish **Ilmarinen** was powerfully armed but ill-suited to open waters.*

HÄMEENMAA, UUSIMAA (400nt, two 4-inch guns, mines, 15 knots, 1917): sloops built for Russia, sisters to the Chilean *Elicura* class. Records disagree on the armament; they likely began with Russian 4/60 guns, possibly switching by 1943 to a 4.1-inch model (FC four or better, a 16,840-yard range. 70° mount).

KARJALA, TURUNMAA (342 tons, two 3-inch guns, 30 mines, 15 knots, 1918): ex-Russian sloops, useful for little besides training; two sisterships in the Polish navy. Their guns fired 15 rpm to 10,500 yards.

Two products of nineteenth-century Russia, *Klas Horn* and *Matti Kurki* (420 tons), remained inactive through the war.

VÄINÄMÖINEN, ILMARINEN (3,900 tons; four 10-inch, eight 4.1-inch DP guns; 15.5 knots, 1932–34): a striking and innovative design. The project took shape around studies of 2,450–4,500 tons with a main battery of 6.7–11-inch guns. One of the larger proposals won out, bearing a heavy armament but lacking in sea-keeping. Undesirable roll behavior necessitated the fitting of bilge keels. The 10-inch guns fired three 496-lb shells per minute, with 45° elevation providing a 33,140-yard range (though some sources give a figure near 39,370 yards). The DP guns fired fifteen rpm (SW 35 lbs; 19,900-yard range; 39,400-foot ceiling). In addition to their coast defense duties, the ships could act as icebreakers.

These ships, and the submarines listed below, demonstrated a domestic shipbuilding industry that was capable, yet restrained by economic and other factors.

TURSAS, UISKO (360 tons, one 3-inch gun, 12 knots, 1933): Belgian-built trawlers used as coast guard vessels.

The navy made a stationary decoy of a former TB (*S5*: 240 tons, 20 knots). The icebreaker *Tarmo* served as an escort (2,300 tons, two 4.7-inch guns?, 12 knots, 1907). The navy converted two merchantmen to gunboats (*Aunus*, *Viena*: one 5.1-inch gun, 4–6 rpm to 26,250 yards?) along with some lesser craft. A previous *Aunus*, a tug and gunboat, became a Soviet prize in 1940 along with four other small craft. The Finns later countered, capturing several Soviet small craft. Four MAL-craft purchased from Germany fell into Soviet hands in 1944.

Minecraft

The Finns converted four merchant vessels to ML, each with a 3-inch gun and 50–60 mines. Also, two auxiliary minelayers operating on Lake Ladoga transferred to the Soviets in 1940.

FINLAND

PAUKKU, LIESKA, LOIMU (60 tons, light guns, 80 mines, 8 knots, 1915–16): from a series of Russian designs, related to the Estonian *Vaindlo* and *Keri*.

POMMI, MIINA (80 tons, light guns, 80 mines, 9 knots, 1916–17): similar to *Paukku*. The Finns rated these five vessels as mining tenders.

VILPPULA, RAUTU (165 tons, one 3-inch gun, 30 mines, 12 knots, 1917): ex-Russian minesweepers. Two others of this type remained in Soviet service.

LOUHI (640 nt, two 3-inch guns, 140 mines, 11 knots, 1917): ex-Russian ML, also used as a submarine tender.

RUOTSINSALMI, RIILAHTI (310 tons, one 3-inch gun, 100 mines, 15 knots, 1941): Finnish-built minelayers and AS escort.

AHVEN class (17 tons, light guns, 10.5 knots, 1936–37): six Finnish-built minesweepers.

SM1-4 (20 tons, light guns, 9 knots, 1939–40): Finnish-built minesweepers.

PUKKIO, PORKKALA (162 tons, light guns, 40 mines, 10 knots, 1939–40): Finnish-built MS.

KUHA 1–6 class (18 tons, light guns, 9 knots, 1941–45): minesweepers. Twelve additional boats entered service postwar.

AJONPÄÄ, KALLANPÄÄ (52 tons, light guns, 10 knots, 1942): Danish-built minesweepers.

NARVI, JURMO (400 tons, light guns, 40 mines, 10 knots, 1944): ordered by the Soviets as tugs, but retained and converted to minesweepers. They transferred to the Soviets in 1944.

At least four other tugs, numbered *761–764* (335 tons, light guns, 10 knots, 1941–42), served as escorts, along with eight icebreakers.

As Finland separated from the failing Russian Empire, it took over a number of small craft, including motor minesweepers, minelayers, and gunboats. At least eleven units served into the 1940s as MMS: the "A" class *A37, 38, 40, 42–45* (13–21 tons); the "MT" class *AF2* (25 tons); *BVA* and *BVD* (23.5nt, two sisters as gunboats in Soviet service); and *Haukka* (12 tons). A miscellany of small and aged craft, known collectively as the *Silmä* class, assisted in minesweeping, as did several tugs as the need arose.

Motor Boats

SISU, HURJA (12 tons, two 17.7-inch TT, 27 knots, 1918): relics bought from Italy (ex-*MAS218* class), stricken during the war; sisters in Chinese and Spanish service.

ISKU (11 tons, two 17.7-inch TT, 31 knots, 1926): Finnish-built, rather worn out. The Finns exuberantly planned 48 MTB for their new republic before the economic realities took hold. *Isku* was their first experiment with MTB construction.

NUOLI class (13 tons, two 17.7-inch TT, 40 knots, 1928–29): four Thornycroft 55-foot CMB, two built in Britain and two in Finland. Despite their age, they served actively and effectively against the Soviets. They carried their torpedoes aft and could land them to accommodate three mines.

J1–4 (25 tons, two 17.7-inch TT, 42 knots, 1939): ex-Italian *MAS526–529*.

H1–5 (20 tons, two 17.7-inch TT, 36 knots, 1941): Italian-built. They served as MTB for only a couple years before the Finns removed their torpedo gear and relegated them to minelaying.

T1–6 (22 tons, two 17.7-inch TT, 48 knots, 1942–43): plus two delivered postwar, an Italian design built in Finland.

The Finns used torpedoes left over from World War I (warheads of 302–375 lbs), plus British models purchased during the Winter War and others captured from the Soviets.

Some captured Soviet boats (three G5 type, one D3 type, one armored MGB, and perhaps one "pocket MTB") served for a short time before being returned in 1944. Finland failed to complete several MTB purchases overseas—six American-made boats (diverted to British service), a replacement order of seven boats (also diverted to British service), and two British-made boats (retained in British service as *MTB67, 68*). There may also have been an order for 10 French MTB.

A clutch of coast guard launches included *VMV1, 2* (30 tons, light guns, 25 knots, 1930), *VMV5, 6* (30 tons, 24.6 knots, 1931), *VMV8–17* (31 tons, light guns, 23.8 knots, 1935), and *VMV18–20* (22 tons, light guns, 11 knots,

The Finnish submarine Vesikko, *now a museum exhibit, resembled the subsequent German Type II submarines.*

1935–43). At various times they carried up to five mines or a pair of 17.7-inch torpedoes. The German-built *VMV101–104* (10 tons, light guns, 7 knots, 1942?) went to the Soviets in the 1944 surrender. Two armed launches were among the vessels seized on Lake Ladoga by the Soviets in 1940.

Submarines

SAUKKO (114/142 tons, two 17.7-inch TT, nine mines, 9/5.7 knots, 1930): a German design built in Finland, the world's smallest true submarine at the time of completion. In fact, the Germans considered her too small, and she proved disappointing in engine performance (seven knots surfaced), seakeeping, and targeting. *Saukko* used Italian torpedoes as well as some Russian WWI leftovers (256-lb warhead, 3,280 yards at 39 knots or 6,560 yards at 29 knots). Modifications in 1939 reduced her to six mines.

VETEHINEN, VESIHIISI, IKU-TURSO (493/716 tons, one 3-inch gun, four 21-inch TT, 20 mines, 14/8.5 knots, 1930–31): another Finnish-built German design, from which the German Type VII was developed. Though somewhat overloaded, they performed well. The torpedoes apparently came from Italy or Britain with warheads exceeding 500-lbs. Captured Soviet torpedoes became available during the war (presumably 21-inch Type 38, for the most part).

VESIKKO (250/300 tons, three 21-inch TT, 13/8 knots, 1936): completed in 1933 in Finland, but not delivered to the Finns until 1936, serving in the meantime as a German training boat. She became the prototype of the German Type II. Unlike previous classes, she had no mine gear, but she could lay German mines through her torpedo tubes.

Foreign markets like Finland allowed the Germans to evade the Versailles restrictions against submarine development. So without producing a domestic design, Finland attained a place in the history of the submarine.

FRANCE

During World War II, the French navy fought engagements against Germany and Japan, against Italy and Thailand, against the British and the Americans—even against the French. The story of the French navy is one of the saddest chapters of the war.

A Bad Start

At the turn of the century, French capital ship design had already begun to lag behind foreign competition, producing a fleet of ugly archaisms. World War I then paralyzed the ship-building industry beyond any remedy available to the postwar economy. Inactivity reigned until the Washington Treaty reduced France to mere parity with Italy.

Though exempt from the treaty's battleship "holiday," the French drowsed until construction in Germany and Italy spurred them to life. Amazingly, French designers emerged from their decades-long hibernation and produced masterpieces like the *Dunkerque* and *Richelieu*. Other designs, however, exhibited less art, and not one modern carrier reached completion.

France declared war in response to Germany's invasion of Poland. The Battle of France began in May 1940 and ended soon after. As the French prepared to surrender, they instituted a plan to prevent any French ships

Ordnance

GUN	SW	RANGE	CEILING	FC	NOTES
15/45	1,949	45,600		25–40	*Richelieus*
13.4/45	1,268	29,090			*Bretagnes*
13/50	1,235	45,600		22–40	*Dunkerques*
12/45	952	25,150			*Courbets*
8/50	295	32,800		12–15	CA
	295	30,180		20	*Surcouf*
6.1/50	125	28,540		12–20	*Béarn, Jean d'Arc, Duguay Trouins*
6/55	119	28,952		7–8	BB, *Émile Bertin, Galissonnières*
5.5/55	87	17,600		10–12	BB, *Arras* class
5.5/50	90	21,870		5	*Le Fantasques, Mogadors*
5.5/40	90	19,900		10–12	*Guépards*
	90	18,150		4	*Plutor., Aigles, Vauquelins, Bougainvilles*
5.1/45	71*	22,820		6	*Dunkerques, Joffres*
	71			6	*Le Hardis*
5.1/40	70	20,670		12–15	*Chacals, Simouns*
	74?	20,450		10–12	*Adroits*
3.9/45	33	17,280	32,280	6	*Algérie, Lorraine, Richelieu*
	33	16,400		6	*Melpomènes, Élans, Commandant Teste*
	33				*Le Fiers, De Grasses*
	32				*Redoutables*
3.5/50	21	16,885	34,800	6	*Bertin, Galissonnières, Jean Bart*, most *Suffrens*
3/50	13	15,420	32,800	4–8	*Suffren*, other cruisers, CV, SS, old BB
3/34.5	14				SS

*A 74-lb shell may also have been available for the 45cal gun.

TORPEDO	WW	RANGE		NOTES
21.7in 19V	525	2,200/43	4,400/35	
21.7in 19D	525	6,560/35	15,300/25	
21.7in 23DT	683	9,840/39	14,200/35	more modern, used by DD
21.7in 23D	683	6,560/43	21,900/29	used by cruisers
21.7in 24M	683	3,300/45	7,650/35	SS model
17.7in M12D	320	8,750/28		very old
15.7in 26	317	2,200/44	3,300/35	in SS, MTB, and aircraft

from falling into German hands. The plan, so extensive it prevented even the Vichy puppetry from ceding the fleet, involved the scuttling of all incomplete and immobile vessels, while the others withdrew to bases well away from German troops.

Too Many Enemies

The British remained uneasy, however, and Churchill initiated Operation Catapult. In British ports, more than 200 French warships and merchantmen were seized. (The British commander in Alexandria more diplomatically interned eleven vessels, several of which became Free French before year's end.) Portions of the Royal Navy then steamed to the French ports of Mers-el-Kebir and Dakar, demanding that the French, in effect, come out and surrender. The French, of course, were not so easily bullied, and the British felt obligated to attack, sinking a battleship and inflicting other damage—all of this despite French assurances that their fleet would remain beyond German grasp.

Operation Catapult accomplished much: men died, profound bitterness arose between former allies, and French ships fled to ports more secure against British attacks—the very ports they had left to escape the Germans. It also set a precedent for attacking the French instead of negotiating. When the Americans and British invaded North Africa, they hoped the French would race to surrender at the first glimpse of American flags. Instead, more troops died and 33 French warships went down, many of them at Casablanca where U.S. forces inflict-

ed the most serious defeat suffered at sea by the French navy in World War II. And again, at Dakar, Syria and Madagascar, the policy continued, and the Free French went into battle against Vichy.

This lethal distrust crippled a powerful fleet that would certainly have returned to Allied operations. Instead, another certainty arose: subsequent to the North African invasion, the Germans swept through Vichy France, reaching toward the French fleet stationed at Toulon. If not for Operation Catapult and the like, Toulon might have been virtually empty, but major portions of the navy had gone there after the attack on Mers-el-Kebir. So at last the French had the opportunity to validate their promise—they scuttled 70 ships.

When all this had ended, the survivors of the French fleet served under Allied command: two incomplete battleships, the old carrier *Béarn*, ten cruisers, and about 115 lesser vessels, all in varying states of disrepair. The French navy never steamed full-strength into battle—a thorough disappointment to the student of naval history.

French warship design had produced significant innovations: the *contre-torpilleur* concept, unorthodox battleship armaments, etc. However, in three areas, the French showed a pronounced weakness: anti-aircraft weaponry, anti-submarine equipment, and carrier aviation.

On January 12, 1945, American airmen in the Far East attacked and sank a cruiser—not a Japanese ship, but the *Lamotte-Picquet*, the last major loss suffered by the French navy in World War II. And so the sad chapter ended.

FRANCE

Contradictory sources cloud some details of French weaponry, for example, describing *Algérie*'s guns as 55cal (for a range increase of 1,000 yards or so). In general, French ordnance shows an interest in heavy shells, with occasional inclination toward high velocity, but little else of note. *Richelieu*'s double malfunction at Dakar was a fluke caused by a batch of faulty ammunition. Some mounts proved less than perfect, as in the *contre-torpilleurs* and battleship DP batteries. The large quad turrets of the *Richelieus* and *Dunkerques* had some shell dispersion problems. Fire control suffered from a lack of radar (a deficiency corrected for ships refitted in the U.S. and Britain) but had some benefit from early forms of remote power control.

The French navy, like all others, entered 1939 relying heavily on machine guns for AA defense, then quickly realized their lack of value. The standard light AA cannon was an obviously inadequate device, a 37mm weapon firing 42 rpm. The 1940 surrender prevented the mounting of more modern batteries, but the ships refitted overseas received Bofors and Oerlikon cannon.

The navy developed an anti-submarine torpedo, but most vessels relied on depth charges for their AS systems.

Naval Aviation

France's combat aircraft compared poorly with the best foreign designs. Dewoitine's parasol-wing D.373/376 fighter (speed: 249 mph; armament: four 7.5mm mg), a plane neither reliable nor modern, had started phasing into retirement prewar, as had Levasseur's PL-7 torpedo biplane (speed: 106 mph; armament: two 7.5mm mg, one 15.7-inch torpedo or 992 lbs of bombs). This left the sole French aircraft carrier, *Béarn,* equipped only with an uninspiring lot of dive-bombers. The Loire-Nieuport LN-401 (speed: 236 mph; armament: one 20mm cannon, two 7.5mm mg, one 496-lb bomb) had the single seat of its fighter ancestry and Stuka-like bent wings, but it lacked a fighter's performance and the Stuka's bombing ability. The search for new planes led to America. An export version of the Vought Vindicator entered service before the 1940 surrender, an event which found *Béarn*

With no carriers more modern than the Béarn, *the French fell behind foreign standards in naval aviation.*

traveling to America to ferry a batch of new SBC-4's. Likewise, an order of Wildcat fighters, marred by a replacement engine and rearmament with 7.5mm guns, never made it to France.

The next generation of carrier planes showed promise but died young. Design work had just begun on Bloch's MB-720, a navalized version of the MB-700 fighter prototype (speed: 342 mph; armament: two 20mm cannon, two 7.5mm mg). A Latécoère torpedo plane (Laté 299, speed: 221 mph; armament: three 7.5mm mg, one 17.7-inch? torpedo or 1,322 lbs of bombs) derived from a successful seaplane. The *Joffre* project inspired bold specifications for a twin-engine torpedo plane, with the Dewoitine D.750 (speed: 222 mph; armament: three 7.5mm mg, one 15.7-inch torpedo or 1,322 lbs of bombs) and C.A.O. 600 (speed: 236 mph; armament: three 7.5mm mg, one 15.7-inch torpedo or 1,322 lbs of bombs) as the competing prototypes.

BÉARN (22,146 tons; eight 6.1-inch, six 3-inch DP guns, four 21.7-inch TT; AC 40, 21.5 knots, 1927): CV built on the converted hull of an incomplete *Normandie*-class battleship. An unsightly ship, too slow and cramped for effective flight operations, she might at least have found some purpose as a test-bed; but because the war halted France's carrier development, *Béarn* simply lingered as testimony to French naval decline. And she qualifies as an oddity, an aircraft carrier fitted with torpedo tubes.

After the fall of France, *Béarn* lay idle in Martinique until 1944 when she underwent conversion in the U.S. for duty as an aircraft transport—humble but important work that suited her well. She landed her old armament, including the hopeless torpedoes, and shipped four American 5/38 DP guns.

The program that proposed the *Béarn*'s conversion also envisioned a hybrid, a catapult-equipped battlecruiser (17,500 tons, two quadruple 12-inch mounts firing 970-lb shells to 48,100 yards, a 5.1-inch DP battery, up to eight aircraft, and a speed of 34–36 knots). The design carried its aircraft facilities fore and aft with the 12-inch guns set in wing turrets amidships, with cross-deck firing arcs—not an appealing layout. Fortunately, the appearance of Germany's pocket battleships caused the French to abandon this project in favor of a dedicated battlecruiser.

Another aviation concept emerged in the 1930s, when the French realized the limitations of their *Duquesne*-class cruisers. Studies began for converting the CA into CV (12,000 tons, twelve 3.9-inch DP guns, AC 12–14), but some of the plans retained one 8-inch turret, creating a cruiser-carrier hybrid.

France maintained a minor interest in hybrids into the war years. A bold merging of carrier with battleship (about 45,000 tons, a 13-inch quad turret mounted aft, twenty-four 4.5-inch DP guns) included extremely heavy armor. A similar but less radical version hovered between 30,000 and 40,000 tons with the 13-inch battery replaced by 11-inch or 12-inch guns.

JOFFRE, PAINLEVÉ (18,000 tons, eight 5.1-inch DP guns, AC 40, 33 knots): plus one other not named. Only *Joffre* herself began construction. The Germans seized her incomplete but made no progress with her.

The design showed a tremendous advance over *Béarn*, mostly due to British input, but some problems remained. The superstructure, cranes, and 5.1-inch gun turrets cramped the flight deck off the centerline. The two-story hangar and small air complement reflect British standards. Despite their shortcomings, the *Joffre*s could have proved useful.

In 1945, Britain transferred the CVE *Biter* to the French, who renamed her *Dixmude*.

FRANCE

COMMANDANT TESTE (10,000 tons, twelve 3.9-inch DP guns, AC 26, 20.5 knots, 1932): seaplane carrier; an intelligent domestic design intended not only for independent operations, but also for the replenishment of cruiser-borne scout planes.

PÉTREL 1–8 (80 tons, unarmed?, 11.5 knots, 1933): tiny seaplane tenders stationed along the French coast. Four served with the Germans in various duties, and one with the Italians.

SANS SOUCI class (1,372 tons, one 3-inch DP, eighteen knots): four seaplane tenders, incomplete when captured. Unable to finish them as seaplane tenders, the Germans turned them into gunboats SG1–4 but disliked their light construction and poor sea-keeping.

The *Arras*-class sloop *Belfort*, the minelayers *Castor* and *Pollux*, the sloop *Diligente*, and some SC could adapt for seaplane tender duty. A transport, *Hamelin*, also operated as a tender (622 tons, two 3.9-inch guns, 12 knots, 1920).

Battleships and Battlecruisers

French battleship design rushed headlong into decline before stumbling into the Great War. The first dreadnoughts represented an improvement, but they aged poorly. Then in the 1930s, with the *Dunkerque* and *Richelieu*, France sprinted to the van of BB design.

Unsightly *Condorcet* (17,599 tons, 16 knots, 1911), the last of six *Danton*-class predreadnoughts, remained as a hulk. Her original weaponry included four 12-inch and twelve 9.4-inch guns.

COURBET, PARIS (22,189 tons; twelve 12-inch, twenty-two 5.5-inch, seven 3-inch DP guns, four 17.7-inch TT, 30 mines; 20 knots, 1913–14): a fairly successful leap from *Danton*s to dreadnoughts, but not adequately modern-ized before 1939. An additional unit, *France*, sank in 1922; another, *Jean Bart*, became a disarmed training ship (renamed *Océan*) in accordance with the Washington Treaty. The Germans expended her in explosives tests in 1944.

The *Courbet*s appear to have had stout hulls; *Jean Bart* survived two torpedoes in 1914, a notable feat at the time. Horizontal protection included an inch or so of armor on each of four deck levels—reasonable by pre-WWI standards, but obsolescent within three years. Armor gives the greatest resistance when configured in a single layer, and long-range gunfire of the sort displayed at Jutland brought a new emphasis on deck protection. The consolidation of deck armor became a hallmark of modern battleship protection.

Dry dock dimensions limited the *Courbet*s' length, making them rather wet forward. Age reduced *Paris* and *Courbet* to training duties in 1939, and both fell captive to the British in Operation Catapult. They gave no further active service, and *Courbet* was expended as a breakwater off the Normandy beachhead.

BRETAGNE, PROVENCE, LORRAINE (22,189 tons; ten 13.4-inch, fourteen 5.5-inch, eight 3-inch DP guns; 20 knots, 1915–16): similar to *Courbet* and similarly wet forward. The design did improve slightly in underwater protection and subdivision, but the armor was actually reduced somewhat to compensate for the main battery's weight. The 13.4-inch guns earned a good reputation.

All units received interwar rebuilds. *Lorraine* changed most dramatically, emerging with eight 13.4-inch, fourteen 5.5-inch, and eight 3.9-inch DP guns. She also embarked four aircraft. Unfortunately, like the *Courbet*s, none of these ships approached modern standards of protection. They fared ill under British gunnery at Mers-el-Kebir. *Bretagne* lasted only 10 minutes before exploding. Gunfire disabled *Provence*; she eventually sailed to Toulon, where the Germans seized her and removed some of her guns for use in shore batteries. More fortunate, *Lorraine* endured internment at Alexandria before joining the Free French in 1943. She reverted to 3-inch DP early in the war, freeing the 3.9-inch guns for installation aboard *Richelieu*.

NORMANDIE, LANGUEDOC, GASCOGNE, FLANDRE, BÉARN (22,230 tons; twelve 13.4-inch, twenty-four 5.5-inch guns, six 17.7-inch TT; 21 knots): laid down prior to World War I, never completed. Two facts made them notable: they pioneered the quadruple-turret main battery, and *Béarn* became France's first aircraft carrier.

The design showed some improvements over the *Bretagnes*, but none of them aesthetic. The armor was thickened, though deck protection remained in layers. The use of quadruple mounts increased the main battery while reducing the number of turrets. Thus, with just one mount forward, *Normandie* would have enjoyed a drier bow. But one mount sat square amidships, when a super-firing position aft would have increased the arcs of fire and decreased the risk of blast damage. The design also had overly complex power plant (*Béarn*, as completed, avoided this problem).

After World War I, the French considered finishing the *Normandies*, modified according to battle experience, but financial realities swallowed what little enthusiasm the project retained. Had the *Normandies* or subsequent *Lyons* reached completion, they might have undergone an interwar refit, gaining DP guns and other modern features.

LYON, LILLE, DUQUESNE, TOURVILLE (26,000 tons; sixteen 13.4-inch, 24 5.5-inch guns, six 17.7-inch TT; 23 knots): as ugly as the *Normandies*, and likewise killed by the Great War. With four quad turrets, *Lyon* boasted more centerline guns than any other dreadnought,

though one mount remained amidships. The navy discussed updating the 13.4-inch model, perhaps by increasing to 50cal or providing a heavier shell (1,411 lbs?).

In 1912, the French began toying with the battlecruiser concept. Several designs took shape around the official specifications (28,000 tons, at least eight 13.4-inch guns, 27 knots), but the navy placed no orders.

DUNKERQUE, STRASBOURG (26,500 tons; eight 13-inch, sixteen 5.1-inch DP guns; AC 4, 29.5 knots, 1937–38): a small but thoroughly modern design. Within the framework of the new treaty restrictions, in 1926 the French began to design their 17,500-ton hybrid, capable of outgunning all treaty cruisers (those with

The all-forward armament introduced in France's Dunkerque *created a "blind spot" aft but also allowed the use of all eight guns over a wide arc.*

10,000 tons and 8-inch guns) and attacking a convoy protected by slow battleships, while also providing a potent scout force. When the particulars of the *Deutschlands* became known, the French completely reworked their design to provide protection against 11.1-inch shells. In the end, displacement grew to 26,500 tons. The *Dunkerque* class embraced modern standards of protection; about 42% of *Dunkerque's* displacement consisted of armor. By comparison, the old *Bretagne* had 34%, and Britain's later *King George V* only 33%. *Strasbourg*, whose construction allowed more time for refinements, increased to 44% protection; for example, the belt armor thickened from 8.9-inch to 11.1-inch.

(Different countries calculated their armor percentages in different ways. The British method ignored turret armor, lowering the total by several percentage points. Comparisons with foreign statistics of all sorts have only limited value, as each navy had its own criteria for ship's range, submarine dive time, tonnage—even the definition of an inch varied among the fleets.)

To complement their mass of metal, the *Dunkerque*s incorporated an underwater protection system never bettered by a ship of like size. Indeed, many larger ships could have envied that protection. During a British air strike at Mers-el-Kebir, a torpedo struck a patrol boat positioned alongside the *Dunkerque* and detonated the boat's load of depth charges—more than 6,000 lbs of explosive. Yet *Dunkerque*'s torpedo bulkhead survived largely intact. Fortunately, the explosion took place adjacent to *Dunkerque*'s citadel, the beamy area boasting the greatest depth of protection; the bow and stern sections of even the most rugged dreadnought cannot be so thoughtfully protected.

Designers further safeguarded the ship's propulsion by a dispersal of machinery into nonadjacent compartments. This reduced the chance of one hit knocking out all the boilers or all the engines.

The *Dunkerque*s were beautiful ships of tight design, but they had their flaws. Concentrating the main armament into two quad turrets, both forward, meant that a single hit might disable the entire battery. The French sought to prevent this by widely spacing the turrets and by installing a thick bulkhead down the middle of each mount, with two guns on each side. In service, this idea worked; at Mers-el-Kebir, a 15-inch shell struck *Dunkerque*'s Turret II, killing all the crewmen on one side of the bulkhead, while the guns on the other side remained in action.

Though avant-garde in its DP capability, the secondary battery came with some bugs. The guns sat in two twin mounts and three quads, the latter proving especially troublesome. This, and the hopelessly deficient light AA of French designs, left the *Dunkerque*s open to air attack—a grievous weakness in a war that often reduced capital ships to the role of AA platforms—but the *Dunkerque*s had little opportunity for such duty.

The 13-inch guns, potent for their size and comparable in penetration to the British 14-inch, nevertheless failed to provide the firepower of a full-sized, modern battleship. Even the armor scheme, expertly planned to defeat 661-lb shells, presented no obstacle to the 1,920-lb rounds that fell on Mers-el-Kebir. Sometimes called battleships, sometimes battlecruisers, *Dunkerque* and *Strasbourg* rate among the most powerful of dreadnoughts, ton for ton; unfortunately, they just didn't have enough tons.

RICHELIEU, JEAN BART (38,000 tons; eight 15-inch, nine 6-inch, twelve 3.9-inch DP guns; AC 5, 30 knots, 1940): plus *Clemenceau* and *Gascogne*, not completed. German construction inspired the *Dunkerque*s, but France's main naval rival was Italy. In 1934, Mussolini revealed his intention to build two 35,000-ton ships with 15-inch guns, forcing France to respond or lose parity in the Mediterranean. The French drew up specifications for a 35,000-ton battleship with guns no smaller than 15-inch, a DP secondary battery, and a speed of about 30 knots. The *Richelieu* resulted, a magnificent and imposing ship, among the best of her type.

The French accepted a 15-inch battery, believing (correctly) that no 16-inch-armed ship at 35,000 tons could combine the desired speed with the necessary armor. *Richelieu* followed the *Dunkerque* example of thick and thoughtful protection (43% of her standard displacement) with a machinery dispersal layout. And the repeat of two forward quadruple turrets allowed for a shortened citadel, saving weight with only one magazine area to protect. Designers eased the risks of this arrangement with the same methods used in the *Dunkerque*s.

The 15-inch gun performed well, out-penetrating even the Italian 15/50 gun at likely battle ranges. The intended DP array of 6-inch guns, certainly effective against surface targets, proved in its AA role to be lacking—or more precisely, useless. Consequently, the 6-inch battery shrank from five triple mounts to three, while a crop of 3.9-inch DP sprang up. All these guns demanded much space in the already cramped superstructure, leaving little room for light AA. So the plan for the *Clemenceau* changed slightly, removing her aircraft facilities and rearranging the armament to allow greater arcs of fire and twelve 6-inch guns. The *Gascogne* design went even further, switching one 15-inch turret aft and re-siting the smaller guns (nine 6-inch and sixteen 3.9-inch), while restoring the aircraft facilities.

Construction of the *Richelieu* and *Jean Bart* had progressed too far to make drastic changes, and the other sisters never commissioned, so it's difficult to gauge the success of the modifications. On paper, they showed promise. Proposals for two further *Gascogne*-type ships crumbled with the 1940 surrender.

The fall of France found *Richelieu* 95% complete and *Jean Bart* 77% complete. *Richelieu* fled to Dakar where she suffered damage, some of it self-inflicted, in action against the British. She eventually joined the Free French and underwent extensive reconstruction in the United States. She had to adapt to new, American-made ammunition; the effect on her gunnery remains unclear, but given the armor-piercing quality of American shells, it may have worked to her benefit. She landed her aircraft and catapult to make room for a powerful light AA battery. This work bloated her up around 40,000 tons, but she emerged as a first-rate battle unit. During 1944 and 1945 she served with

the British Eastern Fleet in the Indian Ocean and Southeast Asia.

The *Jean Bart* lay incomplete in Casablanca harbor, mounting only one main turret and a provisional AA armament of ten 3.5-inch guns. As a floating battery, she opposed the Allied landings with intimidating but inaccurate fire. The Americans responded, hitting her with three bombs and five 16-inch shells.

Assessment of this battle damage has only partial relevance for an understanding of the ship's design, as she was neither complete nor fully manned. The bombs tore large chunks out of the forecastle and quarterdeck and sparked a serious fire. One 16-inch shell passed through some light decking and exited the ship before exploding. A second shell broke apart, having struck the barbette armor at an extreme angle; as a dud, it caused little damage, though it killed the ship's executive officer. Another ricocheting shot continued its flight all the way into Casablanca city, but its impact jammed *Jean Bart*'s only turret. This illustrates the gamble of such a concentrated armament.

The other two hits caused damage that might have proved serious for a ship maneuvering in battle. One shell plunged deep into her fantail, damaging the steering gear and blasting fragments all the way through the ship's bottom. Had *Jean Bart* been at sea, the hit might have compromised her rudder control, but she would have retained some maneuverability with her four propellers.

The deep penetration of this shell resulted partly from the location of the hit: well aft, beyond the protection of the citadel. But more important was the shell itself: a superheavy 16-inch round plunging in from a range near 25,000 yards. This American ordnance scored one other impressive hit, piercing directly into a pair of 6-inch magazines. (Fortunately, *Jean Bart* carried no 6-inch ammunition at the time; the results might otherwise have proved catastrophic.) Secondary batteries presented a vulnerability in all battleships, because no design could afford them the same thick protection given to the main batteries—especially true for the *Richelieus* with their 6-inch guns so far removed from whatever cover the 15-inch turrets and barbettes provided. But French designers did not leave these spaces naked. The incoming shell had to pierce several decks, about 8.8 inches of metal including two armored decks (1.6-inch and 5.9-inch), the same protection given to the machinery spaces. In fact, only *Yamato* had deck protection significantly thicker than *Richelieu's*.

Once the French in North Africa had agreed to rejoin the Allied cause, various plans arose for *Jean Bart's* completion, the most promising of which included thirty-four American 5/38 DP guns and her one 15-inch mount. But the project received low priority, and *Jean Bart* had to wait until 1949 for her completion, with only slight modifications.

The Germans captured *Clemenceau* as a partially formed section of hull and briefly considered using it as a decoy. *Gascogne* was never laid down.

ALSACE, NORMANDIE, FLANDRE, BOURGOGNE, and perhaps two more (45,000 tons; twelve 15-inch, twelve 6-inch, twelve 3.9-inch DP guns; AC 1, 30 knots): projected in April 1940 but never finalized. They might have resembled *Gascogne* with an additional quadruple turret, though various 15-inch and 16-inch layouts received consideration.

Cruisers

All French cruisers were seaworthy, and most proved economic and reliable. The earlier designs lacked protection, but improvements took place, culminating in some of the finest of the prewar cruisers.

The disarmed remains of a few elderly units awaited disposal. The armored cruisers *Guey-* *don*, *Condé*, and *Trémentin* displaced about 9,000 tons each. The hull of the 13,955-ton *Waldeck Rousseau* lasted long enough to serve the Germans as a stationary decoy. A pair of WWI prizes, renamed *Strasbourg* and *Thionville*, avoided scrapping until the 1940s.

DUGUAY TROUIN, LAMOTTE-PICQUET, PRIMAUGUET (7,249 tons; eight 6.1-inch, four 3-inch DP guns, twelve 21.7-inch TT; AC 2, 33 knots, 1926): highly successful ships, from an operational point of view—good seaboats and easy steamers, capable of 30 knots at half power, though they had less range than many wartime destroyers (3,000 miles at 15 knots).

In developing this, the world's first post-WWI CL design, planners had few precedents to draw on. (The greatest weight of inspiration came from the U.S. Navy's *Omaha*—a dubious model.) Their work inevitably showed imbalance: while emphasizing operational virtues, they provided only the slightest armor—nowhere thicker than an inch—with questionable survivability. Both the French and the Italians in their Mediterranean rivalry subordinated protection to other design priorities. France soon discarded this policy.

Duguay Trouin, interned at Alexandria, eventually returned to action with improved light AA and no torpedoes. *Primauguet's* heedless charge against the Americans at Casablanca speaks well of French élan and hints at what the French navy might have accomplished. (The élan and hints did *Primauguet* no good; torrential gunfire smashed her and drove her onto the beach.) *Lamotte-Picquet* also displayed French capabilities, leading four sloops in a surprise strike against a Thai flotilla at Koh-Chang. She then settled into four years of relative inactivity amid lukewarm relations with Japan. Things heated up in the war's last year, though, and the Japanese attempted to seize several French combatants. *Lamotte-Picquet* avoided that fate long enough to fall victim instead to American zeal.

An inspired design made the Algérie *capable of challenging the largest Axis cruisers.*

DUQUESNE, TOURVILLE (10,000 tons; eight 8-inch, eight 3-inch DP guns, six 21.7-inch TT; AC 2, 33.75 knots, 1928): a continuation of *Duguay Trouin* priorities, including good speed even at half power. The design resembled a *Duguay Trouin,* expanded to fill the treaty limits of 10,000 tons and 8-inch guns. Unfortunately, armor thicknesses did not increase, leaving the ships with protection equal to just 4.3% of their standard displacement. No other navy had such an ill-armored heavy cruiser. The design did employ machinery dispersal, but the *Duquesnes* nonetheless rate as the worst of the treaty cruisers.

Both ships proceeded from internment to Free French service, giving up their aircraft to accommodate more light AA, an especially important consideration in view of their weak DP battery. They had 50% more range than *Duguay-Trouin*—still an unimpressive figure.

SUFFREN, COLBERT, FOCH, DUPLEIX (9,938 tons; eight 8-inch, eight 3-inch DP guns, twelve 21.7-inch TT; AC 2, 31 knots, 1930–32): illustrative of the shift in French design priorities. Each ship differed from the previous one, incorporating more protection; *Suffren* had less than 10% armor, while *Dupleix* had almost 16%.

Suffren herself carried the same guns and air complement as the *Duquesne* class, along with 12 torpedo tubes; her sisterships, however, entered service with six torpedo tubes, three aircraft, and a DP battery of eight 3.5-inch guns. *Suffren* alone survived after the Toulon scuttle and became a Free French unit, landing her planes and torpedoes.

PLUTON (4,773 tons; four 5.5-inch, four 3-inch DP guns, 290 mines; 30 knots, 1931): cruiser-minelayer and troop transport, dabbling also in training duties. She would have converted full-time to training, renamed *La Tour d'Auvergne*, but her loss in 1939 preceded the switch. (Nevertheless, the new name appears in some references.) The French approved a replacement for her, but nothing came of it.

JEANNE D'ARC (6,496 tons; eight 6.1-inch, four 3-inch DP guns, two 21.7-inch TT; AC 2, 25 knots, 1931): purpose-built training cruiser with an almost mercantile look and negligible armor. Her aircraft had no catapult. In Free French service, she underwent the usual exchange of aircraft and torpedoes for improved light AA.

FRANCE

ALGÉRIE (10,000 tons; eight 8-inch, twelve 3.9-inch DP guns, six 21.7-inch TT; AC 3, 31 knots, 1934): well armed and well protected, among the best of treaty cruisers. Weight of protection exceeded 20% of her displacement; no wartime CA equaled her 3.1-inch armored deck. Designers worked a relatively extensive torpedo defense into her hull, but since this afforded less room to the power plant and left *Algérie* without the machinery dispersal of earlier designs, it did little to increase survivability.

Algérie had the same economical steaming traits as her predecessors, and her guns, like theirs, elevated to 45°. In most respects, she compared well with larger ships, such as the *Hipper* and *Nachi*. And she was beautiful. Her range—8,700 miles at 15 knots—showed a vast improvement over previous classes and placed her in company with some Pacific designs.

After trading her aircraft for additional light AA guns, *Algérie* fell victim to Toulon.

ÉMILE BERTIN (5,886 tons; nine 6-inch, four 3.5-inch DP guns, six 21.7-inch TT, 200 mines; AC 2, 34 knots, 1935): a development of the *Pluton* concept which, compared to Britain's cruiser-minelayer *Adventure*, placed more emphasis on the cruiser role. This emphasis increased in *Émile Bertin*, which went through the entire war without laying a mine. She proved a speedy ship, reaching almost 40 knots on trials, and this allowed her to operate as a leader for the *contre-torpilleurs*. However, unlike the heavy cruisers, French light cruisers still lacked protection. Furthermore, *Bertin* had a weak hull that required strengthening before she could safely fire all her guns. A 1943 refit in America replaced her aircraft and torpedoes with four more 3.5-inch guns and light AA. The 6-inch guns performed reliably in their 45° mounts.

LA GALISSONNIÈRE, JEAN DE VIENNE, MARSEILLAISE, GLOIRE, MONTCALM, GEORGES LEYGUES (7,600 tons; nine 6-inch, eight 3.5-inch DP guns, four 21.7-inch TT; AC 4, 31 knots, 1936–37): among the best prewar CL. Based on the *Bertin*, they incorporated an intelligent armor scheme and machinery dispersal. Speed remained sufficient, and all attained 35 knots. Likewise, their range exceeded design specifications, almost equaling *Algérie's*. Though outgunned by the *Brooklyn* class, they showed greater design balance on their more modest displacement. During the war, they carried two aircraft, or three at most.

The first three sank at Toulon. Italian salvage teams tried to repair them; the first pair received the names *FR12* and *11*, but neither entered service. The others had American refits that removed their aircraft facilities, improving their already attractive appearance.

DE GRASSE, CHATEAURENAULT, GUICHEN (8,000 tons; nine 6-inch, six 3.5-inch DP guns, six 21.7-inch TT; AC 4, 33 knots): development of the previous class. Details remain unclear, but the added tonnage gained little apparent improvement: protection remained about the same, and the DP battery shrank into a tight crowd on the aft superstructure. The Germans gave some thought to completing the captured *De Grasse* as a carrier, but in the end, only one ship reached completion, postwar with a modified design.

The navy ordered three heavy cruisers of the *St. Louis* class (14,470 tons; nine 8-inch, six 3.9-inch DP guns, six 21.7-inch TT; AC 2, 33 knots) but completed none. Most countries, when not restrained by treaty, produced CA designs of 14,000–17,000 tons—apparently the optimum heavy cruiser displacement.

Destroyers

France pursued two DD types: the *torpilleur*, a conventional destroyer; and the famous *contre-torpilleur* that straddled the line between destroyer and light cruiser. These two types had several characteristics in common. Short-ranged (even by Mediterranean standards), without proper AS equipment, pitifully weak in AA weaponry, the ships themselves showed no eagerness to remain afloat. None of them mounted a DP main battery, and the guns in many cases gave problems: cumbersome mounts, slow rates of fire, inadequate fire control, illogical ammunition handling. Speed ranged from modest to good, and at times, truly remarkable. Some units underwent conversion for escort duty, sacrificing a few knots for added range, while the universal wartime quest for improved AA fire had its usual effects.

Old *Aventurier* (930 nt, 1914) lasted as a hulk until 1940.

SIMOUN, TYPHON, ORAGE, TRAMONTANE, OURAGAN, CYCLONE, TROMBE, TEMPÊTE, MISTRAL, TORNADE, BOURRASQUE, SIROCCO (1298 tons, four 5.1-inch guns, six 21.7-inch TT, 33 knots, 1926–28): rather slow and unsuccessful. Their instability prompted a series of partial remedies—a trimming of the funnels, the removal of a gun or some torpedoes. The 5.1-inch gun performed well, but had a slow rate of fire.

Mistral went into RN service as a gunnery training ship with four 4.7-inch guns, a 3-inch DP gun, and three TT. The British also took *Ouragan*, rearmed her with 4.7-inch guns, and handed her over to a Polish crew, later to Free French. The Italians found *Trombe* at Toulon and managed to repair her for service as *FR31*; after the Italian surrender, she was returned to the French. *Simoun* and *Tempête* were the only others to survive past Toulon.

CHACAL, JAGUAR, LYNX, TIGRE, LÉOPARD, PANTHÈRE (2,126 tons; five 5.1-inch, two 3-inch DP guns, six 21.7-inch TT; 35 knots, 1926–27): first of the *contre-torpilleurs*, or super-destroyers. They lacked maneuverability. Their machinery, though reliable, had aged and by 1939 reduced their speed to 31 knots. The

main battery provoked some criticism—just one gun more than in the *Simoun* class—but at least it caused no stability problems. In fact, the gun armament represented the major weakness in a design intended to provide superior firepower. Even the 3-inch guns proved too slow. Light AA replaced them, along with one main gun and three TT in some ships, while at times a 4-inch DP gun happened aboard. Prewar proposals would have rearmed them as AA escorts with 3.9-inch DP guns—not a bad idea, but the war prevented it.

The French scuttled *Lynx*, *Panthère*, and *Tigre* at Toulon; the last two became the Italian *FR22* and *23*, but only *FR23* entered service. In 1943, she joined *Léopard* as a Free French escort.

L'ADROIT, L'ALCYON, LE FORTUNÉ, LE MARS, LA PALME, LA RAILLEUSE, BASQUE, BORDELAIS, BOULONNAIS, BRESTOIS, FORBIN, FOUDROYANT, FOUGUEUX, FRONDEUR (1,356 tons, four 5.1-inch guns, six 21.7-inch TT, 33 knots, 1928–31): similar to the *Simouns*, but larger and more stable, with slightly better gun mounts. Some landed a gun for further stability, and most replaced some guns or torpedoes with light AA weapons. The *Adroits* exemplify the short "legs" of French destroyers, with an endurance of just 2,150 miles at fourteen knots.

They also illustrate the fortunes of the French navy. One sank after an accidental explosion. Two went down off Dunkirk. Three suffered internment at Alexandria, returning to service in 1943. Five took part in the Battle of Casablanca, where the French flotilla displayed a mastery of light ship tactics, darting in and out of smoke screens to launch their attacks. However, French marksmanship suffered from the smoke almost as much as the enemy's did and, despite all their skill and daring, the attack sputtered against the overwhelming American battle force.

The *Adroits* didn't exhibit much resistance to damage. The battleship *Massachusetts* put a couple of salvos onto *Fougueux*, which sank at once. *Boulonnais* also took four 16-inch armor-piercing rounds, enough to cripple her, and the light cruiser *Brooklyn* finished her off. *Brestois* withdrew after hits from six cruiser shells and slowly sank after being strafed. *Frondeur* suffered severe flooding from an 8-inch hit; strafed later in the harbor, she sank. Only *L'Alcyon* survived, badly damaged. She and the three interned ships were the last of the *Adroit*s after the Toulon scuttling.

France's **Le Fantasque** *had the looks to match her high performance.*

GUÉPARD, BISON, LION, VALMY, VERDUN, VAUBAN (2,436 tons, five 5.5-inch guns, six 21.7-inch TT, 35.5 knots, 1929–31): superdestroyers, showing much improvement over the *Chacal* class. They could reach nearly 40 knots, but ranged only to 3,450 miles at 14.5 knots. Their sluggish guns lacked adequate fire control for targets beyond 14,200 yards. *Bison* survived a prewar collision that sheared off everything forward of the bridge; she later succumbed to air attack. The others became victims of Toulon. Italy seized *Lion* and *Valmy* as *FR21* and *24*, but neither entered service.

AIGLE, VAUTOUR, ALBATROS, GERFAUT, MILAN, ÉPERVIER (2,441 tons, five 5.5-inch guns, six 21.7-inch TT, 36 knots, 1931–34): successors to *Guépard* with a faster gun—up to fifteen rpm, though an inefficient ammunition supply nearly halved that. Good seaboats, they could maintain 37 knots, even fully loaded. The last pair carried an extra torpedo tube and had

improved machinery for better range. A few cruiser shells sent *Milan* and *Albatros* skittering onto the beach at Casablanca. Workers salved *Albatros* as a gunnery trainer (three 5.5-inch and two 3-inch DP guns, 24.75 knots), the last survivor of her class.

VAUQUELIN, TARTU, CASSARD, CHEVALIER PAUL, KERSAINT, MAILLÉ BRÉZÉ (2,441 tons, five 5.5-inch guns, seven 21.7-inch TT, 50 mines, 36 knots, 1932–34): nearly identical to the *Aigle*s without *Milan's* improved machinery, leaving endurance at 3650 miles at 18 knots. None survived past Toulon.

LE FANTASQUE, L'AUDACIEUX, L'INDOMPTABLE, LE MALIN, LE TERRIBLE, LE TRIOMPHANT (2,569 tons, five 5.5-inch guns, nine 21.7-inch TT, 50 mines, 37 knots, 1935–36): the class that secured the *contre-torpilleur* legend. Their machinery inexplicably produced power far in excess of the design figures; each ship topped 41 knots on trials. *Le Terrible* exceeded 45 knots. They gained a reputation as good seaboats, but their range remained modest—4,000 miles at fifteen knots. The British "G"-class destroyers, at about half the French ships' tonnage, reached 5,530 miles at 15 knots.

The 5.5-inch guns had improved fire control and ammunition supply, giving a theoretical (and optimistic) firing cycle of five seconds. *Le Triomphant*, seized in Britain, had one gun replaced by a 4-inch DP. She joined *Le Malin*, *Le Fantasque*, and *Le Terrible* in Free French service. All underwent changes to increase their light AA batteries.

These beautiful, powerful warships compared well with some light cruisers.

MOGADOR, VOLTA (2,884 tons, eight 5.5-inch guns, ten 21.7-inch TT, 40 mines, 39 knots, 1939): little improvement over the *Fantasque*, despite the increase in size and weaponry. They exceeded 43 knots on trials, but experience proved their machinery unsatisfactory, with little increase in range. The placement of their guns in enclosed twin mounts enhanced their impressive appearance, but delicate shell hoists restricted fire to about six rpm until corrected in 1940. Still, the practical firing cycle remained about eight seconds.

French destroyers earned no reputation for durability, but *Mogador* survived serious damage at Mers-el-Kebir. A 15-inch shell landed on her stern, detonating her depth charges. Later towed to Toulon, she underwent repairs and traded an aft turret for light AA. The French completed the work just in time to scuttle her, along with *Volta*.

The navy ordered four improved units (*Kléber*, *Desaix*, *Hoche*, and *Marceau*: possibly 2930 tons, eight 5.1-inch DP or 5.5-inch guns and four 3.9-inch DP guns, six 21.7-inch TT) with six more vessels added later, but no construction took place. They would have had greater range and stronger hulls.

LE HARDI, FLEURET, EPÉE, MAMELUCK, CASQUE, LANSQUENET, LE CORSAIRE, LE FLIBUSTIER (1,772 tons, six 5.1-inch guns, seven 21.7-inch TT, 37 knots, 1939–41): intended to correct the flaws of the *Adroits*. They had more stability and structural strength—and a range of just 2,760 miles at 20 knots. The 5.1-inch guns, the same model as in the *Dunkerque*, had unreliable low-angle mounts. Several units received new names to commemorate ships lost in the early fighting. The Toulon scuttling claimed the entire class. The Italians assigned some new names as they began salvage work:

> *Le Corsaire—Sirocco—FR32*
> *Epée—L'Adroit—FR33*
> *Lansquenet—FR34—TA34* (German)
> Le *Flibustier—Bison—FR35*
> *Fleuret—Foudroyant—FR36*
> Le *Hardi—FR37*

At least one ship, *Bison*, was incomplete when scuttled. She became a smoke-generating platform for the Germans, but no *Hardi*s gave active Axis service.

A group of enlarged *Hardi*s (*L'Intrépide*, *Le Téméraire*, *L'Opiniâtre*, *L'Aventurier*, *L'Eveillé*, *L'Alerte*, *L'Inconstant*, *L'Espiègle*: 2180 tons, six 5.1-inch DP guns, 6–7 21.7-inch TT, 35 knots) never reached completion. The navy had plans to rearm *L'Opiniâtre* (six 5.1-inch low-angle mounts and four 3.9-inch DP).

The French had several other designs under consideration in 1940, but unless they overcame the basic problems of unreliable guns and poor durability, the new ships would have achieved little. Some talks took place with the United States concerning an order of twenty-four *Benson*-class ships. Vichy developed a new design (2,000 tons, four or six 4.7-inch guns, four 21.7-inch TT, 33 knots) but placed no orders.

Submarines

Had circumstances permitted, the French submarine fleet could have excelled. As a group, the boats proved reliable and handy, both on the surface and submerged. The crews enjoyed a high level of training. The torpedoes did have problems. The 15.7-inch model, intended for merchant targets, failed abysmally; the 21.7-incher, otherwise reliable, had gyro troubles that forced the French to retain traversing mounts after other major powers had abandoned them. The boats themselves submerged a bit slowly, a potential hazard in busy Mediterranean and Atlantic waters, but such quirks did little to hamper the fleet's potential.

REQUIN, SOUFFLER, MORSE, NARVAL, CAÏMAN, MARSOUIN, PHOQUE, DAUPHIN, ESPADON (1,150/1,441 tons, one 3.9-inch gun, ten 21.7-inch TT, 15/9 knots, 1926–27): ocean-going boats later deemed unsatisfactory due to poor handling and low speed. Four tubes had traversing mounts. Only two boats served with the Free French. Four went to the Italians: *Phoque, Requin, Espadon,* and *Dauphin* became *FR111, 113–115,* but only *FR111* actually commissioned.

SIRÈNE, NAÏADE, GALATÉE (609/757 tons, one 3-inch DP gun, seven 21.7-inch TT, 13.5/7.5 knots, 1927): good, maneuverable boats, though lacking in habitability and submerged stability. They had two traversing TT and three others mounted externally, which limited reloading. The navy scrapped *Nymphe* of this class in 1938; the other three went down at Toulon. The *Sirène*s were the first of the *600 tonne* classes.

ARIANE, EURYDICE, DANAÉ (626/787 tons, one 3.9-inch gun, seven 21.7-inch TT, 14/7.5 knots, 1928–29): best of the classes built to a common *600 tonne* specification. *Ondine* of this class sank after a collision in 1928. The others became scuttling victims in 1942.

CIRCÉ, CALYPSO, THÉTIS, DORIS (615/776 tons, one 3.9-inch gun, seven 21.7-inch TT, 14/7.5 knots, 1929–30): the final *600 tonne* class. None survived to join the Free French. *Circé,* raised by the Italians as *FR117,* never returned to service.

SAPHIR, TURQUOISE, NAUTILUS, RUBIS, DIAMANT, PERLE (761/925 tons; one 3-inch DP gun, three 21.7-inch, two 15.7-inch TT, 32 mines; 12/9 knots, 1930–37): a good minelaying design with a meager torpedo battery. *Rubis,* operating with the Free French from 1940, became the war's most successful minelayer sub. The first three boats fell under Italian control (*FR112, 116,* with *Nautilus* not renamed), but none saw action.

REDOUTABLE, VENGEUR, ARCHIMÈDE, FRESNEL, HENRI POINCARÉ, MONGE, PAS-CAL, PASTEUR, PONCELET, ACHILLE, AJAX, ACTÉON, ACHÉRON, ARGO, PROTÉE, PÉGASE, PERSÉE; L'ESPOIRE, LE GLORIEUX, LE CENTAURE, LE HÉROS, LE CONQUÉR-ANT, LE TONNANT; AGOSTA, SFAX, CASA-BIANCA, BÉVÉZIERS, OUESSANT, SIDI FER-RUCH (1,570/2,084 tons; one 3.9-inch gun, nine 21.7-inch, two 15.7-inch TT; 17/10 knots, 1931–35): successful subs built in three series. The first series (seventeen boats, plus *Phénix* and *Prométhée,* lost prewar) had a surface speed of 17 knots; the second series (six boats) had 19 knots, and the third series (six boats) had 20 knots. This high speed—along with good maneuverability, range, and armament—made for an excellent class, though slow in diving (about 45 seconds). They had seven external TT. Most boats replaced their 15.7-inch tubes with one 21.7-incher.

Redoutable had her range further augmented in 1941. She and six sisters were scuttled at Toulon. One of them, *Henri Poincaré,* became the Italian *FR118.* Four others had scuttled in 1940, and 10 sank after Allied attacks. One left service in the Far East in 1941.

ARGONAUTE, ARÉTHUSE, ATALANTE, LA VESTALE, LA SULTANE (630/798 tons; one 3-inch DP gun, six 21.7-inch, two 15.7-inch TT; 14/9 knots, 1932–35): the first class designed from a *630 tonne* specification intended to correct the flaws of the *600 tonne* boats. All survived the war except *Argonaute,* sunk by the Allies. Only three tubes were internal.

DIANE, MÉDUSE, AMPHITRITE, ANTIOPE, AMAZONE, ORPHÉE, ORÉADE, LA SYBILLE, LA PSYCHÉ (651/809 tons; one 3-inch DP gun, six 21.7-inch, two 15.7-inch TT; 14/9 knots, 1932–34): much like the *Argonaute*s. Six succumbed to various causes during the North African landings.

ORION, ONDINE (558/787 tons; one 3-inch DP gun, six 21.7-inch, two 15.7-inch TT; 14/9 knots, 1932): the final *630 tonne* class. Both became a source of spare parts for other Free French boats.

SURCOUF (3,250/4,304 tons; two 8-inch guns, eight 21.7-inch, four 15.7-inch TT; 18.5/10 knots, 1934): the only submarine of the war to mount an 8-inch gun, a unique "cruiser sub" intended for commerce raiding. She had an innovative design well-suited to her intended role, with accommodations for forty prisoners. However, her intended role had lost its place in modern war. Her large size dictated a lengthy dive time (two minutes), and after surfacing, her crew needed two and a half minutes to ready her guns for action—a virtual eternity in the burgeoning world of electronics and aviation. *Surcouf* also carried a reconnaissance seaplane, but it required thirty minutes to assemble and prepare for flight. Things could have been worse; the original specifications called for her to carry a motor boat as well.

Though her 15.7-inch tubes and four aft tubes had external mounts, they could be reloaded (if circumstances allowed the surface time). Despite her size, *Surcouf* proved relatively maneuverable with good stability. With sufficient range for the Pacific (10,000 miles at 10 knots, surfaced), she might have had success against Japan's inferior AS effort. Her Free French crew set a course for the Panama Canal, but en route she collided with a merchant ship and sank.

MINERVE, JUNON, PALLAS, VÉNUS, CÉRÈS, IRIS (662/856 tons; one 3-inch DP gun, six 21.7-inch, three 15.7-inch TT; 14.25/9 knots, 1936–39): developed from the *630 tonne* types. They carried no reload torpedoes, which greatly limited their value. The first pair, seized in Britain, quickly entered Free French service. *Iris* endured internment in Spain 1942–45. The other three were scuttled after the North African invasion.

AURORE, LA CRÉOLE, L'AFRICAINE, LA FAVORITE, L'ANDROMÈDE, L'ASTRÉE, L'ARTÉMIS, and eight others not completed (893/1,170 tons, one 3.9-inch gun, nine 21.7-inch TT, 14.5/9 knots, 1940): a much improved *630 tonne* development without the faulty 15.7-inch torpedoes. Three 21.7-inch TT had traversing mounts. *Aurore* barely reached completion in 1940 and gave no service before Toulon. *La Créole*, towed incomplete to Britain, spent the war there. The Germans took over four boats: *L'Africaine, La Favorite*, and *L'Andromède* became *UF1–3*, and *L'Astrée* kept her name. Only *UF2* entered service, as a training boat. France completed the other three and *L'Artémis* and *La Créole* postwar, slightly modified.

ROLAND MORILLOT class (1,817/2,416 tons; one 3.9-inch gun, ten 21.7-inch, two 15.7-inch TT; 22/9 knots): 13 boats not completed. An improved *Redoutable* class.

EMERAUDE class (862/1,119 tons, one 3.9-inch gun, four 21.7-inch TT, 40 mines, 15/9 knots): four boats not completed, with perhaps three more planned, based on the *Saphir* class.

PHÉNIX class (1,056/1,252 tons, ten 21.7-inch TT, 18/9 knots): 13 boats not completed, based on the *Aurore* class.

Britain transferred four boats to Free French crews: *Vox, Vineyard*, and *Vortex* became *Curie, Doris*, and *Morse;* and *P714* (ex-Italian *Bronzo*, captured in 1943) became *Narval*.

Torpedo Boats

The French had little opportunity in either world war to develop an MTB design. They bought *VTB1* (14 tons, two 17.7-inch TT in stern troughs, 38 knots) from Britain in 1922 as a prototype. The subsequent *VTB2* and *VTB3* (10 tons, two 17.7-inch TT, 37 knots) and *VTB4* (11 tons, two 17.7 TT, 44 knots), frail and aging, barely sufficed as trainers into June 1940; *VTB1, VTB2,* and *VTB4* managed to reach Britain (*VTB3* broke down on the way), but gave no further service.

VTB8, 9 (21 tons, two 15.7-inch TT, 46 knots, 1935): French MTB design. Like future classes, they had speed and agility and frailty. One broke apart in heavy seas in August 1939; the other limped to Britain in 1940 and became a Catapult victim, but did little else.

VTB11, 12 (28 tons, two 15.7-inch TT, 45 knots, 1940): built in France, sent to Britain for arming. After Catapult, they became the British *MGB98, 99.* The French planned ten similar boats. *VTB13* perhaps reached completion in occupied France before falling victim to air attack in 1941; *VTB14,* taken by Free French in 1944, entered service as a rescue boat.

France intended *VTB23–40,* ordered from the British, to mount 15.7-inch torpedoes, but they all ended up in RN service (*MGB50–67*) with British weapons. Four similar boats, ordered in Canada with American engines, would have had removable TT to make room for twelve mines.

Britain sent eight MTB to the Free French. France recovered two 65-ton MTB (taken incomplete by Germany) in 1944.

LA MELPOMÈNE class (669 tons, two 3.9-inch guns, two 21.7-inch TT, 34.5 knots, 1936–38): 12 torpedo boats. Their unreliable machinery, lack of stability, and limited range offset their qualities of speed and maneuverability and left them almost useless. Most units landed a 3.9-inch gun for increased light AA. The British seized six of them, one of which served with Polish and Dutch crews, as well as Free French. Five others became *FR41–45* in Italian service, then *TA9–13* (not respectively) with the Germans.

LE FIER class (994 tons, four 3.9-inch DP guns, four 21.7-inch TT, 33 knots): 14 TB planned, designed to correct the flaws of the previous class. They carried all their 3.9-inch guns aft. The French laid down seven, and the Germans took six as *TA1–6,* but none reached completion.

Twenty-four more TB based on *Le Fier* never began construction. France received six *Cannon*-class DE from the United States and one "Hunt" Type III from Britain. An old ex-TB (*T369:* 101 tons, light guns, 25.5 knots, 1907) temporarily emerged from retirement to perform local duties.

The French Melpomènes *illustrated the pitfalls of designing a ship to fit treaty restrictions.*

Minecraft and Escorts

POLLUX (2,463 tons, four 3.9-inch guns, 236 mines, 14 knots, 1915) and CASTOR (3,150 tons, four 3.9-inch guns, 368 mines, 14 knots, 1916): former Russian icebreakers used as minelayers and sometimes as seaplane tenders. *Castor* became the Italian *FR60*.

France also employed a small number of auxiliary minelayers, including a couple of tugs, on temporary duty.

CH25 class (60 tons, one 3-inch gun, 17 knots, 1917–18): eight American *SC1*-class vessels. The navy laid up five of them in 1939. The British seized one unit; the Germans may have taken one.

France maintained a sprinkling of elderly small craft on the brink of retirement. The last of eight British-built "Flower"-class sloops, *Altair*, lasted to 1940.

DÉDAIGNEUSE, ÉTOURDI, TAPAGEUSE, AUDACIEUSE (266–310 tons, two 3.9-inch guns, 14–15 knots, 1917): obsolete sloops from a class of 23, capable of minesweeping. The Axis seized *Dédaigneuse* after her scuttling (Italian *FR56*, German *M6020*).

LURONNE (266 tons, two 3.9-inch guns, 13.7 knots, 1917): differed from *Dédaigneuse* mostly in her machinery.

DILIGENTE, ENGAGEANTE, SURVEILLANTE (315 tons, two 3.9-inch guns, 14.5 knots, 1917): from a class of eight obsolete sloops capable of minesweeping. *Diligente*, converted to a seaplane tender, later went to the British in Catapult. The navy slated *Engageante* for seaplane duty but never started work; she retired by 1944, as *Surveillante* had done prewar. However, a group of sister ships in the Romanian navy had careers lasting decades after the war.

MARNE (601 tons, four 3.9-inch guns, 20.5 knots, 1917): old sloop, similar to *Somme*.

SOMME, YSER (576 tons, four 3.9-inch guns, 20 knots, 1917): old sloops from a class of five. *Somme* mounted an additional 3-inch gun. The Germans raised *Yser* after Toulon and named her *SG37*(?). At least two sisters lingered into German captivity as hulks.

VILLE D'YS (1,121 tons; three 3.9-inch, two 3-inch DP guns; 17 knots, 1917): ex-British decoy vessel with concealed armament, used for fishery protection.

QUENTIN ROOSEVELT (585 tons, one 3-inch gun, 13 knots, 1918): fishery protection vessel, seized by the British.

ASTROLABE class (315 tons, light guns, 10 knots, 1918–20): five survey vessels used as patrol boats.

CONQUÉRANTE (351 tons, two 3.9-inch guns, 15 knots, 1918): one left from a pair of sloops similar to *Diligente*s, declared obsolete but pressed into service. She never underwent a planned conversion to a seaplane tender. The British took her in 1940.

SUIPPE (604 tons, four 3.9-inch guns, 20 knots, 1918): escort sloop seized by the British. Two sister ships retired prewar, but one (*Ancre*) lasted long enough for the Germans to consider her for target duty.

AILETTE (492 tons, four 3.9-inch guns, 20 knots, 1918): PB with concealed armament. A sister retired prewar.

GRANIT (354 tons, light guns, 12 knots, 1919): MS of limited value, four others discarded prewar. Raised after Toulon, *Granit* became *SG26* in German service.

FRANCE

MEULIÈRE (380 tons, light guns, 10.5 knots, 1919): six others discarded prewar, like *Granit* except in machinery.

DUBOURDIEU, ENSEIGNE HENRY (453 tons; one 5.5-inch, one 3.9-inch gun; 16.5 knots, 1919–20): from a class of five PB of mercantile appearance.

ARRAS class (644 tons; two 5.5-inch, one 3-inch DP gun; 20 knots, 1919–24): eleven units left from a class of 30 sloops designed to resemble merchant ships. They could perform various duties; one became a seaplane tender, and two became unarmed surveying vessels. Though notably dry and comfortable, they rolled badly. One became the German *M6060*. Another, discarded and abandoned, was scuttled by the Italians. Two, including the seaplane-tending *Belfort*, went to the British after Catapult.

CH106, 107 (128 tons, one 3-inch gun, 16.5 knots, 1921): SC. The British took *CH106*. Two sisters, listed below, served as river gunboats.

BOUGAINVILLE, DUMONT D'URVILLE, SA-VORGNAN DE BRAZZA, AMIRAL CHARNER, D'ENTRECASTEAUX, RIGAULT DE GENOU-ILLY, LA GRANDIÈRE, D'IBERVILLE, plus two not completed (1,969 tons, three 5.5-inch guns, 50 mines, 15.5 knots, 1931–40): a smart design for a colonial sloop, habitable enough for tropical duty. All of them exceeded their design speed, and they showed good range (7,600 miles at 14 knots). Most units carried an aircraft. *Savorgnan de Brazza* sank her sister *Bougainville* in a duel between Free French and Vichy.

The war prevented the construction of other sloops, possibly equipped as AA vessels with six 3.9-inch DP guns. Of four modern "Flower"-class sloops ordered from British yards, three went to the Royal Navy. Nine other "Flowers" began construction in French yards; the only ones completed served the Germans as *PA1–4*. Eight British "Flowers" transferred to the Free French, along with six "Rivers."

CH1–4 (148 tons, one 3-inch gun, 20 knots, 1933–34): SC also used as MS. *CH4* became the German *Uj6077*.

AMIRAL MOUCHEZ (719 tons, two 3.9-inch guns, thirteen knots, 1937): a surveying vessel used as an escort.

ÉLAN and CHAMOIS classes (630–647 tons, two 3.9-inch DP guns, 20 knots, 1938–44): 22 minesweeping sloops, plus four completed postwar and eleven canceled. The classes differed only in bow form. A few carried 3.5-inch DP guns. Seaworthy, stable, with good range and strong hulls, they made reliable escorts.

Most units operating from Britain switched to two 4-inch DP guns. Italy captured five units; three of those and four others went to the Germans, though not all became operational.

CH5–21 (107 tons, one 3-inch gun, 15.5 knots, 1940–41): SC also used as MS. *CH5–8, 10–15* became Catapult victims, two eventually serving with Polish crews. The Germans captured five as *RA1, 2, 6–8*.

CH41–48 (126 tons, one 3-inch gun, 15.5 knots, 1940–42): SC also intended as MS and seaplane tenders. The first three fell prey to Catapult, the next three became German RA-boats, and the last pair were not completed.

The target ship *L'Impassible*, towed incomplete to England, mounted light guns as a floating AA battery.

The United States supplied 32 *PC461*-class and 50 *SC497*-class escorts during the war, along with five motor launches. Britain transferred 19 Fairmile "B" launches, plus 21–23 Admiralty HDML's.

The French deployed 13 AMC as convoy escorts—most mounting five to eight medium guns (5.5-inch or 5.9-inch) and a couple of 3-inch DP—plus 15 auxiliary sloops (four or five 3.9-inch guns), 44 auxiliary PB (with 3-inch or 3.9-inch guns), and five armed yachts (3-inch guns); one of these became a German auxiliary ML. Two vessels operated with the Poles, while the French received eight trawlers transferred from the British, and six trawlers purchased in America.

France operated approximately 500 auxiliary MS. (The Germans took one for ML duty; another, an old German Type 1915 MS, returned to German service.) The navy also requisitioned 86 trawlers for harbor minesweeping; these received VP-numbers, standard for harbor patrol craft and auxiliaries. Britain supplied seven MMS by war's end, and 31 YMS-craft came from the United States.

Many of France's auxiliaries and small craft fell under Axis control. The Germans assigned new hull numbers according to the ships' anticipated duties, such as Uj-numbers for submarine hunters. The Italians used only the FR prefix and set aside certain numbers for certain vessels: *FR11–19* for cruisers, *FR20–29* for superdestroyers, *FR30–39* for DD, *FR40–49* for torpedo boats, *FR50–69* for sloops, *FR70–79* for minesweepers, *FR80–89* for transports, *FR90–109* for tugs, *FR110–129* for submarines,

and *FR200–259* for yachts and similar craft. Not all these numbers were used.

River Gunboats

DOUDART DE LAGRÉE (183 nt, one 3-inch gun, 14 knots, 1909): despite the age difference, a near-sister to *Balny*.

BALNY (201 nt, one 3-inch gun, 14 knots, 1920): laid up in China in 1940, then perhaps given to China as *San Min*.

AVALANCHE, COMMANDANT BOURDAIS (128 tons, one 3-inch gun, 16.5 knots, 1920): former *CH111, 112*. The Japanese attempted to seize *Commandant Bourdais*, but the French probably succeeded in scuttling her.

ARGUS, VIGILANT (218 tons, two 3-inch guns, 12 knots, 1922): *Argus* laid up in China in 1940. The French probably scuttled *Vigilant* before the Japanese took her.

FRANCIS GARNIER (639 tons; two 3.9-inch, one 3-inch DP gun; 15 knots, 1929): possibly transferred to a Chinese crew.

MYTHO, TOURANE (95 tons, one 3-inch howitzer, 10 knots, 1934): *Mytho* blown up just before or just after capture by the Japanese.

The German Bismarck *as seen from the* Prinz Eugen *shortly before their breakout into the Atlantic.*

GERMANY

Saddled with the entire blame for World War I, Germany shriveled to a third-rate military power beneath the weight of the Versailles Treaty. The High Seas Fleet, formerly second only to the Royal Navy, evaporated into an innocuous Reichsmarine. The treaty allowed the following strength: six pre-dreadnoughts plus two in reserve (10,000 tons each, though this figure applied to replacement construction; the pre-dreadnoughts themselves displaced more); six light cruisers, plus two in reserve (6,000 tons each); 12 destroyers, plus four in reserve (800 tons each); 12 torpedo boats, plus four in reserve (200 tons each); no submarines or naval aviation; 15,000 personnel.

Scenario I: Poland

The treaty barred Germany from projecting a strong naval presence beyond its own coast. The Reichsmarine defined its goals according to its modest capabilities: policing the coastline, guarding the sea lanes (especially to isolated East Prussia), and venturing overseas only for courtesy visits. The most probable war scenario pitted the fleet against the forces of some Baltic country (Poland, perhaps); in such a contest, the Germans had a fair chance for success.

Stagnation set in for a time. The navy yearned to grow, but the treaty terms forbade any build-up; nor did attitudes at home favor it. This encouraged—or perhaps caused—two policy trends. First, the Germans cheated; they understated ship displacements and secretly returned to submarine construction. Second, they crammed the most "bang" into the least size. This begat breeds of ponderous destroyers with peevish machinery, heavy ships without heavy armor, and other freakish hybrids.

Scenario II: France

Poland had close ties to France, and the Reichsmarine began to see the French navy as a likely opponent—again, a potentially winnable scenario, since the 1930s brought widespread change.

The 1935 Anglo-German accord nullified the Versailles restraints. Germany gained the right to a submarine fleet 45% as large as Britain's, plus 35% of the surface ships—virtually the same share given to France at Washington. For the Germans, it equaled approximately:

    184,000 tons in battleships
    47,000 tons in aircraft carriers
    51,000 tons in heavy cruisers
    67,000 tons in light cruisers
    52,000 tons in destroyers
    24,000 tons in submarines

The door had opened.

Scenario III: Great Britain

In 1938, Hitler sketched a new strategic picture, one involving a confrontation with the British. To meet this challenge, the navy developed a construction program known as the "Z Plan." With a target date of 1948, the fleet would swell to:

    6 battleships of 56,000 tons each
    2 battleships of 42,000 tons each
    5 battlecruisers
    4 aircraft carriers
    3 pocket battleships
    5 heavy cruisers
    17 light cruisers
    22 scout cruisers
    68 destroyers
    90 torpedo boats
    249 submarines

A swarm of smaller vessels and auxiliaries accompanied this group—no longer a third-rate navy.

Scenario IV: World War

War inconsiderately overturned the Nazi plan. But even if it hadn't, this German fleet, however impressive, would still have found itself a poor second to the Royal Navy at any given date—a fact apparent to Erich Raeder, commander-in-chief of the Kriegsmarine (as the Reichs-marine was ominously renamed). He believed his surface units would fare best as commerce raiders, rather than as a massed battle fleet. But the island home that left Britain vulnerable to commerce warfare also blessed its fleet with unparalleled freedom of movement, while German ships had to huddle behind the North Sea bottleneck. Any attempt at breakout would attract ravening Royal Navy squadrons. Britain's strategic position confronted the Germans with a problem that they never overcame, even after the conquests of Norway and France.

Ordnance

GUN	SW	RANGE	CEILING	FC	NOTES
16/47*	2,271	40,250		31	"H" class BB
15/47*	1,764	38,880		26	*Bismarck*s, BC
11.1/54	728	44,760		17+	*Scharnhorst*s
11.1/52	661	39,890		24	*Deutschland*s
11.1/40	626	28,040			*Schlesien*s
8/60	269	36,680		12	CA
5.9/60	100	28,100		7.5	*Nürnberg, Leipzig,* "K" class CL
5.9/55	100	25,150		7.5	*Scharnhorst* twin mounts, BB, "M" class cruisers
	100	24,060		7.5	*Graf Zeppelin, Scharnhorst* and *Deutschland* singles
5.9/48	100	24,005			regunned *Emden,* more range in "O"
	88#	25,700		7.5	"SP" class, DD twin mount, less range in DD single
5.9/45	100	21,220			*Schlesien*s, some AMC
	100	18,370			original *Emden*
5/45	62	19,030			*Grille, Bremse,* DD and TB
4.1/65	33	19,360	41,000	3.5	*Graf Zeppelin, Deutschland*s, BB, BC, CA
4.1/45	33	16,595	33,800~		*Emden, Schlesien*s, SS, many TB and others
3.5/76	20	18,800	40,680		*Nürnberg, Leipzig,* "K" class CL
3.5/45	20	13,070			some SS, MS, and SC

*Various lengths are quoted for these guns, 47cal being common.
~At 80°—few mounts elevated so high, nor were all of them DP. U-boat mounts had limited elevation and range.
#All 48cal guns could use 100-lb shells, though destroyers seem to have kept with the lighter ammunition.
Sources disagree with regard to the range of the guns in various mounts and with the differing shells. However, the variation would not be great.

TORPEDO	WW	RANGE		NOTES
21-inch G7a T1	661	6,560/44	15,300/30	general issue
21-inch G7e T2	661	5,470/30		electric model in SS and some MTB
21-inch T5		6,230/25		SS homing torpedo

The Graf Spee's early radar demonstrated the potential of German technology.

In fact, Versailles had already assured the Kriegsmarine's defeat twenty-five years before. The catastrophic cuts in personnel stunted the development of a modern command structure, creating a visionless and ill-organized staff unable to manage an extremely challenging scenario. Like an amputee's obsession, the focus for the high command was the hope of recaptured glory, a new High Seas Fleet, a goal as pointless as it was unattainable. Amid that futility, no one formulated a suitable alternative. Germany had no doctrine for victory.

Thus, the swastika never fluttered over any great battle fleet, and surface ships that did risk the seaways as commerce raiders accomplished little. It was the U-boat that fought Germany's naval war and, by 1943, lost it.

Thanks to superior optical equipment, German marksmanship gained a peerless reputation at the war's start. Germany had also assumed the early lead in electronics, when in 1936 *Graf Spee* mounted the first operational naval radar—a primitive and fragile device. More helpful sets entered service from 1940 onward but, amazingly, the Kriegsmarine consciously chose to neglect radar in favor of passive systems. The Allies' state-of-the-art radars afforded

their fleets an array of new capabilities, while the Germans went to war's end relying on optical fire control.

German ammunition represented a combination of the superior and the poor. The heavier shells showed remarkable performance against vertical armor, but were also plagued with a high percentage of duds. Propellants, on the other hand, consistently showed their resistance to accidental explosion. When a British bomb ignited 23 tons of *Gneisenau's* powder charges, the pressure of expanding gases knocked a main battery turret out of place, but with no catastrophic blast.

The largest DP weapon, the 4.1/65, earned little praise. The older 4.1/45 performed consistently but lacked power. At the war's beginning, the standard 37mm gun fired only 30 rpm; later models had real value (theoretically 250 rpm, 7,100-yard range, 15,750-foot ceiling). A few ships received Bofors guns late in the war. The German 20mm gun developed into a reasonable weapon as well (450–500 rpm, 5,250-yard range, 12,100-foot ceiling). The tandem of 20mm and 37mm guns would have had greater effect if mounted in larger numbers, as in Allied light AA practice.

Since the Germans never concentrated on

AS warfare, their escorts made do with the depth charge. Note that in such constricted areas as the Baltic, the mine became an effective AS device, and Germany was a leader in mine development.

Germany devoted considerable resources to its torpedo program, yet the T1 entered service with a lengthy checklist of flaws. It failed to keep the proper depth, and its magnetic detonator often exploded prematurely. The navy eventually corrected these and other problems, and the weapon performed well. Development of electric drives created weapons that were trackless and quiet, while a host of homing and pattern-running torpedo designs also entered service. The Germans achieved some success with aerial torpedoes, yet never fully grasped their potential. This shows in the failure to pursue a carrier-borne torpedo bomber design.

Aircraft Carriers

The Germans gave low priority to carrier construction and completed none. But the thought of a German CV, loose somewhere among the Atlantic commerce lanes, inspires some intriguing scenarios. Replenished by sub and by air, seeking and striking its targets from a hundred miles away, such a raider might have prospered in 1940.

For the Germans, though, the questions of carrier theory were inconsequential compared to those of carrier design. With no experience and little foreign aid, Germany was doomed to produce obsolete, clumsy designs. Luftwaffe commanders aggravated the problem with their apathy. Though responsible for supplying the carrier planes, they declined to comment on the requirements of air operations. And German pilots often suffered from a scandalously poor training regimen—even when their airfields weren't steaming at 25 knots in heavy swells.

The Luftwaffe had a capable fighter available for carrier use, one of the great planes of the war—the Messerschmitt Bf 109, with its potent, direct-injection Daimler-Benz engine. This celebrated veteran had its flaws: a cramped cockpit with limited visibility, and very narrow landing gear that could only have multiplied the number of deck crashes. The intended carrier model, the Bf 109T (speed: 348 mph; armament: two 20mm cannon, two 7.9mm mg) lacked adequate range (410 miles) and became unwieldy at extreme speeds. But it was a rugged, serviceable plane, vital qualities on a carrier, and through 1941, at least, it could challenge any opponent.

Germany's other premier fighter, the Focke-Wulf Fw 190, had no future as a carrier plane despite its combat prowess. Its landing characteristics, pilot visibility, and undercarriage would have necessitated a thorough redesign, resulting in an almost completely new plane. In any case, the German carrier program had already begun to sputter before the Fw 190 debuted in battle.

Early plans included a Fieseler torpedo biplane (Fi 167, speed: 202 mph; armament: two 7.9mm mg, one 17.7-inch torpedo or 1102-lb bomb). But the Junkers "Stuka" dive-bomber, a proven shipkiller (Ju 87C, speed: 238 mph; armament: four 7.9mm mg, one 1102-lb bomb), came to monopolize the carrier-borne attack role. No other aircraft bettered the Stuka's dive-bombing ability. Handy and pleasant in flight, it needed additional strength in its fixed landing gear to become truly suited to the rigors of a flight deck.

GRAF ZEPPELIN and "B" (23,200 tons; sixteen 5.9-inch, ten 4.1-inch DP guns; AC 42, 33.75 knots): a design with sufficient size and speed, but ill-equipped to handle even its small air group. The Germans complicated matters by insisting on CA-level protection (about 20% armor) with firepower adequate to repel a destroyer squadron. The 5.9-inch guns had twin casemate mounts; no other country had built a carrier with casemate guns since 1928. Such provisions may have made sense for a ship intended to lurk in the North Sea gloom, but the outdated aviation equipment compromised the ship's *raison d'être*.

The design included a unique feature, a pair of small steering propellers forward. These had no function in normal operations at sea but could have provided some maneuverability in the case of battle damage and could even move the ship at 3–4 knots. The main machinery, unfortunately, resembled that in German heavy cruisers and promised the familiar platoon of problems.

A 1942 revision called for a sixth 4.1-inch twin mount, but at that point the ship had no more prospects for completion. Around the same time, the Germans made plans to add hull bulges, a remedy for miscalculations that would have given the ship a 4.5° list when fully loaded.

The original schedule called for *Graf Zeppelin*'s completion by 1940–41. At war's end, she was only 90% finished; meanwhile, her displacement had grown to 28,090 tons. The "B" never proceeded far enough to earn a name (*Peter Strasser*, the probable choice). Tentative plans included two further vessels.

The Germans produced several design schemes for carriers in the neighborhood of 12,000 to 20,000 tons; these featured modest batteries of 4.1-inch DP guns, and some also had casemate weaponry. Larger design studies included one at 30,000 tons and a 58,000-ton behemoth (twenty 5-inch DP guns, 100 aircraft).

Graf Zeppelin's cruiser qualities set her near the hybrid category, and Germany indeed wasted a good deal of paper on hybrid specifications. A series of monstrosities (from around 40,000 tons to 70,000 tons full load displacement) showed little concept of carrier aviation and may not represent a serious effort; all variations had four or six 11.1-inch guns, about sixteen 5.9-inch and sixteen 4.1-inch DP guns, with 24–80 aircraft, and a speed near 34 knots. A more credible project (between 10,000 and 20,000 tons) shipped up to eight 5.9-inch guns and twelve 4.1-inch DP, and carried 10 to 25 planes at around 34 knots. Whatever relevance these ships had to Germany's needs, their aviation deficiencies sapped their potential.

The Luftwaffe had seven merchant-type vessels equipped with catapults for seaplane operations. As many as twelve tug-type units also served as seaplane tenders.

EUROPA (44,000 tons designed, twelve 4.1-inch DP guns, AC 42, 26.5 knots): a liner considered for CV conversion. She had great size but marginal stability. No conversion work took place.

GNEISENAU (18,160 tons designed, twelve 4.1-inch DP guns, AC 24, 21 knots): transport considered for CVE conversion. The Germans would have had little use for a 21-knot ship except in training.

POTSDAM (17,527 tons designed, twelve 4.1-inch DP guns, AC 24, 21 knots): transport considered for CVE conversion.

WESER (13,000 tons, ten 4.1-inch DP guns, AC 24, 32 knots): the incomplete *Hipper*-class CA *Seydlitz* taken in hand for conversion. Her design displacement rose to 18,000 tons while her air group shrank to 18.

The Germans seized France's *Joffre* and Italy's *Aquila* but failed to complete either. They also briefly considered converting the incomplete CL *De Grasse* (11,400 tons designed, twelve 4.1-inch DP guns, AC 23, 32 knots).

Battleships and Battlecruisers

The Battle of Jutland alerted the naval world to the possibilities of long-range gunfire. With guns elevating to reach 20,000 yards and beyond, shells achieved higher arcs before plunging down toward their targets. This plunging fire forced a complete re-evaluation of armor layout as deck hits became increasingly likely. Post-WWI battleships, starting with Britain's *Nelsons*, nearly doubled the former standards of deck thickness. Jutland's lessons fathered a worldwide fleet of modern dreadnoughts covered in five or six inches of horizontal protection.

But somehow the Germans got a different message. Though they rightly appreciated and continued the diligent subdivision that had kept their battered battlecruisers afloat, they persisted in planning, not for long-range glory, but for short-range surprises along the North Sea coasts. This stamped German designs with a set of unique features. Their guns specialized in the high-velocity discharge of relatively light shells at a good rate of fire—a precise equation for short-range accuracy, increasing the likelihood of side hits and the degree of side penetration. Designers made no attempt at maximum elevation in their mounts. Instead, the guns' velocity gave them lengthy reach with their light shells— a precise equation for long-range inaccuracy. Yet here the quality of the guns themselves partly overcame the equation. *Scharnhorst*, in attacking *Glorious*, approximately matched *Warspite's* record with a hit from 26,400 yards away.

A low-angle secondary battery of cruiser-caliber guns seemed the best remedy for a sudden run-in with enemy torpedo craft, but it also necessitated a third caliber for heavy AA fire. The lack of foresight that allowed this weakened AA self-defense likewise failed to provide a suitable protection scheme versus aerial bombs and torpedoes.

Twenty years after *Nevada* and *Oklahoma* revolutionized armor layout, the Germans remained faithful to their pre-Jutland ideals. Ignoring the precedent of deck armor concentrated into a single formidable thickness, they split their protection. One deck sat high in the ship, a barrier to light shells and high-explosive bombs, but no obstacle to heavy weapons. With the upper hull sporting this supposed protection,

the main armor deck shifted down near the waterline, anchored to the bottom of the belt armor—a common arrangement in WWI dreadnoughts. This gave the lower hull tremendous strength and near invulnerability to short-range gunfire, but at great cost. It limited the depth of the belt, increasing the threat posed by underwater hits. More seriously, it hampered resistance to long-range gunnery. Almost everything above the waterline was vulnerable to battleship guns at any range. The end result was a ship undoubtedly difficult to sink, but easy to cripple.

Provisions for the surprise encounter became irrelevant with the advent of radar and the airborne bomb; German designs thus strode first in line on the battleships' march to obsolescence. The virtues the designers gained— buoyancy and strength in the lower hull— proved useless as well, as the ships steamed piecemeal into British guns. Survivability meant little to the lone hunters; *Bismarck* went down with 2,000 men.

SCHLESIEN, SCHLESWIG-HOLSTEIN (13,191 tons; four 11.1-inch, ten 5.9-inch, four 3.5-inch DP guns; 16 knots, 1908): leftovers from the old *Deutschlands*, a class of five pre-dreadnoughts obsolete before their completion. They functioned mostly in training. During the war, they landed their 5.9-inch guns and traded the 3.5-inch battery for six 4.1-inch DP.

A sister ship, *Hannover*, lasted to 1944 vainly awaiting conversion to a target ship. Other predreadnought target ships include *Hessen* (13,200 tons) and *Zähringen* (11,800 tons). A section of old *Preussen's* hull remained for use in experiments.

Some French ships fell under German control. The ex-BB *Océan* served in ordnance tests. The sunken *Provence*, irreparable as a warship, became a source of guns for shore batteries. A hull segment of the newly-begun *Clemenceau* warranted little attention except as a possible decoy.

GERMANY

The Gneisenau *proved that any battleship, even if severely flawed, could be a dangerous opponent.*

SCHARNHORST, GNEISENAU (31,800 tons; nine 11.1-inch, twelve 5.9-inch, fourteen 4.1-inch DP guns; AC 3, 32 knots, 1938–39): BC design formulated around three considerations. First, as outgrowths of the pocket battleships, the *Scharnhorst*s were intended as commerce raiders with modest weaponry and corresponding protection (though this changed with the advent of the *Dunkerque*). Second, international scrutiny disallowed a large dreadnought design with large guns. And third, the determination to squeeze a battle-worthy ship into a modest displacement stretched German ingenuity to its limits. What began as an 18,000-ton raider with six 11.1-inch guns ballooned to 26,000 tons and nine guns, and even then it needed more. The results of all this inflation proved to be unpleasant to operate, terrible seaboats with short range and fickle machinery. The overloaded hulls sat low enough in the water to submerge their armored decks, and waves washing over the bows often interfered with both forward turrets. In turning, the ships wallowed and answered the helm only grudgingly. They were the worst dreadnoughts of their generation.

The most criticized feature, their main guns, gave greater firepower than earlier 11.1-inch marks but looked nonetheless puny. (The world believed these were 26,000-ton battlecruisers similar to the *Dunkerque*s; the 11.1-inch gun hardly compares with the French 13-inch and seems even more toylike in view of

Scharnhorst's true tonnage.) Planners noticed prewar that a twin 15-inch mount would fit nicely atop the triple 11.1-inch barbette—a switch that offered to increase the 6,548-lb broadside to a respectable 10,582 lbs—but the project received low priority. Only in 1942 did *Gneisenau* begin conversion while undergoing repairs, and she never made it back into service.

The secondary battery comprised a curious mix of mounts, enclosed twins and vulnerable singles, all low-angle. The Kriegsmarine's commitment to low-angle secondaries left its ships without a credible heavy AA gun, perhaps a forgivable oversight before World War II revealed the airplane's potential. Yet the Continental powers had to depend on 3.5-inch, 3.9-inch, and 4.1-inch guns firing light shells with little power while America, Britain, and Japan foresaw the need for hefty dual-purpose batteries. Compounding Germany's problem, the 4.1-inch mount moved too slowly to track the newest aircraft. *Scharnhorst*'s menagerie of guns competed for arcs of fire and increased her topweight. She could have shipped twenty or more 5-inch DP for little loss in anti-DD gunfire and a monumental gain in AA power.

The zeal for perfect marksmanship led the designers into a fantastic complexity of fire-control equipment, which ruthlessly complicated gunnery operations. Shortly after the outbreak of war, desperate crews managed to improve the situation by ripping 22,000 yards of wiring out of each ship.

During the war, the navy added six 21-inch torpedo tubes to facilitate the rapid destruction of merchant targets.

The *Scharnhorst*s had a modern tonnage of armor, with 44% of their displacement dedicated to protection, but in an outdated scheme. Despite every effort, designers found it impossible to fit the boilers beneath the lower armor deck and instead had to add a centerline "hump" jutting above both the armor deck level and the top of the belt protection. So instead of enjoying the 13.75-inch thickness of belt protection, the boilers found themselves behind a mere 3.1-inch plate. The hump, only a small target, nevertheless presented an invitation to Murphy's Law, as *Scharnhorst* discovered in her last battle. The Germans doubled this vulnerability by foregoing a modern layout of machinery dispersal for their heavy units. Furthermore, they retained the three-shaft arrangement of the High Seas Fleet battleships. Normally an operational concern, the triple screws had limited use in steering—a grim portent for *Bismarck*.

The anti-torpedo system had to cope with restrictions imposed by the ship's tonnage and speed, which dictated a slim hull. This system, while not as narrow as *King George V's*, lacked the layers characteristic of modern schemes and could resist only 551 lbs of TNT at its thickest point. Survivability thus depended on a high degree of internal subdivision—probably the design's best feature.

Beneath the shadow of her flaws, *Scharnhorst* remained a 32,000-ton warship with great destructive potential. As a combatant, she utterly outclassed her predecessors, the *Deutschland* class, and her machinery placed her among the fastest of dreadnoughts. It would have saved *Scharnhorst* in her last battle, but radar problems and miscommunication let the British repeatedly catch her. She might yet have escaped, but torpedoes and a 14-inch shell in her boilers slowed her. Since heavy weather had forced her escorting destroyers to withdraw, she had no screen to protect her. It would seem that *Scharnhorst's* greatest flaw was finding herself alone against a full-sized battleship.

BISMARCK, TIRPITZ (42,000 tons; eight 15-inch, twelve 5.9-inch, sixteen 4.1-inch DP guns; AC 6, 30 knots, 1940–41): allegedly 35,000 tons. The design began at that displacement with guns not exceeding 16-inch—the same restrictions set for the five treaty powers and accepted by the Germans in their 1935 accord.

The designers, having a 15-inch gun design in hand, thought it suitable for their new ship. The speed of foreign contemporaries forced the high command to insist on 30 knots at overload power. The dimensions of German waterways dictated the maximum draft and beam.

The 35,000-ton limit vanished from consideration as the designers struggled for a balanced plan that met all the specifications. They chose the broadest possible beam to ensure a shallow draft and good stability. The hull form afforded a bit more volume for the anti-torpedo scheme, but the designers repeated *Scharnhorst's* lack of layers. In *Bismarck's* case, no degree of underwater protection could have spared her the crippling hit on her rudder. The propellers and rudders form an Achilles' heel for every ship, and especially for *Bismarck*; though she greatly improved on *Scharnhorst's* handling, she could not steer by her triple screws alone.

The armor scheme generally matched *Scharnhorst's* in thickness and in obsolescence, but *Bismarck* avoided a portion of her predecessor's overloading and over-complexity. Belt protection remained shallow; the dual armor decks remained inadequate.

The traditional virtues also recurred. *Tirpitz* demonstrated great buoyancy; hammered time and again by aircraft and submarines, she finally succumbed when struck by at least two 12,000-lb Tallboy bombs, plus several near misses. The shallow harbor maximized the bombs' effect, barring their explosive force from dissipating downward, and they initiated a serious fire, a turret explosion, and 17,000 tons of flooding. *Bismarck* became a legend by taking up to 400 shell hits and an unknown number of torpedoes before she sank; but the legend neglects to mention how quickly her guns fell silent, scoring not a single hit before British shells demolished her exposed systems.

The guns might have accomplished much if given a chance. The 15-inch model proved capable of rapid fire and excellent belt penetra-

The German Tirpitz *accomplished more by lurking among the fjords than she could have in battle against superior Allied numbers.*

tion at short range. At longer range and against deck armor, however, results were unimpressive. The hull requirements for speed and stability dictated a minor sacrifice in steadiness as a gun platform.

All 5.9-inch guns had armored turrets, giving more protection than *Scharnhorst*'s mounts, but the guns remained low-angle. So the 4.1-incher, neither aircraft-scourge nor killer of ships, appeared again. The airplane's role in sinking the *Tirpitz* and *Bismarck* accents this weakness. The desperate Germans equipped *Tirpitz* with AA shells for her 5.9-inch and 15-inch batteries; what she really needed was a dual-purpose gun.

As standard in German warships, the propulsion machinery was disappointing. Though no breakdowns occurred, fuel consumption rose beyond the design figures. The resulting drop in range may have contributed to *Bismarck*'s loss.

The *Bismarck* underwent few alterations during her brief service. The *Tirpitz* shipped six

21-inch torpedo tubes for merchant targets.

The legend of ruggedness enrobing the *Bismarck*s obscures their grievous flaws and obsolescence. In fact, they rate poorly among the treaty battleships and may be the most overrated warships of all time. Their hopeless solitude canceled any chance they had for long-term success. Yet in drawing the Allies' badly needed resources from other sectors, they did serve a purpose. They became 42,000-ton scarecrows.

"H" class (56,200 tons; eight 16-inch, twelve 5.9-inch, sixteen 4.1-inch DP guns, six 21-inch TT; AC 6, 29 knots): six battleships planned.

By 1939, when Hitler renounced the Anglo-German naval agreement, the Kriegsmarine had already developed a *Bismarck*-like design armed with 16-inch guns. The main battery remained in four twin turrets. Though this disposition demanded more weight and space than triple or quadruple mounts, the Germans claimed it enhanced their fire control. They may also have suffered disappointment in previous experience with triples; the contemporary "M" class cruisers likewise dropped the triples of previous CL in favor of twin mounts.

Apart from its new guns, the "H" design deviated from the *Bismarck* model mainly in its diesel machinery, which promised long range. The deck armor gained a bit in thickness, and the anti-torpedo scheme gained some depth; but the fundamental archaism of both these systems went unchanged. Standards of protection that had made Germany's WWI dreadnoughts remarkably rugged were no longer modern standards—a fact perhaps lost on the harried design teams as they emerged in disarray from the shadow of Versailles.

Ships "H" and "J" began construction in 1939, but neither they nor ships "K" through "N" were launched as the outbreak of war brought the project to a halt. Designers continued their work, modifying the plans according to the lessons of battle. Even after the hulls had been dismantled to make room for U-boat construction, the modifications continued, the statistics inflating steadily from 1939 to 1944.

"H39"   52,643 tons; eight 16-inch, twelve 5.9-inch, sixteen 4.1-inch DP guns, six 21-inch TT; AC 4, 30.4 knots.

"H41"   62,992 tons; eight 16.5-inch, twelve 5.9-inch, sixteen 4.1-inch DP guns, six 21-inch TT; AC 4, 28.8 knots.

"H42"   83,268 tons; eight 16.5-inch, twelve 5.9-inch, sixteen 4.1-inch DP guns, six 21-inch TT; AC 6, 32.2 knots.

"H43"   103,346 tons; eight 19.7-inch, twelve 5.9-inch, sixteen 4.1-inch DP guns, six 21-inch TT; AC 6, 31 knots.

"H44"   122,047 tons; eight 20.1-inch, twelve 5.9-inch, sixteen 4.1-inch DP guns, six 21-inch TT; AC 6, 30.1 knots.

The only constants here are the torpedoes (in anachronistic submerged tubes) and the clutter of 5.9-inch and 4.1-inch guns. Air power's potential had became obvious by 1942, and with Germany's 20mm and 37mm cannon obsolescing, designers persisted with a DP battery less effective than that of an American light cruiser. The navy had a 5-inch, 61cal gun under development, an excellent AA weapon in a twin mount ideal for battleships; but instead the designers considered replacing the 5.9-inchers with 6.7-inch guns firing 159-lb shells—another low-angle battery of even greater weight.

The reworked layouts constituted an exercise in design rather than an actual plan; the navy had officially dismissed the project after "H41." The monstrosities that followed could never have advanced beyond the theoretical—not that they would have lumbered like drunken elephants, but German waterways simply weren't big enough for them. The swelling displacement, not merely prodigal, stemmed from logical decisions concerning protection and the enlarged main battery. The original 16-inch gun design allowed easy conversion to 16.5-inch; and while the Germans never produced a 19.7-inch or 20.1-inch gun, they had a 21-inch weapon firing a 4,850-lb shell beyond 50,000 yards—maybe an "H45" would have included it.

"O," "P," and "Q" (31,152 tons; six 15-inch, six 5.9-inch, eight 4.1-inch DP guns, twelve 21-inch TT; AC 4, 33.5 knots): another BC outgrowth of a pocket battleship, in this case the "Cruiser P" project with more powerful guns. The 15-inch guns gave "O" an edge over previous battlecruisers—in fact, the "O" project delayed, and ultimately prevented, the *Scharnhorst*'s rearmament—but protection dwindled in favor of high speed, the highest for any dreadnought. As in the pocket battleship theory, these ships could outrun anything they couldn't outgun. In reality, they were vulnerable even to cruiser guns, and they lacked the speed to outrun the convoy's newest escort, the airplane, while their inadequate batteries of 5.9-inch and 4.1-inch guns left them ill-equipped for self-defense in either case.

The 5.9-inch twin mounts resembled those in German destroyers, but unlike the destroyers, "O" retained her 100-lb shells. The 65° elevation failed to make AA fire practical.

The armor scheme showed some new thinking—for example, the primary armored deck sat atop the belt—but that deck had only 2.4-inch of metal, setting the "O" in context with the 10,000-ton *Algérie*. The anti-torpedo scheme was even thinner than *Scharnhorst*'s, and a mere 25% of the ships' displacement went to protection.

Hitler, appalled by the *Bismarck*'s loss in 1941, became increasingly reluctant to commit his heavy units to battle; and when *Scharnhorst* went down, he forsook even a fleet-in-being. Only Dönitz's personal intervention prevented the scrapping of all surface ships. So if the "O's" had reached completion, they might never have engaged the enemy—good news for their crewmen.

Cruisers

Germany retained some pre-1914 cruisers, serving in various capacities without their machinery: *Hamburg* and *Berlin* (3,230 tons each) and *Amazone* (2,600 tons) as disarmed accommodation hulks, and *Arcona* and *Medusa* (2,650 tons each) as floating AA batteries with up to six 4.1-inch DP guns. The Yugoslav cruiser *Dalmacija* (ex-German *Niobe*), having become the Italian *Cattaro*, fell into German hands and served for a short time under her original German name, armed with six 3.5-inch DP. None of the captured French, Italian, and Dutch cruisers became operational, though two incomplete Dutch units took names (*KH1, 2*). The antique *Koningin Emma der Nederlanden*, having no combat value, continued as a hulk. The remains of France's old *Waldeck Rousseau* performed decoy duty in Brest harbor.

EMDEN (5,600 tons; eight 5.9-inch, three 3.5-inch DP guns, four 21-inch TT, 120 mines; 29.4 knots, 1925): Germany's first major naval construction after the Armistice. Modeled on WWI cruisers, by 1939 she was just as obsolete. Various update proposals inspired little actual work. Her armament changed somewhat, with 4.1-inch DP replacing her 3.5-inchers and a new 5.9-inch battery of 48cal guns (30° mounts, 100-lb shells). She spent most of the war as a training ship.

KÖNIGSBERG, KÖLN, KARLSRUHE (6650 tons; nine 5.9 in, six 3.5-inch DP guns, twelve 21-inch TT, 120 mines; AC 2, 32 knots, 1929–30): the "K" class, easily identified by their aft turrets, staggered left and right off the centerline. The 5.9-inch guns performed well, capable of 10 rpm or more for short periods under practice conditions. Nine barrels represented worthwhile offense but also contributed to overloading the hull, which thus became an awkward platform. Planners considered building *Karlsruhe* and *Köln* with six 7.5-inch guns to increase their firepower while allowing a return to twin turrets, but the idea foundered amid technical and political factors. The design shared some dubious armor features with German BB projects—a narrow belt, an unassuming thickness of armor, and the downward-sloping deck—which left it less than rugged. Overall, the "K's" were unsuccessful, the obvious victims of a stern treaty and overly ambitious designers.

Diesel engines supplemented the turbines in an attempt to achieve long range. Instead, it achieved needless complexity, and considerations of range became irrelevant—the ships' poor sea-keeping qualities and hull frailty meant they couldn't travel far from port. After venturing overseas prewar and incurring serious damage, *Karlsruhe* had her hull strengthened and bulged. The added weight knocked a couple knots from her speed, but still didn't save her from an early grave, the result of a single torpedo and an ill-trained crew.

The war prevented other refits. Lesser alterations included a reduction in torpedoes. *Köln* gave up her aircraft prewar and served in helicopter trials. Like other German cruisers, the "K's" carried a token stock of depth charges.

LEIPZIG (6,710 tons; nine 5.9-inch, six 3.5-inch DP guns, twelve 21-inch TT, 120 mines; AC 2, 32 knots, 1931): similar to *Königsberg*, slightly improved with better sea-keeping. Hull weakness recurred, however; heavy seas and heavy shells posed an equal threat to German CL, and only the old *Emden* could manage the open Atlantic. *Leipzig*'s hull threatened to collapse after a single torpedo hit in 1939. Faced with the extent of her damage, the Germans made partial repairs (speed 24 knots) and modified her for training duty, later removing her catapult and torpedo tubes. Her hull did manage to hold together after a 1944 collision with *Prinz Eugen* that nearly cut her in two.

Leipzig enjoyed a marginal gain over *Königsberg*'s protection. The belt armor tilted slightly outward at the top, increasing the tendency to deflect shells. (At only two inches thick, the armor needed every advantage.) Designers continued with inclined belts in the *Deutschland* and *Hipper* types.

DEUTSCHLAND, ADMIRAL SCHEER, ADMIRAL GRAF SPEE (11,700 tons; six 11.1-inch, eight 5.9-inch, six 4.1-inch DP guns, eight 21-inch TT; AC 2, 26 knots, 1933–36): the famous "pocket battleships." Their official rating as "armored ships" derived from terminology in the Versailles Treaty, whose authors had in mind the innocuous vessels providing coast defense in several smaller navies. But the *Deutschland*s were not innocuous, and their range (18,650 miles at 15 knots) had nothing to do with coast defense. Their size and intended role as commerce raiders qualify them as cruisers, which title they received in 1940.

Shortly after the Versailles Treaty imposed the 10,000-ton limit, the Germans set about deciding the best way to use that tonnage. They considered two possible types, a monitor-like vessel (four 15-inch guns, 22 knots) and a cruiser with firepower taking precedence over protection (eight 8.3-inch guns, 32 knots). The monitor they eliminated at once, since it would establish the navy as a mere coast defense force. The cruiser design also failed to create any enthusiasm, and the whole project faded.

The German pre-dreadnoughts continued to age, so the task of planning their replacements recurred periodically. A 12-inch battery seemed appealing, as the Germans had a few barrels in reserve. One design showed three twin mounts forward, rather *Nelson*-like; but another had two triples mounted fore and aft. In any event, difficulty in producing further 12-inch barrels fueled the prevailing official indecision, and economic blight put the project back to sleep.

It awoke amid interest in 11.1-inch guns, which were more politically expedient and more likely to produce a balanced design. Some planners dallied with the monitor idea, but a new concept gained momentum—a ship that could outrun anything it couldn't outgun. From this idea sprang the *Deutschland*s.

The first ship in the class displaced 1,700 tons more than the treaty allowed, but the Germans didn't mind cheating to reach a more effective design. When the time came for the next ship, planners voiced some suggestions: increasing the 5.9-inch and 4.1-inch batteries while decreasing the TT; replacement of the main and secondary guns by nine 9.4-inchers and a gain of 1.5–2 knots; a new battery of eight 12-inch guns; enlargement to 15–18,000 tons and nine 11.1-inchers. But the next two units differed only slightly, with more powerful machinery allowing them to exceed 27 knots and an enlarged displacement reaching 12,100 tons.

The 11.1-inch gun was a weapon of modest punch but long range. The 5.9-inch guns, in the same single mounts later used aboard

Scharnhorst, did not perform well in service. *Deutschland* (renamed *Lützow* in 1940) and *Scheer* mounted 3.5-inch DP guns as completed, but received 4.1-inchers early in the war, when *Deutschland* also shipped a load of depth charges. The navy considered more elaborate refits (up to fourteen 5-inch DP replacing the 5.9-inch and 4.1-inch guns, an enlarged hull—adding over 700 tons—to gain two knots and correct deficient sea-keeping), but as with most such plans in Germany, no work took place.

The pocket battleships raised many eyebrows. They fulfilled the "outrun or outgun" concept with their heavy weaponry and long-ranging diesels; of their likely foes, only Britain's three battlecruisers could match them. But of course, the design lacked balance. Its modest protection left it vulnerable to much humbler warships, as *Graf Spee* found out off the River Plate when one of two 8-inch hits punched through her armor, barely missing her diesels. None of the eighteen 6-inch hits defeated her armor (three of them bounced off turrets), and she emerged from the duel without serious damage. *Lützow* showed moderate resistance to underwater damage; a torpedo struck her stern, crumpling the aft structure and letting in 1,300 tons of water. Repairs required nine months.

Near the war's end, some thought went into converting *Lützow* and *Scheer* into aircraft carriers.

The armored ship concept persisted after this class, with additional units anticipated as replacements for retiring pre-dreadnoughts. British treaty proposals for small battleships encouraged German work on a 12-inch gun (915-lb shell) and design studies starting at 17,500 tons (eight 12-inch guns in twin mounts, eight 5.9-inch guns, four 3.5-inch DP, 34 knots) with armor equaling about 30% of the displacement. But rather than build something seen as a challenge to Britain, the Germans began construction of two 18,000-ton ships (a pocket battleship design with thicker armor). The need to match France's *Dunkerque*s sent the project into metamorphosis, until it emerged as the *Scharnhorst*.

The next pocket battleship project, "Cruiser P," hovered around 21,000–31,000 tons (requiring rather large pockets) before settling at 22,145 tons with six 11.1/54 guns, two twin 5.9-inch mounts, eight 4.1-inch DP, six TT, four planes, and about 34 knots. "P1–12" worked their way into the Z Plan and sired the "O" class BC project, but the approaching war pruned away "P9–12," then eliminated "P" and "O" altogether.

NÜRNBERG (6,980 tons; nine 5.9-inch, eight 3.5-inch DP guns, twelve 21-inch TT, 120 mines; AC 2, 32 knots, 1935): a repeat *Leipzig* with only the slightest changes, ordered in the absence of new design. (The leadership wanted an 8,000-ton ship, but with so much attention diverted to CA studies, no one had time for CL work.) *Nürnberg* suffered a torpedo hit on the same day as *Leipzig,* damaging her bow. It posed no serious threat, but the widespread damage reminded the Germans of her weak structure. Half of her torpedoes were transferred to *Scharnhorst* in 1941.

The German light cruisers illustrate a curiosity of the Kriegsmarine—the large crew complements. The *Nürnberg* design called for 896 crewmen; her French counterpart, *Duguay Trouin,* needed only 578. This demand on manpower combined poorly with Germany's lack of trained seamen early in the war.

ADMIRAL HIPPER, BLÜCHER (14,050 tons; eight 8-inch, twelve 4.1-inch DP guns, twelve 21-inch TT, 128 mines; AC 3, 32.5 knots, 1939): Germany's version of the treaty cruiser. The 8-inch cruiser, a rarity before the treaty, began to proliferate in the 1930s. France's *Algérie* pushed the Germans to try their hand at the type, recently legalized for them by agreement with Britain. As things turned out, the *Hipper*s exceeded the tonnage limits more than

Like Germany's other light cruisers, the Nürnberg *spent much of her war service in the Baltic, unchallenged by enemy cruisers or heavy seas.*

the light cruisers or pocket battleships had, yet gained little thereby.

Planners reviewed the 5.9-inch gun, seriously considered a 7.5-inch gun, then settled on the conventional 8-inch caliber. The 10,000-ton limit received hardly a thought; the design began at 12,500 tons and headed immediately upward. The *Hippers* resembled miniature *Bismarcks*, both visually and in several design features, including the deck armor and triple-screw propulsion. Troublesome engines—extremely troublesome—helped reduce their range from a designed 6,500 miles at 17 knots to about 5,000 miles at 15 knots. And for all their size, they had no more combat value than the *Algérie* that inspired their construction.

Despite their formidable appearance, the *Hippers* lacked ruggedness, with only the turrets sufficiently armored. *Hipper* herself, nearly crippled by a few 6-inch rounds at Barents Sea, never returned to operations. *Blücher's* experience earned greater, though not entirely justified, derision. Struck by approximately twenty-five shells (mostly 5.9-inch) from Norwegian shore batteries at Oslo, she suffered a serious fire, and two torpedoes caused further damage. When flames detonated a 4.1-inch magazine, she went down. No design flaw caused this; she would have survived if not for her inexperi-

enced crew and the detachment of soldiers crowded on board with their ammunition.

PRINZ EUGEN, SEYDLITZ, LÜTZOW (14,680 tons; eight 8-inch, twelve 4.1-inch DP guns, twelve 21-inch TT, 128 mines; AC 3, 32 knots, 1940): a modified *Hipper* class, somewhat enlarged. Only *Prinz Eugen* reached completion. Her 1942 experience with a British torpedo testified to continued problems with hull structure. After the war, she started across the Atlantic but suffered a total engine breakdown and completed the journey at the end of a towline.

The navy selected *Seydlitz* and *Lützow* for completion with a main battery of twelve 5.9-inch guns, then switched back to the usual eight 8-inchers. When 90% complete, *Seydlitz* began conversion to an aircraft carrier with room for eight Stukas and ten Bf 109's in a narrow hangar with questionable ventilation. The Soviets purchased *Lützow* incomplete in 1940 and renamed her *Petropavlovsk*; they never got her into service with the fleet but did find time to rename her *Tallinn*.

"M" class (7,800 tons; eight 5.9-inch, four 3.5-inch DP guns, eight 21-inch TT, 160 mines; AC 2, 35.5 knots): twelve unnamed CL, with plans

53

for twelve more. While a thousand tons heavier than their predecessors, the "M's" featured weaker weaponry and no improvement in armor. Yet designers sought greater balance, a ship suited to commerce raiding on the open seas. The combination of diesel and turbine machinery (if it worked properly) would have provided good range and speed, but it had a vulnerable arrangement. The "M's" would have needed all their mobility to avoid battle with foreign rivals like *La Galissonnière*, a ship of equal tonnage but superior in firepower and protection.

Planners considered a 6.7-inch main battery, but the 5.9-inch guns in BB-style twin mounts saved weight. Habitability hardly sufficed for a design intended for long cruises. If not for the war, the navy might have reordered seven units as four "armored ships."

Interest continued in light cruisers. Several designs emerged for a ship of 8,000–9,000 tons

Germany's **Nymphe,** *the ex-Norwegian* **Haarfagre,** *armed with AA guns.*

with eight or nine 5.9-inch guns and a speed of 35–36 knots, but the navy placed no orders.

SP1–6 (4,542 tons; six 5.9-inch, two 3.5-inch DP guns, ten 21-inch TT, 140 mines; 36 knots): begun as a DD project mounting 5.9/48 guns (60° twin mounts), then reordered as "scout cruisers." Displacement rose near 6,400 tons and the DP battery doubled before the plan died.

AA Ships

The Germans renamed and rearmed these captured vessels:

Nymphe, Thetis (ex-Norwegian *Haarfagre* class): seven 4.1-inch DP guns.

Niobe (ex-Dutch *Gelderland*): six 4.1-inch DP guns.

Ariadne (ex-Dutch *IJmuiden*): six 4.1-inch DP guns.

Undine (ex-Dutch *Vliereede*): six 4.1-inch DP guns.

Adler (ex-Danish *Peder Skram*): 5.9-inch guns removed?

Nordland (ex-Danish *Niels Iuel*): three 4.1-inch DP guns.

The Danish ships performed training duties; the details of their rearmament remain obscure. The other five ships served exclusively as AA batteries, usually immobile.

The **Hipper** *had powerful guns, but her handsome appearance masked an overall mediocrity.*

Auxiliary Cruisers

These AMC operated as commerce raiders rather than convoy escorts, using their mercantile appearance to achieve surprise:

ORION (15,000 tons; six 5.9-inch, one 3-inch DP gun, six 21-inch TT, 230 mines; AC 2, 14 knots).

ATLANTIS (17,000 tons; six 5.9-inch, one 3-inch DP gun, four 21-inch TT, 92 mines; AC 2, 16 knots).

PINGUIN (17,600 tons; six 5.9-inch, one 3-inch DP gun, four 21-inch TT, 300 mines; AC 2, 16 knots).

WIDDER (16,000 tons; six 5.9-inch, one 3-inch DP gun, four 21-inch TT, 60 mines; AC 2, 14 knots).

THOR (10,000 tons, six 5.9-inch guns, two 21-inch TT, 40 mines, AC 2, 18 knots).

STIER (11,000 tons, six 5.9-inch guns, two 21-inch TT, 35 mines, AC 2, 14 knots).

KOMET (7,500 tons, six 5.9-inch guns, six 21-inch TT, 270 mines, AC 2, 16 knots).

KORMORAN (19,000 tons, six 5.9-inch guns, four 21-inch TT, 360 mines, AC 2, 18 knots).

MICHEL (11,000 tons; six 5.9-inch, one 4.1-inch DP gun, four 21-inch TT, mines; AC 2, 16 knots).

CORONEL (11,000 tons, six 5.9-inch guns, two 21-inch TT, mines, AC 4, 16 knots).

HANSA (19,200 tons; eight 5.9-inch, one 3-inch DP gun, four 21-inch TT, 150 mines; AC 1, 18 knots).

Despite initial successes and creating much fear, the raiders fared poorly; all were sunk except *Widder* and the last pair, which never completed a patrol. *Komet*, *Kormoran*, and *Michel* carried an MTB on board. *Kormoran* won the most fame, dueling the Australian cruiser *Sydney* to mutual destruction. *Stier* met a similar fate, but ingloriously: attacking an American merchantman armed with a single 4-inch gun, *Stier* suffered 35 hits and sank.

Destroyers

As a group, German destroyers were a failure. Though large—a response to the French *contre-torpilleurs*—they never attained the numbers needed for effective deployment, and after the Norwegian campaign, half of them had sunk. Designers intended their high-pressure boilers to produce maximum power for their weight, but mostly they produced aggravation and short range. Likewise, the 5.9-inch gun supposedly outclassed all enemy weaponry, but the sluggish thing merely added its great bulk to the ships' wallowing movements. Heavy seas forced *Scharnhorst*'s escorting destroyers back to base, deserting her as she steamed to her destruction.

An oddity in German destroyer design was the meager magazine capacity, with only about 120 rounds per gun. British destroyer magazines accommodated 200–250 rounds per gun, while the Americans were most lavish; including ready-use ammo, the *Farragut*s carried up to 300 rounds per gun, and late in the war, the *Fletcher*s topped 500 per gun.

No German destroyers mounted a DP main battery. They did carry mines, and most achieved more success in minelaying than they did in battle.

LEBERECHT MAASS, GEORG THIELE, MAX SCHULTZ, RICHARD BEITZEN, PAUL JACOBI, THEODOR RIEDEL, HERMANN SCHOEMANN, BRUNO HEINEMANN, WOLFGANG ZENKER, HANS LODY, BERND VON ARNIM,

ERICH GIESE, ERICH KOELLNER, FRIEDRICH IHN, ERICH STEINBRINCK, FRIEDRICH ECKOLD (2,230 tons, five 5-inch guns, eight 21-inch TT, 60 mines, 38 knots, 1937–39): the Type 1934 destroyers, also called *Z1–16*. Germany's first modern DD had many bugs, most lodged deeply in the machinery. Time after time, German squadrons had to sortie at partial strength, leaving a ship behind to nurse its boilers. During the Battle of Narvik, *Giese's* port engine decided to stop; the ship sat motionless for 13 minutes. She later got under way, but sank after twenty-some shell hits.

Wetness and structural weakness necessitated alterations. Workers trimmed the funnels to save top-weight. *Z5–16*, sometimes called the Type 1934A, entered service with these changes. Displacements varied as much as 70 tons.

The 5-inch guns threw a heavy shell with good velocity but failed to achieve their designed rate of fire (18–20 rpm).

DIETHER VON ROEDER, HANS LÜDEMANN, HERMANN KÜNNE, KARL GALSTER, WILHELM HEIDKAMP, ANTON SCHMITT (2,411 tons, five 5-inch guns, eight 21-inch TT, 60 mines, 38 knots, 1938–39): Type 1936, also called *Z17–22*, the best German destroyers until the Type 1936B. With improved sea-keeping, they were drier and more agile, and their machinery proved more reliable. *Galster*, being refitted at the time of the Norway invasion, was the only member of the class not sunk there.

Z23–30 (2,600 tons, five 5.9-inch guns, eight 21-inch TT, 60 mines, 38.5 knots, 1939–42): Type 1936A. Knowing that their destroyers would be outnumbered, German designers decided to provide increased firepower. This sound reasoning foundered amid mishandled tests that indicated the 5.9-inch gun would do the job. Plans called for a twin mount forward (with 65° elevation but no AA value) and three single mounts aft (30°). The hull dimensions didn't increase to compensate for the added weight. Consequently, the twin mount drove the bow deep into waves, drenching itself, often to the point of incapacitation. Even when the gun functioned properly, it had a slow rate of fire, and a retreat from 100-lb to 88-lb shells provided only a partial remedy. At least the ships looked impressive.

Production delays postponed the delivery of the twin mounts, and the Type 1936A ships had to start out with four single guns. Only Z23–25, 29 ever received the twin mount. Some units landed a gun to augment their light AA. Z28 converted to a flagship with extra accommodations. Mounting two single guns forward and two aft, she achieved greater seaworthiness than the others and had slightly better range, 2,087 miles at 19 knots. Displacements varied widely in this class, with some topping 3,000 tons.

Z31–34, 37–39 (2,600 tons, five 5.9-inch guns, eight 21-inch TT, 60 mines, 38.5 knots, 1942–43): Type 1936A(mod), repeats of the Type 1936A. All had the twin mount forward, though *Z31* initially had to make do with a single. Workers later removed her twin mount after battle damage and replaced it with a 4.1-inch DP gun. Postwar tests with *Z38* revealed a lack of hull strength, indicating that this issue extended beyond German heavy units.

Z35, 36, 43–45 (2,527 tons, five 5-inch guns, eight 21-inch TT, 76 mines, 38 knots, 1943–44): Type 1936B. The return to a 5-inch battery helped produce a more valuable design. Their range, 2,239 miles at 19 knots, actually was best among German DD. The Allies bombed and sank the incomplete *Z44*; *Z45* also never reached completion.

The fleet reordered the Type 1938A/Ac units *Z40–42* as scout cruisers *SP1–3*, and the order later grew to six ships.

Z46–50 (2,574 tons, six 5-inch guns, eight 21-inch TT, 60 mines, 37.5 knots): Type 1936C, never launched. They would have carried twin mounts with 52° elevation, firing a 62-lb shell to 24,060 yards. Continued tinkering with the design sent the displacement over 3,000 tons.

Z51 (2,053 tons, four 5-inch guns, six 21-inch TT, 40 mines, 36 knots): Type 1942, an experimental ship for trials with diesel engines; sunk while building. The diesels would have given at least 5,500 miles at 19 knots. Displacement rose above 2,300 tons.

Z52–56 (2,818 tons, six 5-inch guns, eight 21-inch TT, 60 mines, 37.5 knots): Type 1942C, developed from the Z51, none completed. The design, topping 3,100 tons, used the same gun as the Type 1936C.

Two other designs went unordered; the Type 1938B (1,971 tons, four 5-inch guns, eight 21-inch TT, 36.5 knots), which makes a curious comparison with the Type 1940 torpedo boat design; and the Type 1945 (2,657 tons, eight 5-inch DP guns, eight 21-inch TT, mines, 40 knots).

Captured destroyers served in a number of roles. The following received a DD rating, but only two became active:

ZH1 (ex-Dutch *Callenburgh*: 1,628 tons, five 4.7-inch DP guns, eight 21-inch TT, 24 mines, 37.5 knots, 1942).

ZF2 (ex-French *L'Opiniâtre*: 2,070 tons, five 5-inch guns, eight 21-inch TT, 37 knots, incomplete).

ZG3 (ex-Greek *Vasilefs Georgios*: 1,414 tons, four 5-inch guns, six 21-inch TT, mines?, 36 knots, 1939): also called *Hermes*.

ZN4, 5: ex-Norwegian, later re-rated as torpedo boats *TA7, 8*.

The poor condition of some sisters of *ZH1* and *ZF2* prevented their entering German service. Likewise, the sunken Polish *Wicher* never completed repairs (under the curious name *Seerose*).

Torpedo Boats

With a shortage of destroyers, the Kriegsmarine had to rely heavily on torpedo boats, which became some of its busiest surface ships. Later designs actually resembled destroyers.

Like so many other German ships, the Albatros *failed to survive the Norway operation.*

GERMANY

Germany's Wolf *and her sisterships execute precise maneuvers past the 11.1-inch guns of old battleships during a prewar exercise.*

MÖWE, ALBATROS, GREIF, SEEADLER, FALKE, KONDOR (924 tons, three 4.1-inch guns, six 21-inch TT, 30 mines, 33 knots, 1926–28): Type 1923, developed from WWI designs. Though not the best seaboats, they saw extensive service. All underwent a reduction in top-weight. The 4.1-inch mountings varied, but most elevated to 50°. *Möwe* differed slightly from the rest and could make only 32 knots.

WOLF, ILTIS, JAGUAR, LEOPARD, LUCHS, TIGER (933 tons, three 4.1-inch guns, six 21-inch TT, 30 mines, 34 knots, 1928–29): Type 1924, based on the previous class. *Luchs* and *Leopard* were rearmed with a main battery of three 5-inch guns in 1934.

T1–12 (844 tons, one 4.1-inch gun, six 21-inch TT, 30 mines, 35 knots, 1939–40): Type 1935. These evolved not from the *Wolf*s, but from the S-type MTB. Designers wanted more range and seaworthiness; instead, the T-boats became best known for their fragile hulls and irksome engines. They were poor seaboats and ugly

besides. Wartime modifications improved them somewhat. Some traded three TT for light AA. The 4.1-inch gun, mounted aft, elevated to 50°.

T13–21 (874 tons, one 4.1-inch gun, six 21-inch TT, 38 mines, 35 knots, 1941–42): Type 1937, similar to the Type 1935 and equally ugly, with even weaker hulls. They underwent similar changes.

T22–36 (1,294 tons, four 4.1-inch guns, six 21-inch TT, 59 mines, 33.5 knots, 1942–44): Type 1939, designed to operate with the fleet. The 4.1-inch guns elevated to 70°, but with no high-angle fire control. The machinery had a dispersed layout but—no surprise—it failed to perform; the ships reached only 31 knots, while their range at 19 knots dropped from the designed 2,400 miles to 2,085 miles.

T37–51 (1,493 tons, four 4.1-inch guns, six 21-inch TT, 30 mines, 34 knots): Type 1941, a Type 1939 derivative with improved machinery. None commissioned with the fleet.

T52–60 (1,418 tons, four 4.1-inch DP guns, six 21-inch TT, 30 mines, 37.25 knots): Type 1944, never built, perhaps never ordered.

T61–84 (1,931 tons, four 5-inch guns, eight 21-inch TT, 50 mines, 35 knots): Type 1940, a powerful design—DD in all but name—for construction in Dutch yards. Three began building, but none were finished.

Germany had some WWI leftovers doing various duties, such as torpedo recovery. All received T-numbers; some also got names:

T139 (533 tons, 1907): named *Pfeil* as a radio control ship.

T151, 153, 155–158 (660 tons, one 3.5-inch gun, 22 knots, 1908): at least one disarmed (*T153*, named *Eduard Jungmann*).

T185 (760 tons, light guns, 25 knots?, 1910).

T190 (755 tons, one 4.1-inch gun, 25 knots, 1911): named *Claus von Bevern*, may have carried two 19.7-inch TT.

T196 (755 tons, two 4.1-inch guns, 25 knots, 1911).

T107, 108, 110, 111 (760 tons, one 4.1-inch gun, three 19.7-inch TT, 25 knots, 1911–12): training vessels, sometimes mounting four TT (three 21-inch and one 19.7-inch).

T123 (640 tons, light guns, 22 knots, 1913): named *Komet* as a radio control ship.

Many captured destroyers and torpedo boats took TA-numbers in German service; a few also received names:

TA1–6 (ex-French *Le Fier* class: 1,087 tons, three 4.1-inch DP, six 21-inch TT, 33.5 knots).

TA7, 8 (ex-Norwegian TB, formerly rated as DD: 1,218 tons, three 4.1-inch DP guns, four 21-inch TT, 32 knots).

TA9–13 (ex-French *La Melpomène* class: 610 tons, two 3.9-inch guns, two 21.7-inch TT, 34.5 knots).

TA14 (ex-Italian *Turbine*: 1,092 tons, four 4.7-inch guns, 6 21-inch TT, 52 mines, 30 knots).

TA15 (ex-Italian *Crispi*: 955 tons, four 4.7-inch guns, four 21-inch TT, mines, 30 knots).

TA16, 19 (ex-Italian *Curtatone* class: 966 tons; 2–4 4-inch guns, six 17.7-inch or two 21-inch TT, 10 mines; 26 knots).

TA17, 18 (ex-Italian *Palestro* class: 862 tons; 3–4 4-inch guns, 0–4 17.7-inch TT, 10 mines; 25 knots).

TA20 (ex-Italian *Audace*: 629 tons, two 4-inch guns, four 17.7-inch TT, 10 mines, 25 knots).

TA21 (ex-Italian *Insidioso*: 542 tons, two 4-inch guns, two 17.7-inch TT, 24 knots).

TA22, 35 (ex-Italian *Pilo* class: 615 tons, two 4-inch guns, two 17.7-inch TT, 23 knots).

TA23, 25, 26 (ex-Italian *Ciclone* class: 925 tons, three 3.9-inch DP guns, four 17.7-inch TT, 20 mines, 25 knots).

TA24, 27–30, 36–42, 45–47 (ex-Italian *Ariete* class: 745 tons, two 3.9-inch DP guns, 3–6 17.7-inch TT, 28 mines, 31.5 knots).

TA31 (ex-Italian *Dardo*: 1,205 tons, four 4.7-inch guns, three 21-inch TT, 54 mines, 38 knots).

TA32 (ex-Yugoslavian *Dubrovnik*: 1,880 tons, four 4.1-inch DP guns, three 21-inch TT, six mines, 31 knots).

TA33, 34 (ex-Italian "Soldati" class: 1,800 tons, one 4.1-inch DP gun, three 21-inch TT, 50 mines, 38 knots).

TA43 (ex-Yugoslavian *Beograd*: 1,210 tons, four 4.7-inch guns, six 21-inch TT, 30 mines, 36 knots).

TA44 (ex-Italian *Pigafetta*: 1,900 tons, six 4.7-inch guns, four 21-inch TT, 104 mines, 29 knots).

TA48 (ex-Yugoslavian *T3*: 240 tons, two 3-inch DP guns, two 17.7-inch TT, 20 knots).

TA49 (ex-Italian *Spica* class: 799 tons, three 3.9-inch DP guns, two 17.7-inch TT, 30 mines, 34 knots).

Many of these vessels never became operational with the Germans: *TA1–8, 12, 13, 33, 34, 46, 47, 49*. Several units that did give service lacked their original speed due to age, a shortage of parts, or modification. *TA15* eventually fell to 15 knots. *TA20* probably traded her TT for 21-inchers. *TA48* provided German and Croatian service. Most of the French and Yugoslav ships came via Italian capture.

Other TB operated as patrol boats, usually without TT and thus not given TA-numbers, though most were renamed:

> Danish: *Hajen, Springeren*—not renamed, used as MS
> Polish: *Podhalanin* class—not in active service
> Italian: one "Generali" class—*SG20*
> Belgian: *West Diep*—*Reiher* (later *Warendorp*), training boat
> *Wielingen*—scrapped
> Norwegian: *Odin, Balder, Tor*—*Panther, Leopard, Tiger*
> *Gyller*—*Löwe*
> *Trygg, Snøgg*—*Zick, Zack*, each later renamed
> *Troll*—not renamed

> *Teist*—various names
> *Lom, Ørn*—*Eidechse, Schlange*
> *Hval, Delfin, Brand*—only *Delfin* not renamed
> *Hauk, Kjæk, Hvas, Falk*—N023–26, all later renamed again
> *Kvik, Lyn, Blink*—KT2–4, all later renamed again

These vessels operated with only light guns except *Löwe* (one 4-inch gun, four 21-inch TT, 24 mines), the *Panther*s (one 4-inch gun, two 21-inch TT, 24 mines), and *KT1* (one 3-inch gun, three 17.7-inch TT).

German torpedo recovery vessels, larger than foreign types, could perform combat duties. German yards built *TF1–8* (381 tons, light guns, 23.5 knots, 1941–42) and *TF9–24* (380 tons, light guns, 24 knots, 1943–44). Some captured vessels received similar designations: *TFA1–6* (ex-Danish *Glenten* and *Dragen*-class TB, rearmed); *TFA7, 8, 11* and *Oxhoft* (ex-Polish *Jaskółka*-class MS); and *TFA9, 10* (ex-Dutch TB *G16, 2*).

Motor Boats

In Germany, the MTB had a development different from that seen in other countries. The S-boat resulted not from a desire for mass-produced expendables, but from a diligent quest for an effective, well-rounded combatant. This led to a large boat—twice as large as foreign counterparts—which was practical only because the Germans produced a line of remarkable, brawny diesel engines. With its enlarged displacement, the S-boat gained more crew comfort and protection, two reload torpedoes, superior sea-keeping, long range (typically 700 miles at 35 knots, versus 480 miles at 28 knots in American PT-boats), along with stealth—a low silhouette and minimal wake. Not surprisingly, S-boats gained the most respect among German surface craft.

The Allies began capturing German small

craft after the invasions of France and Italy, though few of these vessels commissioned for active service.

Note: some German listings give warship displacement in metric tonnes (1 long ton = 1.016 metric tonnes); also, German documents concern themselves more with "design" displacement (in trial condition) than standard displacement. These factors create minor discrepancies among sources, especially for small craft and submarines.

S1 (48 tons, two 21-inch TT, 37 knots, 1939): ex-*F5*, intended for delivery with *F1–4* to Bulgaria, but retained.

S2–5 (49 tons, two 21.7-inch TT, 35.5 knots, 1938–39): the ex-Yugoslav *Orjen* class seized by the Italians, then the Germans. They may have taken on the standard 21-inch tubes.

The original *S1–5* had been sold to Spain in 1938.

S6 (59 tons, two 21-inch TT, 32 knots, 1933): pioneered diesel engines, otherwise inadequate.

S7–13 (75–80 tons, two 21-inch TT, 35–36.5 knots, 1934–35): corrected *S6*'s flaws. Speed varied with different diesel models.

S14–17 (92 tons, two 21-inch TT, 37.5 knots, 1936–38): plus one similar but unarmed boat for target duty. The design included a more reliable engine. These and most subsequent S-boats carried reload torpedoes; in some cases, six mines replaced the reloads.

S18–25 (92 tons, two 21-inch TT, 39.5 knots, 1938–39): based on the previous class.

German S-boats take refuge in a bunker. Their burly hull form and diesel power gave them unmatched sea-going capability.

S26–29 (92 tons, two 21-inch TT, 39.5 knots, 1940): based on *S18*.

S30–37, 54–61 (77 tons, two 21-inch TT, 36 knots, 1939–41): similar to the *S7*, no reload torpedoes. As the only advantage in these smaller boats was the ease of overland travel, the navy built few of them. Germany almost sold *S30–36* to China.

S38–53, 62–99, 101–135, 137, 138 (92 tons, two 21-inch TT, 39.5 knots, 1940–43): introduced an armored bridge. S73, 78, 124-126, 134 transferred to Spain in 1943. Some units had less engine power (38.5 knots).

S100, 136, 139–150, 167–218 (100–105 tons, two 21-inch TT, 42 knots, 1943–45): an improved *S38*. Individual boats differed slightly. Some had extra power (45 knots). *S145* transferred to Spain in 1943. Eight more boats, *S159–166*, remained incomplete at war's end.

S151–158 (57 tons, two 21-inch TT, 35 knots, 1941–42) were the Dutch *TM54–61*, captured incomplete. *S201, 202* (32 tons, two 21-inch TT, 34 knots, 1940—not to be confused with the like-named boats of the *S100* class) were the captured *TM52, 53*; the Germans sent this pair to Bulgaria, then used Dutch materials to make at least five more boats: one for Bulgaria, four for Romania, and possibly some others.

S219–228, 301–305 (107 tons, two 21-inch TT, 42 knots, 1944–45): much like the *S100*, with *S306, 307* finished after the surrender. Planned construction included *S308–500*. Those from *S301* on had more powerful engines (45 knots).

S701–709 (107 tons, four 21-inch TT, eight mines, 42 knots, 1944–45): similar to previous type but with all four torpedoes in tubes. *S710–800* went incomplete.

A prototype semi-submersible, the bizarre *VS5* (two 21-inch TT, 50 knots designed), quickly proved a complete and freakish failure.

LS1–12 (12 tons, two 17.7-inch TT, 42.5 knots, 1942–45): carried aboard commerce raiders. The concept inspired no great zeal, and the boats themselves showed little promise, with quirky machinery and flimsy hulls. The LS-boats thus became something of a miscellany: *LS1* had no armament, *LS2* had three mines instead of TT, *LS3* had four mines and only 38 knots, *LS5, 6* carried only depth charges, and *LS13–34* never reached completion.

KM1–34 (15 tons, 4 mines, 32 knots, 1942): KM 35, 36 incomplete, coastal units intended as offensive ML but later rearmed as TB (two 17.7in) with KS-numbers. Eight units went to Croatian crews. The Soviets captured at least two boats.

KS201–220 (13 tons, two 21-inch TT, 33 knots, 1945): coastal MTB, only seven completed.

Late in the war, the Germans realized the downside of their commitment to the big MTB: its drain on industrial and manpower resources. They threw together a dozen or so small prototypes (the smallest had one crewman, two 21-inch TT, and 21 knots), some with jet or rocket propulsion. One design, which began as a glider-borne MTB, went into production; thirty-nine of these "Hydra" boats (about eight tons, two 17.7-inch TT, 36 knots) were built.

A number of Italian MTB fell into German hands at the time of the Italian surrender. Eight units, five of which went to pro-Fascist forces, suffered no name changes. The remainder, including seven later given to Romania, became *S501–512, 601–604, 621–629* and *SA1–7*. (Some of the S-numbers later changed to SA-numbers.) All had two 17.7-inch TT except *SA1–3* (two 21-inch TT). The Germans also took up construction of Italian MTSMA-boats, completing seventy-eight, including some postwar. A few Italian MTM explosive boats gave service, and the Germans added hundreds of their own "Linse" boats (1.8 tons, one 661-lb or 882-lb charge, 35 knots, 1944).

The Germans used three captured Soviet MTB in trials.

The R-boats, the most prominent motor launches serving the Kriegsmarine, worked mostly as MS, but their versatility and excellent sea-keeping allowed them many roles. All carried light guns and up to 12 mines (or six in smaller boats).

CLASS	TONS	SPEED	YEAR
R1–16	40–50	17–20	1931–34
R17–24	115	21	1935–37
R25–40	105	21	1938–39
R41–129	120	20	1940–43
R130–150	145	19	1943–44
R151–217	105	21	1940–43
R218–270, 272–276, 288–290	135	21	1943–45
R401–424	135	22.5	1944–45

Further plans included at least twenty-two R218- and twenty-four R401-type craft. The need for a more heavily armed convoy escort led to an R301–400 design (165 tons, two 21-inch TT, 23.5 knots, 1943–44), but only the first 12 reached completion, later renamed GR301–312.

Eight commandeered boats received R-numbers as MMS, and the following war prizes received RA-numbers:

> French CH5 class—RA1, 2, 6–8
> French CH41 class—RA3–5
> British Fairmile "B" type—RA9
> British MTB314 (ex-American PT56)—RA10
> British MGB508—RA11

Italian VAS201 class—seven boats, no name changes
Italian VAS301 class—RA251–260, 263, 264
Italian VAS231 class—RA261, 262, 265–268
Dutch Mv I class—RA51–56

Germany may have completed the Dutch Mv V-X. Other captives included up to three British HDML's (one served as KJ25), Norway's MTB631 (MTB345 also?), and nine French and Spanish MTB building in France.

The navy built eight RD101 class launches (93 tons, light guns, 20 knots, 1944–45) in occupied Italy and ordered other MMS from yards in occupied territory: RA101–105 (Danish: 69 tons, six mines, 14.5 knots, 1943–44), RA106–112 (Danish: 80 tons, six mines, 14.5 knots, 1944–45), RA201–204 (Norwegian: 30 tons, light guns, 14 knots, 1943). Domestic yards built the MMS FHR1–6 (13 tons, 13 knots, 1938), FR1–12 (21 tons, 13 knots, 1938–39), MR1–4, 7 (20 tons, 12 knots, 1938–42), and KR1–3 (10–12 tons, 10 knots, 1938).

A series of hydrofoil experiments included TS1–5 (six tons, light guns, 1940–43), VS6 (about 15 tons, four mines, 47 knots, 1941), VS7 (similar to VS6), a second VS7 (13 tons, two 17.7-inch TT, 54.5 knots, 1942), VS8 (96 tons, 45 knots, 1943), and VS10, 14 (about 45 tons, two 17.7-inch or 21-inch TT, 58 knots). These projects showed more innovation than value as combatants.

Minecraft

The old "M" class (525 tons, one 4.1-inch gun, 16 knots, 1916–20): 38 Type 1915 MS—later units modified and called Type 1916—including one barracks hulk and one in Luftwaffe service. Additional units, one an auxiliary MS with the French and two serving Italy as Vieste and Crotone, returned to German command. Crotone became Kehrwieder, but Vieste had to be scuttled.

GERMANY

The development of modern minesweepers began with the M1 and provided the Kriegsmarine with some extremely capable combatants.

Some of these ships continued as MS, but many performed auxiliary duties. The armaments differed; three 3.5-inch was common. During the war, Type 1915/1916 MS served in at least nine different navies.

M1 class (760–763 tons, two 4.1-inch DP guns, 60 mines, 18 knots, 1938–42): 68 Type 1935 MS. Tough and versatile, maneuverable and seaworthy, the design had its shortcomings in range and overly complex machinery. Displacement far exceeded the intended 671–674 tons, and practical considerations made it impossible for them to carry more than 32 mines. Allegedly dual-purpose, most guns had 50° mounts. Improvements worked their way into the production run, creating several subtypes. Spain license-built the design as the *Bidasoa* class.

M261 class (534 tons, one 4.1-inch gun, 17.2 knots, 1942–45): 128 Type 1940 MS, more easily built and longer-ranged than *M1*. Most had 35° mounts, and a few took on a second gun. Optional equipment included 12 mines or two

21-inch TT for training purposes. The Germans intended a few of these ships for Romania; these commissioned postwar.

M601 class (573 tons, two 4.1-inch DP guns, 16.7 knots, 1944–45): 18 Type 1943 MS, further refinement with an eye to rapid production. Different weaponry was installed aboard: two 21-inch TT or 24 mines or a battery of AA rockets (as useless as any other navy's AA rockets). The guns elevated to 70°. Like other German MS, they were good seaboats that handled well.

Though they completed only 214, the Germans had planned 950 of these three modern MS classes.

KSB1–27 (1,588 tons, two 4.1-inch guns, 12.5 knots): MS, canceled.

Germany converted about 126 merchant vessels to act as MS. Several WWI sweepers of the FM-type (about 165–180 tons, originally one 3.5-inch gun, 14 knots, 1918–22) existed in various European waterways; one re-entered German service as a submarine hunter, some others as noncombatants. A dozen or so former F-type motor minesweepers (less than 20 tons, 1917–19) performed miscellaneous jobs: police, customs, etc.

"A" through "H" (5,450 tons, eight 4.1-inch DP guns, 400 mines, 28 knots): ML, none completed.

About 44 merchantmen served in minelaying duties, including some ships taken from France and Italy. About 20 small vessels served as defensive ML and powered mine barges; many became trainers or tenders.

When Germany gained control of Austria and Czechoslovakia, it gained their riverine forces, including minecraft. During the war, many minecraft were captured and renamed:

Italian: *Fasana*—not renamed
    Albona class—two renamed
    five old RD-craft—most given M-numbers
    at least four auxiliary minecraft—most renamed
British: one WWI "Hunt" class—renamed twice
Yugoslavian: *Zmaj*—*Drache*
    two *Malinska* class—served with Italian names
Dutch: three *Jan van Amstel* class—*M551, 553*
    M1, 4—various renamings, used mostly as tugs
Danish: six *Søbjørnen* class—only four served, all renamed
    Lindormen—*Vs1401* (later renamed again)
    Kvintus—*Fürstenburg*
    Lossen, Sixtus, Laaland, Lougen—not renamed
    six *MS1* class—given Vs-numbers
Norwegian: *Otra, Rauma*—*Togo, Kamerun*
    Glommen, Laugen—*NKi01, 05*

Olav Tryggvason—*Albatros* (later *Brummer*)
Greek: three auxiliary ML—*Uj2103, 2106, 2110*

Of these vessels, only *Drache* underwent serious alteration (1,870 tons, two 4.1-inch—later 3.5-inch—DP guns, 400 mines, one helicopter, 15 knots). She should not be confused with the training ship *Drache* (790 tons, six 4.1-inch guns, 13 knots, 1908).

Escorts and Patrol Craft

BEOWULF class (496 tons, one 3.5-inch gun, 10.2 knots, 1912–21): twelve trawlers acquired prewar, also used for minesweeping.

WESER, ELBE (600 tons, one 3.5-inch DP gun, 15 knots, 1931): fishery protection vessels.

BREMSE (1,435 tons, four 5-inch guns, 27 knots, 1931): training ship used for escort and minelaying (maximum load, about 200 small mines).

GRILLE (2,560 tons, three 5-inch guns, 228 mines, 26 knots, 1935): yacht, used as a testbed for the high-pressure boilers that caused so many problems in German ships.

BRUMMER (2,410 tons; four 4.1-inch DP, two 3.5-inch DP guns, 150 mines; 20 knots, 1936): another versatile training ship. She could carry as many as eight DP guns of either caliber.

F1–10 (712 tons, two 4.1-inch guns, 28 knots, 1936): minesweeping escorts. They could also ship a load of 62 mines (or more, depending on the type). Designers managed a machinery dispersal layout, but otherwise they had little success. The unusual requirement for these craft to operate with fleet units resulted in irascible machinery. As minesweepers, they gave mediocre service. As anti-submarine vessels, they proved nearly useless. They lacked range, sea-keeping, steadiness, and stability. The class began conversion for tending and training duties before the war, landing one or both guns.

HELA (2,315 tons, two 4.1-inch guns, 19 knots, 1939): yacht also used as a tender.

KFK1 class (110 tons, light guns, nine knots, 1942–45): 630 units completed of 1,072 planned. The layout, based on a fishing design, allowed for peacetime conversion for fishing work. Construction orders went to yards all over Europe, from the Adriatic to Belgium, even to Sweden. Their versatility left the KFK's susceptible to rampant renaming as the Germans designated them to various tasks: M-numbers for minesweeping, V-numbers for coastal patrol, and so on. Desperation caused many to specialize as SC (given Uj-numbers), the duty which suited them least. Three units transferred to Romania. A number of KFK's were among the small craft captured by the Allies in 1944–45.

MZ1, plus eleven planned (281 tons, two 3.5-inch DP guns, two 21-inch TT, 14 knots, 1944): "MZ" indicating "multi-purpose," with definitely too much "multi." As an escort intended to fend off mines, planes, subs, and motor gunboats, she then took on torpedo weaponry—it was too much for one design. Problems arose at once, and corrective measures added some tons despite all attempts at weight-saving. The machinery was underpowered and left her struggling to hit 13.5 knots.

Designers applied themselves to altering her sisters. Already under construction, *MZ2–4* received minor changes but never reached completion. Thorough redesign gave *MZ5–12* a lengthened hull (359 tons?) with new machinery to add some range and regain the lost speed; these plans never emerged from the drawing board. *MZ1's* range (2,100 miles at 12 knots) sufficed for her coastal duties. Armament included 3.4-inch rockets (mostly for AA), a late-war system that served poorly aboard a few vessels.

Little *UZ32, 33* (60 tons, 14 knots, 1920) and *UZ(S)18* (26 tons, 27 knots, 1929) remained available with their negligible combat value. Another former UZ-boat lasted into the

Small craft form the cornerstone of any fleet. All major navies adapted fishing and trawling designs for military uses, as in the case of this German KFK-craft.

war years as a rescue vessel. With increasing pressure from Allied subs, the Germans started fitting depth charges aboard small transports for escort duty.

KUJ1 class (830 tons, one 3.5-inch DP gun, 12.75 knots, 1943–45): about 42 trawlers planned, only half of them completed.

Requisitions supplemented the navy's *Beowulfs*, Kuj-craft, and KFK-craft. Approximately 2,110 trawlers and fishing vessels served as harbor craft and local patrol boats, 12 as weather ships, 871 as auxiliary minesweepers, 231 as Uj-boats, 801 as auxiliary patrol boats, 473 as auxiliary coastal patrol boats, 198 as coast guard boats, 158 as river security craft, 507 as smoke batteries, 79 as balloon boats, and 252 doubling as smoke and balloon boats. This list includes some duplications, but it gives an idea of the numbers involved. During the war, at least three German trawlers fell into Allied hands, two to the British and one to the Norwegians.

G1–24 (1,324 tons, four 4.1-inch DP guns, 21 knots): none completed; an improvement over the *F1*-class escort. The "G" class showed better sea-keeping, adequate speed for most duties, and a stronger gun armament in DP mounts.

Some of the following war prizes were renamed, and some underwent modifications as noted:

> Danish: *P1–38*, nine *K1* class—not renamed
> > *Hvidbjørnen*—*Vs*?
> > *Freja*—*Südpol*
> > *Hejmdal*—*Nerger*
> > *Ingolf*—*Sleipner* (?)
> British: seven trawlers—all renamed
> French: four "Flower" class—*PA1–4* (930 tons, one 4.1-inch gun, 16 knots)
> > four *Sans Souci* class—*SG1–4* (1,372 tons, two or three 4.1-inch DP guns, 16.72 knots, 1942-43)
> > five *Élan* and *Chamois* class (and two

incomplete)—*SG14* class (590 tons, two 4.1-inch DP guns, 20 knots)
> > *Dédaigneuse*—*M6020* (previously Italian *FR56*)
> > *Yser* (also two hulked sisters)—*SG37*?
> > *Ancre*—not used
> > *Granit*—*SG26*
> > one *Arras* class—*M6060*
> > *CH4*—*Uj6077*
> > perhaps one *CH25* class—?
> > four *Pétrel* class—various designations
> > about 17 auxiliaries—various designations
> Italian: four Japanese-built GB—three given GA-numbers
> > 17 *Gabbiano* class—*Uj201* class
> Polish: *Komendant Pilsudski*—*Heisternest*
> Norwegian: *Gor*, *Tyr*, *Brage*, *Nor*, *Vidar*, *Vale*, and *Uller*—not renamed
> > *Senja*—renamed five times (proving that the Germans could out-rename anyone)
> Dutch: 10 (?) *Braga* class—most scrapped
> > three incomplete GB—*K1–3* (1,200 tons, four 4.7-inch DP guns, 200 mines, 14.5–18 knots, 1942–43)
> Belgian: *Zinnia*—*Barbara* (1,200 tons, 3 4.1 inch guns, 17 knots)
> > *Artevelde*—*Lorelei*, later *K4* (1,640 tons, three 4.1-inch DP guns, 120 mines, 28.5 knots)

Apart from the Dutch and Belgian captives, the Germans planned some K-boats of their own in the late 1930s. Changing priorities led to the cancellation of *K1–4* (1,390 tons, four 4.1-inch DP guns, 18.5 knots) and *K I–IV* (2,100 tons, four 5-inch guns, two 21-inch TT, 24 knots).

Among other surface craft that did see service, the icebreaker *Castor* (plus one sister ship incomplete: 5,150 tons, one 4.1-inch DP gun, 15 knots, 1940) could carry four guns and serve in AA training. Several navies adapted landing craft as GB, but the Germans planned *MAL1–47*

(140–185 tons, 6.5–8.5 knots, 1943–44) with GB duty in mind, mounting 3.5-inch guns (some DP) or sometimes 3-inch or 4.1-inch guns; four transferred to Finland before the Soviets captured them.

The Danube flotilla included many small craft, such as the river GB *FM1, 2* (17 tons, two 3-inch guns, 17 knots); most Austrian and Czech craft continued in German service, among them *Bechalaren* (ex-*Masaryk*, later *GB1*) and *Birago* (ex-*Siofok*). A number of riverine units came by capture in Poland: the gunboat *Nieuchwytny* (renamed *Pionier*), a pair of KU-type launches, a "Z" class gunboat (renamed *91*), and perhaps a *Sierpinek*-class patrol craft—these last two taken from Soviet forces. Many of these vessels, plus some noncombatants, fell into Soviet hands in 1945.

Submarines

The German submarine force, 1,200 units strong, established an impressive record: 2,840 merchantmen sunk (over 14,000,000 gross tons) plus 150 warships. They represented Germany's only hope for naval victory; however, despite the level of destruction they inflicted, they ultimately failed. Their losses reached nearly 800 boats, and three fourths of Germany's submariners died. The two primary factors in this failure were the Allies' ability to sustain heavy losses and the Germans' inability to outpace Allied technology.

Forbidden by the Versailles Treaty to build a U-boat fleet, the Germans in the 1920s and 1930s took advantage of the nations that wanted submarines but lacked experience with their construction. German-led design teams, using WWI boats as models, developed several units, including the Finnish *Vetehinen*, *Vesikko*, and *Saukko* and the Turkish *Gür* and *Birindci Inönü*. This foundation enabled the Germans to prepare successful designs by 1934, when they renounced the ban on U-boat construction.

In the eyes of Karl Dönitz, commander of the submarine fleet, his U-boats' one purpose was the destruction of the enemy merchant fleet. But the first months of the war saw little progress toward that goal. One reason was the small number of boats operational at the time, and many of these boats had been diverted to other operations, especially the Norway invasion. To make matters worse, torpedoes began to malfunction in large numbers. The Germans addressed this problem at once, unlike the Americans who encountered the same situation in 1942.

As these initial difficulties passed, and when the fall of France provided new bases with direct access to the Atlantic, the U-boat threat became truly serious. The Allies responded with new devices and techniques: radar, sonar (asdic), long-range air patrols, escort carriers, Hedgehog and Squid—constant refinements kept the Allies one step ahead.

A decisive factor, of which the Germans remained completely unaware, was the excellence of Allied intelligence—ULTRA changed everything. Supplemented by American efforts, Britain's cracking the enemy's top-secret Enigma code thwarted the Germans' best efforts. A promising idea, like Dönitz's wolf-pack tactics, simply served to gather U-boats where they could be dealt with more easily.

Despite the risks involved, a submarine must surface to recharge its batteries, replenish the crew's air supply, and search effectively for targets, and the Allies' radar-equipped aircraft dramatically heightened the hazard. An increase in U-boat AA weaponry gained nothing, and radar detectors became useless when the enemy changed the radar wavelength. The obvious solution lay in finding a way for the boats to stay submerged indefinitely. By experimenting with equipment seized from the Dutch, Germany perfected the snorkel, allowing free access to air while moving at periscope depth. This gave the U-boats a great advantage, but again, refined radar became sensitive enough to detect even a snorkel. Ultimately, the Germans began to develop boats with machinery nearly independent of the atmosphere. The need for air decreased, while high underwater speed allowed the subs to search while submerged and evade (or even outrun) the surface escorts.

But these advancements came too late. The boats with Walther propulsion and augmented battery power barely had time to debut before the war ended.

This section attempts to list all the U-boats commissioned in the Kriegsmarine. But with numerous subs nearing completion in May 1945, much uncertainty remains about which boats were actually commissioned. The mass scuttling of completed and nearly completed boats adds to the confusion. Also, as designs evolved, their features sometimes overlapped, making it hard to say whether a sub was, for example, a Type IXC or a Type IXC40.

Type IA, two boats: U25, 26 (848/967 tons, one 4.1-inch gun, six 21-inch TT or 28 mines, 17.75/8.3 knots, 1936): development of the *Gür* design and predecessor of the Type IX. Crash dive time was 30 seconds.

Type IIA, six boats: U1–6 (250/298 tons, three 21-inch TT or 12 mines, 13/6.9 knots, 1935); Type IIB, 20 boats: U7–24, 120, 121 (275/324 tons, three 21-inch TT or 12 mines, 13/6.9 knots, 1935–36); Type IIC, eight boats: U56–63 (286/336 tons, three 21-inch TT or 12 mines, 12/7 knots, 1938–40); Type IID, 16 boats: U137–152 (309/358 tons, three 21-inch TT or 12 mines, 12.7/7.4 knots, 1940–41): developed from the *Vesikko* design. These maneuverable boats had strong hulls and good range for their size, but the trends led toward bigger boats better suited to Atlantic patrols. By foregoing their torpedo load, they could lay 12 mines through their torpedo tubes. China ordered *U120, 121,* but the Germans seized them during construction. Three boats—*U9, 18, 24*—having sunk in port, fell into Soviet hands in 1944 but gave no further wartime service.

Type VIIA, 10 boats: U27–36 (616/733 tons, one 3.5-inch gun, five 21-inch TT or 22 mines, 16/8 knots, 1936–37); Type VIIB, 24 boats: U45–55, 73–76, 83–87, 99–102 (741/843 tons, five 21-inch TT or 26 mines, 17.25/8 knots, 1938–40); Type VIIC, 591 boats: U69–72, 77–82, 88–98, 132–136, 201–212, 221–232, 235–291, 301–329, 331–394, 396–458, 465–473, 475–486, 551–683, 701–722, 731–768, 771–779, 821, 822, 825–828, 901, 903–907, 921–930, 951–995, 997–1010, 1013–1025, 1051–1058, 1063-1065 (749/851 tons, five 21-inch TT or 26 mines, 17/7.6 knots, 1940–44); Type VIIC41, 70 boats: U292–300, 1101–1110, 1131, 1132, 1161–1172, 1191–1210, 1271–1279, 1301–1308 (747/847 tons, five 21-inch TT or 26 mines, 17/7.6 knots, 1944–45); Type VIID, six boats: U213–218 (950/1063 tons, five 21-inch TT, 15 mines, 16.7/7.3 knots, 1941–42); Type VIIF, four boats: U1059–1062 (1067/1162 tons, five 21-inch TT, 17/7.6 knots, 1943): developed from the *Vetehinen*, these boats formed the bulk of Germany's underwater fleet. A dozen units mounted only three or four TT.

The Type VII resulted from an order specifying a combination of offensive power with good strength and handling, all in the least possible displacement to facilitate mass production. The final design attained all these virtues (at some expense to habitability), making these among the best submarines of the war—not spectacular, but well balanced. The usual dive time was 30 seconds.

The boats quickly proved popular, though the first group lacked somewhat in range. The B-subtype corrected this while also adding agility with twin rudders. The C's went into mass production only slightly changed. Stronger hulls and lighter machinery distinguished the C41 boats, some of which could not lay mines. The VIIF provided torpedo replenishment for other boats. The VIID functioned mainly as a minelayer capable of enlarging its load with 26 tube-laid mines. The number of tube-laid mines in German subs varied depending on the model, for example, up to 33 small mines for the Type VIIA and up to 39 for the Type VIID.

The Germans planned more than six hundred additional Type VII boats, including many of an improved Type VIIC42 (983/1082 tons). But the rapid advances in submarine technology rendered the design obsolete, and Type VII construction was phased out.

In 1942, those boats with 3.5-inch guns had them removed. The Type VIIs received their first snorkels in 1943.

U428–430, 746–750, and *1161* transferred to Italy as *S1–9* (not respectively). The British captured *U570* and renamed her *Graph*; they also managed to board *U744* and *U1024* but couldn't prevent their sinking. The Soviets salvaged *U250* but didn't make her operational. *U573* suffered internment in Spain; the Spaniards later purchased her as *G7*.

Type IXA, eight boats: U37–44 (1,016/1,135 tons, one 4.1-inch gun, six 21-inch TT or 44 mines, 18.2/7.7 knots, 1938–39); Type IXB, 14 boats: U64, 65, 103–111, 122–124 (1,034/1,159 tons, one 4.1-inch gun, six 21-inch TT or 44 mines, 18.2/7.3 knots, 1939–41); Type IXC, 54 boats: U66–68, 125–131, 153–166, 171–176, 501–524 (1,102/1,213 tons, one 4.1-inch gun, six 21-inch TT or 44 mines, 18.25/7.3 knots, 1941–44); Type IXC40, 87 boats: U167–170, 183–194, 525–550, 801–806, 841–846, 853–858, 865–870, 877–881, 889, 1,221–1,235 (1,126/1,227 tons, one 4.1-inch gun, six 21-inch TT or 44 mines, 18.25/7.3 knots, 1942–44); Type IXD1, two boats: U180, 195 (1,585/1,771 tons, 15.8/6.9 knots, 1942); Type IXD2, 29 boats: U177–179, 181, 182, 196–200, 847–852, 859–864, 871–876, 883 (1,590/1,775 tons, one 4.1-inch gun, six 21-inch TT or 48 mines, 19.2/6.9 knots, 1942–44): excellent seaboats with long range (13,850 miles at 10 knots in the IXC40), Germany's most effective ocean-going boats, more habitable than the Type VII. They could dive in 35 seconds. The mine load could include up to 66

small mines in some boats, though not all had minelaying equipment. Some of the IXD boats carried an FA 330 autogyro kite which, if the wind was right, could lift a lookout up to 300 feet. Most boats with 4.1-inch guns landed them.

The IXD1 boats entered service with the usual weaponry, greater surface speed (20.8 knots), and engine problems; by 1944, disarmed and re-engined, they became freighters. *U883* is sometimes classed as a Type IXD42, an improved Type IXD2.

Planned construction included more than 150 further Type IX subs. Several boats transferred to Japan; *U181, 195, 862, 511, 1224* became *I501, 506, 502* and *RO500, 501*. The Americans captured *U505* and gave her the name *Nemo*. The British boarded *U110* and removed her Enigma code machine and other material before she went down.

Type XB, eight boats: U116–119, 219, 220, 233, 234 (1,735/2,143 tons, one 4.1-inch gun, two 21-inch TT, 66 mines, 16.4/7 knots, 1941–44): ML type chosen over a Type XA design, rather vulnerable due to their size and sluggishness. Most of their careers involved supply runs, and they landed their deck guns. The Japanese took *U219* and renamed her *I505*.

Type XIV, ten boats: U459–464, 487–490 (1,661/1,901 tons, light guns, 14.4/6.3 knots, 1941–43): based on the Type VIIC, "milk cows" used as replenishment boats for other subs. An additional 14 units were planned but not built.

Type XXI, 118 boats: U2501–2546, 2548, 2551, 3001–3035, 3037–3041, 3044, 3501–3508, 3510–3530 (1,595/1,790 tons, six 21-inch TT, 12 mines, 15.5/17.2 knots, 1944–45): arguably the best submarines of the war, fast and quiet. Their underwater speed, slightly less than in the Walther boats, stemmed from less radical measures—streamlining and increased electrical power. Lavishly equipped with radar, sonar, and hydrophones, these boats could prowl for targets while submerged. They could even attack without resorting to a periscope, and then flee at a speed that rendered Allied sonar ineffective. Hydraulic gear greatly speeded torpedo reloading. Intended for lengthy patrols, the boats were quite habitable by German standards. The boats ranged to 15,500 miles at 10 knots and dove in a mere 18 seconds.

However, the design came with several problems, some of them potentially serious. When surfaced, they had a rather wide turning radius and poor sea-keeping—crewmen referred to the bridge as the "bathtub" due to its willingness to collect seawater. The haste which characterized their design and construction compromised their hull strength and hydraulics gear. The need to provide specialized crew training delayed effective deployment long after the first unit reached completion in June 1944. In establishing new standards of underwater speed, the Type XXIs had great significance for submarine design, but their combat service barely rated a footnote.

The Germans set aside an additional 1,144 U-numbers for Type XXI boats, though only a fraction of this number began construction. Planners considered and rejected numerous subtypes (up to XXIT), including milk cows, transports, and boats with enlarged torpedo arrays.

Type XXIII, 62 boats: U2321–2371, 4701–4707, 4709–4712 (230/254 tons, two 21-inch TT, 9.75/12.5 knots, 1944–45): similar in propulsion to the Type XXI, little more than high-performance midgets carrying only two torpedoes. Their range of 4,300 miles at six knots suited them for coastal work only. They had good prospects for success, given their speed and incomparable dive time—a mere nine seconds—but only six boats became operational in the war's last days. U2370 may have scuttled before completion. Construction plans included at least 918 additional units.

Turkey ordered a sub (*Batiray*: 1,044/1,357 tons,

one 4.1-inch gun, six 21-inch TT, 18/8.4 knots, 1939) from a German yard, but with the onset of hostilities, Germany commandeered her and renamed her *UA*. The Kriegsmarine gave new names to the following captured boats:

British: *Seal—UB*
Norwegian: *B5, 6—UC1, 2*
Dutch: *O8—UD1*
　　O12—UD2
　　O25–27—UD3–5
French: *L'Africaine, La Favorite*
　　L'Andromède—UF1–3
Italian: *R10–12, 7–9—UIT1–6*
　　Bario, Litio, Sodio, Potassio, Rame,
　　　Ferro, Piombo, Zinco—UIT7–14
　　Sparide, Murena, Nautilo, Grongo—
　　　UIT15, 16, 19, 20
　　CM1, 2—UIT17, 18
　　Giuseppe Finzi—UIT21
　　Alpino Bagnolini, Reginaldo Giuliani—
　　　UIT22, 23
　　Comandante Cappellini—UIT24
　　Luigi Torelli—UIT25

UF1, 3 and *UIT1–16, 18–20* never became operational, nor did several additional boats captured in damaged condition. Other French units, seized in the Mediterranean in 1942, went to Italian command; in turn, a number of ex-Italian midget boats transferred to Romania following Italy's surrender. The Japanese took *UIT24, 25* as *I503, 504*.

The Germans developed many designs that went unbuilt or unordered or served only in trials (as with many later types featuring high submerged speed due to Walther engines or other means). Note the use below of metric tonnes. In many cases, the tonnage and speed are estimates.

Type III (initially 970/? tonnes, two 4.1-inch guns, six 21-inch TT, 42 mines, 18.5/8 knots; later 1,500/2,000 tonnes, one 4.1-inch gun, six

21-inch TT, 48 mines, 15.5/7 knots): none ordered. This began in 1934 as a development of the Type IA, then grew as planners tried to fit two LS-type MTB aboard in dry hangar spaces.

Type IV (2,500/? tonnes): none ordered; boats designed to supply and repair other U-boats.

Type V (300/320 tonnes, 26/30 knots): the first Walther project; no orders placed.

Type VI (850/? tonnes): no orders; a steam-powered development of the Type IA. Like the previous three designs, it died around 1934.

Type VIII: canceled early, perhaps in favor of the Type IX.

Type XI (3,140/3,630 tonnes, four 5-inch guns, 6–8 21-inch TT, AC 1, 23/7 knots): cruiser-submarines U112–115 ordered and canceled in 1939. Twin mounts carried the standard 5/45 weapon but with a bit more elevation than in DD mounts.

Type XII (2,041/? tonnes, one 4.1-inch gun, eight 21-inch TT, 22/10 knots): nine boats planned in 1939, but none ordered.

Type XIII (400/? tonnes, four 21-inch TT, 15/? knots): no orders, a 1939 development of the Type II.

Type XV (5,000/? tonnes) and Type XVI (3000/? tonnes): none ordered; supply and repair boats, too large and therefore vulnerable.

The boat V80 (73/76 tonnes, 4/28 knots, 1940) was the first completed with Walther engines. With no armament, she served a couple of years in trials. An enlarged prototype named V300 (later U791: 610/655 tonnes, two 21-inch TT, 9.3/19 knots) never reached completion. Construction of the Type XVII family then

German submarines sank unprecedented amounts of shipping and suffered unprecedented losses.

began. First, U792, 793 of the Type Wa 201 (277/309 tonnes, 9/25 knots, 1944) and U794, 795 of the Type WK 202 (plus five not completed: 236/259 tonnes, 9/26 knots, 1944), known collectively as the Type XVIIA, performed trials without ever shipping the two intended TT. The Type XVIIB boats (U1405–1407, plus U1408–1416 not completed: 312/ 337 tonnes, two 21-inch TT, 8.8/25 knots, 1944) had torpedoes but never made any war patrols. The Type XVIIG (U1081–1092: 314/345 tonnes, two 21-inch TT, 8.8/25 knots) and Type XVIIK (U798–800: 308/340 tonnes, unarmed, 14/16 knots) went unfinished. For all its promise, Walther propulsion never proved practical.

Type XVIII (1,485/1,652 tonnes, six 21-inch TT, 18.5/24 knots): U796, 797; large Walther boats begun in 1943, not completed.

Type XIX (2,000 tonnes maximum displacement, light guns, 14.5/6.5 knots): none ordered; a freighter design of 1942.

Type XX (2,708/2,962 tonnes, light guns, 12.7/5.8 knots): a freighter design begun in 1943; U1601–1800 not completed.

Type XXII (155/170 tonnes, three 21-inch TT, 7/20.1 knots): based on V80; U1153, 1154 and seventy others planned, none built.

Type XXIV (1,800/? tonnes, fourteen 21-inch TT, 14/22 knots): a 1943 Walther project; no orders.

Type XXV (160/? tonnes, two 21-inch TT, ?/9 knots): 1943 project for boats with electric propulsion only; none ordered.

Type XXVIA-E (785–1,050/865–1,124 tonnes, 8–12 21-inch TT, 13–15/15.8–22.5 knots): various designs that lost out to the Type XXVIW, but development continued into the Type XXIX.

Type XXVIW (842/926 tonnes, ten 21-inch TT, 11/24 knots): Walther boats *U4501–4600* not completed.

The Type XXVII (*Hecht*) and XXVIIB (*Seehund*) are described in the section on miniature subs. *Seehund* spawned many proposed improvements in 1944, but none were built. *U6251, 6252* were electric-only versions. Project K (16.4/? tonnes, two 21-inch TT, 9.5/10 knots) had closed-cycle diesels; the related Type 227 earned some U-numbers but no completions (*U5188–5193, 6244–6248*: 17/? tonnes, two 21-inch TT, 8/10.3 knots). The Type XXVIIF Walther version (9.2/? tonnes, one 21-inch TT, ?/22.6 knots) aspired to high speed.

Type XXVIII (200/? tonnes, four 21-inch TT, ?/10 knots): Walther boats; none ordered.

Type XXIX, many subtypes (630–1,060/700–1,100+ tonnes, 8–12 21-inch TT, 11.8–18/13.8–21.5 knots): no orders.

Type XXXA (1,180/? tonnes, twelve 21-inch TT, 14.6/15.6 knots) and Type XXXB (1170/? tonnes, twelve 21-inch TT, 14.6/15.8 knots): none ordered.

Type XXXI (1,200/? tonnes, twelve 21-inch TT, 14.3/16.4 knots): rated more highly than the XXX's, but none ordered.

Type XXXII (20/? tonnes, two 21-inch TT): electric *Seehund* again.

Type XXXIII (360/? tonnes, four 21-inch TT, 9.5/11.5 knots): no orders.

Type XXXIV (90/? tonnes, two 21-inch TT, 12/21 knots): no orders.

Type XXXV (1,000/? tonnes, eight 21-inch TT, ?/22 knots) and Type XXXVI (1,000/? tonnes, ten 21-inch TT, ?/22 knots): Walther boats; no orders.

Mounting desperation in 1944 prompted the Germans to develop a series of human torpedoes and midget boats, some large enough to receive U-numbers. The craft managed few successes (perhaps thirty vessels sunk or damaged) and suffered frightful losses. Most of the following descriptions include no distinction between surfaced and submerged displacement.

NEGER type (about 200 boats: 2.75 tons, one 21-inch TT, 4.2/3.2 knots, 1944–45): not completely submersible, little more than two torpedoes slung together, one containing a warhead, the other containing a crewman. A plexiglass dome afforded limited visibility when not completely fouled with oil or debris. It could manage bursts of speed up to 20 knots.

MARDER type (about 300 boats: three tons, one 21-inch TT, 4.2/3.2 knots, 1944–45): a refined *Neger* capable of underwater travel. Without improved visibility, targeting remained a random act.

The Allies captured a few *Marders* and *Negers* but had the good sense not imitate them.

The next *Neger* development (*Hai*: 3.5 tons, 1944) resulted only in the completion of one prototype. The design attempted greater speed and range, but in practice proved nearly unmanageable.

GERMANY

BIBER type (324 boats: 6.2 tons, two 21-inch TT or two mines, 6.5/5.25 knots, 1944–45): more seaworthy design inspired by captured British Welman craft. While it looked more like an actual submarine, its submerged performance remained problematic, and torpedoes had to be launched on the surface. The rudimentary periscope had little value.

The Germans made ambitious plans for the *Biber*. Three U-boats, each fitted with two midgets, tried to attack the BB *Arkhangelsk* in the Kola Inlet but failed. A plan to air-drop a *Biber* into the Suez Canal never went through.

Unlike previous craft, the *Biber* supplemented its electric motor with a gasoline engine; the attendant threat of asphyxia made the *Biber* virtually a suicide weapon. Attempts to improve the design (adding a second crewman, installing a closed-cycle engine) came to an end with the war.

MOLCH type (393 boats: 11 tons, two 21-inch TT or two? mines, 4.3/5 knots, 1944–45): resembled an overgrown torpedo, electric-powered only. Though intended to stay under the surface, the *Molch* had difficulty getting fully submerged.

Molch and *Biber* operations represented considerable risk with little hope for success. In March 1945, for example, 56 sorties led to 42 losses without sinking a single target. They apparently had better luck with mines rather than torpedoes. The torpedoes in fact proved most effective against the midgets themselves, as accidents claimed dozens of boats. A couple of units managed to become Allied trophies.

HECHT type (11.8 tons, one 21-inch TT, 5.75/6 knots, 1944): unsuccessful, but substantial enough for the title Type XXVIIA and the assignment of numbers. Fifty-three boats reached completion, *U2111–2113, 2251–2291* among them. Orders included *U2114–2200, 2205–2250, 2292–2300*.

The first three units were adapted to carry a mine. Another proposal included a capsule for three commandos and a rubber boat. Though inspired by British X-craft recovered in Norway, these two-man electric boats proved so difficult to operate that they served only in training.

SEEHUND type (14.9 tons, two 21-inch TT, 7.75/6 knots, 1944–45): Type XXVIIB5 two-man boats assigned numbers *U5001–U6442* with 285 completions (likely including *U5001–5118, 5251–5394*). Protracted tinkering with the *Hecht* led, for the first time, to a design resembling a scaled-down fleet sub with diesel and electric drives and a worthwhile periscope. This made them the best of Germany's midgets. Even so, 142 Seehund sorties netted at most nine ships at a cost of 35 losses. The boats could dive within three seconds; however, as with previous types, their machinery left them slower than the slowest moving targets.

In an attempt to gain higher speeds, the navy experimented with *Delfin* (two prototypes: 2.8 tons, one 21-inch TT or one 1102-lb mine, 19/15 knots, 1944); a follow-up *Grosser Delfin* (7.5 tons, possibly two 21-inch TT or two mines, 18 knots submerged) went incomplete. The *Schwertwal* prototype (11–14.7 tons, two 21-inch TT or one mine, ?/25–30 knots) may have reached completion; derived from the Type XXVIIF with proposed weaponry to include AS rocket torpedoes, the *Schwertwal* had more speed than its crew could safely manage. Nevertheless, manic designers considered fastening a pair of improved *Schwertwal* hulls together to create a *Manta* (four TT or ? mines, 50/30 knots).

The bizarre two-man *Seeteufel* project (20 tons, two 21-inch TT, 10/8 knots, 1944) equipped a mini-sub with tracks, a sort of submersible amphibian. The prototype showed excellent handling underwater, but land travel (intended to obviate dock facilities) involved some difficulties. Germany's surrender halted further development.

GREAT BRITAIN

(Plus the major Commonwealth combatants, including: **AUSTRALIA, INDIA, NEW ZEALAND, CANADA, SOUTH AFRICA**)

Between the wars, no country strived more zealously for disarmament than Britain, but these noble and largely unilateral efforts also served to compromise the country's war readiness. For example, the British argument for a 14-inch gun limit convinced only themselves, and the *King George V* was thus undergunned.

Nonetheless, when war broke out, the Royal Navy remained the world's largest, armed also with the richest of naval traditions. When the British found themselves alone against the Axis, that great navy was stretched to its limits; but because it was great, it held out until relieved by America's mobilization.

One of the Royal Navy's chief advantages was its technology. Carrier aviation brought the submarine's worst enemy to the farthest reaches of the ocean. Squid, entering service late in 1943, established itself as the war's best AS system. Britain's electronics industry flourished, though its small size left individual ships with outdated equipment right through 1945. Its

Ordnance

GUN	SW*	RANGE	CLNG	FC	NOTES
16/45	2,375	40,560		30	*Lion*s
	2,048	39,780		35–40	*Nelson*s
15/42	1,938	33,550		30	30° mount, *Renown*, *Vanguard*, other BB
	1,938	26,650		30	20° mount, new shell; "R" class, other BB
	1,920	30,180		30	30° mount, old shell; monitors, *Hood*
	1,920	24,350		30	20° mount, *Repulse* and BB
14/45	1,590	38,560		30	*King George V*s
13.5/45	1,400	23,740		40	*Iron Duke*
8/50	256	30,650		11	CA
7.5/45	200	21,110			*Hawkins, Frobisher*
6/50	112	25,480		7.5–10	modern CL
	100	25,800		12	*Nelson*s
	100	16,190		8.5–12	*Eagle*
	100	14,310			some AMC
6/45	100	18,750		8.5–12	old CL, *Effingham*, river gunboats (often)
	100	20,620			*Enterprise* twin mount
	100	15,660			some AMC
	100	13,500		8.5–12	*Queen Elizabeth*s, "R" class BB
	100				*Iron Duke*
5.5/50	82	18,500		5–7.5	*Hood*
	82				*Hermes*, some AMC
5.25/50	80	24,070	46,500	8	*King George V*s, *Bellona*s, most *Dido*s
4.7/50	62	21,240		6	"L" and "M" class DD
4.7/45	50	16,970		5	DD classes: "J," "K," "N," "Tribal"
	50			5–6	"S" to "W" class DD
	50	16,970		6–8	DD classes: "E" to "I," "Q," "R," some "O" (cont...)

GREAT BRITAIN

GUN	SW*	RANGE	CLNG	FC	NOTES
	50			6-8	sloops, "A" to "D" class DD
	50	15,800			*Amazon, Ambuscade, Keppel, Broke, Scotts,* some old "W" class DD, French *Mistral, Ouragan*
4.7/40	50	16,160	32,000	5	*Nelsons, Adventure, Albatross, Courageous* class
4.5/45	55	20,750	41,000	5	CV, *Renown, Savage,* some BB and CL, "Battle" class DD
	55	20,750		5	DD classes: "Z," "Ca," "Ch," "Co," "Cr"
4/45	35	19,850	39,000	5	*Abdiels,* BB, most cruisers, new "Hunts," CVE, monitors, old DD and escorts
	35	19,850	39,000	4	some Australian MS and escorts
	31	13,840			*Repulse* triples, some MS, GB, old DD, most modern "Flowers" and old sloops
	31	16,430	31,000	4	*Repulse,* CV, some cruisers, "O" and "P" class DD, many "Lochs," some old DD
4/40	35	10,450			submarines
	35	9,700			many "Rivers" and "Castles"
	31	13,970			*P614,615*
	31	11,580			some escorts, MS, old DD, and MAC
3/45	17	12,920	25,500		some MS, added to DD
	17				some "S" and "U" class SS
3/40	13	11,750	19,000		some SS and old DD, many others

*The British sometimes added dye packs to their ammunition to aid in spotting their fall of shot. This could increase the shell weight by several pounds, but it had no significant effect on shell performance.

---

greatest achievement was the centimetric radar that plagued German submarine operations. The Royal Navy had exactly what it needed to defeat its arch-rival.

It also had the good fortune to avoid a decisive engagement with the Japanese, whose capabilities meshed precisely with British weaknesses. A British carrier maintained about half as many planes as its Japanese and American counterparts, and the planes it carried were uniquely unimpressive. (Imagine a duel between Fulmar and Zeke. In fact, the two met in major engagements at least twice near Ceylon at the outbreak of the Pacific War. Near Trincomalee, British interceptors shot down one Zeke and five bombers at a cost of eight Hurricanes and three Fulmars; over Colombo, the British lost 19 fighters—many of them Fulmars—while destroying one Zeke and six

bombers.) The fleet lacked AA firepower: destroyers with DP guns were almost unknown, and like all countries, Britain suffered from insufficient light AA, at least initially. As the war dragged on, the Admiralty adopted the Bofors and Oerlikon AA cannon and began to operate American planes. The carrier air complements grew, approaching foreign standards. Through such borrowings, the Royal Navy gained strength, but also underscored its own decline.

Many prewar cruisers had the less powerful 4/45 (31-lb shell), but only *York, Canberra, Sydney,* and the AA cruisers *Curlew* and *Coventry* retained it; most ships took the 39-lb type in its place. (The other "C" class AA cruisers never had the older gun.) Likewise, the river gunboats carried different 6-inch marks at different times. Of course, the greatest variation

The Queen Elizabeth's *modernization provided twin mounts of the new
4.5-inch gun, Britain's best DP weapon.*

shows among the smaller escorts and minecraft, carrying whatever guns were at hand in a miscellany of mounts.

Ammunition varied almost as much. The war's start found the fleet switching from its standard 1920-lb 15-inch shell to a new 1938-lb type giving better performance. Further range increase came from super-charges of propellant (29,930 yards with the new shell at 20°); these became available in 1941 but saw little service, if any. Ships with 30° mounts received the new shell but not the super-charges, which would have provided a 37,870-yard range. Some older 6-inch guns, as in the river gunboats, had superpropellants as well.

Just before World War I, the British scored a brilliant success, matching their 13.5-inch gun with a 1,400-lb shell; the heavy shell and low muzzle velocity created new standards of consistent accuracy and long barrel life. The *Queen Elizabeth*s followed with a 15-inch gun that surpassed those standards and became perhaps the greatest battleship gun ever.

Then came the *Nelson*s. The increase to 16-inch guns raised concerns that a larger shell might break apart against thick armor. Thus the British opted for a light shell at high velocity, which translated into inaccuracy and short barrel life (200 rounds, as opposed to 350 rounds

for the 15-inch). Also, the *Nelson*s gave the fleet its first big triple turret; its weight completely overtaxed British design expertise, and the mounts proved slow and surly. In service, they literally ground themselves to pieces. Persistent tinkering mollified the shortcomings, but could not remove them.

The British repented; their next gun, the 14-inch of the 1930s, had almost the exact shell weight and velocity as their WWI model (as in Chile's *Latorre*). In armor penetration, it barely equaled America's old 14-inch guns; but the barrels' construction provided accuracy with long life—the makings of a successful, if dated, battery. Unfortunately, the turret design left legions of bugs lurking in the works, and if *Nelson*'s triples caused trouble, the 14-inch quads proved ruthless. (The 14-inch twin, a last-minute design, was comparatively tame.)

The fleet's smaller guns warranted little complaint or praise. Unlike the Americans, the British failed to standardize a single DP caliber: 4-inch, 4.5-inch, 4.7-inch, and 5.25-inch, none quite good enough to generate any zeal. The new 4/45 was most in demand, appreciated for its rapid fire and handy twin mount.

The 3/40 DP gun firing a 13-lb shell was called the 12-pounder, naturally.

The standard light AA gun in 1939 was the

TORPEDO	WW	RANGE		NOTES
24.5-inch Mk I	743	15,000/35	20,000/30	*Nelsons*
21-inch Mk IV	515	8,000/35	13,500/25	WWI issue, in old ships and MTB
21-inch Mk VII	740	16,000/33		initially in CA
21-inch Mk VIII	722	5,000/40		SS standard in "O" class and after, MTB, DD
21-inch Mk IX	750	10,500/35	13,500/30	most cruisers and DD
18-inch Mk XII	388	1,500/40	3,500/27	MTB, standard aerial torpedo
18-inch Mk XV	545	2,500/45	3,500/33	replaced Mk XII around 1942

2-pounder, a competent 40mm weapon (115 rpm). The "pom-pom" served in large numbers, but it required attentive maintenance and possessed only a modest muzzle velocity—that is, modest stopping power and a short reach (6,800-yard range; 13,000-foot ceiling). Another 40mm cannon, the Swedish Bofors, impressed the British during service aboard Dutch vessels fleeing the German invasion. Though it obviously outperformed the pom-pom—by some calculations, one Bofors equaled two 2-pounders— the Admiralty remained ambivalent about its safety features. Also, it had a complex mount that was difficult to manufacture. A less precise but simpler version was developed, and America produced thousands more. But despite its capabilities (120–150 rpm; 10,750-yard range; 23,500-foot ceiling), the Bofors never completely supplanted the 2-pounder.

The British also scouted out the 20mm Oerlikon as a replacement for its .50cal machine guns. This Swiss cannon was first brought to British attention by an Austrian engineer marketing the gun to the Japanese. An important weapon when it entered service (465–480 rpm; 4,800-yard range; 10,000-foot ceiling), it obsolesced by 1945, lacking in offensive punch against high-speed, modern opponents.

As did several other countries, Britain toyed with batteries of AA rocket projectors, which proved capable of frightening enemy pilots, if nothing more.

British high-angle gunnery fell below American standards; this persistent AA mediocrity is especially puzzling in view of Allied cooperation in most other areas. (America did provide the proximity fuse.) Britain used radar to bolster its AA efforts, but its peculiar doctrines of engagement placed extra stress on AA gunnery, its weakest link. For example, in the war's early stages, an aircraft carrier that detected incoming bogeys might not send up its fighters to intercept, but rather stow all planes belowdecks and rely on gunfire to drive off the attack. Even in 1945, the fleet used radar more as an early warning system than a vectoring tool for fighter interception.

In contrast, the Royal Navy excelled in anti-ship gunnery, making a close match with the Kriegsmarine early in the war, and then pulling ahead with steady advances in electronics. Some older vessels had to make do with aging fire-control systems, but standards remained high. By 1945, the British outperformed all, save the Americans. Meanwhile, the ghosts of Jutland had spurred the Admiralty's pursuit of consistent, trustworthy ammunition.

Britain defeated the U-boat in World War II. While Allied merchant shipping losses continued at a frightening rate through 1943, in fact the British had already claimed the victory—though they may not have realized it at the time. A U-boat patrolling the North Atlantic in late 1940 could expect to sink about 20,000 tons per month; that figure fell below 2,000 tons in 1942. British AS warfare went well beyond the depth charge. Hedgehog, a spigot mortar hurling 7-inch rounds with contact fuses, went to sea in 1941; it became truly formidable as escorts mastered the proper techniques, including the complementary use of depth charges. Squid, a battery of 12-inch mortars using time fuses, arrived late in the war and immediately proved its superiority. Royal Navy statistics ranked it as one-third more effective than Hedgehog and four times as effective as a pattern of depth charges. Some planning went into developing Squid into a gun with a range exceeding 600 yards. Such a weapon, combined with America's AS proximity fuse, could have been successful even against the fastest U-boats.

Royal surface and air attacks accounted for 475 U-boat kills while the Americans, beneficiaries of British know-how, added another 171.

Only Japan's torpedoes performed better than Britain's. The 1942 development of Torpex—an explosive 50–100% more potent than TNT—gave even the 18-inch torpedoes a considerable punch. (Despite the nomenclature of the period, all 18-inch torpedoes of World War II were in fact 17.7-inch.) Torpex impressed the Americans enough for them to switch from TNT at the end of 1942.

No electric models saw war service. The Mark IV served only in the absence of anything more modern. Few Mark VII's were used before replacement by the Mark IX. Successive improvements traded the Mark IX's 750-lb TNT warhead for 810 lbs of Torpex while also adding about five knots to its speed settings; a 930-lb warhead missed the war. More than half of all British torpedoes expended during the war were Mark VIII's; modifications included an 805-lb Torpex warhead and a slight boost in propulsion.

Naval Aviation

The Royal Navy had pioneered carrier aviation, but its potential fell victim to catastrophic mismanagement in the wake of World War I. The Royal Air Force, enthroned over all military aircraft, exalted itself as the modern alternative to army and navy. From this insular and monolith-

ic organization came leeching an ooze of spurious ideals that, in time, tainted even the Admiralty's thinking despite spirited inter-service sparring. The supposed prowess of attack aircraft stigmatized carrier-borne fighters as pawns of futility, unworthy of cutting-edge design work. Indeed, it became reasonable in the fleet to accept outdated performance from all carrier aircraft. An air of stagnation smothered experimental initiatives, while treaty and financial restraints injected further inertia. The lead in carrier operations and aircraft shifted overseas to America and Japan, where the navies had their own independent air forces. The British Admiralty continued to arm-wrestle the Royal Air Force, but only in May 1939 did the fleet gain control of the Fleet Air Arm.

Despite all this, British carriers weren't ineffective. Air crews proved themselves capable, developing techniques for night operations. The ships had their qualities, including a most handsome appearance, and the units with armored flight decks proved especially survivable against bomb damage. More importantly, the Germans and Italians provided no carriers to oppose them, and in 1940 Axis AA was as primitive as any other.

Prewar air groups had their foundation in time-tested rather than up-to-date aircraft designs—a reality that garnered sudden attention with the approach of war clouds. As an emergency measure, the British navalized a successful land-based fighter; the Gloster Sea Gladiator biplane (speed: 245 mph; armament: four .303cal mg) was extremely agile and battleworthy but, by 1939, no longer modern. An interim design, it nevertheless continued serving into 1941. Fortunately, it spent most of its time dueling Italian planes and rarely saw a Messerschmitt.

The fleet intended the Blackburn Skua (speed: 225 mph; armament: five .303cal mg, one 500-lb bomb) for double-duty. As a fighter replacing the Sea Gladiator, it proved too sluggish; as a dive-bomber, it carried unimpressive bomb loads. Its bombing performance was adequate, but pilots disliked its landings and take-offs. It was retired from front-line service by 1941.

The Blackburn Roc (speed: 194 mph) appeared in 1940 and disappeared soon after. It carried its battery of four .303cal machine guns in a turret, leaving the pilot unarmed.

Another interim fighter that saw lengthy service, the Fairey Fulmar (Mk I, speed: 280 mph; armament: eight .303cal mg) derived from a failed bomber project, and its performance belied that dubious ancestry. The FAA requirement of two seats for its fighters (the Sea Gladiator was an emergency exception) guaranteed their inferiority. The Fulmar simply lacked the performance of its modern, land-based counterparts, being slow in climb-rate and speed and unimpressive in maneuver, but it did have several worthy features. Its eight machine guns matched the firepower of the latest RAF fighters. The Fulmar proved easy to fly, land, and takeoff, while its range (about 800 miles) nearly doubled the Sea Gladiator's. From its introduction in 1940 until its replacement as the navy's premier fighter, it accounted for one third of all FAA aerial kills in World War II. It continued as a night fighter through the war's end.

Experience finally taught the British that they needed a single-seat fighter. Their desperate choice was a good one; as they had done before, they navalized a land-based plane, the Hawker Hurricane. The Sea Hurricane (Mk II, speed: 340 mph; armament: eight .303cal mg) established the viability of a single-seat carrier fighter and, when deployed in 1942, finally gave the fleet a first-class airplane; but it was becoming outdated, and by 1944 was retired from service. The .303cal battery, though numerous, lacked power against modern opponents (many pilots preferred smaller American batteries of .50s), and the later Sea Hurricane models carried four 20mm cannon.

When a Blackburn design, intended as the standard carrier fighter, turned out a disappoint-ment, the British chose once again to shanghai a land plane, this time their classic fighter, the Supermarine Spitfire. The agile and speedy Seafire (Mk III, speed: 352 mph; armament: two 20mm cannon, four .303cal mg) naturally excelled in combat. In carrier operations, however, it had significant problems, and its introduction saw a high incidence of deck accidents. A tricky plane to land, it offered poor visibility on approach and inadequate speed control, compounding the hazard of fragile, bouncy landing gear. The overall structure lacked sturdiness; experience showed that arrester gear could snap a Seafire in two. Takeoff behavior was better, but upon ditching, the plane sank at once. Range never exceeded 800 miles even with drop tanks, and some models needed drop tanks just to reach 300 miles. Thus the magnificent Seafire could not fulfill all the navy's fighter needs, and it often served in fleet defense only.

No other British fighters entered carrier operations before the war's end. A project in development at that time was the Hawker Sea Fury (Mk 11, speed: 460 mph; armament: four 20mm cannon, two 1,000-lb bombs), a cousin of the land-based Tempest and Typhoon. With a maximum range near 1,000 miles, it became the main FAA fighter postwar, a complete success. A twin-engined contemporary, the de Havilland Sea Hornet (Mk 20, speed: 467 mph; armament: four 20mm cannon, two 1,000-lb bombs) had a more useful maximum range, over 1,500 miles. The Sea Hornet evolved from the Mosquito which, in 1944 trials, established the viability of twin-engine carrier planes. A Sea Mosquito design also joined the fleet in 1946, mostly as a torpedo-reconnaissance plane (Mk 33, speed: 385 mph; armament: four 20mm cannon, one 17.7-inch torpedo or 2,000 lbs of bombs).

Britain's most famous carrier aircraft was a torpedo-bomber, the Fairey Swordfish biplane (Mk I, speed: 139 mph; armament: two .303cal mg, one 17.7-inch torpedo or 1,500 lbs of bombs). It epitomized the FAA aircraft: reliable, serviceable, operationally splendid, and achingly antique. Despite its open cockpit and WWI performance, pilots loved the "Stringbag," which handled easily in all aspects of operation.

Admiration, however, could not defy time forever. The fleet made a bid to extend the life of its elderly planes with ventures into nighttime attacks utilizing airborne radar, but strained resources and a lack of opportunity stunted the promise of these early efforts. The Swordfish's last torpedo attack came amid the daylight and Messerschmitts of the Channel Dash in early 1942; none of the attacking Swordfish survived. Yet the Stringbag continued in front-line service up to May 1945, not lugging torpedoes but using the lengthy endurance that suited it well to AS patrol. A Swordfish became the first plane to destroy a submarine by rocket attack. Rockets subsequently became standard in British and American operations, replacing a portion of a plane's bomb load for patrol and attack missions.

The Swordfish's replacement, the Fairey Albacore biplane (speed: 161 mph; armament: three .303cal mg, one 17.7-inch torpedo or 2,000 lbs of bombs), vanished from operations sooner than the plane it was supposed to replace. First deployed in 1941, it quickly displayed its lack of value. It had an enclosed cockpit and more range than a Swordfish, but was otherwise equal in obsolescence and operationally inferior. It was retired in 1943.

Britain then adopted the monoplane Fairey Barracuda (Mk II, speed: 228 mph; armament: two .303cal mg, one 17.7-inch torpedo or 1,500 lbs of bombs), an obvious advance, yet still something of a disappointment. Not an easy plane to fly, it suffered several accidents due to its handling flaws. Its engine lacked power. The meager armament left pilots without a forward-firing gun. Nevertheless, the Barracuda had enough range and maneuverability to be useful, and though it performed only a couple of torpedo operations during the war, it could complete a variety of missions in unspectacular fashion.

A much more successful design, the Fairey Firefly (Mk I, speed: 316 mph; armament: four 20mm cannon, 2,000 lbs of bombs) earned instant favor upon deployment in 1944. Nominally a fighter and successor to the Fulmar, it rarely functioned in that role. (The Firefly was in service for one year before scoring its first aerial victory.) The design included a heavy armament and surprising maneuverability—a Firefly could turn inside a Spitfire. But once again, the inclusion of a second crewman precluded the necessary speed; fighters in 1944 were of the 400-mph variety. Instead the Firefly won its reputation with its excellent handling and deadly attack capability.

Just as the war was drawing to a close, the Blackburn Firebrand entered service. Originally a fighter, the Firebrand proved too heavy, slow, and unmaneuverable (thus forcing the FAA to develop the Seafire). However, its large wings provided good lift, prompting a redesign as a "torpedo-fighter" (Mk V, speed: 350 mph; armament: four 20mm cannon, one 17.7-inch torpedo or 2,000 lbs of bombs), a slow process that kept the plane from seeing any wartime action. Its range of 740 miles suited an attack plane more than a fighter, but operational shortcomings blunted its value in any role.

Two other notable projects barely missed combat. The Fairey Spearfish (Mk I, speed: 292 mph) was a rather conventional torpedo-bomber, canceled postwar. Teething problems in the Westland Wyvern torpedo-strike fighter (Mk I, speed: 456 mph) delayed its introduction and foretold its maintenance woes.

Fortunately, Britain's wartime carrier squadrons fortified themselves with American imports. Among fighters, the Wildcat (or Martlet, in FAA parlance), Hellcat, and Corsair appeared in large numbers. The absence of a modern British torpedo plane made the Avenger the standard. By 1945, one-half of Britain's carrier planes came from America. Note the absence of dive-bombers; the SB2C Helldiver disappointed many on both sides of the Atlantic.

GREAT BRITAIN

The Courageous. The Royal Navy's early lead in carriers became a liability when treaties restricted its production of newer, more efficient designs.

ARGUS (14,000 tons, light guns, AC 20, 20.25 knots, 1918): a converted liner originally fitted with six 4-inch DP. Her narrow flight deck and lack of speed made her inadequate for fleet operations, but her stout construction provided a long career in training.

EAGLE (22,600 tons; nine 6-inch, four 4-inch DP guns; AC 21, 24 knots, 1920): begun as the Chilean battleship *Almirante Cochrane*, sister of the *Latorre*. The Royal Navy commandeered her and converted her into a carrier. The *Eagle* handled well and demonstrated the ability of the large carrier to operate in heavy seas. Though completed without a battleship's heavy belt armor, she had much more protection than Britain's BC conversions. A hangar fire and refit in 1941 reduced her to 20 knots. She sank four minutes after suffering four torpedo hits.

HERMES (10,850 tons; six 5.5-inch, three 4-inch DP guns; AC 15, 25 knots, 1923): the world's first purpose-built carrier, an ugly ship without modern speed. But she held steady with little roll, handling well except in high winds. Designers incorporated *Raleigh*-level protection and provided for emergency conversion into a cruiser (in case the British suddenly

needed a 25-knot CL). This did not make *Hermes* particularly rugged, but even a younger, larger ship would have crumpled beneath the dozens of bombs the Japanese showered on her.

The navy added an extra 4-inch gun prewar and may have removed it shortly thereafter. A wartime plan proposed replacing all guns with a new battery of 4-inch twins, but no such work took place.

FURIOUS (22,450 tons, twelve 4-inch DP guns, AC 36, 30 knots, 1925): begun as a half-sister to the *Courageous* class BC, but completed to a hybrid design in 1917—a single 18-inch gun aft and a flight deck forward. Later another flight deck replaced the big gun. By 1925, she became a functional, flush-deck carrier. In this form, she had value for modern carrier offense due to her speed and size, though her primitive conversion failed to provide room for efficient aircraft maintenance. She had the good fortune to avoid serious battle damage. Aging rapidly, she left front-line service by mid-1944.

British interest in hybrids faded after the *Furious* conversion, lingering only for some scout vessels foreseen by prewar trade protection theorists. Hybrid designs revived amid the war emergency, but none progressed very far. The Admiralty reviewed two cruisers types (18,900 tons; six 8-inch, twelve 4-inch DP guns, six 21-inch TT; AC 14, 30+ knots; and 20,000 tons; nine 8-inch, twelve 4-inch DP guns, six 21-inch TT; AC 12, 30+ knots) and a BB-CV showing obvious relation to the *Lion* (44,750 tons; six 16-inch, sixteen 5.25-inch DP guns; AC 14, 28–29 knots).

COURAGEOUS, GLORIOUS (22,500 tons, sixteen 4.7-inch DP guns, AC 48, 30 knots, 1928–30): completed in 1917 as light BC with four 15-inch guns, converted to carriers 1927–30. This conversion improved on the earlier work done on *Furious*, allowing a larger air group and providing adequate maintenance facilities. The flight deck included two catapults, though not as efficient as in wartime carriers. The ships reached 5,030 miles at 16 knots, which was deemed acceptable until the war began to teach its lessons.

The original *Courageous* design, frightening in its lack of protection, found no improvement in its conversion. The new bulges added seakeeping rather than protection; *Courageous* sank 15 minutes after taking two torpedoes. *Glorious* suffered a more prolonged agony trying to outrun German dreadnoughts and their 11.1-inch shells.

ARK ROYAL (22,000 tons, sixteen 4.5-inch DP guns, AC 72, 31 knots, 1938): Britain's best prewar carrier, habitable and handsome. Foibles included vibration problems and a lack of maneuverability, but design figures doubled the *Courageous* range.

The designers used her flight deck to enhance her structure; not simply an added flattop, it formed an integral part of the framework. This system created the characteristic enclosed hull of modern British carriers. The enclosure inhibited the spread of flame and flammables, like those that doomed the American *Wasp*; but it also complicated re-supply efforts at sea, limited her ventilation (her planes could not warm up in the hangar), and precluded a deck-edge elevator.

The hangar's two-storey layout allowed a large air group (by British standards) and a concentration of armor protection. However, the navy abandoned the official figure of seventy-two aircraft even before the ship's completion; sixty proved a more feasible number. There were two catapults.

Unfortunately, *Ark Royal's* armor and strong hull did not equal watertightness. Late in 1941, a single torpedo struck—a significant hit, but not one that should have endangered a ship of her size. The damage revealed fundamental flaws in design. Her subdivision proved inadequate, and the cramping of her boiler uptakes

The closed-hangar design of Britain's Ark Royal *came with distinct advantages and disadvantages.*

around the double-decked hangar made her boilers susceptible to progressive flooding. A vulnerable communication system hindered damage control. When the ship lost main power, her lack of auxiliary power—a failing common throughout the Royal Navy—left the crew without options. *Ark Royal* sank 14 hours after the attack.

In the mid-1930s, the Admiralty began a project for small CV to provide trade protection. Designs started near 14,500 tons with four 5.25-inch DP guns, 15 aircraft, and 27–28 knots. The need for protection raised the project beyond 17,000 tons before it lost impetus and shrank to 11,000 tons. By then, planners decided that a big ship was what they really wanted.

ILLUSTRIOUS, VICTORIOUS, FORMIDABLE, INDOMITABLE (23,000 tons, sixteen 4.5-inch DP guns, AC 36, 30.5 knots, 1940–41): the ships that made armored flight decks famous. Their three inches of flight deck steel formed the top of an armored box which completely enclosed the hangar space—a feature that appeared only in British carriers. They had better subdivision and communications than *Ark Royal* along with 5000 tons of armor (about 22% of their displacement), a significant amount for a CV and a huge advance over *Ark Royal*'s 2,850 tons. *Illustrious* amply illustrated the benefit of all that metal when attacked by Stukas in January 1941. Hit after hit—four 1,102-lb bombs (one of them a dud) and three 551-lb, plus a near-miss—rocked the ship. Some bombs penetrated to the hangar, but her armor helped to localize the damage, and she struggled into Malta, burning but under her own power. While lying in harbor a week later, she suffered attack again, taking another heavy bomb and several near-misses. The ship survived all this abuse although she was out of action more than 10 months. Never completely repaired, *Illustrious* developed severe vibrations that forced the removal of one propeller and cut her speed to 24 knots.

Her sisters all had their protection tested. A bomb that hit *Victorious* merely skipped off her armor, and two kamikazes caused slight damage. *Formidable* also absorbed two kamikazes; but she took more serious damage back in 1941 from a pair of German bombs that caused some flooding and a permanent distortion of her hull. Not properly repaired, her condition deteriorated. By the end of her career, she had to strain to reach 21 knots. She suffered further indignity in a bizarre landing accident that sparked a fire in the hangar via the elevator opening. The elevator represented a chink in the flight deck armor; three of *Illustrious*'s bomb hits penetrated the elevator well.

But British carrier design retained its true Achilles' heel below the waterline. Poor, hob-

Folding wings couldn't qualify the **Indomitable's** *Albacores as modern planes. However, new stowage techniques did allow British carriers to enlarge their air groups; note the Seafire on a starboard outrigger.*

bled *Illustrious* maneuvered to avoid a kamikaze, but the plane's bomb exploded in the water nearby, splitting her plates and cracking their supports. She could not safely exceed 19 knots, and leisurely repair work dragged out until mid-1946. *Indomitable* had to cope with two bomb hits, one piercing her armored deck, while a near-miss complicated the situation with enough flooding to create an 8° list. Later, in 1943, a single torpedo nearly sank her. It was an aerial torpedo, not large, and it didn't strike an especially vulnerable point, but progressive flooding reached as high as main deck level. The lessons from *Ark Royal* helped, notably in maintaining communication within the ship; however, if not for a calm sea, *Indomitable* might well have sank. This persistent underwater vulnerability—more than a year and a half after *Ark Royal*'s loss—defies explanation.

For all its fame, the armored flight deck was not without drawbacks. Elevators operated more slowly. The cramping of hangar space complicated maintenance, cut air complements by as much as 50%, and even limited the choice of usable aircraft. (The big American Corsair fighter had to be specially modified with clipped wings to fit in *Illustrious*'s hangar.) The flight deck itself tended to be lower and wetter, and on those occasions when it was pierced, it required lengthy repair time. In fact, the armored box had structural consequences not foreseen in the design process; fires within the hangar (as in *Formidable*'s accident) and mining effects (as with *Illustrious*'s near-miss kamikaze) could severely distort the hull, damage that had no remedy short of a complete hull rebuild.

Indomitable differed from her three sisters as designers addressed some of these problems. The flight deck retained its three inches of armor, but other surfaces of the armored box were thinned out. This provided more maintenance room with a double-decked hangar like *Ark Royal*'s. (Unfortunately, one story lacked the headroom necessary for Corsairs, even with clipped wings, so other fighters had to be used.) The original *Illustrious* design accommodated 36 aircraft, later increased to 54 by new storage methods, but the ships didn't carry enough fuel to operate the enlarged group most effectively. *Indomitable* began with 45 planes, later increased to 56 with ample fuel for all. Some accounts show an air group of 60 late in the war, but a proposed expansion to 75 planes remained a pipe dream.

All units showed some operational shortcomings: only one catapult, elevators too narrow for some aircraft, a lack of overhead space in the hangars. Ship's speed, designed at 30.5 knots, lagged behind American standards. Poor maneuverability, a general feature of British triple-screw carriers, created smirks among the Yanks during joint operations.

The *Illustrious* makes an interesting comparison with the *Ark Royal*; by growing from 22,000 to 23,000 tons (in fact, *Illustrious* got up to 26,760 tons), what did the newer design gain? With its inferior operational facilities and smaller air group, it was also (in practice) two knots slower and even less maneuverable. Underwater protection showed a meager improvement. Only in its resistance to bomb damage and gunfire was there a distinct advantage.

UNICORN (14,750 tons, eight 4-inch DP guns, AC 35, 24 knots, 1943): intended as a maintenance ship, given carrier-like performance for emergency use. After one operation as a carrier, she assumed her subsidiary role, for which her speed sufficed. As a ferry, she could carry up to sixty-nine Seafires, while her own air group rarely exceeded twenty. Unbefitting her name, *Unicorn*'s stubby appearance lacked the grace of the big carriers. She shared no design lineage with subsequent light carriers.

Britain, like Japan and the United States, considered plans for converting liners as a wartime emergency measure. The most notable

GREAT BRITAIN

British candidates were the *Queen Elizabeth* (as planned: 72,000 tons, eight 4-inch DP guns, AC 84, 31.5 knots) and the 29-knot *Queen Mary*.

IMPLACABLE, INDEFATIGABLE (23,450 tons, sixteen 4.5-inch DP guns, AC 72, 32 knots, 1944): an improved *Illustrious* class with the same handsome lines. The armor layout compromised between *Indomitable*'s and the original *Illustrious* plan. Though the air complement grew (eventually to 81), the ships lacked sufficient fuel stores for it. They were cramped and could not carry Corsairs.

The cramping derived in part from an enlarged propulsion system with four shafts rather than three, providing good speed. A new and powerful catapult improved operations. Underwater protection included some refinements, but generally resembled earlier schemes. Fortunately, the *Implacables* encountered no hostile torpedoes.

COLOSSUS, GLORY, OCEAN, VENERABLE, VENGEANCE, PIONEER (13,190 tons, light guns, AC 40, 25 knots, 1944–45): plus four additional units completed postwar. This design began with the idea of a specialized fighter carrier to protect the fleet. Hybrid designs appeared impractical, so an "aircraft destroyer" evolved (8,350 tons, four 5-inch DP, AC 12, 31–32 knots). A short-lived idea, it regained support after the *Prince of Wales* debacle, then developed into a more general-purpose design, a simple light carrier to supplement the big ships. A mercantile hull would facilitate production.

The *Colossus* class ships had distinct limitations. With neither a large air group nor an armored flight deck, they lacked speed as well. The absence of armor was almost complete. Survivability rested on machinery dispersal, a small pattern of watertight bulkheads, and the stowage of hollow drums to retain buoyancy in flooded spaces. *Pioneer* was completed as a maintenance carrier, and the entire class had lit-tle contact with the enemy. As combatants, they made a poor comparison with the American *Independence*, which was smaller but superior by several significant criteria. However, the design was cheap, reliable, and roomy, cherished as an operational success, though short on habitability, and not as weather-capable as the big ships.

EAGLE, AUDACIOUS, ARK ROYAL (36,800 tons, sixteen 4.5-inch DP guns, AC 100, 32 knots): only two completed, postwar and much modified. The original plan included even more extensive armor than in *Illustrious* and, finally, a much better underwater scheme reflecting wartime lessons. The machinery showed a good measure of dispersal. Operational facilities—catapults, hangar spaces, etc.—received more attention; maneuverability and fuel stores increased. The air group grew from an originally specified 78 planes.

MAJESTIC class (14,000 tons, light guns, AC 37, 25 knots): six light carriers completed postwar, begun as part of the *Colossus* class but with a stronger flight deck (for heavier aircraft) and less aviation fuel. They boasted improved habitability and a number of operational refinements.

CENTAUR class (18,310 tons, eight 4.5-inch DP guns, AC 45, 29.5 knots): four ships completed postwar, plus four not completed. A much improved descendant of the *Colossus* with operational improvements but only slight advances in protection.

MALTA class (46,900 tons, sixteen 4.5-inch DP guns, AC 120, 32.5 knots): four carriers planned, but none laid down. A handsome and potent design, *Malta* had adequate armor and an underwater layout related to *Eagle*'s. Initial specifications included 81 aircraft and the standard armored box around the hangar, but this changed. The weight devoted to armor shrank from 10,610 to 8,506 tons, as an inch of steel replaced the armored flight deck and the hangar gained open sides—the whole project began to look very American. (Meanwhile, the Americans were busy putting flight deck armor onto their *Midways*.) The 4.5-inch guns, a new model, fired about 25 rpm. If the *Maltas* had reached completion, they would have served long and well.

The British were the first to realize the airplane's value as a convoy escort and AS terror. The Admiralty began, in the mid-1930s, to develop the idea of merchantman-CV conversions for convoy duty and, by 1940, settled on general specifications, blending various ratios of idealism and practicality: Type A (2 4-inch DP guns, 25 aircraft, 20 knots), Type B (2 4-inch DP guns, 15 aircraft, 18 knots), and Type C (1 4-inch DP gun, 10 aircraft, 16.5 knots). In the early years of the war, the demands on merchant shipping allowed for no diversion to CVE construction. So the navy grasped at a crude and desperate alternative, the Catapult-Armed Merchant ships carrying fighters (Hurricanes, or in one case, a Fulmar) on catapults. At the approach of an enemy threat, a fighter would be launched, but the pilot had no way to land back aboard ship—a rather awkward situation unless there was a land base in range. Thirty-five CAM ships entered service before their replacement by the escort carrier.

A similar but more promising system failed to become practical before the war's end. Plans were made to fit merchant ships with helicopter platforms to support an American AS helicopter that never materialized.

AUDACITY (about 9,000 tons, one 4-inch DP gun, AC 6, 15 knots, 1941): one of the most significant ships of the war, though in service a mere six months—the first escort carrier, converted from a captured German merchantman. She fell short of even the Type C specification, rebuilt with such urgency that she had neither an island nor a hangar; her six Martlets were stowed and serviced on deck. *Audacity* established the value of the CVE before U-boat torpedoes ended her short career.

ARCHER (10,220 tons, three 4-inch guns, AC 16, 17 knots, 1941): a merchant design converted in the United States, closely related to the *Long Island* and the *Avenger* class. *Archer* had a hangar and a minimal island. Her displacement included almost 3,000 tons of ballast. CVE displacement is especially confusing, often listed in gross tonnage, and alterations account for a ship's tonnage differing in American and British records.

AVENGER, BITER, CHARGER, DASHER (8,200 tons, three 4-inch guns, AC 15, 16.5 knots, 1942): merchantmen with troublesome engines, converted by the Americans, who retained *Charger* in their own navy. The British sometimes shipped depth charges aboard their CVE, and *Biter* became the first to use them (without success). She later transferred to French command as *Dixmude*.

Unfortunately, the Lend-Lease CVE became a point of friction between the British and the Americans. The British considered the ships unsuitable as delivered—*Dasher* sank as a result of spontaneous explosion—so they carried out extensive alterations, mostly to increase safety and stability. The Americans blamed the accident on British operational practices and complained about British slowness in getting the ships into action. In fact, the delays stemmed as much from the Royal Navy's shortage of manpower and facilities as from its safety standards. And the British units certainly had greater survivability, at least initially.

TRACKER, BATTLER, CHASER, FENCER, HUNTER, PURSUER, RAVAGER, SEARCHER, STALKER, STRIKER, ATTACKER (10,200 tons, two 4-inch guns, AC 20, 16.5 knots, 1942): converted merchant hulls ordered as part of the American *Bogue* class. As in the previous two

The American-built British **Puncher** *carries a deckload of American Corsairs and Avengers.*

classes, the 4-inch gun was American, but *Battler* later took on three British 4-inch DP. *Ravager* served exclusively in training. This design incorporated several lessons in ruggedness and operations, and the ships performed well.

ACTIVITY (11,800 tons, two 4-inch DP guns, AC 15, 18 knots, 1942): cargo ship converted by the British, modeled on the Type C specification. The icy waters of Arctic duty could open cracks in the hulls of merchant conversions; the rivets of British-built ships fared better than American welding.

PRETORIA CASTLE (19,650 tons, four 4-inch DP guns, AC 15, 17 knots, 1943): a liner converted first to an AMC, then a CVE in accordance to Type B specifications. The Allies' largest escort carrier, she seemed too vulnerable for combat duty and served mostly in training amid Britain's manpower shortage.

AMEER, ARBITER, ATHELING, BEGUM, EMPEROR, EMPRESS, KHEDIVE, NABOB, PATROLLER, PREMIER, PUNCHER, QUEEN, RAJAH, RANEE, REAPER, RULER, SHAH, SLINGER, SMITER, SPEAKER, THANE, TROUNCER, TRUMPETER (11,420 tons, two 5-inch guns, AC 24, 17 knots, 1943–44): American-built vessels with improved operational details, more battle-worthy than the *Attackers*, which they resembled. Nine served as trainers to relieve the manpower crisis. *Slinger* and *Thane* survived serious underwater damage, as did *Nabob*; the British felt certain an American CVE would have succumbed in *Nabob*'s situation.

VINDEX (13,455 tons, two 4-inch DP guns, AC 18, 17 knots, 1943): cargo ship converted in England.

NAIRANA (14,050 tons, two 4-inch DP guns, AC 18, 17 knots, 1943): half-sister of *Vindex*.

CAMPANIA (12,450 tons, two 4-inch DP guns, AC 18, 17 knots, 1944): British conversion of a cargo ship. *Campania*'s superior operational features made her the best of the British CVE. Long range was a fundamental requirement for British CVE, and *Campania* had the longest (17,000 miles at 17 knots).

Impatient awaiting the commission of CVEs, the Royal Navy quickly adapted two types of MAC ships. These were fully functional merchant vessels fitted with flight decks—a different sort of hybrid.

RAPANA, MIRALDA, ACAVUS, ADULA, ALEXIA, AMASTRA, ANCYLUS, GADILA, MACOMA (16,600 tons, one 4-inch gun, AC 4, 13 knots, 1942–44): oilers with no hangars. The last pair served with Dutch crews.

EMPIRE MacALPINE, EMPIRE MacKENDRICK (13,000 tons, one 4-inch gun, AC 4, 12.5 knots, 1943): grain carriers. They had shorter flight decks than the oiler types, but included a hangar.

EMPIRE MacANDREW, EMPIRE MacDERMOTT, EMPIRE MacRAE, EMPIRE MacCALLUM (13,000 tons, one 4-inch gun, AC 4, 12.5 knots, 1943–44): nearly identical to previous type, usually considered one class. Some of these vessels mounted a 12-pounder instead of the 4-inch gun.

EMPIRE MACKAY, EMPIRE MacCOLL, EMPIRE MacMAHON, EMPIRE MacCABE (16,967 tons, one 4-inch gun, AC 4, 11 knots, 1943): oilers, again without hangars.

The MAC ships carried Swordfish exclusively. More of these vessels would have entered service if not for the proliferation of American-built CVEs.

At the start of the war, the fleet operated two seaplane carriers. *Albatross* (4,800 tons, four 4.7-inch DP guns, AC 9, 20 knots, 1929) became a repair ship in 1943. *Pegasus* (6,900 tons, four 3-inch DP guns, AC 10, 11 knots, 1914) began as a seaplane carrier but performed a variety of dull tasks before becoming a fighter

catapult ship in 1941, embarking three Fulmars. One Seagoing Auxiliary AA Vessel and three Ocean Boarding Vessels (listed with the escorts, below) also served as fighter catapult ships, similar to the mercantile CAM ships.

A 1939 proposal for modifying merchant ships as seaplane carriers resulted in two conversions (*Engadine* and *Athene*: 10,890 tons full load; one 4.7-inch, one 4-inch DP gun; AC 10, 17 knots, 1941). The latter may have served as a seaplane carrier, but the Admiralty needed both as aircraft ferries.

A pair of requisitioned merchantmen operated as seaplane tenders with the RAF.

Battleships and Battlecruisers

Although the British invented the fast battleship, it did them little good. The speedy *Queen Elizabeth*s should have revolutionized British BB design, but of the thirteen subsequent completions, seven had less speed than *Queen Elizabeth*, and not one matched her success. The culprit here was the old empire's brittle finances. Britannia, crowned with its tradition of naval dominance, exited World War I begging for treaty restrictions and international restraint—the only hope for maintaining its place among the new powers. Design teams created the *Nelson* class, the perfect metaphor of an apparent yet flagging supremacy. But the most spectacular victim of British ambivalence was the *King George V* class, which at least had some speed in an otherwise dismal design.

Nevertheless, His Majesty's dreadnoughts proved equal to the tasks of 1939–45, since the tasks weren't particularly trying. German battleships came out politely one by one for destruction, while the Italian ships refused to come at all. There was some unpleasantness with Japan in 1941, but little came of it.

In addition to a handful of Victorian ironclads gathering barnacles in various ports, a pair of senile dreadnoughts continued their employment with the Royal Navy. *Centurion* (25,000 tons, 16 knots, 1912) of the old *King George V* class was a target vessel rebuilt as a dummy ship to resemble a new *King George V*; for this role, she shipped some light AA and fake big guns. *Iron Duke* (21,250 tons; six 13.5-inch, twelve 6-inch guns; 18 knots, 1914) provided gunnery training.

Paris and *Courbet*, seized in Operation Catapult, served as noncombatants.

QUEEN ELIZABETH, BARHAM, WARSPITE, MALAYA, VALIANT, plus one other canceled (30,600–31,585 tons; eight 15-inch, twelve 6-inch, eight 4-inch DP guns; AC 4, 23.5–24 knots, 1915–16): when first completed, superior to all opponents, with adequate protection, good speed (25 knots), and the wonderful 15-inch gun, its firing cycle as short as 25 seconds. These classic ships continued as important units in the Second World War, sweeping away the German destroyers at Narvik and crushing the Italian cruisers off Cape Matapan. But they had aged; time dimmed the luster from their armor, their speed, even their guns.

Several refits served to enhance their qualities and create considerable variation. All but *Barham* and *Malaya* underwent extensive rebuilding during the 1930s, including a fine tower bridge. Deck protection thickened nicely over the main magazines, somewhat less over the machinery. *Queen Elizabeth* and *Valiant* experienced the most elaborate changes with their 6-inch and 4-inch guns replaced by a dual-purpose battery; the navy wanted the new 5.25-inch DP, but weight concerns dictated something smaller (twenty 4.5-inch guns—adequate weapons, though their low mounts caused some blast concerns). Main battery elevation increased from 20° to 30°, firing the new 1,938-lb shell. *Warspite* received the main battery enhancements but kept eight of her 6-inch guns. (A 3.7-inch howitzer somehow sneaked aboard for a time.) *Barham* shipped the new 15-inch shells by 1940 but retained her 20° mounts; it seems she also kept two of her old

21-inch TT and only one plane. (The others usually carried two.) *Malaya* likely got 1,938-lb shells before 1943.

In wartime, ships discarded some or all of their 6-inchers, along with the aviation facilities. Displacement rose near 34,000 tons.

The class sometimes achieved brilliant gunnery; as early as Jutland, the Germans noted *Valiant*'s consistent fire. At Calabria, *Warspite* planted a shot on the Italian flagship at a range of 26,400 yards, the longest ship-to-ship hit in history, even though the *Queen Elizabeth*s lacked the most up-to-date fire-control equipment.

They also lacked up-to-date durability. *Barham*, struck by three torpedoes, swung into an immediate list, capsized, and blew apart four minutes after first impact. But none of the others were lost. *Valiant* and *Queen Elizabeth* returned to action after damaging attacks by Italian SLC craft. *Warspite* survived a guided bomb of the sort that sank *Roma*; partly repaired, she then triggered a mine. By August 1944, she operated off the French coast with one propeller shaft broken, two damaged, and one undamaged (15.5 knots)—a performance that shows some heart.

The *Queen Elizabeth*s and all British dreadnoughts had more opportunities for action in the Mediterranean than in the Atlantic, with a few operations in the Far East. But their major opponent remained ever the aircraft rather than surface units; such was World War II. The Axis fleet-in-being tied many ships to sectors where no battles developed. This sometimes made for boring duty, but fortunately so; the thought of the *Queen Elizabeth*s steaming into the Pacific to face an aggressive naval foe is not a happy one.

ROYAL SOVEREIGN, RESOLUTION, REVENGE, ROYAL OAK, RAMILLIES (29,150 tons; eight 15-inch, twelve 6-inch, eight 4-inch DP guns; 21.5 knots, 1916–17): the "R" class, with three more units planned, two of them reordered as BC.

Compared with *Queen Elizabeth*, the "R's"

sacrificed some stability to achieve greater steadiness. The armor scheme improved, while speed and underwater protection regressed. Smaller and cheaper, in reality they proved an inferior long-term investment; the money and metal would have been better spent on four more *Queen Elizabeth*s since the lesser speed, stability, and size of the *Royal Sovereign*s made them less worthy of interwar upgrades. They entered the shipyards enough to increase their individuality, but only *Royal Oak* received much improvement, gaining some deck armor and having her four submerged 21-inch TT moved above water. Her sisters landed their torpedoes (*Revenge* perhaps kept two tubes) and went into the war with their original layers of deck plating. Some units shipped a plane and catapult, but only *Resolution* kept them through 1942. Around that time, she landed two 6-inch guns and, with *Royal Sovereign*, also received a token addition of deck armor. *Revenge*, *Royal Sovereign* and *Ramillies* landed four 6-inchers. *Resolution* may have had her 15-inch elevation increased in 1942, but the others remained at 20°. The new, heavier shells became available by 1941–43.

The wartime suggestion to expend the "R's" as blockships reveals their true worth. Operation Catherine, a planned foray into the German-dominated Baltic, changed to include some "R's" instead of the more valuable *Queen Elizabeth*s. *Royal Sovereign* sailed to the Soviet Union in 1944 (renamed *Arkhangelsk*), a substitute for Italian ships awaiting delivery as war reparations.

RENOWN, REPULSE (32,000 tons; six 15-inch, nine 4-inch, six 4-inch DP guns, eight 21-inch TT; AC 4, 29 knots, 1916): BC, originally part of the *Royal Sovereign* program. Their habits gained them the nicknames "Refit" and "Repair."

The design began at a mere 18% protection with 6-inch belt armor. Fortunately, changes came quickly with thousands of tons of armor added. Deck protection thickened to a reason-able degree. Both ships upgraded to 9-inch belts, still meager, and *Renown*'s belt lacked adequate depth. Her armament underwent modernization as twenty 4.5-inch DP guns replaced her 4-inchers and the main battery increased in elevation and shell weight. Speed fell from 31.5 to 30 knots, still enough for her to rate as Britain's fastest dreadnought for most of the war. She landed her aircraft by 1943 and, later, her torpedoes and most of her DP guns, these for use in new CV. Old age had claimed her.

Repulse retained her low-angle secondaries in three awkward triple mounts, one of which gave way to light AA in 1941. (A more ambitious plan would have provided fourteen 4-inch guns, all in DP mounts, with a reduction in torpedoes.) Her speed was 28.3 knots. She sank after taking one bomb and five aerial torpedoes.

Battlecruisers never lacked detractors, even before they sped into obsolescence. And yet, with regard to vessels of WWI vintage, it may be that the battlecruiser made a superior long-term investment. The Japanese *Kongo*s, after a thoughtful interwar reconstruction, transformed from BC to BB with increased armor and speed; meanwhile, the *Fuso*s, battleships derived from the *Kongo* design, transformed into senior citizens that showed up in World War II just long enough to sink. Had *Renown*, *Repulse*, and *Hood* been rebuilt *à la Kongo*, they would have proved more valuable than the "R's" or even the *Queen Elizabeth*s. Not the equal of modern battleships, they nevertheless had the one virtue—speed—that facilitated a primary mission of World War II dreadnoughts: fast carrier escort. Amid the scrappings caused by the Washington Treaty, the British might have done better to retain the battlecruisers *Lion*, *Princess Royal*, and *Tiger*, discarding some "R's" instead.

HOOD (42,100 tons; eight 15-inch, twelve 5.5-inch, eight 4-inch DP guns, four 21-inch TT; 31 knots, 1920): plus three sisterships canceled, the "Admiral" class. Usually rated as a battle-cruiser, *Hood* in many ways resembled a 30-

knot *Queen Elizabeth*, similar in armament and in protection. The fresh ache of Jutland spurred the navy to reject its original BC armor criteria, and *Hood's* designed protection scheme swelled, even as she underwent construction, to about 13,650 tons of armor—near the proportional standard for British battleships. However, this haphazard growth failed to make the most of its metal and couldn't fully incorporate Jutland's lessons.

Her obvious deficiencies prompted criticism—outspoken, repeated and blunt—within the Admiralty. The rest of the world, though, took no notice. Between the wars, *Hood* reigned over the seas, revered as the most powerful warship afloat, the symbol of British naval might. Of course, she wasn't the most powerful; she was merely the heaviest.

Ironically, her inflated reputation did her in, as the demands of a celebrity schedule kept her from a full reconstruction. Any such work would have proved difficult as her altered design had already pushed the hull to its limits. A 1938 suggestion included updating her bulges and deck armor, rearming her with sixteen 5.25-inch DP guns, and replacing her well-worn machinery (top speed was falling under 30 knots); but the war intervened. So, over-weight and sloshingly wet, *Hood* steamed unchanged into World War II, vulnerable according to standards that had been inadequate twenty years earlier. She landed her secondary battery in 1940 and gained six more 4-inch DP. Her main battery had 30° elevation but, like *Repulse*, she sank before shipping the new 15-inch shells.

Inquiries have failed to pin down the exact cause of *Hood's* loss. Her many flaws allow for many theories: an 8-inch shell touching off her torpedoes, a fire amid her 4-inch ammunition, a fiery splinter lancing into her magazines—even self-destruction from a malfunctioning shell hoist. In any case, the proposed changes might have sufficed to save her.

Britain's next BC project, dubbed *Incomparable* (6 20-inch, fifteen 4-inch, four 4-inch DP guns, eight 21-inch TT; about 35 knots), was euthanized following Jutland. It was, in fact, a simple design study rather than a serious effort.

NELSON, RODNEY (33,900 tons; nine 16-inch, twelve 6-inch, six 4.7-inch DP guns, two 24.5-inch TT; AC 1, 23 knots, 1927): misbegotten twins fathered by disarmament. After the Great War, as America and Japan constructed

Arguably the world's most powerful prewar battleship, the British **Nelson** *possessed several revolutionary features and a truly appalling appearance.*

ships with 16-inch guns, Britain realized that
even its 15-inch BB were obsolescing. Wartime
lessons and trials with former German vessels
led to a pair of designs aimed at restoring the
Royal Navy's place of ascendancy. Both designs
had extensive armor and powerful batteries,
with their secondary guns in turrets rather than
casemates.

The G3 design (48,400 nt; nine 16-inch,
sixteen 6-inch, six 4.7-inch DP guns, two 24.5-
inch TT; 31 knots), though called a battlecruiser, fit the description of a fast battleship; the
more conventional battleship N3 (48,500 nt;
nine 18-inch, sixteen 6-inch, six 4.7-inch DP
guns; 23.5 knots) fired shells weighing 2,837
lbs. But the drained English economy couldn't
float such behemoths, and in any case, the
Washington Treaty outlawed them, which is
well; almost surreal in ugliness, they mounted
two triple turrets forward and one amidships,
precisely where it could cause the most blast
damage. Sadly, though they never blighted the
seas with their awkward silhouettes, their lega-
cy did.

The Washington Treaty granted Britain
70,000 tons of new battleship construction to
provide parity with the Japanese *Nagato*s and
American *Colorado*s. Naval designers then pared
down the G3 battlecruiser, saving weight wherever practical and elsewhere besides. The three
turrets were clumped together forward to econ-
omize on armor weight, the machinery shrank
to 28% of its original power, and the hull lost
150 feet of length.

The *Nelson*s were innovative in many ways,
but successful in few. The nine 16-inch guns
seemed a potent battery, but by the time they
worked out all their bugs, they proved no more
effective than the old 15-inchers. In design, the
firing cycle was 30 seconds; in practice, 35 seconds; and for sustained fire, it rose to 60–65
seconds, complicated by poor ammunition handling. A proposed switch to 2,250-lb shells ran
afoul of the austere 1930s. Also, the turret
arrangement severely restricted their arcs of fire,

with blast damage an ever-present hazard. (In
attacking *Bismarck*, *Rodney* damaged herself
badly enough to start rumors she'd taken some
15-inch hits.) The 16-inch guns did have
greater reach than the 15/42, if not accuracy.

The secondary battery had its own list of
problems. Crowded together with no wealth of
armor, they offered a tempting target. The 60°
elevation represented a forlorn hope for dual
purpose. Even the 4.7-inch guns fell short of
expectations; rumors claimed *Rodney* would
replace them with eight 4-inch guns. A wartime
proposal for 12 American 5/38 DP failed
because of the already heavy demand for the
gun.

The design challenged its pilots as well as
its gunners. The ships' superstructure created a
vast sail area, giving winds the license to blow
them off course. The *Nelson*s handled poorly,
and the forward placement of the main battery
forced the bridge back, closer to the stern than
to the stem. But all this might have been forgiv-
en if only the ships had possessed some speed.
At least they handled heavy seas well.

With regard to protection, the design represented one advance of historic significance—its
armored deck more than doubled the Royal
Navy's previous best. Yet only the magazines
enjoyed its 6.75-inch thickness. The poorly
subdivided machinery had only about half that
much. The armor layout represented Britain's
first foray into all-or-nothing, while a newly
developed anti-torpedo system also had the
appeal of novelty, if not improvement. The
inclusion of submerged torpedo tubes brought
an inherent vulnerability, as *Nelson* demonstrated with 3,750 tons of flooding from an aerial
torpedo hit in 1941. During her repairs, workers removed the tubes.

Nelson enjoyed a prewar refit that tinkered
with her protection scheme. *Rodney* began the
war with two aircraft aboard, but landed them in
1943 along with her torpedoes. Defects in her
hull required regular attention, but finances and
wartime crises left her neglected; she fell into dis-

repair and gave no postwar service. The *Bismarck* provided the only excitement for the *Nelson* class, as *Rodney*'s guns proved they could score damaging hits on a disabled, ill-protected target.

KING GEORGE V, PRINCE OF WALES, DUKE OF YORK, ANSON, HOWE (37,000 tons; ten 14-inch, sixteen 5.25-inch DP guns; AC 4, 28 knots, 1940–42): no more successful than the previous class, except with respect to speed. All exceeded the specified 27.5 knots.

Once again, the design killer was the ambivalence inherent in planning a weapon pursuant to disarmament. The British fared poorly with the 35,000-ton limit. The battleship holiday had disrupted their design teams, and the newly-formed teams had to contend with arbitrary restrictions on size and armament. Yet the British wanted even more limits; they wanted smaller, cheaper BB and were prepared to provide the world with an example of self-restraint—as if the world cared. Reams of restrained British designs tumbled forth, displacements ranging as low as 20,000 tons with guns as small as 10-inch. No project could have survived unmangled.

The most restraint that the British could formalize at the Second London Conference was a reversion to 14-inch guns, on the condition that Japan also agree. The United States and Great Britain therefore finalized their BB designs with twelve 14-inch guns or nine 16-inch guns—indeed, hardly "finalized." Neither country had either gun prepared, so both began scurrying lest they incur any delay in construction. The Americans proceeded with a 14-inch design—one they could readily switch to 16-inch if Japan renounced the 14-inch limit. The British considered a similar plan, but the complications of designing a barbette suitable to both calibers proved too intimidating.

Japan renounced the limit; the Americans adopted 16-inch guns; *King George V* got 14-inchers.

The proposed armor and weaponry canceled all hope for 30 knots. With a DP secondary battery considered essential, planners picked the 4.5-inch gun (as in *Queen Elizabeth*), later replaced by a 5.25-inch weapon more potent against surface targets. As deficiencies in protection became apparent, the main battery changed from three quad mounts to three triple mounts, then to two quads and one twin (the quad mount design having neared completion). A twin turret design came quickly, causing no delays. This weakening of the already weak

The **Howe.** *Photographs and statistics don't reveal this design's best features—its armor quality and gun accuracy.*

armament freed several tons of displacement for an increase in armor. The finished ships came in overweight, but the approaching war had nullified all treaties.

Prince of Wales's encounter with the *Bismarck* gave an early indication of problems in the design. Any criticism here must bear in mind that *Prince of Wales* hadn't yet completed trials, entering the battle with civilian workmen still aboard. But the unreliability of the main battery showed itself clearly, as did a lack of protection in the conning tower. (British design had abandoned the idea of a heavy conning tower, a feature American planners considered essential, even if American commanders did not.) The much-reviled 14-inch guns did have a partial vindication, probably scoring the hit that, while not threatening to sink the *Bismarck*, caused a loss of fuel and completely changed the tactical situation.

The subsequent gun duel between *Bismarck* and *King George V* proved little except that British marksmanship could pound a crippled target, while neither the 14-inch shells nor *Rodney*'s 16-inchers could inflict lethal damage at short range. Plunging fire from a greater distance would have had more effect. The main battery continued its unreliability.

Though temperamental weaponry presented a problem, defective protection below the waterline presented an opportunity for disaster. Designers gave *King George V* the slimmest anti-torpedo system of any modern battleship, then boldly claimed it could resist 1,000 lbs of TNT—a hopeless case of optimism. (*Yamato*'s system claimed only 882 lbs.) Furthermore, the system integrated poorly with the ship's structure, not extending high enough in the hull, while defects in watertightness encouraged progressive flooding. These compound flaws seem especially unfortunate, since British designers had compromised the belt protection in their pursuit of flood resistance.

Prince of Wales had the misfortune to demonstrate the full extent of the hazard when attacked by Japanese aircraft in December 1941. Four torpedoes struck the starboard side: one inconsequential hit nipped the bow; two others hit the thickest part of the anti-torpedo system and posed no great threat to the ship; and one struck among her propellers, destroying a shaft and opening a few compartments to the sea. This last hit might have caused some concerns except that events on the port side had already doomed the ship.

A torpedo scored a direct hit on the strut supporting the port outboard propeller shaft. The shaft began to flail, simultaneously ripping into the hull and distorting the shaft tunnel, which allowed flooding straight into an engine room. Damage of this sort could endanger even a ship of thorough watertightness. Meanwhile, another explosion blasted through the side protection closer to midships, causing damage so severe that some believed two torpedoes had struck together—unlikely, but possible. Another theory notes the placement of the hit in a section damaged by a near-miss bomb during the ship's construction; some over-hasty repairs may have left the area weakened. In any event, the inrush of seawater from the two port hits completely overmatched the ships' emergency power and communications systems. This interfered with damage control, disabled many pumps, and set loose a hint of panic in the crew. In the midst of battle, guns began to lose power, while a menacing list restricted their arcs of fire. In the end, inexorable flooding flipped the vessel over and pulled her down, the victim of 331-lb and 452-lb warheads.

This vulnerability derived partly from the limits imposed by treaties and dockyard facilities. But the flooding hazard reached beyond British battleships, affecting carriers and cruisers as well—an unfortunate family trait. The early warning of *Ark Royal*'s experience inspired a sluggish response. Only after the *Prince of Wales* trauma did the Admiralty rouse itself for the serious pursuit of a remedy. Simple but significant changes eventually made their way into the surviving *King George V*s, and by 1945 the 35,000-ton ships reached 40,000 tons (45,000 tons full load). Other wartime alterations included the proliferation of light AA and the removal of the aircraft by 1942.

A bomb that hit *Prince of Wales* in her last battle caused no great damage. Against bombs and against shellfire, the uncomplicated armor layout provided satisfactory protection.

Duke of York's duel with *Scharnhorst* was no equal contest. Poor *Scharnhorst*, with a damaged radar and no escort, was the only modern dreadnought that a *King George V* could clearly outgun. A crowd of British cruisers and destroyers further imbalanced the fight. Three torpedoes and a 14-inch shell that burst in *Scharnhorst*'s boilers cut her speed and ended her hopes. The British 14-inch guns gave no disadvantage against the German 11.1-inchers, but even at this late date (December 1943), the mounts remained troublesome, reducing fire to about two-thirds of its potential volume.

The 5.25-inch secondary battery, while properly intended for DP duty, also proved a disappointment. Designed to fire 10–12 rpm, the guns managed 7–8 rpm at most in their cramped turrets. The mounts lacked the speed necessary for tracking modern aircraft.

The *King George V* design did few things well. Its weapons underperformed. The hull form made for poor seaboats, so wet that waves at times disabled the forward turret. Ship's speed was acceptable, maneuverability less so, and range not at all—7,000 miles at 14 knots as designed (more like 7,000 miles at 10 knots in practice), less than half the range of American battleships. In operations with American units, the *King George V*s required repeated refueling; they could carry only two-thirds as much fuel as a *North Carolina*, and their machinery burned through it quickly. British naval machinery in general proved 25% less economical than the American.

Given the situation the designers faced, the flaws in their work are understandable, but that doesn't make the work any less flawed. On the positive side, the quality of British battleship armor from this period was unexcelled. It's unfortunate that, in a design that made such sacrifice to increase its armor, its protection should fall victim to an underwater oversight. The ships accomplished their duties well enough; but then, their primary duty was to counter an enemy fleet-in-being, which they could accomplish by merely existing.

A peculiar, clandestine scheme arose during the war when a high-ranking American official proposed trading eight American heavy cruisers (presumably CA24–31, 33, 35) for the *Duke of York*. The British recovered from their surprise and expressed some interest, but they lacked the manpower to crew eight new ships. Inspiring more curiosity than enthusiasm, the scheme faded away.

LION, TEMERAIRE, CONQUEROR, THUNDERER (42,550 tons; nine 16-inch, sixteen 5.25 DP guns; AC 2, 30 knots): designed after the Japanese renounced the 14-inch limit, but never completed.

The Japanese decision triggered an escalation clause allowing BB of 45,000 tons with 16-inch guns. Yet the British remained tentative, limiting themselves to a design of 40,550 tons despite the harm their self-restraint had already inflicted on the *King George V* class. Only with the onset of world war did the planners doff their inhibition; *Lion*'s displacement rose to 42,550 tons and, after assimilating some lessons of war, to about 49,000 tons.

The 16-inch gun showed no signs of British hesitancy. The design promised accuracy and reliability with a shell weight of 2,375 lbs. (Later proposals for 2540 lbs and a 20-second firing cycle showed admirable optimism.) In other regards, the *Lion*s look mostly mediocre. Belt and deck thickness showed no increase over *King George V*'s, nor did the designed range, at first; the embarrassment of experience later inspired an enlarged fuel load. After the *Prince of Wales* incident, the underwater scheme improved, though not enough. The scout planes eventually faded from the design, which continued to develop until more urgent projects caused its cancellation. Had the ships been completed, they would have given good service, being roughly equal to analogous foreign designs.

VANGUARD (46,100 tons; eight 15-inch, sixteen 5.25-inch DP guns; 30 knots): an ironic name for Britain's last battleship, completed postwar.

In 1939, the head of British naval construction had a brainstorm: the fleet could hasten one of its fast battleships into service by reusing old parts. Britain had a surplus of 15-inch guns and mounts, including those removed from the *Courageous*-class BC. Obviously not modern weapons, they still had some punch; penetration exceeded that of the new 14-inch gun and, at some ranges, the *Nelson's* 16-inch model. *Vanguard*, laid down in 1941, delayed by more urgent works, missed the war by less than a year.

The British made the most of the old guns by providing remote power control, a first in Royal Navy battleships, and American fire-control systems. The secondary battery enjoyed similar technology. Roomier mounts allowed 18 rpm; though their armor thickened, they achieved quicker training and elevation than in previous battleships. With her powerful array of light guns, *Vanguard* had no superior in AA ability.

The overall design owed much to the two preceding projects, as in her machinery dispersal and the basic protection layout. The armor actually thinned slightly, but refinements made better use of it and enhanced *Vanguard's* resistance to flooding. American standards instigated an upgrade in habitability but no serious increase in range. Hull strength was marginal; speed was good. A handsome ship and a fantastically dry seaboat, *Vanguard* would have estab-

lished an excellent war record despite her range and old guns.

In 1942, a short-lived proposal suggested converting *Vanguard* into an aircraft carrier.

Monitors

The 15-inch monitors had 30° mounts and probably received the 1,938-lb shell by 1943.

MARSHAL NEY, MARSHAL SOULT (6,400 tons; two 15-inch, three 3-inch DP guns; six knots, 1915): a true successor to the original *Monitor*, with a silhouette featuring little more than a turret, a mast, and a funnel. The turret so dominated the design that it affected the magnetic compass. The armor percentage equaled that of a full-sized BB, and exaggerated bulges protected the hull; this protection continued in future designs.

Designed for nine knots, they clearly reflect the difficulty Britain was having with monitor machinery at the time, and the bulged form made steering a challenge. *Ney* was such an annoyance that the navy moved her turret to *Terror* in 1916. Totally disarmed between the wars, she became the hulk *Drake*. The navy wanted to refit *Soult* for combat in 1939, but she proved too decrepit; workers removed her turret and other salvable equipment for installation in the new *Roberts*, and she became a depot ship.

EREBUS, TERROR (7,200 tons; two 15-inch, eight 4-inch, two 3-inch DP guns; 12 knots, 1916): Britain's first big-gun monitors with adequate machinery, and a slight gain in handling as well. *Erebus* mounted a turret from the *Furious* project. *Terror* exemplified the toughness of these ships in 1917 when she survived three torpedo hits. The ships were much older by 1939, but *Terror* still showed some heart before succumbing to a series of mines and near-miss bombs.

War modifications made them more modern but harder to maneuver. Six 4-inch DP replaced the 3-inch and 4-inch guns.

ROBERTS, ABERCROMBIE (7,973–8,536 tons; two 15-inch, eight 4-inch DP guns; 12.5 knots, 1941–43): the world's last big monitors. Britain's unique persistence with monitors provided ships of unquestioned value in fire support. In this role, they often proved the equal of battleships, though with a smaller magazine capacity. By recycling the turrets and guns of older vessels, monitors made a cheap investment, and the navy was delighted to find they cost less than old BB for use as training ships.

Though inexpensive, these last two were distinct from the bare-bones designs of the First World War. In fact, these humble monitors rate among the finest British warship designs of their time. Their main flaw lay in their lack of mobility, a sacrifice that allowed a balance of their other virtues. Faster and more reliable than previous classes, they still couldn't qualify as speedy, and their bulging hulls caused them to lose speed rapidly in conditions of heavy seas, strong wind, and bottom-fouling. This last factor translated into a loss of two knots after six months out of dock, while endurance would fall from 3,600 miles to 2,700 miles at 10 knots. Unlike the WWI types, *Roberts* was maneuverable—but only in the hands of an experienced and determined helmsman.

Both ships had the opportunity to show their ruggedness, and they earned a reputation with their AA outfit; when not shelling enemy shore targets, they often served as AA guardships. Drier than *Erebus*, *Roberts* was however overcrowded and short on habitability. *Abercrombie* had expanded crew accommodations, along with more armor, additional generators, and other details. She mounted the second unused *Furious* turret.

The British considered a few other monitor projects during the war, including a swarm of 6-inch-armed vessels and floating batteries of army howitzers. But the leadership, trying to avoid all the effort of purpose-built designs, settled for the expedient of landing craft modified as gunboats.

Cruisers

The heart of the Royal Navy was its cruiser force. Treaties allowed the rising American fleet a parity in battleships, but when the Americans claimed an equal tonnage of cruisers, the British responded with a bulldog growl. Their years of expertise with successful designs enabled them to avoid the prewar fumbling that plagued the United States. Designers enjoyed a fling with 10,000-ton ships before reverting to their traditional modest types. Having no trans-Pacific commitments, the Admiralty preferred to build the largest possible number of smaller ships.

Britain's hatred of the U-boat and the need of its cruisers to operate alone resulted in unusual provisions for AS warfare. Most British cruisers had depth charge racks and sonar; some even carried depth charge throwers. But they were otherwise a boring lot: reliable rather than radical, functional if not fearsome. No wartime heavy cruisers materialized—a regrettable turn, given the powerful designs being considered.

Like Britain's battleships, the cruisers never carried more than two aircraft, despite their stated maximums.

Three veterans survived in training duty: *Caroline* from the first "C" class (3,750 tons; four 4-inch, one 3-inch DP gun; 29 knots, 1914), *Defiance I* (11,000 tons full load, disarmed?, 1897), and *Philomel* (2,575 tons full load, disarmed, 19 knots, 1891). A few other metal-hulled refugees from the 19th Century—sloops, corvettes, and the like—lingered into the war years.

ADELAIDE (5,100 tons; eight 6-inch, three 4-inch DP guns; 24.3 knots, 1922): in Australian service, last of four old *Birmingham*-class ships. Such an elderly design could function only in convoy escort. She landed a 6-inch and a 4-inch gun to make room for light AA.

CALEDON, CALYPSO, CARADOC, plus one sister ship lost prewar (4,180 tons; five 6-inch, two 3-inch DP guns, eight 21-inch TT; 29 knots, 1917): the third of Britain's "C" classes laid down before World War I. Wet forward, they also rolled badly. *Caledon* became an AA cruiser during the war with an armament of six 4-inch DP and no torpedoes.

The 6-inch guns on old British cruisers (up to the "E" class) sometimes used super-charges of propellant to extend their range to 20,020 yards.

CERES, CARDIFF, CURACOA, COVENTRY, CURLEW (4,190 tons; five 6-inch, two 3-inch DP guns, eight 21-inch TT; 29 knots, 1917–18): improved seaworthiness, but the roll and wetness remained. The last pair underwent a prewar conversion to AA vessels with their original armament replaced by light guns and ten 4-inch DP, some of which they later landed. The navy planned to convert the others (eight 4-inch DP), but because of the war, only *Curacoa* had the work done. *Coventry* survived a torpedo hit, though was later lost to air attack near Tobruk; *Curlew* showed her age by sinking after some bomb near-misses. *Cardiff* provided training through most of the war. *Ceres* landed her TT and in 1944 was retired from active service.

CARLISLE, CAIRO, CALCUTTA, COLOMBO, CAPETOWN (4,290 tons; five 6-inch, two 3-inch DP guns, eight 21-inch TT; 29 knots, 1918–22): the fifth and final "C" class, designed to be drier. The first three underwent conversion at the beginning of hostilities, shipping eight 4-inch DP instead of the previous guns and torpedoes. *Colombo* converted in 1943 with six 4-inch DP. *Capetown* survived a torpedo; *Cairo* did not. *Calcutta* succumbed to two bombs. *Carlisle* shot down a total of 11 aircraft during the war, the most for a British cruiser.

HAWKINS, CAVENDISH, EFFINGHAM, FROBISHER, plus a sistership lost prewar (9,800 tons; seven 7.5-inch, four 4-inch DP guns, six 21-inch TT; 30 knots, 1918–24): sometimes called the "Elizabethans, " a large and unique class designed to hunt commerce raiders, chasing them down at high speed through any sea and weather conditions. Their hulls, based on the *Furious* BC hull form, had extra strength to localize battle damage. Their cumbersome main guns earned some criticism. *Hawkins* experienced few prewar changes except the removal of two TT. *Effingham* traded her original armament for nine 6-inch and eight 4-inch DP guns with four TT and one aircraft. *Frobisher*, disarmed by 1937, regained her torpedoes and five main guns, plus five 4-inch DP. *Cavendish* went through the greatest changes; renamed *Vindictive* in 1918 for duties as an aircraft carrier, she became a training cruiser in 1937 (9,100 tons, two 4.7-inch guns, 23 knots), later a repair ship and transport.

The "Elizabethans" performed a secondary role in wartime, most landing all their torpedoes. Their top speeds varied.

The construction of these ships had far-reaching repercussions. They were the direct cause of Britain's endorsing the 10,000-ton, 8-inch-gun treaty cruiser, a new type of warship which ultimately proved something of a failure. The *Hawkins* provided the basis for the "County" classes and thus gave the British a head start in the development of the heavy cruiser.

DANAE, DRAGON, DAUNTLESS, DELHI, DESPATCH, DIOMEDE, DUNEDIN, DURBAN, plus four additional units canceled (4,850 tons; six 6-inch, three 4-inch DP guns, twelve 21-inch TT; 29 knots, 1918–22): the "D" class, related to the "C" class with increased firepower. The last five had an improved, drier hull form. All were good seaboats.

Prewar plans included rearmament with eight 4.5-inch DP, but the plans never went

*The **Berwick** shows the high freeboard of Britain's "County"-class cruisers.*

through. For most of the class the biggest changes included losing some torpedoes or a main gun, perhaps gaining an extra 4-inch DP. *Delhi*, however, traded her guns in 1941 for five American 5/38 DP. This made her equal in firepower to an American DD, but the British enjoyed the 5/38 almost as much as the Americans and asked to have *Dunedin* so equipped. By then, events had changed American priorities. Besides *Delhi* and a pair of support ships, the only British ships to get the 5/38 gun were the American-built *Ameers*, whose flight deck overhang limited their AA arcs of fire.

Britain's AA conversions represented an intelligent use of cruisers no longer suited to front-line operations. A supply of American 5-inch guns would have further increased their value. The unconverted "D's" suffered fates typical for elderly warships. *Despatch* became a depot ship; *Dauntless* and *Diomede*, training vessels. *Danae* (renamed *Conrad*) and *Dragon* spent time in Polish service. *Dragon* then joined *Durban*, expended as a breakwater off Normandy. *Dunedin* sank from two torpedo hits.

EMERALD, ENTERPRISE, plus one other can-

celed (7,550 tons; seven 6-inch, three 4-inch DP guns, sixteen 21-inch TT; AC 1, 33 knots, 1926): the final development of a lineage that began with *Caroline*. The increase in size gained speed and range (8,000 miles at 15 knots versus 6,700 miles at 10 knots for the "D's"). The design included good sea-keeping and an early form of machinery dispersal.

The "E" class had more torpedo tubes than any other British ship. *Emerald* carried two single guns forward in 30° mounts, but *Enterprise* had a 40° twin mount, the prototype for the higher-angle mounts in the BB *Nelson* (though in *Enterprise's* case the mount proved successful). Wartime changes included removal of eight TT and the aircraft, and the temporary removal of two 6-inchers from *Emerald*. Each ship permanently landed one 6-inch gun. Light AA increased. The "E's" became inactive toward the war's end.

A plan arose in 1942 to fit the ships with flight decks and give them 18 aircraft, at the cost of a reduced power plant.

A development of the "E" class (4 7.5-inch, four 4-inch DP guns, twelve 21-inch TT) appeared too large to be built in sufficient numbers.

KENT, BERWICK, CORNWALL, CUMBER-LAND, SUFFOLK, AUSTRALIA, CANBERRA (9,750–9,870 tons; eight 8-inch, eight 4-inch DP guns, eight 21-inch TT; AC 1–3, 31.5 knots, 1928): the first "County" class. By 1945, their displacements climbed near 11,000 tons. None of them kept their aircraft past 1942, and most landed their torpedoes. *Australia*, after six kamikaze hits, traded two 8-inch guns for more light AA.

The oddest feature of this otherwise mundane design was the 70° elevation given their main battery—a futile bid for AA firepower. The mount produced some initial troubles, but subsequent adjustments made them dependable. In weaponry, the *Kent*s equaled their foreign peers and proved adequate gun platforms. They had plenty of range (13,300 miles at 12 knots, as designed) but not agility. More seriously, they lacked armor.

Prewar British claims about their CA's superior protection showed no acquaintance with reality. Their magazines sat within an armored box (copied from the *Hawkins* design) which served well against plunging shells and bombs, but otherwise the ships lay exposed—as built, totaling less than 10% armor. Prewar modernization added more armor, auxiliary generators, and other improvements. *Cornwall* stood up as well as could be expected amid a crushing air attack; nine bombs scored direct hits, and she sank in 12 minutes. *Kent* required a year of repairs following an aerial torpedo hit. *Suffolk* went out of action for 10 months after one bomb hit and three near misses.

Only *Canberra* went unmodernized, and she suffered the consequences. Japanese cruisers hit her amidships with 27 shells (from 4.7-inch to 8-inch) in the space of about three minutes, causing a sudden and catastrophic loss of power. Since she lagged behind even the British standards for emergency power, her crew had nothing but buckets with which to fight her fires and flooding. The idea that such modest shellfire had crippled a 10,000-ton warship prompted theories of two Japanese torpedo hits,

despite the absence of eyewitness corroboration. Postwar review confirms that no Japanese torpedoes struck *Canberra*, but the sad possibility exists that an American torpedo did. The essential fact is that a neglected "tinclad" incurred a torrent of shell hits around her machinery spaces—explanation enough for her power loss. *Canberra* might well have have survived if not for skittishness among commanders who feared the enemy's return. She lasted for seven hours before scuttling.

The *Kent*s' most visible features were their archaic trio of funnels and their high silhouette. High freeboard made the "Counties" the driest British cruisers, but it also caused complications; despite all attempted remedies, one third of their torpedoes failed to function properly, damaged by the fall from such a great height.

Despite a design resemblance to the *Hawkins*, the "County" classes served as much in fleet scouting as they did in commerce protection. As combatants, they were thoroughly mediocre. Their great virtue lay not in any battle-dominance, but in their reliability. They showed all the flair of a good cart horse, and the steadiness as well. No country built a truly balanced treaty cruiser, and the "Counties" should be viewed in that context.

LONDON, DEVONSHIRE, SUSSEX, SHROP-SHIRE (9,830 tons; eight 8-inch, eight 4-inch DP guns, eight 21-inch TT; AC 1, 32.3 knots, 1929): the second "County" class, differing little from the *Kent*s. They did incorporate a marginal gain in protection, mostly underwater. Their extra fraction of a knot came with a minor loss of range.

All the "Counties" were well built and serviceable, but *London*'s refit (begun in 1939, hastily concluded in 1941) became a disaster. She emerged at 11,015 tons; the extra weight that workers slapped onto her hull created unmanageable stress. When the hull began to crack, the upper portion was reinforced; leaks then opened in the lower portion. Water got into the fuel oil; fuel oil got into the magazines, forming pools deep enough to require bucket brigades. The problem went unchecked until 1943.

London had gained extra armor and two additional aircraft, but the whole class landed their planes during the war. Light AA and other additions pushed each ship over 10,500 tons. The need to reduce top weight led to *Devonshire* sacrificing X Turret, and *Sussex*, a turret and her torpedoes.

NORFOLK, DORSETSHIRE (9,925 tons; eight 8-inch, eight 4-inch DP guns, eight 21-inch TT; AC 1, 32.3 knots, 1930): the final "County" class. Like the previous ships, they entered service with only four single DP guns, but the battery doubled (usually by replacing single mounts with twins) before the war's start or shortly thereafter. The *Norfolk*s showed little change from the *London*s but had simplified shell handling.

Many treaty cruisers lacked protection; the "County" classes certainly did. But while the Italians sacrificed armor for speed and the Americans sought firepower, the British pursued seakeeping and dependability. Despite their thin skins, only three "Counties" became war losses, a commendable record for such an active group. On the other hand, damaged units required lengthy repair times.

YORK, EXETER (8,250–8,390 tons; six 8-inch, four 4-inch DP guns, six 21-inch TT; AC 1, 32.3 knots, 1930–31): sometimes called the "Cathedral" class. In fact, the two ships differed. The heavier *Exeter* had two aircraft and only 50° elevation for her guns (perhaps later increased to the standard 70°). Her DP battery was doubled to eight guns shortly before her loss.

The Admiralty foresaw these ships primarily as commerce protectors, a less demanding role allowing a cheaper design. In trimming down the "County" layout, designers managed to retain several features, though sea-keeping

suffered. Protection also received low priority; the armor scheme (similar in proportion to the "County" type) included some advances, but all in all, the *York*s seemed even more vulnerable, especially in the machinery spaces. *Exeter* took an 8-inch shell in her after boilers at Java Sea with a resulting drop to half speed; two days later, another 8-inch shell struck the forward boiler room and ended her career. Previously, in her duel with *Graf Spee*, seven 11.1-inch rounds all but crippled her. *York* was done in by an explosive motor boat.

SURREY, NORTHUMBERLAND (10,000 tons; eight 8-inch, four 4-inch DP guns, eight 21-inch TT; AC 2, 30 knots): not laid down before the leadership decided to concentrate on light cruisers. Continued work with this canceled design eventually wound its way into the "Town" project.

Surrey resembled a combination of previous types with "County" type armament but *Exeter*'s two stacks and lesser freeboard. An armor increase to about 20% promised good protection. Had the ships commissioned, their DP battery probably would have doubled.

The cancellation of the *Surrey*s in 1930 closed the book on British heavy cruisers. New designs arose during the war, but none got far. Some WWI surplus 9.2-inch guns with 380-lb shells inspired studies for a nine-gun ship, while a 22,000-ton version mounted 12 guns. The 8-inch proposals topped out at 16,100–18,740 tons (about 20% armor) with four ships planned to carry nine new 8/50 guns (290-lb shell, 31,300-yard range at 45° elevation) plus eight to sixteen 4-inch DP guns (or a 4.5-inch DP battery) with six 21-inch TT, three aircraft, and 35.25 knots.

LEANDER, ACHILLES, AJAX, NEPTUNE, ORION (6,985–7,270 tons; eight 6-inch, eight 4-inch DP guns, eight 21-inch TT; AC 2, 32.5 knots, 1933–35): varying tonnage due to development of weight-saving measures such as welding. War service sent the ships as high as 7,600 tons.

The *York*s evolved amid Britain's desire for larger numbers of cheaper ships, but the result left the navy disappointed. The logical next step was to try an even smaller but more balanced design. Some thought went into a four-gun CA before common sense settled on light cruisers, whose 6-inch guns sufficed against armed merchant cruisers and had the added appeal of an increased rate of fire—better for driving enemy light forces away from the fleet. The success of *Enterprise*'s twin mount won approval for a similar mount in this new class. The guns in the *Leander*s elevated to 60° but had no AA value. As the heavy cruisers also had done, the *Leander*s commissioned with only four single DP; *Achilles* didn't get her twin mounts until 1943. As a rule, they carried just one aircraft, until its removal during the war. *Achilles* and *Leander* landed a main turret as well to accommodate more light AA.

By foregoing the full 10,000-ton and 8-inch allowance, the British created an all-around successful class. The *Leander*s had adequate range (10,300 miles at 12 knots) and proved handy in service. Ton for ton, they compare well with ships like Italy's "Condottieris," but the advent of the 15-gun CL made them seem insignificant. In fact, *Leander*'s modest armament corresponded properly to her size. The problem lay in providing the small ships with adequate protection.

The design included 845 tons of armor—not a negligible total, but not sufficient either—and the *Leander*s had no machinery dispersal, the last British cruisers to lack it. *Orion* and *Ajax* suffered greatly from just one or two bombs. *Neptune*'s loss after striking four mines is understandable, but only one crewman survived. *Leander*, hit by a Long Lance, needed two years of repair, an absurdly long time; perhaps a backlog in the yards caused some delay.

ARETHUSA, GALATEA, PENELOPE, AURORA (5,220–5,279 tons; six 6-inch, eight 4-inch DP

guns, eight 21-inch TT; AC 1, 32.3 knots, 1935–37): weight later up to 6,000 tons. Having built a successful light cruiser, the British decided to try something weaker. As successor to the C-type classes, *Arethusa* had humble requirements, intended to operate in conjunction with destroyers. A quest began for the smallest possible cruiser (studies as small as 3,000 tons) with suitable sea-keeping and crew accommodation. Apparently the outcome pleased no one, and *Leander* had more prominence in later design development.

The *Arethusa*s, with only four-fifths the range of their predecessors, were even less suited to the Pacific. The armor percentage remained about the same, so despite their machinery dispersal, survivability in the smaller ships decreased. They did prove extremely maneuverable. *Aurora* had no aircraft, and the others landed theirs by 1941. *Arethusa* had only single DP guns until 1942.

PERTH, HOBART, SYDNEY (6,980 tons; eight 6-inch, eight 4-inch DP guns, eight 21-inch TT; AC 1, 32.5 knots, 1935–36): *Leander* repeats, named *Amphion*, *Apollo*, and *Phaeton* until transferred to Australia. Apart from their machinery dispersal, which left them somewhat cramped, they resembled the earlier ships. A proposed increase to ten 6-inch guns would have caused complications in the proven design. Apparently *Perth* received her scout plane but not its catapult. *Sydney* sank before doubling her DP battery. *Hobart* required 17 months of repair after one torpedo hit.

SOUTHAMPTON, GLASGOW, SHEFFIELD, BIRMINGHAM, NEWCASTLE (9,100 tons; twelve 6-inch, eight 4-inch DP guns, six 21-inch TT; AC 3, 32 knots, 1937): first of the "Town" classes. Aware of Japanese and American decisions to build large "light" cruisers, the British reluctantly admitted their ships had begun to look puny. (*Arethusa* had a broadside of 672 lbs; *Brooklyn* had 1,950 lbs.) They

The appearance of Japan's powerful Mogami *spurred Britain toward larger light cruisers, such as the* Sheffield (above).

therefore developed the *Perth* design into a powerful, solid CL capable of taking the same role as a "County."

The *Southamptons* gave good service. They had the range of a *London* and almost as much seaworthiness. Main battery elevation reverted from 60° to 45°, which became standard until the postwar *Tiger*. During the war, light AA replaced the aircraft and one main turret. Protection totaled about 15% of displacement, and though *Southampton* sank after only two bomb hits, the "Town" classes in general showed commendable ruggedness. They did suffer some lack of hull structure, and *Glasgow* had her back broken by two aerial torpedoes, yet she survived.

GLOUCESTER, LIVERPOOL, MANCHESTER (9,400 tons; twelve 6-inch, eight 4-inch DP guns, six 21-inch TT; AC 3, 32.3 knots, 1938–39): modified *Southamptons* with improved protection and fire control. Only *Liverpool* survived long enough to exchange her aircraft and a turret for light AA. She had an experience usually reserved for aircraft carriers when a torpedo hit caused a leak of aviation fuel. The fumes spread, then detonated and blew off her bow.

EDINBURGH, BELFAST (10,550 tons; twelve 6-inch, twelve 4-inch DP guns, six 21-inch TT; AC 3, 32.5 knots, 1939): the final "Town" class and Britain's finest cruiser design. The initial plan included a main battery of four quadruple turrets, but troubles with the turret design caused a return to triples—a fortunate choice. Sixteen guns would have provided impressive firepower and many problems.

Compared to the previous class, the *Edinburghs* were better seaboats but less maneuverable. The primary difference lay in an improved protection scheme, which topped 18% of their displacement; no British cruiser bettered their 4.5-inch belt and 4-inch turret armor. Both ships endured severe damage. *Belfast* survived the war, having traded her catapult and four DP guns for additional light AA.

DIDO, ARGONAUT, BONAVENTURE, CHARYBDIS, CLEOPATRA, EURYALUS, HERMIONE, NAIAD, PHOEBE, SCYLLA, SIRIUS (5,600 tons, ten 5.25-inch DP guns, six 21-inch TT, 32.2 knots, 1940–42): an *Arethusa* development. The project began, much as *Arethusa* did, with a request for a small fleet cruiser, but with increased antiaircraft capability. The plan then wallowed amid low priorities until it began to seem as useful as a conventional CL. The 5.25-inch guns hampered a promising design; in cramped mounts like those aboard the *King George V*, their theoretical firing cycle of five seconds became eight seconds in service, and

there was a problem with jamming. Fire control showed some over-complexity, while the layout did not provide the steadiest gun platform. The ships did prove maneuverable and seaworthy. Their looks were graceful rather than strong, and appropriately so; a weakness in the hulls necessitated additional strengthening. Improved subdivision would have helped, as wing passages encouraged uneven flooding. This made an unfortunate combination with the *Didos*' top-heaviness—alterations had loaded the design well above the intended 5,450 tons—and the class gained a reputation for rapid capsizing. *Naiad* and *Hermione* sank after single torpedo hits. The design was 12% protection.

British gun supply fell well behind demand. *Dido*, *Phoebe*, and *Bonaventure* entered service with only four turrets; *Dido* later got her fifth. On the other hand, some ships mounting all 10 guns later landed two. *Scylla* and *Charybdis* had no 5.25-inch guns at all; they went to sea with a makeshift battery of eight 4.5-inch DP. The two were well regarded despite their lighter armament since it made them less crowded and top-heavy. Still, *Charybdis* reached 5,582 tons. Some *Didos* carried a 4-inch star shell gun—rather prodigal for ships with too much top-weight and not enough light AA.

The Belfast. *Though lacking in hull strength, the "Town" series culminated in Britain's finest cruisers.*

GREAT BRITAIN

The *Didos*' closest counterparts were the American *Atlantas*, which displaced 1,000 tons more. An enlargement of the British design could have made the ships more battle-worthy; a *Dido* would have disintegrated under the pounding the *Atlanta* received.

Wartime ideas for a small cruiser included a *Dido* enlargement featuring seven (or more) 5.25-inch twins, plus eight 4-inch DP guns with six 21-inch torpedo tubes, one or two scout planes, and 31.75 knots—never practical for a lineage already blighted by top-heaviness, and ultimately dismissed in preference of a 6-inch armament's punch (hence the *Fijis*). Nevertheless, initial enthusiasm greeted a proposal mounting *Vanguard*-type 5.25-inch guns despite its top speed of just 28 knots. A most aberrant proposal, and duly short-lived, involved a "torpedo cruiser" of 4,900 tons with 35 knots, slight armor, light guns, and six bow torpedo tubes.

FIJI, MAURITIUS, BERMUDA, GAMBIA, JAMAICA, KENYA, NIGERIA, TRINIDAD, CEYLON, NEWFOUNDLAND, UGANDA (8,525 tons; twelve 6-inch, eight 4-inch DP guns, six 21-inch TT; AC 2, 33 knots, 1940–43): the "Colony" class. The Second London Conference limited CL to 8,000 tons, prompting a series of *Dido*-ish studies. However, the prospects of combat against heavy cruisers sent the 5.25-inch gun into disfavor, and the Admiralty resolved to squeeze a "Town" into 8,000 tons.

Designers did their best. A refined hull form afforded greater speed despite a smaller power plant. Armor thinned out by an inch or two, and there were no torpedo tubes (they could be added for war service). The stunted design came close to its 8,000-ton target (8,170 tons) before the war's approach summoned the TT and some other features back on board. *Fiji* entered service at 8,631 tons.

All this sleight-of-hand could not reproduce the success of the *Edinburghs*, though the *Fijis'*

displacement over time expanded to 9,200 tons. Efforts began early to relieve their crowding and excess top-weight. (One proposal would have removed the center gun from each mount.) Some ships never took on their X turret, and by war's end, only *Gambia* and *Nigeria* retained theirs. Likewise, those ships completed with aircraft facilities had them removed by 1944.

Fiji's reduced armor scheme filled about 15% of her displacement, more than acceptable since the Admiralty saw her as successor to *Leander*; in ruggedness, she approximated the *Southamptons*. She survived a torpedo but succumbed to one bomb hit and three near misses. A German guided bomb plunged all the way through *Uganda* before exploding; she survived and was renamed *Quebec* for Canadian service in 1944.

Purse strings often reined Britain toward small designs, following a successful class with a dwarfish imitation. This provided a larger number of ships, even admitting their inferiority. *Fiji* after *Edinburgh*, *Arethusa* after *Leander*, the cut-rate "O" class destroyers after the muscular "L's"—the compromise between quality and quantity, a factor in every navy, proved especially compromising for the fleet upon which the sun never set.

BELLONA, BLACK PRINCE, SPARTAN, ROYALIST, DIADEM (5,950 tons, eight 5.25-inch DP guns, six 21-inch TT, 32 knots, 1943): a slightly altered *Dido* class. Designed at 5,770 tons, they began their service at 6,018. Often referred to as AA cruisers, the 16 *Dido* type ships shot down a grand total of 15 enemy planes. The entirety of British cruiser-dom accounted for only 97 planes, while enemy planes accounted for 11 British cruisers.

SWIFTSURE, ONTARIO, plus one ship reordered as part of the *Tiger* class (8,800 tons; nine 6-inch, ten 4-inch DP guns, six 21-inch TT; 31.5 knots, 1944–45): modified *Fijis* with added beam for stability.

TIGER class (8,885 tons; nine 6-inch, ten 4-inch DP guns, six 21-inch TT; 31.5 knots): six ships planned. One ship reached completion postwar to the original design, similar to the *Swiftsure*. Three ships were reworked to completely new specifications including 6-inch DP guns in twin mounts, which proved unsuccessful. The navy reordered one incomplete vessel with the *Neptune* class.

Britain's final CL project of the war included six *Neptune*-class ships. The navy drafted a general layout but placed no orders: 15,280–15,700 tons; 10 or twelve 6-inch guns in 80° twin mounts; 12 smaller DP guns (3-inch or 4.5-inch?); sixteen 21-inch TT; 32.25 knots.

Destroyers

Like Britain's cruisers, the destroyers were notably nondescript; yet they ventured repeatedly into harm's way, often sustaining heavy losses, always performing valiantly in the best traditions of the Royal Navy. They had few opportunities for glorious torpedo charges, flinging themselves heedlessly against enemy heavy ships. Instead they subsisted on grittier work: sudden submarine confrontations and incessant air attack. Mediterranean attrition chewed its way through the British destroyer alphabet, but the ships persevered.

Designs were spartan even before the crowd of wartime personnel reduced their habitability. While the United States, Japan, and Germany opted for ships exceeding 2,000 tons, Britain resolved to save money with designs below 1,800 tons.

The most regrettable flaw in these ships was their weak AA. The navy that thought DP mounts were perfect for its 8-inch cruiser weapons also thought its destroyermen could get by with 40° or 50° guns; later, a fit of frenzied magnanimity gave rise to 55° elevation. This official contentment with low-angle DD guns evolved within the context of prewar fleet AA doctrine, a pleasant but impractical notion

in which destroyers needed only to account for torpedo planes and other low-altitude aircraft while the high-angle guns of heavier ships dealt with targets overhead. (Apart from its other failings, this plan offered few options to destroyers operating on their own.) The severity of losses couldn't hasten a practical DP gun through the processes of design, testing, and production, so not until the "Battle" class of 1945 did such a weapon go to sea. The Royal Navy lost 120 destroyers in the war; the greatest single cause was air attack, accounting for forty-six ships.

SKATE (900 tons; one 4-inch, one 3-inch DP gun; 36 knots, 1917): lone survivor of the Admiralty "R" class, serving as an escort and MS. The "R" classes originally included sixty-two ships.

SABER, SALADIN, SARDONYX, SCIMITAR, SCOUT, SHIKARI, TENEDOS, THANET, STRONGHOLD, STURDY, THRACIAN (905 tons; one 4-inch, one 3-inch DP gun; 36 knots, 1918): Admiralty "S" class, from sixty-seven ships (plus two canceled) of the "S" classes. The last three listed above served as ML with a gun armament of two 4-inch. Most of the others performed escort duty. *Thracian*, beached after battle damage, was salvaged by the Japanese as patrol boat *101*.

The "R" and "S" types, smaller than the "V's" and "W's" that followed, couldn't manage ocean-going work or carry a heavy AS outfit. They sufficed for coastal and North Sea duty.

VANESSA, VANOC, VANQUISHER, VELOX, VERSATILE, VIMY, VIDETTE, VESPER; VIVACIOUS, VAMPIRE, VENDETTA, VENETIA, VORTIGERN; VALENTINE, VALOROUS, VANITY, VEGA, VERDUN, VIMIERA, VIVIEN (1,090 tons, four 4-inch guns, six 21-inch TT, 34 knots, 1917–18): Admiralty "V" class. The last seven listed above had DP guns and no TT. The first eight became escorts with two 4-inch guns and one 3-inch DP, no TT, and 25 knots.

Vivacious had three 4-inch guns and three torpedoes. In other cases, a 3-inch DP replaced three TT. *Vortigern* and *Venetia* could carry sixty mines. Displacement in all the old "V" and "W" classes rose near 1,200 tons.

WALKER, WARWICK, WATCHMAN, WESTCOTT, WINCHELSEA, WRESTLER; WALPOLE, WINDSOR, WATERHEN, VOYAGER, WAKEFUL, WESSEX, WHIRLWIND; WESTMINSTER, WHITLEY, WINCHESTER, WOLFHOUND, WRYNECK (1,100 tons, four 4-inch guns, six 21-inch TT, 34 knots, 1917–18): Admiralty "W" class. The last five on the list had DP guns and no TT. The first six became escorts with two 4-inch guns and one 3-inch DP, no TT, and 25 knots. *Walpole* and *Windsor* had two 4-inch guns, three TT, and numerous light weapons for combating S-boats. Some others took on a 3-inch DP. *Whirlwind* carried sixty mines.

VISCOUNT, VICEROY (1,120 tons, four 4-inch guns, six 21-inch TT, 35 knots, 1918): Thornycroft "V" class. *Viceroy* had DP guns and no TT. *Viscount* became an escort with two 4-inch guns, one 3-inch DP, no torpedoes, and 26 knots. Production of the "V" classes originally included thirty ships.

WOLSEY, WOOLSTON (1,120 tons, four 4-inch DP guns, 35 knots, 1918): Thornycroft "W" class, used as AA escorts. *Woolston* may also have mounted two 3-inch DP.

KEPPEL, BROKE, WALLACE, plus two canceled and two scrapped prewar (1,554 tons; five 4.7-inch, one 3-inch DP gun, six 21-inch TT; 36 knots, 1919–25): last of the *Shakespeare* class. *Wallace* became an AA escort, her armament replaced by four 4-inch DP. The other two became escorts, retaining one gun and all torpedoes. They began their careers as flotilla leaders, a type that continued in British doctrine through World War II.

BRUCE, CAMPBELL, DOUGLAS, MACKAY, MALCOLM, MONTROSE, STUART, plus two canceled and one sunk prewar (1,580 tons; five 4.7-inch, one 3-inch DP gun, six 21-inch TT; 36.5 knots, 1918–19): the *Scott*-class leaders. The navy expended *Bruce* as a target in November 1939. *Stuart* became a fast transport for the Australians, armed with one 4-inch DP gun and no torpedoes. The others landed one to three guns but kept their TT, and some gained another 3-inch DP.

WANDERER, VANSITTART, VENOMOUS, VOLUNTEER, WHITEHALL, VERITY; WREN, WILD SWAN; WHITSHED, VETERAN, WIVERN, WITHERINGTON, WOLVERINE, WORCESTER (1,120 tons, four 4.7-inch guns, six 21-inch TT, 34 knots, 1919–24): Admiralty Modified "W" class. The last six served as escorts with two guns and three torpedoes, some with a 3-inch DP gun. The first six became escorts with two 4.7-inch guns and 25 knots. *Wren* and *Wild Swan* traded three TT for a 3-inch DP.

WITCH, WISHART (1,140 tons, four 4.7-inch guns, six 21-inch TT, 35 knots, 1920–24): Thornycroft Modified "W" class. Both became escorts with three main guns, a 3-inch DP, and six TT. Production for all "W" classes totaled thirty-six with forty canceled.

As the Battle of the Atlantic began to expose Britain's lack of ocean-going escorts, Churchill proposed a deal with the United States: fifty old destroyers from America's reserve fleet in exchange for bases in the West Indies. After some official hesitation, President Roosevelt bypassed Congress and instituted the plan himself. The fifty *Wickes*-, *Clemson*-, and *Caldwell*-class DD could never be ideal AS platforms. Unstable, unmaneuverable, plummeting ever deeper into antiquity, they could at least carry a full load of depth charges well beyond coastal waters. The British reduced their top-weight by trimming the funnels and landing some weapons. A typical armament became one 4-inch gun and one 3-inch DP, an enlarged array of light guns and AS weaponry, and some torpedoes. They served until new construction allowed their retirement. As a group, the ships were called the "Town" class, most bearing names common to cities on both sides of the ocean. Five "Towns" served with Norwegian crews in 1940–42. Nine transferred to the Soviets as they awaited delivery of Italian war booty. For more details, see the section on American destroyers.

AMBUSCADE (1,173 tons, four 4.7-inch guns, six 21-inch TT, 37 knots, 1927): a prototype for future designs. She traded three TT for a 3-inch DP gun, and later landed the 3-incher and two main guns during conversion to escort vessel.

AMAZON (1,352 tons, four 4.7-inch guns, six 21-inch TT, 37 knots, 1927): another prototype. A 3-inch DP temporarily replaced three TT. As an escort, she carried two 4.7-inch guns and six torpedoes.

Amazon and *Ambuscade* established the lineage that ran from the "A" to the "I" classes and formed the bulk of British fleet DD strength at the war's beginning. The modest range of the prototypes (about 3,350 miles at 15 knots) increased in future designs.

ACASTA, ACHATES, ACHERON, ACTIVE, ANTELOPE, ANTHONY, ARDENT, ARROW, SAGUENAY, SKEENA (1,350 tons, four 4.7-inch guns, eight 21-inch TT, 35.25 knots, 1930–31): "A" class with a range of 4,800 miles at 15 knots. The poor habitability of these ships became a theme in British DD design. A 60° gun elevation received consideration, but the navy accepted 30° instead—a lamentable precedent. Like many later ships, the "A's" could act as MS, though they did so rarely. *Acheron* had experimental high-pressure boilers, but the project died out. This left British DD machinery less powerful than German and American types. The Royal Navy did gain a reputation for reliability in its power plants; however, this derived not from high standards of design but from strenuous programs of maintenance. Even so, British crews dealt frequently with steam and oil leaks that the Yanks would have viewed as novelties.

The "A" class illustrates standard destroyer deployment in the Royal Navy: a flotilla of eight ships (*Saguenay* and *Skeena* were extras built for Canada) plus one ship as the leader (*Codrington*, below). This system continued with little exception up to the "J" class. The "A's" received typical wartime modifications, most landing half their torpedoes and one main gun while taking on a 3-inch DP, light AA, and improved AS gear.

CODRINGTON (1,540 tons, five 4.7-inch guns, eight 21-inch TT, 35 knots, 1930): "A" class leader. She sank early in the war, but not before trading four TT for a 3-inch DP. Her displacement and wide turning radius differentiated her from her flotilla mates, and future leaders performed more like their followers.

KEITH, BASILISK, BEAGLE, BLANCHE, BOADICEA, BOREAS, BRAZEN, BRILLIANT, BULLDOG (1,360 tons, four 4.7-inch guns, eight 21-inch TT, 35.25 knots, 1931): the "B" class. At 1,400 tons, the leader *Keith* more closely matched the performance (and cost) of the others.

These ships differed only slightly from the "A's." *Bulldog* tested a 60° mount but unsuccessfully. The usual changes took place during the war. *Boreas* became the Greek *Salamis*.

ASSINIBOINE, FRASER, OTTAWA, RESTIGOUCHE, ST. LAURENT (1,375 tons, four 4.7-inch guns, eight 21-inch TT, 35.5 knots, 1932): the "C" class, formerly named *Kempenfelt*, *Crescent*, *Crusader*, *Comet*, and *Cygnet*. This demi-flotilla resulted from another British gesture of self-restraint. But since the fleet had no use for a smaller group, Britain offered the "C's" to Canada. The transfer took place in 1937–38, with the Canadians supplying suitably

Canadian names. The TT gave way to light guns and a DP (4-inch for *Fraser*, 3-inch for the others). The leader *Assiniboine* displaced 15 more tons; she tested a 5.1-inch gun prewar, but it proved a failure.

DUNCAN, DAINTY, DARING, DEFENDER, DELIGHT, DIAMOND, DUCHESS, DIANA, DECOY (1,375 tons; four 4.7-inch, one 3-inch DP gun, eight 21-inch TT; 36 knots, 1932–33): "D" class, nearly identical to the "C's," leader *Duncan* with 25 extra tons. She landed one gun and half her TT during the war. The others all sank by 1941. A near-miss bomb broke *Defender's* hull, and she had to be scuttled. The British DD never distinguished themselves in ruggedness, partly because of their size. The later, larger designs fared better, but high costs precluded a serious increase in displacement (and durability). Machinery dispersal appeared only in 1945 as designers labored to arrange the bulky British power plants within such modest hulls.

The "D's" ranged to 5,870 miles at 15 knots. The last pair listed above transferred to Canada as *Margaree* and *Kootenay*.

EXMOUTH, ECHO, ECLIPSE, ELECTRA, ENCOUNTER, ESCORT, EXPRESS, ESCAPADE, ESK; FAULKNOR, FAME, FEARLESS, FIREDRAKE, FORESIGHT, FURY, FOXHOUND, FORTUNE, FORESTER (1,375 tons, four 4.7-inch guns, eight 21-inch TT, 36 knots, 1934–35): "E" and "F" classes, leaders *Exmouth* and *Faulknor* (1495 tons, five guns). The "E's" had a touch more displacement than the "F's," though in service they both weighed about 1,405 tons before wartime additions. *Esk* and *Express* could be quickly converted for minelaying duty, landing two guns and shipping sixty mines. *Echo* became the Greek *Navarinon*; *Express*, *Fortune*, and *Foxhound* became *Gatineau*, *Saskatchewan*, and *Qu'Appelle* with the Canadians.

These ships closely resembled the "D" class with increased subdivision. Design teams con-

sidered including a 3-inch DP gun, but instead the 4.7-inch guns received an awkward 40° arrangement, which still left them useless against aircraft. Most ships took on a 3-inch DP later upon removal of some TT.

By the mid-1930s, destroyer armament had become a point of concern for the Admiralty. Although the 4.7-inch gun earned nothing but praise, larger calibers had entered service with the French and the Americans. Yet the British, optimistic and not fully aware of the power of Japan's "Special Type" ships, decided to forego such escalation rather than encourage it abroad. Their self-restraint brought an end to the 5.1-inch project, and it wasn't until the "Tribal" class of 1938 that they made any attempt at increased firepower.

GRENVILLE, GALLANT, GARLAND, GLOWWORM, GRAFTON, GREYHOUND, GIPSY, GRENADE, GRIFFIN (1,335 tons, four 4.7-inch guns, eight 21-inch TT, 35.5 knots, 1936): "G" class, leader *Grenville* (1,465 tons, five guns). The reason for this return to a larger leader is unclear.

The "G's" could act as ML or MS if necessary. In other regards, they resembled the previous class in design and modifications. *Glowworm* had 10 TT and 10 extra tons. *Garland* transferred to the Poles with no name change; *Griffin* became a second Canadian *Ottawa*.

HARDY, HASTY, HAVOCK, HEREWARD, HERO, HOSTILE, HOTSPUR, HUNTER, HYPERION (1,340 tons, four 4.7-inch guns, eight 21-inch TT, 35.5 knots, 1936–37): "H" class, leader *Hardy* (1455 tons, five guns), repeats of the "G" class with improved gun mounts (still 40°, unfortunately). They underwent the usual changes; some landed two guns to increase their AS gear, *Hero* became the Canadian *Chaudière*. Shortly after the "H's" went into service, the Brazilian government expressed interest in the design.

HARVESTER, HAVELOCK, HESPERUS, HIGH-LANDER, HURRICANE, HAVANT (1,340 tons, three 4.7-inch guns, eight 21-inch TT, 35.5 knots, 1939–40): repeat of the "H" class intended for Brazil as the *Juruena* class but taken over by the Royal Navy. None was a leader. Originally they showed little difference from the previous "H's" except for the smaller armament and an improvement of their fire control equipment. The navy rushed them into service, some without torpedoes or the complete fire control layout. Most took on four torpedoes and a 3-inch DP gun.

INGLEFIELD, ISIS, ILEX, IMOGEN, IMPERI-AL, IMPULSIVE, ICARUS, INTREPID, IVAN-HOE (1,370 tons, four 4.7-inch guns, ten 21-inch TT, 36 knots, 1937–38): "I" class, leader *Inglefield* (1,544 tons, five guns). The major difference from the "H" class was the quintuple torpedo mounts in place of the previous quads. This compromised stability somewhat, and the ships sometimes landed one torpedo from each mount. The "G's" and "H's, " capable of serving as minecraft, rarely did so. But the last four of the "I" class often converted into ML, exchanging their torpedoes, two guns, and other gear for sixty mines. On the eve of war, Turkey decided to go ahead with plans to purchase some modern DD, and ordered four from the British.

ITHURIEL, INCONSTANT (1,370 tons, four 4.7-inch guns, eight 21-inch TT, 35.5 knots, 1940–42): plus two more, repeat "I's" built as *Gayret*, *Muavenet*, *Sultanhisar*, and *Demirhisar* for Turkey, with only the last pair delivered. None was a leader. Except for their torpedo battery, they closely resembled the earlier ships; but as with the repeat "H's, " they had improved fire control of a sort that wasn't planned for His Majesty's ships until the "L" and "M" classes. It's unclear why Britain retained two ships but delivered two others.

Imperial, near-missed by a bomb, had to be scuttled; this illustrates the fragility of the "A" through "I" destroyers as well as their vulnerability to air attack. Britain's realization that their smaller ships were being outclassed abroad (Japanese *Fubuki* and American *Porter*) inspired a growth in design displacement and capabilities, which in turn produced tougher, more battle-worthy ships, yet did little to remedy their lack of AA. Thus, while a 1,900-ton "L" class DD could spit individual 4-inch rounds at attacking aircraft, an older, 1,500-ton American *Mahan* could blast away with five 5-inch guns.

AFRIDI, ASHANTI, BEDOUIN, COSSACK, ESKIMO, GURKHA, MAORI, MASHONA, MATABELE, MOHAWK, NUBIAN, PUNJABI, SIKH, SOMALI, TARTAR, ZULU (1,854 tons, eight 4.7-inch guns, four 21-inch TT, 36 knots, 1938–39): the British-built "Tribal" class, none especially equipped as a leader. With no design ancestors and no descendants, the "Tribals" stand solitary among Royal Navy destroyers.

Britain's old friend, Japan, had raised a distinctly unfriendly gaze across the waters of the Far East where its powerful "Special Type" DD carved menacing wakes. To counter this threat, the Admiralty resolved to use the full treaty allowance of 1,850 tons per destroyer, calling for a battery of five twin 4.7-inch mounts and a dispersal of machinery. Designers couldn't manage the machinery dispersal, and they found room for only eight guns. Maneuverability was poor, and the hulls proved weak enough to require strengthening.

Yet the "Tribals" garnered success. The potent gun battery, their *raison d'être*, gave them the heaviest broadside ever in a British DD. But they continued with the 40° mountings and their negligible AA potential. (When the Americans designed 1,850-ton DD with heavy firepower, their *Porter* and *Somers* classes also lacked DP guns—the only modern American designs to do so.) However, the "Tribal" design included two important features: a stronger light AA battery and—a first among British

*A depiction of the Canadian **Haida** in action against German units.*

DD—fire control for its AA gunnery. The "Tribals" that survived past June 1940 traded a twin 4.7-inch for a twin 4-inch DP. With a true DP main battery, the "Tribals" could have formed the basis of a design equal to the big ships employed in the Pacific by Japan and the United States.

In the eyes of the British, the "Tribals" were too large (expensive), their gun mounts too complex (expensive to maintain), and their torpedo armament too small (torpedoes were expensive, yes, but British torpedoes were quite good and worth the cost). Nevertheless, Canada and Australia knew the value of the big ships, and they wanted some of their own.

ARUNTA, KURNAI, WARRAMUNGA; ATHABASKAN, HAIDA, IROQUOIS, HURON (1,927 tons; six 4.7-inch, two 4-inch DP guns, four 21-inch TT; 36.25 knots, 1942–45): Commonwealth "Tribals": the first three built in Australia, the other four built in Britain for the Canadians, plus four more completed postwar in Canada. *Kurnai* was renamed *Bataan* while under construction to honor General MacArthur. The four postwar completions had eight 4-inch DP and no 4.7-inchers, but there were no other major differences from the earlier "Tribals."

JERVIS, JACKAL, JUPITER, JAGUAR, JAVELIN, JERSEY, JANUS, JUNO; KELLY, KANDAHAR, KASHMIR, KHARTOUM, KIMBERLY, KINGSTON, KIPLING, KELVIN; NAPIER, NERISSA, NONPAREIL, NIZAM, NOBLE, NEPAL, NORMAN, NESTOR (1,690 tons, six 4.7-inch guns, ten 21-inch TT, 36 knots, 1939–42): the "J," "K," and "N" classes. Many naval leaders criticized the "Tribals" as having too many guns and too few torpedoes. But the earlier classes were clearly undersized. The "J's" presented a compromise. Their size gave them improved sea-keeping and allowed three twin turrets. Some accounts describe the aft mount as an oddity, trained forward with a 20° "blind spot" aft—in other words, incapable of firing directly astern at pursuing warships, but fully capable of lobbing shells into the forward superstructure whenever the need arose. Fortunately, this was mere myth.

The "K" class was a repeat, as were the "N's." Since the ships had much more room than the earlier type, an enlarged leader became unnecessary, and flotillas shrank to eight ships total. (A ninth "J," *Jubilant*, was therefore canceled.) The flagships *Jervis*, *Kelly*, and *Napier* differed little from the others.

Structural collapse precipitated 41% of the losses among Britain's smaller warships, most of them sinking in less than 10 minutes. However, the "J's" introduced an advance in hull strength. When torpedoes knocked both bow and stern off *Javelin*, she stayed afloat. Of course, for destroyers in general, the extremities proved expendable; the true test came from a hit amidships. *Kelly* took a torpedo right in her boilers. With no machinery dispersal, she lost all power but was successfully towed home and repaired. Ironically, she later succumbed to a single bomb hit. *Khartoum's* loss was even odder; she sank after suffering a lucky shot from the deck gun of an Italian submarine—a fluke indeed, but such anecdotes indicate the continued vulnerability of British designs.

Modifications in these ships differed from those in earlier types. They lost no main guns, and when the time came to replace some TT with a DP gun, it was a 4-incher instead of 3-inch. This left the ships with five torpedoes, just one more than in the criticized "Tribals."

Nerissa became the Polish *Piorun; Noble* and *Nonpareil* became the Dutch *Van Galen* and *Tjerk Hiddes*.

LAFOREY, LANCE, GURKHA, LEGION, LIGHTNING, LIVELY, LOOKOUT, LOYAL; MILNE, MAHRATTA, MARTIN, MATCHLESS, MUSKETEER, MYRMIDON, MARNE, METEOR (1,920 tons, six 4.7-inch guns, eight 21-inch TT, 36 knots, 1940–42): "L" and "M" classes, flagships *Laforey* and *Milne* (1935 tons). *Gurkha* (ex-*Larne*) was renamed to commemorate a lost "Tribal." *Myrmidon* became the Polish *Orkan*.

Debate over the "Tribals" and the "J's" had remained inconclusive. Some in the Admiralty wanted to pursue a large design armed with six 5.25-inch guns, like a miniature *Dido*—an expensive proposition. Instead the designers modified the "J" layout with a new 4.7-inch mark; most of the weight increase in the "L's" stemmed from this updated gun with its weather-proof mount (the first in a British DD) and heavier shell. The mounts had 50° elevation, still no good against airplanes. The turret's complexity created delays, so *Lance*, *Gurkha*, *Lively*, and *Legion* went to sea armed with eight 4-inch DP guns—all in all, not a bad trade, though losing somewhat with regard to surface gunfire. The other sisterships exchanged four TT for one 4-inch DP.

ONSLOW, ORIBI, ONSLAUGHT, OFFA, ORWELL, OBEDIENT, OBDURATE, OPPORTUNE; PAKENHAM, PALADIN, PANTHER, PARTRIDGE, PATHFINDER, PENN, PETARD, PORCUPINE (1,610 tons, four 4.7-inch guns, eight 21-inch TT, 36 knots, 1941–42): "O" and "P" classes, with no major differences in *Onslow* and *Pakenham*. Concerned about the trend toward big designs, the Admiralty switched direction as war approached, looking for something economical like a "Hunt" but nearer the capabilities of a fleet destroyer.

Simplicity allowed the "O's" and "P's" to hurry into service. (*Oribi*, laid down around the same time as *Milne*, commissioned a year earlier.) This hurry banished all pretensions, so the 4.7-inch guns had only 40° elevation. At first this battery was to fire 62-lb shells (as in the "L's"), but that too would have caused delays.

With the outbreak of war, the British finally realized the disadvantage of their low-angle weapons, and they decided on DP guns for their fleet units. The new specification called for eight 4-inch DP (as in some of the "L's"), but the "Hunts" claimed all the available twin mounts. The first four "O's" listed above commissioned with the original 4.7-inch battery. The last four "O's" and first four "P's" had five single 4-inch DP and four TT. The last four "P's" had four 4-

inch guns and eight TT. *Oribi* traded four torpedoes for a 4-inch DP.

QUILLIAM, QUADRANT, QUALITY, QUEEN-BOROUGH, QUIBERON, QUAIL, QUENTIN, QUICKMATCH; ROTHERHAM, REDOUBT, ROEBUCK, RAPID, ROCKET, RACEHORSE, RELENTLESS, RAIDER (1,705 tons, four 4.7-inch guns, eight 21-inch TT, 36 knots, 1942–43): "Q" and "R" classes, *Quilliam* and *Rotherham* 20 tons heavier. They resembled the "J" class armed with available 4.7-inch singles. While slightly wet forward, they were quite stable, and they incorporated a substantial increase in fuel. No TT-for-DP exchanges took place.

SAUMAREZ, SAVAGE, SCORPION, SCOURGE, SERAPIS, SHARK, SWIFT, SUCCESS; TROU-BRIDGE, TEAZER, TENACIOUS, TERMA-GANT, TERPSICHORE, TUMULT, TUSCAN, TYRIAN; GRENVILLE, ULSTER, ULYSSES, UNDAUNTED, UNDINE, URANIA, URCHINE, URSA; HARDY, VALENTINE, VENUS, VERU-LAM, VIGILANT, VIRAGO, VIXEN, VOLAGE; KEMPENFELT, WAGER, WAKEFUL, WESSEX, WHELP, WIZARD, WRANGLER, WHIRLWIND (1,710 tons, four 4.7-inch guns, eight 21-inch TT, 36 knots, 1943–44): "S" through "W" classes, all virtually identical, except "T's" and "U's" not suited to Arctic service. The hull form

resembled the "J" type again, but with a "Tribal" bow which was drier. Nominal displacement in the "U" class was 1,777 tons, and 1,808 tons for the "V" class. *Saumarez* and *Troubridge* displaced about 20 more tons than their letter-mates. *Shark* and *Success* became the Norwegian *Svenner* and *Stord*. *Vixen* and *Valentine* transferred to Canada as *Sioux* and *Algonquin*.

Designers no longer doubted the necessity of high-angle guns, but time hadn't yet allowed completion of the DP project. Options included 4-inch twins as in the "Hunts" and 5/38 guns from America; but the Admiralty's roving eye came home to rest again on 4.7-inchers (now graced with 55° mounts) and thought they looked perfect. *Savage* at least betokened a brighter future; she carried an experimental twin 4.5-inch DP mount forward (80°), as later appeared in the "Battle" class, with two 55° single 4.5-inch mounts aft.

At this point, the British alphabet ran out of famous seamen with names appropriate for their flagships. The Royal sense of adventure never dared an entire class of "X's" or "Y's."

MYNGS, ZAMBESI, ZEALOUS, ZEBRA, ZE-NITH, ZEPHYR, ZODIAC, ZEST; CAVENDISH, CAESAR, CAMBRIAN, CAPRICE, CARRON, CARYSFORT, CASSANDRA, CAVALIER (1,710 tons, four 4.5-inch guns, eight 21-inch TT, 36

The British DP gun project started too late to help the wartime destroyers. The Crystal was commissioned in 1946, still with 55° mounts.

knots, 1944–45): "Z" and "Ca" classes with *Myngs*, *Cavendish*, and *Caesar* fitted as flagships. They were visually indistinguishable from the previous classes except for their main battery which, unfortunately, remained in 55° mounts.

CHAPLET, CHEVRON, COMET, CRESCENT, plus 20 others completed postwar (1,825 tons, four 4.5-inch guns, four 21-inch TT, 36 knots, 1945): the "Ch," "Co," and "Cr" classes, none equipped as leaders. Similar to the "Z" class but with fewer TT, they used the top-weight savings to add more gunnery equipment. Even these late arrivals—too late to see war service—had 55° mounts.

ARMADA, BARFLEUR, TRAFALGAR, HOGUE, CAMPERDOWN, plus 11 others postwar (2,315 tons, four 4.5-inch DP, eight 21-inch TT, 35.75 knots, 1945): the "Battle" class with the first three fitted as leaders. Finally, after six years of war and dozens of losses, the Royal Navy got a ship with a genuine DP battery. But, arranged in two twin mounts forward, it was a small, ill-placed battery; a little creativity would have enabled the planners to fit another mount aft, but they were simply unused to accommodating full-sized DP guns on a destroyer. A 4-inch star shell gun sat amidships, a waste of five tons and valuable centerline space. A second group of eight "Battles" began commissioning in late 1946; they replaced the star shell gun with a 4.5-incher (in a 55° mount).

Their hefty displacement afforded the "Battles" improved fire control and seaworthiness, larger fuel stores, and their DP guns. They re-introduced high-pressure boilers; Britain's failure to pursue this concept after the experimental *Acheron* contributed to the general inefficiency of naval power plants and the designers' inability to employ machinery dispersal. British electrical systems were likewise obese, often adding tons to a design.

The British had several projects in the works in 1945. The "Weapon" class (1,955 tons, six 4-inch DP guns, ten 21-inch TT, 34 knots) produced four completions postwar and 15 cancellations. The use of 4-inch guns earned criticism, as it should have, but the ships did include a machinery dispersal layout. Eight "D" class units (2,610 tons, six 4.5-inch DP guns, ten 21-inch TT, 34.75 knots) were designed by 1945 but commissioned around 1950, displacing 2830 tons. They represent the sort of ship the Royal Navy needed in wartime. None of the eight "G" class ships (1,995 tons, four 4.5-inch DP guns, ten 21-inch TT, 33.75 knots) reached completion. They had twin mounts fore and aft on a hull similar to the "Weapon" type.

The French destroyers *Mistral* and *Ouragan* entered British service after France's defeat, rearmed by the British.

Submarines

Britain's submarine fleet hasn't won much ink from historians. The spurts of interest that do arise tend to focus more on the exploits of the few midget subs than on the day-to-day operations of the two hundred full-sized boats. This anonymity hasn't resulted from any failing among the crewmen; British submariners were probably the best trained in the world. But throughout the war, they suffered from a lack of juicy targets: no plodding convoys sprawled upon the ocean, no massed battle fleets to engage, just a steady stream of heavily defended merchant traffic in coastal waters always within range of land-based aircraft. Even so, the British boats emerged from the war with the lowest loss-to-kill ratio of all submarine forces, except the American.

Britain quickly developed a few successful designs, then duplicated them in large numbers. Strong and simple boats with heavy torpedo armaments and rapid diving, they had the qualities necessary for the sort of warfare they waged. Technology became a strong suit, as illustrated by *Venturer* when her submerged attack sank the submerged *U864*, a feat unique in World War II.

Compared with American boats, British designs lacked habitability and range, and thus couldn't join the Americans in their Pacific feeding frenzy. Only with the "A" class did the Admiralty give much thought to deployment against Japan.

H28, 31–34, 43, 44, 49, 50 (440/500 tons, four 21-inch TT, 13/10.5 knots, 1918–20): highly successful American design, in service during the war with the British, Dutch, Chileans, Italians, and Soviets. Age had turned the British boats into trainers, though some were forced into war patrols. The original design included a 3-inch gun and 17.7-inch tubes.

L23, 26, 27 (890/1,080 tons, one 4-inch gun, four 21-inch TT, 17.5/10.5 knots, 1924–26): another good design grown old.

OBERON (1,598/1,831 tons, one 4-inch gun, eight 21-inch TT, 13.75/7.5 knots, 1927): the first "O" class, an unsuccessful long-range prototype. Being heavy for her dimensions, she was neither maneuverable when submerged nor buoyant at any time. She never reached her designed speed (15/9 knots), and by 1944 the navy retired her.

OXLEY, OTWAY (1,636/1,872 tons, one 4-inch gun, eight 21-inch TT, 15/8.5 knots, 1927): somewhat improved, as in speed, but retaining *Oberon*'s major flaws.

ODIN, OLYMPUS, ORPHEUS, OSIRIS, OSWALD, OTUS (1,781/2,038 tons, one 4-inch gun, eight 21-inch TT, 17.5/8 knots, 1929–30): the last "O's." Enhanced speed and range failed to address the type's fundamental shortcomings.

PARTHIAN, PANDORA, PERSEUS, PHOENIX, POSEIDEN, PROTEUS (1,775/2,040 tons, one 4-inch gun, eight 21-inch TT, 17.5/8.6 knots, 1930–31): the "P" class developed from the "O's." The same problems recurred, and these boats, which weren't even safe to operate, did nothing to forecast Britain's future success. The first two listed above were altered, acting as transports to supply Malta.

This class introduced a system for carrying mines (in this case 18 mines) instead of torpedoes.

RAINBOW, REGENT, REGULUS, ROVER, plus two canceled (1,772/2,030 tons, one 4-inch gun, eight 21-inch TT, 17.5/8.8 knots, 1930–32): "R" class, based on the "P" class but hardly improved. They too could carry 18 mines in their torpedo tubes.

THAMES, SEVERN, CLYDE (2,206/2,723 tons, one 4-inch gun, six 21-inch TT, 22/10 knots, 1932–35): also called the "River" class. They were intended for operations in concert with the fleet, and thus required high speed. The overgrown power plant left no room for torpedoes aft; British submarine design then abandoned internal stern tubes until the "A" class of 1945. The "Rivers" could carry 12 mines instead of their torpedoes.

Thames differed from the rest (2,165/2,680 tons, 22.5/10 knots). The other pair had additional buoyancy tanks. The design had sufficient speed and endurance (6,260 miles at 12.4 knots) for its role, but lacked maneuverability and armament. In fact, the intended role was ill conceived; tying a sub to the fleet's movements could only limit its effectiveness. The Japanese, dedicated to submarine–fleet coordination, met with only the barest success; the Americans, waging unrestricted anti-commerce warfare, had warships handed to them while on patrol stations (as in the battles of Savo Island, Philippine Sea, and Leyte Gulf).

SWORDFISH, STURGEON, SEAHORSE, STARFISH (737/927 tons, one 3-inch gun, six 21-inch TT, 13.75/10 knots, 1932–33): the first "S" class. Meant as replacements for the old "H" class, they required the same virtues of maneuverability and quick diving. But the Admiralty wanted more—improvements in range, armament, and surface speed. The "S" types became a pillar of His Majesty's submarine force; not remarkable in any respect, rather they performed all tasks at acceptable levels, a class of well balanced and workmanlike boats that proved safe and easy to operate. Dive time was good: 25–30 seconds.

These first four boats, however, had serious stability problems. To reduce top-weight, *Sturgeon* and *Swordfish* switched their 3-inch gun from a complicated disappearing DP mount to a simpler low-angle mount. (Few if any subsequent "S" class boats had DP mounts.) The *Swordfish* design never fully overcame its woes, leaving it to subsequent classes to establish the concept's worth. *Sturgeon* served as the Dutch *Zeehond*.

PORPOISE (1,782/2,053 tons, one 4-inch gun, six 21-inch TT, 50 mines, 15/8.75 knots, 1933): successful minelaying design. An additional 12 mines could take the place of her torpedoes.

SHARK, SNAPPER, SUNFISH, STERLET, SEALION, SPEARFISH, SALMON, SEAWOLF (768/960 tons, one 3-inch gun, six 21-inch TT, 13.75/10 knots, 1934–38): second "S" class, an improvement with a less complicated layout. The "S's" became progressively simpler to mass-produce. *Sunfish* managed 15 knots on the surface. She and *Seawolf* sometimes carried 12 mines instead of their torpedoes. *Sunfish* transferred to the Soviets as *B1* but was accidentally sunk en route.

GRAMPUS, NARWHAL, RORQUAL, CACHALOT, SEAL (1,810/2,157 tons, one 4-inch gun, six 21-inch TT, 50 mines, 15.75/8.75 knots, 1936–39): often classed with *Porpoise*, but possessing less fuel and more buoyancy and stability. *Seal* became a German captive, renamed *UB*.

The navy began a new minelayer project in 1938 (four boats, 1,755 surface tons, 50 mines, 15.75 surface knots), then swayed toward a cheaper "S"-like foursome (820/1,030 tons, one 3-inch gun, six 21-inch TT, 12 mines, 14/9 knots). This plan also faded, along with a proposal for three replacement *Grampus* types, and the British built no more minelayer designs; TT-laid mines made specialized boats unnecessary. Later in the war, the fleet considered a combined minelayer and replenishment boat (like a German "milk cow") for Pacific operations, possibly refitting some elderly units. Planners dropped the mining role and concentrated on a replenishment design (2,494/2,914 tons, no TT or mines, 14.5 knots surfaced) before dropping the project entirely.

TRITON, THUNDERBOLT, TRIBUNE, TRIDENT, TRIUMPH, TAKU, TARPON, THISTLE, TIGRIS, TRIAD, TRUANT, TUNA, TALISMAN, TETRARCH, TORBAY (1,326/1,575 tons, one 4-inch gun, ten 21-inch TT, 15.25/9 knots, 1938–41): first series of the "T" class. The Admiralty wanted replacements for their "O," "P," and "R" classes and set about deciding the best way to use their treaty allotment of SS tonnage. In this instance, British designers transcended the displacement restrictions and produced a boat that was stronger, safer, more heavily armed, more maneuverable, and quicker in the dive than its predecessors. The loss of two knots on the surface didn't hinder the "T's" in service.

Originally, all 10 TT fired forward. The British emphasis on bow armament stemmed from a respect for modern AS systems; it was thought that attacks would have to take place from a greater range, necessitating a concentration of torpedoes to get the job done. The boats of this series had four external tubes, which

The British submarine Ursula *had humble origins, but the*
"U" classes outgrew their intended role.

caused turbulence at periscope depth. This prompted *Triumph* and *Thunderbolt* to land two tubes. Other boats had two tubes repositioned to fire aft, and some of them received a third external aft tube (as became standard in later series). The mine load varied from 14 to 18, depending on the number of TT.

Triton displaced 1,331/1,585 tons. *Thunderbolt* (ex-*Thetis*) sank in a 1939 accident but returned to service with her new name. *Torbay*, *Tetrarch*, and *Talisman* served in unsuccessful tests with a system of mine rails.

UNDINE, URSULA, UNITY (630/730 tons, six 21-inch TT, 11.25/10 knots, 1938): the first "U" class, intended to replace the "H's" in their training duty, with local patrol as a secondary function. But they proved so maneuverable and versatile, the Admiralty started them on missions in the North Sea. They had two external tubes and could replace their torpedoes with six mines. *Ursula* mounted a 3-inch, 45cal gun. She transferred to the Soviets as *B4*. These vessels were not good seaboats.

UTMOST, UMPIRE, UNA, UNBEATEN, UNDAUNTED, UNION, UNIQUE, UPHOLDER, UPRIGHT, URCHIN, URGE, USK, ULTIMATUM, ULTOR, UNBROKEN, UMBRA, UNBENDING, UNISON, UNITED, UNRIVALLED, UNRUFFLED, UNRULY, UNSEEN, UNSHAKEN, UPROAR, UREDD, UNIVERSAL, UNSPARING, UNTIRING, UNSWERVING, UPSTART, USURPER, UTHER, VANDAL, VARANGIAN, VARNE, VITALITY, VOX, P32, P33, P36, P38, P39, P47, P48, P52 (646/732 tons, one 3-inch DP gun, four 21-inch TT, 11.25/10 knots, 1940–43): second series of "U's," improved over the *Undines*. The external tubes had caused problems (as in the *Tritons*), so only *Utmost*, *Upright*, *Unique*, and *Upholder* kept them in this design, a total of six TT. The bow form in the others made them easier to handle at periscope depth. All boats could ship six mines instead of torpedoes. In many boats, a 45cal gun replaced the DP weapon.

Given their size, the "U" classes inevitably had flaws: limited range (4,050 miles at 10 knots), weak armament, awkward operation of the deck gun, etc. But they possessed the qualities the Admiralty held most dear—a small price tag, safety and reliability, ease of maintenance. They proved ideal for operations in the Mediterranean, where submarines could not afford mistakes.

Britain's submarine nomenclature wavered during the war; the boats received a name, then switched to one or two P-numbers, then recovered their names again. *Vitality* (ex-*Untamed*) got her new name after salvage from an accidental sinking. *P47* became the Dutch *Dolfijn*; *P52* became the Polish *Dzik*. The others with P-numbers were lost before reclaiming their names. *Uredd* and *Varne* went to Norwegian control, the latter as *Ula*. *Vox* became the French *Curie*; *Urchin* became the Polish *Sokół*. *Unbroken* and *Unison* went to the Soviets as *B2, 3*.

THRASHER, TEMPEST, THORN, TRAVELLER, TROOPER, TRUSTY, TALLY HO, TURBULENT, TACTICIAN, TANTALUS, TANTIVY, TRESPASSER, TAURUS, TEMPLAR, TRUCULENT, P311 (1,327/1,575 tons, one 4-inch gun, eleven 21-inch TT, 15.25/9 knots, 1941–43): a second, improved "T" class. They included no dramatic changes, though details differed, and displacements varied a few tons. *P311* sank before getting back her original name.

With only six internal tubes, the "T's" carried fewer torpedoes than might be expected, just 17. (American fleet boats with 10 TT carried twenty-four torpedoes.) They had an alternative load of 18 mines.

P611, 612, 614, 615 (683/856 tons, one 4-inch gun, five 21-inch TT, 13.7/8.4 knots, 1941–42): built for Turkey as *Oruç Reis*, *Murat Reis*, *Burak Reis*, and *Uluc Ali Reis*. As with the Turkish "I" class DD, the first pair went right to Turkey, but British kept the other two for war service. One tube was external.

SERAPH, SEA ROVER, SEA NYMPH, SEADOG, SAFARI, SAHIB, SATYR, SARACEN, SCEPTRE, SHAKESPEARE, SIBYL, SICKLE, SIMOOM, SPITEFUL, SIRDAR, SPLENDID, SPORTSMAN, SCOTSMAN, SCYTHIAN, SHALIMAR, SEA DEVIL, SPARK, SPIRIT, STATESMAN, STOIC, STONEHENGE, STRATAGEM, STORM, STRONGBOW, STUBBORN, SURF, SYRTIS, P222 (842/990 tons, one 3-inch gun, seven 21-inch TT, 14.75/9 knots, 1942–45): another of the "S" series, including one external tube except in *Safari*, *Strongbow*, *P222*, *Scotsman*, *Scythian*, and *Sea Devil* (only six TT; those last

three boats also had a 4-inch gun in place of the 3-inch). The mine load was 12. Some boats displaced just 814/990 tons. *Seraph* became a high-speed target boat in 1944 with 16.75/12.5 knots.

VENTURER, VAMPIRE, VELDT, VIGOROUS, VIKING, VISIGOTH, VOX, VIRTUE, UPSHOT, URTICA, VAGABOND, VARIANCE, VENGEFUL, VINEYARD, VARNE, VIRULENT, VIVID, VOLATILE, VORACIOUS, VORTEX, VOTARY, VULPINE (670/740 tons, one 3-inch gun, four 21-inch TT, 11.25/10 knots, 1943–45): plus twenty more canceled, the last "U" class—or the "V" class as some called it. The most significant design development was an increase in hull strength. None are listed as having laid mines. *Veldt* and *Vengeful* became the Greek *Pipinos* and *Delfin*; *Vineyard* and *Vortex*, the French *Doris* and *Morse*; and *Variance*, the Norwegian *Utsira*.

STURDY, STYGIAN, SUBTLE, SUPREME, SAGA, SANGUINE, SCORCHER, SPUR, SEA SCOUT, SELENE, SENESCHAL, SENTINEL, SIDON, SPEARHEAD, SLEUTH, SOLENT, SPRINGER (814/990 tons, one 4-inch gun, six 21-inch TT, 14.75/9 knots, 1943–45): the final "S" class. There was some overlap between this design and the previous "S's." *Sturdy* and *Stygian* displaced 842/990 tons; they and *Subtle* had a seventh tube, externally aft, with only a 3-inch deck gun. They could carry 12 mines. *Selene*, *Solent*, and *Sleuth* became high-speed target boats.

TUDOR, TACITURN, TAPIR, TARN, TELEMACHUS, TERRAPIN, TIPTOE, THULE, THOROUGH, TIRELESS, TRADEWIND, TRENCHANT, TRUMP, TURPIN, TOTEM, TRUNCHEON, TALENT, TALENT (1,321/1,571 tons, one 4-inch gun, eleven 21-inch TT, 15.25/9 knots, 1943–45): plus four completed postwar and five others canceled, the final "T" class. The first *Talent* became the Dutch *Zwaardvisch*, with the English name recycled for a second boat.

GREAT BRITAIN

Tarn became the Dutch *Tijgerhaai*. These boats could carry 12 mines (*Zwaardvisch* alone was credited with 18).

Compared to other British subs, the "T's" had exceptional range, especially in this last series (about 11,000 miles at 10 knots).

AMPHION, ASTUTE (1,385/1,620 tons, one 4-inch gun, ten 21-inch TT, 18.5/8 knots, 1945): with 14 more completed postwar and thirty others not completed; the "A" class. This design provided sufficient range and habitability for the Pacific. The "A's" tended to roll and required alterations to gain stability. They could carry 18 mines. Four tubes were external.

The Royal Navy commissioned four captured boats: *Graph* (ex-German *U570*), *P711*, *P712*, and *P714* (ex-Italian *Galileo Galilei*, *Perla*, *and Bronzo*). The last two transferred to Greece and France respectively as *Matrozos* and *Narval*. British sailors managed to board some other U-boats but managed only to seize some materials before the boats went down. America lent nine boats for training: *R3, 17, 19* and *S25, 1, 21, 22, 24, 29* became *P511, 512, 514, 551–556*; *P551* then became the Polish *Jastrząb*. Many submarines from defeated Allies and Italy served under Royal Navy command.

Italy's SLC human torpedo inspired a copy, the Chariot (one 700-lb charge, 3.5 knots). Intended for use against the *Tirpitz*, the craft proved unsuitable for cold fjord waters and achieved its only success with Anglo-Italian teams raiding Italian ships under German control.

The navy ordered 150 Welman craft, tiny subs (2.5 tons, one 1,200-lb charge, three knots surfaced, 1943) with one crewman, no periscope, and a proven ability to implode. The decision to halt construction at twenty craft came too late; completions exceeded 100, including prototypes. Efforts to find some use for the design led to a "Welfreighter" (at least eight completed), but the only Welman operation sent four armed boats against German facil-

ities in Norway. None of the boats managed to enter the target area. The Germans recovered one of them, and the Welman's only contribution to the war effort came in inspiring the enemy to build similarly useless craft.

The X-craft, however, met with success. The prototypes *X3* (22/24 tons, 6/5 knots, 1942) and *X4* (23/25 tons, 6/5 knots, 1942) established the standard armament, a pair of 2-ton explosive charges. *X5–10, 20–25* (27/30 tons, 6.25/5.75 knots, 1942–43) executed raids against the Germans, who recovered *X6, 7* for examination as models for their own midget sub program. *XE1–9, 11, 12* (plus seven canceled: 30/34 tons, 6/5 knots, 1945) had increased habitability for work in the Far East. All units had exceptional agility and three or four crewmen. *XT1–6* (plus 12 canceled: 27/30 tons, 6.6/6.1 knots, 1944) were unarmed training boats.

Minecraft

MEDUSA, MELPOMENE, MINERVA (535 tons, 52 mines, 10 knots, 1915): the last of five "M" class monitors, converted to ML between the wars when they became the primary minelaying trainers. During the war, *Medusa* served as a depot ship, sometimes under the names *Talbot* and *Medway II*. *Melpomene*, later renamed *Menelaus*, mounted one or two 21-inch TT for torpedo training. *Minerva* became a hulk and floating workshop.

Another former monitor, *Claverhouse*, served as a stationary drill ship.

ADVENTURE (6,740 tons, four 4.7-inch DP guns, 340 mines, 28 knots, 1927): rated as a "cruiser-minelayer," but lacking the speed, armor, and weaponry of a cruiser. She also served as a fast transport before becoming a repair ship in 1944.

PLOVER (805 tons, one 3-inch DP gun, 100 mines, 14.75 knots, 1937): coastal minelayer and workhorse of the fleet. *Plover* single-handedly accounted for more than 15,000 of the nearly 300,000 mines Britain deployed in wartime.

LINNET, REDSTART, RINGDOVE (498 tons, 12 mines, 10.5 knots, 1938): controlled minelayers.

M1–8 (346 tons, 10 mines, 10 knots, 1939–44): controlled ML.

Eight merchantmen served as mine tenders and base ships; one of them, *Matai*, worked temporarily as a controlled minelayer; another, *Rhu*, went to the Japanese. The Royal Navy employed eleven auxiliary ML (244–560 mines) as well as many of its trawlers and motor launches. One fishing vessel and four tugs (two of them seized from France) became observation minelayers.

ABDIEL, WELSHMAN, MANXMAN, LATONA, APOLLO, ARIADNE (2,650 tons, six 4-inch DP guns, 156 mines, 40 knots, 1941–44): ML, much more successful than the *Adventure*. The term "cruiser-minelayer" referred only to their relatively great size and speed. In combat prowess, they more closely resembled destroyers with minimal AS gear and no torpedoes. Their high speed (about 35 knots when loaded) suited them well to fast supply runs. The last pair had only four 4-inch DP guns, but in improved mounts.

Old "Hunt" class (710 tons; one 4-inch, one 3-inch DP gun; 16 knots, 1917–19): 28 former minesweeping sloops in various configurations for various duties, plus an incomplete unit serving as a drill ship. The navy had planned 151 vessels, of which 113 entered service. One unit operated with the Thai navy. The Germans captured a "Hunt" and renamed her *Uj2109* as a submarine-chaser.

At the time of the Great War, the Admiralty envisioned three types of sloop: minesweeping

(as the old "Hunts"), ocean-going escorts (as the old "Flowers"), and coastal patrol (P-boats and PC-boats). The terminology continued to a certain degree, but design specifications and assignments blurred all distinctions.

HALCYON class (815 tons, two 4-inch guns, 17 knots, 1934–39): 22 MS. One gun (or sometimes both) had a DP mount.

BANGOR class (590–680 tons, one 3-inch DP gun, 16.5 knots, 1940–44): 113 minesweepers built in three slightly differing series. They had some problems with top-weight, and one remedy included the removal of minesweeping gear—an unusual modification for a minesweeper, but the need for escorts early in the war placed a greater emphasis on the type's modest AS ability. Though too small for some duties, the *Bangor*s were useful. The Japanese captured four ships under construction at Hong Kong.

BATHURST class (650 tons, one 4-inch gun, 15 knots, 1940–44): sixty MS, an Australian design unrelated to other Royal classes, similar to the *Bangor*s but a bit superior, especially as AS craft. The initial batch had 15 knots, but most subsequent completions had 16. Some had a 3-inch DP gun, a variation typical in small warships.

ALGERINE class (940–1,030 tons, one 4-inch DP gun, 16.5 knots, 1942–45): 104 MS including 15 intended for the United States but handed back to the British. As many as 21 more were canceled. Construction included two series differing mostly in their engines. Bigger and better than the *Bangor*s, they excelled as AS vessels, and some entered service with no MS gear. Still, as ocean-going escorts, they lagged behind dedicated designs like the "Flowers."

CATHERINE class (890 tons, one 3-inch DP, 18 knots, 1942–43): twenty-two ex-American *Auk* class MS armed with the American 3/50 gun. Original plans included up to eighty transfers.

Australia's Bathurst-class Whyalla *shows part of her gun armament,
a 4/40 forward and an Oerlikon cannon in the superstructure.*

The British adapted many of their small craft for minesweeping, including *ZZ1–30* (ex-landing craft, 360 tons) used for riverine duty. Approximately 41 tugs helped to sweep and destroy mines. The Japanese captured at least three incomplete tugs, one of which, *Grinder*, commissioned as the minecraft *Nagashima*. The Japanese also salved a sunken "Bar"-class harbor craft for mine duties.

Mercantile conversions totaled at least 114 (plus seven seized from the French); some of them switched to auxiliary patrol duties. Two units, *Jeram* and *Han Wo*, fell captive to the Japanese. Two others transferred to American forces. About 18 craft served as "mine destructors."

MMS1 class (255 tons, light guns, 11 knots, 1940–44): about 292 motor minesweepers completed and 27 not completed. Many transferred to foreign service: ten to the Netherlands, nine to Belgium, seven to France, three to the Soviet Union, and one to Greece.

MMS119–122 (216grt, light guns, nine knots, 1941–42): merchant vessels requisitioned in Canada.

MMS1001 class (360 tons, light guns, 10 knots, 1943–45): 96 vessels, plus ten canceled. Twelve went to the Soviet Union, eight to the Netherlands, and two to Norway.

MMS2001 class (260 tons, one 3-inch DP gun, 15 knots, 1942–45): 152 American-built *YMS1*-class vessels. While British types resembled fishing craft, this class had a more naval design. Twelve units went on to the Greeks.

Britain built four additional MMS for Greece.

Escort Vessels

Old "Flower" class (1,175 tons, two 4-inch guns, 16 knots, 1915–18): six WWI sloops performing various duties, plus two still afloat as drill ships. One of the active units, *Cornwallis*, served in the Royal Indian Marine and displaced 1,383 tons. The navy had built 112 "Flowers" in five series, and the type went on to serve in Belgium, Portugal, Japan, Italy, China, and Egypt during World War II, though mostly in non-combatant roles.

The design ran along mercantile lines, a standard British practice to allow mass production in numerous shipyards. During World War II, Britain built very few escorts of true warship design because of the cost, the labor-intensive construction, and the small number of capable yards. Types based on merchant hulls could be churned out by many builders.

PC69, 74 (610–661 tons; one 4-inch, two 3-inch guns; 20 knots, 1918): patrol vessels from a class of twenty. *PC69* took the name *Pathan*. *PC74* served temporarily as a Q-ship.

Three escort sloops of the old "Racehorse" class (also called the "24" class, though only 22 reached completion: 1320 tons, 17 knots, 1918) continued in service, one as an immobile drill ship, two still active as survey vessels; *Moresby* went on to function as an escort, but

The Sackville *of the "Flower" class, now a memorial in Halifax. She carries Hedgehog mortars beside her 4-inch gun.*

the Japanese sank *Herald* and salved her as *Heiyo*.

Another survey vessel (*Investigator*: 1,572 tons, one 4.7-inch gun, 12.5 knots, 1925) also performed as an escort.

LAWRENCE (1,210 tons, two 4-inch guns, 15 knots, 1919): old sloop.

CLIVE (1,748 tons, two 4-inch guns, 14.5 knots, 1920): old sloop.

BANFF class (1,546 tons; one 4-inch DP, one 3-inch DP gun; 17 knots, 1927–31): ten American "Lake" class Coast Guard cutters transferred in 1941. Note the change in armament.

BRIDGEWATER, SANDWICH (1,045 tons, two 4-inch DP guns, 16 knots, 1929): sloops with minesweeping gear. At first only one gun was DP, then both, and then one was removed.

HASTINGS, FOLKESTONE, SCARBOROUGH, PENZANCE (1,045 tons, two 4-inch DP guns, 16 knots, 1930–31): similar to the *Bridgewaters* with an even greater variety of guns. *Hastings* could lay 22 mines.

HINDUSTAN (1,190 tons, two 4-inch guns, 16.25 knots, 1930): the *Hastings* design adapted for service in India. Dual-purpose guns replaced her original weapons in 1943.

SHOREHAM, ROCHESTER, FOWEY, BIDE-FORD (1,105 tons, two 4-inch DP guns, 16 knots, 1931): sloops with the usual gun variations.

FALMOUTH, DUNDEE, MILFORD, WESTON (1,060 tons, two 4-inch DP guns, 16 knots, 1932–33): repeats of the *Shoreham*.

GRIMSBY class (990–1,070 tons; two 4.7-inch, one 3-inch DP gun; 16.5 knots, 1934–40): 12 heavily armed sloops. Weaponry varied widely. Some units had three or four 4-inch guns, probably DP. Two were listed with 40 mines.

INDUS (1,190 tons, two 4.7-inch guns, 16.25 knots, 1935): an up-gunned development of the *Hindustan*.

BITTERN, STORK, ENCHANTRESS (1,190 tons, six 4-inch DP guns, 18.75 knots, 1935–38): a quantum leap in sloop design, establishing a lineage that culminated in the *Black Swan* class. *Enchantress* functioned as a yacht (1,085 tons; two 4.7-inch, one 3-inch DP gun).

The volume of their AA fire (if not the accuracy) created a high demand for Britain's Flamingo *and the other* Black Swans. *This, and their warship origins, won them regard as prestige ships.*

KINGFISHER, MALLARD, PUFFIN (510 tons, one 4-inch DP gun, 20 knots, 1935–36): rated as patrol vessels, a type the Admiralty soon abandoned because its warship nature prevented mass production. Later re-designated as corvettes, they provided local patrol more than ocean escort where the slower "Flowers" made their mark.

KITTIWAKE, SHELDRAKE, WIDGEON (530 tons, one 4-inch DP gun, 20 knots, 1937–38): patrol vessels.

EGRET, PELICAN, HERON (1,250 tons, eight 4-inch DP guns, 19.25 knots, 1938–39): enlarged *Bitterns*. The heavy AA batteries of these sloops shows a foresight the Royal Navy should have applied to its destroyers.

GUILLEMOT, PINTAIL, SHEARWATER (580 tons, one 4-inch DP gun, 20 knots, 1939): last of the *Kingfisher*-type patrol vessels. The 4-inch gun in these classes was probably low-angle at first, later given DP mounting.

BLACK SWAN class (1,300 tons, six 4-inch DP, 19.5 knots, 1939–45): 32 sloops built in two series, plus five ships postwar and five others canceled. The first series (four ships) included MS gear. The second series had more depth charges and more beam, displacing up to 1,490 tons. The *Black Swans* and the "Hunt" type escort destroyers were Britain's only wartime escorts of warship derivation. And like the "Hunts," the *Black Swans* were ill-suited to ahead-throwing weapons (like Hedgehog). They sufficed as AS escorts but excelled against aircraft.

"Flower" class (900–1,110 tons, one 4-inch gun, 16 knots, 1940–44): 267 corvettes (plus at least 13 cancellations and about 50 more planned completions) built in two series for the Allies, including four units built for France but not the four captured incomplete and finished by the Germans. The design developed from a commercial whaler. Transfers numbered 18 to the Americans, eight to the Free French, one to the Dutch, four to the Greeks, and one to the Yugoslavians.

The "Flowers" epitomize Britain's mass production of cheap, simple vessels with modest capabilities. It was the quantity of "Flowers" that made them so important—decisive, by some accounts—rather than any quality. Intended for coastal work, the AS emergency in the Atlantic forced them into mid-ocean where they displayed their ability to gather seawater, roll excessively, and discomfort their crews. Improvements worked their way into the design during its long production run, but it lacked the size to mount Squid mortars. The 4-inch gun, usually low-angle, was often supplemented or replaced by a 3-inch DP.

While the naval leadership was removing MS gear from *Bangor*s needed as AS escorts, it was placing MS gear aboard some "Flowers" needed for local minesweeping. Australia proposed turning some "Flowers" into flying-boat tenders with lower speed and no 4-inch gun.

SUTLEJ, JUMNA, GODAVARI, NARBADA (1,300 tons, six 4-inch DP guns, 19 knots, 1941–43): developed from *Bittern* for Indian service.

"Hunt" class, Type I (1,000 tons, four 4-inch DP guns, 27.5 knots, 1941–42): 20 escort destroyers. Planners wanted a ship capable of doing everything a destroyer could do, except cover the fleet. In addition to its AA and AS equipment, the plan originally included MS gear, four torpedoes, and a total of six guns. At a late stage, designers realized they'd completely miscalculated the ship's stability, and they had to undertake a series of drastic alterations. In service, the Type I proved unwieldy and short-ranged (2,300 miles at 20 knots). But in combat, the "Hunts" had indisputable worth, especially in dealing with E-boats and aircraft. Only

21% of "Hunt" losses stemmed from air attack. (The figure for British fleet destroyers was 38%.) Against submarines, the 86 "Hunts" had to manage with depth charges alone. They accounted for 21 enemy subs, but the 78 American "Captains, " with their ahead-throwing weapons, destroyed 35 subs in a shorter amount of time.

"Hunt" class, Type II (1,050 tons, six 4-inch DP guns, 27 knots, 1941–43): 36 ships. Their increased beam allowed for more stability and three 4-inch twin mounts. Difficulty in operating the aftermost mount led to its elimination from the Type III. Three ships transferred to Poland, two to Greece, and one to Norway.

"Hunt" class, Type III (1,050 tons, four 4-inch DP guns, two 21-inch TT, 27 knots, 1942–43): 28 ships, similar to Type II except in armament. Four went to the Greeks, two to the Norwegians, and one to the French.

"Hunt" class, Type IV (1,175 tons, six 4-inch DP guns, three 21-inch TT, 26 knots, 1942–43): two ships. As Thornycroft's variation on the "Hunt" specifications, they were least like the others. They had stronger, drier hulls, but were harder to handle. With more guns and torpedoes, they had fewer depth charges. They showed the least speed but the most range (2800 miles at 20 knots). Since their abilities suited them best to the Mediterranean, the "Hunts" had little trouble with their short range.

"River" class (1,310–1,537 tons, two 4-inch DP guns, 19–21 knots, 1942–45): 136 frigates built in Britain, Canada, and Australia, plus three more completed postwar. Cancellations totaled almost 110 as construction priorities shifted from AS escorts to landing craft late in 1943. Six transferred to France, and one to the Netherlands. Two went to the United States as *Asheville* and *Natchez*, forming the basis for the *Tacoma* class.

The design began as an effort to improve on the sea-keeping, speed, habitability, and weaponry of the "Flowers." The navy initially rated the "Rivers" as corvettes before adopting the frigate title to distinguish them from the smaller ships. As in other merchant-derived classes, individual variations stemmed from the large number of builders. Occasionally a 3-inch DP gun happened aboard. Some units entered service carrying MS gear.

As ocean-going escorts, the "Rivers" certainly proved successful, if not perfect. Endurance was 7,200 miles at 12 knots. As emphasis shifted from the Atlantic to the Pacific, projects began for possible conversions, such as doubling the 4-inch armament (for fear of kamikazes), replacing the AS gear and 4-inch battery with two 6-inch guns (for use in shore bombardment), and total disarmament (for duty as supply ships). None of these plans went into practice.

"Castle" class (1,060 tons, one 4-inch gun, 16.5 knots, 1943–45): 39 corvettes, plus 53 canceled and five built as armed rescue vessels. They showed much improvement over the "Flowers" in both sea-keeping and AS gear—they could carry Squid. The 4-inch mount usually had 60° elevation. The navy considered the "Castles, " along with the "Rivers" and "Hunts, " for conversion into fire support vessels armed with 6-inch guns.

Despite their advances, the "Castles" and improved "Flowers" remained inferior to frigates. Yet their production continued in yards that couldn't build the bigger ships.

"Kil" class (640 tons, one 3-inch DP gun, 15.5 knots, 1943–44): 15 ex-American *PCE827*-class escorts renamed *Kilham*, *Kilmore*, etc. Experience showed them superior to "Flowers" for coastal work but not for mid-ocean.

As many as five of the WWI "Kil" class (895 tons, 13 knots) served in various roles.

"Colony" class (1,500 tons, three 3-inch DP

guns, 20 knots, 1943–44): 21 ex-American *Tacomas* received in 1944.

Bayntun class (1,140 tons, three 3-inch DP guns, 21 knots, 1943–44): the first "Captain" class, 32 ex-American *Evarts*-class destroyer escorts. The Royal Navy rated them as frigates. Like the "Kil" and "Colony" classes, they mounted American 3/50 guns.

Bentinck class (1,400 tons, three 3-inch DP guns, 24 knots, 1943–44): the second "Captain" class, 46 ex-American *Buckley*-class destroyer escorts. The British at first requested 520 "Captains" prior to Pearl Harbor, supplying only the most general specifications. The American-built DE, warships through and through, out-performed the merchant-type frigates and became perhaps the best AS vessels of the war, despite the lack of 5/38 guns. Amid preparations for the Pacific show-down, Britain hoped to rearm the "Captains" with two 5-inchers since the gun shortage had ended; instead, a time shortage prevented it.

"Loch" class (1,435 tons, one 4-inch DP gun, 19.5 knots, 1944–45): 26 frigates, plus two postwar, the best of the merchant-type AS ships. In fact, with Squid as a standard feature, the "Lochs" matched or surpassed even the American destroyer escorts as killers of submarines. The design improved on its "River" predecessor with better seaworthiness, one third more range, and the latest AS equipment.

"Bay" class (1,580 tons, four 4-inch DP guns, 19.5 knots, 1945): seven frigates, plus 12 completed postwar. With an eye on the shift to the Pacific, the Admiralty ordered modification of the "Lochs" then under construction, with the intent to improve their AA abilities. The "Bay" design consequently sacrificed some of its AS value.

Britain canceled 55 (or as many as 155) "Lochs" and "Bays" and completed eight postwar as yachts, depot ships, etc.

In 1940, several Dutch torpedo boats escaped to England and came under Royal Navy command. *G13*, *G15*, and *Z6–8* were scrapped during the war or immediately thereafter. *Z5*, renamed *Blade*, became a tender for British submarines. Six ex-French *Melpomène*-class TB went on to serve at various times with British, French, Dutch, and Polish crews; the ships had little value as combatants and acted mostly in training and miscellaneous duties. Other French captives included *CH5–8, 10–15* (two of which went to Polish crews), *CH41–43* and two older sub-chasers; *Quentin Roosevelt*, *Conquérante*, *Suippe*, *Diligente*, and two *Arras*-class sloops (including the seaplane tender *Belfort*); various auxiliary patrol vessels (two served with the Poles), and dozens of tugs and harbor craft.

The Admiralty operated more than 200 large yachts (with swarms of smaller ones), not all of them combatant or even commissioned. Fifteen acted as MS, 64 became AS escorts (most armed with a 3-inch gun, with one later converting to a coastal auxiliary AA vessel), and many others performed local patrols.

A miscellany of converted vessels received official designations, mostly for convoy duty:

Fifty-six AMC (plus one that never completed conversion), many later switched to other duties (mostly transports, one CVE, one auxiliary AA) as their lack of value became apparent; armament consisted six to eight 6-inch guns and two 3-inch DP; a couple of ships carried a seaplane.

Sixteen Ocean Boarding Vessels, smaller than AMC and armed with a pair of 6-inch guns; later converted to other uses (three became fighter catapult ships).

Nine "Q-ships" (not including *PC74*), decoy ships armed with four to nine 4-inch guns and some TT; one carried two planes and *MTB105* aboard.

Thirteen Armed Boarding Vessels, smaller than Q-ships, most carrying 4-inch guns; two became auxiliary AA vessels.

Approximately 104 Auxiliary Patrol Vessels (plus five seized from the French) with one or two 4-inch guns; some switched to MS duty, one (*Kelena*) went to the Japanese.

Eight Seagoing Auxiliary AA Vessels (including ex-AMC) with six to ten 4-inch DP guns, good fire control facilities, and a warlike appearance; one vessel doubled as a fighter catapult ship; these were among the most useful conversions.

Thirty-two Coastal Auxiliary AA Vessels (including twenty former auxiliary MS) armed with light guns and perhaps a 3-inch DP gun or two.

Two Convoy Escorts with one 4-inch DP gun.

The navy adapted three ships—a former auxiliary patrol vessel, the ex-French *L'Impossible*, and a merchant conversion—as AA guardships. Three dummy warships, *Mamari*, *Pakeha*, and *Waimana*, bravely impersonated *Hermes*, *Revenge*, and *Resolution* respectively.

Few craft translated as readily from civilian to naval life as the trawler and its relatives. Well suited to coastal work, they could also cope with mid-ocean waters; so while they lacked the speed of SC, their excellence in rescue work made them valuable to convoys. The Royal Navy, capitalizing on the yards that built only trawlers, ordered a fleet of these versatile vessels. Many veterans of the first war served again in the second; some had passed into commercial use and had to be re-commissioned.

Old "Military" class (294–297 grt, light guns, 10.5 knots, 1915): two trawlers left from a batch of ten. Each may have carried a 12-pounder.

AXE class (390 tons, one 3-inch gun, 10.5 knots, 1916): six trawlers.

STRATH class (311 tons, one 3-inch gun, 24 mines, 10.5 knots, 1916–19): 76 trawlers in service during World War II (originally 167 ordered and 149 completed, including noncombatants). This was one of three standard trawler classes ordered during World War I. The French also requisitioned some commercial *Strath*s.

MERSEY class (438 tons, two 3-inch guns, 11 knots, 1917–19): 44 trawlers, the second standard design (156 ordered, 112 completed). Requisitioned *Mersey*s also gave service in Belgium, Germany, Greece, and France.

"Castle" class (360 tons, one 3-inch gun, 10.5 knots, 1917–20): at least 128 trawlers, and perhaps 50 more after all the requisitions, the third standard class (286 ordered, about 266 completed). Some "Castles" also served with the French.

ARMENTIERS class (440 tons, one 3-inch gun, 10.5 knots, 1917–18): eight trawlers.

Admiralty drifters (175–190 tons, light guns, 9 knots, 1918–20): 104 steel-hulled vessels (170 ordered, 123 completed) plus 60 wooden-hulled (209 ordered, 188 completed).

BASSET class (520 tons, one 4-inch gun or one 3-inch DP gun, 13 knots, 1935–44): 25 craft made in Britain, Canada, and India; 27 not completed. The *Basset* became the prototype for most wartime trawlers.

"Lake" class (560 tons, one 3-inch DP gun, 13.75 knots, 1939): six whalers serving exclusively as AS vessels with their relatively high speed.

"Tree" class (530 tons, one 3-inch DP gun, 11.5 knots, 1940): 20 trawlers, virtually identical to the subsequent "Dance," "Shakespearian," and "Isles" classes. Like other trawlers, they could function as minecraft, convoy escorts, and patrol boats.

"Dance" class (530 tons, one 4-inch gun, 11.5 knots, 1940–41): twenty trawlers.

"Shakespearian" class (545 tons, one 3-inch DP gun, 12 knots, 1940–42): 12 trawlers.

"Isles" class (545 tons, one 3-inch DP gun, 12 knots, 1941–45): 145 trawlers. The 3-inch gun in these and most other trawlers was the 12-pounder, a handy weapon of limited power placed in DP mounts whenever possible.

KIWI, MOA, TUI (600 tons, one 4-inch gun, 14 knots, 1941): a New Zealand AS trawler design; in appearance and capabilities, seemingly half-trawler and half-corvette.

"Port" class, wooden hull (525 tons, one 3-inch DP gun, 11 knots, 1941): six Portuguese-type trawlers, also known as the first "Professor" class.

"Port" class, steel hull (550 tons, one 3-inch DP gun, 11 knots, 1941–43): six Portuguese-type trawlers, plus two canceled and two completed as commercial trawlers; the second "Professor" class.

"Castle" class (447 tons, one 3-inch DP gun, 10 knots, 1941–44): 14 trawlers, four canceled, similar to the WWI "Castles."

"Hills" class (750 tons, one 3-inch DP gun, 12 knots, 1941–42): eight trawlers used for AS duty.

Brazilian-type (680 tons, one 3-inch DP gun, 12.5 knots, 1942): six trawlers ordered from a Brazilian yard and handed over to the Brazilian Navy while under construction.

"Fish" class (590 tons, one 4-inch gun, 11 knots, 1942–43): ten trawlers.

"Round Table" class (440 tons, one 3-inch DP, 12 knots, 1942–43): eight trawlers used for minesweeping only.

"Military" class (830 tons, one 4-inch gun, 11 knots, 1943–44): nine trawlers used for AS duty. This largest design had the most naval appearance.

In addition to these naval orders, the British requisitioned more than 2,000 vessels, about 360 drifters among them. Operation Catapult netted about 55 French trawlers, including some *Strath*, *Castle*, and *Mersey* units. Britain also captured a Vichy trawler and two German trawlers; in addition, the Norwegians turned over a German unit they had captured. The British in turn gave at least 31 vessels (mostly whalers built in Norway) to the Norwegians. Other transfers include the following vessels, probably more: nine to Poland, three to Turkey, 18 to the Netherlands, nine to Portugal (eight being renamed *P1–8*), eight to France (one thence to Norway), nine to the Soviet Union, four to Greece (plus more Norwegian vessels reassigned), and 22 to America. At least seven trawlers fell into German hands.

Motor Boats

Between the wars, British yards supplied MTB to the United States, Japan, Greece, France, China, Sweden, Yugoslavia, the Netherlands, the Philippines, Finland, Thailand, and (unintentionally) the Soviet Union. This was mostly an independent effort by Thornycroft, based on their CMB of World War I; the Royal Navy had abandoned such craft, not regaining interest until 1935. At that time, British Power Boat (BPB), Vosper, White of Cowes, and others poured out designs to fill a sudden international demand. Great Britain stood atop the world market, yet failed to produce adequate powerplants, and the best prewar engines in England were Italian. The hunt for engines caused variations in otherwise standard classes and limited the performance of many boats. Packard engines from America became the norm whenever available; but in all cases, the engines ran on petrol. The British made but one stab at diesel power—an unsuccessful one.

Early units had only .303cal weapons as their gun armament. Wartime escalation provided .50cal guns, Oerlikons, and pom-poms (sometimes equipped with star shells—a special hazard for wooden targets). A power-operated 57mm gun entered service in 1944, its 6-lb shell providing lavish firepower. The 6-pounder had some drawbacks: low elevation (a range of just 6,200 yards and no AA value) with a low rate of fire (one third that of a Bofors). Few Royal Navy motor boats carried Bofors guns.

Air-sea rescue designs formed the basis for combatant types, and the rescue boats themselves became increasingly combatant as the navy found they needed AA self-defense. Some American boats, mostly 63-footers with their theoretical AS ability, transferred to British service.

The Admiralty, in ordering its combatants, numbered the MTB in one sequence, and the gunboats and AS boats together in another. The inadequacy of the AS types led to their redesignation; the smaller units retired to rescue duty while the larger ones became gunboats with MGB-numbers. The navy later opted to clump all remaining combatants together under the heading of MTB, despite the fact they used their guns much more often than their torpedoes. This chapter will include all Britain's combatants, but without tracing all the name changes.

MASB1–5 (19 tons, light guns, 25 knots, 1938–39): BPB; based on *MTB1* (below). Most of this class converted for work as rescue boats.

MASB6–21 (23 tons, light guns, 27 knots, 1939–40): BPB; converted to MGB with Packard engines (about 30 tons, 38 knots).

MASB22–39 (23 tons, light guns, 33–40 knots, 1941): BPB. Their displacement increased as they switched to gunboat duty, and they later became rescue craft.

MGB40–45 (24 tons, light guns, 40 knots, 1940): BPB; intended as MTB for Norway and Sweden, but retained by the Royal Navy. Polish crews manned two craft as *S2, 3.*

MGB46, built by BPB as the Dutch *TM51*, entered British service without torpedoes, though temporarily designated *MTB433.*

MGB47, 48 (35 tons, light guns, 41 knots, 1940): White; intended for Poland, the former eventually delivered as *S1.*

MAS49 (20 tons, light guns, 25 knots, 1941): became a rescue boat.

MGB50–67 (28 tons, light guns, 37 knots, 1940–41): based on BPB's *PT9*, intended for France as *VTB23–40.*

Operation Catapult netted *VTB8, 11, 12;* the latter two became *MGB98, 99.*

MGB68 was the ex-American *PT6.*

MGB69–73 (30 tons, light guns, 27 knots, 1940): built in America, intended for Finland, diverted to Britain.

MGB74–81 (46 tons, light guns, 40 knots, 1942): BPB; later named *MTB412–418* with two 17.7-inch TT. One boat went to the Dutch.

MGB82–93 (45 tons, light guns, 40 knots, 1941): ex-American *PTC1–12.*

MGB100–106 (30 tons, light guns, 27 knots, 1941): more American-built boats intended for Finland.

Of *MGB177–192* (ex-American *PT201,203–217,* not respectively), eight went to Yugoslavian crews.

MGB312–335 (69 tons, light guns, 27 knots, 1941): Fairmile "C" type, developed from the "A's" to take advantage of the pre-existing assembly equipment. While sharing some "A" defects, the "C's" proved more satisfactory. Germans boarded the damaged *MGB335* and recovered her electronics.

MGB501 (95 tons, two 21-inch TT, 30 knots, 1942): from Camper & Nicholson; an experimental wood and steel composite design like the S-boats it imitated. The original plan included a 3-inch gun.

MGB502–509 (87 tons, two 21-inch TT, 28 knots, 1942): similar to the previous boat. This was Britain's one attempt at diesel propulsion, and its unimpressive speed underscores the superiority of German diesels. Turkey had placed the order for these boats, but the British took them, some as MGB (without their TT); others specialized as blockade runners, one of which (ex-*MGB508*) fell into German hands.

MGB510 (75 tons, two 17.7-inch TT, 35 knots, 1943): experimental.

MGB511–518 (93 tons, four 17.7-inch TT, 31–33 knots, 1944): a petrol-powered development of *MGB501,* later renamed *MTB511–518.* These boats could ship two 6-pounders while retaining all their torpedoes, ranking them among the war's most heavily armed MGB. Some units took on an ingenious, light-weight 4.5-inch gun (SW: 15 lbs; FC: 4–6 seconds; range: 3300+ yards) but not until the war had ended.

MGB2001 (80 tons, light guns, 30 knots, 1943): Fairmile "F, " a project that lapsed due to the boat's overweight (99 tons) and the lack of suitable engines.

MTB1–12, 14–19 (18 tons, two 17.7TT, 35 knots, 1936–39): from BPB. Developed from a rescue boat design, these were Britain's first modern MTB, though they entered service with their torpedoes in distinctly archaic stern troughs.

The switch in designation from CMB to MTB indicates the boats were expected to operate well away from shore. In fact, a few CMB remained from World War I, and the Admiralty recalled at least two from retirement.

MTB20–23, 29, 30 (36 tons, two 21-inch TT, four mines, 42 knots, 1939–40): Vosper boats based on *MTB102.* Romania bought *MTB20, 21, 23* in 1940.

MTB24, 25, 28 (37 tons, two 21-inch TT, 42 knots, 1939–40): Thornycroft. Ireland bought six more of this type.

The British confiscated China's 55-foot Thornycroft *Kuai 1,2* for service as *MTB26,27.*

MTB31–40, 57–66 (about 35 tons, two 21-inch TT, four mines, 25–40 knots, 1940–42): plus one similar boat in auxiliary service. This and subsequent Vosper classes had the best reputation among British MTB. Note the speed variation caused by Britain's engine shortage. Four of the boats listed above were lost incomplete.

MTB41–48, 201–212, 246–257 (37–41 tons, two 21-inch TT, four mines, 28–36 knots, 1940–43): White. Three boats went to the Dutch.

MTB49–56 (52 tons, two 21-inch TT, 29 knots, 1941): slow Thornycrofts used for target towing. Five of them spent time with Norwegian crews.

MTB67, 68, 213–217, 327–331 (17 tons, two 17.7-inch TT, 40 knots, 1940–41): Thornycroft's 55-foot version of its 45-foot CMB. The

GREAT BRITAIN

Royal Navy had rightly dismissed the outdated design but requisitioned these boats ordered by Finland and the Philippines.

MTB69, 70, 218–221 (32–35 tons, two 21-inch TT, 28 knots, 1940–41): a different Vosper type ordered by the Greeks. The inability to secure suitable engines left the boats well below their designed speed of 40 knots.

MTB71, 72 (25 tons, two 17.7-inch TT, 41 knots, 1940): Vosper type built for Norway, plus two sisters that actually were delivered. *MTB71* did transfer to the Norwegians for a time.

MTB73–98 (about 38 tons, two 21-inch TT, 38–40 knots, 1941–43): Vosper. Six went to the French. One *MTB75* replaced an earlier twin, bombed incomplete.

MTB100 (18 tons full, 22 knots, 1938): formerly rated as a motor minesweeper, soon became a target vessel.

MTB101 (22 tons, two 21-inch TT, 42 knots, 1939): unsuccessful experimental hydrofoil, intended for speeds as high as 60 knots.

Vosper's prototype *MTB102* (31 tons, two 21-inch TT, 43.7 knots, 1937) beat out BPB's entry in official trials—a much debated decision—before the BPB boat went on to success in the United States. Other experimental units were *MTB103* (Vosper: 32 tons, 1941), *MTB104–107* (various Thornycrofts as small as nine tons for transport aboard other ships), and *MTB109* (an incomplete hydrofoil: nine tons, two 17.7-inch TT). Spain ordered a dozen boats of Anglo-French construction; the only completed unit served for a time as *MTB108* (23 tons full, two 17.7-inch TT, 40 knots, 1940) before going to minesweeper duty. Neither of two subsequent experimental *MTB108*s reached completion.

Perhaps inspired by Italian explosive boats, Vosper built 17 small (16-foot) craft for para-chute-drop into fjords, but none saw action. Vosper also built *Bloodhound* (35 tons, 25 knots, 1938) as a torpedo test vessel mounting one trainable 21-inch tube with two reloads. Another *Bloodhound*, ordered from Thornycroft in 1941, failed to survive the fall of Singapore. A 1940 experiment with diesels and a steel hull, *Tarret* attempted 30 knots at 80 tons but reached only 23.5 knots.

MTB222–245 (about 38 tons, two 21-inch TT, 34–39.5 knots, 1942): Vosper; two to France, six to the Netherlands.

The American *PT3–19, 49–58, 88, 90–92, 94, 384–399* and *BPT21–68* transferred to the Royal Navy as *MTB258–316, 363–378, 396–411, 419–423* (not respectively), and *PT93, 198* became target boats; in fact, a few of these boats remained in American hands. *MTB363–370* went on to the Soviets. The Germans captured *MTB314* (renamed *RA10*).

MTB332–343 (32 tons, four 17.7-inch TT, 45 knots, 1941): BPB; probably carried four mines instead of torpedoes. The prototype for this class, *CMTB1*, provided training duty in Canada.

MTB344–346 were experimental Thornycroft boats (two 17.7-inch TT, about 40 knots) meant for shipboard transport. *MTB345* transferred to Norway and may have become a German prize.

MTB347–362 (about 37 tons, two 21-inch TT, 35–39.5 knots, 1943–44): Vosper.

MTB379–395 (about 37 tons, four 17.7-inch TT, 34–39.5 knots, 1944–45): Vosper boats with a new armament and hull form. *MTB379*, the prototype, differed in detail.

MTB424–429 (39 tons, two 17.7-inch TT, 40 knots, 1944): White; transferred to Poland as *S5–10*.

MTB430–432, 434–500, 502–509, 519–522 (37–44 tons, two 17.7-inch TT, 39 knots, 1942–45): BPB; sisters of the *MGB74*, some originally named *MGB107–176*. The Dutch received three, and the Poles one (as *S4*).

MTB523, plus 11 postwar and three canceled (about 40 tons, two 17.7-inch TT, 38–40 knots, 1945): final Vosper series.

MTB601–800, 5001–5003, 5005–5026, 5028, 5029, plus one postwar and one canceled (102 tons, two 21-inch TT, 29 knots, 1942–44): Fairmile "D." These "dog boats" began as an MGB (90 tons, up to 31 knots) capable of mounting two 6-pounders. The torpedo armament varied; some boats had two or four 17.7-inch TT. Norway received 23 transfers, one of which the Germans captured. Thirty-nine units entered RAF rescue service.

Three Dutch *TM22* class vessels escaped to England in 1940 and served as target towers. After the capture of the Italian *MAS452*, an enlightened individual renamed her *XMAS*.

SGB3–9 (175 tons, one 3-inch DP gun, two 21-inch TT, 10 mines, 34 knots, 1941–42): steam-powered gunboats, a unique design that proved vulnerable to light gunfire. When sufficiently armored, the extra weight made them too slow to be useful (205 tons, 30 knots).

PAHLAWAN class (60 tons, light guns, 16 knots, 1939): four Thornycroft launches.

Fairmile "A" type (66 tons, light guns, nine mines, 25 knots, 1940): 12 launches. Not well liked, the "A's" proved most helpful in pioneering mass-production techniques.

Fairmile "B" type (75 tons, light guns, 18 knots, 1940–44): about 654 motor launches completed, plus 18 more canceled or destroyed incomplete in the Far East. To hasten production, the "B's" took on only two engines instead of the intended three. Despite their loss of speed, they delighted the navy with their performance. Supremely versatile, they could ship a variety of guns, up to nine mines, even (amid the fear of a invasion in 1940) a pair of torpedoes, using tubes taken from ex-American destroyers. Transfers sent at least four "B's" to Greek crews, while the French got 19, the Norwegians nine, the Dutch five, and the Americans eight. One entered German captivity as *RA9*. The Japanese salvaged a sunken "B" and finished at least one incomplete wreck captured in 1941–42.

Admiralty harbor defense motor launches (46 tons, light guns, 11.5 knots, 1940–45): another great success, similar to the Fairmile "B's" in seakeeping and reliability. The navy set aside hull numbers ML1001–1600 and achieved 454 completions (including 70 built in American yards), plus five postwar, with 45 more canceled or lost incomplete. The most important mission for the HDML's was local AS patrol; 20 specialized as a counter to German midget subs. Wartime transfers included at least 21 to France, one to Greece, and nine to Turkey (one sank before delivery). The Germans captured as many as three, and the Japanese one (plus some irreparable wrecks).

LEELO class (150 tons, light guns, 10 knots, 1941): six launches.

Two vessels transferred to Turkey as the *Kavak* class just after the outbreak of war.

Dozens of requisitioned launches gave wartime service.

The navy acquired 20 motorized fishing vessels as *MFV501–520* and built four major classes: *MFV1* class (289 units, plus 65 postwar and 105 canceled: 50 tons, 8.5–9 knots), *MFV601* class (259 units, plus 74 postwar and 69 canceled: 29 tons, 7.5 knots), *MFV1001* class (159 units, plus 57 postwar and 38 canceled:

114 tons, 8.5 knots), and *MFV1501* class (47 units, plus 35 postwar and 26 canceled: 200 tons, 9.25 knots). The figures listed here are approximate, and completions include those for commercial use. Combatants carried a small machine gun. They performed numerous services, many as tenders. Six vessels transferred to the French and three to the Americans. The names *MFV2001–2047* were assigned in 1943 to vessels already in naval service.

The United States sent the British a miscellany of 54 small craft.

River Gunboats

"Insect" class (625 tons; two 6-inch, one 3-inch DP gun; 14 knots, 1915–16): 10 heavily armed and successful gunboats from a class of 12. *Moth* became the Japanese *Suma*.

TERN, SEAMEW (262 tons, two 3-inch DP guns, 14 knots, 1928): designed with increased habitability.

PETEREL, GANNET (310 tons, two 3-inch DP guns, 16 knots, 1928): similar to previous class. *Gannet* transferred to China as *Ying Shan*.

FALCON (372 tons, one 3.7-inch howitzer, 15 knots, 1931): transferred to China as *Lung Huan*.

SANDPIPER (185 tons, one 3.7-inch howitzer, 11.25 knots, 1933): shallow draft GB, transferred to China as *Ying Hao*.

ROBIN (226 tons, one 3.7-inch howitzer, 12.75 knots, 1934): used as a depot ship from 1941.

SCORPION (700 tons, two 4-inch guns, one 3.7-inch howitzer, 17 knots, 1938): good habitability. *Scorpion* was selected for conversion to an AS vessel, but no work took place.

DRAGONFLY, GRASSHOPPER, LOCUST, MOSQUITO (585 tons, two 4-inch guns, 17 knots, 1939–40): plus one unit canceled. The first pair mounted an additional 3.7-inch howitzer.

The four Iranian *Charogh*-class gunboats were seized and assigned to the Royal Indian Navy as *Nilam*, *Hira*, *Moti*, and *Lal*.

GREECE

Hitler schemed to bring Greece under his control without a fight, but Mussolini ruined the plans when his troops invaded from Albania on October 28, 1940.

The Greek Navy nearly acquired some powerful units just prior to World War I. Construction began in a German yard on the battleship *Salamis* (19,500 nt; eight 14-inch, twelve 6-inch, twelve 3-inch guns, five 19.7-inch TT; 23 knots). *Vasileus Konstantinus* (23,500 nt; ten 13.4-inch, twenty-two 5.5-inch, twelve 3-inch guns, four 17.7-inch TT; 23 knots) was a copy of the *Bretagne* design ordered from a French yard. The outbreak of war terminated both projects. Thus the only Greek battleships in 1940 were a pair of ex-American pre-dreadnoughts: *Lemnos* (ex-*Idaho*) as a hulk in reserve and *Kilkis* (ex-*Mississippi*) as a floating battery. A pair of cruisers ordered from a British yard in 1914 (*Antinavarhos Kontouriotis* and *Lambros Katsonis*: 5,200 nt; ten 5.5-inch, one 3-inch DP gun, two 21-inch TT; 25.5 knots) became the British *Birkenhead* and *Chester* and never entered Greek service.

GEORGIOS AVEROFF (9,450 tons; four 9.2-inch, eight 7.5-inch, eight 3-inch, four 3-inch DP guns; 22.5 knots, 1911): armored cruiser. Her shells weighed 380 lbs (9.2-inch), 200 lbs

(7.5-inch), 14 lbs (3-inch), and 13 lbs (3-inch DP). The number of 3-inch guns (single- and dual-purpose) varied during the war.

HELLE (2,115 tons; three 6-inch, two 3-inch DP guns, two 17.7-inch TT, 110 mines; 20.5 knots, 1913): American-built half-sister of China's *Chao Ho* down to just 18 knots. The 6-inch shells weighed 100 lbs. An Italian sub sank *Helle* prior to Greece's entry into the war.

HYDRA, PSARA, KONDOURIOTIS, SPETSAI (1,389 tons, four 4.7-inch guns, six 21-inch TT, 40 mines, 38 knots, 1932–33): Italian-built DD based on the *Freccia* class, but credited with much longer range (5800 miles at 20 knots). The guns fired 52-lb shells. The last pair operated with the Royal Navy after the Greek surrender, trading one gun and half their TT for a 3-inch DP and extra AS gear, a standard modification for the destroyers that worked with the British.

VASILEFS GEORGIOS, VASILISSA OLGA (1,350 tons, four 5-inch guns, eight 21-inch TT, 36 knots, 1938–39): British-built DD based on

the "G" class, with German-made guns firing 62-lb shells to 19,030 yards. The Germans captured *Vasilefs Georgios* and renamed her *ZG3*, later *Hermes*. *Vasilissa Olga* served in modified form with the British.

AETOS, PANTHIR, IERAX, LEON (1,050 tons, four 4-inch guns, six 21-inch TT, 32 knots, 1912): British-built DD, originally ordered by Argentina. The 4-inch shells weighed 33 lbs. The first pair could carry 40 mines. All but *Leon* served under British command with the usual modifications.

In 1914, Greece ordered four *Kriti*-class destroyers (1,000 nt, three 4-inch guns, four 21-inch TT, 32 knots), but the British took them.

During the war, the British DD *Echo* and *Boreas* transferred to Greece as *Navarinon* and *Salamis*.

PROTEUS, TRITON, GLAVKOS, NEREUS (750/960 tons, one 3.9-inch gun, eight 21-inch TT, 14/9.5 knots, 1928): French-built SS based on *Katsonis*. All four survived to operate with the British.

The Greeks retained the Averoff *in active service after hulking their old battleships.*

GREECE

Though derived from the Freccia *design, Greece's* Hydra *and her sisters bore little resemblance to their Italian cousins.*

KATSONIS, PAPANICOLIS (605/778 tons, one 3.9-inch gun, six 21-inch TT, 14/9.5 knots, 1927): French-built SS, went on to operate with the British.

World War I prevented Greece's purchase of two French-built subs (457/670 tons, four 17.7-inch TT, 17.5/11 knots) and five German-built subs (685/878 tons, one 3.5-inch gun, four 19.7-inch TT, 16.4/9.7 knots) which might have remained in service into 1940.

The Italian submarine *Perla*, captured by the British, transferred to the Greeks as *Matrozos*. Other British transfers were *Pipinos* (ex-*Veldt*) and *Delfin* (ex-*Vengeful*).

THYELLA, SPHENDONI (305 tons, two 3.5-inch guns, two 17.7-inch TT, 29 knots, 1907–8): last of four British-built TB. *Sphendoni* switched to 3-inch guns in service with the British.

KIOS, KYZIKOS, KIDONIA (270 tons, four 17.7-inch TT, 12 mines, 28.5 knots, 1915–16): the "K" class, ex-Austrian TB.

PERGAMOS, PROUSA (266 tons, four 17.7-inch TT, 28 knots, 1916): the "P" class, ex-Austrian TB. Sisterships operated with the Portuguese, Romanian, and Yugoslavian navies.

NIKI, ASPIS (275 nt, two 3.5-inch guns, two 21-inch TT, 29 knots, 1906–7): last of four German-built TB, shells weighed 18 lbs.

AIGLI, DORIS, ARETHOUSA, ALKYONE (120 nt, two 17.7-inch TT, 24 knots, 1912–13): last of six German-built TB.

T1, 2 (11 tons, two 17.7-inch TT, 37 knots, 1929): Thornycroft 55-foot CMB.

Greece ordered six more MTB, but they wound up in the Royal Navy (*MTB69, 70, 218–221*). The British did supply the following vessels: two "Hunt" Type II and four Type III escorts, four "Flowers," at least four trawlers and whalers (plus about six formerly Norwegian craft), one *MMS1*-class and 12 American-built *MMS2001*-class vessels, one HDML, four or more Fairmile "B's," and perhaps some other small craft. The Americans provided a *PC461*-class escort.

Greek light forces including two British-built *Mersey*-class trawlers. Eight vessels of about 450 tons served as ML with 40–52 mines each; Germany captured three and assigned them Uj-numbers.

GUATEMALA

Though lacking a navy, Guatemala followed up its 1941 entry into the war by making base facilities and natural resources available to the Allies.

HAITI

Haiti also declared war on the Axis after Pearl Harbor. The Haitians operated a few small boats and later received an 83-foot Coast Guard cutter from the United States.

HONDURAS

The Hondurans declared war on the Axis in 1941. They had no navy, but their tiny air force performed local anti-submarine patrols.

HUNGARY

As Germany began to carve up the continent, Hungary found an opportunity to acquire more territory, and so became a German ally in November 1940. German influence pervaded the country and chained Hungary to Germany's ultimate fate. Though dubious political entities produced a declaration of war against Germany on January 20, 1945, Hungarian troops continued fighting the Soviets into May.

Hungary's navy, mostly Austro-Hungarian leftovers, operated along the Danube.

SOPRON, DEBRECEN (140nt, two 3-inch guns, 18.6 knots, 1918:): river patrol boats.

KECSKEMET, SZEGED, BAJA, GYOR (127 tons, light guns, 17.3 knots, 1918): river patrol boats similar to previous class.

GODOLO (60 nt, light guns, 13.8 knots, 1915): river patrol boat, sister to Austrian *Siofok*.

A variety of small craft operated along the river. The PB *Honved*, *Huszar*, and *Tuzer* were Austro-Hungarian veterans used also for minesweeping. The Soviets seized two MS launches, one armed motor boat, and other craft (including noncombatants).

ICELAND

An interwar treaty established Iceland as an independent republic under the King of Denmark. As German occupation crushed Danish autonomy, the Icelandic parliament distanced itself from continental ties, and in 1944 Iceland declared itself completely independent, electing its own president. The country made no declarations of war. The defense of Iceland had already been entrusted to Great Britain and the United States, and the only armed vessels employed by the local government were a few trawlers and such, armed with light guns.

IRAN

The political winds in Iran gusted in a distinctly Axis direction. To secure this strategic sector, Great Britain and the Soviet Union launched an invasion on August 25, 1941. The Iranians surrendered within a week and eventually declared war on Germany and Japan.

IRAQ

BABR, PALANG (950 tons, three 4-inch guns, 15 knots, 1932): Italian-built sloops sunk in the Allied conquest.

CHAROGH, CHANBAAZ, KARKASS, SIM-ORGH (331 tons, two 3-inch guns, 15.5 knots, 1932): Italian-built PB, renamed *Nilam*, *Hira*, *Moti*, and *Lal* when captured by the British, who found them too lightly built for anything but coastal work.

SHAHIN (170 tons, one 3.5-inch gun?, 14 knots, 1919): ex-German *FM1*-class MS used as a gunboat, left active service in 1941.

AZERBAIJAN class (28 tons, light guns, 14 knots, 1935): six Italian-built motor launches. Three entered Soviet service.

IRAQ

Like its neighbor to the east, pro-Axis Iraq suffered an Allied conquest in 1941 and declared war on the Axis in 1943.

1–4 (67 tons, one 3.7-inch howitzer, two 3-inch mortars, 12 knots, 1937): British-built patrol boats.

FAISAL I (1,025 tons, 1923): royal yacht.

Regolo, one of Italy's "Capitani Romani" class cruisers.

ITALY

In May 1940, Mussolini reviewed a list of Hitler's European conquests in Austria, Czechoslovakia, Belgium, Norway, Denmark, the Netherlands, Luxembourg, Poland, Lithuania, and France. Then he scanned his own list: Albania. On June 10, Italy made its entry into World War II.

But the country was neither prepared for nor desirous of a prolonged military action. The meager gains in Abyssinia and Albania quickly paled beneath glaring setbacks in Greece, North Africa, and the Mediterranean, portending an early Italian surrender.

It came in the summer of 1943. Mussolini fell from power, and his successors sued for peace. The Germans, not at all surprised, had already occupied a large portion of the peninsula, which they proceeded to fortify. They seized numerous ports and the vessels in them. The ships seeking escape to Allied custody underwent Luftwaffe attack, the most significant loss being the new battleship *Roma*. Surviving units showed up in a few Allied actions after Italy declared war on Germany (October 13), but for the most part they sat and waited for the victors to divide them as spoils—the logical end for a navy widely reviled as timid.

Il Duce's hooliganism in the 1930s had isolated Italy from foreign influences, including technical advances and trends. Left to themselves, Italian designers produced few successful novelties, but harped on dubious ideals like the quest for speed and extreme muzzle velocity. Italian warships in general lacked true depth and balance, and the navy never obtained modern radar, AS gear, or AA weaponry. Meanwhile, as Italy was busy offending other nations, it remained dependent on foreign oil. The navy feared its fuel needs more than it feared the British fleet.

Ostracized from the community of nations, Italy also suffered from internal noncommunication. The navy, without a carrier to provide air support, had to rely on the air force, a distant entity with concerns of its own. Participation by the Luftwaffe hardly helped. Thanks to ULTRA, the British often kept in closer touch with the Italian fleet than the Italians' own fighter cover.

The navy drifted into World War II with little hope for success. A fleet without tradition (it hadn't fought a major engagement since Italian Unification in 1870), it saw its high command fall victim to politics, cronyism, and self-deluding propaganda. This inbred pack of drones, in considering a strategy against the British, rehashed the experience of World War I, when battleships countered the Austrian fleet-in-being while small craft executed daring strokes and garnered the glory. So in 1940, in the critical days following France's fall, when the Italian naval presence outweighed the Allies in the Mediterranean, when a strike westward against Gibraltar or eastward against Alexandria would have confronted an outnumbered and isolated enemy, when Malta sat alone amid the Roman Lake—the Italian battle fleet waited. Critics usually condemn this inaction as a lack of initiative; rather, it was simply the Italian navy doing what it did best. There was nothing timid about the human torpedo attacks at Alexandria or the motor boat raids against Crete. But the Italians had never learned that capital ships were the things that had to be risked to win a campaign.

Italian fire control aspired to mediocrity, and radar remained novel. Ammunition performed poorly. Anti-aircraft gunfire suffered from shells of insufficient fragmentation. In surface gunfire, faulty fuses led to an excessive dud rate, and the lack of stringent manufacturing standards compromised gun accuracy. This became obvious after experience with vessels like *Bari* and *Taranto*, ex-German ships that showed excellent gunnery until their original ammunition ran out. The switch to Italian-made ammunition saw their formerly tight salvoes degrade into casual scatterings. Many Italian designs aggravated the problem by mounting their gun muzzles too closely, with a subsequent increase in shell dispersion.

The quest for a remedy centered around trials with various shells and propellant charges; these never fully succeeded but did manage to confuse the records of service ammunition. All heavy cruisers were capable of firing 276-lb shells, to ranges beyond 37,000 yards for the 8/53 and 34,000 yards for the 8/50, but the figures listed in the table more accurately reflect wartime practice. The 6/53 and 6/55 could both fire the 110-lb shell, but the shorter gun regressed to the lighter shell and a lower muzzle velocity, cutting its range, which originally exceeded 31,000 yards. Even the relatively small 4.7/50 had troubles; some records indicate a 49-lb shell.

It was high muzzle velocity that distinguished Italian guns. *Littorio*'s 15-inchers thus had impressive range and excellent belt penetration, but the increased wear necessitated frequent barrel replacement to avoid a drop-off in accuracy. *Littorio*'s guns lasted only half as many rounds as *Yamato*'s or *Iowa*'s.

Rate of fire seems to have been a low priority, even in the case of DP guns, which also lacked agile mounts. This left the modest 3.5-inch gun as the best heavy AA weapon. Light AA did show potential. The 20mm Breda (240 rpm; 6,000-yard range; 9,500-foot ceiling) and 37mm Breda (120 rpm; 8,530-yard range; 16,400-foot ceiling) could have developed into a successful tandem, especially against British carrier aircraft; but at the time of the armistice, the fleet had only a few examples at sea.

Though Italy's war plans relied heavily on its submarines, AS warfare received little attention, with the depth charge the only noteworthy weapon. Mediterranean waters made submarine duty especially hazardous, and Italian escort skippers often displayed skill and persistence in their attacks; but without sophisticated equipment they achieved relatively few kills.

Ordnance

GUN	SW	RANGE	FC	NOTES
15/50	1,951	46,216	45	*Littorios*
15/40	1,929		50	*Caracciolos*
12.6/43.8	1,157	31,280	30	old BB
10/45	500	27,300	22	*San Giorgio*
8/53	276	34,520	16	*Bolzano, Zaras*
8/50	260	30,620	18-40	*Trentos*
7.5/45	200	24,000	19	*San Giorgio*
6/55	110	28,150	13-15	*Littorios, Duca degli Abruzzis*
6/53	105	24,710	12	most CL
6/45	104		18	*Caracciolos*
5.9/43	100	21,220	8.5	*Bari, Taranto*
5.3/45	72	21,430	8-10	*Regolos, Dorias*
4.7/50	52	21,430	10	*Freccias, Folgores*, "Navigatoris," some "Soldatis"
	52	21,000	10	*Cavours*, some "Soldatis"
	52	19,400	10	*Maestrales, Orianis*
4.7/45	51	16,950	8.5	*Turbines, Sellas, Sauros*
	49	15,850	7.5	*Balillas, Fieramosca, Micca, Calvis*
	49		8.5	*Eritrea, Leones*
4/45	30	16,400	8.5	many TB
	30		8.5	*Mirabellos*
4/35	30	12,800	8.5	*Diana, Audace, Pilos*, SS
3.9/47	30	16,670	6-7.5	*Cavours*, most cruisers
	30	16,850	7	modern TB, *Gabbianos*
	30	13,800	7	SS
3.9/43	30	12,000		*Focas, Brins*
3.5/50	22	14,215	5	*Littorios, Dorias**

*Ceiling: 35,400

TORPEDO	WW	RANGE		NOTES
21-inch W270	595	4400/50	13,100/30	SS
21-inch W250	551	3300/43	10,900/28	
21-inch SI270I	595	4400/49	8,750/38	SS
21-inch SI270	595	4400/46	13,100/29	standard in DD, CL, and CA
21-inch SI250	551	3300/40	13,100/26	older model
17.7-inch W200	441	3300/44	8,750/30	*Cagnis*, usable in 21-inch tubes
17.7-inch SI200	441	at least 2200/44		MAS-boats
17.7-inch W110	243	2200/43		MAS-boats

Italian torpedoes derived in part from British design, and as a group they enjoyed a good reputation, even if they didn't deserve it. While the 50-knot speed was excellent, imprecise manufacture caused irregularities. Warheads were comparatively small. In battle, the weapons proved merely satisfactory.

Naval Aviation

Financial considerations curtailed naval construction in Italy as they did in every other country. Since its leadership subsisted on recycled doctrines, the navy disliked gambling its limited liras on an untried weapons system (aircraft carriers) when it had designs of proven merit (such as cruisers). And with the fleet expected to operate within easy reach of base facilities, certain sacrifices seemed apt. Planners gave low priority to habitability and range—and carrier aviation.

The confidence in land-based aircraft led to disaster for the navy. The planes themselves fared poorly in combat against Allied designs, especially with regard to fighters, but this was secondary. The catastrophe lay in the lack of coordination between the planes and the fleet they were supposed to support. An admiral's request for fighter cover might go unanswered; his call for a bomber strike might be ignored; his order for aerial reconnaissance might come to nothing, and any information he did gain might be old or misleading. The Battle of Cape Matapan became a one-sided rout when misinformation led to the loss of two destroyers and three beautiful cruisers. Such failures had grave ramifications for a navy whose doctrine often dangled its proud battle fleet as bait, luring the enemy into the twin jaws of submarine and air attack—jaws that consistently failed to close. Italy placed its heaviest burden on its Achilles' heel.

A minute portion of Italian air strength was under direct naval command, and some thought went into bringing that strength to sea. A 1925 design specified a 12,480-ton carrier hybrid with eight 8-inch guns in quadruple mounts, plus six 3.9-inch DP. In 1932, a 15,000-ton design had four 6-inchers and seven 3.9-inch DP to supplement its 45 aircraft. This step in the right direction was not followed by another until war had broken out.

Some carrier construction neared completion by 1943. The most likely aerial candidate for sea duty was some version of the Reggiane Re 2001 Falco II fighter (speed: 337 mph; armament: two 12.7mm mg with two 20mm cannon or two 7.7mm mg), which had proved its superiority over the Sea Hurricane, if not more modern opponents. In typical Italian fashion, it had short range (466 miles). A fighter-bomber version carried a 1,410-lb bomb, and a torpedo-bomber was in the works (the Re 2001G).

AQUILA (23,130 tons, eight 5.3-inch guns, AC 66, 30 knots): former liner requisitioned when Italy entered the war. The 5.3-inch guns elevated to 45°, inadequate for AA. The originally intended armament consisted of eight 6-inch guns and twelve 3.5-inch DP.

The conversion involved stout bulges, reworked subdivision, and a bit of armor plating. The overall design had sufficient speed and stability but, understandably, without the operational niceties provided by more experienced navies. Had she reached completion early enough, *Aquila* might have had a profound impact; a carrier didn't fit into the usual regurgitated thinking of the high command, and she might have inspired a new boldness within the battle fleet.

She was nearly complete at the time of the surrender. The Germans took her, but Allied attacks (including a Chariot raid) managed to keep her inoperative.

SPARVIERO (20,000 tons; six 6-inch, four 4-inch DP guns; AC 20, 18 knots): another liner intended as an auxiliary carrier, but conversion work didn't progress far. The design included no island.

There was a short-lived plan to fit a flight deck onto the cruiser *Bolzano* while retaining four 8-inch guns. Another plan would have rearmed her (ten 3.5-inch DP guns and light AA only) and equipped her to launch, but not recover, 12 fighters during transport runs to North Africa.

GIUSEPPE MIRAGLIA (4,880 tons, four 4-inch DP guns, AC 20, 21 knots, 1927): a merchant design converted as a seaplane carrier. Some sources credit her with a 3-inch DP battery (as many as 11 guns). She served mostly as an aircraft transport, then became a depot ship at Malta after the surrender.

Battleships

Because of their finances, the Italians were slow to utilize the battleship tonnage allotted to them by the Washington Treaty. They had 70,000 tons immediately available, inspiring design schemes of 35,000 tons, 23,000 tons, and 17,000 tons. But the navy contented itself at first with rebuilding their old ships to counter France's small *Dunkerques*. It wasn't long before mere parity with the French became insufficient.

The inactivity of Italy's battleships was an obvious factor in the country's defeat. From June 1940 to September 1943, the seven BB steamed a total of 80,000 miles; by contrast, the *New Jersey* covered 220,000 miles from May 1943 to the war's end, a feat by no means unique in America's far-ranging navy. Instead of pressing home an attack against the British in 1940, Italy let the Mediterranean campaign degenerate into a duel of convoys, a meatgrinder from which the Royal Navy's greater resources would emerge more intact.

The hull of the pre-dreadnought *Ruggiero di Lauria* (10,824 tons full load, 1884) served as a fuel hulk, numbered *GM45*.

CONTE DI CAVOUR, CAIO GIULIO CESARE (25,902 tons; ten 12.6-inch, twelve 4.7-inch, eight 3.9-inch DP guns; 28 knots, 1914–15): with one sister sunk in 1916. By the 1930s, these ships were decrepit, and the French had begun their *Dunkerques*. Italy had to respond. A plan to build a pair of *Dunkerque*-like ships gave way instead to an intensive renovation program. From 1933 to 1937, the *Cavour*s were completely rebuilt.

Their original battery consisted of thirteen 12-inch guns in five turrets; workers removed the midship turret and rebored the remaining guns to 12.6 inches. This enlargement furnished more firepower, though still less than the French 13-incher. The provision of a DP secondary battery would have been a boon, but like the Germans, the Italians stayed with low-angle guns.

The removal of the midship turret made room for an expansion of the machinery which, along with a lengthening of the bow, increased ship's range (6,400 miles at 13 knots) and added six knots to the original speed, rating the *Cavour*s among the world's fastest battleships at the time. They were also among the loveliest, with a silhouette of refined and delicate beauty.

Unfortunately, they were as delicate as they looked. Even after reconstruction, their armor scheme barely topped 6000 tons—less than

Italy's **Cavour** *retained her good looks even with awning material partly rigged fore and aft.*

24% of their displacement, about the same proportion as in the *Abruzzi*-class light cruisers. Although their watertight subdivision improved and they received a new type of underwater protection, the original design had doomed them to everlasting vulnerability. Britain's raid on Taranto revealed the fragility of these old ships; though never called battlecruisers, they should have been.

While anchored at Taranto, *Cavour* sank from a single aerial torpedo hit. The Italians raised her and planned to refit her with a battery of twelve 5.3-inch DP guns, but the armistice halted work.

The *Cavour*s, as useful as their vintage and vulnerability allowed, were certainly superior to their French contemporaries. Their speed allowed them to operate with the newest units in the fleet, and they might have proved excellent AA escorts for a fast carrier, if they'd mounted better AA weapons and if there had been a fast carrier for them to escort. But in one-on-one duels against the *Dunkerque*s, which had inspired their reconstruction, they'd have been wrecked.

ANDREA DORIA, CAIO DUILIO (26,100 tons; ten 12.6-inch, twelve 5.3-inch, ten 3.5-inch DP guns; 27 knots, 1915–16): similar to the *Cavour*s in their design and reconstruction. Not quite as fast or as handsome—but equally naked of armor—the *Doria*s also shipped some different weaponry. The triple 5.3-inch turrets were cramped, but the 3.5-inch guns were almost adequate in their uneconomical single mounts. *Doria*'s 12.6-inch battery elevated to 30° (with a 33,100-yard range) rather than 27° as in the other three ships.

The *Doria*s' reconstruction finished in 1940. *Duilio* survived a torpedo in the Taranto raid and was repaired. None of these old ships provided service after Italy's surrender.

FRANCESCO CARACCIOLO, CRISTOFORO COLOMBO, MARCANTONIO COLONNA, FRANCESCO MOROSINI (31,000 tons; eight 15-inch, twelve 6-inch, eight 4-inch guns, eight 17.7-inch TT; 28 knots): begun in 1914–15, but incomplete due to wartime priorities and shortages. Their speed far exceeded that of any contemporary battleship. They had thicker armor than the previous classes, but they might be better labeled battlecruisers nonetheless. There's no doubt about their firepower. Some of their guns entered service aboard hastily prepared monitors, including *Faà di Bruno*.

If the ships had reached completion, they might have been rebuilt like the *Cavour*s and *Doria*s, depending on allowances in the Washington Treaty. Improvements might have included the removal of torpedoes, the mounting of DP guns, an increase in armor (especially deck armor, which was a bit thin even by pre-Jutland standards), higher elevation for the main battery, and updated machinery (original range, 8,000 miles at 10 knots).

LITTORIO, VITTORIO VENETO, ROMA (40,700 tons; nine 15-inch, twelve 6-inch, twelve 3.5-inch DP guns; AC 3, 30 knots, 1940–42): plus another (*Impero*) not completed. In the late 1920s, Italy gave serious thought to the best use of its 70,000-ton allotment of BB construction. Britain's initiative toward smaller dreadnoughts helped make a 23,000-ton design attractive, and a 1928 study foresaw six 15-inch guns, eight 6-inch guns, twelve 3.9-inch DP guns, four aircraft, and a speed of 28–29 knots. But the London Conference failed to lower the 35,000-ton limit, so Italy abandoned its 23,000-ton project. International hubbub surrounding the German *Deutschland* and the French *Dunkerque* prompted a new plan, seemingly a marriage of the two foreign ships, carrying its main battery in two turrets, fore and aft (18,000 tons; six 13.5-inch, eight 6-inch,

twelve 3.9-inch DP guns, ten 21-inch TT; AC 4, 26 knots). The heavy armament, dictated by *Dunkerque*'s weaponry, left little weight available for armor—an obvious imbalance that sent the design teams to a higher displacement.

The 1933 project (26,500 tons; eight 13.5-inch, twelve 6-inch guns; AC 4, 29 knots) had BC-level protection. But the leadership tired of trifling with humble designs; Italy would counter the *Dunkerque* by refitting its old BB, while designers indulged in the treaty's maximum tonnage.

The new specifications called for 30 knots and, therefore, 15-inch guns. (All navies realized the impossibility of a 30-knot, 35,000-ton ship armed with 16-inch guns. The French reacted by accepting 15-inch guns. The Americans accepted 27.5 knots. The British accepted 14-inch guns and 27.5 knots.) The Italians, to compensate for foregoing the 16-inch maximum, developed a battery of ultra-high-performance guns, powerful weapons, if slow-firing. The ship swelled toward 40,000 tons as designers tried to tweak the imperfections from their work.

Like other Italian heavy units, the *Littorio*s possessed an airy elegance. For the most part, their flaws were no more glaring than those in foreign designs. Protection totaled less than a third of their displacement, but a cunning armor scheme sought to make the most of it.

No battleship mounted sufficient deck armor to defeat the sort of weapon that destroyed the **Roma**.

The belt protection showed particular quality, surpassing *Richelieu*'s. But in planning the deck armor, designers seem to have out-thought themselves, as their complex layout included ominous gaps. *Roma*'s decks did nothing to protect her against the two guided bombs that sank her. (In fairness, not much could be done against a bomb weighing more than 3,400 lbs dropped from a height exceeding 12,000 feet— a weapon that could threaten even *Yamato*.)

The underwater scheme remains a topic of debate. The Pugliese system, one of the few examples of Italian innovation in the 1930s, positioned a large, hollow cylinder in a fluid-filled chamber running down the ship's side beneath the belt armor. The explosion of a torpedo or mine would lose much of its energy in crushing the cylinder, sparing the hull the worst of the blow—in theory. War experience failed to show its claimed superiority over conventional schemes, though sloppy workmanship contributed to flooding that the design might otherwise have prevented. The Pugliese system saved weight, but its bulk dominated a large portion of the hull, limiting the possibilities of machinery dispersal. It also limited the depth to which the belt armor could extend, increasing the danger from shells that struck below the waterline. The rebuilt *Doria*s and *Cavour*s, even with a compressed and modified version of the system, had their machinery dangerously exposed by it.

During the Battle of Cape Matapan, an aerial torpedo struck *Veneto* near her stern. The relatively small warhead caused 3,500 tons of flooding, and with a pump room out of action, the influx of water outpaced her auxiliary systems. In regard to flooding, *Bismarck* managed better with her torpedo damage. But *Veneto*, with four screws and three rudders, never lost her ability to maneuver; so despite her uninspired subdivision, she survived.

Like many contemporaries, the *Littorio*s were ill-equipped to deal with aircraft. The 6-inch guns provided good anti-ship firepower, but their 45° elevation posed no threat to air-craft. The 3.5-inch battery, sophisticated but not reliable, sat in single mounts hogging deck space.

The failure to deploy a medium-caliber DP gun constituted a critical miscalculation. Certainly, a 6-inch shell will do much more to stop an attacking destroyer than a 4.7-inch shell weighing half as much; but hindsight has established the airplane, not torpedo craft, as the battleship's true nemesis. *Roma*, *Cavour*, *Tirpitz*, *Bismarck*, *Prince of Wales*, *Repulse*, *Arizona*, *Oklahoma*, *Yamato*, and *Musashi* testify to the need for a potent DP armament; only *Hiei*, *Fuso*, and *Scharnhorst* argue for maximized gunnery versus cruisers and destroyers, and we should note that these ships' low-angle secondary batteries did not save them. The *Littorio*s would have benefited from a deckful of 3.5-inch DP twin mounts, eliminating the 6-inchers altogether. A DP battery of 4.7-inch or 5.3-inch guns would have been even better, but no such weapons existed. (A 5.3-inch DP project was just under way at the time of surrender.) In fact, the ships did take on four 4.7-inch guns, but amazingly, these were for star shell only. Air defense desperation led to trials in 1942 with a catapult version of Reggiane's Re 2000 fighter (speed: 329 mph; armament: two 12.7-inch mg). In the end, as the ships spent more time in port and less at sea, they received special 6-inch and 15-inch shells for use against planes.

The *Littorio*s of course had limited endurance (4,580 miles at 16 knots), and their triple rudder arrangement failed to provide much maneuverability. *Littorio* became *Italia* in 1943.

Coast Defense

A former Austro-Hungarian vessel, *Buttafuoco* (about 5,800 tons, 1874), existed as a hulk.

SAN GIORGIO (9,470 tons; four 10-inch, eight 7.5-inch, eight 3.9-inch DP guns; 22 knots, 1910): former armored cruiser of limited value. With two additional 3.9-inch DP, she spent most of her time as a floating battery. Her sistership, *San Marco*, served as an unarmed target ship (8,600 tons, 18 knots).

GM194 (2,796 tons; two 15-inch, six 3-inch guns; 3.3 knots, 1916): ex-monitor *Faà di Bruno*, used as a floating battery. The 15-inch mount apparently had limited elevation (range near 21,870 yards).

The Italians assigned GM-numbers to various old hulls and pontoons. Several gave service as floating batteries with guns up to 7.5-inch, though at least two had 12-inch guns.

Cruisers

Part of an old "Regioni"-class cruiser (possibly *Puglia*, 2,498 nt, 1901) served as floating battery *GD32*, armed with six army-type 3.9-inch AA guns (SW: 22 lbs; FC: 3–4 seconds). The old scout cruiser *Quarto* (3,229 nt, 1913), though stricken from the navy list, continued to serve in tests.

TARANTO (3,184 tons; seven 5.9-inch, two 3-inch DP guns, 120 mines; 21 knots, 1912): formerly the German *Strassburg*, WWI booty. Her best service speed was 19 knots. She still had some value as a colonial gunboat, but within the Mediterranean confines, even escort duty would have been hazardous.

BARI (3,248 tons; eight 5.9-inch, three 3-inch DP guns, 120 mines; 27 knots, 1914): ex-German *Pillau*, still capable of 24 knots. Her loss in an air attack halted plans to convert her to an AA escort. The Italians raised her, then sank her again to keep her from the Germans.

TRENTO, TRIESTE (10,340 tons; eight 8-inch, twelve 3.9-inch DP guns, eight 21-inch TT; AC 3, 35 knots, 1928–29): Italy's first treaty cruisers and, like most nations' first effort, inadequately armored. The design combined an 8.5% protection scheme with a lightly built hull. This vulnerability, part of the payoff in a class designed for high speed, recurred in many subsequent cruisers. Other, more desirable features which also became standard were the use of machinery dispersal and a main battery elevation of 45°. As mentioned previously, shell dispersion hampered the 8-inch guns. Endurance was 4160 miles at 16 knots.

ALBERTO DI GIUSSANO, ALBERICO DA BARBIANO, GIOVANNI DELLE BANDE NERE, BARTOLOMEO COLLEONI (5,109–5,169 tons; eight 6-inch, six 3.9-inch DP guns, four 21-inch TT, mines; AC 2, 37 knots, 1931–32): first of the "Condottieri" classes.

Of all a ship's qualities—protection, firepower, endurance, and so forth—speed would seem the most straightforward, a concept quantified with a single number. The Italians seized upon this simplicity and sacrificed much in pursuit of it. In the end, the sacrifice proved too great. The *di Giussano*s weren't the only design disfigured by speed-lust, but they became its most famous victims.

Speed is not, in fact, all that straightforward; the trial figures for all the *di Giussano*s neared or exceeded 40 knots, but they achieved these numbers for only short bursts with the machinery forced beyond its normal, safe output. The rationale for this policy remains unclear. The intention may have been for publicity to lure foreign customers to Italian yards. The Swedes apparently acquired an unmerited regard for Italian designs, as did the Soviets, as did the Italians themselves. But war experience would change the reputation for speed into a legend of frailty; *di Giussano*'s protection equaled only 11% of the displacement and the hull lacked adequate structure. Heavy seas weakened *Bande Nere* before torpedoes flicked her in two. The name ship of the class succumbed to a single torpedo and 4.7-inch gunfire. Ironically, by 1940 top speed had fallen to 30 knots. *Colleoni* was chased down and destroyed by *Sydney*, a ship supposedly four knots too slow to catch her.

The design's faults constitute a lengthy list. Cramped and wet, the tumblehome form compromised stability and produced a serious

"Condottieri"-class ships like the Colleoni *initially gained fame with their high speed, but the war tarnished their reputation.*

rolling action. This in turn interfered with gunnery, which already had problems; the overly complex 6-inch guns suffered from salvo dispersion and shell irregularities, and 10% of the rounds failed to fire. Each misfire might effectively plug its gun for the duration of a battle. The 3.9-inch guns were consistent but outdated. In view of this, and because the ships had aged rapidly, the Italians planned to reconstruct them for AA duty, a less challenging and more suitable role. The revised armament would have included four 5.3-inch guns and twelve 3.5-inch DP (or simply sixteen 3.5-inch DP) with no torpedoes. Since the 3.5-inch gun barely out-performed the old 3.9-incher, Italy slogged through the war without a quality DP weapon, and a rebuilt *di Giussano*'s potential decreased. The war prevented conversion, and all four ships sank in their original CL guise.

The *di Giussano* design came in response to France's super-destroyers. On paper, the Italian ships seem capable of overwhelming the *Chacals* and *Guepards*; in the real world, they were vulnerable to the French guns even at maximum range. Future "Condottieri" classes improved in many respects, including their stability and gunfire. Most of them shared the ability to lay mines (*di Giussano* herself had no mines) and to attack submarines with a complement of depth charges.

ZARA, FIUME, POLA, GORIZIA (11,327–11,713 tons; eight 8-inch, twelve 3.9-inch DP guns; AC 3, 32 knots, 1931–32): a victory for Italian cruiser design. The *Zara*s, by overstepping the treaty limits, balanced their speed, armor, and weaponry. They were handsome ships, dry and stable, with the most endurance among Italian cruisers (5,000+ miles at 16 knots). With 13% of their tonnage devoted to protection, they showed an excellent concentration of metal; only American cruisers had thicker belt armor. The guns were again paired too closely, but they otherwise performed well. If the Italians had persisted in designs like this one, they could have deployed a powerful fleet indeed.

Despite their potential, the *Zara*s earned no battle-glory. The first three were shattered in an instant, caught unaware beneath the point-blank fire of British 15-inch guns. *Gorizia* fell temporarily into German hands only to suffer destruction in a Chariot raid.

LUIGI CADORNA, ARMANDO DIAZ (5,232–5,321 tons; eight 6-inch, six 3.9-inch DP guns, four 21-inch TT, 138 mines; AC 2, 36.5 knots, 1933): the second "Condottieri" class. These ships had stronger hulls with no tumblehome and less top-weight, improving stability. Slight modifications to the 6-inch guns and mounts created only slight improvement. The *Cadorna*s retained more speed than the *di Giussano*s, but protection remained marginal; *Diaz* sank in six minutes after one torpedo hit. Endurance in all "Condottieris" was short (in this case, about

3000 miles at 16 knots). *Cadorna* landed her TT and aircraft during the war.

BOLZANO (10,890 tons; eight 8-inch, twelve 3.9-inch DP guns, eight 21-inch TT; AC 3, 36 knots, 1933): after the balanced design of the *Zara*s, a reversion to speed-over-protection. *Bolzano* resembled the *Trento* with even less armor but some improved subdivision; twice she survived torpedoes. While under repair the second time, planners considered converting her to a cruiser-carrier, but no such work began. The Germans had her for a while before some Chariots got to her.

RAIMONDO MONTECUCCOLI, MUZIO ATTENDOLO (7,406 tons; eight 6-inch, six 3.9-inch DP guns, four 21-inch TT, 96 mines; AC 2, 37 knots, 1935): the third "Condottieri" class. By increasing displacement 40%, planners allowed themselves leeway to consider protection. This class had twice as much armor as the *Cadorna*s—1350 tons, or 18% of their displacement—a great advance, though the design did not yet qualify as truly rugged. Wartime speed was 34 knots. *Montecuccoli* landed her tubes and aircraft in 1943.

EMANUELE FILIBERTO DUCA D'AOSTA, EUGENIO DI SAVOIA (8,317–8,612 tons; eight 6-inch, six 3.9-inch DP guns, six 21-inch TT, 185 mines; AC 2, 36.5 knots, 1935–36): the fourth "Condottieri" class, with protection increased to 22%. As with other cruisers, light AA guns replaced the aircraft and torpedoes.

LUIGI DI SAVOIA DUCA DEGLI ABRUZZI, GIUSEPPE GARIBALDI (9,050–9,441 tons; ten 6-inch, eight 3.9-inch DP guns, six 21-inch TT, 108 mines; AC 4, 34 knots, 1937): the fifth "Condottieri" class. By accepting a 31-knot sea speed, the Italians at last produced a top-quality cruiser. The protection scheme came to 22%, as in the *Duca d'Aosta*s but with a more advanced layout. The 6-inch guns, an improved model also adopted for the *Littorio*s, were more powerful and free of dispersion problems. The DP battery had grown, but still relied on the old 3.9-incher. Apart from poor AA and short "legs" (4125 miles at 12.7 knots), these ships equaled or surpassed most foreign contemporaries.

Italy's Fiume and her sisterships achieved thick protection by foregoing high speeds and exceeding the treaty limits.

ATTILIO REGOLO, SCIPIONE AFRICANO, POMPEO MAGNO (3,686 tons, eight 5.3-inch guns, eight 21-inch TT, 130 mines, 40 knots, 1942–43): the "Capitani Romani" class; one additional ship completed postwar and eight others never completed, including *Ulpio Traiano* (sunk by Chariots while nearing completion in German control) and *Caio Mario* (used from 1943 as a fuel storage hulk). The 5.3-inch guns elevated to the standard 45°. Each ship carried depth charges, and the original plans included a plane (without a catapult). Two 4.7-inch star shell guns were planned, then deleted. The torpedo tubes sat in unique double-decker quad mounts, which proved unreliable in service.

As the first "Condottieris" had been a counter to early French super-destroyers, these ships came in response to the *Fantasque* class. But unlike the "Condottieris," they had genuine speed: 43+ knots in service. They featured a destroyer-ish look and destroyer-ish protection, with armor intended merely to stop splinters. Even so, they were well liked and might have met with success, if circumstances had allowed. Dual-purpose guns would have made them truly valuable.

COSTANZO CIANO, LUIGI RIZZO (9,615 tons; ten 6-inch, eight 3.5-inch DP guns, six 21-inch TT; AC 4, 33 knots): the final "Condottieri" class, never laid down. The design resembled an improved *Duca degli Abruzzi*. Some sources show *Rizzo*'s name changed to *Venezia*, a switch that never took place.

ETNA, VESUVIO (5,906 tons, six 5.3-inch DP guns, 28 knots): ordered by Thailand as *Taksin* and *Naresuan*, taken over the Italians, not completed. Like all Italian cruiser designs, the *Etna*s included machinery dispersal. However, they seem unimpressive compared to the *Dido*s. Designers never finished the 5.3-inch DP project.

The Italians tried to recover two French cruisers scuttled at Toulon. *Jean de Vienne* and *La Galissonnière* were raised and renamed *FR11* and *FR12*, but neither entered service. The Germans also failed to get them into action before Allied bombs finished them off.

Destroyers

Intended for Mediterranean operations, Italian destroyers had little endurance (usually less than their French rivals) and relatively light structure. They screened the fleet and faced the convoy duel without DP guns or adequate light AA while air attack drove them toward extinction: of the 59 ships in service in June 1940, only seven survived the war.

CARLO MIRABELLO, AUGUSTO RIBOTY (1,811 tons, eight 4-inch guns, four 17.7-inch TT, 100–120 mines, 35 knots, 1916–17): and one sister ship lost prewar. Originally classed as "scouts," they were much larger than contemporary destroyers and heavily armed (including a 6-inch gun, later removed as it overstressed the hull). By 1940, they were obsolescent. *Riboty* landed four guns and her TT to enhance her AS and light AA gear.

LEONE, PANTERA, TIGRE (1,743 tons, eight 4.7-inch guns, four 21-inch TT, 60 mines, 34 knots, 1924): improved *Mirabello*s also classed as scouts; two additional sister ships not built. They introduced the twin-mounted main battery that became standard in Italian DD.

QUINTINO SELLA, FRANCESCO CRISPI, BETTINO RICASOLI, GIOVANNI NICOTERA (970 tons, four 4.7-inch guns, four 21-inch TT, 32 mines, 35 knots, 1925–27): derived from the *Palestro* class TB. They were pushed to 38 knots on trials, but in wartime they couldn't exceed 33 knots. Their unreliable engines gave a meager range of 1,800 miles at 14 knots. Sweden considered *Ricasoli* and *Nicotera* worth buying in 1940 but must have regretted it soon after; the pair retired in 1947. The other two served the Italians as ML and convoy escorts. In 1941, they transported MTM craft for the attack on

ITALY

The **Pancaldo** *of the "Navigatori" class, a departure from Italy's modest destroyer designs.*

Crete that destroyed *York*. The Germans took *Crispi* in 1943 and deployed her as *TA15*.

NAZARIO SAURO, DANIELE MANIN, CESARE BATTISTI, FRANCESCO NULLO (1,058 tons, four 4.7-inch guns, six 21-inch TT, 52 mines, 35 knots, 1926–27): similar to the *Sella*s. Their machinery showed no improvement; *Battisti*, unable to keep up with her squadron mates, had to be scuttled during African operations. *Nullo* was lost due, in part, to steering problems. None could manage more than 31 knots.

TURBINE, AQUILONE, BOREA, ESPERO, EURO, NEMBO, ZEFFIRO, OSTRO (1,070 tons, four 4.7-inch guns, six 21-inch TT, 52 mines. 36 knots, 1927–28): further development of the *Sella* type. In service, they topped out at 33 knots. Few lasted past the first four months of the war. *Euro* was lucky. She survived having her bows blown off in 1940; the next year, she was hit by six 6-inch shells that failed to explode; at the surrender, she avoided German capture and served with the Allies for about a month before the fragments of near-miss bombs sent her to the bottom. *Turbine* landed half her torpedoes and later became the German *TA14*.

ALVISE DA MOSTO, ANTONIO DA NOLI, NICOLOSO DA RECCO, LEONE PANCALDO, GIOVANNI DA VERAZZANO, LANZEROTTO MALOCELLO, EMANUELE PESSAGNO, AN-TONIO PIGAFETTA, LUCA TARIGO, ANTO-NIOTTO USODIMARE, UGOLINO VIVALDI, NICOLO ZENO (1,913 tons, six 4.7-inch guns, six 21-inch TT, 104 mines, 38 knots, 1929–31): the "Navigatori" class, classified for a time as scouts. The French *contre-torpilleurs* caused the Italians great concern, instigating the "Condottieri" project and frightening the naval planners out of their DD rut. The powerful "Navigatoris" became a one-shot departure from Italian design evolution, unique in their machinery dispersal and their six-gun battery. The new 4.7-inch model did become standard.

Time reduced their top speed to 32 knots, but the machinery itself proved reliable. The design turned out wet and lacking in stability, which prompted a reduction in top weight (shortening the funnels, removal of two torpedoes, etc.). Eventually all but *Da Recco* and *Usodimare* had their beams widened. The results were satisfactory, but speed fell to just 28 knots. Some units regained their two lost torpedoes; others served with only two or three tubes. The original 1870-ton ship had become 2,125 tons.

Despite the increase to six main guns, the "Navigatoris" retained the curiously small torpedo battery, a standard Italian DD feature that became especially pronounced as ships lost tubes during modification.

The "Navigatoris" had successful careers, providing rigorous service throughout the war. *Da Recco* had no minelaying gear. The Germans took *Pigafetta* as *TA44*.

FRECCIA, DARDO, SAETTA, STRALE (1,205 tons, four 4.7-inch guns, six 21-inch TT, 54 mines, 38 knots, 1931–32): a return to the *Sella* type with unreliable engines, four guns, and no machinery dispersal. Endurance increased to 4600 at 12 knots. The ships were not particularly seaworthy, and their instability necessitated some changes. Speed fell to 30 knots. Most of the class exchanged torpedoes for light AA. The Germans captured *Dardo* and renamed her *TA31*.

FOLGORE, FULMINE, LAMPO, BALENO (1,220 tons, four 4.7-inch guns, six 21-inch TT, 54 mines, 38 knots, 1932): similar to the *Freccia*. The design featured a smaller beam to help maintain high speed. Of course, it also reduced fuel loads and sea-keeping, so the *Folgore*s had to undergo the same changes as the *Freccia*s and likewise fell to 30 knots. The machinery remained troublesome.

Apart from the "Navigatoris," Italian designs thus far looked small even in comparison with British contemporaries, which were faster, better armed, more reliable, and no less durable. Like the "Tribals," the "Navigatoris" could have provided a starting point for developing a truly impressive design, but planners contented themselves with more modest aspirations.

MAESTRALE, GRECALE, LIBECCIO, SCIROCCO (1,417 tons, four 4.7-inch guns, six 21-inch TT, 56 mines, 38 knots, 1934): planned as slightly enlarged *Folgore*s. Designers remedied some of the flaws and sent the displacement to about 1619 tons. The *Maestrale*s became effective combatants.

On trials, *Libeccio* topped 41 knots; in service, the class managed 32 knots, an acceptable figure. They ranged to 4,000 miles at 12 knots. Some units traded torpedoes for light AA, and some shipped a 4.7-inch star shell gun, one of the war's more dubious items. *Grecale* survived to join the Allies and launch the assault craft that attacked *Bolzano* and *Aquila*.

ALFREDO ORIANI, VITTORIO ALFIERI, GIOSUE CARDUCCI, VINCENZO GIOBERTI (1,688 tons, four 4.7-inch guns, six 21-inch TT, 56 mines, 38 knots, 1937): repeat *Maestrale*s with a 1-knot increase in sea speed. They endured the usual alterations, including the star shell guns. (Star shells did little to transform the fleet's tragicomic performance in night engagements; to say that Italian night training was inferior would be to imply it existed.) All four ships were at Cape Matapan: *Alfieri* fired only four salvoes before shellfire smashed her; *Carducci* was battered and sunk; *Oriani* and *Gioberti* escaped, the former with serious damage. She was repaired, eventually serving with the Allies.

ARTIGLIERE, BERSAGLIERE, CORAZZIERE, FUCILIERE, GRANATIERE, ALPINO, AVIERE, GENIERE, CARABINIERE, LANCIERE, ASCARI, CAMICIA NERA; BOMBARDIERE, CORSARO, LEGIONARIO, MITRAGLIERE, VELITE, plus SQUADRISTA and CARRISTA incomplete (1,620–1,830 tons, four 4.7-inch guns, six 21-inch TT, 48 mines, 38 knots, 1938–42): the "Soldati" class, built in two series. These series differed little, but with several builders involved, the individual units varied.

This was a tough, effective development of the *Maestrale* lineage. They could make 34 knots in service but with a range of only 2,000 miles at 20 knots. These ships all had a fifth gun, at first a star shell piece; but for the second series (except *Velite*) and the last five of the first series, it was a genuine 4.7/50 in a single mount. In many cases, this gun and some torpedoes later gave place to increased light AA.

Camicia Nera was renamed *Artigliere* after the original sank. The incomplete *Squadrista* likewise became a second *Corsaro* before the Germans made her *TA33*. Parts of *Carrista* entered service, her bow repairing the damaged *Carabiniere* and her stern repairing the damaged *Velite*; the Germans named the remainder *TA34* but never got it afloat. Seven "Soldatis" joined the Allies.

In weaponry, Italian destroyer armament had changed little since 1927. In genuine combat prowess, however, "Soldati"-class ships like the Alpino *far exceeded the likes of the* Sauros.

"Comandante Medaglie d'Oro" class (2,067 tons, four 5.3-inch DP guns, six 21-inch TT, 35 knots): 24 DD planned. One unit was set aside to include a dispersed machinery layout as in the "Navigatoris," but neither that ship nor any others reached completion. The 5.3-inch battery began with five guns in low-angle mounts; then the fleet took the opportunity to address its shameful AA performance and switched to four single DP mounts. This battery, if provided with suitable mounts and firing cycles, would have made for a capable group of gunfighters. Their size promised good durability, especially if combined with machinery dispersal. Against smaller British units in the Mediterranean, they might have prospered. But all in all, the big Pacific destroyers appear superior. In range and torpedo armament at least, the Italian ships remained subpar.

The Italians took over several Allied destroyers. They gave the Yugoslavian *Split* the name *Spalato* but never completed her. *Dubrovnik* became *Premuda*; she landed her 3.3-inch guns, and plans were made to rearm her with 5.3-inch low-angle guns. She served a short while before

the Germans took her as *TA32*. *Beograd* and *Ljubljana* became *Sebenico* and *Lubiano* with few changes; *Sebenico* went to the Germans as *TA43*. The French *Lion, Panthère, Tigre, Valmy, Trombe, Sirocco, L'Adroit, Lansquenet, Bison, Le Foudroyant,* and *Le Hardi* became *FR21–24, 31–37*, but only *FR21, 23* and *31* were commissioned. *FR23* and *FR31* returned to French control in 1943.

Submarines

The predatory partnership of Italy's air force and submarine fleet proved a toothless one. Both hunters fell prey to poor inter-service liaison, inferior equipment, and incompetence in the high command.

Italy began the war with 115 submarines, a number exceeded only by the Soviets, but the designs fell short of foreign standards. Somehow, the navy that obsessed on the high speed of its surface ships was content to watch its submarines drag along. Slow in the dive with their large silhouettes, the boats also proved clumsy underwater. Their poorly trained crews had no sophisticated detection or fire-control equipment, and only the most primitive methods of engagement: that is, to lie submerged and wait for targets to happen by. The glassy Mediterranean then exposed every flaw. The subs indeed accounted for several Allied cruisers and other warships, plus a modest amount of shipping, but they did this while losing half their numbers. Construction programs couldn't hope to match the losses. Only 30 new boats entered service before the surrender, thanks to the war's disruptive effects—the work force shrank, air attacks played havoc with industry in general, and raw materials remained in perpetual short supply. Though relatively well stocked with oil, the sub fleet had no true wealth; some boats resorted to mixed loads of 17.7-inch and 21-inch torpedoes.

H1, 2, 4, 6, 8 (355/434 tons, four 17.7-inch TT, 12/11 knots, 1916–18): from the famous American-designed "H" class, with three others sunk or stricken prewar. Excellent but elderly, they performed some patrols before relegation to training duty. In a navy that tended to wear out its subs in a hurry, the longevity of the "H's" is noteworthy, though they must have been in truly sad condition by 1943. At times, they mounted a 3-inch deck gun. *H1* served under British command after the surrender.

X2, 3 (397/460 tons, one 3-inch gun, two 17.7-inch TT, 18 mines, 8.2/6.3 knots, 1918): ungainly sluggards with few virtues, used only for training. The Italian navy had little success with minelaying subs, and their minelaying techniques proved dangerous.

BALILLA, ENRICO TOTI, ANTONIO SCIESA, DOMENICO MILLELIRE (1,427/1,874 tons, one 4.7-inch gun, six 21-inch TT; 16/7 knots, 1928–29): the first large subs built in Italy, intended for patrols from African colonies. They included an auxiliary diesel engine providing a range of 13,000 miles at seven knots, a fair total, but designers abandoned the idea in future classes. The *Balillas* had stability problems and never reached their designed speed of 17.5/8.9

knots. They executed only a few war patrols before their reassignment. *Sciesa* could carry four mines.

GOFFREDO MAMELI, PIER CAPPONI, GIOVANNI DA PROCIDA, TITO SPERI (812/993 tons, one 4-inch gun, six 21-inch TT, 15/7.25 knots, 1929): good short-range boats, though needing additional bulges for buoyancy. This cut their speed from 17.2/7.7 knots. They proved tough and handy. Those that survived to 1942 received new engines capable of 17 knots. *Mameli* served with the Allies after the Italian surrender.

VITTOR PISANI, GIOVANNI BAUSAN, MARCANTONIO COLONNA, DES GENEYS (866/1,041 tons, one 4-inch gun, six 21-inch TT, 15/8.2 knots, 1929): with buoyancy problems like *Mameli*'s, but without many virtues. As in many other Italian designs, the need for bulges canceled any hope of achieving their designed speed (17.25/8.75 knots). The class didn't last long in combat service.

ETTORE FIERAMOSCA (1,531/2,094 tons, one 4.7-inch gun, eight 21-inch TT, 15/8 knots, 1930): intended as a long-range cruiser-submarine housing a scout plane in a hangar. Planners deleted the aircraft and hangar, but the conning tower remained large, contributing to a slow dive time and poor maneuverability. The deck gun failed to match the caliber seen in foreign cruiser-types. Designed speed was 19/10 knots, and endurance (5300 miles at eight knots) barely surpassed *Pisani*'s. *Fieramosca* was taken out of service in 1940 following a battery explosion.

FRATELLI BANDIERA, SANTORRE SANTAROSA, CIRO MENOTTI, LUCIANO MANARA (925/1,080 tons, one 4-inch gun, eight 21-inch TT, 15/8 knots, 1930): derived from the *Pisani* with little improvement. Designed speed was 17.5/9 knots, but bulges and wear had their way. Italian submarines suffered from inadequate upkeep, with the result that many were forced out of service and into yards for refit.

ITALY

To improve their performance as seaboats, the *Bandiera*s had their bows stepped up, also improving buoyancy. With all the modifications, displacement varied among the four boats (some at 1,135 tons submerged). Like many old boats, they served mostly as trainers and transports. *Menotti* differed in mounting a 3.9-inch gun; she went on to join the Allies.

SQUALO, NARVALO, DELFINO, TRICHECO (919/1,125 tons, one 4-inch gun, eight 21-inch TT, 15/8 knots, 1930–31): similar to the *Bandiera*s, including the bulges and bows. The lineage had yet to develop into an effective design, so these boats became trainers and transports. Transport runs to North Africa became an important task for Italian subs.

MARCANTONIO BRAGADIN, FILIPPO COR-RIDONI (966/1,068 tons, one 4-inch gun, four 21-inch TT, 24 mines, 11.5/7 knots, 1931): short-range minelayers, but even modifications to the mine gear failed to make it practical. The *Bragadin*s switched to secondary duties, and the design underwent no further development. Both boats edged past their design speed, but that still left them capable of little more than a crawl. *Bragadin* served with the Royal Navy.

ARGONAUTA, FISALIA, MEDUSA, SALPA, SERPENTE, JANTINA, JALAE (650/800 tons, one 4-inch gun, six 21-inch TT, 14/8 knots, 1932–33): the first "600 class." These small boats were less expensive and more effective in the Mediterranean. They handled well and had strong hulls, but only *Jalae* survived to serve with the Allies.

LUIGI SETTEMBRINI, RUGGIERO SETTIMO (938/1,135 tons, one 4-inch gun, eight 21-inch TT, 17.5/7.7 knots, 1932): derived from *Mameli* with no need for bulges. Strong and maneuverable, they were almost as successful as the original *Mameli*s.

SIRENA, NAIADE, NEREIDE, AMETISTA, ZAFFIRO, RUBINO, TOPAZIO, ANFITRITE, GALATEA, ONDINA, DIAMANTE, SMERAL-DO (680/837 tons, one 3.9-inch gun, six 21-inch TT, 14/7.7 knots, 1933–34): the second "600 class," enlarged *Argonauta*s. In some, the needlessly large conning tower gave place to a smaller one. Displacements varied (829–846 tons submerged). *Galatea* operated with the Allies after 1943.

GALILEO GALILEI, GALILEO FERRARIS (969/1,239 tons, two 3.9-inch guns, eight 21-inch TT, 17/8 knots, 1934–35): the *Archimede* class, with *Archimede* herself and *Evangelista Torricelli* transferred to Spain, 1937. These were good boats based on the *Settembrini* but enlarged for long-range patrol (10,500 miles at eight knots). *Galilei* met with misfortune on her first war patrol, suffering an air conditioning malfunction that threatened to asphyxiate the crew. When she surfaced, British units captured her. Renamed *X2*, she served the Royal Navy as a training boat.

GLAUCO, OTARIA (1,054/1,305 tons, two 3.9-inch guns, eight 21-inch TT, 17.1/8 knots, 1935): ordered for Portugal as *Delfim* and *Espadarte* but taken over by Italy. Based on the *Squalo* design, they became successful long-range boats.

PIETRO MICCA (1,545/1,939 tons, two 4.7-inch guns, six 21-inch TT, 20 mines, 15.5/8.5 knots, 1935): a "cruiser-minelayer" with relatively long range (12,000 miles at eight knots). A good seaboat, she also showed some agility.

PIETRO CALVI, GIUSEPPE FINZI, ENRICO TAZZOLI (1,526/2,028 tons, two 4.7-inch guns, eight 21-inch TT, 17.1/7.9 knots, 1935–36): based on the *Balilla*, including similar range without needing an auxiliary engine. They performed well for the most part, though they never reached their designed speed (in service, 16.8/7.4 knots). *Finzi* and *Tazzoli* became specialized as transports. The Germans took *Finzi* as *UIT21*.

PERLA, BERILLO, CORALLO, DIASPRO, GEMMA, MALACHITE, ONICE, TURCHESE, AMBRA, IRIDE (687/844 tons, one 3.9-inch gun, six 21-inch TT, 14/7.5 knots, 1936): the third "600 class," fairly successful descendents of the *Sirena*. Some of them had their conning towers reduced. With their deck guns removed, *Ambra* and *Iride* were modified to carry three and four SLC craft respectively. The British captured *Perla*, renamed her *P712*, and transferred her to the Greeks as *Matrozos*. *Onice* became an Allied training boat after Italy's surrender.

ADUA, ALAGI, ARADAM, ASCIANGHI, AXUM, BEILUL, DAGABUR, DESSIE, DURBO, GONDAR, LAFOLE, MACALLE, NEGHELLI, SCIRE, TEMBIEN, UARSCIEK, UEBI SCEBELI (680/844 tons, one 3.9-inch gun, six 21-inch TT, 14/7.5 knots, 1936–38): the fourth "600 class," also called the "Africans." Three other boats (also named *Gondar*, *Neghelli*, and *Ascianghi*) were sold prewar to Brazil and replaced by like-named boats. In appearance and performance, they resembled the *Perla*s and achieved some success. Several had their conning towers reduced. *Gondar* and *Scire* exchanged their guns for three SLC mountings. *Gondar* then launched the famous raid against Alexandria, disabling *Valiant* and *Queen Elizabeth*. *Alagi* served with the Royal Navy.

ARGO, VELELLA (781/1,002 tons, one 3.9-inch gun, six 21-inch TT, 14/8 knots, 1937): ordered by Portugal, seized by Italy. These well-liked boats formed the basis of the wartime *Flutto* classes.

FOCA, ATROPO, ZOEA (1,305/1,621 tons, one 3.9-inch gun, six 21-inch TT, 36 mines, 16/8 knots, 1937–39): Italy's last minelaying subs. Though built in the same yard, their displacements varied (up to 1633 tons submerged). The original 3.9-inch gun in the conning tower was replaced by a 3.9-inch, 47cal weapon mounted on the deck.

MARCELLO, BARBARIGO, DANDOLO, EMO, MOCENIGO, MOROSINI, NANI, PROVANA, VENIERO, COMANDANTE FAÀ DI BRUNO, COMANDANTE CAPPELLINI (1,043/1,290 tons, two 3.9-inch guns, eight 21-inch TT, 17.4/8 knots, 1938–39): developed from the *Glaucos*. The large conning tower caused problems, including instability, but the class on the whole met with success. They were maneuverable and, rare in Italian submarines, got a touch past their design speed (listed above). The last pair, ordered separately, differed in detail. *Barbarigo* and *Cappellini* converted for transport duty. The Japanese seized *Cappellini* in 1943 and

*Several Italian submarine designs, such as the **Pietro Calvi**, had large conning towers that impeded their mobility and produced a large radar echo.*

gave her to the Germans (*UIT24*) until she went back again to the Japanese (*I503*). The Germans replaced her deck gun with a 4.1-inch piece.

BRIN, GALVANI, ARCHIMEDE, TORRICELLI, GUGLIELMOTTI (1,000/1,246 tons, one 3.9-inch gun, eight 21-inch TT, 17.3/8 knots, 1938–39): long-range boats derived from the original *Archimede* class. This *Archimede* and *Torricelli* replaced the earlier ones transferred to Spain. The *Brins* proved successful despite minor sea-keeping troubles. Their gun armament changed as in the *Foca* class. *Brin* served with the British in training duty.

CONSOLE GENERALE LIUZZI, CAPITANO TARANTINI, ALPINO BAGNOLINI, REGINALDO GIULIANI (1,148/1,461 tons, one 3.9-inch gun, eight 21-inch TT, 18/8 knots, 1939–40): improvement of the *Brin* design, but with the same sea-keeping troubles. They were among the fastest Italian subs. The group converted for transport work, and the last two became the German *UIT22, 23* in 1943.

GUGLIELMO MARCONI, LUIGI TORELLI, LEONARDO DA VINCI, MICHELE BIANCHI, MAGGIORE BARACCA, ALESSANDRO MALASPINA (1,176/1,466 tons, one 3.9-inch gun, eight 21-inch TT, 17.8/8.2 knots, 1940): among Italy's best submarines. Based on the *Marcellos*, they had all the virtues of that class plus longer range and, with a smaller conning tower, they had better stability. *Leonardo da Vinci* undertook tests with the CA-type midget subs, temporarily trading her gun for mounts to transport a CA-boat (to America or Africa, in theory). *Torelli* became a transport sub; seized by the Japanese, she served as the German *UIT25*, then the Japanese *I504*.

AMMIRAGLIO CAGNI, AMMIRAGLIO SAINT-BON, AMMIRAGLIO MILLO, AMMIRAGLIO CARACCIOLO (1,654/2,136 tons, two 3.9-inch guns, fourteen 17.7-inch TT, 17/8.5 knots, 1941): with good sea-keeping, habitability, and range, intended for extended anti-commerce patrols. *Cagni's* first mission lasted 137 days. The size of the design did not prevent good maneuverability. By selecting 17.7-inch torpedoes (adequate against merchantmen), the designers found room for 14 tubes; this was a constructive and innovative reversion.

Only *Cagni* had the opportunity to demonstrate her abilities; the other three became casualties on transport runs. *Cagni* provided Allied training after the armistice.

ACCIAIO, ALABASTRO, PLATINO, ASTERIA, AVORIO, GIADA, GRANTO, PORFIDO, COBALTO, NICHELIO, ARGENTO, BRONZO, VOLFRAMIO (697/850 tons, one 3.9-inch gun, six 21-inch TT, 14/7.7 knots, 1941–42): the final "600 class," a successful design. They could hit 15 knots on the surface, but submerged they fell short of the design figure. The last three entered service with four TT and more powerful surface engines for an extra half knot. *Bronzo* encountered ill luck; she surfaced to approach Syracuse harbor unaware the British had just captured it. The British renamed her *P714*, then gave her to the French as *Narval*. *Giada* and *Platino* served with the Allies after the surrender.

FLUTTO, VORTICE, TRITONE, MAREA, GORGO, SPARIDE, MURENA, NAUTILO, GRONGO (930/1,093 tons, one 3.9-inch gun, six 21-inch TT, 16/8.5 knots, 1942–43): plus three others not launched. These were Italy's best medium-sized boats, but no better than foreign designs. They had the strong hulls and small conning towers that had finally become standard features. Dive time was 30 seconds. The class handled well under water but never topped eight knots.

In *Murena* and *Grongo*, four SLC mounts replaced the deck gun, but the Italians scuttled *Grongo* incomplete. In fact, only the first five listed above saw any active service before Italy surrendered. The others, all scuttled, fell into German hands as *UIT15, 16, 19, 20*.

The navy ordered a second series of *Fluttos* (24 boats: 913/1,113 tons), but none of the boats reached completion. Germany captured *Bario, Litio, Sodio, Potassio, Rame, Ferro, Piombo,* and *Zinco* (renamed *UIT7–14*) but couldn't complete them.

No units from the third group of *Fluttos* (12 boats, identical to the second series) were laid down.

ROMOLO, REMO, R3–12 (2,155/2,561 tons, light guns, 14/6.5 knots, 1943): designed solely for transport work. Some were planned for completion with two 17.7-inch TT; in fact, only the first two were completed at all. The Germans took six other boats and renamed them *UIT1–6,* but none reached completion.

CM1 class (90/112 tons, three 17.7-inch TT, 14/6 knots): 19 boats planned, a design intended for coastal defense. Germany captured *CM1, 2* as *UIT17, 18,* but only the first was completed (in 1943).

CC1 class (98/115 tons, three 17.7-inch TT, 16/9 knots): 37 boats, none completed. The design came as part of the same program as the *CM1.*

The Italians captured and renamed three Yugoslav boats: *Smeli, Osvetnik,* and *Hrabri* became *Francesco Rismondo, Antonio Bajamonti,* and *N3* (which was in such poor condition that she gave no service).

In 1942, Germany transferred several captured French boats to Italy. *Phoque, Saphir, Requin, Espadon, Dauphin, Turquoise,* and *Circé* became *FR111–117; Henri Poincaré* may have received the name *FR118; Calypso* and *Nautilus* weren't renamed. Of these boats, only *FR111* commissioned (largely disarmed for cargo-carrying).

Nine German boats transferred to Italy to compensate for Italian boats converted as transports. *U428–430, 746–749, 1161, 750* became *S1–9. U1162* would have become *S10* if not for Italy's surrender.

CA1, 2 (13.3/16.1 tons, two 17.7-inch TT, 6.25/5 knots, 1938): two-man midgets intended for use against enemy ports, modified in 1941 to carry eight 220-lb charges instead of the torpedoes. This shaved a couple tons from their displacement and raised their speed to 7/6 knots. In this form, they resembled the subsequent *CA3.* Tests took place with *Leonardo da Vinci* acting as transport for a planned mission against New York; but *da Vinci*'s loss, and then Italy's surrender, prevented operations.

CB1–22 (35/44 tons, two 17.7-inch TT or two mines, 7.5/6.6 knots, 1941–43): plus 50 more planned for harbor defense and coastal patrol, well designed. They had a crew of four. Five boats operating on the Black Sea became highly successful, sinking at least two Soviet submarines.

When Italy surrendered in 1943, five boats managed to turn themselves over to Allied forces in the Mediterranean. The Black Sea boats entered Romanian service, then became Soviet captives. Most of the others continued in Axis service; British forces and Yugoslav partisans each captured one.

CA3, 4 (12.6/13.8 tons, eight 220-lb or 20 4-lb charges, 7/6 knots, 1943): three-man design developed from the *CA1.*

The Italians deployed a human torpedo called the SLC or *Maiale.* With two crewmen, this craft moved at 4.5 knots carrying a 485-lb explosive charge to be affixed to a target and detonated by timer. The SLC, ranging to about four miles at top speed, had to be launched close to its target by a submarine fitted with watertight cylinders. Later models had a 551-lb charge; one development, the SSB, carried a 661-lb charge. The SLC's success prompted the British to make their own version, the Chariot.

At least one other human torpedo of a type used in World War I lingered long enough to become a museum piece after 1945.

ITALY

Torpedo Boats

The Italian navy loved its torpedo craft, the heroes of that David-and-Goliath drama which was *War!*—as the naval leadership saw it. Deploying more torpedo boats than any two rivals combined, Italy cast them center stage in a daring naval strategy. This strategy succeeded completely, yet failed utterly; the smaller warships indeed bore a fleet-full of responsibility, but not for the sort of action that displayed their histrionic flair. Convoy attrition meant that Davids dueled Davids, with great slaughter and no theatrics.

INSIDIOSO (542 tons, one 4-inch gun, 24 knots, 1914): last of six "I" class units, originally rated as DD good for 30+ knots. At some point, she mounted two torpedo tubes. The Germans took her as *TA21*.

ROSOLINO PILO class (615 tons, five 4-inch guns, four 17.7-inch TT, 10 mines, 25 knots, 1915–16): seven former DD, plus one sister stricken prewar. Age had stripped five knots from their original 30. Most were modified with the removal of three guns and some TT. two boats became the German *TA22, 35*.

AUDACE (815 tons, seven 4-inch guns, 27 knots, 1916): ex-*Kawakaze*, sister of the Japanese *Urakaze*, purchased during World War I. Between the wars, she served as the control ship for the target *San Marco*. She originally had four 17.7-inch tubes and 30 knots. By 1942, her armament shrank to two guns. The Germans renamed her *TA20*.

GIUSEPPE SIRTORI, FRANCESCO STOCCO, VINCENZO GIORDANO ORSINI, GIOVANNI ACERBI (669 tons, six 4-inch guns, four 17.7-inch TT, 10 mines, 25 knots, 1917): four former 30-knot destroyers similar to the *Pilo* class in design and modification.

GIUSEPPE LA MASA class (650 tons; four 4-inch, two 3-inch DP guns, four 17.7-inch TT; 27 knots, 1917–19): seven former DD plus one lost prewar, basically a repeat of the *Sirtori* design. They endured much juggling of weaponry; light AA usually replaced the TT, the 3-inch guns, and some main guns.

PALESTRO, CONFIENZA, SAN MARTINO, SOLFERINO (862 tons; four 4-inch, two 3-inch DP guns, four 17.7-inch TT, 10 mines; 27 knots, 1921–23): former DD designed for 32 knots. Some landed two 4-inch guns. The last pair became the German *TA17, 18*.

"Generali" class (635 tons; three 4-inch, two 3-inch DP guns, four 17.7-inch TT, 10 mines; 25 knots, 1921–22): six ships, an improved *La Masa* design. Light AA replaced the 3-inch guns and perhaps some torpedo tubes. The Germans put one unit in service with light guns under the name *SG20*.

CURTATONE, MONZAMBANO, CASTELFI-DARDO, CALATAFIMI (876 tons; four 4-inch, two 3-inch DP guns, six 17.7-inch TT, 16 mines; 28 knots, 1923–24): former 32-knot DD. Light AA replaced the 3-inch guns; some gave up a 4-inch gun and traded in their old TT for two 21-inchers. The last two became *TA16, 19* in German service.

ALBATROS (334 tons, two 4-inch guns, two 17.7-inch TT, 24.5 knots, 1934): a submarine-chaser, rerated as a torpedo boat.

SPICA class (620–670 tons, three 3.9-inch guns, four 17.7-inch TT, 20 mines, 34 knots, 1935–38): 32 TB built in four series, each increasing in displacement. As torpedo boats, the *Spica*s were a failure, with short range (1,200 miles at 20 knots) and poor stability; as AS escorts, they sufficed, hampered by a lack of proper equipment. The gun mounts varied from 45° to 60° elevation. Sweden bought two boats in March 1940 as *Romulus* and *Remus*. One *Spica* became the German *TA49*.

One of the Italian Spica-class ships in Swedish service as the Romulus.
Not all Italian designs worked well when outside the Mediterranean.

ORSA, ORIONE, PEGASO, PROCIONE (840 tons, two 3.9-inch guns, six 17.7-inch TT, 20 mines, 28 knots, 1938): useful vessels rated variously as escorts and TB. In fact, Italian TB spent most of their time as AS craft, a role in which they proved effectively greedy.

CICLONE class (910 tons, two 3.9-inch guns, four 17.7-inch TT, 20 mines, 26 knots, 1942–43): 16 modified *Orsas*, designed to escort African convoys. They sacrificed range and speed for stability and AS weaponry. Some carried a third 3.9-inch gun. The Germans captured three ships and renamed them *TA23, 25, 26.*

ARIETE class (745 tons, two 3.9-inch guns, six 17.7-inch TT, 28 mines, 31.5 knots, 1943–45): 42 vessels planned, a development of the *Spica* but larger to provide all-around defense against aircraft, submarines, and surface ships. Only *Ariete* commissioned with the Italian navy, but the Germans completed 13 more as *TA24, 27–30, 36–42, 45; TA46, 47* remained incomplete at war's end.

Yugoslavia's six old TB became Italian war prizes, some rearmed with two 3-inch DP. *T1, 5* returned to the Yugoslavians in 1943. The Germans got *T3, 7* and handed both over to Croatian forces, the former renamed *TA48.* The Italians scuttled *T6,* and the Germans sank *T8* while still in Italian control.

The Italians took three French *Melpomène* class TB in 1942, renaming them *FR41–43,* but failed to make them operational before Germany took them as *TA9–11.*

Minecraft

Old "RD" class (200 tons, one 3-inch gun, 13 knots, 1917–24): 38 MS assigned RD-numbers. The individuals varied in speed, displacement, etc. The Germans captured five of them.

VIESTE, CROTONE (539 tons, two 4-inch guns, mines, 14 knots, 1919): German-built Type 1915 MS. The Germans captured both, *Vieste* in irreparably damaged condition.

The six Yugoslav *Galeb*-class ships, also Type 1915 MS, became the Italian *Selve* class. Only one returned to the Yugoslavians in 1943.

ALBONA, LAURANA, ROVIGNO (113 tons, one 3-inch gun, 34 mines, 11 knots, 1920): built as minesweepers for the Austrians. Each entered Croatian or German service (two renamed as net tenders).

Yugoslavia had five vessels of the same type, the *Malinska* class. The Italians captured them as the *Arbe* class. Three made it back to Yugoslavian control after 1943.

ITALY

The number of auxiliary minesweepers reached 983 (approximately—records of Italian auxiliary warships remain imprecise), many of which also provided other duties. R-numbers and G-numbers indicated sea-going units, B-numbers and F-numbers indicated coastal craft, and DM-numbers went to magnetic sweepers.

OSTIA, AZIO, LEGNANO, LEPANTO (615 tons; two 4-inch, one 3-inch DP gun, 80 mines; 15 knots, 1925–28): ML used also for sweeping. Venezuela bought two sisterships prewar. The Japanese seized *Lepanto* and renamed her *Okitsu.*

FASANA, PELAGOSA, DURAZZO, BUCCARI (531 tons, one 3-inch gun, 54 mines, 10 knots, 1925–26): ML also used as MS. *Fasana* fell into German hands.

The Italians converted few vessels specifically as auxiliary minelayers—among them, four railway ferries—but instead used their auxiliary minesweepers in that role, along with some convoy escort ships. One auxiliary minelayer entered German service. A water tanker equipped with mine rails also went to the Germans, along with two mine transporters that the Germans used as auxiliary ML.

VEDETTA, VIGILANTE (70 tons, one 3-inch gun, 12.3 knots, 1937): minesweepers.

RD1 (188 tons, one 3-inch gun, 10 knots, 1939): MS, not to be confused with the old RD-boats.

The *RD101* class was a minelayer design built under German supervision in northern Italy. (See the section on German minecraft.)

Escorts and Gunboats

AURORA (935 tons, light guns, 14.7 knots, 1905): old yacht.

VALOROSO (338 tons, one 3-inch DP gun, 10 knots, 1908): former British vessel used as a gunboat.

SEBASTIANO CABOTO (778 tons, six 3-inch guns, 13 knots, 1912): gunboat; taken by the Germans after scuttling, not repaired.

ERMANNO CARLOTTO (180 tons, two 3-inch DP guns, 14 knots, 1921): river gunboat; later taken by the Japanese as *Narumi.*

ERNESTO GIOVANNINI (211 tons, two 4-inch guns, two 17.7-inch TT, 12 mines, 23 knots, 1922): the last of six gunboats derived from a small TB design and intended to escort coastal convoys.

SAVOIA (5,280 tons, four 3-inch DP guns, 22.4 knots, 1924): yacht.

ERITREA (2,200 tons, four 4.7-inch guns, mines, 20 knots, 1937): colonial sloop. A planned sister ship, *Etiopia*, was not built.

DIANA (1,735 tons, two 4-inch guns, mines, 32 knots, 1940): yacht; originally planned to mount two 3.5-inch DP. She also acted as a fast transport and carried eleven motor boats to Malta in a dramatic but fruitless raid.

GABBIANO class (660 tons, one 3.9-inch gun, two 17.7-inch TT, 19 knots, 1942–43): 29 corvettes completed by the Italians (four went to the Germans) plus ten completed by the Germans. Intended as cheap escorts easily mass-produced, they fared well in their AS role. They had no use for their torpedo tubes, and only a few ever shipped them. All German vessels received Uj-numbers.

After scuttling, the French sloop *Dédaigneuse* joined the Italians as *FR56*, then the Germans as *M6020*. Five *Élan-* and *Chamois*-class sloops became *FR51–55*, and three went on to the

Germans. An *Arras*-class sloop, found abandoned, was simply scuttled. One French *Pétrel*-class vessel performed coastal duties for Italy, and the ML *Castor* served as escort *FR60*. Albania's small patrol boats probably remained in service after the country's annexation. The former Yugoslavian *Beli Orao* operated for two years as the *Alba*.

Unlike the British, the Italians never ordered large, standardized classes of trawlers. They did retain at least nine fishing vessels (300–400 tons, 1–2 3-inch DP guns, 9–13 knots) from a batch of 47 purchased from Japan in 1916; some functioned as minecraft, and Germany seized four of them. A total of 260 vessels of various types labeled with V-numbers provided coastal patrol, and 66 served as submarine-chasers. Thirty-six larger vessels commissioned as convoy escort ships, most with D-numbers and 4.7-inch guns, the closest Italy came to AMC. (Three of these vessels entered German service as auxiliary ML.)

The Italian customs service operated a collection of 156 vessels in 1940 (87 for harbor duty and local patrol, 38 as coastal craft, and 31 for offshore work, including 12 of the navy's auxiliary minelayers) with eight more units added during the war. However, the bulk of this force found itself absorbed among the larger numbers of naval auxiliary types; 52 local, 40 coastal, and 29 offshore vessels transferred to naval command. The navy also took control of numerous launches from the Port Captains Corps.

Motor Boats

The navy's leaders saw its heavy units as potential losses and its small craft as expendable war-winners. They had some precedent for this belief; in World War I, torpedo boats sank the Austrian battleships *Wien* and *Szent Istvan*; and just after the war, frogmen sabotaged *Viribus Unitis*. Meanwhile, the only exciting thing any Italian dreadnought did was blow up. One old battleship watched her hope of glory fade with

the Great War's close: *Re Umberto*, saved from the scrap yard, was intended to spearhead a charge into Pola harbor, supported—not by the battle fleet—but by dozens of motor torpedo boats. Italian strategic thinking had begun to crystallize.

It was inevitable that the Italians would play a major role in the inter-war MTB trade. Their boats appeared in many navies, and their engines in many more. Unfortunately, designers committed themselves to the MAS-boats. Among the smallest MTB in the world, these craft proved neither rugged nor seaworthy. They carried a farcical gun armament (usually one machine gun or 20mm cannon) and lacked the size to ship the growing array of modern equipment. Even their torpedoes were tiny. Experience with big German boats inspired a change in thinking, and the resulting MS-types proved a major but belated advance.

Germany seized many MTB after the 1943 surrender. Some they commissioned, and others they gave to Fascist forces continuing the fight in northern Italy. The Germans disliked the Italian boats, which is no surprise, accustomed as they were to their peerless S-boats.

Two WWI veterans were being preserved: *MAS15* (12 tons, two 17.7-inch TT, 24 knots, 1916) and *MAS96* (12 tons, two 17.7-inch TT, 27 knots, 1917).

MAS204, 206, 210, 213, 216 (13 tons, one 3-inch gun, two 17.7-inch TT, 26 knots, 1918): the last of 14 boats. They landed their 3-inch guns in 1940, by which time their top speed was 15 knots.

MAS423, 426 (13.8 tons, two 17.7-inch TT, 40 knots, 1929–30): plus two sisters lost prewar, derived from WWI designs. The 40 knots were only a memory. *MAS423* became the German *S604*.

MAS430, 432–434, 437 (13–14 tons, two 17.7-inch TT, 40 knots, 1929–34): plus *MAS435, 436* given to Spain during the Civil War. They resembled *MAS423*, though *MAS437* differed from the rest of the class with a displacement nearer 18 tons and an unsuccessful diesel plant. *MAS430, 437* became the German *S602, 625*.

There had been another class (*MAS427–429*, 31 tons, 26 knots), but its lack of speed led to early retirement, and Italy stayed with its small designs.

MAS431 (16 tons, two 17.7-inch TT, 41 knots, 1932): similar to *MAS430*, became the German *S603*.

MAS438–441 (40 tons, one 3-inch gun, 32 knots, 1934–35): renamed *AS25–28*, used as AS escorts. The MAS designation originated with the type's intended AS function, but the small boats were never satisfactory in that role. The leap to 40 tons provided more capability, but no further growth took place until 1942.

A metal-hulled experiment, *Stefano Turr* (58 tons, four 17.7-inch TT, mines, 24 knots, 1937), had diesel engines designed to produce 35 knots. However, the engines failed so completely that Italy abandoned its diesel MTB program; Germany became the only country to benefit from the diesel's noncombustibility. Engine failure and hull corrosion kept *Stefano Turr* out of operations until discarded in 1941.

MAS424 (19 tons, two 17.7-inch TT, 40 knots, 1937): named after an accidentally lost predecessor, later became the German *S624*.

MAS451, 452 (24 tons, two 17.7-inch TT, 42 knots, 1940): intended for diesels, but delayed until fitted with petrol engines. The Japanese H1 type was similar. The British salvaged *MAS452*, sunk at Malta, and cheerfully provided the name *XMAS*.

MAS501–525 (about 22 tons, two 17.7-inch TT, 44 knots, 1937): various builders producing minor variations in design. *MAS525* had a metal hull. Sweden bought four, *MAS506, 508, 511, 524*. The Germans took five in 1943; *MAS525, 502, 504, 505* became *S508, 626–628*, while *MAS522* served with the Fascists.

MAS526–550 (25 tons, two 17.7-inch TT, 43 knots, 1939): various builders. Typical of Italy's MTB, they lacked seaworthiness but had good maneuverability. *MAS550* (21 tons) had a metal hull. Finland bought *MAS526–529* in June 1943 as the "J" class. *MAS549, 542, 550* went to the Germans as *S509, 601, 622* (some later given SA-numbers), and *MAS531* went to the Fascists.

MAS551–554 (28 tons, two 17.7-inch TT, 43 knots, 1941): a failed attempt to increase hull strength and seaworthiness. Experience with *MAS525, 550* prodded the navy to try this metal-hulled design. Ironically, it turned out more susceptible to sea damage. *MAS551, 553, 554* became *S510, 512, 623* in German service and later received SA-numbers.

A previous *MAS551* (19 tons, two 17.7-inch TT, 39.5 knots, 1939) was an experimental boat—new engines in an incomplete WWI hull—used for torpedo tests and discarded in 1941.

MAS555–564, 566–576 (28 tons, two 17.7-inch TT, 43 knots, 1941): reversion to wood hulls, an *MAS526* repeat carrying the smallest possible torpedoes. In May 1943, *MAS566–570, 574, 575* transferred to Germany as *S501–507*, then went to the Romanians who eventually scuttled them. Italy's surrender saw Germany take *MAS557, 558, 561* as *S511, 629, 621*, and Fascist forces got *MAS556, 562*.

The conquest of Yugoslavia brought several boats into Italian control. The *Cetnik* class became *MAS1D, 2D*, and the six *Orjen*-class boats became *MAS3D–8D*. *MAS1D* sank, and the others were renamed *MS47, 41–46*. Four *Orjen*s went on to German service as *S2–5*. The German-built *Orjen*s completely overturned Italy's MAS tradition; their sea-keeping and combat abilities prompted immediate copies and a flight from small designs. The navy did order 30 more MAS-boats, but only because the war had approached Italy's coast. The order was canceled in 1943.

MS11–16, 21–26, 31–36 (62 tons, two 21-inch TT, 32 knots, 1942): far superior to the MAS-boats, based on the *Orjen*s. The AA battery of one or two cannon remained unfortunately small. The design included two reload torpedoes. The Italians looked askance at these boats with their limited speed until combat experience established their advantages. The Germans, for their own impenetrable reasons, refused to supply Italy with diesel engines or plans, thus limiting the MS-boats. *MS16, 34, 36* became the German *SA1–3*.

MS51–56, 61–66, 71–76 (67 tons; two 21-inch, two 17.7-inch TT; 31 knots, 1943): similar to *MS11*, with two 21-inch reloads. *MS75, 76* were altered (70 tons, 29 knots) to carry human torpedoes, explosive boats, or small MTB. *MS51, 63, 71, 76* became the German *SA4–7*, and *MS74, 75* served with Fascist crews.

The navy placed a large order (*MS81–86* plus many more) based directly on Germany's *S38* (105 tons, 39 knots), armed as the *MS51* class or perhaps with fewer TT and more guns. Plans for further MS-boats included six of 120 tons, three of 105 tons, and 26 of 60 tons.

VAS201–230 (63 tons, two 17.7-inch TT, 20 knots, 1942): Type I anti-submarine boats based on Yugoslavia's *Orjen*s. The provision of torpedoes made for a more versatile escort, but with few opportunities for their use, many VAS-boats landed them in 1943. Seven of these boats entered German service, none renamed.

VAS231–248 (68 tons, two 17.7-inch TT, 21 knots, 1942–43): the Type II AS boats, similar to the Type I but with different power plants. The first six operated as MS without TT.

VAS242–244 commissioned just after the surrender. *VAS236, 239–243* became the German *RA261, 262, 265, 268; VAS238* wasn't renamed.

VAS301–312 (90 tons, two 17.7-inch TT, 18–19 knots, 1942–43): Type III AS boats, the last six completed by Germany. The entire class entered Germans service: *RA251–260, 263, 264*.

Italian plans to build 24 more VAS-boats never went through.

A number of smaller vessels served in experiments or in action. The explosive MAT-boats (about one ton, one 727-lb charge, 32 knots, 1936–40) had one crewman who would aim the boat at its target, then abandon it. The specifications called for transport by seaplane, which proved impractical, so only three (?) MAT-boats were completed.

By enlarging the MAT design, the Italians developed the MTM (28 completed: about 1.5 tons, one 661-lb charge, 33 knots, 1940–41), a craft useful enough to sink the heavy cruiser *York* near Crete. Some entered German service.

A submarine-portable version, the MTR (one ton, one 661-lb charge, 29 knots), never became operational.

Four MTS-boats (1.75 tons, two 17.7-inch TT, 28 knots, 1940) carried an especially effete torpedo (WW: 330 lbs; range: 1090 yards at just 12 knots). The design evolved into the MTSM (over 100 built: three tons, one 17.7-inch TT, two depth charges, 32 knots) which used its depth charges for their concussive effect against surface targets. The Italians didn't complete any MTSMA (4 tons, one 17.7-inch TT, two depth charges, 29 knots), but the Germans made 78 of them from 1944 into January 1946. The MTL design (7 tons, five knots) was intended to transport two SLC, but no production took place.

Italy also employed the usual multitude of more conventional launches. Records indicating four oar-powered R-boats, each armed with a 485-lb explosive charge, may be as fictional as they are amusing.

JAPAN*
(Plus Chinese units under Japanese control.)

Shortly after Perry's expedition forced the Japanese to acknowledge the outside world, they set about conquering it. The Russo-Japanese War confirmed Japan as a major military power, and the Empire's participation in World War I fixed its place as an international leader. Expansionism continued in the one available direction; by the 1930s, war with China had become a habit.

On the infamous day in 1941, Japan attacked Pearl Harbor and Allied holdings in the Far East. Within five months, after an unbroken series of victories, the Imperial Japanese Navy became the most powerful in the world, a concentrated force of matchless carrier strength and muscular surface units. That supremacy wilted within the space of 48 hours near Midway Island, and though the Japanese retained some advantage over the Allied Pacific contingent, they could no longer defend their vast perimeter. The Americans started pecking away at it with a steadily growing fleet. The fighting came to an end in August 1945, with Japan's official surrender following on September 2.

Combat Skill

The Japanese navy entered the war with the highest level of training in the world, and a correspondingly high morale. In the Russo-Japanese War, the navy had suffered some messy attrition but no decisive defeats, while the Great War had provided great returns for little effort. These successes, combined with an

*The scope of this section is expanded to include the ships extant during the periods of warfare in the 1930s.

Oriental strain of Manifest Destiny and a *bushido* mentality, generated a willingness to accept the most extreme standards of training. Exercises took place under weather conditions that would have canceled American fleet maneuvers, and fatalities became almost common. The superiority of Japanese training was most pronounced in night combat. The Solomons campaign became a showcase for Japanese skill as Allied ships blundered into accurate gunfire and torpedo spreads. The quality of Japan's designs was a significant factor, but not as important as the expertise of the crews and their well-developed doctrines of engagement. But because the Americans could sustain heavy losses, their defeats yielded valuable lessons, and the march of Allied technology soon provided a margin of superiority. Near Vella Lavella in October 1943, the Japanese eked out a slight victory—and their last.

There were gaps in the quality of training among submarine crews, in damage control, and in anti-submarine warfare. These deficiencies had far-reaching consequences.

Ship Design

Japan began the century dependent on British construction, and this continued to lessening degrees until the 1920s. After that, the navy struck out on its own, sometimes without clear direction. Planners viewed the treaty restrictions as an opportunity to outwit foreign designers, forcing a gallon of firepower into a pint-sized displacement. The famous foundering of the *Tomozuru* in 1934 illustrates the results, and the Japanese came to understand that a warship's first job is to stay afloat. Design policy reversed course, with treaty restrictions now viewed as an opportunity to cheat. The Japanese slapped modifications onto existing vessels and designs in progress. This produced ships that were battle-worthy beyond doubt, but hardly economic in weight. The cruiser

Mogami, laid down in 1931, began as an 8,500-ton design loaded with fifteen 6.1-inch guns; she had little stability and a flimsy hull that warped and prevented her turrets from turning. By 1940, she displaced 12,400 tons, one of the toughest CA in the world.

Such haphazard growth was only one of the reasons behind Japan's illegally high displacements. A mysterious, recurring corrosion problem prevented widespread use of aluminum. Welding techniques produced inferior work. Designers pursued extremely long hull forms with overweight structural members, but because displacement limits were of no concern, the lack of weight economy rarely caused a problem. As a rule, Japanese warships were well built. Older vessels refused to act like the senior citizens they were. New ships like *Musashi* and *Akizuki* withstood horrific punishment before sinking. The quality of its front-line units affirmed Japan's confidence in ultimate victory.

The navy's greatest strength in 1941 was its carrier fleet, equipped with the world's best

Ordnance

GUN	SW	RANGE	CEILING	FC	NOTES
18.1/45	3,219	45,960		30–40	*Yamato*s
16.1/45	2,249	42,000		25	*Mutsu*s, canceled designs
14/45	1,485	38,770		30	*Kongo*s, *Fuso*s, most *Ise* guns
10/40.3	500	19,700		20+	*Kasuga*
8/50	277	32,150		12–15	*Tone*s, *Takao*s, *Ibuki*s, *Mogami*s, *Furutaka*s
	277	31,600		12–15	*Aoba*s, *Myoko*s
8/45	250	19,700		12+	armored cruisers
7.9/50	243	24,700			*Akagi*, *Kaga*
6.1/60	123	29,960		12	*Yamato*s, *Oyodo*
6/50	100	22,970		6–10	*Agano*s
	100	19,685		10–15	*Fuso*s, *Kongo*s
6/45	100?	16,185			old *Chikuma* class
6/40	100			7.5+	armored cruisers
5.5/50	84	21,600		6–10	*Mutsu*s, *Katori*s, *Nisshin*
	84	20,890		6–10	*Yubari*, *Sendai*s, *Okinoshima*, *Ise*s, *Jingei*s
	84	19,140		6–10	*Kuma*s, *Nagara*s
	84	17,280		6–10	*Tenryu*s
5.5/40*	84	17,500		12	SS
5/50	51	20,100		6–12	various DD
5/40	51	16,075	30,970	5-7	many escorts, BB, CV, CA
4.7/45	45	17,500	32,800	6	*Akagi*, some CA, CVE, and escorts
	45	17,500		12	TB
	45	16,400		12	SS, old DD
3.9/65	29	21,320	42,650	3–4	*Taiho*, *Oyodo*, *Akizuki*s
3.9/50	29	17,700	36,750	5–10	*I165-170*
3/60	13	14,870	29,850	2.4	*Agano*s
3/40	13	11,800	22,310	3–5	various units, SS Types K5 and K6, prewar in CL

*Most subs had single mounts. The range figure cited here probably applies to the twin mount with its slightly higher elevation.

JAPAN

TORPEDO	WW	RANGE		NOTES
24-inch Type 90	860	7,650/46	16,400/35	*Fubukis*, some CA early in war
24-inch Type 8	763	10,900/38	21,900/27	some old CL and DD
24-inch Type 93	1,080	21,900/48	43,700/36	the "Long Lance"
21-inch Type 6	448	7,650/37	16,400/26	some old RO-boats, CL
21-inch Type 89	650	6,000/45	12,600/36	SS early in the war
21-inch Type 92	661	7,650/29		electric model for SS
21-inch Type 95	893	9,850/49	13,100/45	oxygen torpedo for SS
17.7-inch Type 97	772	5,450/45		midget subs
17.7-inch Type 02	772	3,300/40		midget subs

ship-borne aircraft and flown by an elite corps of airmen from a suitable set of fast carriers. Its greatest weakness was its inability to sustain losses. After one year of combat, the American and Japanese fleets had suffered nearly identical losses, but the former was growing and the latter was not. The Imperial Japanese Navy was a historical marvel; no other fighting force possessed so much glory for so short a time.

Japanese nomenclature has baffled researchers with its imprecision. All "8-centimeter" guns were 3-inch; "10-centimeter" guns ranged from 3.9-inch to 4.1-inch. Postwar analysis has clarified most issues, but many relevant documents were destroyed in the war.

Japan's most famous gun, the 18.1-inch model mounted aboard the *Yamato* class, generated an impressive set of statistics, though its relative performance was mediocre. Japanese shells tended to be on the light side, with no attempt at extravagant velocities. This followed the British example, pursuing reliability rather than hyper-performance. The 3.9-inch, 65cal gun provides an exception; it served admirably in its AA role, but its high muzzle velocity led to short barrel life.

In the night battles of 1942–43, Japanese gunnery proved effective. Enhanced optical equipment, more reliable than the radar of that time, gave early and accurate detection; superior tactics and Long Lance torpedoes then finished the job, producing such one-sided triumphs as Savo Island, Tassafaronga, and Kula Gulf. But American technology and tactics grew increasingly effective and culminated in Surigao Strait, where the Japanese sank nothing but a lonely PT-boat.

In daylight, Japanese gunnery suffered some lapses. It failed to inflict significant damage on the beleaguered *Salt Lake City* near the Komandorski Islands; and in the running fight off Samar, the American CVE escaped, some with hardly a scratch, though Japanese cruisers were closing the range from only 10,000 yards. The primitive state of Japanese radar caused part of the problem. Another factor may have been the excessively tight shellfire patterns, delivering few hits unless the gunner scored a bull's-eye.

Ammunition gave consistent performance for the most part. (Some concern arose over the number of 8-inch duds.) An interesting feature was the special cap fixed on some rounds to preserve their trajectory underwater; such a shell, if it landed short, could continue its path into the target's hull and inflict serious damage—as *Boise's* crew discovered. This solitary success failed to justify the technique, which degraded the shells' penetration against thick armor; in the same battle, a direct hit on one of *Boise's* turrets caused no damage at all. Meanwhile, designers tinkered with *Yamato's* armor to counter such ammunition, which led directly to the flaws in her belt design.

Japan manufactured antiaircraft rounds for

all calibers. This reflects a surprising weakness of the Japanese navy; the fleet that based its success on its air power was ill-equipped in air defense weaponry. High-angle fire control was mediocre, and the techniques outdated. American seamen in the battle off Samar scoffed at the Japanese barrage patterns, abandoned years earlier by the United States.

Japan put all its light AA eggs in one basket, the Hotchkiss 25mm Type 96 (8,200-yard range; 17,220-foot ceiling), chosen over the 20mm Oerlikon in a prewar competition—a decision that enhanced the life expectancy of many Allied airmen. Theoretically capable of 220–240 rpm, in practice it managed only half that rate of fire due to its magazine arrangements. The mounts and gun sights couldn't cope with high-speed targets, and the gun itself proved too small to succeed on its own. There had been another weapon, a 40mm gun similar to the British 2-pounder, but that was the gun that the Hotchkiss replaced. A new 40mm model based on the Bofors never made it into service. With American airmen battering the life out of the Imperial battle fleet, the only supplement Japan gave its too-small 25mm cannon was the 13.2mm Type 93—a machine gun. Long after other major navies had abandoned machine guns as AA weapons, the Japanese embarked them in ever-growing batteries, and their fleet continued to shrink.

From mid-1944, the Japanese deployed sets of AA rocket fixtures, each firing twenty-eight 4.7-inch projectiles. Not one Allied plane fell to this weapon.

The 4.7-inch DP gun, adequate when introduced, seemed less so by the late 1930s. New propellants introduced late in the war lengthened its reach by 25%, using a 50-lb shell. But the 5/40 gun had long since become the fleet standard and replaced the 4.7-inch aboard several classes. Its handy mount and rapid fire made it a crew favorite, despite its modest range. Unfortunately, few destroyers had high-angle

mounts, and in those that did (75° maximum), the 5/50 turrets and firing cycles were too slow for effective AA fire. The 3.9-inch gun corrected these problems, though less than ideal as an anti-ship weapon.

The weakness of air defense hardly compares with the scandalous ineptitude in AS warfare, a primary cause of Japan's defeat. The navy never developed any advanced systems; even its depth charge designs were outdated. Some AS mortars entered service, a 3.2-inch model aboard several escort classes and a 5.9-inch model for merchant use. The fleet also distributed special AS shells in 1943 for guns up to 6-inch bore. The absence of effective sonar canceled the slight value these weapons might have had. A pair of howitzer-like weapons aspired to defend merchantmen from air, surface, and submarine attack: the 8-inch, 12cal gun (SW: 104 lbs; FC: 13; 6,890-yard range; 10,830-foot ceiling) and the 4.7-inch, 12cal gun (SW: 29 lbs; FC: 7.5; 5,800-yard range; 9,190-foot ceiling).

Worse than any equipment shortcomings was the fleet's standardization of amateurish tactics; escort skippers failed to press home their attacks, and for years no one bothered to assign adequately deep settings to the depth charges. This allowed many Allied submarines to escape. Japanese surface units sank only 23 American, British, and Dutch subs—about the same number those countries lost to friendly fire and other accidents.

Mine warfare was not a Japanese strength. Their torpedoes, though, brought results that were literally beyond belief.

In conventional torpedoes, a flask of air allows the engine to burn its fuel. However, pure oxygen, used in place of air, increases engine performance and forms a less visible wake—a widely understood principle. But given oxygen's habit of exploding, most navies (including Japan's) gave up on their pure-oxygen experiments. Then rumors popped up about

England's 24.5-inch torpedoes, and Japan resumed its testing. The willingness to shovel mounds of money into this research won the Japanese a huge reward—the Long Lance, indisputably the best torpedo of the war.

A 1940 project envisioned a 28.3-inch oxygen torpedo (WW: 1874 lbs; range: 29,520/55 and 59,050/40), but planners concentrated on work that promised more immediate dividends. In 1943, new versions of the Type 93 and Type 95 sacrificed as much as 40% of their range to carry extra-heavy warheads (up to 60% heavier). Not all Japanese torpedoes used pure oxygen, but the chart above shows the high standards that prevailed.

The Japanese combined these excellent weapons with effective tactics, bewildering the Allied commanders who thought they had run onto minefields when in fact they were being hit by torpedoes launched from unprecedented range. The Long Lance was carried by most Japanese cruisers and destroyers, but only in the last year of the war did the Americans come to understand its capabilities.

Naval Aviation

Just six months after Pearl Harbor, the Battle of Midway snatched away four of Japan's premier carriers. From that point on, the Japanese completed only four more purpose-built CV. They added other ships: inadequate conversions such as the mutilated *Ise*, *Hyuga*, and *Mogami*. This compares poorly with the parade of American opponents: the brawny *Essex* class, the herds of escort carriers, the no-nonsense *Independence* class, and the looming silhouettes of the *Midway*s.

For Japan, nevertheless, the loss of aircraft carriers was a flea bite compared to the loss of air crews. The Japanese training system yielded a crop of aviation elite, but at a rate of just 100 pilots per year—a figure they could not increase without a sharp decline in quality. The dead of Coral Sea and Midway included the aerial *crème*

de la crème; their replacements, unable to match such high standards, thus fell more readily to Allied guns. The cycle continued up to the Battle of the Philippine Sea, dubbed the "Marianas Turkey Shoot." There the Japanese lost 476 planes with 445 airmen, while the Americans lost 130 planes (only 50 in combat) with 76 airmen. In the next battle, Leyte Gulf, the Japanese could muster only 116 carrier aircraft—and the kamikaze made its debut.

In 1941, the Japanese equipped their warrior aristocracy with the world's finest carrier aircraft, and the most famous of these—the most famous carrier plane of the war—was Mitsubishi's A6M Zero fighter (A6M2, speed: 332 mph; armament: two 20mm cannon, two 7.7mm mg, two 132-lb bombs). The "Zeke," as the Allies called it, created an oxymoronic legend of invincibility and inflammability. The design emphasized maneuverability almost to the point of caricature, its performance shocking the Chinese when it first appeared, then shocking the Americans in the opening phase of the Pacific War. At high altitudes, no carrier fighter could match its dogfighting ability; and at low altitudes, it could tangle with even the best land-based planes. Operationally, the Zeke's behavior in landing and take-off seemed almost loving. It awed its opponents as much with its range (a maximum of almost 2,000 miles) as with its combat prowess.

Its foibles included a lack of dive acceleration and an unimpressive rate of roll. The armament earned some criticism, as initially the 20mm gun fired too slowly. But the Zeke's spectacular defect was its vulnerability. No armor, no bullet-proof glass, no self-sealing fuel tanks—one well-placed burst from American .50cal guns could turn a Zeke into a high-performance coffin. The Americans realized this weakness and began, even before the recovery of Koga's Zero from the Aleutians, to devise effective counters to the plane's strengths. Team tactics gave the Americans an edge, and here the Zeke's lack of a radio represented another severe

*Though its performance shocked opponents at the start of the Pacific War,
Japan's Zeke failed to keep pace with advances in Allied designs.*

disadvantage. Wildcats successfully stood up to the Zeke until the Hellcat arrived and seized control of the Pacific skies.

As the Zeke began to give way before new American designs, Japan struggled to produce a successor. The navy issued specifications, but amid the urgency to churn out large numbers of planes, new design work received low priority. So the Zeke, instead of retiring, endured a prolonged process of revisions which indeed improved the airplane but never made the quantum leap to parity with the Hellcat and Corsair. The A6M5 (speed: 351 mph) had improved diving, but the most heavily armored variant arrived just in time for the Turkey Shoot.

The Zeke's vulnerability has created a false impression of Japan's attitude toward its pilots. They were not seen as expendables, nor as fragrant petals scattered on the breeze. The guiding principal in the A6M design was pilot survivability via attack and maneuver, an aggressive concept that met with great initial success, and within this concept the plane was nearly flawless. Of course, the concept itself was severely

flawed, and Japan proved unable to adjust in time. Tough planes like the Mitsubishi J2M "Jack" had to evolve from scratch; the Jack suffered endless teething problems, and few units made it into combat before the surrender. Meanwhile, the Zero's reputation for expendability increased as it became the most commonly encountered kamikaze. But after all, the Zeke was the most common Japanese plane.

The Japanese had two fighter projects under way at the close of the war. One was a carrier version of the Kawanishi N1K "George" (N1K1-J, speed: 363 mph; armament: four 20mm cannon, two 7.7mm mg, two 132-lb bombs), a land-based fighter which had earned the respect of Allied pilots. But the George's history of bugs in its engine and landing gear made it a dubious prospect for carrier use. The Zero's true successor was the Mitsubishi A7M "Sam" (A7M2, speed: 390 mph; armament: four 20 mm cannon or two 20mm cannon and two 13.2mm mg, two 551-lb bombs). The Sam lingered in limbo while designers sought a suitable engine, their quest endlessly delayed by earthquakes and Allied bombing. Only 10 Sams were completed.

Japanese fighter design had shown great promise during the 1930s in China. A Nakajima model (A4N1, speed: 219 mph; armament: two 7.7mm mg, two 66-lb bombs) was Japan's first entirely home-grown fighter. It hurried into service as a stopgap, performing adequately without gaining its pilots' affection. It was maneuverable but short-ranged (526 miles maximum). In 1937, airmen received the plane they'd been waiting for, the Mitsubishi A5M "Claude" (A5M4, speed: 270 mph; armament: two 7.7mm mg, two 66-lb bombs). Despite its old-fashioned fixed landing gear and open cockpit, the Claude got the best of its opponents, due in part to pilot skill. It was a rugged aircraft, but the army thought it regressed in maneuverability; future designs like the Zeke and Oscar sacrificed all for utmost agility, and Japan's air power began its descent into thoroughbred vulnerability.

The Americans, negligently unaware of the Zeke's existence, thought the Claude remained Japan's primary navy fighter. In fact, it had reverted to secondary duties, retiring completely from carrier service early in 1942.

Contemporary with these early fighters was the Aichi D1A dive-bomber (D1A2, speed: 192 mph; armament: three 7.7mm mg, one 551-lb bomb, two 66-lb bombs), nicknamed "Susie" by the Allies. The Susie equipped front-line units from 1934 up to around 1940 and became famous as the plane that sank the American gunboat *Panay*. Its replacement was the Aichi D3A "Val" (D3A2, speed: 267 mph; armament: three 7.7mm mg, one 551-lb bomb, two 132-lb bombs), an excellent airplane with dive characteristics almost as good as a Stuka's. The Val's fixed undercarriage gave the impression of a Stuka clone; the design did owe some features to German work, but the inspiration came more from the Heinkel He 70's wing than the Ju 87's landing gear. Vals also showed German-like toughness and surprising maneuverability; they

could, if needed, operate as fighters, though hampered by a weak gun armament. It was with their bombs that the Vals made their mark, sinking more ships than any other Axis aircraft. In the 1942 attacks against *Hermes*, *Dorsetshire*, and *Cornwall*, Vals made hits with 85% of their bombs. They had sufficient range (a maximum over 900 miles), and they remained in service for years aboard small carriers that couldn't handle the new, faster models.

The Yokosuka D4Y "Judy," really a lovely aircraft, became the standard dive-bomber starting in 1943 (D4Y1, speed: 343 mph; armament: two 7.7mm mg, one 7.92mm mg, one 1,102-lb bomb, two 66-lb bombs). Its speed and great range (up to 2417 miles) exceeded the Val's; otherwise it provided no improvement, fitting well within the stereotype of the sporty Japanese disposable, with the added dimension of engine maintenance troubles.

During the fighting in China, Japan introduced Mitsubishi's B2M torpedo biplane (B2M1, speed 132 mph; armament: two 7.7mm mg, one 17.7-inch torpedo or 1070 lbs of bombs) which proved difficult to service. It retired by 1940, too soon to receive an Allied nickname. In the absence of a definitive replacement, the navy deployed the Yokosuka B4Y "Jean" (B4Y1, speed: 173 mph; armament: one 7.7mm mg, one 17.7-inch torpedo or 1102 lbs of bombs) as a stopgap. Another open-cockpit biplane, it left front-line service in 1940 and, by the time of Pearl Harbor, had all but disappeared from the carrier fleet.

When the Jean began operations in 1937, the navy had already begun searching for a torpedo-bomber it really liked. Mitsubishi developed the B5M "Mabel" with fixed landing gear and pleasant take-off characteristics (B5M1, speed: 237 mph; armament: one 7.7mm mg, one 17.7-inch torpedo or 1,764 lbs of bombs). The navy considered it an adequate plane, but when Nakajima's design appeared, the B5M order was canceled, and the type left combat operations by 1942.

The B5N "Kate" (B5N2, speed: 235 mph; armament: one 7.7mm mg, one 17.7-inch torpedo or 1,764 lbs of bombs) equaled or excelled the B5M in all areas except take-off and range (1,237 miles maximum, versus about 1,400). Both models, with their anemic gun armament (one machine gun in the rear cockpit), were vulnerable. But the Kate proved itself well suited to its role—in December 1941, the world's most modern torpedo-bomber. Like all prewar designs, it soon became outdated; the Kate lasted into 1944.

Its replacement, the Nakajima B6N "Jill" (B6N2, speed: 299 mph; armament: two 7.7mm mg, one 17.7-inch torpedo or 1764 lbs of bombs), had more speed and range, plus a gun for its pilot. Its high landing speed limited its use to big fleet carriers, and the Jill never demonstrated any real superiority to the Kate. Its first major operation was at Philippine Sea.

The Japanese decided to try an all-purpose attack design, a big plane to replace both the Jill and the Judy. Aichi's B7A "Grace" (B7A2, speed: 352 mph; armament: two 20mm cannon, one 13mm mg, one 17.7-inch torpedo or 1,764 lbs of bombs) featured inverted gull wings to help shorten its landing gear, as in America's Corsair. The design had excellent handling characteristics, but it showed up too late to see carrier service. In comparison with the big American

attack planes, its weapons load seems modest. Japan had long since ceased to deploy the best carrier-borne aircraft.

HOSHO (7,470 tons, four 5.5-inch guns, AC 21, 25 knots, 1922): an oiler converted to a carrier with help from British technicians. The planned conversion of a sister ship never took place. By 1941, *Hosho* had little value as a combat unit. She spent most of the war as a trainer, with light AA replacing the 5.5-inch battery.

AKAGI (36,500 tons; six 7.9-inch, twelve 4.7-inch DP guns; AC 91, 31.2 knots, 1927): with sister ship *Amagi*, selected for conversion from BC to CV. An earthquake damaged *Amagi's* hull, so *Kaga* took her place. (For information on the original *Akagi* and *Kaga* designs, see the section below on battleships.)

As built, *Akagi* had a flush deck and platforms for take-offs from the hangar. Her main battery included four twin turrets, later removed during reconstruction. This left her with six casemate guns. Workers also improved the underwater scheme, lengthened the flight deck, removed the flying-off platforms, and raised a small island on the port side. This port-side arrangement met with failure, and only *Hiryu* repeated it.

Reconstruction couldn't offset Japan's sub-

*The **Akagi** in 1939. Originally a battle cruiser, the **Akagi** was converted to an aircraft carrier.*

standard damage control or anticipate the war's lessons on fuel storage safety. In the Pacific, several carrier losses stemmed from leaks of aviation fuel. When the Japanese realized the extent of this hazard, they performed makeshift precautions, such as surrounding the storage spaces with layers of concrete. But *Akagi* sank before receiving these changes; indeed, her loss helped to inspire them. With her air group preparing for take-off, she suffered two bomb hits, not normally a threat to a ship her size. Yet the first bomb alone sufficed to destroy her, exploding amid the crowd of torpedoes, bombs, and gassed-up aircraft; the resulting blaze consumed the ship. The other three Midway victims succumbed under similar circumstances. This risk, an inherent feature in all carrier designs, continues even to this day. The aircraft is a splendid weapon, and equally good kindling.

Akagi's maximum of 91 planes meant a practical limit of 72; at Midway she carried 61. Few carriers shipped their maximum air group, except when serving as ferries.

KAGA (38,200 tons; ten 7.9-inch, sixteen 5-inch DP guns; AC 90, 28.3 knots, 1928): converted BB. She bore some similarity to the *Akagi* and experienced similar modifications. However, she had her turret guns remounted in new casemates, proving just as useless as any other casemate guns. Pelted by American bombs at Midway—perhaps 11 hits and numerous near misses—*Kaga* burned for nine hours, then exploded and sank.

RYUJO (10,600 tons, eight 5-inch DP guns, AC 48, 29 knots, 1933): a good example of Japanese displacement inflation. As completed, *Ryujo* displaced only 8000 tons with little hull strength, little stability, and little freeboard forward. A refit gave her bulges for stability and a higher forecastle to keep her dry. She lost four of her 12 DP guns, gained more hull structure,

and emerged as a fairly balanced unit. She carried a good air complement for her size (usually 37 planes) but was short on protection. Four bombs and one torpedo did her in.

SORYU (15,900 tons, twelve 5-inch DP guns, AC 71, 34.5 knots, 1937): begun as a cruiser-carrier project (17,500 tons, six 8-inch guns). Fortunately, the planners abandoned the cruiser function and created a high-speed carrier with a large air group—the sort of ship that would emerge dominant from World War II. However, *Soryu* achieved these qualities at the expense of protection, especially underwater. A single torpedo hit might have crippled her, but she encountered no torpedoes, just three bombs.

HIRYU (17,300 tons, twelve 5-inch DP guns, AC 73, 34.3 knots, 1939): enlarged *Soryu* with port-side island and increased (not yet adequate) protection. She usually carried 64 planes.

Japanese carrier design tended to side with the British preference for enclosed hangars. Along with aesthetic benefits, this provided more safeguards against the spread of flames between decks, while American open-sided hangars allowed better ventilation.

ZUIHO, SHOHO (11,262 tons, eight 5-inch DP guns, AC 30, 28 knots, 1940–42): originally *Takasaki* and *Tsurugisaki*, submarine support ships, a type of vessel that proved unsuccessful. Consequently, *Takasaki* was converted to a flush-deck carrier while building. Her sister ship, already completed in 1939, underwent a reconstruction that lasted into 1942; less than four months later, as *Shoho*, she suffered 12 bomb hits and seven torpedoes—enough to sink a ship thrice her size—and disappeared in 10 minutes. *Zuiho* shipped eight AA rocket mounts in 1944, which did her no good at Leyte Gulf, where air attacks overwhelmed her.

Prior to this class, the Japanese had yet to

complete any carrier sister ships. Presumably, they were waiting for a design of distinctive merit before they started duplication. As for the *Zuiho*s, their only merit lay in their availability.

SHOKAKU, ZUIKAKU (25,675 tons, sixteen 5-inch DP guns, AC 84, 34.2 knots, 1941): handsome, battle-worthy vessels evolved from the *Hiryu*. They were, along with their descendent *Taiho*, Japan's best carriers. Their excellent speed helped in operating a respectable air group (usually no more than 72 planes). The design included arrester wires at both ends of the flight deck; those at the bow proved superfluous.

Shokaku improved on *Hiryu*'s protection, supplemented after Midway by concrete around the fuel stores, but some underwater vulnerability may have remained. *Shokaku* twice survived serious bomb damage, on one occasion incurring six hits. But three or four submarine torpedoes sufficed to sink her at Philippine Sea. The attack came during flight operations with planes refueling on deck. The warheads struck with particular savagery, simultaneously igniting her avgas stores, knocking out her power, and letting in tons of water. The results could not have gone worse. Without power for her pumps, she couldn't manage the flooding in her bow; her fires never came fully under control; and her stuffy hangar filled with volatile fumes. *Shokaku*

was triply doomed. Improvements in subdivision and machinery arrangement might have allowed her crewmen some chance to overcome the flames and flooding. But instead, as they prepared to abandon ship, a *Taiho*-type explosion ripped her to pieces.

In the same battle, several bombs struck *Zuikaku*, and her captain ordered her abandoned. However, before the order was carried out, damage control managed to secure the ship. Four months later, despite her newly-installed rocket batteries, planes sank her with seven bombs and six torpedoes.

JUNYO, HIYO (24,140 tons, twelve 5-inch DP guns, AC 53, 25.5 knots, 1942): former liners. Italy, Germany, Britain, and the United States all had plans for liner conversions. Only Japan brought its plans to completion, but the *Junyo*s proved a dubious effort. Blessed with the look of a purpose-built CV, they lacked the more important qualities. Their machinery, while not as troublesome as sometimes alleged, rarely pushed the ships past 24 knots. This complicated their assignments with fast fleet units and interfered with air operations as more of the flight deck had to function as a runway, a problem aggravated by the total absence of flight deck catapults from the Imperial Japanese Navy. Crewmen had little room for arranging aircraft

Japan's Shokaku *combined ruggedness with a large air group.*

on deck, while the hangar space too was cramped. The problem increased as aircraft designs grew.

The flight deck had some metal, but the *Junyo*s had no actual armor on board. Subdivision was minimal. Each ship survived one torpedo attack, but *Hiyo* later blew up after a pair of aerial torpedo hits. Fuel vapors helped destroy her.

RYUHO (13,360 tons, eight 5-inch DP guns, AC 31, 26.5 knots, 1942): converted from the submarine tender *Taigei*. As in the *Junyo*s, the design speed remained beyond reach. Protection and subdivision were similarly poor, and *Ryuho* had a delicate hull besides. She served mostly in training.

Plans for five more submarine support ships came to nothing. The navy had some conventional submarine depot ships, including *Jingei* and *Chogei* (6,600 tons; four 5.5-inch, two 3-inch DP guns; AC 1, 18 knots, 1923–24), whose humble machinery and success as depot ships made them poor carrier candidates. Their biggest alteration was trading the DP guns for AS and light AA weapons.

TAIHO (29,300 tons, twelve 3.9-inch DP guns, AC 84, 33 knots, 1944): derived from *Shokaku* with a thickly-armored flight deck, an even thicker hangar deck, and a grand total of 8,800 tons of armor. The designers combined this mass of steel with a viable air group (a practical maximum of 75 planes), a formidable DP defense, and a sufficiency of speed—an excellent piece of work.

The armor scheme showed an *Illustrious* influence, and *Taiho* had an enclosed hull form as well. This gave her an attractive and British appearance, but it also contributed to her loss. A hit by a submarine torpedo caused minor initial damage, but jammed an elevator in the up position. The Japanese probably considered this

fortunate since it allowed continued flight operations, but it also eliminated a major source of ventilation to the enclosed hangar. The ship, forced by circumstance to run on unrefined fuel oil, began to fill with the crude's fumes as the torpedo had opened tiny cracks in the fuel spaces. The ventilation system then carried the fumes throughout the ship in an exact repeat of the *Lexington*'s experience. *Taiho* became a giant gas bomb. The subsequent blast flung the flight deck up at an angle and ripped through the ship's bottom. A well-protected ship thus fell victim to a most intricate misfortune.

The *Taiho*'s completion followed *Zuikaku*'s by more than two and a half years. During that time, the Americans completed 18 fast carriers. Japan should have been churning out *Shokaku*s, but its shipyards could barely churn out submarine-chasers. And the leadership had some difficulty assigning construction priorities, as with the *Yamato* class BB—peerless ships indeed, but the logistics, work force, and material that went into them dominated the industry. Even the use of sisal matting to screen their work areas from view created a widespread shortage.

A proposal for two refined *Taiho*s eventually expanded to include five ships (30,360 tons, 16 3.9-inch DP guns, AC 53, 33 knots), but no construction took place. The desire for larger air groups prompted a look into 50,000 ton possibilites.

SHINANO (62,000 tons, sixteen 5-inch DP guns, AC 47, 27 knots, 1944): the war's largest CV, converted from a *Yamato*-class hull. The carrier retained heavy armor and the *Yamato*'s underwater flaws.

The air group (42 planes ready plus five unassembled) seems insignificant for such a large ship, but the Japanese had decided to employ her as a support ship for front-line units, capable of ferrying 25 additional aircraft—a bizarre decision, considering the paucity of fleet carriers. The design included lots of AA rockets and a set of arrester wires at each end of the armored flight deck. Concrete encased the fuel stores. *Shinano* would have been a rugged ship, had she become operational; by that time, though, the lack of pilots would have left her jobless. She had more habitability than the *Yamato*s, but inside Japan's shrinking empire, with fuel supplies dwindling, she would have made no long cruises.

After an American reconnaissance plane flew over the *Shinano* work site, the leadership decided to hurry her completion and transfer her out of harm's way to the Inland Sea, where she could undergo final touches. At the time of her departure, she lacked four of her boilers and a number of pumps. Shipyard laborers, whose hurried workmanship was substandard, hadn't sealed the holes for pipes and cables. Most of her crew had no sea experience, and many civilian technicians remained on board. Manholes and hatches lay open for convenience. Poor *Shinano* could hardly have been more vulnerable.

Shortly after exiting Tokyo Bay, the ship took four torpedo hits from the American submarine *Archerfish*. All four torpedoes defeated the protection system, but would have caused only moderate damage to a complete vessel. The skipper in fact assumed the damage posed no serious danger; he maintained the ship's speed, and the resulting water pressure hastened the spread of flooding. A green crew, panicked civilians, and incomplete construction made the outcome inevitable.

UNRYU, AMAGI, KATSURAGI (17,150–17,460 tons, twelve 5-inch DP guns, AC 64–65, 32–34 knots, 1944): based on the *Hiryu* with little improvement. Three more ships were begun (*Kasagi*, *Aso*, *Ikoma*: 17,150 tons, AC 53–64, 32–34 knots), but the Japanese abandoned their construction in 1945. The original project included 11 further units with a new DP battery of 50cal guns (SW: 60 lbs; FC: 3–5 seconds;

24,820-yard range; 53,150-foot ceiling). Variations among the individuals resulted not from design development as much as difficulties in securing the needed materials.

The vulnerability of these ships shows clearly in *Unryu*'s loss. An American sub stopped her with a single torpedo; before she could withdraw, a second attack scored a hit that triggered a catastrophic blast, aggravated by a load of suicide boats and *Ohka* bombs crowded into her hangar.

Some analysts have theorized the Japanese accepted this lightly-built design expecting to use it in anti-commerce warfare rather than battle fleet operations, which seems improbable. Yet in dedicating giant *Shinano* to non-fleet duties, the leadership indeed showed a strange set of priorities at a time when it was replacing its lost fleet units with converted merchant ships.

IBUKI (12,500 tons, four 3-inch DP guns, AC 27, 29 knots): the conversion of an improved *Mogami*-class hull, never completed. It was a homely design, but if it retained the *Mogami*'s durability, it could have had a long career. The planned armament included AA rockets and depth charges—a testimony to desperation.

For other relevant vessels, see the *Ise* class BB, the cruiser *Mogami*, and the seaplane carriers *Chitose* and *Chiyoda*.

TAIYO, UNYO, CHUYO (17,830 tons, eight 4.7-inch DP guns, AC 27, 21 knots, 1941–42): flush-decked escort carriers converted from liners. The concept of qualitative superiority played a defining role in Japanese ship design; given the fact that American and British fleets would always possess greater numbers, Japan could achieve parity only by the superiority of individual ships. This instigated ultra-compact designs like the ill-fated *Tomozuru* and the illegally large units that followed. The *Taiyo*s qualify as a humble example of this policy, outclassing their Allied counterparts. Their advantages, however, went largely unused as the ships functioned mostly as ferries rather than anti-submarine units as Allied CVE did. There was certainly a need for aircraft ferries, but Japan lost the war because it lacked submarine-killers. In the end, submarines killed all three *Taiyo*s.

The weaponry varied in these ships, sometimes four to eight 4.7-inch DP, sometimes eight 5-inch DP.

KAIYO (13,600 tons, eight 5-inch DP guns, AC 24, 23.75 knots, 1943): another liner converted to flush-decked CVE. She acted as an aircraft ferry and training ship. Wishful thinkers armed her with depth charges and AA rockets. Submarine torpedoes sank a sister ship, *Brazil Maru*, preventing her conversion. *Kaiyo* became the only Japanese CVE not to fall prey to American SS.

SHINYO (17,500 tons, eight 5-inch DP guns, AC 33, 22 knots, 1943): escort carrier, ex-*Scharnhorst*, sister to the liner *Gneisenau* considered for conversion by the Germans.

Planners wanted to convert the liner *Kamakura Maru* (16,800 tons, eight 5-inch DP guns, AC 38, 20 knots), but a sub got to her first.

The Japanese selected two tankers, *Shimane Maru* and *Otakisan Maru*, for modification as merchant aircraft carriers (11,800 tons, two 4.7-inch DP guns, AC 12, 18.5 knots). A mine sank *Otakisan Maru* before her completion. *Shimane Maru* reached completion in 1944, but the navy had no air group available for her. Her loss to air attack prevented a reconversion. Two additional sister ships and a similar tanker never underwent their planned modifications. These vessels would have served as AS escorts, equipped with a dubious batch of depth charges.

The Japanese Army, ever impatient with the navy's failings, picked two tankers of their own to convert (15,864 nt, four 3.9-inch DP guns and some depth charges, AC 8, 15 knots). With no planes to carry, *Yamashiro Maru* sank in an air raid before reconverting; *Chigusa Maru* never completed her conversion. The army also toyed with the idea of converting some coal-burning freighters.

Three landing ships came equipped with flight decks: *Akitsu Maru* and *Nigitsu Maru* (11,800 tons; ten 3-inch, two 3-inch DP guns; AC 30, 20 knots, 1942–43) and *Kumano Maru* (8000 tons, eight 3-inch DP guns, AC 37, 19 knots, 1945). The number of aircraft depended on the number of landing craft the ships had to accommodate. The original layout allowed for no recovery of aircraft; it served for ferrying only. Circumstances prevented modification to permit landings.

NOTORO (14,050 tons; two 4.7-inch, two 3-inch DP guns; AC 10, 12 knots, 1920): completed as an oiler, converted to a seaplane carrier in 1924, used also as a transport, reconverted to an oiler in 1942.

KAMOI (17,000 tons; two 5.5-inch, two 3-inch DP guns; AC 22, 15 knots, 1922): an oiler converted to seaplane carrier in 1933, usually with 12 planes. She reconverted in 1943.

CHIYODA, CHITOSE (11,023 tons, four 5-inch DP guns, AC 24, 29 knots, 1938): smart-looking vessels with a unique history. Built as conventional seaplane carriers, they underwent modification in 1941 to transport 12 midget subs, with their air group cut in half. After Midway, they changed again, this time to aircraft carriers (11,190 tons, eight 5-inch DP guns, AC 30, 28.9 knots). This razed their attractive lines with a flush-deck layout. In none of these forms did the ships achieve anything of note. They had negligible protection but good range, longest for a Japanese CV (11,000 miles at 18 knots).

MIZUHO (10,929 tons, six 5-inch DP guns, AC 24, 22 knots, 1939): a *Chiyoda* development that combined the previous design's lack of protection with a lack of speed. This might have prevented her conversion to aircraft carrier if a submarine hadn't already sunk her in 1942. She could carry 12 midget subs with half her air complement.

NISSHIN (11,317 tons, six 5.5-inch guns, AC 20, 28 knots, 1942): seaplane tender capable of handling a variety of cargos: 20 aircraft, or 12 aircraft with either 12 midget subs or 700 mines.

Two enlarged *Nisshin*s (13,500 tons) never began construction.

AKITSUSHIMA (4,650 tons, four 5-inch DP guns, AC 1, 19 knots, 1942): rated as a seaplane tender or flying boat support ship.

Plans included four more *Akitsushima*s and seven other flying boat tenders (11,000 tons).

Nine merchant ships served temporarily as seaplane carriers with eight to 12 floatplanes (up to 24 when ferrying).

The tanker and seaplane carrier *Hayasui* (plus one incomplete sister: 18,300 tons, four 5-inch DP guns, 16.5 knots, 1944) could service six planes. The navy canceled seven similar *Tamano*-class ships (15,600 tons, four 5-inch DP, AC 14, 17 knots). Japan operated a few dozen aircraft salvage vessels developed from tugs (100–300 tons, with little or no armament and 13–14 knots). They used their one or two floatplanes in harbor duties rather than combat.

Battleships and Battlecruisers

Japan founded its considerable naval might on its carriers, not its battleships. A Japanese fleet built around battleships would have been easy meat for the Americans; the navy began the war with just ten dreadnoughts, and the only reinforcement came from the two *Yamato*s—impres-sive individuals, but no match for the ten modern battleships completed in the United States.

The old dreadnought *Settsu* (16,914 tons, light guns, 18 knots, 1912) acted as a wireless-controlled target ship. A few veterans of the Russo-Japanese War remained extant. Of three hulked ex-Russian ships (*Okinoshima*, 4,126 nt; *Mishima*, 4,165 nt; *Suwo*, 12,674 tons), only the third lasted into the 1940s. Two Japanese ships (*Fuji*, 9,179 tons; *Shikishima*, 11,275 tons) also remained as hulks. The disarmed *Asahi* (11,441 tons, 12 knots) served as a submarine depot ship. *Mikasa* (15,140 nt; four 12-inch, fourteen 6-inch guns, four 17.7-inch TT; 18 knots, 1902) was a war memorial.

KONGO, HIEI, KIRISHIMA, HARUNA (32,100 tons; eight 14-inch, fourteen 6-inch, eight 5-inch DP guns; AC 3, 30.3 knots, 1913–15): a British BC design. *Kongo* was Japan's last major warship built abroad, her three sisters coming from domestic yards.

Between the wars, the *Kongo*s underwent a carefully considered modernization, arguably the most successful refit carried out by any navy. New machinery raised them from their original 27.5 knots, making them the fastest of the old dreadnoughts and, with a range of 10,000 miles at 18 knots, the best suited to carrier escort duty. They became Japan's most active dreadnoughts.

Unlike the Italian *Cavour*s and *Duilio*s, the *Kongo*s managed to combine their speed increase with a significant gain in protection. The weight of armor more than doubled, raising their protection level to 32% of displacement and changing their rating from BC to BB. But while the deck armor grew to worthwhile thickness, belt armor remained at 8-inch—the thinnest belt on any dreadnought in World War II. *Hiei*, peppered by as many as 85 shells (5-inch to 8-inch), suffered widespread but manageable damage until an 8-inch round disabled her steering gear. Thus crippled, she fell afoul of air attack (four bombs and four torpedoes) and was scuttled.

Modernization gave the Fuso *a hideous pagoda superstructure. Note the 5-inch DP guns in their lofty perch aft.*

The Japanese subsequently modified other old units, with a layer of concrete encasing the steering compartment. *Kirishima* never received this upgrade, nor would it have helped; she caught nine 2,700-lb shells from *Washington* at close range, plus dozens of 55-lb shells—enough to threaten a much newer ship. *Haruna* eventually succumbed to air attack while lying in harbor without a full crew. As for *Kongo*, her age and inadequate damage control must have factored in her loss to two torpedoes—an incident that might pass as a fluke if not for *Fuso's* similar sinking.

The main battery remained that of a pre-WWI battlecruiser, with a broadside totaling only 11,880 lbs. Most of America's old BB fired broadsides around 18,000 lbs. Britain's modern *King George V*, whose weaponry earned repeated snickers, had a 15,900-lb broadside.

The refits provided 5-inch DP guns but could have gone further with the complete replacement of the 6-inch battery. The two ships that survived to 1944 cut back to eight 6-inch guns, with twelve 5-inch DP. *Haruna* later took on some depth charges, a fair measure of Japan's AS futility.

Hampered by age and thin armor, the modernized *Kongos* nevertheless represented a commendable achievement, as revealed by their war record.

In accordance with the Washington Treaty, *Hiei* spent some time as a "demilitarized" training ship, but was restored to full strength by 1940.

FUSO, YAMASHIRO (34,600 tons; twelve 14-inch, fourteen 6-inch, eight 5-inch DP guns; AC 3, 24.75 knots, 1915–17): the *Kongo* BC design bulked up to BB standards with 12-inch belt armor. Yet horizontal protection remained marginal with a pair of armored decks (1.4-inch and 4.5-inch maximum).

The *Kongos* emerged from their refits as fast, valuable fleet units; the *Fusos* came out as the ugliest warships on the face of the earth. They had only a slight speed advantage over their American contemporaries, whose degree of protection they never approached. *Yamashiro*, slowed to five knots by two torpedoes, crumpled under an avalanche of heavy shellfire. *Fuso* didn't last as long, blown apart after one or two torpedo hits.

These ships mounted six twin turrets, two of them amidships with restricted arcs of fire. The Japanese could have adopted four triples as in American ships, but they felt that twin mounts allowed more flexibility in engaging multiple targets. Any such advantage, slight at best, hardly merited the cost, as it required much more armor to achieve the same level of protection; six twin turrets far outweigh four triples of equal armor thickness, not to mention the weight of two extra barbettes and ammunition spaces and the lengthened citadel necessary to cover those spaces. This represents poor economy of design.

The *Fusos* had range comparable to *Kongo's*; a comparable speed would have made them useful. Modernization had added a few knots, but it's doubtful the Japanese ever considered the Italian model of removing a midships turret to provide more machinery space.

ISE, HYUGA (35,800 tons; twelve 14-inch, sixteen 5.5-inch, eight 5-inch DP guns; AC 3, 25.25 knots, 1917–18): similar to the *Fusos*, slightly improved and not as ugly.

The after pair of turrets in the *Ises* had less elevation and range (35,420 yards). With the midship turrets set in a superimposed position, designers were able to improve the internal layout. The reversion to a 5.5-inch secondary battery mirrors a British practice, as in *Hood* and *Birkenhead*. The level of protection paralleled *Fuso's*, but range seems to have lagged (7,870 miles at 16 knots).

Following the Midway debacle, desperation for new aerial platforms spurred the leadership to study possible conversions; designers estimated they could fit 30 planes onto a converted CA (*Myoko* through *Tone* classes), while the old BB might take 54. Work began on the *Ises*, but with 18 months needed for a complete CV conversion, the design changed. The air facilities, exiled aft, handled only 22 floatplanes, much less effective than wheeled aircraft. (One suggestion called for Judy bombers, capable of taking off but not landing.) Various studies deleted as many as eight main guns, but the *Ises* landed only four, along with all their secondaries. The DP battery grew to 16 guns supplemented by AA rocket gear. Range rose to 9,449 miles at 16 knots. By the time the ships returned to service (at 35,350 tons), the pilot shortage prevented their serving as carriers (and canceled similar conversions of *Fuso* and *Yamashiro*). As for the *Ises* themselves, obsolescent as battleships, they had even less value as demi-carriers.

MUTSU, NAGATO (39,100 tons; eight 16.1-inch, eighteen 5.5-inch, eight 5-inch DP guns; AC 3, 25 knots, 1920–21): an entirely Japanese design with excellent all-around qualities. The first battleships to carry 16-inch guns, they also reached 26.7 knots on trials, a fact the Japanese kept to themselves. The protection scheme showed a considerable advance over previous designs in an arrangement that verged on the all-or-nothing principle. Though lacking in endurance, the *Mutsus* represented a well-rounded design.

Interwar reconstruction had a less dramatic effect than in the *Kongos*. The new machinery failed to rejuvenate their speed (due in part to a displacement increase exceeding 6,000 tons) when an additional knot or two would have suited them to carrier escort duties and matched them to the modern *Yamatos*. Range did increase, but only to 8,650 miles at 16 knots. The most interesting changes took place in the protection scheme. The magazines gained a modern thickness of plating overhead and a truly startling mass of side armor, almost equal to a second belt. Yet the machinery armor went almost unchanged, inferior by *Colorado* standards.

The main turret plates thickened considerably, and the gun elevation provided long range. The guns themselves had a firing cycle of just 21.5 seconds at low elevation, but the sustained ammunition supply was nearer 1.5 rpm.

The two ships had little opportunity to

shine in combat; the *Kongo*s were the only Japanese BB mobile enough to experience active careers throughout the war. *Mutsu* met a gloriless end in 1943 when she exploded in harbor. Lucky *Nagato* avoided the perils of American bombs and her own ammunition until late in the war, and thus survived. She landed two 5.5-inch guns and added some light AA. The highlight of her career came off Samar where one of her shells may have struck an escort carrier.

KAGA, TOSA (38,500 tons; ten 16.1-inch, 20 5.5-inch, four 3-inch DP guns, eight 24-inch TT; 26.5 knots): BB, part of the Japanese "8–8 Fleet" program intended to provide 16 dreadnoughts. The Washington Treaty killed the plan, and the *Mutsu*s (the basis for the *Kaga* design) were the only survivors.

Had the *Kaga* plan gone through, the ships would have undergone extensive prewar changes as their fleet-mates did, landing their torpedoes and shipping a modern DP battery of 4.7-inch or 5-inch guns. *Kaga* instead converted to an aircraft carrier, while *Tosa*'s incomplete hull served in ordnance and armor experiments.

AMAGI, AKAGI, ATAGO, TAKAO (40,000 tons; ten 16.1-inch, sixteen 5.5-inch, six 4.7-inch DP guns, eight 24-inch TT; 30 knots): canceled BC. Since the treaty allowed America to build two *Lexington*-class CV, the Japanese got permission to convert two *Amagi*s, but only *Akagi* reached completion.

KII, OWARI, plus "11" and "12" (41,400 tons; ten 16.1-inch, sixteen 5.5-inch, six 4.7-inch DP guns, eight 24-inch TT; 29.75 knots): fast BB, never laid down.

"13" through "16" (47,500 nt; eight 18.1-inch, sixteen 5.5-inch, eight 4.7-inch DP guns, eight 24-inch TT; 30 knots): BC, the final "8–8" victims, canceled even before receiving names. Details of the main battery remain uncertain, but the guns differed from the model later used aboard *Yamato*.

YAMATO, MUSASHI (64,000 tons; nine 18.1-inch, twelve 6.1-inch, twelve 5-inch DP guns; AC 7, 27 knots, 1941–42): the most powerful battleships of all time, unexcelled in firepower or protection, designed to confront a numerically superior enemy. Even so, while Admiral Yamamoto admitted their battle-line supremacy, he also opposed their construction, likening them to samurai swords on a modern battle-

Japan's incomparable Yamato *inherited her 6.1-inch guns and 1-inch turret armor from the* Mogami *project.*

field—precise insight from the man who would later make *Yamato* his flagship. Yet he knew that Japan needed fewer behemoths and more *Shokakus*.

As the battleship holiday neared its end in the early 1930s, Japanese designers huddled to consider the treaty limits. Despite their tendency toward overloading, they came to agree with the Western teams that 30 knots and 16-inch guns could not coexist within 35,000 tons. Their labors produced more pain than success, yielding misshapen twins: one design (35,000 tons; ten 16-inch, sixteen 6-inch, eight 4.7-inch or 5-inch DP guns, two 24-inch TT; AC 2, 26.3 knots) featured a cramped superstructure not unlike the one that later stuck up atop *Yamato's* deck; the other (35,000 tons; nine 16-inch, twelve 6-inch, eight 4.7-inch or 5-inch DP guns; AC 2, 25.9 knots) mounted its secondary guns before and after its main battery, where they and their ammunition could be most vulnerable.

By the time construction became legal in 1936, the Japanese had adopted their cheating philosophy. The old designs lost favor (as they should have), and work began on a design that would outclass everything American. The designers hoped to take advantage of America's need to fit its ships through the Panama Canal. (Actually, the United States went ahead with the beamy *Montana* design while planning to widen the canal.)

As design work began, the 18.1-inch gun established itself as the weapon of choice, and hopes for a 30-knot ship consequently died. The number and placement of guns remained a question. Most early schemes stacked everything forward to save weight, as in Britain's *Nelson*. Further work abandoned the ugly handicap of an all-forward armament, and for the first time the Japanese accepted triple mounts, requiring fewer turrets. Unfortunately, a single-purpose secondary battery also lasted into the final draft, with 6.1-inch guns available after the *Mogami* class conversions. Construction began in 1937.

Descriptions of the *Yamato*s require repeated superlatives. However, they showed little economy of design, and a ship of equal strength might have displaced 4,000 tons less. The design flaws were distinct, yet not severe enough to dislodge the ships from their place in history. The biggest mistake was the decision to build them.

The virtues of the class need little explanation. Their broadside equaled almost 29,000 lbs. Protection constituted an adequate 35% of displacement, with armor concentrated in lavish thickness; the 25.6-inch turret faces rate as the toughest protection ever mounted afloat. However, Japanese armor was decades behind foreign standards, and other problems lay in the details of protection and weaponry.

All things gave way to considerations of the main battery. The turrets, each weighing as much as a destroyer, required tons of elaborate strengthening in the hull; these monoliths cramped the superstructure but also cleared large portions of deck space perfect for light AA guns—except that one 18.1-inch salvo would have made them molten. Even the guns that designers squeezed onto the upper works needed shields (added weight). Blast from the main battery threatened everything; the aircraft and boat facilities found themselves banished to the extreme stern.

The big guns elevated and depressed quickly enough to keep the maximum FC near 40 seconds, and despite their size, the weapons performed smoothly even at maximum elevation (usually 41°, adjustable to 45°). The turrets, however, trained as slowly as WWI types. Of other modern designs, only the *King George V*s showed such inertia, while America's new 16-inch mounts had twice the speed. *Yamato's* 3,219-lb ammunition, the heaviest ever fired by a battleship, matched proportions with the old 14-inch, 1,485-lb shell—in other words, it was rather light.

The 6.1-inch guns, suitable anti-ship weapons, had an entirely theoretical AA capacity (55° elevation). Workers removed the midship mounts from both ships in 1943; *Yamato* then took on 12 more 5-inch DP, but *Musashi* sank before receiving them. The enlarged DP battery made for a better ship; as trained fighter pilots became a rarity, surface units had to rely on gunfire for air defense. *Yamato* eventually mounted 150 25mm guns in her more blast-free areas. But the combination of inferior high-angle fire control, a marginal DP gun, and an overmatched light AA design left even these great ships unable to defend themselves. The series of attacks that wrecked *Musashi* dragged out over six hours; during that time, the Japanese task force of 29 ships (including five BB) shot down only 18 planes. By comparison, the *South Dakota* in one engagement claimed 26 Japanese planes—an optimistic figure, but indicative of the ship's capability. The Japanese tried to compensate by issuing time-fused AA rounds for the 6.1-inch and 18.1-inch guns. The sight of gunfire from *Yamato*'s main battery impressed the American airmen as they sank her.

The *Yamato* design had a short armored citadel due to its triple turrets and compact superstructure. This saved weight but left great lengths of the bow and stern unprotected. All battleships share these Achilles' heels, but in *Yamato*'s case, the heels represented 46.5% of her total length (about the same as in the two-turret *Richelieu*).

Designers strove to protect the vitals from plunging shells and bombs. The *Yamato*s never dueled an enemy dreadnought, but they did suffer some bomb hits. Bombs, for the most part, had to content themselves with inflicting casualties, putting smaller guns out of action, and damaging the upper works and the sensitive systems there. They had no hope of penetrating a main turret, but they did at times strike damaging blows. In *Musashi*'s last battle, a bomb penetrated deeply enough to start fires in two boiler rooms and an engine room (which its crew had to abandon). On the same day, two

bombs struck *Yamato*'s long bow, opening the hull to 3,300 tons of water—not an immediate threat to the ship, but certainly an undue amount of flooding. The air attacks that destroyed *Yamato* in 1945 included bomb hits that touched off a blaze in the after 6.1-inch mount. The fire defied all damage control for more than three hours and was extinguished only when the ship went down.

The primary agent in each ship's loss was the aerial torpedo. But *Musashi* withstood repeated hits, a total of 20 torpedoes along with 17 bombs and 18 near misses. This performance astonished the American pilots, especially since they mistook the *Yamato*s for a 45,000-ton design with 16-inch guns. *Musashi* endured because the torpedo hits came almost equally to port and starboard; flooding evenly, the ship settled with just a slight list. The airmen learned this lesson, and of the 13 torpedoes that sank *Yamato*, 11 struck the port side. Note also that 1,023 of *Musashi*'s 2,399 seamen survived, while *Yamato* went down with 3,063 of her 3,332-man crew.

The protection scheme had a weakness underwater. *Musashi* once suffered a submarine torpedo hit on her bow that let in 4,000 tons of water, more than four times as much flooding as a Japanese torpedo inflicted on *North Carolina*. These two hits weren't entirely comparable because of their locations, but they illustrate the consequences of a short citadel and poor subdivision. The *Yamato* designers addressed this flooding hazard with a novel safeguard, a vast reserve of buoyancy—the ship could survive the flooding of all areas outside the citadel. An admirable achievement, this feature nonetheless presupposed the citadel's ability to defeat all attacks. The metal had great thickness—perhaps too much, creating a rigid system that lacked the necessary structure. As a result, underwater detonations could displace long sections of the armor belt, swinging it inward as the line of joints failed. This collapse then sent bits of metal through the inboard bulkhead. In

December 1943, a submarine torpedo struck *Yamato* abreast the aft 6.1-inch mount; the armor joint split, opening a long wound along the hull, and 3,000 tons of water poured in. Only the ship's great size allowed her to absorb such damage without serious danger. The incident sparked a series of proposals to strengthen the side protection and increase subdivision. This was one case when Japanese ineconomy of design had long-term consequences; for a hull constructed with prodigal masses of metal, the added weight of improvements would have pushed the ship too deep into the water—just like the flooding they sought to prevent. Designers wrestled with this problem without success, and no major work took place. In *Yamato*'s loss, most of the torpedoes striking abreast the citadel penetrated the defenses to flood some outer compartments. Those striking the bow or stern sometimes reached the inner compartments. It does credit to the design that the ships maintained stability for so long after absorbing so much battle damage.

The *Yamato* hull, a masterpiece of streamlining, gave the equivalent of a 10% boost in the power plant. Two rudders served to guard against a loss of steering. But being mounted on the centerline instead of side-by-side, they provided less than the maximum maneuverability. Even so, the ships were quite handy for their size.

They also had marvelous habitability—by Japanese standards. The designers who packed too much into limited displacements also packed too many sailors into limited crew space. This feature became especially pronounced in the vast Pacific. Even *Yamato*'s relatively palatial accommodations declined as the complement rose from 2,200 men to 3,300.

The *Yamato*s might have made more of their combat abilities if not for their machinery. While both ships easily matched the design speed of 27 knots, their inefficient power plants wasted many tons of displacement and provided only limited range: 7,200 miles at 16 knots,

half of *North Carolina*'s endurance. While the Guadalcanal campaign was deciding the war's outcome, the *Yamato*s spectated. The high command balked at the thought of sending its most valuable units to their limits of endurance in the confined Solomons waters; this completely subverted the design's *raison d'être*. In the Battle of Guadalcanal, when two American battleships confronted one Japanese battleship, that ship should have been *Yamato*, designed to fight superior numbers. But no, it was *Kirishima*, designed to fight World War I.

Two intended sisterships, *Shinano* (completed as a carrier) and the unnamed "111," gained some refinements. Their plans showed a new DP battery (16–20 3.9-inch guns) and a thinner but smarter armor scheme. After Midway, though, Japan lost interest in its BB projects.

The *Yamato* and *Musashi* were the ultimate development of an obsolescent ideal. No other dreadnoughts matched their power, and by that yardstick, they measure as a success. But they showed little economy of design and they failed to fulfill their mission against numerically superior battle lines.

Designers began further BB plans, none less ambitious than *Yamato*. Warship "797" would have resembled "111" but without the 6.1-inch guns amidships, allowing up to twenty-four 3.9-inch DP. The Type A150 warships "798" and "799" were similar, equipped with a new main battery in three twin turrets (probably 20.1-inch guns with 4,409-lb shells).

"795," "796" (31,495 tons; nine 12.2-inch, sixteen 3.9-inch DP guns; eight 24-inch TT; AC 3, 33 knots): the Type B65, planned in anticipation of large American cruisers (the *Alaska*s), which had in fact been intended to counter vessels like the Type B65. Unlike *Alaska*, the Japanese ships included an underwater protection system, qualifying them as genuine dreadnoughts. (The Japanese rated them as "super heavy cruisers.") Even an underwater scheme with *Yamato*-type flaws would have provided superiority over the American design. But like the *Yamato*s, the B65's lacked machinery dispersal.

As design work never progressed beyond the preliminary stages, many details remain in doubt. Sketchy reports credit the main guns with a firing cycle of 20 seconds and a range of 36,000 yards at 45° elevation. A claim of absurdly heavy shells (1,265 lbs, comparable to an 18.1-inch shell of 4,130 lbs) cannot be right. Later proposals to augment the margin of superiority over the *Alaska*s (six 14-inch guns, no torpedo tubes, thicker armor) would likely have proved impractical.

Cruisers

Unlike Japan's CV and BB construction, the cruiser program produced designs that matched the navy's needs. The heavy cruisers combined durability with great ship-killing potential. The light cruisers, though they looked like refugees from World War I, proved no embarrassment in World War II, managing to pull their weight as destroyer leaders. Later designs showed a flair for innovation, but the most unusual ships had the least success: *Tone, Katori, Oyodo*.

The Long Lance handed several victories to the Japanese before American air power and technology took control. The cruiser fleet succumbed ultimately to the scourge-in-general of the Imperial Japanese Navy: limited numbers. Japan didn't complete a single heavy cruiser during World War II.

Four venerable veterans retired during the 1930s. The ex-*Chitose* (4,760 nt, disarmed, 22.9 knots, 1899), the ex-*Tone* (3,760 tons; two 6-inch, ten 4.7-inch, two 3-inch guns, three 17.7-inch TT; 23 knots, 1910), and the Russian prize ex-*Aso* (7,726 nt, disarmed, 21 knots, 1903) became hulks *Haikan 1, 2,* and *4* until expended as targets by 1933; *Tsushima* (3,120 tons, disarmed, 20 knots, 1904), renamed *Haikan 10* in 1930, survived at least to 1944.

Japan retained its armored cruisers in active service longer than any other major power, designating them for coast defense. These ships all came from European yards, but the rise of domestic shipbuilding kept subsequent cruiser programs at home.

ASAMA, TOKIWA (9,240 tons; four 8-inch, eight 6-inch, two 3-inch, one 3-inch DP gun; 16 knots, 1899): armored cruisers. After a grounding incident in 1935, *Asama* became an immobile training ship, eventually landing all weapons except some light AA. *Tokiwa* became a minelayer (300 mines) with two main guns removed; by 1940, her gun armament had shrunk to four 6-inch guns and one 3-inch DP. Her mine load increased to 500, with some depth charges thrown in as well, and her speed fell to 12 knots.

YAKUMO (9,010 tons; four 8-inch, eight 6-inch, four 3-inch, one 3-inch DP gun; 16 knots, 1900): armored cruiser, then coast defense vessel, then training ship. By 1945, she mounted just four 6-inch guns with DP batteries of one 3-inch and four 5-inch guns and a speed of nine knots.

ADZUMA (8,640 tons; four 8-inch, eight 6-inch, four 3-inch, one 3-inch DP gun, two 17.7-inch TT; 16 knots, 1900): armored cruiser, became a training ship in 1914, hulked in 1941.

IDZUMO, IWATE (9,180 tons; four 8-inch, eight 6-inch, four 3-inch, one 3-inch DP gun; 16 knots, 1900–1): armored cruisers. *Iwate* became a training ship in 1923, but *Idzumo* continued to serve as a coast defense vessel in China until 1943. Three of *Iwate*'s five 3-inch guns were DP. The armament in both ships shrank to four 6-inch guns and four 5-inch DP along with the 3-inch DP battery. Speed fell to 12 knots.

KASUGA, NISSHIN (7,080 tons; one 10-inch, two 8-inch, four 6-inch, four 3-inch, one 3-inch

DP gun, four 17.7-inch TT; 20 knots, 1904): armored cruisers still serving as trainers. *Nisshin* (mounting two additional 8-inch guns instead of the 10-incher) went down as a target in 1936. *Kasuga* became a hulk in 1942.

The Japanese raised the scuttled Dutch coast defense ship *Soerabaia*, but used her only as a blockship.

CHIKUMA, HIRATO, YAHAGI (4,400 tons; eight 6-inch, two 3-inch DP guns, four 21-inch TT; 26 knots, 1912): protected cruisers (10% armor), a modernization of the old *Tone*. Japan's early cruisers derived directly from British designs, an influence that carried through into the 5,500-ton CL types. The navy discarded *Chikuma* in 1931 and disarmed the others as hulks *Haikan 11* and *12* before Pearl Harbor.

TENRYU, TATSUTA (3,230 tons; four 5.5-inch, one 3-inch DP gun, six 21-inch TT; 33 knots, 1919): Japan's first light cruisers, conceived as flotilla leaders but immediately overtaken by new, faster DD. They did give wartime service as leaders, but mostly in convoy escort. Britain's AA conversion of "C"-class cruisers inspired a similar plan for the *Tenryu*s (a new gun armament of eight 5/40 DP or the new 3/60, no TT, and an AS outfit); this low-priority project got lost in the prewar construction frenzy, and the ships experienced few changes. They landed their 3-inch guns by early 1941, and probably their minelaying gear (48 mines) as well.

Armor protection, intended only to defeat the 4-inch guns of American destroyers, amounted to 5.4% of the ships' displacement. Their limited endurance (6,000 miles at 10 knots) and their size did not work well in the Pacific.

Since the "3,500-ton" class (the *Tenryu*s, designed at 3,495 normal tons) lacked the speed to match the newest destroyers, studies began for a series of three "5,500-ton" types, ships that could act as flotilla leaders or operate

independently. The *Kuma*, *Nagara*, and *Sendai* classes closely resembled each other, and they went through similar modifications. The *Tomozuru* and Fourth Fleet incidents led to an increase in stability and hull strength. (Hull reinforcement became habitual for the 5,500-tonners.) All units gained several hundred tons before the outbreak of war, and most showed a decline in service speed to 32–33 knots, hampering their coordination with DD flotillas. However, they always demonstrated laudable sea-keeping.

The enlargement of the *Tenryu* design permitted more weaponry, but two guns found themselves in wing positions, and all of them mimicked *Tenryu*'s single mounts on a single deck level with open shields. This stamped the ships with a distinct obsolescence. The navy removed their token DP battery—two 3-inch guns—before Pearl Harbor. The original layout called for a large mine load (as many as 150 mines), later reduced to 48 by the addition of aircraft facilities. Some units retained their mine rails into 1940.

KUMA, KISO, TAMA, OI, KITAKAMI (5,100 tons, seven 5.5-inch guns, eight 21-inch TT, AC 1, 36 knots, 1920–21): the first 5,500-ton class, actually 5,580 normal tons. Before they began to gain weight, they could exceed their designed range of 5,000 miles at 14 knots.

Because of their age and their 21-inch torpedoes, the fleet used the *Kuma*s less aggressively than their later semi-sisters. The idea of converting them to secondary duties became attractive amid the interwar treaty situation. Designers prepared several layouts, including an AA version armed with 3.9/65 guns; the provision of 300 mines for *Kuma* and *Tama* as fast minelayers (no TT, 25 knots); and the relegation of *Kuma*, *Tama*, and *Kitakami* to training duty with four main guns, two 5-inch DP, no TT, and 25 knots. The navy opted for something more warlike, selecting *Kiso*, *Kitakami*, and *Oi* for conversion to torpedo cruisers armed with eight

5-inch DP guns and forty-four 24-inch torpedo tubes (Long Lances). The plan went ahead in 1941, but including *Oi* and *Kitakami* only, their redesign tempered by a shortage of materiel (5,860 tons, four 5.5-inch guns, forty 24-inch TT, 31.7 knots). This established the two ships as front-line battle units. But the start of American operations in the Solomons overturned the scenario for which the pair were intended, prompting the leadership to order a new conversion into fast transports—an interesting and debatable decision. The ships lost 16 of their torpedoes while embarking two landing craft and a load of depth charges. (Almost all 5,500-tonners carried depth charges at some point during the war.) The navy canceled a more thorough change (four 5-inch DP guns, sixteen 24-inch TT, 29 knots), and a single torpedo sank *Oi* before further work took place. *Kitakami* survived a pair of torpedoes; her repairs turned into a conversion to kaiten carrier (5,640 tons, four 5-inch DP, eight kaiten, 23.8 knots).

The other *Kuma*s had more conventional alterations. Like *Oi* and *Kitakami*, they landed their aircraft, but they kept their original TT. *Tama* and *Kiso* traded two guns for a pair of 5-inch DP; *Kiso* also mounted, temporarily, an army-type 3-inch AA gun. *Kuma* landed one main gun, and all units sprouted new 25mm and machine-gun mounts.

NAGARA, ABUKUMA, KINU, ISUZU, YURA, NATORI (5,170 tons, seven 5.5-inch guns, eight 24-inch TT, AC 1, 36 knots, 1922–25): completed at 5,570 normal tons, nearly identical to the *Kuma* except for their torpedoes. The 24-inch tubes could not fire Long Lances, but *Abukuma* received Long Lance tubes in 1941, as did at least two others (*Nagara* and *Isuzu*) by 1944. Typical wartime changes included removal of their aircraft and the replacement of two main guns by a pair of 5-inch DP. By 1944, *Nagara* displaced 6,050 standard tons with a top speed of 33.4 knots. *Isuzu* became an AA cruiser with a new main battery of six 5-inch DP guns; she also served as a flagship for AS craft until a submarine sank her.

Natori illustrated the need for hull strengthening in the 5,500-tonners when a pair of dud torpedoes knocked off a 65-foot section of her stern.

SENDAI, NAKA, JINTSU, plus one other canceled (5,195 tons, seven 5.5-inch guns, eight 24-inch TT, AC 1, 35.25 knots, 1924–25): designed at 5,595 normal tons, completed at 5,900. They differed from the previous two classes in their machinery arrangement (giving four funnels instead of three) and the higher elevation of their main guns. Ordered before *Yubari*, they didn't reach completion until after the smaller vessel.

The Naka. *Japan's 5,500-tonners sufficed as flotilla leaders but hardly compared with modern cruisers.*

All three units sank before experiencing much modification, though at least two embarked depth charges and two received Long Lance tubes. They kept their planes and at least six main guns; *Naka* mounted two 5-inch DP.

The 5,500-ton designs followed the same protection guidelines as *Tenryu*, with a 4–5% armor scheme intended to defeat American 4-inch shells. Some units survived single torpedoes; some did not. *Kinu* succumbed to one bomb hit and several near misses. One bomb and one torpedo sufficed to snap *Naka* in two. The 5,500-tonners did not go gentle into those cold depths, but they couldn't deny their vintage and vulnerability.

The Japanese planned four more 5,500-tonners, then reordered them as part of a CA program.

YUBARI (2,890 tons, six 5.5-inch guns, four 24-inch TT, 35.5 knots, 1923): an experimental attempt to squeeze the 5,500-ton type down to about half size. Designed before the Washington Treaty, *Yubari* foreshadowed Japan's policy of overloading. Planners hoped to match 5,500-ton type range (5,000 miles at 14 knots) and speed, but unexplained miscalculations left her vastly overweight—at 3,387 tons, she made only 34.8 knots with her range dropping to 3,300 miles. Otherwise the design proved a significant success, pioneering design techniques that played an important part in subsequent cruiser classes.

Despite having one less gun than her predecessors, *Yubari* actually had a superior main battery; disposed fore and aft on the centerline with two superimposed twin mounts, the guns had wide arcs of fire and a simpler ammunition supply for a higher practical rate of fire. Such traits might qualify *Yubari* as the world's first modern cruiser, if only she had a more cruiser-like size. In fact she was little more than a destroyer, a fair match to some German and French DD, which points out how under-gunned the 5,500-tonners were. *Yubari* did have

an undestroyerlike amount of armor—349 tons, much more than in the 5,500-tonners, yet still a deterrent only to 4-inch shells. This armor didn't prevent her sinking in destroyerly fashion after a single torpedo hit.

The two single guns retained open-backed shields as in previous cruisers, but the twin mounts had enclosed gunhouses. Their thin plating kept out the weather, but had no value against shells. Even when the Japanese resolved to produce rugged CA designs, they never supplied more than an inch of turret protection, sufficient against splinters only. Thus, mighty *Myoko* could have her guns knocked out by an American destroyer from almost any possible range.

A curiosity of *Yubari*'s design was the inclined belt; tilted inward at the top rather than outward, it stood more perpendicular to the path of incoming shells, making it easier to penetrate. No subsequent design copied this mis-inclined belt. On the contrary, all Japanese heavy cruisers used an outward tilt to maximize their modest belts.

The original *Yubari* layout included a 3-inch DP and 48 mines, discarded by 1934. In wartime, she landed her two 5.5-inch singles and gained a 4.7-inch DP, more light AA, and depth charges. Now 3,510 tons, she reached 32 knots. She may have retained her Type 8 torpedoes throughout her career.

FURUTAKA, KAKO (9,150 tons; six 8-inch, four 4.7-inch DP guns, eight 24-inch TT; AC 2, 33 knots, 1926): the world's first "treaty" cruisers. In fact, the project began before the treaty, employing many protection and weight-saving measures developed in *Yubari*. Like *Yubari*, the ships turned out overweight, 1,000 tons above the design figure of 7,100 tons. The original order included four ships (see *Aoba* class, below).

The *Furutaka*s experienced widespread changes during the 1930s as Japan sought to standardize its CA force. The original main battery (six 7.9-inch guns in obsolete single gun-houses) gave way to twin 8-inch turrets with 55° elevation; 4.7-inch DP guns replaced the original 3-inch battery. The navy later upgraded most heavy cruisers to eight 5-inch DP in twin mounts, but the *Furutaka*s couldn't handle such a large battery.

The Long Lance started to replace earlier CA torpedoes by 1940, though some units retained conventional 24-inchers for a time. The decision to equip the CA force with torpedoes came after some argument among planners. The Long Lances could inflict great harm, but not only on the enemy; the detonation of their warheads helped sink or heavily damage Japanese heavy cruisers on at least six occasions during the war.

Like many of their fleet-mates, the *Furutaka*s had their strength and stability augmented after the *Tomozuru* and Fourth Fleet incidents. By the time of Pearl Harbor, they topped 9,000 tons, though the navy continued to list them at 7,100 tons, a figure that never was correct.

AOBA, KINUGASA (9,000 tons; six 8-inch, four 4.7-inch DP guns, eight 24-inch TT; AC 2, 33.4 knots, 1927): *Furutaka* class ships altered while building to correct shortcomings seen in the first two units. They entered service with 4.7-inch and 8-inch guns (the latter in 40° mounts) plus other refinements, but had less extensive alterations during the 1930s. By the outbreak of war, the two classes formed a more or less homogeneous group.

Though designed pre-treaty, the four *Furutaka* type ships compare well with many treaty cruisers. Protected only against 5.9-inch shells, they still had more armor (a protection scheme near 13%) than the Mediterranean tin-clads. They also had more range (about 8,000 miles at 14 knots), though falling short of the great distances achieved by some British and American types. In displacement, they correspond to the *Pensacola*s and *Northampton*s,

which boasted much more firepower but less balance. In armament, they compare with the *York* and *Exeter*, but there the comparison ends; the British ships were brittle combatants. The *Furutaka*s, despite their age, showed some toughness under fire. Off Cape Esperance, cruiser gunfire struck *Furutaka* and ignited her torpedoes, making her an easy target for additional shells; she sank two and a half hours after the first hit. In the same battle, *Aoba* suffered twenty-four 6-inch and 8-inch hits. She survived but never fully recovered. Her aft turret required such lengthy repair that she had to operate without it for several months. As with the old light cruisers, the main vulnerability lay beneath the waterline. Three small torpedoes sank *Kako* in five minutes. *Aoba*, struck by one bomb and near-missed by others, survived only by beaching. Her engines defied repair, and she thereafter managed only 28 knots.

The navy began issuing AS gear to its heavy cruisers in 1942. *Aoba* embarked depth charges, but her sisters probably sank before doing so.

Japan had considered building two more *Furutaka* type ships, but the Washington Treaty enthroned a 10,000-ton specification. Subsequent designs inherited *Furutaka*'s graceful hull structure with its undulating sheer line that helped reduce tonnage, but the inexplicable overweight recurred as well. Crew space and ventilation received low priority; improvements in the 1930s failed to bring these up to Western standards. Endurance remained adequate, but DP batteries grew into something more useful, and protection became a hallmark. The 10,000-ton limit and the navy's willingness to exceed it gave Japan some of the war's best heavy cruisers.

MYOKO, HAGURO, NACHI, ASHIGARA (13,380 tons; ten 8-inch, eight 5-inch DP guns, sixteen 24-inch TT; AC 3, 33.75 knots, 1928–29): begun with specifications for 10,000 tons, four 7.9-inch twin mounts (three forward), and four 4.7-inch DP guns. The main battery soon gained an extra turret aft to assure superiority over foreign designs. The only Allied CA to carry 10 guns, the 9,100-ton *Pensacola*s, had no hope of equaling the all-around capabilities of a ship with 45% more tonnage.

Arrogance speaks for itself. Japanese designers felt they had the power to enlarge their ship's main battery by 25% without adding to its tonnage. The same weight-saving techniques that failed to keep *Yubari* and *Furutaka* at their design displacements also left the *Myoko*s with several hundred surplus tons. This initial overweight resulted from miscalculation rather than intended illegality. But the high command, in seeking to regain the loss in performance, chose a series of additions, deliberately pushing the ships further beyond the 10,000-ton limit; and while this work was taking place, the navy decided to tack on a few extras and a few more tons.

The *Myoko*s entered service with six 4.7-inch DP. They received their 5-inch and 8-inch guns before Pearl Harbor, along with their Long Lance torpedoes. Japan's 8-inch gun, while potent, was not the fleet's most successful weapon, performing poorly against heavy armor. Intended to fire 4–5 rpm, in service it never bettered 2–3 rpm.

Japan's refusal to develop an 8-inch triple mount detracted from the economy of design. Designers also made no attempt to utilize machinery dispersal. The machinery performed well enough, but *Myoko*'s obesity dropped her endurance to about 7,500 miles at 14 knots— the only lingering consequence of her overweight; prewar refits had ironed out the other wrinkles.

The *Myoko*s had a powerful appearance and great combat potential. They carried about 2,100 tons of protection, twice as much as the rival *Pensacola*s. The original layout included bulges to counter the underwater vulnerability of previous CA; refits then added another set of overlapping bulges, partly for stability, but they also formed an extra layer of protection. Yet no amount of metal could have saved *Nachi* from

the air attack that hit her with at least nine torpedoes, 20 bombs, and 16 rockets; she broke into three pieces and sank.

During the war, the *Myoko*s landed half their torpedoes to make room for light AA.

TAKAO, ATAGO, MAYA, CHOKAI (11,350 tons; ten 8-inch, four 4.7-inch DP guns, eight 24-inch TT; AC 3, 35.5 knots, 1932): similar to *Myoko*, but the designers thought they could fit extra armor and improved gun mounts onto a lower displacement, 9,850 tons. (The overweight problem of previous designs had not yet become apparent, and the next class, the *Mogami*s, would attempt even more on just 8,500 tons.)

In imitation of Britain's "Counties," the main battery elevated to 70°. Gunnery at extreme elevation proved impractical, so *Maya*'s guns had only 55° (the subsequent CA standard).

Like *Myoko*, the *Takao*s needed alterations shortly after completion. In 1938–39, the navy gave *Takao* and *Atago* a thorough reconstruction along the same lines as *Myoko*'s, providing the double-layer bulges and a doubling of their torpedo tubes to 16; but they had to wait until early 1942 for their DP battery of eight 5-inch guns. At that time, they displaced 13,400 tons (18% protection) with a speed of 34.25 knots. The onset of war prevented similar work for *Maya* and *Chokai*, and they experienced only minor changes. In fact, they probably served for some time without Long Lances. In 1944, *Maya* underwent alteration as an AA cruiser. She landed one forward turret and embarked a new DP battery of twelve 5-inch guns. She also gained additional bulges and eight more torpedo tubes. Her speed fell to 34.25 knots at 12,000 tons. The navy planned to modify *Chokai* as well, but never had the opportunity.

The Battle of Leyte Gulf brought an end to the *Takao* class. *Maya* and *Atago* each took four hits from submarine torpedoes and went down immediately. Avenger pilots, desperately de-

The Takao displays her imposing profile. Otherwise powerful, she relied on 1-inch turret armor.

fending their escort carriers, bombed *Chokai* into a ruin. *Takao* survived two sub torpedoes, one in her boilers and the other well aft, but never again became operational.

No cruiser had a more imposing or handsome visage than the *Takao*s. Japan shelved plans for four improved ships (better protection and 5-inch DP guns) after the London Conference.

MOGAMI, MIKUMA, SUZUYA, KUMANO (12,400 tons; ten 8-inch, eight 5-inch DP guns, twelve 24-inch TT; AC 3, 34.9 knots, 1935–37): a revolutionary design. The London Treaty allowed Japan no further tonnage for CA construction. However, the Japanese saw in their CL allotment an opportunity to build CA-sized ships armed (temporarily) with CL-type guns. Though nominally 8,500 tons, but the project actually began at 9,500 tons and instantly started to grow.

The *Mogami*s were commissioned with five triple turrets of 6.1-inch guns (replaceable, in the event of war, by the usual 8-inch twins). Initial studies for the 6.1-inch mount showed high elevation as in the *Takao*s, later reduced by practicality to 55°. Ironically, the temporary 6.1-inch battery introduced triple mounts to the Japanese navy, and the only subsequent ships

with triple mounts—the *Oyodo* and *Yamato* classes—featured guns removed from *Mogami*s.

Weight-saving mania gave the design a frighteningly frail hull; the simple action of full-speed trials distorted the structure badly enough to put the main turrets out of action. Furthermore, unforeseen overweight threatened to flip the ships over. As corrected, they displaced 11,200 tons.

Having begun the revolution in "light" cruiser design, the *Mogami*s took on their 8-inch twin mounts during 1939 refits. Their guns, bulges, and 12,400 tons marked their kinship with Japan's other heavy cruisers.

Mogami herself exemplified the family's ruggedness. During the Battle of Midway, she lost her bows in a collision with *Mikuma*. The pair then fell afoul of American dive-bombers. At first, *Mogami* incurred only slight damage from near misses. Then she took two hits; and another, killing everyone in no. 5 turret; then two more hits; and finally, a bomb that killed everyone in one engine room. Much mangled, she managed to crawl home.

Mikuma did not. With only slight damage from the collision, she fared well in the subsequent air attacks until a dive-bomber crashed into her, igniting a fire that wiped out the crew of the starboard engine room. This slowed her, and she sustained at least five bomb hits before a fire detonated her torpedoes.

Eleven months later, *Mogami* returned to duty, but in the guise of a cruiser-carrier hybrid similar to the converted *Ises*, or perhaps more like the *Tone* class; she was intended as a scout rather than a supplement to the fleet carriers. Retaining six main guns and the rest of her armament, she embarked up to 11 floatplanes. Her displacement dropped to 12,206 tons, allowing 35 knots. Despite a 1943 collision with an oiler, *Mogami* survived up to the Battle of Leyte Gulf, where five American 8-inch shells set her afire. With her steering damaged, she steamed into yet another collision, this time with *Nachi*. As many as 20 more cruiser shells and two bomb hits forced her crew to scuttle.

Suzuya and *Kumano* experienced few wartime changes, though radical suggestions for AA conversions included the replacement of some or all 8-inch guns by 5-inch DP. Misfortune sank *Suzuya;* a near-miss bomb ignited her torpedoes.

TONE, CHIKUMA (11,231 tons; eight 8-inch, eight 5-inch DP guns, twelve 24-inch TT; AC 8, 35 knots, 1938–39): a design that sprang from the treaty-induced effort to squeeze a *Mogami* into 8,450 tons. Apart from the impossibility of such a notion, the leadership also had new ideas for a dedicated scout design. Japan's impending renunciation of the treaties removed all tonnage limits, allowing the *Tone*s to gestate healthily on the drawing board rather than suffer a series of post-completion corrections. And since the designers had finally mastered their weight calculations, the ships came out just a bit above their design displacement (about 11,450 tons). They entered service with 8-inch guns and never required additional bulges; in fact, they hardly changed at all during their careers, not even gaining a depth charge battery as most Japanese heavy cruisers did.

The primary feature of the *Tone* design was its all-forward main battery, an unsightly queue of twin mounts. The planners did this to free the stern for scout plane operations and to reduce shell dispersion problems experienced by *Tone*'s weak-hulled predecessors. (The Japanese proved zealous and successful in their quest for tight salvoes.) Such an arrangement had its advantages, and its drawbacks.

The absence of barbettes in the hull's aft portion allowed the pleasant consequence of enlarged crew spaces, creating the most comfortable of Japan's heavy cruisers. Meanwhile, the forward concentration of main guns dictated a similar concentration of protection, allowing a slight increase in deck thickness while keeping the armor weight similar to *Mogami*'s. Near the Solomons, *Chikuma* survived three bomb hits and a damaging near miss; her wounded captain's timely orders prevented the explosion of her torpedoes. But off Leyte, an aerial torpedo stopped her dead in the water, and she had to be scuttled.

The crowding of turrets limited their arcs of fire, and while the crews liked their roomy *Tone*s, the navy considered them unsuccessful. The *Tone*s suffered more than any other class from Japan's bias against triple mounts. Three triples would have provided more firepower, better arcs of fire, and a savings in weight. Even a reduction to two triples would have provided improvement. Six guns might seem a small armament for a ship weighing 11,000 tons, but several British "Counties" found it sufficient. The CL *Oyodo* managed with a similar arrangement; in fact, a six-gun battery represented no handicap to a vessel intended as a scout plane carrier (consider *Mogami*), while the savings in weight and space might have accommodated four more 5-inch guns and some light AA.

The *Tone*s never carried eight planes: their service maximum was six, with a normal listing of five, though three or two became standard, or only one by the war's end. As semi-hybrid floatplane carriers, they performed adequately for the most part, and they had the most endurance among Japan's heavy cruisers (12,000 miles at

14 knots). On the other hand, it was *Tone's* malfunction at Midway that set the stage for catastrophe.

KATORI, KASHIMA, KASHII, plus one not completed (5,890 tons; four 5.5-inch, two 5-inch DP guns, four 21-inch TT; AC 1, 18 knots, 1940–41): intended as warships, but classified separately from true cruisers. The navy specified extensive accommodations and communications equipment for peacetime training work and wartime flagship duties. The design included a sampling of weapons and other gear, but its lack of speed set distinct limits on its combat value. The stout hull, atypically strong for Japanese ships, provided the only hint of durability. *Katori* survived an aerial torpedo only to crumple beneath cruiser gunfire.

The ships saw wartime service in a number of roles. By 1944, the high command ordered the surviving units to undergo modification as AS escort flagships with four additional 5-inch DP guns, a heavy load of depth charges, and no torpedoes.

The *Katori*s represent a prodigal diversion of resources on the eve of war, though in fact they cost only a quarter as much as an *Agano*. A 1942 study for four similar vessels armed with eight 3.9-inch DP led to nothing.

AGANO, NOSHIRO, SAKAWA, YAHAGI (6,652 tons; six 6-inch, four 3-inch DP guns, eight 24-inch TT; AC 2, 35 knots, 1942–44): successors to the old CL as destroyer leaders. Initial specifications called for six 6.1-inch guns (*Mogami* turrets?) and eight 3-inch DP squeezed into 5,000 tons, but the design staff headed off any overload by reducing the weaponry and increasing the tonnage. Unfortunately, the final design failed to ship adequate armor; protection totaled not quite 10% of displacement, insufficient to cope with shells greater than 5-inch. Designers shielded the magazines as best they could, but *Agano* failed to match the durability of like-sized American cruisers.

The 6-inch twin mounts had enclosed gunhouses with 55° elevation, a futile attempt to allow AA fire. Depth charges formed part of the standard weaponry. No major changes took place, despite a proposed switch to eight 3.9-inch DP.

The navy planned as many as seven improved *Agano*s (8,520 tons; eight 6-inch, eight 3-inch DP guns, eight 24-inch TT; AC 2, 37.5 knots).

IOSHIMA, YASOSHIMA (2,200 tons; six 5.5-inch guns, 3–6 3-inch DP guns; 22.25 knots, 1932–36): the captured *Ning Hai* and *Ping Hai* (see Chinese section). For four years after their 1938 salvage, they sat inactive while the Japanese leadership wondered what to do with "cruisers" that lacked the speed, armor, and sea-keeping of fleet units. They returned to duty in 1944 as escorts, equipped also to serve as transports and seaplane tenders. They received their new names and a complete rearmament—two single 4.7-inch DP guns backed by light AA and depth charges—with the removal of all previous guns and aircraft. The navy rated both ships at 22 knots, despite their differing machinery.

OYODO, plus one sister ship never begun (8,164 tons; six 6.1-inch, eight 3.9-inch DP guns; AC 2, 35 knots, 1943): unique but irrelevant. The hull form and other features derived from *Agano*, but *Oyodo's* nearest ancestor was probably the *Jingei*-class submarine depot ships. Between the wars, Japan developed an unusual doctrine of submarine deployment involving fast surface vessels acting as flagships. The doctrine began to crumble before Pearl Harbor with the failure of support ships like *Taigei* and *Takasaki*, but the leadership continued its studies for designs ranging from a 5,000-ton almost-cruiser to a 16,000-ton hybrid (six 6.1-inch, eight 3.9-inch DP guns; AC 49). The final design moderated between these extremes, a cruiser with an all-forward main battery and seaplane facilities aft. These facilities included an oversized catapult for use with a new aircraft, a high-speed reconnaissance type. *Oyodo* would have carried six such scouts, but since their design never made it into operations, she instead mounted a conventional catapult and two mundane seaplanes. Like the *Aganos*, *Oyodo* carried depth charges and an inadequate protection scheme. She did have excellent endurance, totaling 10,600 miles at 18 knots.

IBUKI, plus one unnamed (12,220 tons; ten 8-inch, eight 5-inch DP guns, sixteen 24-inch TT; AC 3, 35 knots): begun as a *Tone* follow-up until *Tone* revealed her shortcomings. The design then evolved from *Suzuya* with more TT. One proposal involved replacing the aircraft with an enlarged torpedo battery (five quintuple mounts). But *Ibuki* instead began a CV conversion that never reached completion.

Destroyers

At the time of the Washington Conference, Japan's destroyer fleet was even more archaic than America's flush-deckers; but by the start of the next meeting in London, the Japanese destroyer had become the pace-setter. This about-face grew out of the navy's resolve for qualitative superiority.

The modern destroyers were indeed powerful vessels with illegally high tonnage, enclosed gun mounts, and of course, the 24-inch torpedo. To capitalize on this key weapon, many layouts featured a quick reloading system that, in effect, doubled the torpedo armament. But the Long Lance couldn't shoot down Allied aircraft or hunt a lurking submarine; few destroyers shipped adequate DP guns, and none proved adept at AS warfare. They did, however, withstand brutal punishment despite their lack of machinery dispersal. In any case, their losses utterly outpaced Japanese industry. The Americans built 175 wartime *Fletcher*-class

ships, a number equal to all Japanese DD production from 1928 to 1945.

The following ships served during prewar operations against China but retired before Pearl Harbor:

UMIKAZE, YAMAKAZE (1,150 nt; two 4.7-inch, five 3-inch guns, four 17.7-inch TT; 33 knots, 1911): converted to MS in 1929 (one 4.7-inch, four 3-inch guns; 24 knots), stricken 1936.

SAKURA, TACHIBANA (605 nt; one 4.7-inch, four 3-inch guns, four 17.7-inch TT; 30 knots, 1912): broken up 1933.

KABA class (665 nt; one 4.7-inch, four 3-inch guns, four 17.7-inch TT; 30 knots, 1915): ten DD, stricken 1931.

URAKAZE (907 nt; one 4.7-inch, four 3-inch guns, four 21-inch TT; 30 knots, 1915): sister-ship of the Italian *Audace*, hulked in 1936 as *Haikan 18*, sunk in 1945.

AMATSUKAZE class (1,227 nt, four 4.7-inch guns, six 17.7-inch TT, 34 knots, 1917): four DD stricken 1935, one of them retained as hulk *Haikan 20* until 1948.

ENOKI class (850 nt, three 4.7-inch guns, six 17.7-inch TT, 31.5 knots, 1918): four DD stricken 1932, plus two ships altered as MS (one less gun) and stricken 1938.

TANIKAZE, KAWAKAZE (1,300 nt, three 4.7-inch guns, six 21-inch TT, 37.5 knots, 1918–19): stricken 1934–35, the former hulked as *Haikan 19.*

The statistics listed above refer for the most part to the ships as built; their speed sagged over the years, a trait inherited by future classes right up to the *Mutsukis*.

In 1937, the Japanese captured *Chien Kang* from the Chinese and renamed her *Yamasemi*

(390 nt, two 3-inch guns, two 17.7-inch TT, 20 knots, 1912). She served a year or two before her scrapping.

MOMO, KASHI, YANAGI, HINOKI (755 tons, three 4.7-inch guns, six 17.7-inch TT, 31.5 knots, 1916–17): elderly things developed from *Kaba*. Between 1937 and 1943, *Kashi* served the puppet government of Manchukuo as *Hai Wei*, then returned to the Japanese as *Kaii* for escort duty. *Momo* and *Hinoki* went to the scrap yard in 1940, but *Yanagi* lingered as an unarmed training hulk.

MOMI, NASHI, KAYA; NIRE, ASHI, KAKI, SUMIRE, TAKE; HASU, KURI, TSUGA; KIKU, AOI, HAGI, SUTSUKI, TSUTA, FUJI, HISHI, YOMOGI, TADE (770 tons, three 4.7-inch guns, four 21-inch TT, 36 knots, 1919–23): plus *Warabi*, sunk in a 1927 collision. Derived from *Enoki*, these ships had a clearly obsolete appearance with one gun wedged between the stacks and a torpedo mount between bridge and forecastle—recurrent themes in later designs. But the raised forecastle also increased seaworthiness and agility in rough seas. The first three units listed above were scrapped in the 1930s. The next five, disarmed in 1939, resumed duty the following year as tenders (755 tons, 1–2 4.7-inch guns, two 21-inch TT, 14 knots); all of them but *Take* then shifted to training as *Tomariura 1* and *2*, *Osu*, and *Mitaka* (this last pair disarmed). In 1939, the last nine ships converted into patrol boats numbered *31–39* (935 tons, two 4.7-inch guns, 18 knots); most of these also functioned as fast transports. *Hasu*, *Kuri*, and *Tsuga* continued as DD, trading one gun for light AA. Their best speed was 31.5 knots.

MINEKAZE, AKIKAZE, HAKAZE, HOKAZE, NADAKAZE, NAMIKAZE, NOKAZE, NUMA-KAZE, OKIKAZE, SAWAKAZE, SHIOKAZE, TACHIKAZE, YAKAZE, YUKAZE, SHIMAKAZE (1,215 tons, four 4.7-inch guns, six 21-inch TT, 20 mines, 39 knots, 1920–22): contemporary with *Momi*s and visually similar. Advancing age and the advent of "Special Type" destroyers caused the *Minekaze*s to convert for secondary duties. *Yakaze* gave up two guns and her TT in 1937 to serve as control vessel for the target ship *Settsu*, then became a target herself with only light guns and 24 knots. Her sisters had their hulls strengthened and their range reduced (it was only 3,600 miles at 14 knots to begin with) in the late 1930s. In 1940, *Shimakaze* and *Nadakaze* became patrol boats *1* and *2* (2 4.7-inch DP, two 21-inch TT, 20 knots), and a year later they landed another gun to act as fast transports. *Sawakaze* spent some time as an aircraft rescue ship before her conversion in 1941 to a patrol vessel (two DP guns, no TT); late in the war, with a top speed of 16 knots, she exchanged another gun for an experimental 5.9-inch AS rocket launcher.

The other sisterships worked mostly as escorts mounting one or two guns. With about 200 added tons, they could manage 34–35 knots. After damage reduced *Namikaze* to 28 knots, she became a kaiten carrier (no TT, two kaiten); the damaged *Shiokaze* also converted (four kaiten) but never became operational.

WAKATAKE, KURETAKE, SANAE, SAWARABI, ASAGAO, YUGAO, FUYO, KARUKAYA, plus five canceled (820 tons, three 4.7-inch guns, four 21-inch TT, 35.5 knots, 1922–24): an improved *Momi* design. *Sawarabi* sank in a storm in 1932. *Yugao* became patrol boat *46* (two guns, no TT, 18 knots) in 1942, by which time all eight landed the gear they had carried for laying and sweeping mines. They also gave up one gun, and *Asagao* landed two TT. For some of these ships, top speed fell as low as 31 knots.

KAMIKAZE, ASAKAZE, HARUKAZE, MAT-SUKAZE, HATAKAZE, OITE, HAYATE, ASANAGI, YUNAGI, plus two canceled (1,270 tons, four 4.7-inch guns, six 21-inch TT, 37.25 knots, 1922–25): improved *Minekaze*s. As the

Pacific War began, the design underwent modification, losing a gun and three TT; displacement neared 1,400 tons while speed sank below 35 knots. The ships performed fleet duties early in the war until replaced by newer units. Only two of this class survived the war; and yes, one of them was *Kamikaze*.

MUTSUKI, KISARAGI, YAYOI, UZUKI, SATSU-KI, MINAZUKI, FUMIZUKI, NAGATSUKI, KIKUZUKI, MIKAZUKI, MOCHIZUKI, YUZU-KI (1,313 tons, four 4.7-inch guns, six 24-inch TT, 16 mines, 37.25 knots, 1925–27): improved *Kamikaze* capable of minesweeping. This design, the last in a lineage that never graduated from World War I, persisted with siting its torpedoes between the bridge and forecastle, though with one important difference—the 24-inch tubes. They didn't carry Long Lances, but they did have four reloads. The top speed of just 33.5 knots at full load (1,772 tons) left the navy disappointed, and by 1941 several units went into the yards for conversion to lesser duties; as fast transports with an increase to 1,590 tons, they retained two guns, possibly dual-purpose. (A number of Japan's old destroyers may have received 4.7-inch DP guns of the model mounted in *Aoba* class CA.)

Unlike later classes, the *Mutsuki*s showed

little durability. It appears that none of them, when struck directly by a functioning bomb or torpedo, survived the incident. The Americans found the sunken *Kikuzuki* and raised her for intelligence purposes.

FUBUKI, SHIRAYUKI, HATSUYUKI, MIYUKI, MURAKUMO, SHINONOME, USUGUMO, SHIRAKUMO, ISONAMI, URANAMI; AYANA-MI, SHIKINAMI, ASAGIRI, YUGIRI, AMAGIRI, SAGIRI, OBORO, AKEBONO, SAZANAMI, USHIO (1,750 tons, six 5-inch guns, nine 24-inch TT, 18 mines, 38 knots, 1928–32): the first class of Special Type destroyers. These brawny ships created a sensation with their powerful gun armament and enclosed twin mounts, but not with their torpedoes; the world remained unaware of Japan's 24-inch models. The *Fubuki*s entered service with conventional torpedoes, but some units may have switched to Long Lances during the war.

For the first 10 ships listed above, the main battery elevated to 40°; the other 10 had sufficient elevation (75°) for AA fire. But DP or not DP, these mounts—not the same type used for AA in larger ships—tracked too slowly to engage modern aircraft. Records disagree on the precise firing cycle, listed between six and 12 seconds—again, too slow for use against air-

*The **Mutsuki**s introduced the 24-inch torpedo but didn't match later standards of ruggedness. Here the **Kikuzuki** undergoes salvage by the Americans.*

The Kagero-*class* Amatsukaze, *like so many other Japanese destroyers, fell victim to air attack.*

craft. No one criticized this since, at that time, no other destroyer had a DP main battery.

Like the *Mogami*s, the *Fubuki*s inspired the construction of large designs in England and America. And, like the *Mogami*s, the *Fubuki*s gained their combat superiority at a high cost. Though more seaworthy than previous classes, they lacked stability and strength. A year after the *Tomozuru* Incident, another typhoon bowled into the Japanese fleet, bruising almost every ship it encountered. In this Fourth Fleet Incident, 10 *Fubuki*s suffered significant hull damage; two of them had their bows torn off. The entire class therefore underwent reconstruction in 1935–37, raising displacement to 2,090 tons. Range remained near 4,700 miles at 15 knots, but speed fell to 34 knots. The number of reload torpedoes shrank from nine to three, while some of the ships with DP guns may have traded them for the 55° type that became standard from the *Hatsuharu* class to the *Kagero*s.

Thus improved, the *Fubuki*s became excellent combatants. In wartime, light AA replaced one main turret. *Miyuki* failed to see war duty, sinking after a 1934 collision; only *Ushio* survived to see the war's end.

AKATSUKI, HIBIKI, IKAZUCHI, INAZUMA (1,680 tons, six 5-inch DP guns, nine 24-inch TT, 18 mines, 38 knots, 1932–33): the second Special Type design. They needed the same refit as the *Fubuki*s, which made them 1,980 tons with 34 knots. The 5-inch mounts were the 75° type used in the later *Fubuki*s. This left the ships dependent on light AA, and 25mm guns replaced one main turret early in the war.

HATSUHARU, ARIAKE, NENOHI, HATSUSHI-MO, WAKABA, YUGURE (1,490 tons, five 5-inch guns, nine 24-inch TT, 36.5 knots, 1933–35): the first DD to enter service with Long Lances. After the London Treaty fixed destroyer limits at 1,500 tons, the Japanese set out to compress a Special Type ship into that size. An impossible task, yet the designers did it—with predictable results. The typhoon experiences prompted a thorough reconstruction, more dramatic than in the Special Types: a growth to 1,715 tons, a loss of 3.2 knots, a turret rearrangement (the single mount crowded aft with one of the twins), and a reduction to six TT (but with six reloads and improved gear). In wartime, light AA took over the single mount's position aft.

As designed, the ships had excellent endurance, 6,000 miles at 15 knots.

SHIRATSUYU, SHIGURE, MURASAME, YUDA-CHI, SAMIDARE, HARUSAME, YAMAKAZE,

UMIKAZE, SUZUKAZE, KAWAKAZE (1,685 tons, five 5-inch guns, eight 24-inch TT, 34 knots, 1936–37): ordered as part of the *Hatsuharu* class, but redesigned after *Tomozuru* capsized. Apart from their quad-mounted torpedoes (each with a reload), they resembled the rebuilt *Hatsuharu*s. They had the same gun disposition and likewise traded the single mount for light AA. Wartime displacement rose by 100 tons.

Only one unit lasted past 1944: *Shigure*, the luckiest ship of the war. Twice—at Vella Gulf and at Surigao Strait—she was the only member of her task force to escape an American ambush. At Vella Lavella, a torpedo punched right through her rudder without exploding. But her luck ran out in 1945 amid a spread of submarine torpedoes.

ASASHIO, ARARE, ARASHIO, ASAGUMO, KASUMI, MICHISHIO, MINEGUMO, NATSU-GUMO, OSHIO, YAMAGUMO (1,961 tons, six 5-inch guns, eight 24-inch TT, 35 knots, 1937–39): designed after Japan decided to disregard tonnage limits. The *Asashio*s thus had a Special Type gun armament without the Special Type's lack of strength and stability. Unfortunately, the engines played host to tenacious bugs, evicted at last in 1943. Steering problems also required correction, and the figure listed for range (5,700 miles at 10 knots) seems curiously low. Wartime alterations sent the displacement to 2,000 tons as AS and light AA weaponry replaced a turret and the torpedo reloads.

KAGERO, KUROSHIO, OYASHIO, HATSU-KAZE, NATSUSHIO, YUKIKAZE, HAYASHIO, MAIKAZE, ISOKAZE, SHIRANUI, AMAT-SUKAZE, TOKITSUKAZE, URAKAZE, HAMA-KAZE, NOWAKI, ARASHI, HAGIKAZE, TANI-KAZE, AKIGUMO (2,033 tons, six 5-inch guns, eight 24-inch TT, 35 knots, 1939–41): improved *Asashio*s, a blend of the virtues of previous designs. The specifications, unhindered by treaty, called for the weaponry and dimensions of a Special Type ship, combined with superior range and speed. The *Kagero*s fulfilled all these requirements except speed. Powerful vessels with an improved reloading layout, they ranged to 5,000 miles at 18 knots. Light AA replaced one turret by 1943–44.

YUGUMO, AKISHIMO, ASASHIMO, FUJINA-MI, HAMANAMI, HAYANAMI, HAYASHIMO, KAZEGUMO, KISHINAMI, KIYONAMI, KIYOSHIMO, MAKIGUMO, MAKINAMI, NAGANAMI, OKINAMI, ONAMI, SUZUNAMI, TAKANAMI, TAMANAMI, plus eight units canceled (2,077 tons, six 5-inch DP guns, eight 24-inch TT, 35 knots, 1941–44): much like the *Kagero*s. The main guns had the same 75° mounts that provided inadequate AA in the Special Types. Light AA batteries increased, but a change in the 5-inch weaponry (a mount replaced by a 5/40 DP twin, as reported in some references) appears to be fictitious.

Not a single *Yugumo* survived the war, and air attack accounted for nine of them. In 1928, the Special Type's lack of a true DP gun seemed no great flaw; after all, its overseas rivals were the American flush-deckers, the British "A" class, the French *L'Adroit*s, and so on. But 15 years later, the Emperor's new ships depended on the same slow weapon to counter growing swarms of hungry American Dauntlesses. The failure to provide modern AA and AS armament left a capacious chink in the armor of these otherwise splendid warriors.

AKIZUKI, FUYUZUKI, HANAZUKI, HARUZU-KI, HATSUZUKI, NATSUZUKI, NIIZUKI, SHI-MOTSUKI, SUZUTSUKI, TERUZUKI, WAKAT-SUKI, YOIZUKI (2,701 tons, eight 3.9-inch DP, four 24-inch TT, 33 knots, 1942–45): plus four not completed. Twenty-two similar ships and 16 of enlarged design (2980 tons) never began building.

The *Akizuki*s started out as an AA mini-cruiser design with depth charges and torpedoes thrown in for general escort duties; the final product resembled nothing more closely than the cruiser *Yubari*. The two designs had similar dimensions and torpedo armament. At full load as built, the destroyers' displacement (3,700 tons) topped the cruiser's design figure (3,587 tons). However, *Akizuki*'s modest speed belied its standard DD machinery trying to push a cruiser-like bulk. Also, the 3.9-inch caliber makes an embarrassing comparison with *Yubari*'s 5.5-inchers. In these two regards, the new destroyer was rather a lot of ship for a little capability.

Nevertheless, the *Akizuki*s rate as a complete success, one of the top DD types of the war. The only Japanese destroyers with a practical DP gun, they also had relatively elaborate high-angle fire control; only two of them succumbed to air attack. They did lack anti-ship firepower, firing up to 4,640 lbs of metal per minute versus 6,050 lbs for a *Fletcher*, though the better ballistics of the Japanese gun largely compensated for the disadvantage. Also, the *Akizuki*s packed four reload torpedoes, and in any case, surface combat was not their mission. The tonnage that made their armament look so small gave the ships a remarkable range (8,300 miles at 18 knots) and made them the toughest of Japan's destroyers—a notable achievement, as the post-*Mutsuki* DD were an extremely hardy bunch. Despite the expense and commitment of resources, Japan could have done with more *Akizuki*s.

SHIMAKAZE (2,567 tons, six 5-inch DP guns, fifteen 24-inch TT, 39 knots, 1943): built with experimental high-pressure boilers, perhaps a German influence. Fortunately, *Shimakaze* didn't cause the problems that German destroyers did. She reached 40.9 knots on her trials, and designers began work on a 2,750-ton derivative; however, this class of 16 ships offered little advantage over smaller designs, and the project fell through.

Shimakaze's guns had the semi-useless 75° mount. Despite reports to the contrary, she did not land any of her turrets before her loss to aerial attack.

Three Allied DD, captured during the opening phase of the war, entered service as PB (described in a later section).

Submarines

Japan vehemently opposed prewar initiatives to abolish the submarine. The navy, facing the numerically superior Americans, looked to its undersea fleet to level the odds prior to a decisive surface battle. But by the time war actually broke out, this reasonable strategy had mutated into a suffocating dogma; the submarines found themselves tethered to the surface fleet's movements and leashed to one overriding mission— to target the enemy's capital ships. The high command, lest anyone misunderstand this mission, issued explicit orders forbidding the subs to waste more than three torpedoes on a mere cruiser. Destroyers and large merchantmen warranted a single shot at most. As for small merchant ships—that's what deck guns were for.

Subtler errors whittled away at the submarine fleet's potential. In pursuing a large number of classes, the Japanese forewent the standardization of successful types that might have produced more completions and simplified training. And as the war dragged on, supply and kaiten missions created a further diversion of resources.

The utter failure of submarines in the Pearl Harbor raid and other early operations led the skippers to advise a new doctrine emphasizing merchant targets. But the leadership, despite all urging and a changing war situation, never quite gave up its ideals.

The vast Pacific created long lines of communication, as vulnerable as they were vital; the decision to ignore this wealth of targets must have been complicated. It was certainly inexcusable. Perhaps commerce warfare lacked glory. But while the Japanese hesitated, the submarine—the weapon they'd struggled so hard

Dozens of Japanese midget subs, most of them Type D, lie in a Kure drydock.

to retain in their arsenal—became the sword the Americans used to gut the Empire in a relentless anti-commerce campaign, not a pursuit of glory but of victory.

During the war, Japanese submarines sank less than a million gross tons of shipping, plus a handful of warships. Casualties ran high, though in this case new construction matched most of the losses—in raw numbers, at least. The submarine fleet of 1945 consisted of the war-weary, the obsolete, and the noncombatant.

The mission of fleet support placed heavy demands on submarine designers and forced them to create large boats. These large boats attracted attention with their obvious radar and sonar signatures. When attacked, they were slow in diving, unwieldy beneath the surface, and plump as targets. Like other Japanese vessels, they lacked up-to-date electronics.

A more surprising problem lay in the poor quality of crew training. Most exercises took place in the immediate vicinity of the home islands, which left the crewmen unprepared for long-range patrols. It also led to the acceptance

of meager habitability, a surprising flaw given the size of the boats. Crew efficiency slumped as long cruises dragged on, and when circumstances forced the boats to act as transports, sometimes unarmed, morale plummeted.

On the positive side, the submariners had an excellent weapon, a 21-inch version of the Long Lance. They also had the sort of night optics that benefitted the surface fleet. Some boat designs showed originality, featuring high speed or a complement of aircraft; a floatplane operating from *I25* became the only airplane ever to bomb the continental United States (a strange choice of targets, though—a forest in Oregon).

Japanese submarines achieved a few notable successes, such as sinking the *Wasp* and the *Indianapolis*. But while the Americans couldn't ignore the underwater threat, they found it easy to manage. The following boats served into the 1930s:

RO11, 12 (735/1,030 tons, one 3-inch DP gun, six 17.7-inch TT, 18/9 knots, 1919): Type K1, stricken 1931.

JAPAN

RO13–15 (755/1,050 tons, one 3-inch DP gun, six 17.7-inch TT, 17/8 knots, 1920): Type K2. *RO13* was a training hulk from 1931 to postwar, the others sold in early 1930s.

RO51, 52 (902/1,195 tons, one 3-inch DP gun, six 17.7-inch TT, 17/8 knots, 1920): Type L1, stricken 1940 and 1932 respectively.

RO16–25 (755/1,050 tons, one 3-inch DP gun, six 17.7-inch TT, 17/8 knots, 1920–23): Type K3, stricken 1932–36, but *RO18* lasted to postwar as hulk *Haikan 4*.

RO53–56 (902/1,195 tons, one 3-inch DP gun, four 17.7-inch TT, 17/8 knots, 1921–22): Type L2; all stricken by 1940.

RO3–5 (689/1,047 tons, one 3-inch DP gun, five 17.7-inch TT, 14/8 knots, 1922): Type F2; stricken in 1930.

RO26–28 (770/1,070 tons, one 3-inch DP gun, four 21-inch TT, 16/8 knots, 1923–24): Type K4; stricken 1940, not broken up until postwar; five further boats canceled after 1922 treaty.

Japanese nomenclature assigned I-numbers to long-range boats, RO-numbers to short-range boats, and Ha-numbers to coastal boats.

RO57–59 (897/1,195 tons, one 3-inch DP gun, four 21-inch TT, 17/8 knots, 1922–23): Type L3, served in training from 1941 until hulked in 1945. The L-types all derived from the British "L" class.

RO60–68 (996/1,322 tons, one 3-inch DP gun, six 21-inch TT, 16/8 knots, 1923–27): Type L4, relegated to training in 1943.

RO29–32 (665/1,000 tons, one 4.7-inch gun, four 21-inch TT, 13/8 knots, 1923–24): Type KT, based on French designs. They aged quickly; *RO29* retired in 1936, and the others served as trainers until hulked during the war.

The Washington Treaty curtailed further L and KT construction.

I51 (1,500/2,430 tons, one 4.7-inch gun, eight 21-inch TT, 20/10 knots, 1924): Type KD1, inspired by British subs. The design originally included a second deck gun, a 3-inch DP. *I51* served in training from 1930 until stricken in 1941. All KD-types were intended for operations with the surface fleet.

I52, plus five sisters canceled after the Washington Treaty (1,500/2,500 tons, one 4.7-inch gun, eight 21-inch TT, 22/10 knots, 1925): Type KD2, based on a WWI German design. Like *I51*, she entered service with a 3-inch DP gun. In 1940, she began training duty.

The navy made a naming change in 1942, adding 100 to some I-numbers: *I52* became *I152* and soon retired to become a source of spare parts.

I1–4 (2,135/2,791 tons, two 5.5-inch guns, six 21-inch TT, 18/8 knots, 1926–29): Type J1, based on another WWI U-boat. The J1's had lightly armored upper surfaces for their work as cruiser-subs, but they wound up in a different role, as transports, with *I1, 2* landing one gun to free up more cargo space. Like future J-type boats, they performed well on the surface but not underwater; and like most of Japan's big boats, they dove slowly but had long range (in this case, 24,400 miles at 10 knots).

I53–60, 63 (1,800/2,300 tons, one 4.7-inch gun, eight 21-inch TT, 20/8 knots, 1927–30): Type KD3. The boats showed variations in detail; some lists classify *I53–55, 58* as a separate group. An accident claimed *I63* in 1940. After *I60*'s early wartime loss, the others became *I153–159* and served in training. In 1945, two kaiten mountings replaced the deck gun on *I156–159*.

I21–24, plus perhaps two others planned (1,383/1,768 tons, one 5.5-inch gun, four 21-inch TT, 42 mines, 14.5/7 knots, 1927–28): Type KRS, a copy of a WWI U-boat. The lack of submerged stability made the design a failure, so no further development took place. The navy didn't wait until 1942 to rename the boats; they became *I121–124* prewar and were converted as tankers for long-range reconnaissance aircraft. By 1942, they served mostly in training.

I61, 62, 64 (1,720/2,300 tons, one 4.7-inch gun, six 21-inch TT, 20/8.5 knots, 1929–30): Type KD4. The Japanese raised *I61* after her loss to collision in October 1941, then scrapped her. *I62*, renamed *I162*, became a training boat in 1944, but returned to combat duty with two kaiten replacing her deck gun.

I5 (2,243/2,921 tons, one 5.5-inch gun, six 21-inch TT, AC 1, 18/8 knots, 1932): Type J1M, similar to the Type J1 but equipped with aviation facilities. In 1936, *I5* temporarily traded her 5.5-inch gun for a 5-inch DP. The aircraft equipment performed poorly; by 1940, a second 5.5-inch gun took its place.

I65–67 (1,705/2,330 tons, one 3.9-inch DP gun, six 21-inch TT, 20.5/8.2 knots, 1932): Type KD5, similar to KD4 but with a stronger hull. *I67* sank in a 1940 accident; the others became *I165, 166*, and the former lasted long enough for conversion to kaiten carrier (two craft).

I68–75 (1,785/2,440 tons, one 3.9-inch DP gun, six 21in TT, 23/8.2 knots, 1934–38): Type KD6, enlarged from KD5 with some individual variations. Only the first three carried a 3.9-inch DP; the rest had a 4.7-inch gun. The final pair, sometimes classed separately, displaced 1,810/2,564 tons with a strengthened hull and mar-

ginally decreased speed underwater. The survivors in 1942 had their I-numbers increased by 100, and some went on to serve as transports with no deck gun.

I6 (2,243/3,061 tons, one 5-inch DP gun, six 21-inch TT, AC 1, 20/7.5 knots, 1935): Type J2, similar to J1M with more speed and less range. The design repeated *I1*'s light armor. The 5-inch gun, like that in *I5*, was a "wet" version of the standard DP weapon with less elevation (only 75°, thus a lower ceiling). *I6*'s flight equipment sufficed and remained throughout her career.

RO33, 34 (940/1,200 tons, one 3-inch DP gun, four 21-inch TT, 19/8.2 knots, 1935–37): Type K5, a successful development from the previous K's and KT's, built as a prototype for wartime mass production. They showed good sea-keeping qualities.

I7, 8 (2,525/3,538 tons, 1–2 5.5-inch gun, six 21-inch TT, AC 1, 23/8 knots, 1937–38): Type J3, derived more from KD's than from J's. The aircraft facilities showed no operational advances. *I8* traded her plane for four kaiten in 1944. *I7* apparently had only one single-mount gun, making *I8* the only sub with the 5.5-inch twin mount.

I16, 18, 20, 22, 24 (2,554/3,561 tons, one 5.5-inch gun, eight 21-inch TT, 23.6/8 knots, 1940–41): Type C1, developed from KD6. Despite having a smaller conning tower, these boats still tended to wallow underwater. But in general, the various C-types proved reliable and combat-worthy, among the better I-boats. Each Type C1 boat could transport a Type A midget submarine on deck. *I16* became a transport boat with no deck gun.

I15, 17, 19, 21, 23, 25–39 (2,589/3,654 tons, one 5.5-inch gun, six 21-inch TT, AC 1, 23.6/8 knots, 1940–43): Type B1, an adequate scouting design with a streamlined conning tower for better submerged performance. Some boats traded the seaplane for a second gun. *I36, 37* landed gun and aircraft to accommodate six and four kaiten, respectively. *I34, 35* began modification for launching balloon bombs, but the work went incomplete.

I9–11, plus two others planned but not completed (2,919/4,149 tons, one 5.5-inch gun, six 21-inch TT, AC 1, 23.5/8 knots, 1941–42): Type A1, intended as flagships for submarine flotillas. Their new aviation equipment at last proved practical.

I76–85, plus 10 others planned (1,833/2,602 tons, one 4.7-inch gun, six 21-inch TT, 23/8 knots, 1942–43): Type KD7, renamed *I176–185*. They were typical big boats with good range, speed, and surface performance, but poor habitability and submerged performance. Some functioned as gunless transports.

RO100–117, plus nine others planned (601/782 tons, one 3-inch DP gun, four 21-inch TT, 14.2/8 knots, 1942–44): Type KS. Their smaller size made these boats faster in a dive and more agile underwater at a cost in speed and range (just 3500 miles at 12 knots).

RO35–50, 55, 56, plus 70 others planned (1,115/1,447 tons, one 3-inch DP gun, four 21-inch TT, 19.75/8 knots, 1943–44): Type K6, wartime emergency construction based on the K5's. These boats handled quite well, and they rate among Japan's best, but they accomplished little; only *RO50* survived the war.

I40–45, plus eight more planned (2,624/3,700 tons, one 5.5-inch gun, six 21-inch TT, AC 1, 23.5/8 knots, 1943–44): Type B2, similar to the 31's with characteristics typical of the big boats. Some B2's gave up their aircraft for another gun. *I44* shipped four kaiten.

I52, 53, 55, plus 17 others planned (2,564/3,644 tons, two 5.5-inch guns, six 21-inch TT, 17.7/6.5 knots, 1943–44): Type C3, sacrificing speed for increased range (21,000 miles at 16 knots). *I53* landed one gun and embarked as many as six kaiten.

I46–48, plus six others planned (2,557/3,564 tons, one 5.5-inch gun, eight 21-inch TT, 23.5/8 knots, 1944): Type C2, derived from the C1 but without mounts for midget subs. Six kaiten replaced the deck gun aboard *I47, 48*. The C2 project preceded the C3 but entered service later. With the typical high-speed machinery, the C2's had less endurance than the C3's; but 14,000 miles at 16 knots was still an excellent figure, and typical of the I-boats.

The Type C4 design (25 boats: 2,756 standard

One of Japan's large submarines, the newly renamed I176 *in 1942.*

tons surfaced, one 5.5-inch gun, eight 21-inch TT, 20.4 surface knots) barely started building before getting canceled.

I54, 56, 58, plus 18 others planned (2,607/ 3,688 tons, one 5.5-inch gun, six 21-inch TT, AC 1, 17.7/6.5 knots, 1944): Type B3, similar to previous B's but given the endurance and speed of C3. *I56, 58* gave up their planes and deck guns for six kaiten, with an alternative load under consideration: the Type 4 tractor (19.2 tons, two 17.7-inch TT, 5 knots, 1944), an amphibious jalopy intended to raid enemy bases, though it had no value in this or any other role. At most, 18 Type 4's were built, and none entered service.

The navy canceled its order for 18 Type B4 submarines (2,800 standard tons surfaced, one 5.5-inch gun, eight 21-inch TT, eight mines, AC 1, 22.5 surface knots).

I12 (2,934/4,172 tons, one 5.5-inch gun, six 21-inch TT, AC 1, 17.7/6.2 knots, 1944): Type A2, like the A1 but trading speed for range.

I361–372, plus ninety-two planned (1,779/ 2,215 tons, one 5.5-inch gun, 13/6.5 knots, 1944): Type D1, designed specifically as transport subs of simple construction. The original provision of two 21-inch TT created handling problems. Eight boats traded their deck guns for five kaiten.

Ha101–109 (429/493 tons, light guns, 10/5 knots, 1944–45): Type SS, a no-frills transport design. The conning towers had a special coating intended to reduce their radar echo.

The large orders of transport types reveals the depth of Japanese desperation late in the war. Plans included 100 Type SS boats, but only the first nine reached completion, plus *Ha111*, scuttled postwar in a semi-complete state.

I13, 14, plus five others planned (3,603/4,762 tons, one 5.5-inch gun, six 21-inch TT, AC 2, 16.7/5.5 knots, 1944–45): Type AM, based on the Type A2 with one additional seaplane. The design featured a crude (and unsuccessful) snorkel.

I400–402 (5,223/6,560 tons, one 5.5-inch gun, eight 21-inch TT, AC 3, 18.7/6.5 knots, 1944–45): Type STo, the *Yamato*s of the undersea fleet, behemoths intended to combine reconnaissance, attack, flag, and seaplane carrier functions. The initial order included 18 boats. *I404* (and perhaps *I403*) sank in an air raid prior to completion. *I402* reached completion modified to act as a tanker, but none of the STo boats performed a patrol.

The navy classified many I-boats as cruiser-submarines, but the STo's actually had a cruiser's displacement. When first allowed into public view, they masqueraded as surface ships with their lofty conning towers and a set of fake funnels. Even without the funnels, their silhouette bulged with a corpulent hangar crowding the conning tower off the centerline, and they had a snorkel mast as well. The engines labored to shove this water-resisting mass along its course, and they couldn't match the speed of the typical I-boat. But otherwise, *I400* had the shortcomings and virtues one might expect from the biggest of the big. She possessed great surface stability and matchless range: 37,500 miles at 14 knots.

Foreign rivals never approached this figure: America's *Balao* had 11,800 miles at 10 knots; Italy's *Cagni*, 10,700 miles at 12 knots; Britain's *Amphion*, 10,500 miles at 11 knots; Germany's Type XXI, 15,500 miles at 10 knots; and France's *Surcouf*, 10,000 miles at 10 knots.

Admiral Yamamoto had wanted the Type STo for air attacks against the Panama Canal, but after his death and other naval setbacks, the plan lost its impetus.

I351 (3,512/4,290 tons, four 21-inch TT, 15.75/6.3 knots, 1945): Type SH, intended as seaplane tenders servicing up to three flying boats. The design included a 5.5-inch gun, but with none available, a pair of 81mm mortars took its place. I352 sank incomplete during an air raid, and four others never began building.

From 1938 to 1940, the navy experimented with submarine 71 (213/240 tons, three 17.7-inch TT, 18/25 knots designed). Manufacturers could not supply the desired engines, and speed fell to 13.1/21.3 knots. Successful trials paved the way for the Types ST and STS.

I201–203, plus ninety-five others planned (1,291/1,450 tons, four 21-inch TT, 15.8/19 knots, 1945): Type ST, combining high underwater speed with rapid construction. They had snorkels. While generally inferior to analogous German types, the ST's showed promise and would have given the Allies a nasty shock if they'd entered service early enough to see action.

I373, plus 145 others planned (1,926/2,240 tons, one 5.5-inch gun, 13/6.5 knots, 1945): Type D2, a D1 derivative. I373 may have switched from transport to kaiten-carrying duty before her loss.

Ha201–205, 207–210, 216 (377/440 tons, two 21-inch TT, 10.5/13 knots, 1945): Type STS, simple to build, highly maneuverable—a good design for local defense. The design included a snorkel; though lacking German refinements, it still gave the boats a theoretical ability to stay submerged up to 15 days.

With several STS boats were nearing completion at the war's end, there's some confusion over which units actually entered service. Production plans included Ha201–279 plus 10 unnamed, but the number commissioned could be as few as seven. In any case, none of the boats saw any action.

The malcontent Japanese Army decided to clutter the yards with its own transport designs based on the Type SS: Yu1–12 (273/370 tons, light guns, 10/5 knots, 1943–45) and Yu1001–1014 (about 392/500 tons, unarmed, 12/5 knots, 1944–45). Plans for a Yu2001 class ended with the war.

Eight former German and Italian boats entered Japanese service: U511, 1224 became RO500, 501; U181, 862, 219, 195 became I501, 502, 505, 506; UIT24 (ex-Cappellini), UIT25 (ex-Torelli) became I503, 504 (all respective).

A salvaged Dutch wreck, K XVIII, served as a radar hulk. The American Sealion, found sunken at pier-side at Cavite, earned only a cursory examination.

Japan invested much hope and effort in its midget submarines. The program began with a pair of two-man prototypes completed around 1934. Without a conning tower, they topped 24 knots submerged, but the conning tower proved necessary despite the two knots it cut off the speed. Two more units were built—Ha1, 2—followed by a production order (Ha3–52, 54–61?: 46 tons submerged, two 17.7-inch TT, 23/19 knots, 1938-42). The prototypes apparently carried 21-inch Type 89 torpedoes; production boats began with Type 97 17.7-inchers, but Type 02 proved less troublesome.

Initially intended for open-sea battle, the boats were transportable via seaplane carriers or fleet subs, but not even their refined layout could make such a mission practical. A persistent desire for offensive weapons then cast them in the role of covert attack craft, a ridiculous choice for torpedo-armed craft. They were eventually reassigned to local defense, prompting the Type B design, better suited but still unsuccessful in the face of Allied superiority. From the start of the Pacific War, examples of the boats began to fall captive to the Allies, who apparently saw them as nothing more than a novelty.

The three-man Type B Ha53 (50 tons submerged, two 17.7-inch TT, 6.5/18.5 knots,

1943) served as the model for the Type C *Ha62–76* (1943–44). This design (which by some accounts included *Ha54–89*) introduced a battery-charging capability, and one similar boat was modified as a minelayer with four mines replacing the torpedoes. This *M-Kanamono* might have had the greatest potential among the IJN midgets, but the concept was not pursued. The navy planned more than 600 of the five-man Type D or *Koryu* boats (59 tons submerged, two 17.7-inch TT, 8/16 knots, 1945) but completed only 115. The *Koryu* had more range, habitability, and seaworthiness than previous types. Some were deployed aboard *T1*-class landing ships.

The more midget-like, two-man *Kairyu* design (19/19 tons, two 17.7-inch TT or one 1,322-lb charge, 7.5/10 knots, 1945) resulted from whittling down a 45-ton prototype based on the Type A. Intended for local defense, the *Kairyu* became a suicide craft as torpedoes became scarce. Production totaled only 212 of a planned 760 boats. An enlarged version (40 tons) never started construction.

The army tried its hand at a similar project, building three prototypes for semisubmersible attack craft (5–6 tons, eight knots, 1944–45). They carried one or two crewmen and an armament of two torpedoes or an explosive charge (possibly exceeding one ton).

The midgets accomplished little; the kaiten accomplished little more. The first batch of these human torpedoes came with escape hatches, but they soon took on the suicide role. The following list shows the approximate number of completions:

Type 1 (330 craft: 8–9 tons, one 3,420-lb charge, 30 knots, 1944–45)

Type 2 (two craft: 18.4 tons, one 3,420-lb charge, 40 knots, 1945)

Type 3 (one craft: 18.3 tons, one 3,310-lb charge, 30 knots, 1945)

Type 4 (50 craft: 18.2 tons, one 3,967-lb charge, 40 knots, 1945)

There were also perhaps five Type 10's with seven knots. None of these designs were reliable or successful; more than 50 kaiten missions managed to sink only two vessels.

The Japanese had a miscellany of minor underwater craft. The *U-Kanamono* (14 craft: about 15 tons, one 17.7-inch TT, three knots, 1944–45) was only partly submersible. The one *Shinkai* type midget (11.5 tons, nine knots, 1944) carried an explosive charge instead of a torpedo. At least two submersibles (about 20 tons) served in research and rescue missions. The army adapted Germany's Walther technology in one *Maru-Se* craft (two 17.7-inch TT, 15/20 knots, 1945). The effort to resupply beleaguered garrisons prompted the production of underwater cargo containers, most of them unpowered and unmanned, but one type (44 tons) employed torpedo-like propulsion with a two-man crew.

Torpedo Boats and Escort Destroyers

The captured Chinese *Fu Ngo* served as *Kawasemi* for a time before her scrapping.

TOMOZURU, CHIDORI, MANAZURU, HAT-SUKARI (600 tons, three 4.7-inch guns, two 21-inch TT, 28 knots, 1933–34): a design instigated by diplomacy.

When the 1922 treaty defined capital ships as exceeding 10,000 tons, the world's navies produced a flurry of imbalanced 10,000-ton cruisers; but when the London Conference left 600-ton TB unrestricted, the results were even worse. Fortunately few fleets wanted a 600-ton TB design, but the Japanese considered it a promising idea. *Tomozuru* squeezed three 5-inch guns and four TT into her 535 tons. Overloaded, unstable, frail—she capsized in a 1934 typhoon and sparked a complete reassessment of Japanese warship design. After *Tomozuru*'s salvage, she and her sisters underwent reconstruction. The main battery gave way to 4.7-inch guns in 55° mounts; half of the torpedo tubes went ashore; further top-weight reductions and the addition of ballast provided stability, making the boats seaworthy at 600 tons. Early in the war, they landed one gun for more AS and AA weaponry.

OTORI, KASASAGI, HIYADORI, HAYABUSA, HATO, SAGI, KARI, KIJI (840 tons, three 4.7-inch guns, three 21-inch TT, 30.5 knots, 1936–37): an improved *Tomozuru*, altered while building to conform with lessons of the 1934 storm. They landed one gun in wartime, while their displacement rose above 1,000 tons.

The *Otori*s, with almost 60% more tonnage than the original *Tomozuru*s, presented a more balanced design and highlighted the folly of the 600-ton TB. In fact, the TB concept itself had become obsolete. The Japanese abandoned it and canceled a batch of eight additional *Otori*s in favor of eight submarine-chasers.

MATSU, MOMO, TAKE, UME, KUWA, MAKI, KIRI, SUGI, MOMI, KASHI, HINOKI, KAYA, KAEDE, SAKURA, NARA, TSUBAKI, KEYAKI, YUNAGI, plus 11 others canceled (1,262 tons, three 5-inch DP guns, four 24-inch TT, 27.8 knots, 1944–45): escort destroyers, the virtual equal of some fleet DD. Though they lacked the speed, torpedo battery, and enclosed turrets of a Special Type, they also had significant advantages. Their 5/40 guns were legitimate DP pieces, and their internal layout included machinery dispersal and extensive subdivision. The *Matsu*s, while easy to build, were disturbingly difficult to sink. They ranged to 4,680 miles at 16 knots.

TACHIBANA, NIRE, TSUTA, HAGI, KAKI, SHII, NASHII, SUMIRE, ENOKI, KUSUNOKI, ODAKE, HATSUZAKURA, KABA, HATSU-YUME, plus 19 others not completed (1,289 tons, three 5-inch DP guns, four 24-inch TT, 27.8 knots, 1945): a further simplified *Matsu* design, the largest ships in the Imperial Japanese Navy to benefit from machinery dispersal.

The American destroyer Nicholas *encounters Japan's* Hatsuzakura *while en route to the surrender ceremony.*

The navy gave up plans for 80 units of improved design.

Minecraft

NATSUSHIMA class (405 tons, two 3-inch DP gun, 45 mines, 12.75 knots, 1911–20): originally 13 coastal ML, but *Natsushima* and one other scrapped in the 1930s. They could also act as MS. They landed a gun in 1941–42 and raised their mine load to 120.

KATSURIKI (1,540 tons, three 3-inch guns, 150 mines, 13 knots, 1917): minelayer and survey vessel.

SHIRATAKA (1,345 tons, three 4.7-inch DP guns, 100 mines, 16 knots, 1929): minelayer and netlayer; converted for escort duty during the war with the replacement of a gun and mine gear by AS weaponry.

ITSUKUSHIMA (1,970 tons; three 5.5-inch, two 3-inch DP guns, 300 mines; 17 knots, 1929): ML and netlayer. Light AA replaced the 3-inch guns; the mine load grew to 400. Displacement became 2330 tons.

KAMOME, TSUBAME (450 tons, one 3-inch DP gun, 120 mines, 19 knots, 1929): ML and netlayers, then escorts with no mine gear.

YAEYAMA (1,135 tons, two 4.7-inch DP guns, 185 mines, 20 knots, 1932): ML and netlayer, later an escort with no mine gear.

NASAMI, NATSUSHIMA (450 tons, two 3-inch DP guns, 120 mines, 19 knots, 1933–34): similar to the *Kamome* class.

SARUSHIMA (566 tons, two 3-inch DP guns, 120 mines, 18 knots, 1934): similar to *Kamome*, became an escort.

OKINOSHIMA (4,470 tons; four 5.5-inch, two

3-inch DP guns, 500 mines; AC 1, 20 knots, 1936): cruiser-minelayer used also for escort duty.

SOKUTEN class (720 tons, 120 mines, 20 knots, 1938–40): five vessels used as ML and netlayers, changing later to escorts.

HATSUTAKA, AOTAKA, WAKATAKE, plus one canceled (1,608 tons, 360 mines, 20 knots, 1939–41): attractive and versatile ML design. In addition to her light guns, *Wakatake* also mounted two 3-inch DP. All three units converted for escort work.

One improved vessel (1,650 tons) never began building.

HIRASHIMA class (720 tons, one 3-inch DP gun, 120 mines, 20 knots, 1940–42): nine ML plus one canceled; nearly identical to *Sokutens*.

HATSUSHIMA, ODATE, TATEISHI, TSURUSHIMA (1,564 tons, one 3-inch DP gun, 12 mines, 14 knots, 1940–41): built as cable ships, used for various duties. They became minelayer escorts in 1944, perhaps with 120 mines.

TSUGARU, plus two more planned (4,000 tons, four 5-inch DP guns, 600 mines, AC 1, 20 knots, 1941): a compact *Okinoshima* design.

MA1–4 (215 tons, one 3-inch DP gun, 40 mines, 9.5 knots, 1942): auxiliary ML, similar to *Wa1* class MS.

AJIRO (720 tons, one 3-inch DP gun, 120 mines, 20 knots, 1943): another repeat *Sokuten*. The navy canceled 21 additional ships, along with 12 vessels of improved design.

KAMISHIMA, plus one completed postwar and 18 canceled (766 tons, 120 mines, 16.5 knots, 1945): simplified ML design.

About 50 tugs and a dozen merchant ships functioned as auxiliary minelayers, along with a captured British tug *Grinder* (renamed *Nagashima*). As many as 33 minelaying trawlers remained from WWI service. Japan seized the British harbor craft *Barlight* for service as *Ma101* (730 tons, one 3-inch DP gun, mines, 10 knots, 1938). *Col. George F. E. Harrison*, an American army mine-planter captured in the Philippines, performed various duties as *Harushima* (700 grt, one 3-inch DP gun, mines, 11 knots, 1919). The Chinese ML *Tung Hsin* and *Tung Teh* apparently fell into Japanese hands in 1937.

W1–4 (600 tons; two 4.7-inch, one 3-inch DP gun; 20 knots, 1923–25): MS, most becoming escorts with one gun (4.7-inch) and no mine gear.

W5, 6 (620 tons; two 4.7-inch, one 3-inch DP gun; 21 knots, 1929): enlarged version of *W1*, likewise converted.

W13–16 (691 tons, two 4.7-inch guns, 18 knots, 1933–34): MS rebuilt after *Tomozuru's* capsizing (designed for 500 tons and 20 knots). Only *W15* survived long enough to trade the MS gear for AS gear.

W17, 18 (578 tons, two 4.7-inch guns, 19 knots, 1936): MS similar to previous class, became escorts.

W7–12 (630 tons, three 4.7-inch guns, 20 knots, 1938–39): MS like previous class. As escorts they had two guns and no mine gear.

W19–30, 33, 34, 38, 39, 41, plus 63 planned (648 tons, three 4.7-inch guns, 20 knots, 1941–44): MS, almost identical to *W7* in design and conversion.

The Japanese captured four incomplete *Bangor*-class MS from the British. Two became MS *W101, 102* (590 tons, one 4.7-inch gun, 15.75

knots, 1944); one became a GB (*Nanyo*: 1,200 tons?, two 4.7-inch guns, 13 knots, 1943); and one served as a noncombatant.

WA1–22 (215 tons, one 3-inch DP gun, 9.5 knots, 1942–43): auxiliary MS adapted from trawler design, similar to *Ma1* class ML.

The navy converted 112 merchant ships into auxiliary MS. Three captured Dutch *Merbaboe*-class MS and at least four *Djember*s went into Japanese service, seven of them under the names *Wa101–107*.

Escort Vessels

CH1, 2 (300 tons, light guns, 21 knots, 1934): sub-chasers. Post-*Tomozuru* alteration changed them from 266 tons and 24 knots.

CH3 (270 tons, light guns, 20 knots, 1936): modified *Ch1*.

CH51–53 (170 tons, light guns, 23 knots, 1937): SC, later re-rated as auxiliary SC *Ch251–253*, later re-rated as tugs.

CH4–12 (291 tons, light guns, 20 knots, 1938–39): a return to the *Ch1* type.

CH13–27 (438 tons, one 3-inch DP gun, 16 knots, 1940–42): an enlargement of previous SC designs. Notably seaworthy, they showed that the designers had learned their stability lesson.

SHIMUSHU, HACHIJO, KUNASHIRI, ISHIGA-KI (860 tons, three 4.7-inch guns, 19.7 knots, 1940–41): Type A "coast defense ships." The Japanese used this curious rating to indicate a multi-purpose craft—intended first for patrol and fishery protection, then for minesweeping, and lastly for convoy escort—with a simple design to facilitate wartime mass production. However, over-zealous designers submitted a complex plan, which the navy casually accepted with an order for just four units in its 1937 Program. At that time, the leadership clearly had no grasp of the potential of American submarines.

The *Shimushu*s proved a capable class, strong and stable, ably freeing fleet destroyers for more demanding duties. They had good range, 8,000 miles at 16 knots. The navy ordered four more units, then canceled them in pursuit of a revised version.

TSUKUSHI (1,400 tons, four 4.7-inch DP guns, AC 1, 19.75 knots, 1941): survey vessel used as an escort.

The Japanese captured a British survey vessel, the former sloop *Herald*, and used her in various roles as *Heiyo* (1,320 tons, one 3-inch DP gun, 17 knots, 1918). The Dutch survey vessel *Tydeman* and the tender *Poolster* entered Japanese service, but probably not as combatants.

CH28–58, 60, 61, 63, plus twenty-eight more planned (420 tons, one 3-inch DP gun, 16 knots, 1942–44): a *Ch13* repeat.

ETOROFU class (870 tons, three 4.7-inch guns, 19.7 knots, 1943–44): 14 repeat *Shimushu*s, also called Type A coast defense ships. The design included slight simplification and a vague emphasis on AS and AA firepower. The *Etorofu*s formed part of an order for 30 escorts, a number the high command in 1941 apparently considered sufficient for dealing with Allied subs.

CHA1–100, 151–250 (130 tons, light guns, 11 knots, 1943–45): auxiliary SC based on a tug design, built in commercial yards. Several of them converted to tug duty, and one additional unit provided fishery protection.

The navy made auxiliary SC from three tugs and about 105 trawlers, whalers, etc. Eighteen captured Dutch small craft became *Cha101–118* (see the Netherlands section). The Japanese also captured one British HDML (plus three they scrapped on the stocks), two Fairmile "B" launches (plus others not completed), an auxiliary ML, an auxiliary MS, and a ferry undergoing conversion to patrol craft; these units provided harbor defense.

HAKACHI (1,641 tons, two 4.7-inch DP guns, 19.3 knots, 1943): target ship used as an escort.

MIKURA class (940 tons, three 4.7-inch DP guns, 19.7 knots, 1943–44): eight Type B coast defense ships based on *Etorofu*. Planners finally settled on AA and AS abilities as the first priority, though the *Mikura*s retained some minesweeping gear until late in the war. Endurance dropped to 5,000 miles at 16 knots. This class proved easier to build than the *Etorofu*s, but the navy needed further simplification.

UKURU class (940 tons, three 4.7-inch DP guns, 19.5 knots, 1944–45): 29 Modified Type B escorts completed, with 113 others incomplete or canceled. The design derived from *Mikura* but much simplified with minimal habitability. Escort functions received added emphasis, and while the ships commissioned with MS gear, they soon landed it. A diesel shortage slowed production.

T1–21, plus 25 more planned (1,500 tons, two 5-inch DP guns, 22 knots, 1944–45): landing ships designed after experience with destroyer-transport conversions. This gave the ships a striking appearance and a respectable combat potential. They could perform AS duty or transport small attack craft (two Type D midget subs or six kaiten).

Like the other naval powers, Japan modified some landing craft for gunboat duty; these *daihatsus* became prominent in China and the

*The **Shisaka** of the **Ukuru** class. Note the guns in one single and one twin mount, a feature introduced in the **Mikuras**.*

Solomons. The navy's limited resources pushed this policy one step further, and some *daihatsus* shipped depth charges for AS patrol. A few even embarked a pair of torpedoes; the torpedo-capable craft include the 17-meter Type (about 35 tons and nine knots) and the 14-meter Type (about 20 tons and eight knots).

CD1 class (745 tons, two 4.7-inch DP guns, 16.5 knots, 1944–45): 300 Type C coast defense ships planned, 53 of them completed in wartime and three soon thereafter. Using the *Sokuten*-class ML as a model of the smallest possible ocean-going warship, the navy simplified its *Ukuru* design. The Type C's (all assigned odd numbers) inherited their strength and sea-keeping from earlier ships, but nose-heaviness made them wet forward.

CD2 class (740 tons, two 4.7-inch DP guns, 17.5 knots, 1944–45): 203 Type D coast defense ships planned, 63 completed in wartime and four afterward. Similar to the Type C's, the Type D's (given even numbers) had turbine engines due to the lack of diesels. This provided more speed, but range shrank to 4,500 miles at 14 knots.

The navy planned to build 675 coast defense

ships of all types but completed only 171 before the surrender—a glaring contrast to the Allies' AS programs. To supplement these meager numbers, planners adapted two designs (intended as mass-produced kaiten carriers) to serve as "coast defense boats," but no units reached completion. The steel-hulled Type A (20 planned: 278 tons, light guns, 15 knots) originally carried two kaiten, and the wooden Type B (perhaps 100 planned: 280 tons, light guns, 12.5 knots) carried one.

OHAMA (2,560 tons, two 4.7-inch DP guns, 32.5 knots, 1945): target ship used as an escort.

The navy planned four additional vessels of similar design.

PA1 class (238 tons, light guns, nine knots, 1945): 33 auxiliary PB, 247 more planned, intended for postwar use as fishing vessels. They came from commercial yards and could operate under sail. Some functioned as MS. The original design included an incongruous pair of TT.

The following captured vessels entered service as patrol boats:

British DD *Thracian*—*P101* (905 tons, two 4-inch guns?, 25 knots)

American DD *Stewart*—*P102* (1,270 tons, two 3-inch DP guns, 26 knots)

American MS *Finch*—*P103* (980 tons, two 3-inch DP guns, 13 knots)

Dutch patrol vessel *Valk*—*P104* (1,011 tons, one 3-inch DP gun, 15 knots)

American *Arayat*—*P105* (1,200 tons)

Dutch DD *Banckert*—*P106* (1,316 tons, two 3-inch DP guns, 30 knots)

American tug *Genesee*—*P107* (1,000 tons, two 3-inch DP guns, 15 knots)

Dutch patrol vessel *Arend*—*P108* (954 tons, one 3-inch DP gun, 15 knots)

Dutch patrol vessel *Fazant*—*P109* (592 tons, one 3-inch DP gun, 12 knots)

Note that some of these vessels had undergone considerable alteration. *P106* was also modified to carry two landing craft. *Arayat*, something of a mystery, may have been a Spanish gunboat (launched 1888) taken by the Americans as a war prize, sold into commercial use around 1910, and seized during Japan's conquest of the Philippines. Five other Dutch patrol vessels became Japanese merchantmen.

Japan deployed 13 or 14 AMC armed with medium-caliber guns (mostly 5.5-inch to 6-inch), some with a pair of aircraft, a torpedo battery, or up to 500 mines. They served as raiders more than escorts, but all left combat duty by 1943.

Gunboats

The following gunboats, sloops, and dispatch vessels left active service in the 1930s. Many of these names quickly revived.

YAMATO (1,478 nt, 1887): became a survey vessel, stricken 1935, extant 1945; sistership *Haikan 5* (ex-*Musashi*) scrapped 1931.

CHIHAYA (1,243 nt, 1901): a training ship until 1939.

UJI (620 nt, four 3-inch guns, 13 knots, 1903): a coastal gunboat broken up in 1932.

SUMIDA (126 nt, light guns, 13 knots, 1906): river gunboat broken up in 1935.

FUSHIMI (180 nt, light guns, 14 knots, 1906): river gunboat broken up in 1935.

YODO (1,250 nt, two 3-inch guns, 22 knots, 1908): a survey vessel until hulked in 1940 as *Haikan 13*, extant 1945.

MOGAMI (1,350 nt, 23 knots, 1908): *Yodo*'s half-sister, *Haikan 3* until broken up in 1931.

Most of Japan's gunboats operated along Chinese coasts and rivers, often under puppet Chinese rulers. In addition to the units specified here, 87 merchant ships converted to auxiliary gunboats, 31 of them capable of laying mines.

LICHI (362 tons, one 3-inch gun, seven knots, 1896): a prize from the Russo-Japanese War.

TOBA (215 tons, two 3-inch DP guns, 15 knots, 1911): river gunboat, disarmed in 1945.

SAGA (685 tons; one 4.7-inch, three 3-inch guns; 15 knots, 1912): 3-inch battery became DP before Pearl Harbor.

ATAKA (725 tons; two 4.7-inch, two 3-inch guns; 16 knots, 1923): rebuilt in 1937. She landed one 4.7-inch gun, traded her 3-inchers for DP guns, and gained a couple hundred tons.

SETA, HIRA, HOZU, KATATA (305 tons, two 3-

inch DP guns, 16 knots, 1923): river gunboats, survivors disarmed in 1945.

ATAMI, FUTAMI (206 tons, one 3-inch DP gun, 16.75 knots, 1929–30): river gunboats, disarmed 1945.

KOTAKA (50 tons, light guns, 15.5 knots, 1930): river GB.

Japan's building programs had to meet domestic needs plus those of the Manchukuo puppetry, which maintained its own hodgepodge of small craft. Incomplete records inject uncertainty into any listing of Manchukuo vessels.

HAI KUANG class (45 tons, light guns, 12 knots, 1933): listed as four Manchukuo patrol vessels used for policing.

HAIFENG, HAILUNG (200 tons, two 3-inch guns, 14 knots, 1933): likewise listed as patrol vessels.

TATUNG, LIMIN (65 tons, light guns, 10.5 knots, 1933): GB.

EMIN class (15 tons, light guns, 8.5 knots, 1933): three GB.

CHIMIN (20 tons, light guns, 8.5 knots, 1934): gunboat.

SHUN TIEN, YANG MIN (270 tons, three 4.7-inch DP guns, 12.5 knots, 1934): heavily armed river gunboats.

TING PIEN, CHIN YEN (290 tons, three 4.7-inch DP guns, 13 knots, 1935): similar to previous class.

Most or all of these vessels came from Japanese yards. They were joined in service by other minor combatants and possibly three ex-Tsarist gunboats: *Chiang Ching* and *Chiang Pien* (360

tons, one 3-inch gun, 7.5 knots, 1897–1900) and *Chiang Tung* (250 tons, one 3-inch gun, 4.5 knots, 1903?).

SUMIDA, FUSHIMI (304 tons, one 3-inch DP gun, 17 knots, 1939–40): Japanese river gunboats. The navy abandoned plans for two similar boats.

HASHIDATE, UJI (999 tons, three 4.7-inch guns, 19.7 knots, 1940–41): meant for combat in China, later given depth charges.

The following craft, captured during the 1930s and 1940s, entered Japanese (or Manchukuo) service as gunboats, while others served as noncombatants:

Chinese *Yat Sen—Atada* (1,520 tons, three 3-inch DP guns, 16 knots, 1930).

Chinese *Yung Chien, Yung Chi–Asuka, Hai Hsing* (860 tons; one 4-inch, one 3-inch gun; 13 knots, 1915): the former became a repair ship, then an AA ship (3-inch DP and light guns).

Chinese *Kiang Chen, Kiang Heng, Kiang Li*—not renamed (550 tons; one 4.7-inch, one 3-inch gun; 13 knots, 1907).

Six Chinese *Ning* class(?)—*Bunsei* class (400 tons, light guns, 12 knots, 1932–36).

Chinese *Chen Shen*—not renamed (275 tons, one 3-inch gun, 10 knots, 1900).

Chinese *Li Chieh*—*Lisui* (266 tons, light guns, 13 knots, 1903).

Chinese *Kiang Hsi, Kiang Kun*—not renamed (150 tons, one 3.4-inch howitzer, 10 knots, 1911–12).

British *Moth*—*Suma* (625 tons; two 6-inch, one 3-inch DP gun; 14 knots, 1916).

American *Wake*—*Tatara* (370 tons, two 3-inch guns, 14.5 knots, 1927).

American *Luzon*—*Karatsu* (560 tons, two 3-inch guns, 16 knots, 1928).

Dutch *Regulus*, *Ram*—*Nankai*, *Nanshin* (2,200 tons, three 3-inch DP guns, mines, 18 knots, 1944): begun as ML; the latter never completed but would have mounted four 4.7-inch guns.

Portuguese *Macau*—*Maiko* (95 tons, light guns, 11.75 knots, 1910): seized in 1943 due to Portugal's pro-Allied policies.

Italian *Lepanto*—*Okitsu* (615 tons; two 4-inch, one 3-inch DP gun, 80 mines; 14 knots, 1927): scuttled by Italians in 1943, raised by Japanese in 1944 and rearmed with one gun (3-inch DP).

Italian *Ermanno Carlotto*—*Narumi* (180 tons, two 3-inch DP guns, 14 knots, 1921): disarmed 1945.

French *Mytho*—captured just before or just after sinking.

Twenty-seven of Japan's small combatants (minor gunboats and armed launches) fell into Soviet hands in 1945.

Motor Boats

Japan's motor boat program got its start in 1920 with the purchase of four Thornycroft CMB (14 nt, two 17.7-inch TT, 40 knots). These craft, at least one of which survived the 1930s, failed to inspire further development. In 1940, the Japanese made another purchase, this time from Italy: one H1-class boat, creatively named *1* (18.5 tons, two 17.7-inch TT removed by 1941, 33 knots, 1940). This MGB entered a series of comparative trials with a pair of MTB seized in China (*Kuai 1, 2?*: 13 tons, 1918) and the first Japanese-built boat (19 tons, two 17.7-inch TT,

36 knots, 1940). On the basis of these trials, a production program took shape. The initial surge of Pacific conquest provided for further comparison with the capture of the Filipino *Q111* (renamed *114*) and the Dutch *TM3–21* (renamed *101–113, 115–120,* not respectively; few entered service). This mass of foreign input, however, profited nothing. Japanese motor boats proved inferior to all others.

T1 class (17 tons, two 17.7-inch TT, 38.5 knots, 1941): six MTB based on the comparative trials, numbered *1–6*.

Under German influence, the navy built a large prototype, *10* (80 tons, four 17.7-inch TT, 30 knots, 1942).

T51 class (75 tons, two 17.7-inch TT, 29 knots, 1943–45): based on *10*, 35 MTB planned (*11–27, 5441–5458*) but only the first seven completed. These were intended as leaders for MTB flotillas, but their fragility and dimensions left them unsuited to the open waters of the Pacific. Their armament (three 25mm guns and two small torpedoes) and their speed put them in a much lower class than the S-boats that inspired them. They spent most of the war in AS escort and patrol work with their speed reduced.

The navy lost interest in large designs and focused on developing smaller craft of the Italian lineage. Planners issued a 20-ton specification based on the T1 class, and construction began in 1943 with about 800 boats planned. Due to the differing facilities of individual builders and a constant search for adequate engines, the single specification fragmented into several variants. Armament remained constant at one light gun and two 17.7-inch torpedoes. The listings below indicate possible hull number assignments and a rough estimate of completions. These boats, of dubious ancestry and disparate in quality, had no hope of countering the sting of American PT-swarms.

T23 class (17 knots): 19–23 boats, *201–207, 401–410, 451–456*.

T25 class (21.5 knots): 6–55 boats, *468, 484–488*.

T31 class (20 knots): 14–33 boats, *208–240*.

T32 class (21.5 knots): 8–12 boats, *301–308*.

T33 class (21 knots): 6–39 boats, *500–505*.

T34 class (27.5 knots): 6–15 boats, *151–165*.

T35 class (35 knots): 8–55 boats, *469, 482, 483, 494–499, 529–537, 801–837*.

T36 class (21.5 knots): 44 boats, *411–450, 470–473*.

T37 class (25 knots): perhaps 23 boats, *327-?*

T38 class (27.5 knots): 80 boats, *241–286, 457–467, 506–528*.

T39 class (27 knots): 2–8 boats, *474–481*.

The number of completions neared 300, with at least 238 as MTB and others as simple launches.

T14 class (15 tons, two 17.7-inch TT, 33 knots, 1944–45): the first of two coastal MTB classes. At least 47 T14 boats (*538–555, 839–848, 871–889*) reached completion; about 14 others did not.

T15 class (15 tons, two 17.7-inch TT, 35 knots, 1944–45): similar to the previous class. At least 29 boats reached completion: *1001–1008, 1011–1031*. These boats carried the same armament as the 20-ton type with a good turn of speed, but their size restricted them to coastal work.

Including the Italian-built H1 type, the navy deployed 106 MGB. All could take on a battery of two 17.7-inch torpedoes.

H2 class (25 tons, light guns, 33.5 knots, 1942–43): eight MGB based on the H1 design, numbered *2–9*.

H35 class (25 tons, light guns, 34 knots, 1943–44): MGB with T35 class hulls. The Japanese assigned numbers *27–32, 201–217* but completed only about 12 or 13 boats, plus three unarmed craft used for training and torpedo recovery.

H38 class (25 tons, light guns, 27 knots, 1943–44): MGB with T38 hulls. Of boats *10-26, 51–100*, about 40 entered service.

H61 class (26 tons, light guns, 17.5 knots, 1944–45): MGB equipped with wheezing diesel engines. Orders for boats *33–46, 101–124, 218–245* produced about 54 completions.

The army built some vessels along similar lines but without torpedoes. The Type I (about 60 boats: 80 tons full load, light guns, 23? knots, 1944–45), intended for transport duty, instead provided AS work. Thirty or so smaller boats (18 tons, light guns, 37.3 knots) commissioned before war's end.

The navy developed few standard launch designs. Plans for a hundred multi-purpose craft (9.5 tons, nine knots, 1945) turned into just 27 completions. Some designs for ships' boats also served in local AS patrols: the 17-meter (23 tons full, 10.5 knots), 15-meter (12 tons full, 13.5 knots), and 12-meter Types (8 tons full, 10.5 knots). Three riverine designs operated in China; the 19-meter (48 boats?: 19 knots, 1936–38) and 15-meter Types (38 boats?: 11 knots, 1938–39) both mounted one machine gun and displaced about 10 tons, while the 25-ton Type (77 boats?: 11 knots, 1940–44) had two guns and thin armor to guard against small arms. Desperation sometimes forced the 25-tonners into AS escort. The army had its own 17-meter armored GB design (13 knots) and a smaller wooden type (11 knots), both armed with machine guns.

The *Shinyo* boats (1–2 tons, 18–30 knots, 1944–45), suicide craft carrying two depth charges or a contact explosive (usually 551 lbs), sometimes mounted a pair of 4.7-inch rockets as well. The navy built 6,200 units, and the army added 3,000 similar craft, some with rockets providing spurts of 50–60 knots.

LATVIA

Like its Baltic neighbors, Latvia found itself and its navy absorbed into the Soviet Union in 1940.

RONIS, SPIDOLA (390/514 tons, one 3-inch DP gun, six 17.7-inch TT, 14/9.25 knots, 1926): French-built SS with traversing mounts for four tubes. They retained their Latvian names in Soviet service.

VIRSAITIS (539 tons, two 3.5-inch DP guns, 16 knots, 1916): GB, a former German Type 1915 MS. The guns may have been 3-inchers. In Soviet service, she became *T297*.

IMANTA, VIESTURS (256 tons, one 3-inch DP gun, 30 mines, 14 knots, 1927): French-built MS. Under the Soviets, they became *T299, 298*.

The navy had other small craft, including a coast guard vessel and some launches. Most of these vessels, perhaps all, continued in Soviet service.

LEBANON

The only naval presence in Lebanon belonged to the French, as did Lebanon itself by mandate.

The struggle between Vichy and the British-backed Free French ended in an Allied victory prompting Lebanon to declare war against Germany and Japan in 1945.

LIBERIA

The Liberians lacked a navy of their own, but they made bases available to the Americans in 1942. An official declaration of war came in 1944.

LITHUANIA

After losing some of its territory to Germany, Lithuania lost itself completely, annexed by the Soviet Union in 1940. The tiny Lithuanian navy became Soviet property. The largest vessel, the patrol boat *Primunas* (ex-*Antanas Smetona*: about 500 tons, 16 knots, 1917), was a former German Type 1915 MS carrying two guns (4-inch or 4.1-inch). The Soviets—those inveterate renamers—dubbed her *Otlichnik*, then *Korall*. The only other vessels were some small motor boats.

LUXEMBOURG

Luxembourg vanished beneath a carpet of German panzers on May 10, 1940. The land-locked country lacked even a riverine flotilla.

MEXICO

Mexico declared war on the Axis on May 22, 1942, and took an active role in the hostilities, though its navy had only local capabilties.

BRAVO (1,227 tons, two 4-inch guns, 12.25

knots, 1903): old gunboat; sistership *Blanquet* was discarded prewar.

PROGRESO (1,590 tons, light guns, 13 knots, 1907): gunboat and transport used for training.

ACAPULCO, MAZATLÁN, VERA CRUZ (486 tons, light guns, eight knots, 1918): ex-Canadian trawlers.

GUANAJUATO, POTOSÍ, QUERÉTARO (1,300 tons, three 4-inch guns, 20 knots, 1934): Spanish-built sloops.

G20–29 (130 tons, light guns, 26 knots, 1935): gunboats designed in Britain with French guns and German machinery.

DURANGO (1,600 tons, two 4-inch guns, 20 knots, 1935): gunboat and transport built in Spain; sistership *Zacatecas* was retained there as *Calvo Sotelo*. The design provided transportation for 490 personnel and 80 horses.

Mexico received six vessels from the United States: three *SC1466* class vessels and three 83-foot type cutters.

MONACO

Monaco spent much of the war under Axis occupation. The Monegasques had no navy or military of any sort, but after the liberation in summer 1944, individuals had the opportunity to join Allied forces.

MONGOLIA

Straddling the border between Japanese and Soviet spheres of influence, Mongolia had no independent policy and no navy.

THE NETHERLANDS

The Dutch managed to navigate around the First World War, but Hitler had no intention of letting them miss the Second. His troops attacked the Netherlands as part of the Western Offensive in May 1940.

In its European deployment, the Dutch navy was a humble coast defense force, mostly minecraft and gunboats, powerless against the great threat that lay overland. In the Far East, however, the navy stood in position to oppose enemy movement through the Indies. Unfortunately, the Indies defenses never grew into a significant obstacle to the Japanese onslaught.

Though few in number, Dutch warships embodied a rich maritime tradition. Designers combined their penchant for innovation with a readiness to follow foreign successes. It was the Dutch who introduced the world to the Swedish Bofors gun and installed it in a new mount, unexcelled in performance though too complex for mass production. Dutch fire-control equipment displayed a similarly high degree of sophistication, and the Dutch invented an air-intake apparatus for submarines which the conquering Germans developed into the snorkel.

Naval Aviation

The Dutch lagged behind premier naval powers in the area of naval aviation, neither designing nor operating a fleet carrier during the war. While some thought went into modifying merchant ships as carriers after the German conquest, the exiled government had no such resources. However, Dutch crews did man two Royal Navy MAC ships, *Gadila* and *Macoma*.

Coast Defense and Dreadnoughts

The accommodation vessel *Koning der Nederlanden* (5,285 tons, disarmed, 11.75 knots,

Ordnance

GUN	SW	RANGE	NOTES
11.1/50	694	46,590	Design 1047
11.1/42.5	595	17,600	*Soerabaia*
9.4/40	375		*Vlieereede, IJmuiden*
5.9/50	103	23,200	*Sumatra*s
	103		*Tromp, De Ruyter, Flores* class, *van Nassau*
4.7/50	53	21,300?	*Van Ghent*s
	53		*Van Galen*s, *van der Zaan, Van Kinsbergen*
4.7/45	45		*Tjerk Hiddes* class, *K1–7*
4.7/40?	52		*Gelderland*
4.1/50	40		*Brinio*s
3.5/45	22		*O21* class, *K VIII* class
3/55	13		*Jan van Amstel*s
3/30	13		old TB, *K VII*

Dutch weaponry performed well, but some issues remain unclear. For example, the slightly differing batteries on *Van Ghent* and *Van Galen* elevated to either 30° or 35°, and thus may have had different ranges.

TORPEDO	WW	RANGE		NOTES
17.7-inch III45	364	2,200/40		mostly in SS
21-inch I53	551	4,400/39	10,900/26	early SS model
21-inch V53	661–771	4,400/45	13,100/28	SS model introduced shortly before war

A few elderly 17.7-inch torpedoes (187-lb warheads, range near 1,100 yards at 30 knots) served mostly in practice and could be fired from 21-inch tubes. Dutch units operating from American and British bases sometimes resorted to American, British, and German torpedoes.

1875) formerly mounted four 11.1-inch and four 4.7-inch guns as a turret ship.

VLIEEREEDE (4,560 tons; one 9.4-inch, four 5.9-inch, two 3-inch guns; 16 knots, 1903): a battery ship laid up for disposal in 1939, but seized by the Germans and renamed *Ariadne* as an AA vessel.

IJMUIDEN (4,445 tons, two 9.4-inch guns, 16 knots, 1907): a battery ship that became the German AA ship *Undine*.

SOERABAIA (5,644 tons; two 11.1-inch, two 3-inch guns; 16 knots, 1910): a coast defense vessel providing gunnery training in the Far East. After her scuttling, the Japanese raised her for use as a blockship.

These coast defense ships showed relatively good sea-going characteristics, but their 16 knots made them easy targets for the dreadnoughts emerging in major navies. A proposal for enlarged "armored ships" to serve in the Far East included an increase in firepower, resembling Sweden's later *Sverige*-class armored ships, but with little increase in speed. The idea sputtered amid admiring glances toward Spain's humble *España* design which, slightly enlarged, seemed a good match to Dutch needs. As wing turrets revealed their shortcomings, the navy specified a centerline armament, toying with quad mounts before settling on conventional superimposed twins, resulting in a modern battleship that featured modest armor with excellent underwater protection and good habitability. The Dutch approached foreign firms for as many as nine units. German builders submitted the most promising design (24,606 nt; eight 14-inch, sixteen 5.9-inch, twelve 3-inch guns, five 21-inch? TT; 22 knots). Questions remain about the torpedo armament; German ships at that time were escalating from 19.7-inch to 23.6-inch. Planners scheduled the first keel-laying for December 1914, but the guns of August shot the plan to pieces.

In the late 1930s, Japanese belligerence caused the Dutch much concern. In reviewing their position, they reasoned that any aggression in the Pacific would pit Japan's dreadnoughts against those of Britain and America, leaving the Dutch to cope only with cruisers. That called for a design impervious to 8-inch shellfire and equipped with a gun no cruiser could withstand. Planners wanted three such vessels, with the first completion to come in 1944.

Designers received assistance from Italian and German sources, especially the latter, and Design 1047 (27,988 tons; nine 11.1-inch, twelve 4.7-inch DP guns; AC 3, 34 knots) looked distinctly *Scharnhorst*ian, as in its main battery. However, the 11.1-inch guns differed from German models and had 45° elevation. Antiaircraft fire would have benefited from the 40mm Bofors and dual-purpose secondaries. Details of the 4.7-inch model remain uncertain (possibly 10–12 rpm and a range of 21,870 yards with 80° elevation).

Planners never finalized the protection scheme. The armor had enough thickness to manage 8-inch shells but little else. Yet in other regards, Design 1047 surpassed *Scharnhorst*. The anti-torpedo system had greater depth, and would likely have benefitted from the layers that bolstered most non-German systems. Deck protection, concentrated atop the belt, accommodated the boilers with no vulnerable "hump." The machinery itself showed better dispersal. In specifying a reliable and serviceable power plant, the Dutch wisely rejected German specifications, which would likely repeat the typical German machinery problems.

Design 1047 met Dutch requirements quite well, but even if the German invasion hadn't interfered, the three ships would have arrived too late to save the Indies. Their presence in 1942 would have transformed the strategic picture and forced Japan to redeploy for the East Indies campaign; the Emperor's CA could not match the Dutch BC. Design 1047 belonged in the same class as the French *Dunkerque* and the American *Alaska*; while lacking in firepower compared to those two rivals, the Dutch ship was in some ways a more balanced combatant.

The exiled Dutch mulled over the idea of acquiring *Texas* and *New York* for their East Indies defenses, though common sense likely prevented their broaching the subject with the Americans.

Cruisers

The relic *Koningin Emma der Nederlanden* (3,528 tons, disarmed, 15 knots, 1880) had been a cruiser mounting six 6.7-inch and eight 4.7-inch guns; a hulk since 1900, she continued as such after her capture by the Germans.

GELDERLAND (3,542 tons; eight 4.7-inch, four 3-inch guns; 16 knots, 1899): cruiser used for gunnery training until 1939. The navy then disarmed her and considered using her as an accommodation ship. Of her five sister ships, only *Noord Brabant* remained, disarmed prewar. The Germans took both ships; a fire destroyed *Noord Brabant*, but *Gelderland* became an AA vessel. Renamed *Niobe*, she showed some spunk; swarmed over by bombers, she lasted for nine hits and two hours, while her German gunners shot down nine planes.

SUMATRA, JAVA (6,670 tons, ten 5.9-inch guns, 12 mines, AC 2, 31 knots, 1925–26): designed in 1915 and scheduled for a 1918 completion, but greatly delayed by the war. The program included a third unit, *Celebes*, but the Dutch canceled her in favor of future construction, which they then put off for ten years.

Mounting her intended battery of 5.9-inch guns, the Dutch Tromp *ranked among the best of the small cruisers.*

Powerful ships at the time of their design, they were irredeemably obsolete when completed, among the last of the WWI-style light cruisers. A refit replaced the original secondary battery (four 3-inch DP) with a batch of 40mm guns. Subsequent designs also chose the 40mm in place of DP guns, but as good as the Bofors was, it couldn't fully substitute for heavy AA. The Dutch tried providing high elevation for CL main batteries, but this halfway measure proved futile.

A well-worn *Sumatra* lay awaiting refit at the time of the German invasion. She managed to withdraw to Britain and eventually made her way to the Far East, where she lay in neglect until the Japanese attacked. Barely escaping the war zone with a partial crew and power plant, she crawled back to Britain. Her guns transferred to *Flores* and *Soemba*, and *Sumatra* ended her career sunk as a breakwater off Normandy.

DE RUYTER (6,450 tons, seven 5.9-inch guns, AC 2, 32 knots, 1936): a replacement for the *Celebes*. The initial design featured a main battery in three twin turrets on a 5,250-ton displacement; this qualified as a modern layout, but not one likely to impress an enemy. Despite later growth, the plan never met contemporary standards of firepower or protection. It did show Dutch technical expertise in its fire control and light AA outfit.

Cruiser shells and a Long Lance wrecked *De Ruyter*. She was the first Dutch design to mount a 60° main battery and the last to lack torpedoes.

TROMP, JACOB VAN HEEMSKERCK (3,787 tons, six 5.9-inch guns, six 21-inch TT, AC 1, 33.5 knots, 1938–40): conceived as 2500-ton flotilla leaders, enlarged into scout cruisers retaining a load of depth charges. Both ships fled to England in 1940, *Heemskerck* still without her main battery. The British armed her with ten 4-inch DP guns and no torpedoes. *Tromp* later took on four American 3/50 DP. The original layout had no catapult, and neither ship spent much time with a plane aboard.

Displacing less than 60% of *De Ruyter's* tonnage, *Tromp's* design improved on the larger ship in almost every way. With only one less main gun, *Tromp* had a similar 40mm battery, plus six torpedoes. Protection amounted to 13% of displacement, but a thoughtful armor scheme provided as much durability as such small warships could hope for. However, they lacked *De Ruyter's* AA fire control. In general, the *Tromp*s proved successful, superior to any like-sized rivals, and they saw extensive service.

DE ZEVEN PROVINCIËN, EENDRACHT (8,350 tons, ten 5.9-inch guns, six 21-inch TT, AC 2, 32 knots): a much improved development of the *De Ruyter*. Armor thickness doubled in some areas and tripled in others. A combination of twin and triple turrets provided good firepower.

The war interrupted construction. Germany gave some thought to completing the ships as *KH1, 2*. The 5.9-inch mounts, on order from Sweden, remained there and later went to sea aboard the Swedish *Tre Kronor* class. Ultimately, the Dutch completed the ships postwar with extensive alterations and new names.

Destroyers and Torpedo Boats

G2 (144 tons, light guns, 25 knots, 1905): TB no longer on active list, usable for patrol work only. The Germans renamed her *TFA10* and may have given her three 17.7-inch TT. *G1, 3–12* left service by 1919.

CHRISTIAAN CORNELIS (48 tons, light guns, 18 knots, 1906): former TB, last of three sisters, didn't survive 1940.

G13, 15, 16 (180 tons, two 3-inch guns, three 17.7-inch TT, 25 knots, 1914): TB, *G14* scrapped prewar. *G16* became the German *TFA9*, but the other two escaped to the British, who scrapped them in 1943.

In 1914, Germany seized four TB, *Z1–4*, under construction for the Netherlands. (One of them became Poland's *Mazur*.) The Dutch then set out to build their own copies, but material shortages delayed their completion until post-war. Three retired in the 1930s, and *Z3* (277 tons, two 3-inch guns, four 17.7-inch TT, 27 knots) lasted only to 1940.

Z5–8 (263 tons, two 3-inch guns, four 17.7-inch TT, 27 knots, 1915–16): TB, entered service before *Z1–4*. *Z5* became a PB prewar with 22 knots and no TT. She escaped to England with her sisters and commissioned with the Royal Navy as *Blade*, used mostly as a submarine tender. The British scrapped two of the others.

Armed with British 4-inch guns, the Dutch Isaac Sweers *arrives at Malta after victory in the Battle of Cape Bon.*

VAN GHENT, EVERTSEN, KORTENAER, PIET HEIN (1,310 tons; four 4.7-inch, two 3-inch DP guns, six 21-inch TT, 24 mines; 36 knots, 1928): Dutch-built DD based on a British design similar to *Ambuscade*. Each ship originally carried one seaplane.

VAN GALEN, WITTE DE WITH, BANCKERT, VAN NES (1,316 tons; four 4.7-inch, one 3-inch DP gun, six 21-inch TT; 36 knots, 1929–31): only slightly different from previous class, fitted for minesweeping instead of minelaying. Endurance was 3,300 miles at 15 knots, a marginal increase. The designed range of the 4.7-inch model indicates a powerful weapon. However, it may be that the guns suffered neglect, as some accounts say *Van Galen* had her gunnery limited to about 15,000 yards by barrel erosion.

Though modern in design these ships lacked the numbers to confront their powerful enemies. The Japanese captured *Banckert* after her scuttling and renamed her *P106*, but they never got her back into service.

TJERK HIDDES, GERARD CALLENBURGH, ISAAC SWEERS, PHILIPS VAN ALMONDE (1,604 tons, five 4.7-inch guns, eight 21-inch TT, 24 mines, AC 1, 37.5 knots, 1940–42): a powerful design with eight more units planned. The increased tonnage made them more seaworthy than previous DD and provided good endurance, 5,400 miles at 19 knots. The 4.7-inch guns resembled those in gunboats *K1–7*. Questions persist about these weapons; they ranged to about 17,500 yards, but their mounts (two twins and one single) probably lacked elevation for AA fire.

The German invasion found the ships incomplete. Workmen wrecked *Callenburgh*, *Hiddes*, and *Almonde*. The Germans salvaged only *Callenburgh* and put her into service as *ZH1*. *Sweers*, semi-complete, made it to England at the end of a towline. Since she hadn't received her main battery, she took on six

British 4-inch DP guns. However, she came equipped with four Bofors, and these garnered instant envy from British DD crews. Neither she nor *ZH1* ever shipped a seaplane.

As the Dutch destroyer force dwindled—only *Sweers* survived past February 1942, and sank the following November—the government purchased two British ships under construction. *Noble* and *Nonpareil* became *Van Galen* and *Tjerk Hiddes*. The old *Campbeltown* (ex-American flush-decker *Buchanan*) and an ex-French *Melpomène*-class TB also served temporarily with the Dutch.

Submarines

After some early, lackluster designs, the Dutch submarine force matured into a menacing opponent, the most dangerous arm of the Netherlands navy. Strong and reliable, well armed, fast with good sea-keeping, the boats showed good balance of design. They overcame their limited numbers and a lack of proper facilities, and operated effectively until they wore out.

Until 1937, O-numbers indicated boats intended for European waters while the K-boats and their Roman numerals kept to the Far East.

O7 (176/206 tons, three 17.7-inch TT, 11.5/8.5 knots, 1916): decommissioned November 1939.

O8 (343/433 tons, four 17.7-inch TT, 11.5/8 knots, 1916): ex-British *H6*, one of the ubiquitous American-designed H-boats, interned in Dutch waters in 1916. The Germans took her in 1940 and used her for training, renamed *UD1*.

During World War II, the British submarines *Sturgeon*, *Talent*, *Tarn*, and *P47* were transferred to the Netherlands as *Zeehond*, *Zwaardvisch*, *Tijgerhaai*, and *Dolfijn*. Apart from the British units, all Dutch boats came from domestic yards.

K VII (507/639 tons, one 3-inch gun, six 17.7-inch TT, 13/8 knots, 1922): the last of three sisters, aged and small. Two tubes sat in an external traversing mount.

K VIII–X (521/712 tons, one 3.5-inch DP gun, four 17.7-inch TT, 15/9.5 knots, 1922–23): developed from American designs. The 3.5-inch shells weighed 22 lbs. Two of these old boats escaped to Australia in 1942 but gave no further active service.

Modern Dutch submarines like O15 rivaled the designs of the major fleets in quality, but not in numbers.

K XI–XIII (611/815 tons; one 3.5-inch DP gun, two 21-inch, four 17.7-inch TT; 15/8 knots, 1924–25): based on the *K VIII* but with a stronger hull and heavier armament—the first hint of Dutch sub potential. Two of these boats operated from Australia until 1944.

O9–11 (483/647 tons; one 3.5-inch gun, two 21-inch, three 17.7-inch TT; 12/8 knots, 1926): a reduced *K XI* design. The first pair escaped to operate from Britain; the Germans captured and scuttled *O11*.

O12–15 (546/704 tons, five 21-inch TT, 15/8 knots, 1931–32): a much improved design. They introduced a light AA battery of two "wet" 40mm Bofors guns, standard on all subsequent designs. Their range, 3,500 miles at 10 knots, was average among Dutch boats. The Germans captured *O12* and used her as *UD2*.

K XIV–XVIII (771/1,000 tons, one 3.5-inch DP gun, eight 21-inch TT, 17/9 knots, 1933): based on *O12* with two TT in a revolving external mount. The last pair had a slightly higher tonnage. The Japanese raised the scuttled *K XVIII* for use as a radar hulk.

O16 (896/1,170 tons, one 3.5-inch DP gun, eight 21-inch TT, 18/9 knots, 1936): similar to the previous class, including external TT.

O19, 20 (998/1,536 tons, one 3.5-inch DP gun, eight 21-inch TT, 40 mines, 19.25/9 knots, 1939): based on *Orzeł* class built for the Polish navy. A blend of the archaic and the futuristic, this design retained outdated external tubes while introducing the primitive proto-snorkel. The Dutch originally named the boats *K XIX, XX* before deciding to discontinue the use of K-numbers.

O21–27 (881/1,186 tons, one 3.5-inch DP gun, eight 21-inch TT, 19.5/9 knots, 1940–41): an *O19* design modified with no mines but still two external TT. Range grew to 7,100 miles at 10 knots. Germany took the last three boats incomplete and finished them as *UD3–5*.

Minecraft

HYDRA, MEDUSA (593nt, three 3-inch DP guns, 70 mines, 12 knots, 1911): coastal ML.

DOUWE AUKES, VAN MEERLANT (687 tons, three 3-inch DP guns, 108 mines, 13 knots, 1921–22): improved *Hydra*s. In 1941, *Aukes* became a convoy leader with one 3-inch DP.

PRO PATRIA (537 tons, one 3-inch DP gun, 80 mines, 10 knots, 1922): coastal ML, perhaps with only 60 mines.

KRAKATAU (982 tons, two 3-inch DP guns, 150 mines, 15.5 knots, 1924): ML.

NAUTILUS (800 tons, two 3-inch DP guns, 40 mines, 15 knots, 1930): patrol vessel and minelayer. Some sources list her with 60 mines.

PRINS VAN ORANJE, GOUDEN LEEUW (1,291 tons, two 3-inch DP guns, 150 mines, 15 knots, 1931): ML.

JAN VAN BRAKEL (740 tons, two 3-inch DP guns, 80 mines, 15 knots, 1936): similar to *Nautilus* in design and function.

WILLEM VAN DER ZAAN (1,267 tons, two 4.7-inch guns, 120 mines, AC 1, 15.5 knots, 1939): ML also used for training. The seaplane had no catapult. Like most Dutch ML in home waters, *van der Zaan* escaped to England. There she gave the Royal Navy its first demonstration of the 40mm Bofors. Some records list her as carrying 92 mines, probably her load while serving with the British.

RAM, REGULUS (2,400 tons, three 3-inch DP guns, 80 mines, 18 knots): ML with perhaps up to 160 mines, both incomplete in 1942, sabotaged prior to capture. The Japanese renamed them *Nanshin* and *Nankai* but completed only the former.

The Dutch had just begun another minelayer in the Far East (about 2000 tons, two 4-inch guns, mines, 19 knots) before having to wreck her. Five auxiliary ML were commissioned for war service.

M1–4 (205–238 tons, light guns, 10 knots, 1916–18): coastal MS, converted tugs. In German service, *M1, 4* performed various duties under various names before being sold for commercial use.

A–D (179 tons, light guns, 14.5 knots, 1929–30): coastal MS. The first three became Japanese submarine-chasers *Cha113, 112, 116*.

JAN VAN AMSTEL class (460 tons, one 3-inch gun, 15 knots, 1936–40): nine MS, plus five more canceled. One unit struck a mine and sank in September 1939. The Germans captured three (including one they had to complete themselves) as *M551–553*.

ARDJOENO class (75 tons, light guns, 15 knots, 1937): five coastal MS. All became Japanese: *Cha102, 104, 109, 110, 118*.

MERBABOE class (80 tons, light guns, 10 knots, 1937): three coastal MS.

ALOR class (131 tons, light guns, 12 knots, 1938): seven coastal MS. One became the Japanese *Cha117*.

DJEMBER class (175 tons, light guns, 12.5 knots, 1940–43): nine coastal MS planned in two slightly differing series. The Dutch completed only six units; the Japanese got seven into service, assigning them hull numbers *Wa101–107*.

MERAPI class (65 tons, light guns, 10 knots, 1942): three coastal MS scuttled incomplete, one salvaged by Japan as *Cha101*.

Mv I–IV, XI, XII (49 tons, light guns, 10 knots, 1940): MMS, in German service as *RA51–56*.

Fragmentary records refer to the German-built *Mv V-X* (55 tons, light guns, 24 knots, 1940). If completed, they may have served with the Germans.

The British transferred 10 *MMS1*-class and eight *MMS1001*-class vessels to the Netherlands. The Dutch deployed 34 of their own auxiliary MS, mostly trawlers and the like (100–400 grt) plus some tugs.

Gunboats

BRAGA class (223–244 tons, light guns, 4–7 knots?, 1878–79): originally a class of 16 ships, at least 12 still extant in 1939, 10 in active service. When first built, they mounted an 11-inch muzzle-loader.

Five of these vessels converted to ML with 24 mines. One became a minesweeper. The others remained as gunboats, some with a 3-inch or 4.7-inch gun. The Germans seized or salvaged all of them, then set about scrapping the lot. One, *Tyr*, may have given some service before her scrapping.

Two similarly aged GB, *Sperwer* and *Brak*, existed as hulks.

SERDANG (680 tons, light guns, 13 knots, 1898): old sloop, built with three 4.7-inch guns. She may have retained one 3-inch gun. She served for a time as a minelayer, then a depot ship.

BRINIO, FRISO, GRUNO (542nt, four 4.1-inch guns, 14 knots, 1913): armored gunboats intended to guard the coast against raiding destroyers. They lacked the necessary speed for this role and, by 1940, the necessary firepower. Only *Gruno* escaped to Britain.

THE NETHERLANDS

The Soemba *underway with awnings rigged. The Dutch were quick to grasp the importance of habitability in their ships.*

FLORES, SOEMBA (1,457 tons; three 5.9-inch, one 3-inch DP gun; AC 1, 15 knots, 1925): for reconnaissance and harbor defense. They landed the DP gun and seaplane during the war and replaced their main battery with guns removed from *Sumatra*.

JOHAN MAURITS VAN NASSAU (1,520 tons, three 5.9-inch guns, AC 1, 15 knots, 1932): a *Flores* repeat; probably did not carry a plane.

VAN KINSBERGEN (1,760 tons, four 4.7-inch guns, 25.5 knots, 1939): sloop used for training and escort. In operations with the Royal Navy, she shipped British AS gear.

Britain gave the Dutch a "Flower"-class corvette, a "River" class frigate, and 18 trawlers. The Americans supplied a PC-craft. The Dutch themselves had several designs in the works when Germany invaded: seven GB planned (*K1–7*: designed as 1,180 tons, four 4.7-inch guns, 19 knots—only first three completed, by the Germans), four 328-ton SC (none completed: one 3-inch gun, 24 knots), and eighteen 395-ton SC (none completed: light guns, 24 knots).

The Dutch employed 44 auxiliary PB (mostly pilot boats and tugs with BV-numbers).

The following vessels served in the East Indies for administration and law enforcement in peacetime and patrol duty in war. A rather merchant-like group, most captured units gave mercantile service with the Japanese.

ALBATROS (807 tons, light guns?, 12.25 knots, 1912): salvaged by Japan.

ALDEBARAN (725 tons, light guns?, 12.25 knots, 1913).

BELLATRIX, CANOPUS, DENEB (763–773 tons, light guns?, 12.25 knots, 1914–15): first pair salvaged by Japan.

GEMMA (795 tons, light guns?, 12.25 knots, 1919): salvaged by Japan.

ERIDANUS (926 tons, light guns, 12 knots, 1918): salvaged by Japan.

SIRIUS, WEGA (936 tons, one 3-inch gun, 12.25 knots, 1922–23).

FOMALHOUT (800 tons, light guns?, 13.5 knots, 1923).

MEREL (592 tons, light guns?, 12 knots, 1928).

AREND, VALK (775 tons, two 3-inch guns, AC 1, 18 knots, 1929–30): sloop-like rather than mercantile in nature; became Japanese patrol boats *P108, 104.*

FAZANT, REIGER (592 tons, one 3-inch gun, 12 knots, 1930): the former salvaged as the Japanese patrol boat *P109.*

RIGEL plus one more planned (1,631 tons, two 3-inch DP guns, 150 mines, 12.5 knots, 1931): yacht and ML scuttled by the Dutch, raised by the Japanese but not placed in service.

A handful of other craft provided miscellaneous services. The most warlike were two survey vessels, *Willibrord Snellius* (930 tons, one 3-inch gun, 10.5 knots, 1928) and *Tydeman* (1,160 tons, one 3-inch gun?, 10 knots, 1916). In addition to *Arend* and *Valk*, a few others may have serviced seaplanes: *Fazant, Reiger, Sirius*, and the lighthouse tender *Poolster* (1,565 tons, two 3-inch guns, 12 knots, 1939). The Japanese captured *Tydeman* and *Poolster.*

Motor Boats

TM3 (13 tons, two 17.7-inch TT, 32 knots, 1938): MTB with endless engine troubles, gladly scuttled in 1942. Salvaged and renamed *101* by the Japanese, she didn't work for them either.

TM51 (32 tons, two 21-inch TT, 42 knots, 1939–40): British-built. The Dutch brought her home incomplete, lest Britain seize her as the war began. Completed in time to fight the Germans, she had to flee back to Britain where she eventually joined the Royal Navy as *MGB46.*

The Dutch had intended to build as many as 19 additional units. *T52, 53* began construc-

tion but reached completion under the Germans as *S201, 202.* They were then transferred to Bulgaria. Four further completions went to the Romanians.

TM4–21 (18 tons, two 17.7-inch TT, 33.25 knots, 1940–42): MTB. The Dutch completed only a dozen, then scuttled the whole class. The Japanese gave them hull numbers *102–113, 115–120.* Apparently most of them entered service, but grudgingly, fitted with troublesome aircraft engines.

TM54–61 (57 tons, two 21-inch TT, 34 knots, 1940–41): incomplete MTB similar to Germany's *S2.* The Germans finished them as *S151–158*, then transferred the last four to Bulgaria.

The identities and fates of the boats the Germans built (*TM51* and *TM54* types) remain unclear. The Romanians got four, and the Bulgarians as many as eight.

TM22–37 (32 tons, four 17.7-inch TT, 45 knots, 1942): American- and Canadian-built MTB similar to *TM51.* The Americans retained four (*PT368–371*), and the Royal Navy took three as target boats.

Britain supplied the Netherlands with 13 MTB and five Fairmile "B" launches.

Four standard motor launch designs commissioned in wartime:

P1–8: 23–26 tons, light guns, 9–12.5 knots, 1939–40.

P9–16: 26 tons, light guns, 13 knots, 1941.

P17–23: 40 tons, light guns, 18 knots, 1941–42.

B1–16: 130 tons, one 3-inch gun, 18 knots, 1942.

Four tugs took P-numbers as well (*P37–40*: about 30 tons, light guns, 10 knots, 1942). The Japanese took several P-boats and renamed one *Cha111* for active service. They also re-engined seven captured B-boats (most gained a knot or two) as *Cha103, 105–108, 114, 115*.

A 95-ton, 18-knot AS craft may have begun building in the Far East. Other motor AS boats entered service with light guns, including *S3–6* (26 tons, 30 knots, 1942), *S1, 2* (American-built: 15 tons, 28 knots, 1942), and *H7, 8* and *OJR1–6* (American-built: 48 tons, 24–32 knots, 1941–42).

NICARAGUA

The Nicaraguans declared war on the Axis in December 1941. The only significant vessel was an ex-American cutter.

NORWAY

Germany brought the war to Norway on April 9, 1940. At that time, the Norwegian navy totaled 62 war vessels (only 19 of them post-WWI) plus 49 steamers, whalers, and trawlers—a minor obstacle even for the modest Kriegsmarine.

Armored Ships

HARALD HAARFAGRE, TORDENSKJOLD (3,350 tons; two 8.2-inch, six 4.7-inch, six 3-inch, two 3-inch DP guns; 14 knots, 1897–98): steady seaboats, but otherwise obsolete. Inactive by 1940, they may have begun disarming. The 8.2-inch shells weighed 313 lbs; the 4.7-inch shells weighed 45 lbs. The Germans took both ships and turned them into AA vessels *Thetis* and *Nymphe*.

NORGE, EIDSVOLD (3,645 tons; two 8.2-inch, six 5.9-inch, eight 3-inch guns; 15 knots, 1900): good seaboats like their elder comrades, and in slightly better condition. The Germans sank them both. The 5.9-inch shells weighed 99 lbs.

Prior to World War I, Norway ordered two coastal battleships from Britain, but the Royal Navy requisitioned *Bjorgvin* and *Nidaros* (4,807

The Norwegian **Tordenskjold** *as built. The Germans converted her into an AA ship.*

tons; two 9.4-inch, four 5.9-inch, four 3.9-inch guns, two 17.7-inch TT; 15 knots) for service as the *Gorgon*-class monitors.

Torpedo Boats

The world's first torpedo boat, the British-built *Rap* (10 tons full load, 12.25 knots, 1873), retired from patrol duties in 1920 and lingered in storage until made a museum exhibit postwar.

KVIK, LYN, BLINK, DJERV, DRISTIG (45 tons, light guns, 19 knots, 1898): from the eight-boat *Varg* class. The first three served as PB; the Germans took them, perhaps installed two 17.7-inch TT, and began a series of renamings (starting with *KT2–4*). The last pair, capable of minesweeping, no longer served actively.

HVAL class (90 tons, light guns, 19 knots, 1897–1901): six TB, plus four decommissioned prewar. The Germans put three captured units to work as PB under various names.

HVAS, KJÆK, FALK, HAUK (64 tons, light guns, 19 knots, 1902–1904): used as MS, in German service; repeatedly renamed.

RAVN, JO, GRIB, ØRN, LOM (70 tons, two 17.7-inch TT, 25 knots, 1906): TB. The Germans took the last pair as *Schlange* and *Eidechse*, possibly removing their TT.

TEIST, SKARV, KJELL (92 tons, light guns, three 17.7-inch TT, 25 knots, 1908–12): equipped for minesweeping. *Kjell*, slightly larger than the others, mounted a 3-inch gun. All three underwent capture and a series of German renamings.

DRAUG, GARM, TROLL (540 tons, six 3-inch guns, three 17.7-inch TT, 27 knots, 1909–14): rated initially as DD, but no longer modern. The Germans captured *Troll*. *Draug* escaped to operate temporarily from Britain before decommissioning.

TRYGG, SNØGG, STEGG (200 tons, two 3-inch guns, four 17.7-inch TT, mines, 25 knots, 1919–21): TB. Germany seized the first pair.

SLEIPNER, ÆGER, GYLLER (597 tons, three 4-inch guns, two 21-inch TT, 24 mines, 30 knots, 1937–39): a modern design, if not powerful. The 4-inch model fired one 31-lb shell every four seconds. *Gyller* mounted four TT; she became the German *Löwe* with two guns removed. *Sleipner* operated with the Royal Navy, mounting two 4-inch DP.

*Four **Hval** class torpedo boats in 1900. Norway's warships were woefully overage at the start of World War II.*

NORWAY

ODIN, BALDER, TOR (632 tons, two 4-inch guns, two 21-inch TT, 30 knots, 1939–40): improved *Sleipner* design—a dubious concept. Only *Odin* was complete when the Germans invaded; they seized her and completed the others. As *Panther*, *Leopard*, and *Tiger*, they mounted one gun and two torpedoes.

Norway began construction of two destroyers (1,220 tons, four 4.7-inch guns, four 21-inch TT, 34 knots) which almost approached the capabilities of foreign designs. The Germans captured them on the stocks and named them *ZN4, 5* (later *TA7, 8*), but sabotage kept them from completion.

The Norwegians went through the war without a destroyer of their own, but the Royal Navy transferred some units; *Success* and *Shark* became *Stord* and *Svenner*, and five ex-American flush-deckers kept their British names. Some "Hunts," two Type III and one Type II, were also transferred to Norway.

Minecraft

VALE, ULLER, BRAGE, NOR, VIDAR (236–250 tons, one 4.7-inch gun, 50 mines, eight knots, 1874–82): ML captured by Germany. The gun in *Nor* (at least) was a 5.9-incher.

GOR, TYR (294 tons; one 4.7-inch, one 3-inch gun; 55 mines; 10 knots, 1886–87): ML captured by Germany.

FRØYA (870 tons; four 4-inch, one 3-inch DP gun, two 17.7-inch TT, 180 mines; 21.8 knots, 1917): ML. The 4-inch model resembled that in *Odin* and *Sleipner*.

GLOMMEN, LAUGEN (335 tons, two 3-inch guns, 120 mines, 9.5 knots, 1917–18): ML captured by Germany as *NKi01* and *NKi05*.

OLAV TRYGGVASON (1,596 tons; four 4.7-inch, one 3-inch DP gun, 280 mines; 23 knots,

1934): ML, captured as *Albatros*, later *Brummer*. The main guns elevated to 45° and fired 46-lb shells.

OTRA, RAUMA (320 tons, one 3-inch gun?, mines, 13.5 knots, 1939–40): MS captured and renamed *Togo* and *Kamerun*.

The Norwegians converted about 25 whalers into MS. Britain supplied two *MMS1001*-class vessels, and four YMS came from the United States.

Miscellaneous

Norway received three British subs during the war: *Variance* (renamed *Utsira*), *Varne* (renamed *Ula*), and *Uredd* (not renamed).

A2–4 (268/355 tons, three 17.7-inch TT, 14.5/9 knots, 1914): SS built in Germany, *A5* retained there. Summoned from reserve at the war's outbreak, they required several minutes to submerge. Their advanced senility left them capable of little beyond scuttling. *A2* fell into German hands but merely became scrap.

B1–6 (420/545 tons, one 3-inch DP gun, four 17.7-inch TT, 14/11 knots, 1923–30): aging SS with dive time exceeding one minute. *B1* escaped to Britain and served in a training capacity for a few years. The Germans captured *B2, 4–6* but commissioned only the last two as *UC1, 2*.

FRIDTJOF NANSEN (1,275 tons, two 4-inch guns, AC 1, 15 knots, 1931): well-liked patrol boat capable of light ice-breaking. A planned sistership was replaced by the *Nordkapps*.

NORDKAPP, SENJA (266 tons, light guns, 13.7 knots, 1938): PB equipped as MS, cheaper than *Fridtjof Nansen* but decidedly inferior. The Germans captured *Senja* once and renamed her five times.

The navy retained two old sloops, *Michael Sars* (226 tons, light guns, 1900) and *Heimdal* (640 tons, four 3-inch guns, 1892), with trawlers assisting in patrol duty. Norwegian forces captured a trawler during the German invasion and handed it over to the British. After that campaign came to a close, the British reciprocated, giving at least 31 whalers and trawlers (most built in Norway) to the Norwegians; one of these craft had been in French service, and six later went on to serve with the Greeks.

The Norwegians received many other transfers: from the United States, one PC-craft and three SC-craft; from Britain, nine Fairmile "B" launches, one "Castle"-class and six "Flower"-class corvettes, and 30 MTB (*MTB50–52, 54, 56, 71, 345, 618–620, 623, 625-627, 631, 653, 688, 704, 709, 711–713, 715–717, 719–723*), one or two of which fell into German hands. Norway had ordered four Vosper MTB, but the British delivered only boats *5* and *6* and kept the other two as *MTB71, 72*. Four more boats ordered from BPB became the British *MGB40–43*.

PANAMA

Panama declared war on the Axis in December 1941. The United States gave Panama a pair of small patrol craft.

PARAGUAY

Landlocked Paraguay didn't join the Allies until 1945. Naturally, the only Paraguayan vessels were a few river gunboats: *Capitán Cabral* (180 tons, one 3-inch gun, 12.5 knots, 1907), *Tacuarí* (150 tons, two 3-inch guns, 10 knots, 1910), and *Humaitá* and *Paraguay* (745 tons; four 4.7-inch, three 3-inch DP guns, mines; 17 knots, 1931).

PERU

Peru also waited until 1945 to declare war on the Axis.

Peru discarded the old cruiser *Lima* (1,790 tons, three 4-inch guns, mines, 14 knots, 1881) in 1940 and the TB *Rodríguez* (490 tons, three 17.7-inch TT, 25 knots, 1911) in 1939.

ALMIRANTE GRAU, CORONEL BOLOGNESI (3,200 nt; two 6-inch, four 3-inch, two 3-inch DP guns, two 17.7-inch TT; 24 knots, 1906–7): old British-built cruisers. They may have landed their torpedoes and taken on depth charges. The 6-inch shells weighed 100 lbs.

GUISE (1,354 tons, five 4-inch guns, nine 17.7-inch TT, 60 mines, 28 knots, 1917): ex-Estonian DD of the Russian *Novik* Type III class.

VILLAR (1,260 tons, four 4-inch guns, nine 17.7-inch TT, 60 mines, 24 knots, 1917): ex-Estonian DD of the *Novik* Type IV class, same 4-inch guns as in *Guise* (10 rpm, 39-lb shells, 16,400-yard range).

R1–4 (576/755 tons, one 3-inch gun, four 21-inch TT, 14.5/9.5 knots, 1926–28): plus two others planned but not built. Submarines, constructed in America and based on small American designs, they remained sufficient for Peru's local requirements.

LORETO, AMAZONAS (250 tons, four 3-inch guns, 15 knots, 1935): American-built river gunboats.

AMÉRICA (240 tons, light guns, 14 knots, 1905): river GB.

Peru received six 83-foot type cutters from the United States.

POLAND

History regards the German invasion of Poland on September 1, 1939 as the starting point of World War II.

Shortly after achieving independence in 1920, the Poles sketched out an ambitious naval program, headed by a pair of cruisers. The newborn economy, however, viewed Poland's short coastline in a stingier light. The navy had to venture abroad for its first warship purchases, but domestic facilities soon blossomed, spicing the air with a giddy optimism that proposed the impossible. One plan called for three 25,000-ton battleships (nine 12-inch, twelve 5.9-inch, ? DP guns, six TT; 30 knots—rather a lot on the given tonnage), one CV or two 10,000-ton cruisers (nine 8-inch, nine 4.7-inch DP guns), 12 destroyers, 18 torpedo boats, 12 escorts, 21 submarines, 16 minesweepers, and one minelayer. Such a fleet would have outweighed any opponent in the Baltic, but the navy the Poles actually built by 1939 could only hope to escape the Germans and find asylum with the British.

Ironically, once in exile, this humble navy began to grow as the Poles proved worthy of many British transfers (most renamed): cruisers *Dragon* and *Danae* (*Conrad*); destroyers *Garland*, *Nerissa* (*Piorun*), and *Myrmidon* (*Orkan*); submarines *Urchin* (*Sokół*) and *P52* (*Dzik*); plus three "Hunt" Type II escorts, nine MTB and MGB, and nine trawlers. The British also provided, at least temporarily, some ex-French vessels in their custody: the destroyer *Ouragan*, a *Melpomène*-class torpedo boat, a pair of auxiliary patrol craft, and the escorts *CH11, 15*. An ex-American sub, *P551* in British service, became the Polish *Jastrząb*.

WICHER, BURZA (1,540 tons, four 5.1-inch guns, six 21.7-inch TT, 60 mines, 33 knots, 1930–32): French-built DD of an improved

Simoun design, but retaining a serious stability problem. The builders butchered the project with endless delays and faulty workmanship—just one of several misadventures with French yards. The 5.1-inch guns fired a 77-lb shell to 20,450 yards at 5–6 rpm. The TT had adapters for 21-inch and 17.7-inch torpedoes, a standard feature among Polish destroyers and subs.

The Germans, having sunk *Wicher* in port, intended to make use of her as *Seerose* but never completed repairs. *Burza* managed to escape to the Britain. Subsequent changes included the removal of one gun, then another; the removal of three tubes, then the other three; the removal of her mine rails and the addition of a 3-inch DP and British AA and AS weaponry.

GROM, BŁYSKAWICA (2,144 tons, seven 4.7-inch guns, six 21.7-inch TT, 60 mines, 39 knots, 1937): big, handsome DD built in Britain, whither they fled in 1939. The Poles planned to build two additional units, *Huragan* and *Orkan*, in a domestic yard, but the war prevented it. Designed endurance was about 3,500 miles at 15 knots. The 4.7-inch guns fired a 53-lb shell to 21,300 yards.

During operations from England, the ships revealed some top-heaviness and deficient seakeeping not previously apparent in the Baltic. But they left no doubts about their combat ability. The British removed three torpedoes to make room for a 4-inch DP, and after *Grom's* loss, *Błyskawica* underwent complete rearmament: eight 4-inch DP guns, with sometimes three, sometimes six torpedoes.

MAZUR, plus one lost prewar (360 tons, four 3-inch guns, 27 knots, 1914): ex-German TB of the Dutch *Z1* type, used for gunnery training.

PODHALANIN, ŚLĄZAK, KUJAWIAK, plus one unit scrapped prewar (330 nt, two 3-inch guns, two 17.7-inch TT, 28 knots, 1918): ex-German TB. They lingered in noncombatant

Powerful in appearance and weaponry, Poland's Błyskawica
survived the war to become a museum.

decrepitude, awaiting their final duty as scrap metal. Their fate remains a mystery, but it came at the hands of their German captors.

Poland ordered at least two MTB (35 tons, two 21-inch TT, 45 knots) from Britain, but the Royal Navy took them as *MGB47, 48;* the first did eventually go to the Poles as *S1,* while nine other British MTB transfers became *S2–10.*

WILK, RYŚ, ŻBIK (980/1,250 tons, one 3.9-inch gun, six 21.7-inch TT, 38 mines, 14/9 knots, 1929–30): French-built SS, unsuccessfully based on *Saphir.*

ORZEŁ, SĘP (1,110/1,473 tons, one 4.1-inch gun, twelve 21.7-inch TT, 40 mines, 19/9 knots, 1939): Dutch-built SS of high quality, with more than enough range for the Baltic (7,000 miles at 10 knots). The 4.1-inch shells weighed 35 lbs.

GRYF (2,227 tons, six 4.7-inch guns, 600 mines, 20 knots, 1938): ML; another French work with predictably poor results.

Politics dictated a continued patronage of amateurish French yards. The next SS order (two improved *Orzeł* units: 1,175/1,550 tons, light AA instead of a heavy deck gun, twelve 21.7-inch TT, 20/9 knots) went not to the *Orzeł*'s Dutch builders, but to a French firm. In any case, the outbreak of war ended the project.

GENERAŁ HALLER, KOMENDANT PIŁSUDSKI (342 tons, two 3-inch guns, 30 mines, 14 knots, 1921): ex-Russian GB, sisters to the Finnish *Karjala* class. *Piłsudski* became the German *Heisternest.*

JASKÓŁKA class (183 tons, one 3-inch gun, 20 mines, 18 knots, 1936–39): six MS, Poland's first major domestic construction. Some had DP mounts, but AA fire proved impractical. The design turned out a complete success and would have achieved more in 1939 if not overwhelmed by the invasion. Four captured units performed secondary duties for the Germans as the *Oxhoft* class (three later given TFA-numbers), probably without their 3-inch guns.

The Poles built the *Jaskółkas* as replacement for four ex-German *FM1*-class MS (about 165 tons, 20 mines, 14 knots, 1918), two of which lasted into 1939 as noncombatants, only to be sunk in the invasion.

WARSZAWA, PIŃSK, TORUŃ, HORODYSZCZE (110 nt, three 3-inch guns, 9.1 knots, 1921): river monitors; scuttled but salvaged for Soviet use as the *Smolensk* class.

KRAKÓW, WILNO (70 nt, three 3.9-inch guns, 7.5 knots, 1926): river monitors. Poland's modest first step in domestic building. *Kraków* became the Soviet *Bobruisk*.

ZARADNA, ZAWZIĘTA, ZUCHWALA (32–35 tons, one 3.9-inch howitzer, 5.6 knots, 1933–35): "Z" class river gunboats. *Zawzięta* became *Trudowoj* in Soviet service, and *Zaradna* became *Belorus* before the Germans took her and named her *91*. Both captives probably switched to an armament of two 3-inch guns.

The Poles planned a class of four river gunboats, then canceled three when the first proved a disappointment (*Nieuchwytny*: 38 tons, light guns, 12.9 knots, 1934). She gave German service as *Pionier*. A gaggle of smaller launches (27 craft under 15 tons, many with KU-numbers) became a source of plunder; at least 16 went to the Soviets, and two to the Germans.

A collection of ex-Russian paddle-wheelers (sometimes called the *Admirał Sierpinek* class: 64–236 tons, most with light guns, about eight knots), served ostensibly in river patrol, but also in a number of other capacities—hospital ship, torpedo tender, target ship, floating casino, etc. Five of them went to the Soviets, who in turn lost one to the Germans.

Riverine minecraft included old *Mątwa*

(later the Soviet *Pina*: 60 tons, 160 mines, seven knots) and the minelaying launches *T1–3* (10 tons, four mines, 6.5 knots, 1935). Of the minesweeping launches *T4–7* (5 tons, light guns, 5.4 knots, 1928–30), three went to the Soviets.

PORTUGAL

The Portuguese, though neutral, maintained a sympathy with Britain. This helped stabilize the strategic situation in Iberia, and made possible the deployment of Allied AS aircraft from the Azores during the height of the U-boat crisis. But Portugal had no direct confrontation with the Axis, apart from a few scrapes with the Japanese in the Far East.

The navy never transcended its role of coast defense. At various points in the dreadnought era, planners toyed with the idea of building or buying some battleships; suggestions included a *Minas Gerais*, a British *Orion* or *Queen Elizabeth*, or an old American ship. None of these plans became practical. A more realistic program in 1930 included two 5,000-ton cruisers, but even that proved too great a stretch, and the navy had to content itself with sloops, gunboats, and destroyers. With a few British exceptions, most Portuguese ships came from Portuguese yards.

DOURO, DÃO, LIMA, TEJO, VOUGA, plus two others also named DOURO and TEJO sold prewar to Colombia (1,219 tons, four 4.7-inch guns, eight 21-inch TT, 20 mines, 36 knots, 1933–36): DD based on *Ambuscade*; two built in Britain, the rest in Portugal. The 49-lb shells had a 21,300-yd range. Half of the TT went ashore by 1943.

The destroyer *Tâmega* (515 tons; one 4-inch, two 3-inch guns, four 17.7-inch TT; 27 knots, 1923) followed her three sisters into retirement in the mid-1940s. Likewise, *Sado* and *Ave* (195 tons, four 17.7-inch TT, 28 knots, 1915), the last of six ex-Austrian TB, left their training duties in 1940. They had sisterships still in service with Greece, Romania, and Yugoslavia.

In 1938, the Portuguese approached Germany concerning some MTB armed with two 17.7-inch tubes, but nothing came of it.

Portugal had two minelayers. *Vulcano* (129 tons, 12 knots, 1910) served mostly as a training vessel, and as such could mount three torpedo tubes. The army's little *Mineiro* (77 tons, eight knots, 1892) retired around 1943.

DELFIM, ESPADARTE, GOLFINHO (800/1,092 tons, one 4-inch gun, six 21-inch TT, 16.5/9.25 knots, 1935): British-built SS. The 4-inch shells weighed 31 lbs. The navy ordered these subs after canceling four units ordered from Italy in 1931. (The Italians completed their boats as the *Argo* and *Glauco* classes.)

GONÇALO VELHO, GONÇALVES ZARCO (950 tons, three 4.7-inch guns, 16.5 knots, 1933): British-built sloops based on *Bridgewater*; could act as minesweepers.

AFONSO DE ALBUQUERQUE, BARTOLOMEU DIAS (1,780 tons; four 4.7-inch, two

After canceling an order with Italian builders, Portugal ordered the **Albuquerque** *and a sistership from the British and received two excellent general-purpose ships.*

3-inch DP guns, 40 mines; 21 knots, 1935): British-built sloops; originally fitted with a seaplane.

PEDRO NUNES, JOÃO DE LISBOA (1,090 tons, two 4.7-inch guns, 16.5 knots, 1935–37): Portuguese-built sloops.

The navy also had two British "Flower"-class sloops purchased in 1920, *República* (963 tons; two 4-inch, two 3-inch DP guns; 16.5 knots, 1915—discarded in mid-war) and *Carvalho Araújo* (converted prewar as a survey vessel). During the war, Britain transferred nine trawlers (eight renamed *P1–8*) to the Portuguese.

MACAU (95 tons, light guns, 11.75 knots, 1909): river gunboat, seized by Japan and renamed *Maiko*.

BEIRA, IBO, MANDOVI, plus two discarded prewar (397 tons, two 3-inch guns, 13 knots, 1910–18): GB. *Mandovi* carried only light guns, and *Beira* also had reduced armament after a 1936 conversion to survey vessel.

TETE (100 tons, light guns, eight knots, 1918): river gunboat.

ZAIRE, DAMAO, DIO (397 tons, two 3-inch guns, 13 knots, 1925–29): a *Beira* repeat.

FARO, LAGOS (295 tons, light guns, 13 knots, 1927–30): fishery protection.

TORRES GARCIA (250 tons, light guns?, ? knots, 1928): PB.

AZEVIA class (230 tons, light guns, 17 knots, 1941–42): six patrol vessels.

During the war, the navy discarded the gunboat *Limpopo* (288 tons, 1891), the river gunboat *Rio Minho* (38 tons, 1904), and the patrol vessel *Lince* (77 tons, 12 knots, 1911).

ROMANIA

The spread of German and Soviet influence isolated Romania from its Western allies. From the Baltic to the Balkans, countries began to vanish, and the Romanians watched as their own borders started to shrink. Political order degenerated into a German puppetry, and Romanian troops joined the Germans in their Eastern Offensive. The rising Soviet tide prompted a new government to declare war against Germany on August 24, 1944. Romania and its navy became a Soviet appendage.

Like many other countries, Romania preceded the world wars with ambitious naval programs. A 1912 proposal called for six 3,500-ton cruisers, while some planners requested a coast defense battleship (13,000 tons; four 12-inch, four 8-inch, twelve 5.9-inch guns). Reality stepped in, and nothing larger than a DD began construction. The interwar economy squelched all talk of battleships and reduced the cruiser advocates to a whisper, though some consideration went to buying Britain's monitor *Gorgon*. Again, little construction took place, so the Romanian navy of World War II consisted largely of Austro-Hungarian veterans from World War I.

Destroyers and Torpedo Boats

MĂRAŞTI, MĂRĂŞEŞTI (1,410 tons; five 4.7-inch, two 3-inch DP guns, four 17.7-inch TT; 34 knots, 1917–18): ordered from Italy with two other sisters. The Italians requisitioned all four; the Romanians accepted delivery of two after World War I. (Spain bought the others.) Their size and firepower, impressive by WWI standards, allowed the ships to continue as valuable units 25 years later. During the war, they landed one main gun and the two DP to make room for more AS and light AA weaponry. The Soviets took them as *Lovkiy* and *Logkiy*.

REGELE FERDINAND, REGINA MARIA (1,400 tons; five 4.7-inch, one 3-inch DP gun, six 21-inch TT, 50 mines; 37 knots, 1930): a compact and warlike British design built in Italy, the most significant interwar project. The original plan included four ships. They carried a strong armament for their tonnage, and some dispersal of machinery enhanced their ruggedness. The

Though designed in Britain, the Romanian **Regina Maria** *had a feature unknown among British destroyers—machinery dispersal.*

main battery elevated to 45°. Each ship landed the 3-inch and one 4.7-inch gun, but later gained a 3.5-inch DP. The Soviets renamed them *Likhoi* and *Letuchyi*.

SBORUL (262 tons, four 17.7-inch TT, 28 knots, 1914): ex-Austrian TB, sister to the Yugoslav *T1, 3*. Three other units retired in 1932. The Romanians modified *Sborul* for escort duty with two 3.5-inch guns and no TT. She became *Musson* in Soviet service.

NĂLUCA, SMEUL (266 tons, four 17.7-inch TT, 28 knots, 1915–16): ex-Austrian TB, with an additional unit sunk prewar. These were sisters to the Greek "P" class, Yugoslavia's *T5–8*, and the Portuguese *Sados*. Both ships were converted to escorts (no TT, two 3.5-inch guns), and *Smeul* went on to serve as the Soviet *Toros*.

The navy bought three *MTB20*-class craft from Britain in 1940 and renamed them the *Viforul* class. The Soviets got one of them in 1944. Germany completed four Dutch *TM51*-class MTB for the Romanians; this *Vantul* class was capable of only 34 knots due to the lack of proper engines. All four boats went to the Soviets. Germany also provided seven ex-Italian MTB, *S501–507*.

Submarines

During World War I, Romania ordered three boats from France (342/513 tons, four 17.7-inch TT, 14/8 knots) but never received them.

DELFINUL (650/900 tons, one 4-inch gun, eight 21-inch TT, 14/9 knots, 1931): Italian-built, rarely active, not operational when seized by the Soviets as *TS4*. The 4-inch gun fired a 30-lb shell to 12,800 yards at 45° elevation.

MARSUINUL (620/? tons, one 4.1-inch gun, six 21-inch TT, 16/9 knots, 1942): a German-Dutch project built in Romania. Delayed in entering service, she performed only one patrol before becoming the Soviet *S4*. The 4.1-inch shells weighed 32 lbs.

REQUINUL (645/870 tons, four 21-inch TT, 40 mines, 17/9 knots, 1942): another German-Dutch project that entered service in 1944. She went to the Soviets as *S3*.

Five Italian midget submarines seized by the Germans (*CB1–4, 6*: 35/44 tons, two 17.7-inch TT or two mines, 7.5/7 knots, 1941) were transferred to Romania. Eventually the Soviets took them.

Miscellaneous

ARDEAL (450 tons; two 4.7-inch, one 3.5-inch DP gun; 10 knots, 1904): ex-Austrian river monitor, later the Soviet *Azov*. The 4.7-inch guns fired 52-lb shells.

CĂPITAN NICOLAE LASCAR BOGDAN class (45 nt, light guns, 18 knots, 1906–7): seven PB plus one sunk prewar; originally built as river TB. The Soviets operated three, renamed with SKA-numbers.

ION C. BRĂTIANU, ALEXANDRU LAHOVARI, LASCĂR CATARGIU, MIHAIL KOGĂLNICEANU (680 tons; three 4.7-inch, one 3-inch DP gun; 13 knots, 1907–8): river monitors; four more planned but not built. The first pair became the Soviet *Mariupol* and *Berdyansk*.

BASARABIA (590 tons, two 4.7-inch guns, three 4.7-inch howitzers, 12 knots, 1915): ex-Austrian river monitor, sister of Yugoslavian *Drava*; later became Soviet *Kerch*.

BUCOVINA (550 tons, two 4.7-inch guns, two 4.7-inch howitzers, 12 knots, 1915): ex-Austrian river monitor, sister of Yugoslavian *Vardar*; later became Soviet *Izmail*.

SAN MARINO

LOCOTENANT-COMANDOR STIHI EUGEN class (351 tons, two 3.9-inch guns, 15 knots, 1917): four GB of the French *Diligente* class. The Soviets took three and renamed them. A fifth, similar vessel may have been used non-operationally as a source of spare parts.

LUCEAFĂRUL (2,050 tons, light guns?, 17.5 knots, 1930): British-built patrol boat and yacht.

AMIRAL MURGESCU (812 tons, two 4.1-inch DP guns, 135 mines, 16 knots, 1940): ML and escort, three additional units planned. The 4.1-inch model had a 33-lb shell with a range of 16,595 yards and a ceiling of 33,800 feet. *Murgescu* became the Soviet *Don*.

Two auxiliary ML served in wartime; one of them went to the Soviets. Romania planned the construction of several MS based on the German *M261* class, but they didn't reach completion until postwar (the *Democratija* class).

The navy operated numerous small craft along the Danube and the Black Sea coast. The Germans supplied three *KFK1*-class patrol craft and several ex-Czech vessels, including *FM1, 2*. Some minor vessels went to the Soviets, including four or five MS.

SAN MARINO

The formality of San Marino's 1944 declaration of war against Germany came with no military significance. There was no San Marino navy.

SAUDI ARABIA

The pro-Allies Saudis made room for Americans to establish airbase facilities but had no navy to commit to the war effort. An official declaration of war against Germany and Japan came only in 1945.

SOVIET UNION

The Soviets invaded Poland on September 17, 1939. In the following year, they set about recapturing escapees from the Tsarist realm: the Baltic States, Bessarabia, and part of Finland. This new, bloated empire spread itself out beneath the sun only to fall under the shadow of Operation Barbarossa, the German invasion in June 1941.

Soviet Handicaps

For the part it played in the advent of Leninism, the Russian navy would doubtless have enjoyed the new leadership's favor. But then came mutiny and paranoia, and the navy toppled from its pedestal to land at the feet of its new master, the army. Stalin then purged the last traces of initiative and insight from the command structure.

Saddled with this dubious hierarchy, the fleet faced numerous hurdles. The interwar economy stunted development for all navies, but the Soviets faced a unique set of woes in the aftermath of civil war, with their design teams dissolved and their shipbuilding industry slumped into disuse. The Soviet Union, internationally isolated and domestically disrupted, faced the 1920s without experience in modern designs and out of touch with advancing technology.

The leadership's initial response to this situation showed good common sense. With no attempt to reassert itself among the major powers, the navy maintained only its most modern units while scrapping the incomplete, the elderly, and the damaged. By 1924, this reduced the fleet to less than 100,000 tons of warships. But conservative growth plans followed, projecting the construction of small craft and submarines, and slowly reviving the domestic industries.

Then, however, the priorities shifted. Stalin watched his foreign rivals shackling themselves with treaty limitations, and his gleeful imagination began to sparkle. His dream-fleet swelled to include 19 dreadnoughts, 20 cruisers, 18 flotilla leaders, 145 destroyers, 341 submarines, 44 river monitors, 105 submarine-chasers, 514

Ordnance

GUN	SW	RANGE	CEILING	FC	NOTES
16/50	2,443	49,945		23-35	incomplete BB
14/52	1,649	25,415		20	*Izmail*s
12/54	1,036	52,030		18.5–30	*Kronshtadt*s
12/52	1,038	25,400		35–45	old BB
9.4/60	518	45,930		22.5	Cruiser project
7.1/57	215	41,000		10	CA
6/57	121	33,045		8	*Chapayev*s, modern BB and BC
6/50	104	19,010		15	river monitor *Sverdlov*
5.1/55	81	20,690		7.5–12	CL, gunboats, some mounts had less range (16,800 yards)
5.1/50	74	28,140		6–10[1]	modern DD, *Khasan*s
4.7/50	45[2]	15,860		7.5	old BB; GB and monitors
4.7/45	51	14,000			river gunboats
4/60	39	17,600[3]		6	old DD, various escorts and GB
4/45[4]	39				some SS?
3.9/56	34	24,320	49,000?	5	standard in many classes[5]
3.9/51	34	16,400[6]		5	*Fugas*, many SS
3.9/50	31	16,670?		5	Italian gun in *Svetlanas*[7]
3.3/52	20	17,020		3.3–4	*Ognevoi*s, *Albatros*, some CA and DD, various escorts
	20	14,100		3–10	GB with T34/85 tank turrets
3/55	15[8]	14,760	30,180	3.5	GB, newer DD, old BB
3/50	13				old SS
3/41.6	14	12,240		7.5–15	GB with T34/76 tank turrets
3/30.5	12	10,940		5–6	older AA gun
3/23.5	14			6	GB with T28 tank turret

[1] The twin mountings may have fired somewhat faster.

[2] Some records show a much heavier shell, 63 lbs, fired to a maximum 15,000 yards.

[3] Older mounts may have given less range (16,400 yards?).

[4] According to some sources, the only 4-inch gun in Soviet war service was the 60cal model, meaning the submarines actually carried one of the 3.9-inch weapons.

[5] It appears that time fuses restricted the ceiling to 32,460 feet. The mounts planned for new dreadnoughts allowed a firing cycle of 3.75 seconds.

[6] Two versions of this gun existed, a 51cal and a 56cal, and both versions may have had the same performance as the above 56cal gun.

[7] The degree of modification from the Italian 47cal gun remains unclear.

[8] Ordnance records also show an extremely heavy shell, 25 lbs, with a range of 9,810 yards.

SOVIET UNION

TORPEDO	WW	RANGE		NOTES
21in 27K	584	4,600/43	16,400/25	surface ships
21in 27P	639	4,400/43	9,840/32	SS
21in 38	661	4,400/43.5	13,100/28.5	wartime standard, surface and SS
21in d4	595	4,400/50		some Project 7 DD
17.7in 12F	309	3,300/38	6,560/29	old TB and SS
17.7in 36	441	3,300/41	6,560/31	

MTB—all for completion before 1943. It's unclear how seriously Stalin took this fantasy. What is certain is that such a program far exceeded the nation's industrial capacity, and the leadership never identified any mission for the huge fleet.

The very process by which new ships entered service wallowed in futility. Specifications had as much to do with political caprice as they did with perceived naval needs. Designers, often novices, rose to prominence, merely to suffer removal and replacement by the less expert. Construction trudged amid intermittent supplies of materiel, and projects suffered repeated interruptions to accommodate the latest design notions. Soviet industries delivered defective products, which unskilled workmen zealously assembled into an overweight but under-performing medley of metal. Trials dragged along as designers labored to correct the problems, or at least minimize them; sometimes they succeeded.

Foreign Assistance

The Communists paused amid their rhetoric of global revolution to nose around for some bourgeois shipbuilders they hadn't overly offended. As it turned out, Italy's craving to sell matched the Soviets' longing to buy, so the two countries managed some cooperation within an otherwise icy relationship. The Italians gladly handed weapons, ships, and fire-control gear to their future enemy.

One of the most glaring weaknesses of Soviet industry was its inability to produce heavy guns. This prompted a deal with Czecho-slovakia for the construction of guns of 11-inch and up, a plan thwarted by the German takeover. When the Soviets solicited ship designs in America, all discussion ended after it became clear their interest lay not in the ships but in the guns. A tentative proposal to French gun makers met with utter silence.

The British supplied the Soviet navy with some involuntary technical advice. Their submarine L55 had sunk off Kronstadt during the Intervention; the Soviets raised her and studied her in detail. Other sub data came from companies in the Netherlands—companies that were in fact German. As the war erupted, the Soviets made proposals directly to Germany, requesting plans for the *Scharnhorst*, the *Bismarck*, even the carrier *Graf Zeppelin*, herself the product of hopeless inexperience. The Germans did eventually hand over an incomplete heavy cruiser while promising further designs and guns, which they never bothered to deliver.

Great Patriotic Brawl

Unable to produce or procure its desired designs, the Soviet navy had to form a battle fleet around obsolete veterans and a trickling reinforcement of modern but modest newcomers, all under the command of parading yes-men. Conditions deteriorated with the German capture of important facilities, and ships suffered increased unreliability. In all this, the saddest feature was the level of training; Soviet sailors simply didn't know what they were doing. (When a destroyer managed a three-day stay at sea, the achievement received nationwide acclaim.) In the standard, tragicomic deployment of naval personnel, destroyer crews spent less time depth-charging U-boats than they did lugging machine guns through the streets of Sevastopol.

The lack of a respectable surface fleet had one significant result: while Stalin whined about inadequate Allied support, the Soviets abdicated all responsibility for escorting convoys to Murmansk, the one sector where Soviet fleet units had much relevance; warships bottled in the Baltic and Black Seas found themselves relegated as artillery for the army and targets for the Luftwaffe. The Soviets did have a submarine arm, remarkable both for its size and for its lack of success. Ultimately, the story of the Soviet navy in World War II became the story of its small craft: the river gunboats, the MTB, the coastal escorts. While major units lay at anchor, half-sunk in besieged harbors, motor boats harried the enemy endlessly everywhere—a pedestrian role for a fleet with grand pretentions, but an appropriate role for the sort of warfare the Soviets had to fight. The navy had truly become a branch of the army.

Information on Soviet warships and weapons remains a mystery within an enigma. The Soviets' own records are confused and contradictory. For example, shell weight for the new 12-inch gun may have gone as high as 1,058 lbs with a variety of range figures (47,300–52,660 yards). Definitive statistics may prove nonexistent, as the gun never entered fleet service and may never have reached a final design. Further complications derive from similar guns serving in coast defense mountings with special ammunition.

The new medium- and large-caliber guns promised long range and impressive hitting power by following the Italian example of high velocity, but with heavier shells. The practicalities of this combination remain conjectural for guns like the 16-inch and 9.4-inch models that never went to sea. Barrel wear and dispersion problems would seem a certainty, and the 7.1-inch model gave a sobering indication as it initially attained a barrel life of just 55 rounds. A new barrel liner and a reduction in muzzle velocity lessened the problem, but a reputation for unreliability persisted. The switch to 6-inch guns in later cruisers may indicate the navy's final opinion.

Likewise, the stated firing cycles arouse suspicion, especially in their contrast to old Russian and modern Italian models. The 7.1-inch design attempted six rpm, but the single mount achieved only four rpm in service, and the cramped triple mount, only two rpm.

The fleet's inactivity leaves historians guessing pessimistically at the qualities of Soviet gunnery. A lack of technology, with a nearly total absence of radar, indicates primitive fire control, especially with regard to AA defense. The standard light AA gun in 1939, a 45mm model, fired 25–30 rpm (11,680-yard range; 18,040-foot ceiling). The 37mm gun that replaced it at least managed 160–180 rpm with slightly less reach. Another weapon appeared in 1944, a 25mm gun firing 250–260 rpm to a practical limit of 2,600 yards. The Soviet navy fared ill against air attack.

It also had no effective AS system—no modern weapons or detection gear. (The Soviets sank a grand total of seven U-boats.) Nor did the torpedoes, based on Italian models, earn any distinction.

The Russians in the First World War had great success in mine warfare; the Soviets in the Second did not. Though most Soviet vessels could lay mines, their fields had almost no effect on Axis movements and they claimed few victims, nothing more significant than a TB, except the Finnish *Ilmarinen*. In fact, the Germans suffered as much from their own mines as they did from the Soviets'. And yet the Soviet navy sank more enemy targets with their mines than they did with gunfire, torpedoes, and depth charges.

Transfers to Soviet Command

The United States and Britain supplied the Soviets with a near-fleetful of transfers, mostly as a voluntary measure; but in 1943, the Soviets laid claim to a portion of the surrendered Italian navy. Given the impossibility of delivering the ships immediately, the Western Allies substituted units of their own, which the Soviets diligently renamed but failed to employ in any significant way. The British transferred the BB *Royal Sovereign* (renamed *Arkhangelsk*), nine ex-American flush-deck DD (all renamed), one "S"-class and three "U"-class SS (*V1–4*), three *MMS1* and 12 *MMS1001*-class craft (*T108–110* and *T121, 122, 193–202*), and nine minesweeping whalers. The United States provided the CL *Milwaukee* (*Murmansk*), 43 *YMS1*- and 34 *Admirable*-class MS (*T151* and *T111* classes), 28 *Tacoma*-class frigates (*EK1–28*), three "Wind"-class coast guard vessels (*Severni Veter, Severni Polius, Kapitan Belusov*), 78 SC-craft (*BO201–246, 301–332*), the 63-foot type anti-submarine boats *RPC1–16, 30–49* and *PTC37–49, 54–66* (given MO-numbers?), 90 *Vosper* MTB (A1 type), 55 *Higgins* MTB (A2 type), and 60 *Elco* MTB (A3 type).

Other units came less willingly. The Baltic annexations provided new submarines and surface craft. (See the sections on Lithuania, Estonia, and Latvia.) Armed conquest also brought a sizeable collection of prizes. Upon Romania's defeat in 1944, the remnants of its navy became Soviet. The Finns endured the distinction of surrendering twice to the Soviets, ceding some vessels on each occasion. This chapter will specify the more significant prizes. Captured small craft, usually of little consequence, held disproportionate significance for a Soviet navy subsisting on such vessels, and the final offensive through the Danube valley yielded a great harvest, both combatant and non-combatant; Hungarian, Bulgarian, Yugoslav, and German units entered Soviet service.

Naval Aviation

Early carrier proposals included converting an unarmed training ship *Komsomolets* (planned for 11,811 normal tons, sixteen 4-inch guns, AC 42, 15 knots, 1902) and the semi-complete BC *Izmail*, but naval aviation never tickled Stalin's imagination—hence, the absence of carriers from his grand schemes. Still, hopes arose that German assistance might produce a pair of flattops by 1942.

Prewar specifications for a *Chapayev*-class CL conversion evolved into the Project 71 (10,433 tons, eight 3.9 DP guns, AC 30, 35 knots) before vanishing. A wartime initiative, dubbed Project 72 (30,271 tons; 12–16 5.1-inch DP, twenty-four 3.3-inch DP guns; AC 62, 30 knots), included worthwhile protection but limited capability. A hybrid proposal (27,000 tons; nine 12-inch, sixteen 5.1-inch DP? guns; AC 62, 36 knots) sputtered prewar, as did an American-designed BB-CV (see below).

A plan for converting the cruisers *Rurik* (15,190 tons, 1908) and *Komintern* into sea-plane carriers ended amid the pair's antiquity; *Rurik's* old hull proved best suited to prewar scrapping, and *Komintern* finished her days in cruiser-form. A proposal for two new seaplane carriers proved equally futile. Even cruiser-borne scout planes received little attention.

Battleships and Battlecruisers

A few relics survived the scrappings of the 1920's; *Barrikada* lasted as a mine hulk (9,665 tons, 1876) and three ancient monitors as blockships (1,460–2,000 tons, 1865–66). Fanciful Soviet ambitions anticipated as many as 24 new dreadnoughts.

PARIZHSKAYA KOMMUNA, MARAT, OKTYA-BRSKAYA REVOLUTSIA, FRUNZE (23,000 tons; twelve 12-inch, sixteen 4.7-inch guns, four 17.7-inch TT; 23 knots, 1914): commissioned as *Sevastopol, Petropavlovsk, Gangut,* and *Poltava,* but renamed to sound more revolutionary. The first pair recovered their original names in 1943. The project forged a tortuous path back and forth among numerous builders, foreign and domestic, and the final layout showed

Late in the war, the Soviet Oktyabrskaya Revolutsia *sports her 3-inch twin mounts and British radar.*

the work of too many hands. With their armor spread in meager thickness, the *Sevastopol*s are sometimes labeled battlecruisers; but at 23 knots, they equaled BC only in their ability to sink.

Frunze, ravaged by fire and neglect, left service in 1919. Official ambivalence left her sometimes decaying and sometimes subject to imaginative plans, including a series of BC reconstruction schemes (nine 12-inch guns—one midships turret removed, the other placed in a super-firing position forward—plus sixteen 5.1-inch guns and eight or ten 3.9-inch DP, three planes, and 27 knots). A more realistic proposal envisioned her as a mobile battery capable of 12–16 knots. Instead, fate had her linger into the war years as a hulk, stripped for spare parts.

Minimal freeboard and an icebreaker bow (a frivolity repeated in all Imperial dreadnought projects) contributed to a wet and wallowing design, further detracting from its scanty habitability. The three active ships received modest refits that included machinery updates and vain attempts at improved sea-keeping. They probably retained their torpedoes, and *Parizhskaya Kommuna* may even have upgraded to 21-inch tubes. She underwent further change with a set of anti-torpedo bulges and a couple inches added to her negligible deck armor. Displacement rose near 30,000 tons, while her

speed fell to 21.5 knots. Her gun elevation increased, allowing a range of 31,400 yards. Trials with a fantastically heavy shell—1,281 lbs—failed when the range shrank to just 16,000 yards at the new elevation.

Armament began to change on the eve of war. All three units shipped six single-mount 3-inch DP guns. *Marat* got four additional guns in twin mounts, with two 4.7-inch guns going ashore. *Oktyabrskaya Revolutsia* traded eight secondary guns for three twin DP mounts (3-inch guns rather than 3.9-inch as sometimes reported).

Despite their shortcomings as battle-line brawlers, the *Sevastopol*s' size and 12-inch battery—a good one for its caliber and its age—constituted a major threat to any naval force the Axis could muster. However, the suddenness of Barbarossa stole the ships' ability to maneuver, and they spent the war confined behind minefields, subject to repeated bombing. Even so, they provided valuable service as artillery platforms. *Marat* earned special distinction; after a magazine explosion obliterated her forward section, she continued as a "floating" battery (though in fact she rested on the shallow bottom) with three of her turrets returning to action against enemy troops around Leningrad. The navy later outlined Project 27, a plan for her rehabilitation with new weaponry (nine 12-inch guns, sixteen 5.1-inch DP? guns, twelve 3.3-inch DP guns) and portions of *Frunze* grafted onto her hull, but the plan foundered in apathy.

After the *Sevastopol*s, the Russians built three BB with armor supplanting some speed (*Imperatritsa Mariya* class: 22,600 nt; twelve 12-inch, 20 5.1-inch, eight 3-inch guns, four 17.7-inch TT; 21 knots, 1915–17); none of them survived the transition to Soviet rule. An enlarged design followed, a single ship with much more armor (*Imperator Nikolai I*: 25,000 tons; twelve 12-inch, 20 5.1-inch, four 4-inch DP guns, four 17.7-inch TT; 21 knots); renamed *Demokratiya*,

The lucky Soviet battleship Parizhskaya Kommuna *gained extra armor before the war, and regained her original name,* Sevastopol, *during the war.*

she was destroyed incomplete by the Allies during the Intervention.

IZMAIL, BORODINO, KINBURN, NAVARIN (32,500nt; twelve 14-inch, 24 5.1-inch, four 4-inch DP guns, six 21-inch TT; 26.5 knots): BC begun in 1913 but never completed, due to production problems and revolution. Of the four ships, only *Izmail* received any attention after launching. A Communist suggestion for converting her to an aircraft carrier came to naught, and she followed her sisters to the scrap yard.

The 14-inch guns promised impressive firepower with their heavy shells. The 1,649-lb figure seems correct since it corresponds exactly to the proportions of the 1,038-lb 12-inch shell. However, many details of the gun's shipboard service remain theoretical, and much of the 14-inch data derives from its land-based use. The stated firing cycle of 20 seconds seems unlikely in context with other Russian weapons.

In fact, the *Izmail*s may never have mounted this battery. The Russians experienced difficulty with the supply of heavy guns, a situation predating World War I and lasting through World

War II. The *Sevastopol*s brought their 12-inch guns to sea at a time when other navies were adopting 14-inchers. The *Imperatritsa Mariya*s too had to go with 12-inch guns because the Russians couldn't handle anything larger. The *Izmail* upgrade to 14-inch stretched Russian capabilities, with only eight guns completed before the project met its premature end.

The final Tsarist dreadnought proposal (about 44,000 nt, eight to twelve 16-inch guns, twenty 5.1-inch guns, a speed of 25–31.5 knots) faced similar troubles. Nevertheless, ambitious planners anticipated a 16-inch shell weight as high as 2,461 lbs.

By the mid-1930s, the leadership began to dream of modern dreadnoughts. Preliminary sketches for a 33,000-ton, 30-knot BB had no realistic future; the only hope for immediate production lay with foreign designers and, possibly, foreign yards.

The Soviets went to America, claiming an interest in battleships, destroyers, and support craft. The negotiations degenerated into a comedy of international intrigue, highlighted by a proposed hybrid known as Project 10581, a flamboyantly grotesque creation carrying thirty-six carrier planes, four floatplanes, and battleship artillery. One variation mounted eight 18-inch guns, but the most promising plan (61,840 tons; twelve 16-inch, 28 5-inch DP guns; AC 40, 34 knots) would probably have had the same 16-inch model as in *Washington*. The ship had tremendous endurance for use in commerce warfare (29,000 miles at 12 knots).

At this point, the United States government stepped in to invoke the 45,000-ton treaty limitation, and the project deflated to a hybrid with 28 aircraft or a conventional BB with ten 16-inch guns, twenty 5-inch DP, and 31 knots. The episode ended amid mutual mistrust and the invasion of Poland.

The Italians suggested a practical design, Project U.P. 41 (42,000 tons; nine 16-inch, twelve 7.1-inch, 24 3.9-inch DP guns; AC 4, 32 knots). Similar to *Littorio*, it had improved protection but retained the clutter of secondary and DP turrets and housed its aircraft in an open hangar directly beneath the guns of Y Turret.

After the 1939 accord with Germany, the Soviets requested plans for a 50,000-ton "Neo-*Bismarck*" and various naval guns. The final German response came in the summer of 1941.

SOVYETSKIY SOYUZ, SOVYETSKAYA UKRA-INA, SOVYETSKAYA RUSSIYA, SOVYETSKAYA BYELORUSSIYA (58,219 tons; nine 16-inch, twelve 6-inch, eight 3.9-inch DP guns; AC 4, 28 knots): Project 23, magnificent ships laid down 1938–40 but not completed. It may be that only the Soviet inability to procure heavy guns kept the first ship from commissioning.

Obvious clues indicate some Italian design collaboration, as in the low-angle secondary guns and the Pugliese underwater protection. Armor layout also reflected Italian practice, but in a simplified form. The deck armor improved on *Vittorio Veneto*'s, though belt protection regressed somewhat. In general, the ships would likely have proved more rugged than their Mediterranean cousins.

The main battery allowed 45° elevation. Muzzle velocity matched that of Italy's 15-inch model until trials revealed wear problems and prompted a propellant reduction. Another echo of Italian misfortune, inferior ammunition manufacture led to excessive dispersion, with unflattering implications for Soviet gunnery in general. The 3.9-inch battery performed well enough, but eight guns of such modest caliber left the ship ill equipped to deal with air attack.

The *Sovyetskiy Soyuz* design warrants comparison with the other behemoths, *Yamato* and *Montana*. The power of the Soviet guns couldn't fully compensate for their lesser broadside of 21,984 lbs (*Yamato* had 28,968 lbs; *Montana* had 32,400 lbs), a disadvantage compounded by the Soviets' outdated fire control. Durability is difficult to gauge, but the design's Italian heritage gives a discouraging hint. If the three titans met in a theoretical gun duel, the outcome might have rested with the details of design and workmanship; the Russians hadn't completed a battleship since 1917.

Planners identified several of Project 23's shortcomings and formulated the Project 23bis redesign; this came too late for the first four vessels but would have influenced subsequent construction. Speed increased to 30 knots. The Pugliese torpedo defenses, revealed as defective, gave way to a more conventional layered system. The 3.9-inch battery grew to 12 guns, still not enough, while the number of scout planes shrank to three. The six 6-inch twin mounts switched to four triples, the same mount as in the postwar *Chapayev* (45–50°).

Further studies made their way beyond 73,500 tons with 12 main guns; while these represented mere design exercises rather than candidates for construction, the Soviet navy was alone among the world's fleets in sustaining strong dreadnought ambitions throughout the war years, even initiating a BC project postwar (the never-completed *Stalingrad* class, Project 82).

SOVIET UNION

KRONSHTADT, SEVASTOPOL (34,685 tons; nine 12-inch, eight 6-inch, eight 3.9-inch DP guns; AC 4, 32 knots): Project 69, BC begun in 1938 but never launched. Various plans included as many as 15 units.

The Soviets toyed with a number of studies mounting 9.4-inch to 12-inch guns until construction of the *Scharnhorst*s spurred a more serious effort. Nevertheless, *Kronshtadt*'s protection hardly matched that of the German design, carrying 13% less armor on an 11% greater displacement. The armor belt had a 9.1-inch thickness, thinner than *Strasbourg*'s and *Cavour*'s. Horizontal protection looked even skimpier; the *Des Moines*-class cruisers had thicker decks.

In firepower at least, *Kronshtadt* surpassed *Scharnhorst* with high-performance 12-inch guns in 45° mounts capable of lobbing shells far beyond the limits of Soviet fire control. The low-angle secondaries give an additional hint of Italian influence, but a slim hull crowded the Pugliese system out of consideration, replaced by layered bulkheads. A curiosity in *Kronshtadt* and *Sovyetskiy Soyuz* was their triple-shaft propulsion; designers foresaw identical engines for the two classes.

The irony of wartime goodwill with Hitler carried over into this project. With the ships' already under construction, the leadership dictated replacement of the main battery with German 15-inch twin mounts, the exact change planned for the rival *Scharnhorst*s. This would have further bloated the design to 35,846 tons, if the Germans had proved as accommodating as their promises.

In weaponry, the *Kronshtadt*s compare with *Alaska*, *Scharnhorst*, and Japan's Type B65. In protection, though, they seem frighteningly like the "O"-class BC. Ultimately, their tonnage ranks them with *Richelieu*, *South Dakota*, and *King George V*, in whose company they look truly feeble.

Cruisers

At the outbreak of World War II, the Soviet cruiser force amounted to one modern ship, plus the few old units that had survived the revolution and down-sizing. Wartime production contributed only five more completions, ships of doubtful utility but some apparent resistance to damage.

The hulk *25 Oktyabrya*, a former armored cruiser and minelayer (4,500 tons, 1873), survived to the 1950s; other projects died amid the Great War. In 1914, Germany seized two *Muravev Amurski*-class ships (4,500 nt, eight 5.1-inch guns, five 17.7-inch TT, 150 mines, 27.5 knots) building in a German yard; one of them wound up in the Italian navy in World War II as *Bari*. Plans for four minelaying cruisers (4,000–5,000 tons, six or eight 5.1-inch guns, 350–450 mines) never reached a final design.

AVRORA (5,622 tons; ten 5.1-inch, two 3-inch DP guns; 18 knots, 1902): last of three sisters, serving in training duty. Sunk in shallow water by German bombers, she landed most of her guns for use by ground troops.

KOMINTERN (6,338 tons; eight 5.1-inch, six 3-inch, three 3-inch DP guns; 12 knots, 1905): from the *Bogatyr* class of four ships, plus one

The Soviet cruiser Avrora, *shown as preserved with her original 6-inch battery rather than the 5.1-inch guns she mounted during World War II.*

not completed. As built, she had twelve 6-inch and twelve 3-inch guns, six torpedo tubes, 23 knots, and the name *Kagul*. She spent some time as *Pamiat Merkuriya* until 1923 when the Soviets, who never met a ship they didn't rename, settled on a title they found politically correct. Age relegated her to training, but in 1941 she became a minelayer (6 5.1-inch, four 3-inch DP guns, 195 mines).

KRASNYI KRYM (6,693 tons; fifteen 5.1-inch, six 3.9-inch DP guns, six 21-inch TT, 100 mines; 29 knots, 1927): formerly named *Svetlana* and *Profintern*, and possibly *Sovnarkom* and *Klara Zetkin*. The Russians began four *Svetlana*-class ships in 1913; apparently two completed as tankers, one languished for possible completion as a training cruiser until broken up in the 1950s, but *Krym* entered service. A frontline unit early in the war, by 1941 she could make only 24 knots. She shipped a pair of 3-inch DP to bolster her Italian-type 3.9/50 guns.

CHERVONA UKRAINA (7,480 tons; fifteen 5.1-inch, six 3.9-inch DP guns, twelve 21-inch TT, 100 mines; 29 knots, 1928): *Krym*'s half-sister, from a class of four repeat *Svetlana*s. Of these four, two never reached completion, one became *Kasnyi Kavkaz* (see below), and one eventually received the name *Chervona Ukraina*—the world's final WWI-type cruiser. A refit, completed in 1941, reduced her to six torpedoes and gave her one or two seaplanes, at least temporarily. She may not have carried any mines. After her loss, she became a source of spare parts for *Kavkaz*.

KRASNYI KAVKAZ (7,560 tons; four 7.1-inch, six 3.9-inch DP guns, six 21-inch TT, 120 mines; AC 2, 29.5 knots, 1932): another rebuilt *Svetlana*, Project 815. *Kavkaz* rarely carried two aircraft, and by 1944 she carried none. The DP battery may have begun with four guns, but certainly increased to a maximum of 12 with guns removed from *Chervona Ukraina*, plus a pair of 3-inch DP.

Planners first intended a battery of eight 8-inch guns, then retreated to six 7.1-inch guns, then decided she couldn't carry more than four. The centerline turrets made *Kavkaz* more modern than her half-sisters in both layout and looks, but a main battery of four barrels left her profoundly undergunned. Her broadside of 860 lbs hardly compares with foreign CA firepower: *Suffren* had 2,363 lbs; *Bolzano*, 2,210 lbs; *Exeter*, 1,536 lbs; *San Francisco*, 2,340 lbs; *Aoba*, 1,665 lbs. Even the humble CL *Leander* had 896 lbs. The Soviets may have felt the potent 7.1-inch gun gave their aged ship the semblance of offensive power, but the effort seems misguided; Britain made its old cruisers useful by down-gunning to DP batteries. No records indicate a similar plan for *Kavkaz*, but one wartime proposal would have replaced the 7.1-inchers with eight 5.1/50 guns. (This 7.1-inch gun differed from that used aboard later ships. Nominally a 60-caliber weapon, it elevated perhaps as high as 60° in single mounts, but otherwise gave similar performance.)

KIROV, VOROSHILOV (7,800 tons; nine 7.1-inch, six 3.9-inch DP guns, six 21-inch TT, 90 mines; AC 2, 35 knots, 1938–40): Project 26, Soviet-built but very Italian, beginning as a 7,200-ton CL based on *Montecuccoli* with three 6-inch twin mounts and much Italian equipment, including boilers and turbines. An early switch to 7.1-inch guns had few complications, but the decision for 48–50° triple turrets came late enough to force the designers to fit the mounts into the same space as a twin. The designers met this challenge, but only by severely crowding the guns—while Italy's too-close 8-inch gun axes were 39.4-inch apart, *Kirov*'s margin shrank to 32.3-inch—which aggravated their dispersion problems.

The ships benefitted from the Italian model of machinery dispersal, but their performance reflected Soviet inexperience more than Italian expertise. Overweight exceeded 10%, and *Kirov*'s speed remained one knot short of the design figure. Delays in *Voroshilov*'s construction, lengthy even by Soviet standards, allowed enough corrections to get her speed near 37 knots, while she also gained 90 tons and a mine load of 164. During the war, *Kirov* shipped two additional 3.9-inch DP.

The hull structure involved uniquely Soviet framing, complex but relatively strong—a fortunate change from Italian practice. Less conscientious work in DD hulls led to critical defects.

The *Kirov*s correspond in tonnage to contemporary French CL mounting nine 6-inch guns and thus appear well armed, but overloaded as well. Some compensation may have come in a thinness of armor (a 2-inch belt versus 4-inch for *Galissonnière*).

MAXIM GORKIY, MOLOTOV, KALININ, KAGANOVICH (8,048 tons; nine 7.1-inch, six 3.9-inch DP guns, six 21-inch TT, 100 mines; AC 2, 35 knots, 1940–44): Project 26bis, a *Kirov* slightly improved with 2.8-inch belt armor. Some gained an extra pair of DP guns. The last two ships had eight 3.3-inch DP instead of 3.9-inch.

Seaplane operations for the *Kirov/Gorkiy*-types became practical only in 1945. In the meantime, some units landed their planes to accommodate extra AA and depth charges.

Unfettered by treaties, the navy saw its opportunity to make a ship that could prowl the sea lanes and outfight any 8-inch cruiser or pocket battleship. This "Cruiser X" (15,275 tons;

Maxim Gorkiy. *A handsome appearance gave no hint of the design's tortured gestation.*

twelve 9.4-inch, twelve 5.1-inch DP guns, six 21-inch TT, 100 mines; AC 9, 38 knots) enlisted a platoon of design extremes, squeezing machinery more powerful than *Iowa*'s into a cruiser hull while mounting thinner belt armor than a *Brooklyn*-class CL. The main battery (45° mounts) showed the usual lust for performance, implying the usual consequences. As its final oddity, the ship could carry a pair of "Bloha" craft (an improbable design for submersible torpedo boats, none completed: 35/73 tons, two 17.7-inch TT, 11/33 knots.) The project withered as the *Kronshtadt*-class BC began development.

A series of "MK" CL studies (about 6,100 tons; six 6-inch, six 3.9 inch DP guns, ten 21-inch TT, 90 mines; AC 2-3, 36+ knots) featured modest armor, long range, and depth charges. A final draft suggested an armament of ten 5.1-inch DP guns before the project ended.

CHAPAYEV class (10,620 tons; twelve 6-inch, eight 3.9-inch DP guns, six 21-inch TT, 200 mines; AC 2, 33.5 knots): Project 68, with *Kirov*'s Italian elegance but thickened armor for a better design balance. Desperate for guns, the Soviets negotiated a deal in 1940 for German 5.9-inch and 4.1-inch weapons, despite the extra 730 tons this wedged into the design. Seven of twelve planned *Chapayev*s began building. The Germans scrapped two they found lying damaged and incomplete on the slips. The other five were commissioned postwar, updated and mounting Soviet guns.

TALLINN (14,800 tons; eight 8-inch, twelve 4.1-inch DP guns, twelve 21-inch TT; AC 3, 32 knots): Project 83 *Lützow* of the German *Prinz Eugen* class, purchased incomplete in 1939. The Soviets never finished her but found time to rename her *Petropavlovsk*, then *Tallinn*. She served as a floating battery with her four German 8-inch guns. The navy showed little interest in altering the original design, except a possible switch to 3.9-inch DP guns, though a postwar suggestion included ten 7.1-inch guns.

Destroyers

Tsarists and Soviets both found their DD programs snarled by world war. The units in operation in 1939–45 suffered heavy losses and accomplished little, even when presented with opportunities.

Old *Zheleznyakov*'s hulk (570 tons, 1907) lasted through the war.

BAKINSKIY RABOCHIY, ALTFATYER, MARKIN (750 tons, three 4-inch guns, 15 knots, 1905): last of eight *Ukraina*-class DD. They outlived several names while on patrol duty in the Caspian. *Altfatyer* later became *Sovyetskiy Dagestan*.

ARTEMEV, MARTINOV (350 tons, two 3-inch guns?, 20 knots, 1906): last of 10 *Bditelnyi*-class DD serving in secondary duties. The Soviets scrapped *Martinov* in 1940.

KONSTRUKTOR (625 tons, three 3.9-inch DP guns, 20 knots, 1906): last of four *General Kondratenko*-class DD, used as a GB. Battle damage amputated 20 feet of her bow, and workers returned her to service without replacing it.

YAKOV SVERDLOV (1,271 tons; five 4-inch, one 3-inch DP gun, nine 17.7-inch TT, 60 mines; 30 knots, 1913): ex-*Novik*, Type I; at the time of completion, the world's most powerful destroyer. *Novik* became the prototype for several future classes, and her influence continued into the modern *Leningrad*s. All told, the Russians planned 66 *Novik* type units; 36 eventually reached completion. By 1939, 17 of them continued as Soviet fleet units, while two others served in the Peruvian navy.

The initial layout specified two 4-inch guns, but more weapons wandered aboard; this led to an unappealing feature of the type, a crowding of its guns. Two 4-inchers sat side-by-side on the forecastle while the other three huddled aft.

The situation became even more awkward with the addition of the 3-inch DP.

The *Novik*s played an important role in Russia's WWI mining success, but World War II saw the roles reversed. Soviet *Novik*s performed little minelaying, while six of them ran afoul of Axis minefields.

Upon completion, *Novik* attained 36 knots. Endurance may have shrunk from its original 1,800 miles at 16 knots.

FRUNZE (1,100 tons; four 4-inch, one 3-inch DP gun, nine 17.7-inch TT, 60 mines; 28 knots, 1915): *Novik* Type II, with eight sister ships no longer in service. *Frunze* had only one bow gun but retained the collection on her stern.

KARL MARX, KALININ (1,354 tons; five 4-inch, one 3-inch DP gun, nine 17.7-inch TT, 80 mines; 28 knots, 1916–27): *Novik* Type III, planned as a class of five. The ships as completed could make 33 knots. *Marx* mounted only six TT and perhaps no 3-inch gun, while *Kalinin* may have had two 3-inchers. Both ships may have landed one forward gun.

KARL LIBKNECHT, VALERYAN KUIBISHEV, LENIN, VOIKOV (1,260 tons; four 4-inch, one 3-inch DP gun, nine 17.7-inch TT, 60 mines; 24 knots, 1916–28): *Novik* Type IV, planned as a class of eight. *Kuibishev* and *Voikov* each had four previous names. Not one *Novik* served in World War II under its original name.

ARTIOM, ENGELS, STALIN, URITSKIY, VOLODARSKIY (1,440 tons, four 4-inch guns, six 17.7-inch TT, 60 mines, 24 knots, 1915–16): *Novik* Type V, originally a class of eight. *Engels* performed mid-1930s trials with a new 12-inch muzzle-loading recoilless gun (SW: 728 lbs; range: 15,010 yards; FC: 30). Stalinistic politics removed the originator of this project before it could fully display its absurdity.

SOVIET UNION

Though the Novik *destroyers entered service with potent weaponry,
the gun placement was not necessarily efficient.*

DZERZHINSKIY, NYESAMOZHNIK, SHAU-
MYAN, ZHELEZNYAKOV (1,308 tons, four 4-
inch guns, six 17.7-inch TT, 45 mines, 26
knots, 1917–25): *Novik* Type VI, planned as a
class of eight.

The Russians ordered three more batches of
Noviks, totaling 27 ships. (Only three of them
reached completion, and they sank in 1919.)
This concentration on the *Noviks* preempted a
project for 36 TB (500 nt, three 4-inch guns,
four 17.7-inch TT, 30 knots). The navy also
planned a much larger type (2,500 tons) but
never began construction.

LENINGRAD, MOSKVA, KHARKOV; MINSK,
TBLISI, BAKU (2,032 tons; five 5.1-inch, two 3-
inch DP guns, eight 21-inch TT, 84 mines; 36
knots, 1936–40): Project 1, the first fleet project
undertaken by Soviet shipbuilders. The last
three units, called Project 38/38bis, had a
refined layout (1,952 tons, 124 mines). *Baku*
first entered service under the name *Kiev*.

The design shared some features with
Uragan, but also showed the influence of old
Novik and contemporary French *contre-
torpilleurs*. Rated as flotilla leaders, the
*Leningrad*s attempted a pointlessly high speed—
40 knots, far exceeding the speed of the ships
they were intended to lead.

Leningrad somehow reached completion at
her intended displacement, perhaps a unique
achievement for the Soviets, but she couldn't
escape the other standard pitfalls of delay and
deficient manufacture. Launched in 1933, she
lingered semi-complete awaiting her main guns,
whose design received official approval only in
1936. The 5.1-inch design derived from
attempts to get 55cal performance from a 45cal
gun, which naturally proved impossible, and
lengthening to 50cal failed to prevent rapid barrel erosion. In its scramble for a cure, the fleet
distributed a variety of new liners, which
improved the situation but also meant that not
all guns could use the same ammunition or fire-
control input.

The gun went on to serve successfully. It
provided good firepower from a simple mount
easily adapted to a number of platforms.
Unfortunately, the 45° elevation prevented
effective fire against aircraft. Some *Leningrad*s
traded one mount for light AA. No Soviet
destroyers mounted a DP main battery, which
had predictable results in an environment dominated for so long by the Luftwaffe.

Stability and sea-keeping in the *Leningrad*s
rated as marginal. Despite initial trouble with
some machinery components, trial speeds
reached as high as 43 knots. Machinery dispersal enhanced survivability, an advantage largely

248

negated by inordinate susceptibility to shock effects.

GNEVNYI, BODRYI, BYSTRYI, BEZUPRECH-NYI, BDITELNYI, BOIKIY, BESPOSHCHAD-NYI, GORDYI, GROMKIY, GROZNYI, GREM-YASHCHIY, GROZYASHCHIY, SMETLIVYI, SOKRUSHITELNYI, STEREGUSHCHIY, STRE-MITELNYI, REZVYI, RYANIY, RASTROPNYI, REDKIY, RETIVYI, RAZIASHCHIY, RESHITEL-NYI, REZKIY, REVNOSTNYI, RAZYARYON-NYI, RAZUMNYI, REKORDNYI (1,695 tons; four 5.1-inch, two 3-inch DP guns, six 21-inch TT, 60 mines; 38 knots, 1938–41): Project 7. The program included 53 units: these 28, plus a previous *Reshitelnyi* lost incomplete in a pre-war accident; 18 converted to the Project 7U; and six others not completed.

The project began with the purchase of *Oriani* drawings from Italy. The *Oriani*s themselves were overweight, and the problem increased in Soviet hands. An initial estimate of 1,388 tons gave way to a revised 1,524-ton figure, which the completed ships exceeded. Wartime displacement rose above 1,850 tons. Vibration problems necessitated corrections in the machinery. Designed for 2,600 miles at 19 knots, in service the ships achieved 1,700 miles at 16 knots. The need for AA fire prompted some units to take on a third 3-inch DP. At least five Project 7's fell victim to Axis aircraft, and four to mines.

Not as stoutly reinforced as the *Kirov*s, the ships showed frailty at their ends; a storm removed *Gromkiy*'s bow, and *Sokrushitelnyi* went down when her stern broke away. Hull strengthening prevented further losses, but the design's inferior sea-keeping remained. The navy ultimately preferred its elderly *Novik*s to the Project 7's.

TASHKENT (2,893 tons, six 5.1-inch guns, nine 21-inch TT, 110 mines, 42 knots, 1939): Project 20; beautiful flotilla leader built in Italy, perhaps the finest design to serve with the

The stylish Tashkent *awaits her main battery.*

Soviets in World War II. Due to delays with her twin mounts, she commissioned with a temporary trio of singles. Her most significant short-coming, a lack of DP guns, led to her mounting a pair of 3-inch DP. Aircraft did her in. Bombs opened her for 1,900 tons of flooding; the Italian hull held together long enough to allow a tow back to port, but there she foundered. Workers removed her guns, and two mounts went to sea again aboard *Ognevoi*.

The navy ordered at least eight ships of modified design (2,600 tons; six 5.1-inch, two 3-inch DP guns, 8–10 21-inch TT, 80 mines; 38 knots). Construction began on four of them, but none reached completion.

OPYTNYI (1,570 tons, three 5.1-inch guns, eight 21-inch TT, 60 mines, 42 knots, 1941): Project 45, the Soviets' first solo effort at DD design. They completed the ship (without her guns) in 1939 but retained her in trials for two years before the German invasion prompted her official commissioning. Despite her machinery dispersal, *Opytnyi* was a failure. She struggled to reach 35 knots, hampered by impractical boilers and massive overweight beyond her designed 1,570 tons. Ironically, attempts at weight-saving left her flimsier than the Project 7's, and though her design included three 5.1-inch twin mounts, her hull could barely support singles. Since the vibration and stress of high-speed steaming rendered her guns inoperative, she spent the war as a floating battery.

SOVIET UNION

STOROZHEVOI, SILNYI, SUROVYI, SERDI-
TYI, SMELYI, STOIKIY, SLAVNYI, STRASHNYI,
SKORYI, STATNYI, SVIREPYI, STROGIY,
STROINYI, SMYSHLENNYI, SOOBRAZITEL-
NYI, SPOSOBNYI, SVOBODNYI (1,686 tons;
four 5.1-inch, two 3-inch DP guns, six 21-inch
TT, 60 mines; 36 knots, 1940–42): Project 7U.
Another unit, *Sovershennyi*, struck a mine while
running trials and was never commissioned for
service.

The design arose from Project 7 after Stalin
declared his destroyers needed machinery dispersal. Designers achieved the admirable feat of
accommodating this change within the existing
hull lines; unfortunately, another case of mistaken weight calculations masked the fact that
the ships had risen past 1,800 tons. The alterations came at a slight cost of speed and range.
Several units took on a third DP gun. Nine ships
became war losses, most due to mines or
bombs.

OGNEVOI (1,800 tons; four 5.1-inch, two 3.3-
inch DP guns, six 21-inch TT, 80 mines; 36
knots, 1943): Project 30, a Project 7U improvement, more seaworthy and stable. Designers
saved top-weight with twin mounts for the
main and DP guns. Thirty units began building; only *Ognevoi* was commissioned in
wartime, but fourteen modified sisterships followed postwar.

The Soviets took Romania's four DD; *Regele
Ferdinand, Regina Maria, Mărăşeşti,* and *Mărăşti*
became *Likhoi, Letuchyi, Logkiy, and Lovkiy.*

Submarines

In 1939, the Soviet submarine force was the
world's largest; by 1945, almost 300 boats gave
service. Yet this undersea powerhouse under-
achieved. Its torpedoes sank only 20 warships,
eight small craft, and 91 merchant ships
(231,058 grt). Submarine-laid mines added 13
more warships, two tugs, and 18 merchantmen

(38,291 grt). Meanwhile, Soviet losses topped
100 boats. The blame for this record lies not
with the designs, nor with their weapons. In
fact, because submarine production resumed
soon after the revolution, the designs evolved
with continuity—a Soviet rarity. Salvage of the
British *L55* added important input. The Soviets
thus built boats that were modern, though in
many cases glaringly deficient.

Submarine production suffered from the
same incompetence and inferior components
that plagued the surface ships. So worn by prolonged trials, some boats entered service in
need of a refit, while still harboring some of
their bugs.

Submarine duty highlighted the comedy of
Soviet training. Stalin's gutting of the officer
corps elevated fledglings to captaincy, while his
lackeys in the high command stumbled visionless through the war. They responded to a low
initial success rate by threatening the submariners; this produced instant claims of multiple sinkings.

Even without the incompetence that saturat-
ed all levels of the Soviet navy, the submarines
faced a challenging and hazardous scenario. In
the Baltic and Black Seas, the juiciest targets
skulked behind a shield of waspish escorts and
swarming aircraft. The Soviets chanced this
environment without adequate communications, equipped with only the most rudimentary technology. No submarines carried radar
until at least November 1944, if at all.

The Soviets, specialists in confusing records,
perfected their name-changing skills on their
submarines and small craft. This section
attempts to account for each Soviet submarine,
if not for each of their various names.

B2 (664/753 tons, two 3-inch guns, six 21-inch
TT, 11.4/6.8 knots, 1916): last of 24 *Bars*-class
boats. Three or four sisters lingered as battery-
charging hulks; *B2* became one in 1942. The
design had little value when completed, much
less 25 years later, with unreliable engines and a

dive time exceeding three minutes. The 3-inch guns elevated to 60°.

A1–5 (360/470 tons, four 17.7-inch TT, 12/10 knots, 1918–23): from an order that originally included 17 units. These boats, though built in Russia, had the same American "H" class design that served in navies all over the world. *A1–5* each had at least three previous names. They remained in service through most of the war.

L55 (954/1139 tons, two 3-inch guns, six 21-inch TT, 13.5/8.2 knots, 1918): ex-British boat, raised in 1928 and commissioned under the same name with the Soviet navy in 1931. Her value lay not in her combat abilities but in her use for trials and design lessons. She became a battery-charging hulk after a 1941 accident.

The civil war afforded the Soviets the modern *L55* to tinker with, but it also interfered with local construction. The Russians had projected 45 boats of the "B," "G," and "V" classes (920–971/1140–1289 tons, two 3-inch guns, sixteen 17.7-inch TT, 10 mines, 13–17/9–10.5 knots) along with *Z1–4* (230/368 tons, 10/5 knots) carrying no torpedoes but 20 mines. More than 20 completed boats of various classes were scuttled or discarded between 1919 and 1922. Also, two boats ordered prewar from Italian builders went instead to the Italian navy.

The final Tsarist project, which never began production, involved a cruiser-type (1,998/2,725 tons; two 5.1-inch, two 3-inch guns, fourteen 17.7-inch TT; 21/10 knots).

D1–6 (933/1,354 tons, one 3.9-inch gun, eight 21-inch TT, 14/9 knots, 1930–31): Project 6 Series I, also named *Dekabrist, Narodovolets, Krasnogvardeyets, Revolutsioner, Spartakovets,* and *Yakobinets.* Referring to *Balilla* plans purchased in Italy, designers copied some features without understanding their functions. The boats handled well enough on the surface, reaching 15.7 knots, but failed to dive in the designed 30 seconds (as commissioned, 180 seconds). Once underwater, they topped out at 8.7 knots, and bigger problems arose: a lack of stability and a recurrent malfunction threatening to flood their tanks without warning—a submariner's nightmare. *D1* failed to surface after a dive in 1940. At least three others became war losses. The deck gun elevated to 60°.

L1–6 (1,051/1,327 tons, one 3.9-inch gun, six 21-inch TT, 20 mines, 13.8/8.4 knots, 1933): Project 6 Series II, also named *Leninets, Stalinets, Frunzovets, Garibaldyets, Chartist,* and *Karbonariy.* This first "L" class derived in part from the salvaged *L55* but showed no great virtue, and the build-up of engine gases created a hazard. However, the diesels in the "L" classes

The Estonian submarine **Lembit** *came under Soviet command in 1940.*

gave reasonable performance, permitting refinement of the basic type, though the boats always kept their crews busy with maintenance while on patrol. The guns elevated to 60°.

SHCH301–304 (578/704 tons, six 21-inch TT, 13/8.5 knots, 1933): Series III, also named *Shchuka*, *Okun*, *Yorsh*, and *Komsomolets*. They changed numbers at least twice (previously *Shch1–4*, then *Shch31–34*). Their maneuverability, rapid diving (80 seconds—better than previous types), and small size made them effective, despite some flaws. They reached only 11.2 surface knots. Their success prompted five further series showing similar virtues and a persistent lack of speed.

P1–3, plus one not completed (1,200/1,870 tons, two 3.9-inch guns, six 21-inch TT, 18.8/7.7 knots, 1936): Series IV, also named *Pravda*, *Zvezda*, and *Iskra*; poor seaboats that proved slow in the dive. Last-minute alterations for strengthened hulls led to serious overweight, compensated for by removal of some propulsion machinery and by a change of gun armament. Originally intended to carry the new 5.1/50, the boats reverted to the lighter 3.9-inch model (45° elevation) and may have had one mount removed. The machinery change eliminated any hope of reaching the designed 20/10 knots, yet the boats remained among the fastest in the fleet. This failed to make them useful, and their war service consisted of transport duty. The Soviets declined further P-type development.

SHCH101–112; SHCH113–120, 201–204, 305, 308; SHCH121–125, 205–208, 306, 307, 309-311 (586/702 tons, six 21-inch TT, 14/8 knots): Series V (1933–34), Series Vbis (1934–35), and Series Vbis-2 (1935–37): These three classes all derived from the Series III, with a steady trend of mild improvement, gaining some weight (up to 617 tons surfaced) but losing some speed (as low as 12/6.7 knots). The subtle differences in the *Shchuka*s hamper attempts to distinguish among their sub-classes. Boats went through as many as four number changes, and some had names as well.

M1–28, 51, 52 (161/202 tons, two 21-inch TT, 13/6 knots, 1934–35): Series VI.

M53–56,71–86 (161/201 tons, two 21-inch TT, 13/6 knots, 1935–36): Series VIbis, with more streamlining and better workmanship.

The old Holland boats had many good qualities, but not youth. The Soviets set out to replace them, designing the coastal M-types with good underwater handling. Unfortunately, their tiny size limited more than their range; with no space available for reload torpedoes, they had all the offensive ferocity of a midget sub. Yet the Soviets were satisfied with the M-boats, looking to them only for humble duties such as coast defense. Later boats remedied the sea-keeping problems of these first two series.

S1–3 (840/1,070 tons, one 3.9-inch gun, six 21-inch TT, 19.5/9 knots, 1936–37): Project 9 Series IX, the first "S" or "Stalinets" class (not to be confused with the "L" class *Stalinets*—the Soviets weren't shy about using the same name simultaneously on two or more vessels.) All S-boats had 45° gun mounts except perhaps *S1* (4-inch gun in a 60° mount?).

The design looked distinctly German; in fact, it was a German design prepared in the Netherlands, similar to the layout for the Turkish *Gür* and the German Type IA. This heritage made the S-boats the best prewar Soviet design—strong, reliable, and seaworthy. They had a dive time of 30 seconds.

S4–22, 31–34, 50–56, 101–104 (856/1,090 tons, one 3.9-inch gun, six 21-inch TT, 18.9/8.8 knots, 1939–45): Project 9 Series IXbis, some also with names. Additional orders of the Series IXbis and the similar Series XVI totaled about 23 boats; 10 or so reached completion postwar. A key advantage of the foreign design was its quietness. All through the war, domestic designs were audible at five or six times as great a distance as German boats.

SHCH126–134, 139, 141, 209–215, 317–320, 322–324, 401–404, 421, 422, 424; SHCH135, 137, 138, 216, 405–410, 426, 428 (590/705 tons, six 21-inch TT, 13.6/8 knots): Series X (1936–39) and Series Xbis (1941–45), the two groups differing mostly in the manner of construction. Quieter than previous *Shchukas*, they also regained some speed. Orders for about 17 more boats resulted in perhaps 13 postwar completions.

L7–12 (1,025/1,321 tons, one 3.9-inch gun, six 21-inch TT, 20 mines, 14/9 knots, 1936–38): Project 6 Series XI, an improved Series II. Three of the boats also had names. These and subsequent L-boats had 45° mounts for their deck guns.

M87–90 (205/256 tons, two 21-inch TT, 14.1/8.2 knots, 1937–38): Series XII. Their meager range (3,440 miles at 8.3 knots) more than doubled that of earlier M-boats.

The "M" concept became subject to experimentation. The navy built at least two boats to test the viability of adapting diesels for submerged propulsion, but the systems proved impractical. Another submerged-diesel craft that never reached completion, *M400*, was not part of the "M" class sub series, but a prototype for the "Bloha" TB project.

M31–36, 57–63, 91–108, 111–122, 401 (225/275 tons, two 21-inch TT, 14/8.5 knots, 1938–43): Series XIIbis, with a further increase in range.

L13–19 (1,099/1,399 tons, one 3.9-inch gun, eight 21-inch TT, 20 mines, 13.7/8.5 knots, 1938–39): Project 6 Series XIII, showed improvement with more firepower and range (10,000 miles at 8.6 knots).

L20–25 (1,108/1,399 tons, one 3.9-inch gun, eight 21-inch TT, 20 mines, 18/8.5 knots, 1941–43): Series XIIIbis, given more efficient machinery.

K1–3, 21–23, 51–53, 55, 56 (1,480/2,095 tons, two 3.9-inch guns, ten 21-inch TT, 20 mines, 21/10 knots, 1939–44): Series XIV, or the "Katyusha" class, intended specifically for Arctic patrols. As many as six more reached completion postwar, with one cancellation. The design improved on the "P" boats and became the best Soviet wartime class, despite a dive time of 50 seconds. Early design work included a seaplane in a hangar. Though the boats never reached their design speed (22.5 knots), they had good range (15,000 miles at nine knots). The 3.9-inch mounts allowed 45° elevation.

Low expectations helped make a success of the Soviet M35 and her sisters.

M200–203 (283/350 tons, four 21-inch TT, 15.7/7.8 knots, 1943–44): Series XV, with perhaps 56 units following postwar. With two more TT than previous "M's, " they still had no reloads.

In 1936, the Soviets built a midget boat named *Pigmei* and an 8-ton human torpedo. Neither project enjoyed further development, nor did the idea of a 15-ton flying submarine.

The Romanian surrender provided the Soviets with three full-sized boats, *Requinul*, *Marsuinul*, and *Delfinul* (renamed *S3*, *S4*, and *TS4*), plus the ex-Italian midgets *CB1–4, 6*. Some recovered U-boats (including three Type II's and a Type VII) proved too badly damaged for further use.

Minecraft

ZAPAL (185 tons, one 3-inch gun, 32 mines, 11.5 knots, 1911): MS from a class of five. (One sister, named *Minrep*, probably lasted into the war years, possibly renamed *Zmey*, later with a TShch-number.) *Zapal* carried AS gear, but with her top speed fallen near nine knots, even a submerged sub could outrun her.

UDARNIK, KLUZ (190 tons, one 3-inch gun, 36 mines, 9–12 knots, 1917): MS, perhaps renamed with TShch-numbers. They resembled *Zapal* in their AS capability. Two sisterships served as the Finnish *Vilppula* class.

DOROTEYA (443 tons, light guns, eight knots, 1924): coastal MS.

DZHALITA (470 tons, light guns, eight knots, 1926): coastal MS.

FUGAS class (441 tons, one 3.9-inch gun, 31 mines, 18 knots, 1935–42): Project 3/53 also called the *Tral* class, 49 MS given names and T-numbers. The 3.9-inch guns had 45° elevation.

VLADIMIR POLUKHIN class (700 tons, one 3.9-inch DP gun, 15 mines, 24 knots, 1942–45): Project 73, six MS derived from *Fugas*, also with names and T-numbers. The Soviets planned at least 24 of these ships; a dozen or so reached completion postwar.

T301 class (130 tons, mines, 12.5 knots, 1943–44): simple MS for mass production.

T371 class (150 tons, 18 mines, 14 knots, 1944–45): a second *T301* series but further simplified. Wartime production of the two series totaled 92 units, with another hundred completed by 1956.

Auxiliary warships attained an unprecedented status among the Soviets. Military unpreparedness and the Eastern Front's demand for riverine combatants prompted wholesale conversions for every type of duty. The navy adapted a throng of auxiliary minesweepers (283 vessels converted, many of them former tugs or trawlers), then supplemented this throng with a swarm of minesweeping launches, including 475 requisitioned motor boats as well as those purpose-built to one of the navy's standard designs (the R, MSV, K, KM4, and KM2 types etc. listed in the motor boats section below). This throng and swarm gathered together to form an abounding, minesweeping multitude which the Soviets further augmented with a crowd of captured vessels, many of them previously noncombatant. Among the combatants seized were two MS launches from Hungary, four or five auxiliary MS from Romania, plus six riverine MS from Bulgaria and three from Poland. The Finns, in their 1944 surrender, ceded *Jurmo* and *Narvi*.

Since virtually all Soviet warships could carry mines, few designs specialized in the task. Two old ships, *Gidograf* (1380 nt, two 3-inch guns, 250 mines, 10.5 knots, 1893) and 9 *Yanvarga* (1711 nt, light guns, 230 mines, 13 knots, 1905), no longer served actively. The sisters *Berezina* and *Yauza* (380 nt; two 4-inch, one 3-inch DP gun, 90 mines; 8.5 knots, 1917) acted as ML, MS, depots, and trainers.

AMUR (3,020 tons; one 4.7-inch, one 3-inch DP gun, 360 mines; 17 knots, 1909): ML from a class of two; disarmed and hulked in 1940.

MARTI (5,664 tons; four 5.1-inch, seven 3-inch DP guns, 780 mines; 14 knots, 1936): the former imperial yacht. Built in 1896, converted in 1936 (Project 40), but ill-suited to the ML role. She laid a total of 3,159 mines.

ONYEGA, VYATKA (530 tons, mines, eight knots, 1941): barges converted to netlayers; equipped with mines.

The Soviets deployed about 56 auxiliary ML. Two Finnish auxiliary ML entered Soviet service, as did the Romanian *Amiral Murgescu* (renamed *Don*) and one Romanian auxiliary ML. Poland's riverine *Mątwa* took the name *Pina* in Soviet service.

Gunboats and Escorts

The old GB *Terets* (renamed *Znamya Sotsialisma*?: 1,284 tons, 1888–89) avoided scrapping until the 1940s; her sister *Kubanets* probably didn't. The former torpedo gunboat *Abrek* (535 tons, 1897) served throughout the war as a depot ship.

KRASNOYE ZNAMYA (1,794 tons; five 5.1-inch guns, 50 mines; 14.5 knots, 1897): armored gunboats. Some records mention a DP battery of three 3-inch guns.

VOROVSKIY (2,100 tons, two 4-inch guns, 10 knots, 1901): former yacht in imperial and communist service used for patrol and escort.

DOZORNYI, RAZVEDCHIK (100 tons, light guns, 16 knots, 1904): dispatch vessels used as patrol boats.

KHIVINETS (1,340nt, four 5.1-inch guns, 12 knots, 1906): renamed *Krasnaya Zvezda, an* ex-gunboat used for training until scrapped in 1944.

MONGOL, BURYAT (315 tons, two 3-inch gun, 80 mines, 9.1 knots, 1907): river gunboats related to the subsequent *Krasnaya Zvezda*, one sister scrapped prewar.

KRASNAYA ZVEZDA, PROLETARIY, KRASNOYE ZNAMYA (333–337 tons, three 3.9-inch guns, 40-80 mines, 10 knots, 1908): from a class of seven river GB. *Proletariy* had a 4.8-inch howitzer instead of a third gun.

LENIN, KRASNYI AZERBAIDZHAN (700 tons, three 3.9-inch DP guns, 14 knots, 1910): GB. The guns may have been 4-inch, 60cal in low-angle mounts.

SUN YAT SEN, LENIN, KRASNYI VOSTOK, SVERDLOV, DZERZHINSKIY, KIROV, DAL-NEVOSTOCHNOI KOMSOMOLETS, plus one lost prewar (965 tons; 6–8 4.7-inch, two 3-inch DP guns; 15 knots, 1910): well-armed and armored river monitors, disparate in weaponry. Some units had 3.3-inch DP guns. Some received a main battery of four 6-inch guns, though perhaps only *Sverdlov* retained them into the war years. Records disagree on the caliber of the 4.7-inch guns.

KRASNYI VIMPEL (700nt, four 3-inch guns, 11.5 knots, 1911): dispatch vessel.

PIONYER, KOBCHIK (530 tons, two 4-inch guns, 100 mines, 14 knots, 1916): guardships; the latter out of service around 1940, perhaps scrapped prewar.

MOGILEVSKIY (168 tons, one 3-inch gun?, 11 knots, 1916): last of seven dispatch vessels.

During World War I, the navy ordered dozens of *Elpidiofor*-type vessels, primarily for amphibious landing, but also capable of mine work and other tasks. Most of the completed units went into commercial service between the wars. The navy retained four or five for service in World War II as gunboats and minelayers (1,100 tons; three 5.1-inch, two 3-inch DP guns, 380 mines; eight knots).

URAGAN class (463 tons, two 4-inch guns, three 17.7-inch TT, 48 mines, 25 knots, 1931–38): Project 2/4 (?), 18 guardships, an inauspicious first step for Soviet domestic construction. Designers miscalculated the displacement at 395 tons, an error of 17%. The engines failed to provide the designed speed of 29 knots. The ships turned out top-heavy, weak-hulled, and wet. They did have some endearing qualities, such as good habitability prior to wartime crowding. They should have provided lessons for the Soviet shipbuilding industry, yet the design and construction blunders became standard.

Light AA increased during the war, at times replacing the TT. Some units had a main battery of 3.9-inch guns, capable of AA fire but otherwise inferior to the 4-inchers.

UDARNYI (385 tons, two 5.1-inch guns, 13 knots, 1932): river monitor.

AKTIVNYI (262 tons, two 5.1-inch guns, nine knots, 1934): river monitor.

DZERZHINSKIY, KIROV (810 tons, three 4-inch guns, 24 mines, 18.5 knots, 1934): Project 19, Italian-built guardships.

ZHELEZNYAKOV class (263 tons, two 4-inch guns, 7.6 knots, 1936): six river monitors.

RUBIN, SAPHIR, BRILLIANT, ZHEMCHUG (550 tons, one 4-inch gun, 17 knots, 1936–39): Project 43, guardships similar to the *Fugas*-class MS.

ARTILLERIST class (240 tons, one 3.3-inch gun, 22.3 knots, 1941–45): 23 SC, plus perhaps 43 or more completed postwar.

KHASAN, PEREKOP, plus SIVASH postwar (1,677 tons, six 5.1-inch, four 3-inch DP guns, 29 mines; 15.1 knots, 1942–44): Project 1190, powerfully armed and stoutly armored monitors. Rated as river gunboats, they had the appearance of fleet units, as well as true seagoing capabilities and AS weaponry.

YASTREB, plus twenty-nine additional units planned (906 tons, three 3.9-inch DP guns, three 17.7-inch TT, 24 mines, 31 knots, 1944–45): Project 29 guardships, an attempt to improve the *Uragan* design. As many as eighteen sisterships began construction, six of which the Germans captured and scrapped incomplete. The original design mounted a trio of 3.3-inch DP guns, but the escalation to 3.9-inch guaranteed a repeat of *Uragan*'s top-heaviness. Designers tried to restore stability by setting two guns low on the quarterdeck where their crews could crowd each other.

ALBATROS, CHAIKA, KORSHUN, ORYOL, plus one other unit (920 tons, three 3.3-inch DP guns, three 17.7-inch TT, 24 mines, 31 knots): Project 29K, five postwar completions of *Yastreb*-class hulls with few changes. The navy grudgingly accepted the regression to a smaller main battery because of a gun shortage, but this actually improved the design balance.

The number of auxiliary patrol ship conversions reached 69, many of them ex-tugs and like-sized craft, along with 43 additional units converted as antiaircraft vessels. The navy operated a total of 78 auxiliary gunboats, including eleven former dredging vessels of the *Moskva* class (1,083 tons; two 5.1-inch or three 3.9-inch, two–four 3-inch DP guns, 8.75 knots, 1941). A solitary icebreaker converted to serve as an AMC (10,827 tons; three 5.1-inch, four 3-inch DP? guns; 15.5 knots, converted in 1941). *Aunus* and four other Finnish captives entered Soviet service. (The Finns reciprocated with a few minor captures of their own.) The Soviets deployed the following prizes under new names:

Romania: *Smeul—Toros*
      Sborul—Musson
      three *Eugen* class—*Akhtuba, Angara, ?*
      three *Bogdan* class—*SKA754–756*
      Bucovina—Izmail
      Basarabia—Kerch
      Ardeal—Azov
      Brătianu, Lahovari—Mariupol, Berdyansk
Poland: *Warszawa* class—*Vinnica* class
      Kraków—Bobruisk
Bulgaria: three *Smely* class—*Derski* class
      two *Belomorec* class?

The Soviets also took five of Poland's *Admirał Sierpinek*-class vessels, then apparently lost one to the Germans.

Motor Boats

Soviet waterways teemed with small craft. The navy deployed more than 500 launches to its fleet sectors, with hundreds more operating on lakes and rivers. These numbers included requisitioned craft (324 boats for patrol and AA duty) and, especially from 1944 on, captured units: German, Hungarian, and so on, along with three Iranian *Azerbaijan*-class launches, at least 16 Polish river craft, and 27 small craft seized from Japanese forces in 1945.

Some Soviet launches were little more than barges with a small anti-tank piece lashed on deck; others specialized as minecraft. The navy had a few standardized designs, some of which are listed below. Production neared 900 units.

All carried light guns, plus depth charges or MS gear as needed.

R type, 44 units (26 tons, 9.3 knots, 1936-37): minesweeping design.

ZK type, 15 units (19 tons, 16 knots, 1930-31): patrol design.

BK type, 3 units (20 tons, 32 knots, 1939-41): patrol design.

PK type, 7 units (23 tons, 27 knots, 1927-35): patrol design.

MKM type, 6 units (18 tons, 21 knots, 1939-41): patrol design.

R type, 36 units (30 tons, 9 knots, 1937): patrol, unrelated to R type MS above.

K type, 7 units (14-17 tons, 7-11 knots 1928-32).

MSV type, 25 units (16 tons, 8.5 knots, 1940-44): minesweeping design.

KM4 type, 184 units (12 tons, 10 knots, 1938-44).

KM2 type, 72 units (12 tons, ? knots, 1934-40): patrol design.

Some reports allude to *VMV201–212,* similar to Finnish VMV-craft, but this appears incorrect. The Soviets seized *VMV101–104* from the Finns in 1944, having already taken two launches among other craft in 1940.

The Soviets expanded their "MO" designation (for submarine-chasers) to include many of these minor launches as well as a clutch of larger vessels (11 units, 50-75 tons). It seems a 47-ton design entered production (103 wartime completions).

A few SC of WWI vintage may have lasted to join the modern classes.

MO2 type (51 tons, light guns, 14 knots, 1935): 27 unsuccessful vessels that never neared their designed speed of 25 knots.

MO4 type (51 tons, four mines, 24–26 knots, 1937–45): Project 199 (?), 263 submarine-chasers of an improved design. Their superiority to the MO2's didn't qualify them as effective anti-submarine vessels, and range was just 367 miles at 15 knots.

BMO type (52 tons, mines, 20 knots, 1942–45): 66 submarine-chasers completed during the war. They shared the previous SC designs' inadequate endurance.

TK type (38 tons, light guns, 24 knots): 56 underpowered D3 type MTB converted to SC before or after completion. Too slow for torpedo attacks, they also had little value as AS craft.

The Soviets had great success with armored motor gunboats, most operating exclusively on rivers. The Finns captured one boat of unknown type.

KOPYE, PIKA (23.5nt, one 3-inch gun, 14.5 knots, 1910): elderly river gunboats from a class of 10. The Soviets renamed them with BK- or BKA-numbers. Two sisters served in the Finnish navy.

BKA71–74 (25nt, two 3-inch guns, 12 knots, 1917): from a class of nine river gunboats built in America to a rugged design. The Soviets scrapped one in 1940, and the others became *BK72–74*.

The *BKA71* design, also known as the K class, was contemporary with the similar N class (three units: one 3-inch gun, 7 knots). Both types could carry mines.

1124BKA type (97 units: 42 tons, two 3-inch guns, 28 knots, 1935–45): armored MGB.

1125BKA type (151 units: 29 tons, one 3-inch gun, 20 knots, 1935–45): armored MGB.

Nine similar MGB with 3-inch guns entered service prewar. Early BKA units used T28 tank turrets but T34 turrets became standard. Some units carried rocket launchers as well. Simple and sensible, these two designs rated among the most important in the Soviet fleet.

MBKA type (150 tons, two 3.3-inch guns, 18 knots, 1943–44): an enlargement of the 1124BKA with seagoing capability. An initial series of 20 craft mounted 3-inch guns, while 8 slightly different boats went to the larger caliber; more completions followed postwar. Some units also carried rockets.

The Finns surrendered four German-built MAL-craft in 1944. Two of Poland's "Z" type river GB became the Soviet *Trudowoj* and *Belorus*; the latter eventually went to the Germans as *91*, and both apparently rearmed with two 3-inch weapons at some point.

The Soviet Union's MTB led careers of ceaseless activity. Their skippers laid claim to sinking or damaging 250 warships plus 200,000 gross tons of shipping; in fact, they accounted for only 30 vessels. Even so, in the eyes of the Germans, the Soviets' greatest naval threat came from their MTB.

Most Soviet MTB received TKA-numbers; some also had names. Prewar plans to carry MTB aboard battleships were not pursued in wartime.

SKA211–217 (35 tons, light guns, 16 knots, 1905): primitive craft serving as patrol vessels without their torpedoes. After scrappings in 1940, only one remained as *MO312*.

PERVENETS (9 nt, one 17.7-inch TT, 54 knots, 1927): ANT3 type, prototype based on British CMB seized during the Intervention. She proved a poor seaboat, top-heavy and wet, and yet showed promise. The excellent speed had certainly declined by 1939; deemed unusable in 1941, she was scrapped.

TUPOLEV (10 nt, two 17.7-inch TT, 50.4 knots, 1928): ANT4 type, an attempt to correct *Pervenets*'s flaws.

SH4 type (11 nt, two 17.7-inch TT, 44–50 knots, 1928–32): based on the two prototypes. The navy built 55 units, but they required too much maintenance. Only 10 remained in service by 1939, only three by July 1941, their speed slumping below 30 knots.

The Soviets continued experimenting with a series of four SM-boats: SM1 and SM2 type (25 tons, two 21-inch TT, 30 knots, 1931), SM3 type (26 tons, two 21-inch TT, 35 knots, 1932), and SM4 type (11 tons, two 17.7-inch TT, 44 knots, 1932). The first pair, though completed in 1931, became operational only in 1941, possibly with three tubes and only 26 knots; they saw little use. The SM3 boat may not have reached completion; her specifications possibly included spurts of 45 knots. The navy purchased some Italian engines during the 1930s and perhaps developed a G4 type based on the Italian *MAS431*. The preference for high speed and small size in Soviet designs may reflect Italy's input.

G5 type (14–16 tons, two 21-inch TT or four mines, 45–56 knots, 1933–45): Project 116, 293 MTB built in five slightly differing series, plus four boats built for Spain. All but 39 units had entered service by the time of Barbarossa. The design resembled the Sh4 with improved seaworthiness. However, the boats needed diligent upkeep, and their metal hulls could start to corrode after a week or two in salt water. Some boats had engine problems; maximum service speeds perhaps ranged from 40 to 48 knots. A quirk in the design gave the boats a minimum speed of 18 knots, which often made for anxious docking. The placement of torpedoes in stern troughs rather than modern side mounts (a holdover from the CMB) reduced accuracy and lengthened exposure to enemy fire. Nevertheless, the light and sturdy G5's met with fair success. Some units carried a dozen 82mm or 132mm rockets. At least four boats fell into enemy hands, one to the Germans and three to the Finns. Germany captured a total of three Soviet MTB, which they used for trials only.

The G6 prototype (Project 116bis: 85 tons, three 21-inch TT, 49.8 knots, 1939) could carry

Stern-mounted torpedoes reveal this Soviet MTB's kinship with the British CMB.

an additional three torpedoes in a pivoting mount. Practical concerns ended the project, and the G6 served as a refueling boat. Residual interest in large designs brought six 50-ton units into service, but the smaller types remained preeminent, as shown by the next two prototypes, the G8 (26 tons, two 21-inch TT, 47 knots, 1938) and the D2 (17 tons, light guns, 50 knots, 1939).

D3 type (32 tons, two 21-inch TT, 35 knots, 1939–45): 119 boats in all, an important improvement. With wooden hulls, they avoided the corrosion troubles of the G5. They proved superior seaboats, and they had side mounts for their torpedoes as well. Some D3's may have achieved 42 knots with a new engine design, while others used Packards from America. But a scanty engine supply left many units lacking horsepower; underpowered as MTB, they converted to TK type submarine-chasers. Finnish forces captured one D3 boat.

The Soviets built several prototypes in 1940, including one D4 type (22 tons, two 21-inch TT, 39 knots) and the diesel-powered *TKA13* (15 tons, two 21-inch TT, 56 knots). A replacement for the G5, the *Komsomolets* class (15 tons, two 17.7-inch TT, 46 knots), trickled into service; about 32 commissioned by 1945.

Finnish forces claimed the capture of a "pocket MTB" armed with one torpedo—something of a mystery as no such design entered production. Four air-cushion craft entered service with two 17.7-inch TT and extraordinary speed (70 knots). The Soviets took seven Bulgarian and five Romanian MTB (TKA958–964, TKA951–955).

SPAIN

Franco remained aloof from his Axis benefactors when he might have profoundly altered the strategic balance, *vis-à-vis* Gibraltar and Portugal. Most likely, his inaction stemmed from Spain's weakness following its civil war (July 1936 through March 1939) and from the apparent inevitability of Germany's triumph. As that inevitability evaporated, Allied diplomacy and military strength became the deterrent.

The Spanish navy entered the modern era modestly enough, building the world's smallest dreadnoughts (three *España* class, 15,452 nt, all discarded by 1939) suitable for coast defense. A proposal for three larger ships (*Reina Victoria Eugenia* class: 21,000 nt; eight 13.4-inch, twenty 6-inch guns; 21 knots) fell apart amid the Great War, and postwar plans never matured despite obvious Spanish ambition. One project, Design 778A, called for a 45,000-ton BC with nine 15-inch guns, 7-inch deck armor, and 33 knots.

Franco envisioned a new armada of four battleships, two armored cruisers, 12 light cruisers, 54 destroyers, and 50 submarines, along with a host of small craft and new facilities—a pleasant notion but ultimately nonsense. The most likely BB candidate derived from the Italian *Littorio* with additional deck armor and 4.7-inch DP guns replacing the faulty 3.5-inch battery (correctly addressing *Littorio's* two most serious shortcomings). The armored cruiser layout revealed a Spanish interest in Germany's pocket battleships; a 1938 specification (17,500 tons; twelve 8-inch, twelve 3.5-inch DP guns; 36 knots) evolved within a year into something quite *Deutschland*ly (19,000 tons; six 12-inch, twelve 3.5-inch DP guns; 34 knots), and later the main guns changed to 11.1-inch.

Such vanities threaten to overshadow Spain's proven shipbuilding industry. Most of Spain's warships were domestic products. Although no large ships entered service after the mid-1930s, the smaller vessels exhibited sound design and workmanship, equal to their counterparts in the major fleets, though lacking in cutting-edge technologies.

Cruisers

NAVARRA (4,857 tons; six 6-inch, four 3.5-inch DP guns, four 21-inch TT; 25.5 knots, 1923): laid down during World War I as a copy of the British *Birmingham* CL design, and consequently obsolete upon completion. A 1937–38 refit removed three of her original nine main guns and repositioned the remaining six on the centerline. She also received a handsome tower bridge that recurred in subsequent classes.

MÉNDEZ NÚÑEZ (4,650 nt, six 6-inch guns, twelve 21-inch TT, 29 knots, 1924): one sistership lost prewar, two others canceled. The design resembled the British "C" classes. (All Spanish cruiser designs emigrated from England, but the construction took place in Spain.) *Nuñez* retained her WWI appearance until 1944 when she entered the yard for conversion to an AA cruiser. The work lasted until 1947. She emerged at 4680 standard tons with eight 4.7-inch DP guns and six TT, a fair employment of her old hull.

GALICIA, ALMIRANTE CERVERA, MIGUEL DE CERVANTES (7,475 tons; eight 6-inch, four 4-inch DP guns, twelve 21-inch TT; 33 knots, 1925–31): a transitional design derived from the British "E's" but with an all-centerline main battery, including three twin mounts. The 6-inch model, as in the previous classes, fired a 100-lb shell at 10 rpm, but the mount allowed increased elevation (22,300-yard range).

All three ships went through wartime changes. *Cervera* traded the 4-inch for 4.1-inch DP (33lb shells; 16,595-yard range; 33,800-foot ceiling) and grew to 7,976 tons. The others replaced their TT and DP with an airplane and eight 3.5-inch DP; they also set their main battery in a modern disposition (two twin mounts forward and two aft) while their displacement became 8,250 tons.

CANARIAS (10,113 tons; eight 8-inch, eight 4.7-inch DP guns, twelve 21-inch TT; 33 knots, 1934): based on the *Kent*, improved but still vulnerable (a mere 6.6% protection). A sistership, *Baleares*, sank in the Civil War after a single torpedo set off her forward magazine. The original plans included a seaplane. The main guns elevated to 50°, firing a 256-lb shell to 32,530 yards, allegedly at six rpm. The DP battery, as in the rebuilt *Núñez*, fired twelve 49-lb shells per minute.

Destroyers

HUESCA, TERUEL (1,028 tons, four 4-inch guns, four 17.7-inch TT, 42 mines, 32 knots, 1915): ex-Italian ships transferred in 1937. Their age and a 1938 collision kept them from active service during the 1940s.

CEUTTA, MELILLA (1,410 tons; four 4.7-inch, two 3-inch DP guns, four 17.7-inch TT, 50 mines; 34 knots, 1917–20): Italian-built, ordered by Romania with *Mărăşti* and *Mărăşeşti*. They gave little service after the Civil War.

ALSEDO, VELASCO, LAZAGA (1,044 tons, three 4-inch guns, four 21-inch TT, 34 knots, 1924–25): obsolete but active.

CHURRUCA, SÁNCHEZ BARCAIZTEGUI, LEPANTO, JOSÉ LUIS DÍEZ, ALCALÁ GALIANO, ALMIRANTE VALDÉS, plus two others also called CHURRUCA and ALCALÁ GALIANO sold to Argentina in 1927 and one other sunk in the Civil War (1,536 tons, five 4.7-inch guns, six 21-inch TT, 36 knots, 1930–32): first series, based on British *Scott* but built in Spain. The ships enjoyed great popularity and long careers. The 4.7-inch shells weighed 49 lbs. Several units landed one gun.

Spain's entire "C" class fell victim to war or accident except C2, seen here.

ALMIRANTE ANTEQUERA, ALMIRANTE MI-
RANDA, JORGE JUAN, GRAVINA, ESCAÑO,
ULLOA, CÍSCAR (1,590 tons, five 4.7-inch
guns, six 21-inch TT, 36 knots, 1936–37): sec-
ond *Churruca* series, nearly identical to the first.
Some of them landed a gun.

ALAVA, LINIERS (1,650 tons, four 4.7-inch
guns, six 21-inch TT, 36 knots): third *Churruca*
series, laid down in 1936, not completed until
1951 due to the war and economic problems.
Gun elevation increased to 45°, but this did
nothing to improve their AA value.

OQUENDO class (1,940 tons, eight 4.1-inch
DP guns, seven 21-inch TT, 39 knots): three DD
authorized in the mid-1940s but completed 15
years later with much-altered specifications.
The DP battery represents a significant advance.
In size and weaponry, this design resembled the
postwar Canadian "Tribals."

Submarines

The entire "B" class (*B1*–*6*: 491/715 tons, one 3-
inch gun, four 17.7-inch TT, 16/10 knots,
1922–25) fell victim to the Civil War either in
action or in scuttling, but the Spanish raised *B2*
for use as a generator plant.

C2, 4 (916/1,290 tons, one 3-inch DP gun, six
21-inch TT, 16/8.5 knots, 1928–29): American
design built in Spain. The Civil War accounted
for *C1, 3, 5, 6*.

GENERAL MOLA, GENERAL SANJURJO (969/
1,239 tons, two 3.9-inch guns, eight 21-inch
TT, 17/8 knots, 1934–35): ex-Italian *Torricelli*
and *Archimede*, transferred in 1937.

G7 (769/871 tons, five 21-inch TT or 14 mines,
17/7.5 knots, 1942): German *U573*; interned in
1942 and later purchased.

D1–3 (1,065/1,480 tons, one 4.7-inch gun, six 21-inch TT, 20.5/9.5 knots): construction begun by 1933 but completed postwar.

Miscellaneous

1 class (177 nt, three 17.7-inch TT, 26 knots, 1914–18): six TB left of 22 built, plus two canceled. Each boat landed some or all torpedoes and functioned as a minelayer.

AUDAZ class (1,227 tons, three 4.1-inch DP guns, four 21-inch TT, 40 mines, 31.6 knots): nine TB derived from the French *Le Fier* design with machinery dispersal. Construction began in wartime, then dragged on into the 1950s.

ALCÁZAR, LARACHE, TETUÁN (400 tons, one 3-inch gun, 10 knots, 1918): ex-French trawlers.

XAUEN, ARCILLA, UAD QUERT (438 tons, two 3-inch guns, 11 knots, 1918): ex-British *Mersey*-class trawlers.

UAD MARTIN (360 tons, one 3-inch gun, 10.5 knots, 1918): ex-British "Castle"-class trawler; four others lost prewar.

CÁNOVAS DEL CASTILLO, CANALEJAS (1,314 tons, four 4-inch guns, 15 knots, 1923–24): Spanish-built gunboats, plus one sister sunk in 1936. *Castillo* shipped a pair of 3-inch DP; *Canalejas* may have had them as well, but certainly got a new main battery of four 4.1-inch DP guns.

CALVO SOTELO (1,600 tons; four 4-inch, two 3-inch DP guns; 20 knots, 1936): GB; sistership of Mexican *Durango*.

JUPITER, VULCANO, MARTE, NEPTUNO (2,100 tons; four 4.7-inch, two 3-inch DP guns; 264 mines; 18.5 knots, 1937–38): escort and minelaying design. They had the same 4.7-inch model as the *Canarias* but in low-angle mounts. *Vulcano's* DP guns may have been 3.5-inch.

EOLO, TRITÓN (1,500 tons, four 4.1-inch DP guns, 170 mines, 19.5 knots, 1942–43): a scaled-down *Jupiter* with the same 4.1-inch mark as in *Canalejas* and *Cervera*.

The Spanish also had 12 *Aldebaren*-class gunboats (500 tons, one 3-inch gun) and numerous small craft. War delayed the completion of the eight *Pizarro*-class gunboats (1,710 tons, six 4.7-inch guns, 40 mines, 18.5 knots), a powerful and handsome derivative of the *Eolos* that began service in 1947. Seven German-designed *Bidasoa*-class MS (550 tons, one 4.1-inch gun, 16.5 knots) came just after the war's end.

The navy operated several MTB, all from foreign sources:

M1–6 (30 knots, 1922): Thornycroft CMB, probably out of service.

DAR1, 2 (15 tons, two 21-inch TT, 50 knots, 1935): plus *DAR3, 4* sunk in the Civil War, ex-Soviet G5 type.

name? (14 tons, two 17.7-inch TT, 40 knots): ex-Italian *MAS435*.

LT11–15: not respectively, ex-German *S1* (39 tons, two 19.7-inch TT, 34.2 knots, 1930) and *S2–5* (46.5 tons, two 19.7-inch TT, 33.8 knots, 1932).

LT17 (12 tons, two 17.7-inch TT, four mines, 27 knots, 1918): ex-Italian *MAS100*.

LT18 (12 tons, two 17.7-inch TT, 27 knots,

1918): ex-Italian *MAS223*, stricken in 1941, sisters in service in China and Finland.

Germany transferred *S73, 78, 124–126, 134* in 1943 as *LT21–26*. Local yards finished six German diesel boats postwar (*LT27–32*: 120 tons, two 21-inch TT, 41 knots). The Germans seized seven MTB building in France.

SWEDEN

With allies on each side of the war, Sweden struggled to straddle the fence. Fortunately for the Swedes, Hitler felt no need to conquer those he could bully. He extracted several concessions before setbacks reduced German hubris.

The Swedish navy began the interwar period as the strongest force in the Baltic, but visions of utopia let it slip into decline. The delusion began to fade in the mid-1930s, and the Winter War brought reality into stark focus. The navy augmented its domestic shipbuilding with overseas purchases, especially from Italy—a triumph of marketing. Italian designs, barely suited to their native Mediterranean, had no place in the bleak Baltic.

The Swedish firm of Bofors supplied almost all Sweden's guns. During the war, most ships took on a battery of the famous 40mm Bofors gun, and a 25mm model as well. The typical Swedish torpedo had a 551-lb warhead with a range of 5,470 yards (40 knots) or 21,900 yards (26 knots).

Coast Defense

A few elderly hulks lingered, either serving in auxiliary roles or awaiting disposal: *Svea* and *Göta* (3,100 tons, 1888–90) and *Oden, Niord,* and *Thor* (3,400 tons, 1898–1899). *Dristigheten* had become a seaplane tender (2,218 tons, four 3-inch DP guns, mines, AC 3, 16 knots, 1901), providing experience later incorporated in the *Gotland* design. Two ancient monitors somehow avoided the scrap yard: *Folke* (451 tons, 1875) and *John Ericsson* (1,508 tons, 1865).

Sweden founded its formidable seaward defenses on unpretentious but capable designs like the Drottning Victoria.

ÅRAN, TAPPERHETEN, MANLIGHETEN (3,650 tons; two 8.3-inch, six 6-inch guns, two 17.7-inch TT; 17 knots, 1902–4): plus sistership *Wasa* out of service (used temporarily as a dummy *Drottning Victoria*). The other three, despite wartime refits that added 35 tons, served mostly as mobile gun batteries.

OSCAR II (4,273 tons; two 8.3-inch, eight 6-inch guns, mines; 18.3 knots, 1907): modernized on the eve of war; used for gunnery training.

SVERIGE, GUSTAF V, DROTTNING VICTORIA (6,852–7,125 tons; four 11.1-inch, six 6-inch, four 3-inch DP guns; 22.5 knots, 1917–22): handsome warships—typical in the Swedish navy—though differing in appearance after several refits. *Drottning Victoria* and *Gustaf V*, heavier than *Sverige*, could act as icebreakers. Protection comprised 20% of their displacement in a layout clearly intended for short-range encounters (7.9-inch belt, 1.8-inch deck). The main turret design proved somewhat cramped, and a reported increase to the gun elevation (for a range of 31,700 yards) appears unlikely.

The navy rated these three classes as armored ships, perhaps influencing the Germans' title for their pocket battleships. Coincidentally, when Sweden began considering new construction in the late 1930s, an Italian proposal (about 16,000 tons with 29 knots) called for six 10-inch or 11-inch guns. However, most designs lay near the 8,000-ton mark. Possible main batteries ranged from three twin 8.3-inch mounts to two 11-inch twins, with speeds between 23 and 29 knots. If not for the war, the Swedes might have gone ahead with a pair of ships (8,000 tons; four 10-inch, six 4.7-inch DP guns; 23 knots) carrying their dual-purpose battery in triple mounts.

Cruisers

FYLGIA (4,310 tons, eight 6-inch guns, two 21-inch TT, 21.5 knots, 1907): small armored cruiser used for training.

GOTLAND (4,775 tons; six 6-inch, four 3-inch DP guns, six 21-inch TT, 100 mines; 28 knots, 1934): an international sensation at a time when the hybrid concept was *très chic*. The project began as a seaplane carrier, but its front end turned into a light cruiser with all its 6-inch guns in enclosed 60° turrets. When financial concerns caused a shortening of the design, two guns moved to 30° casemate mounts. Aviation facilities took up the stern of the ship. The maximum air group of 11 seaplanes became a more realistic six in practice. Machinery dispersal in-creased crew survivability.

For all its novelty, the design had little value as an aviation platform. By 1944, she ceased to carry aircraft and instead became an antiaircraft cruiser with enlarged batteries of light guns.

Ordnance

GUN	SW	RANGE	FC	NOTES
11.1/45	672	27,300	20	*Sverige*s
8.3/44.4	276			*Åran*s, *Oscar II*
6/55	101	26,700		*Gotland* (less range for casemate guns)
6/50	101	17,500		*Sverige*s
6/50	101			*Oscar II, Fylgia*
6/44.4	100			*Åran*s, *Älvsnabben*
4.7/50	46			*Clas Fleming*
4.7/45	51			*Psilander*s
	46	21,100		*Visby*s, *Göteborg*s, *Ehrensköld*s, *Klas Horn*s
4.1/50	36			*Mode*s
4.1/41	36			*Arholma*s
	35			*Draken*s
3.9/47	30	16,670		*Romulus* class
3/60	12			*Gotland*
3/42.5?	12			*Valen, Dristigheten, Sverige*s

SWEDEN

TRE KRONOR, GÖTA LEJON (8,200 tons, seven 6-inch guns, six 21-inch TT, 160 mines, 33 knots): laid down in 1943 and completed postwar. Their main guns, utilizing materials intended for Dutch ships, elevated to 70° in one triple and two twin turrets; this, of course, did not make them practical AA weapons. The ships included a thorough armor scheme (26% protection).

Destroyers and Torpedo Boats

Old *Magne* (430 tons, 1905) was a British-built DD prototype; inactive from the mid-1930s, she went to the scrappers around 1943. Two TB flotilla leaders, *Örnen* (844 tons, 1896) and *Jacob Bagge* (835 tons, 1898) continued in training. Sweden had ended its TB program; at most 25 of the 29 *Komet*- and *Plejad*-class units (around 100 tons, built 1896–1910) survived as minesweeping PB armed only with light guns, as did some smaller ex-TB of similar age (perhaps 10 units, about 60 tons).

WALE; SIGURD, RAGNAR, VIDAR; HUGIN, MUNIN (430–446 tons, four 3-inch guns, four 17.7-inch TT, mines, 30 knots, 1907–1912): a developing series of DD designs based on *Magne*. *Wale*, a close copy of *Magne*, had only two guns; she left active service by 1940. The others, no longer useful as DD, landed one gun and functioned as escorts, minelayers, and patrol boats. The last pair introduced turbine engines into the Swedish navy. *Munin* left service early in the war.

WRANGEL, WACHTMEISTER (465 tons, four 3-inch guns, four 17.7-inch TT, 34 knots, 1918): plus two others not built. The class represented an improvement of the *Wale* type, but foreign destroyers had grown (two or three times *Wrangel*'s displacement). The 3-inch guns, a new model, fired 14-lb shells. A 1940 refit removed two TT and raised the ships to 498 tons.

EHRENSKÖLD, NORDENSKJÖLD (974 tons, three 4.7-inch guns, six 21-inch TT, 20 mines, 36 knots, 1927): also numbered 1 and 2. By doubling *Wrangel*'s tonnage, the designers nevertheless produced something rather puny. The 4.7-inch guns became standard in 45° mounts, with one gun crowded between the funnels.

A Baltic coast defense force had no need for muscular, ocean-going ships, but the Swedes persisted with their destroyer nomenclature, inviting unfavorable comparisons; *Ehrensköld* was commissioned just a year before *Fubuki*.

KLAS HORN, KLAS UGGLA (1,020 tons, three 4.7-inch guns, six 21-inch TT, 20 mines, 36 knots, 1932): numbered 3 and 4, an improved *Ehrensköld* design.

GÖTEBORG, STOCKHOLM, MALMÖ, KARL-SKRONA, GÄVLE, NORRKÖPING (1,040 tons, three 4.7-inch guns, six 21-inch TT, 20 mines, 39 knots, 1936–41): hull numbers 5–10, a further development of the *Ehrensköld*. The ships showed good speed, all exceeding 40 knots in service, but their design remained at a WWI displacement.

MODE, MAGNE, MUNIN, MJÖLNER (750 tons, three 4.1-inch DP guns, three 21-inch TT, mines, 30 knots, 1942–43): hull numbers 29–32, torpedo boats in all but name. The *Mode*s carried the title of coastal destroyers—a title more apt for the *Ehrensköld*s—though the navy intended them more as convoy escorts than fleet units. The design derived from experience with Italian TB, which were faster but less seaworthy.

VISBY, SUNDSVALL, HÄLSINGBORG, KAL-MAR (1,135 tons, three 4.7-inch guns, six 21-inch TT, 20 mines, 39 knots, 1943–44): numbered 11–14, an improved *Göteborg*, contemporary with American designs twice their

*The Swedish **Malmö** was much smaller than foreign destroyers.*

tonnage with six 5-inch DP guns. None of the *Ehrensköld* types had endurance exceeding 1,600 miles at 20 knots.

ÖLAND, UPPLAND (1,880 tons, four 4.7-inch DP guns, six 21-inch TT, 60 mines, 35 knots): numbers 16 and 17, a monumental advance in DD capability. Endurance increased to 2,500 miles at 20 knots. The 4.7-inch guns, in twin mounts fore and aft, had 80° elevation. These ships had a modern, powerful look; laid down in 1943, they reached completion well after the war.

March 1940 saw one of the war's more curious acts of diplomacy. With domestic yards unable to meet an immediate need for escort vessels, Sweden found Italy willing to sell four warships: two *Sella*-class DD and two *Spica*-class TB. The destroyers, renamed *Psilander* and *Puke* (1,250 tons, four 4.7-inch guns, four 21-inch TT, 32 mines, 35 knots, 1926–27), had a terrible time in the choppy Baltic waters, and retired by 1947. The navy reclassified the *Spica*s as destroyers *Romulus* and *Remus* (870 tons, three 3.9-inch DP guns, four 17.7-inch TT, mines, 34 knots, 1935); this pair fared relatively well after assuming their new Swedish tonnage. Their guns may have had 60° elevation.

Sweden began its MTB program with foreign purchases. A pair of Italian boats retired prewar, while two Thornycroft CMB (*MTB3, 4*: 13 tons, two 17.7-inch TT, 40 knots, 1925), served until 1940. In that same year, the navy accepted delivery of two Vosper boats (*T3, 4*: 20 tons, two 17.7-inch TT, 40 knots, 1939), but *T1, 2* from British Power Boat went instead to the Royal Navy as *MGB44, 45*. Also, a month before the bizarre DD deal with Italy, the Swedes bought *MAS506, 508, 511, 524*, renaming them *T11–14*. The leadership decided to pursue a much larger type, about 150 tons, but couldn't find the necessary engines. Two small designs entered service as an interim measure, Swedish-built but Italian-engined: *T15–18* (23 tons, two 17.7-inch TT, 45 knots, 1941) and *T21–31* (27 tons, two 21-inch TT, 49 knots, 1942–43).

Submarines

HAJEN, SÄLEN, VALROSSEN (392/600 tons, four 17.7-inch TT, 15/9 knots, 1917–18): removed from service by 1943.

A previous *Hajen* (107/127 tons, 1908) retired in 1922 but survived long enough to become a museum. Two other inactive boats, *Svärdfisken* and *Tumlaren* (252/370 tons, 1915), served as AA platforms.

SWEDEN

BÄVERN, ILLERN, UTTERN (429/640 tons, four 21-inch TT, 15/9 knots, 1922): removed from service by 1944.

VALEN (548/730 tons, one 3-inch DP gun, four 17.7-inch TT, 20 mines, 14.8/7.4 knots, 1925): minelaying boat stricken in 1944.

DRAKEN, GRIPEN, ULVEN (667/850 tons, one 4.1-inch gun, four 21-inch TT, 13.8/8.3 knots, 1929–30): served throughout war except *Ulven*, sunk by a German mine.

DELFINEN, NORDKAPAREN, SPRINGAREN (540/720 tons, four 21-inch TT, 20 mines, 15/9 knots, 1936–37): minelaying boats.

SJÖLEJONET, SJÖBJÖRNEN, SJÖHUNDEN, SVÄRDFISKEN, TUMLAREN, DYKAREN, SJÖ-HÄSTEN, SJÖORMEN, SJÖBORREN (580/760 tons, six 21-inch TT, mines, 16.2/10 knots, 1938–42): had two of their TT in revolving deck mount.

U1–9 (367/450 tons, four 21-inch TT, 13.8/7.5 knots, 1942–45): one tube in revolving deck mount.

NEPTUN, NAJAD, NÄCKEN (550/730 tons, five 21-inch TT, 20 mines, 15/10 knots, 1943): minelaying boats.

Miscellaneous

MUL 9 (120 tons, mines, 9.1 knots, 1913): coastal ML.

CLAS FLEMING (1,750 tons, four 4.7-inch guns, mines, 20 knots, 1914): generously rated as a "cruiser-minelayer." As rebuilt in 1939–40, she carried a mine load in excess of 100.

MUL 10 (166 tons, mines, 9.5 knots, 1939): coastal ML.

ÄLVSNABBEN (4,250 tons, four 6-inch guns, mines, 14 knots, 1943): ML converted from a merchant hull.

SÖKAREN, SPRÄNGAREN, SVEPAREN (227 tons, light guns, 10 knots, 1918): MS used for various duties.

ARHOLMA class (365 tons, two 4.1-inch DP guns, mines, 17 knots, 1937–41): 14 mine-

The Arholma-*class* Bremön, *preserved in WWII form. The design achieved commendable versatility in mining and escort duties.*

sweepers built in two series, also equipped as escorts with good AS and AA weaponry.

M1, 2 (61 tons, light guns, 17 knots, 1937): MS.

M3–14 (50 tons, light guns, 13 knots, 1940–41): MS.

M15–26 (70 tons, light guns, 13 knots, 1941): MS.

A gunboat from the 1870s, *Blenda*, lasted as a blockship; the slightly younger *Skuld* was a heating ship for submarines.

SVENSKSUND (415 tons, light guns, 12.5 knots, 1892): old sloop, converted to survey vessel in 1942.

ASKÖFJÄRD, BAGGENSFJÄRD, NÄMDÖF-JÄRD (25 tons, light guns, 11.5 knots, 1931–32): patrol boats.

EDÖFJÄRD, KANHOLMSFJÄRD, LIDÖFJÄRD (28 tons, light guns, 11.5 knots, 1933): patrol boats.

JÄGAREN, KAPAREN, SNAPPHANEN, VÄK-TAREN (310 tons, two 3-inch guns, 23 knots, 1933–34): patrol boats.

SVK1–5 (19 tons, light guns, 10.5 knots, 1944): coastal patrol boats.

V51–56 (145 tons, light guns, 11 knots, 1944–45): patrol boats.

Numerous armed whalers and trawlers functioned as patrol boats and minecraft.

SYRIA

The war years saw Syria's transition to indepen-dence from the French, and the new government joined the Allies in 1945.

THAILAND

Thailand saw in the fall of France an opportunity to seize disputed areas along the Indochina border. Hostilities began in November 1940, and Thai forces secured some gains before signing an armistice in January. The government then focused on the threat posed by Japan. This threat turned into an invasion in the wake of Pearl Harbor, and Thailand quickly acquiesced. Under duress, the government declared war against Britain and America, an act without popular support or practical application; the United States refused to recognize it.

Coast Defense

Shortly after World War I, Thailand approached the British about buying some heavy units (the battlecruisers *Princess Royal* and *Lion*), but a lack of funds reduced the plan to a single destroyer.

RATANAKOSINDRA, SUKHOTHAI (886 tons; two 6-inch, four 3-inch DP guns; 12 knots, 1925–30): British-built gunboats, extremely compact and more thickly armored than many cruisers (2.5-inch belt armor, for example). The 6-inch guns fired 100-lb shells to 20,430 yards. Despite its odd appearance, the design proved a complete success.

SRI AYUTHIA, DHONBURI (2,265 tons; four 8-inch, four 3-inch DP guns; 15.5 knots, 1938): Japanese design from the same theory as the *Ratanakosindra*s and similar in appearance, but much enlarged. The 8-inch mounts may have had 45° elevation; with 4-inch turret armor, they quadrupled the thickness given to Japanese cruiser turrets.

THAILAND

TAKSIN, NARESUAN (5,500 tons; six 6-inch, six 3-inch guns, six 21-inch TT; AC 2, 30 knots): CL design from Italy (retained there as *Etna* and *Vesuvio*) with armor thinner than in the gunboat classes. The 6-inch guns would probably have been the latest Italian 55cal model.

The Thai leadership, adept at ordering vessels well-suited to the country's needs, had to place its orders overseas. No major warships of this period came from a domestic yard.

Miscellaneous

SINSAMUDAR, VILUN, MACHANU, BLAJUN-BOL (370/430 tons, one 3-inch DP gun, five 21-inch TT, 14.5/8 knots, 1938): Japanese-built coastal subs; four additional units planned but not built. Their gun armament may have consisted of light weapons only.

TACHIN, MEKLONG (1,400 tons, four 4.7-inch guns, four 21-inch TT, 17 knots, 1937): Japanese-built sloops used for minesweeping and training, a sluggish but otherwise sound design. The 4.7-inch shells weighed 45 lbs.

PHRA RUANG (1,035 tons; three 4-inch, one 3-inch DP gun, four 21-inch TT; 35 knots, 1917): Thornycroft "R"-class DD purchased after World War I. The main guns fired 31-lb shells.

CHOW PHRAYA (840 tons, light guns, 16 knots, 1918): ex-British "Hunt" class sloop used as a gunboat.

BANGRACHAN, NHONGARHAI (368 tons, two 3-inch DP guns, 142 mines, 13 knots, 1936): Italian-built ML.

TRAD class (318 tons, three 3-inch DP guns, six 17.7-inch TT, 31 knots, 1935–38): nine Italian-built TB; one of the only Thai orders with high speed.

SRIYA MONTHON (225 tons, light guns, 14 knots, 1908): coast guard vessel.

KANTAN, TAKBAI, KYLONGYAI (110 tons, one 3-inch DP gun, two 17.7-inch TT, 19 knots, 1937): Japanese-built TB. The Thais built one additional unit postwar. Apparently, they saw little value in speed.

SARASINDHU, THIEW UTHOCK, TRAVANE VARI (50 tons, light guns, nine knots, 1936): fishery protection vessels designed in Italy but built in Bangkok.

Thailand bought two batches of 55-foot Thornycroft boats, *1–5* (11 tons, two 17.7-inch TT, 37 knots, 1922) and the slightly updated *6–9* (16 tons, two 17.7-inch TT, 40 knots, 1935). The Thais themselves may have completed boats numbered *10–12* to a Thornycroft design.

The Turkish submarine Saldiray *was designed and built in Germany.*

TURKEY

Turkish neutrality blended equal measures of animosity toward the Soviets and anxiety about the Germans. But, safely into 1945, Turkey declared war on Germany and Japan.

Surface Vessels

YAVUZ (23,100 tons; ten 11.1-inch, ten 5.9-inch, six 3.5-inch DP guns, two 19.7-inch TT; 27.1 knots, 1912): ex-German BC *Goeben* which survived into the 1970s. She suffered a period of neglect and then a series of refits. Protection never approached post-Jutland standards, with just two inches of armor atop the magazines. The main battery fired 666-lb shells to 23,730 yards at three rpm. The 5.9-inch shells weighed 100 lbs.

The Ottomans tried to obtain dreadnoughts as early as 1911 with two *Reshadieh*-class BB ordered from British yards (23,000 nt; ten 13.5-inch, sixteen 6-inch, four 3-inch guns, four 21-inch TT; 21 knots). The British completed only one, then kept it for themselves as *Erin*. An order for a slightly enlarged design (*Fatieh*: 24,700 nt) also failed to produce a completion. The Turks then purchased the half-finished *Rio de Janeiro* (renamed *Sultan Osman I*) under construction in Britain for Brazil, but the British took her as well, as *Agincourt*.

The Great War canceled several other orders in Britain: two scout cruisers (3,550 nt; two 6-inch, six 4-inch, two 3-inch guns, two 21-inch TT; 27 knots), four 1,100-ton destroyers (plus two sisters to be built in Turkey), and a pair of submarines. Likewise, the French left six Turkish destroyers unfinished (1,040 tons, five 3.9-inch guns, six 21-inch TT, 32 knots), and Italy never delivered four 700-ton DD. The Turks even had to abandon their own construction of six destroyers authorized in 1917.

HAMIDIEH (3,830 tons; two 5.9-inch, eight 3-inch guns, 70 mines; 17 knots, 1904): British-built cruiser used for training and minelaying.

MEDJIDIEH (3,330 tons; six 5.1-inch, four 3-inch guns; 18 knots, 1903): American-built cruiser used for training, formerly mounting two 17.7-inch TT. She later landed two main guns.

GAYRET, MUAVENET, DEMIRHISAR, SULTANHISAR (1,360 tons, four 4.7-inch guns, eight 21-inch TT, 35.5 knots, 1942): British-built DD of the "I" class. Once again, war interfered with the project, though for some reason Britain delivered the second pair while retaining the first two as *Ithuriel* and *Inconstant;* the former became a war loss, but Turkey received *Muavenet* postwar.

KOCATEPE, ADATEPE (1,250 tons, four 4.7-inch guns, six 21-inch TT, 36 knots, 1931): Italian-built DD derived from the *Folgore* class.

TINAZTEPE, ZAFER (1,206 tons, four 4.7-inch guns, six 21-inch TT, mines, 36 knots, 1932): Italian-built, also derived from *Folgore*.

Three inactive *Samsun*-class destroyers (284 tons, 1907–8) remained until postwar.

ERTUGRUL (900 tons, light guns, 21 knots, 1904): old yacht.

BERK, PEYK (840 tons, two 3.5-inch guns, 25 mines, 22 knots, 1907): former torpedo gunboats modified as ML. *Berk* retained three 17.7-inch TT.

ATAK (500 tons, 40 mines, 13 knots, 1938): minelayer.

KEMAL REIS, HIZAR REIS, ISA REIS (413 tons, three 3-inch guns, 14 knots, 1912): ex-GB converted for minesweeping, surveying,

TURKEY

The reputation for ruggedness in German World War I battlecruisers did not help Turkey's Yavuz *in combat 25 years later.*

etc. The conversion apparently reduced them to two 3-inchers; some accounts claim they carried only light guns.

Another former gunboat, *Aydin Reis* (502 tons, light guns, 14 knots, 1913), acted as a survey vessel.

NUSRAT (364 tons, 40 mines, 15 knots, 1913): minelayer.

An old ex-tug (*Uyanik*: 616 grt, one 3-inch gun?, 50 mines, 12 knots, 1886) performed minelaying duties.

SIVRIHISAR, TORGUD REIS (350 tons, one 3-inch gun, 40 mines, 15 knots, 1940): ML.

DOGAN, MARTI (32 tons, one 3-inch gun, two 17.7-inch TT, 34 knots, 1930): Italian-built motor boats renamed *HB1, 2*, with one additional unit no longer in service.

HB3–8 (30 tons, two 17.7-inch TT, 35 knots, 1942): Turkish-built MTB of British design.

The Turks had other motor boats, including at least one veteran from a class of 21 British-built launches (12 tons, light guns, 11 knots, 1912). Britain supplied *LM1–8* (British HDML, with a ninth craft lost before delivery) and the MMS *Kavak* and *Canak* (32 tons full, light guns, 15 knots, 1938), as well as three trawlers. Another

order for eight large boats was diverted to Royal Navy service (*MGB502–509*).

Submarines

BIRINDCI INÖNÜ, IKINDCI INÖNÜ (505/620 tons, one 3-inch gun, six 17.7-inch TT, 13.5/8.5 knots, 1928): a German design built in the Netherlands. To circumvent the Versailles restriction forbidding U-boat construction, German design teams transplanted themselves into foreign firms; thus, when Hitler ordered the resumption of the submarine program, he could call on experienced designers with fresh ideas.

SAKARYA (710/940 tons, one 3.9-inch gun, six 21-inch TT, 16.5/9.5 knots, 1931): Italian-built.

DUMLUPYNAR (920/1,150 tons, one 3.9-inch gun, six 21-inch TT, 17.5/9 knots, 1931): Italian-built.

GÜR (750/960 tons, one 4.1-inch gun, six 21-inch TT, 20/9 knots, 1934): German design built in Spain, forerunner of the Type IA.

ATILAY, SALDIRAY, YILDIRAY (934/1,210 tons, one 4.1-inch gun, six 21-inch TT, 20/9 knots, 1939): designed and built in Germany except *Yildiray*, built in Istanbul under German supervision. *Atilay* sank in a 1942 accident.

BATIRAY (1,044/1,357 tons, one 4.1-inch gun, six 21-inch TT, 18/8.4 knots, 1939): German-built, requisitioned by the Germans as *UA* and never delivered. Apparently the 4.1-inch model in all Turkish subs fired a 32-lb shell from a 45° mount.

ORUÇ REIS, MURAT REIS, BURAC REIS, ULAC ARI REIS (624/861 tons, one 3-inch gun, five 21-inch TT, 13.75/10 knots, 1941–42): built in Britain and seized there as *P611, 612, 614, 615*. As with the *Gayret*-class DD, the British delivered the first two immediately, while retaining the others for war service. They lost *P615*, then delivered *Burac Reis* in 1945.

UNITED STATES

In 1937, Japanese planes sank the American gunboat *Panay* on the Yangtze. A lather of diplomatic toil, sweat, and ink prevented an escalation toward war.

Four years later, after Roosevelt's pro-Allied diplomacy gave Britain 50 old destroyers and a pledge to assist with Atlantic convoys, a spread of German torpedoes obliterated the *Reuben James*. Diplomats watched their hopes for peace fading away.

There was nothing diplomatic about Japan's visit to Pearl Harbor on December 7, 1941. World War II had its way with the diplomats until September 2, 1945, when they finally wrestled it onto the pages of history. By that time, the United States Navy had become history's most powerful fleet.

Two Oceans

The Spanish-American War confirmed the United States as a global naval power as the nineteenth century drew to a close. Twentieth century developments forced the navy to define its role *vis-à-vis* a new cast of potential opponents: ocean-going fleets from a foreign hemisphere.

Germany seemed the most likely adversary, a threat that the Great War ended—temporarily. Only in 1940 did America identify the continued danger, cloaked in the form of the commerce-raiding submarine, an enemy the fleet was unready to face. With the transfer of destroyers to Britain, the American situation became grave. The navy had few suitable AS escorts, and few designs in the works.

On the other side of another ocean, Japan arose as an obvious rival after World War I. American planners foresaw—with startling precision—the Japanese intention to use submarine and air attack to wear down the superior numbers of America's battle fleet prior to a decisive engagement. To counter this strategy, the Americans laid the foundation for an unprecedented logistics effort to span the vast Pacific. They nurtured naval aviation (especially in the form of seaplanes and their tenders) while cultivating their own anti-aircraft capability. Though American light AA at first revealed no special potential, high-angle control became highly refined. And American ships mounted the 5-inch, 38cal gun, years in advance of foreign equivalents. No other navy equaled the American ability to shoot down aircraft.

From Weakness to Strength

Peacetime couldn't fully prepare the United States for war. In the Atlantic, this meant a lack of AS escorts and technology. Fortunately, British experience had already established the specifications for escort vessels which American yards could mass-produce. This ceaseless stream of warships slowly overwhelmed the U-boats, and by 1943, Allied AS craft began to dominate.

However, the British found themselves helpless in the sort of warfare forced on them by the Japanese fleet; here the Yanks had to hold the line. The Pacific campaign strayed far from the details of America's prewar scenario; but with the ships and techniques derived from that scenario, the navy turned the tide against the Japanese offensive, thanks in large part to the miracle at Midway. And though it would be simplistic to claim that Guadalcanal decided an ultimate Allied victory, the duel in the Solomons began the attrition that eliminated the Japanese fleet—quite the opposite of what the Japanese had planned.

This was the vital quality of the United States Navy in World War II: irresistible growth. Unsurpassed standards of damage control kept prewar designs in action until reinforced by a new generation of warships unshackled by treaty restrictions and modified in light of battle experience.

American overabundance gave shape to the three-pronged strategy that toppled Imperial Japan. The first prong—an island-hopping amphibious campaign—lies beyond the scope of this book. Let it suffice to note that America's old battleships and supporting units rained torrents of fire support against enemy positions while raising an umbrella against the enemy's response.

The second prong consisted of unrestricted submarine warfare that eliminated the enemy's ability to maneuver, depriving his ships of fuel and making every excursion a gamble. America didn't have the largest submarine fleet or the finest designs; it did have a body of consistent performers that, once equipped with a reliable torpedo, capitalized on Japan's laughable AS tactics.

But the most spectacular feature of America's effort was its wide-ranging carrier task groups. Supplied by a highly developed fleet train, the carriers launched ship-killing firepower to the farthest reaches of the Pacific. The navy had established the basis for successful carrier design by 1941. Though Japanese aircraft initially outperformed their American opponents, the appearance of the *Essex*-class CV with its lethal complement of planes signaled an ultimate Allied victory.

Virtues and Vices

As late entrants into the war, the Americans could peaceably consider the lessons Britain obtained in bloodshed. Close cooperation with the British contributed to America's excellence in technology. As radar emerged from its infancy, British experience and innovation meshed with the huge electronics industry in the United States, producing rapid advances and upgrades. Not all ships had the latest models (illustrated well at Surigao Strait), but American warships avoided the long waits their British cousins endured. Navy AA doctrine, emphasizing the interception of incoming bombers, spurred the development of precise shipborne radars, along with early warning sets mounted in carrier planes. Perhaps the premier achievement for American radar was the proximity fuse, which capitalized on the already superior AA gunnery.

Such advances came at a cost. The segue to reliance on radar aggravated American unreadiness for night combat and initiated a series of stinging defeats. Through 1942, Japanese night optics routinely outperformed American technology, and Japanese tactics left American commanders in stunned confusion. The American ability to sustain losses allowed the navy to correct its mistakes and improve its equipment, and by the time the fleet had climbed the Solomons ladder to Empress Augusta Bay, it had gained nighttime superiority.

The advance in technology created a drawback that grew worse as the equipment got better. Warships, weighed down by the addition of electronics, light AA weaponry, and fire control gear, could become critically top-heavy; the experiences of *Reno* and *Indianapolis* underscore the danger. The new equipment also required more crewmen, which effected habitability. Fortunately, designs began with high standards of habitability as well as long range—prerequisites for Pacific duty.

American wealth allowed the navy to "spare no expense" in its construction, making the ships far more costly than most foreign types. A British team observing American construction reacted with unmasked envy to the routine luxuries they saw: elaborate fittings, widespread use of armor-grade steel for non-armored surfaces, efficient electrical systems. Such features, not apparent in design statistics, nevertheless can make the difference in a ship's ability to complete its mission and bring its crew back home.

The United States Navy swaggered into World War I with a smug grin for its marksmanship, only to suffer humiliation in gunnery exercises with the British. The dispersion patterns of American battleships spread far beyond the target area. Part of the problem lay in simple inexperience, and before the fading of wartime cooperation, the Americans began to approach British gunnery standards.

A more serious flaw lay in an emphasis on high muzzle velocity with light shells—a com-

Ordnance

GUN	SW	RANGE	CEILING	FC	NOTES
16/50	2,700	42,345		30	*Iowas*, *Montanas*
16/45	2,700	36,900		30	*North Carolinas*, *South Dakotas*
	2,240	35,000		30[1]	*Colorados*
14/50	1,500	36,300		30	*New Mexicos*, *Tennessees*
14/45	1,500	34,300		30	*Pennsylvanias*, *Nevadas*
	1,500	23,000		30	*New Yorks*
12/50	1,140	38,573		20–25	*Alaskas*
	870	23,500		30	*Wyomings*
8/55	335	30,050		13–15	*Baltimores*
	260	31,860		13–15	*Lexingtons*, most CA
6/53	105	25,300		10–15	*Omahas* (turrets)
	105	23,300			SS
	105	21,100			*Omahas* (casemates)
6/47	130	26,118		6–8	*Brooklyns*, *Clevelands*
	105	19,800			*Eries*
5/54	70	25,909	51,600	4	*Midways*, *Montanas*
5/51	50	17,300		7	some *Tambors*
	50	15,850		7	old BB, *Bogues*, *Sangamons*
	50	14,050		7	some old DD and cutters
5/38	55	18,200	37,200	3[2]	standard fleet DP gun
	55	17,414		3	*Porters*, *Somers* class
	55	15,892		4	CVE
5/25	54	14,500	27,400	3–4	*Ranger*, *Lexingtons*, prewar cruisers, old BB
	54	14,500		3–4	SS
4/50	33	15,920		7	Eagle boats, old DD, some SS
3/50	13	14,590	29,800	3–4	DE, many old or small units
3/23	13	10,100	18,000		some old DD, cutters, other small vessels

[1] Many accounts credit the old BB with firing cycles of 40–45 seconds or more, but prewar exercises established the typical performance of two rounds per minute.

[2] FC 2.7 seconds in DD single mounts, 4 seconds in CV singles.

UNITED STATES

TORPEDO	WW	RANGE		NOTES
18-inch Mk 7	326	6,000/35		oldest SS
19-inch Mk 27	95	5,000/12		homing
21-inch Mk 8	466	16,000/26		in old DD and some MTB
21-inch Mk 10	497	3,500/36		"S" class subs
21-inch Mk 11	500	6,000/46	15,000/27	in some DD
21-inch Mk 14	643	4,500/46	9,000/31	standard SS mark
21-inch Mk 15	825	6,000/45	15,000/26.5	standard DD mark
21-inch Mk 18	575	4,000/29		electric for SS
22.4-inch Mk 13	401*	6,300/33.5		in aircraft and MTB

*Early version only, later increased to 600 lbs.

bination likely to disappoint, as the British later found out. Between the wars, American priorities swung to the opposite extreme. The old 1,400-lb 14-inch shell left service, replaced by a 1,500-lb shell with 4% less velocity. A 1,500-lb shell is not particularly heavy, but even that slight change increased the accuracy and barrel life with no significant loss in range. New guns showed a rabid devotion to shell weight, as in the 6-inch, 8-inch, and 16-inch marks. Though *North Carolina* and *Colorado* had nearly identical guns, the modern version surpassed its elder in all categories, even in range—not that 36,900 yards was particularly good.

American ammunition excelled at armor-piercing. The shift to heavier shells underscored an increasing emphasis on deck penetrations, at which the Americans surpassed all others. The 2,700-lb 16-inch shell exemplifies this; not even *Yamato*'s mammoth shells achieved greater deck penetration.

The 5/38 gun had neither a heavy round nor remarkable ballistic performance, but it became the most important naval gun of the war. Its high rate of fire (nominally 15 rpm, but more like 25 rpm in service) and handy mount made it perfect for AA fire. Japanese pilots called it the "5-inch machine gun."

The American fleet lagged in light AA weaponry, and the outbreak of war found it still relying on the .50cal machine gun. The 1.1-inch gun (150 rpm, 7400-yard range, 19,000-foot ceiling), while not as useless as is sometimes depicted, did not provide the weapon the fleet needed, producing more maintenance woes than hitting power. Fortunately, American factories had begun supplying 20mm Oerlikons to Britain; the navy detoured some for their own use, fitted with improved sights. The Oerlikon supplanted the .50cal gun and became instantly popular. From Pearl Harbor to September 1944, the Oerlikon accounted for 32% of AA kills in the United States Navy. But October 1944 brought the kamikaze and the realization that the 20mm's small shell and short range gave little hope of breaking a plane apart before it struck its target. Against kamikazes, more success came from the 40mm Bofors, another gun recommended by the British. The navy adopted it as the 1.1-incher's replacement after seeing a 1940 demonstration by the Dutch. The Bofors could shred any Japanese airplane, but the Oerlikon remained in service because its single mounts required no external power source and could engage surprise attackers without delay.

A new "light" AA gun arrived just after the war to replace the Bofors—a version of the 3/50 firing 50 rpm. It more than compensated for its slower rate of fire with its longer range and heavier shell, large enough to house a proximity fuse.

American high-angle control, superior to foreign systems and increasingly so as the war progressed, made the most of these potent weapons. Surface gunnery likewise showed improvement. American fire control in 1939 performed near the British and German standards, with wide variations in individual performance. Accounts of the bombardment of Casablanca harbor give the impression of a random flinging of shells, but moments later, direct fire against the charging French warships struck with great effect. American commitment to remote power control helped to integrate guns and directors in the fire-control process while new radars made targeting practical even to the farthest reaches of big guns. Advances in radar and in the doctrine for its use overcame Japan's night-fighting superiority, leading to the one-sided victories at Vella Gulf and Cape Saint George. As late as Empress Augusta Bay, however, an overconcentration on the most obvious radar blip left much of the Japanese force unengaged, while Surigao Strait showed the continuing danger of friendly fire. Ultimately, American fire control outstripped foreign systems, allowing American ships to maintain their fire-control solutions even during radical maneuvers.

In its anti-submarine efforts, the United States benefited from extensive British input; all British techniques and devices found their way into American service except the Squid mortar. But the Americans did more than mimic. They developed the air-dropped Mark 24 "mine"; actually a 19-inch homing torpedo, it excelled in service with both navies. The Mousetrap system, intended for vessels unable to carry Hedgehog, proved less effective. Light and simple, it had longer range than the Hedgehog but less accuracy. Other systems under development by the war's end include sono-buoys, anti-submarine helicopters, and a depth charge with a proximity fuse.

Among the hundreds of AS craft built in American yards, the destroyer escorts established themselves among the finest submarine-killers in the war. The *Buckley*-class DE *England* set a record with six kills in eight days.

American torpedoes earned their abominable reputation, the major culprit being the Mark 14 that frustrated so many submarine skippers. The Mark 14 incorporated all the flaws that dogged early German torpedoes; but unlike the Germans, the American leadership discounted the reports about malfunctions. The most ironic episode came during the battle of Midway when *Nautilus* fired three torpedoes at the damaged *Kaga*. One torpedo struck, but instead of exploding, it broke apart and sank. Its air flask remained at the surface, providing Japanese sailors with a flotation device. Corrections gradually jostled their way into the Mark 14's design until, by the end of 1943, it became a capable weapon. But it could never outlive its reputation.

A different problem marred early operations with the Mark 13 aerial torpedo, whose delicate mechanism required the low-and-slow torpedo run that proved fatal for both Devastators and Avengers at Midway. Further development gave the weapon sufficient ruggedness, and it performed well with its potent warhead. Initial models, armed with TNT, saw service to the end of 1942. The warheads grew, and with the adoption of British Torpex, American aerial torpedoes became as destructive as a Long Lance. (Of course, this came too late to save the Devastator's reputation.) The war's end halted development of a new mark (725-lb warhead).

The navy began a promising experiment with hydrogen peroxide torpedoes. The 21-inch Mark 17 had excellent performance (WW: 880 lbs; range: 18,000/46) but failed to generate interest among the leadership. The project revived after the fleet started running into Japanese Long Lances. A small production order got underway, but none of the Mark 17's made it into combat. The related Mark 16 carried a 920-lb warhead (range: 11,000/46).

The 19-inch Mark 27 fired from the 21-inch tubes of fleet submarines for attacks against Japanese escorts. During its short period of service late in the war, it proved a complete success.

Naval Aviation

As carriers established their relevance in fleet operations, the leadership set down exactly what it wanted in their design—big ships with 30-plus knots and lots of planes. These standards seem the obvious choice in retrospect, but the priorities and balance instituted in prewar designs gave the Americans an early edge over their Japanese and British rivals. Wartime developments then made the American carrier force the strongest in the world.

Backwards thinking in the Royal Navy stunted its carrier fleet. Overly aware of the fire hazard inherent in carrier aviation, British planners obsessed about safety and assigned second priority to the aircraft carrier's aircraft. They consequently sent to sea a group of planes that no modern foe feared. While Britain labored to make the most fire-resistant hangars in the world, America focused on large air groups, training, and complete operational efficiency.

The Japanese matched American doctrine more closely than the British, but in the development of ship design and procedures, they lagged. The country least able to sustain heavy losses allowed too many vulnerable designs into service. However, in December 1941, Japan's carrier force had no superior. This strength derived not from the carriers themselves as much as from their planes and pilots—a short-lived advantage.

American carriers possessed durability and a large offensive hammer in the form of capable aircraft and air crews. As combat eroded the supply of personnel, training programs accelerated in output without compromising on pilot quality. The shipbuilding industry made good the lost carriers, replacing them with more modern designs. A key factor in the carriers' continued success came from the superiority of new aircraft designs, specifically the fighters, specifically the Hellcat.

World War II began amid a period of transition in the carrier fleet; on the day Germany invaded Poland, America's navy had five different dive-bomber designs in service, none of them distinctive enough to crowd the others out. Two biplanes showed the clearest obsolescence: the Great Lakes BG-1 (speed: 188 mph; armament: two .30cal mg, one 1,000-lb bomb) and the Vought SBU-1 (speed: 205 mph; armament: two .30cal mg, one 500-lb bomb). Another biplane, the Curtiss SBC-3 (speed: 220 mph; armament: two .30cal mg, one 500-lb bomb), gave a perkier performance derived from its fighter ancestry. France ordered an updated model (the SBC-4, armed with a 1,000-lb bomb), and American SBC squadrons remained active into 1942.

Vought's SB2U-1 Vindicator (speed: 250 mph; armament: two .30cal mg, one 1,000-lb bomb) boasted modern features like upward-folding wings, but it never caught on with its American pilots, who enjoyed calling it the Wind Indicator. The French liked it enough to use it in combat in 1940, but it retired from Pacific carrier duty before Pearl Harbor. The fifth type, Northrop's BT-1 (speed: 222 mph; armament: one .50cal mg, one .30cal mg, one 1,000-lb bomb), won little fame of its own, but it opened a chapter of great importance to American naval aviation.

Douglas Aviation acquired Northrop and continued developing the BT-1. With modernized landing gear and other improvements, a new plane emerged, the Douglas Dauntless (SBD-3, speed: 250 mph; armament: two .50cal mg, two .30 cal mg, one 1,600-lb bomb). The SBD joined the fleet in 1940 as a carrier-borne scout and dive-bomber, and by 1942 it displaced all other models. A lack of engine power made for ponderous take-off and climb, but the serviceable design had long range—beyond

1,200 miles—and superb landing characteristics. Pilots lauded its handling; at Coral Sea, it even acted as an interceptor. While the SBD never equaled a Stuka in bomb delivery, it became one of the war's most successful naval planes, with a string of achievements stretching into 1944. Generous statisticians credit the rugged, reliable Dauntless with an unsurpassed loss-to-kill ratio.

Starting late in 1942, a new machine began to supplant the SBD, a malevolent Curtiss creation officially nicknamed the Helldiver, or unofficially the Beast (SB2C-3, speed: 294 mph; armament: two 20mm cannon, one .50cal mg, 2,000 lbs of bombs or a 22.4-inch torpedo). The Helldiver possessed more horsepower, more firepower, and a rancorous glee for torturing its pilots. Airmen longed to regain their departed Dauntlesses, but the navy had already committed itself to the Curtiss.

The Douglas TBD-1 Devastator (speed: 206 mph; armament: two .30cal mg, one 22.4-inch torpedo or 1,000 lbs of bombs) thrilled the fleet with its modern features in 1938; it then bypassed obsolescence and hurtled straight into paleontology. The design allowed for uncomplicated flight and an easy landing. If left alone, it had no trouble delivering its payload; but in hostile air space, it offered meager hope for survival. The Devastator's replacement, Grumman's huge Avenger (TBF-1, speed: 271 mph; armament: one .50cal mg, two .30cal mg, one 22.4-inch torpedo or 2,000 lbs of bombs) represented a considerable advance. An Avenger's belly could accommodate its entire bomb load internally. This bloated mass gave stable flight and landing and attack, but like its predecessor, the TBF presented a steady target—more robust and better armed, but still plodding. (In fact, it was the torpedo bomber in general—rather than the Devastator in particular—that was losing its worth in modern warfare.) Avengers provided a valuable platform for radar and AS patrols, and they inflicted critical blows on Axis targets through the war's end—

when escorted by swarms of fighters.

Martin developed a new design to replace all attack planes. The AM-1 Mauler (speed: 367 mph; armament: four 20mm cannon, three 22.4-inch torpedoes or 3,000 lbs of bombs) dispensed with the second crewman and performed more like a fighter. It could carry huge loads; one test flight carried 10,689 lbs of ordnance. Unfortunately, it arrived too late for war service. Such aircraft, like Britain's Firebrand, brought an end to the lumbering bomber designs with their obvious vulnerability. Japan had already opted for high-performance attack planes, but they impressed no one with their durability or bomb loads.

Douglas competed against the Martin design with its BTD-1 Destroyer (speed: 344 mph; armament: two 20mm cannon, two 1,600-lb bombs or two 22.4-inch torpedoes). The project proceeded sporadically—ordered in 1942, then canceled, a few units completed in 1944—but after all the false starts and a series of redesignations, the plane metamorphosed for postwar service as the Skyraider (AD-1, speed: 366 mph; armament: two 20mm cannon, 4,000 lbs of bombs or torpedoes) and eventually replaced the Mauler. A late-model Skyraider got into the air lifting a 14,940-lb load.

Despite its lack of a powerful engine and folding wings, the Dauntless *scored major successes in the Pacific.*

UNITED STATES

Navy fighter squadrons in 1939 comprised a pair of similar Grumman designs, the F2F and F3F biplanes (F3F-3, speed: 264 mph; armament: one .50cal mg, one .30cal mg, two 110-lb bombs), rugged and agile, roughly equal to their contemporaries, though lightly armed. A possible successor, the Brewster Buffalo monoplane (F2A-3, speed: 321 mph; armament: four .50cal mg, two 100-lb bombs), raised naval eyebrows with its potential. Yet somehow, as designers fine-tuned their work, domino effects turned the Buffalo into a wallowing cow. Improvement of the armor and landing gear added weight that strained the engine; this loss in performance then swallowed the plane's handling and maneuverability. The F2A, ruined by refinement, had a short term of naval duty starting in 1939.

Grumman design teams, spurred by Brewster's monoplane, decided to remove a wing from their proven biplane layout. This resulted in the stubby but nimble F4F Wildcat (F4F-3, speed: 328 mph; armament: four .50cal mg, two 100-lb bombs). Operationally, the fighter suffered from a narrow landing gear and some mischief in take-off, but it otherwise proved easy to fly and equal to the rigors of carrier duty, with a maximum range of 1,150 miles. America sent the Wildcat to sea in 1940, and it became the standard carrier-borne fighter before Pearl Harbor. The British viewed the Wildcat (which they renamed Martlet) with such enthusiasm that they made it the first plane to serve aboard an escort carrier.

History remembers the F4F in contrast to its arch-rival, the Japanese Zeke, which surpassed it in range, maneuverability, ceiling, and climb. But after the initial shock of the Zeke's performance, the Wildcat gave a good account of itself as pilots learned to capitalize on its greater durability and firepower. The fact is that American pilots outperformed their Japanese opponents. They did this, not by surpassing them in individual skill, but by embracing a mind-set of teamwork, a concept foreign to the samurai they dueled—few Japanese planes even carried a radio. This difference had a profound effect in the first year of the war.

Strangely, the team mentality failed to pervade American operations, and a lack of coordination reduced the effectiveness of air strikes all during the war.

Wildcats served aboard escort carriers into 1945, but by 1943 the fleet carriers took on the Grumman Hellcat (F6F-3, speed: 376 mph; armament: six .50cal mg, two 1,000-lb bombs). The Hellcat resembled its older kin and displayed the same operational virtues. But the new design's performance made it the top carrier fighter of the war. Of the 6,477 aerial victories claimed by American carrier pilots, the Hellcat accounted for 4,947, attaining a loss-to-kill ratio of 1:19. As a counter to the Zeke, it had more speed, more armor, greater weaponry, and superior dive characteristics. At high altitudes, the advantages increased, and the Hellcat actually possessed more maneuverability and climb. Many Hellcats operated with the British, who sometimes called them Gannets.

The Americans developed another fighter contemporary with the Hellcat, Vought's F4U Corsair (F4U-1A, speed: 417 mph; armament: six .50cal mg). Arguably the most deadly prop fighter to operate from an aircraft carrier, the Corsair also became the most recognizable, with its bent wings and huge propeller, its cockpit pushed back and its fin pushed forward. No one doubted the Corsair as a weapon, but it came with logistical and operational concerns; limited forward visibility and a manic demeanor at low speed made the "hosenose" a horror to land, difficult even to taxi. The British helped develop techniques to tame the Corsair, going so far as to operate some from their CVE. Finally approved for American carriers, the F4U showed its admirable heavy-lift capability, lugging drop tanks for a maximum range of 2,220 miles or striking surface targets with a pair of 1,000-lb bombs (up to 1,600-lb in later models). Charles Lindbergh himself flew a Corsair in combat and demonstrated its versatility by executing a 65° dive-bomb attack. This capability became especially important late in the war as the kamikaze threat forced American carriers to enlarge their fighter groups at the expense of the dive bombers. Sailors appreciated the shield of Corsairs, and no one missed the Helldivers.

Two contrasting Grumman fighters entered service just as the war came to an end. The Tigercat (F7F-1, speed: 427 mph; armament: four 20mm cannon, four .50cal mg, two 1,000-lb bombs or one 22.4-inch torpedo) featured excellent pilot visibility, daunting weaponry, and tremendous power in its twin engines; but operational problems, including size considerations and poor landing characteristics, kept it out of carrier service. In utter contrast, the tiny Bearcat (F8F-1, speed: 421 mph; armament: four .50cal mg, two 1,000-lb bombs) used its light weight to attain extreme maneuverability and climb—an about-face in American design theory that produced a lethal combatant and a well-rounded carrier aircraft.

The following section lists the hull numbers of major warships as part of official United States Navy nomenclature:

LEXINGTON, SARATOGA (CV2, 3: 36,000 tons; eight 8-inch, twelve 5-inch DP guns; AC 90, 33 knots, 1927): begun as battlecruisers but converted to aircraft carriers under a special provision of the Washington Treaty allowing the two CV at 33,000 tons. The Americans then manipulated some wording in the treaty to give the ships 3,000 extra tons—probably the closest any of the Allies came to outright cheating on the treaty. *Saratoga* grew near 38,000 tons by war's end, more than 50,000 tons full load. (Meanwhile, the navy continued to describe her as a 33,000-ton ship. For some reason, the Americans insisted on listing a ship's initial design displacement without regard to its actual tonnage.)

With their enclosed bow and stern, the *Lexington*s had the same graceful lines as a modern British CV. But as in the British ships, the enclosed hangar put limits on ventilation, a

A late-war photo of the USS Saratoga. *Twin DP guns have replaced her 8-inch battery.*

restriction not experienced in the open-sided hangars that became a standard feature of subsequent American designs.

The design had acceptable endurance (about 9,500 miles at 15 knots) but little agility; these were the least maneuverable ships in the fleet. Their high speed derived from a formidable turbo-electric power plant. This arrangement, with a series of engine rooms positioned down the centerline between pairs of boiler rooms, provided useful machinery dispersal and increased subdivision; no wartime carriers surpassed the *Lexington*s in their ability to survive torpedo damage (except a completed *Shinano*). Yet torpedoes made *Lexington* the first victim of a new naval phenomenon, fumes spreading from ruptured fuel stores. Japanese air attack struck her with two torpedoes and two or three bombs, with at least three near misses. The bombs caused minor damage and fires, setting off some 5-inch ammunition. Flooding started the ship into a list, but damage control crews quickly compensated. *Lexington* proceeded at 24 knots, recovering her aircraft; all seemed well. But the torpedoes had opened subtle leaks in her avgas storage, and fumes began to fill large portions of the ship. An otherwise insignificant spark, probably from a generator, detonated the fumes and initiated widespread fires that eventually consumed the ship.

This scenario never recurred in an American carrier, but the hazard of aviation fuel and ordnance later claimed the *Wasp* and *Princeton*, plus several escort carriers.

Saratoga survived the war. Twice she suffered submarine attack, single hits that posed no immediate threat. But one of these torpedoes revealed the potential vulnerability of a turbo-electric ship by overcoming the original provisions insulating the system from shock effects. A shipwide electrical short left the carrier dead in the water. Subsequent remedies went untested, as *Saratoga* endured no more torpedo hits. But she did have one more chance to show her ruggedness, when in 1945 she took four bombs

and three kamikazes; she resumed her air operations an hour after the attack but had to withdraw for permanent repairs.

As an early design and a conversion, the *Lexington*s showed several design ineconomies. Ninety aircraft constituted a modest complement for such a large carrier—the subsequent *Ranger* almost matched that number on less than half the displacement—and by war's end, practical considerations lowered the number near 70. Sluggish elevators slowed operations.

The original layout favored a gun armament of 6-inch guns, but the Washington Treaty gave Americans an 8-inch fever; all carrier designs under consideration at that time switched to 8-inch batteries. With a relatively elaborate fire-control layout, *Lexington* had her main guns in turrets with wide arcs of fire, rather than in casemates (as *Akagi* and *Kaga*), distinguishing the American design as the most powerful gunship CV ever built. (Fortunately, a battery of four 21-inch torpedo tubes worked its way out of the design prior to construction.) Whatever their disposition, the 8-inch guns had no value. Both ships landed them in 1942 for replacement by eight 5-inch, 38cal DP guns. *Lexington* went down at Coral Sea before shipping the new battery, but *Saratoga* received it and later traded her 25cal guns for 38cal, a total of twenty 5/38 DP.

RANGER (CV4: 14,575 tons, eight 5-inch DP guns, AC 86, 29.25 knots, 1934): America's first purpose-built carrier. Planners began with the concept of the smallest practical ship with the largest possible air group. The *Ranger* succeeded in shipping a healthy load of aircraft, easily operating groups in excess of 70, but navy trials would soon reveal the advantages of big designs, especially in conditions of harsh weather. Thus, the purpose-built ship, with its limited size and speed, turned out operationally inferior to the converted *Lexington*s.

The project began flush-decked with its smoke vented through three hinged stacks on each side of the flight deck. Designers added an island but retained the hinged stacks, which caused problems in service. The navy quickly recognized *Ranger*'s inferiority and restricted her wartime service to the Atlantic. By 1944, she became a trainer minus her 5-inch battery—in the American fleet, even a second-line unit could become top-heavy.

Around 1939, the navy considered refitting *Ranger*'s power plant for 30.7 knots, then decided she didn't warrant the effort. A 1943 proposal involved large-scale operational improvements, including catapults, and new provisions for survivability. (As built, she had minimal protection.) Again, the navy declined since the changes would have cut her speed to 28 knots and interfered with *Essex* class production.

YORKTOWN, ENTERPRISE, HORNET (CV5, 6, 8: 19,900 tons, eight 5-inch DP guns, AC 100, 32.5 knots, 1937–41): the best CV design to enter service prewar, later to form the basis of the *Essex* class. The *Ranger* was commis-

sioned before the fleet made its assessment of *Lexington*'s performance. Experience with both types allowed the navy to incorporate the best features from each. The new design had the speed and island-side stack of the conversions, but a large air group as well; it repeated *Ranger*'s open-sided hangars but added cruiser-level armor. Armored flight decks didn't interest the Americans because of the demands they made on the rest of the design. And no American carrier ever had a British-type armored box for the hangar, since it complicated ventilation and, later, would preclude a deck-edge lift.

The *Yorktown*s had about 20% more range than the previous ships, and they routinely operated air groups of 96 planes. (*Enterprise* returned to service after her 1943 refit still carrying 91 planes, including Hellcats and Avengers.) The design took a crucial step in the development of air operations with the installation of two modern catapults (plus a third in the hangar, never used in wartime). America took the lead in providing catapults for its carriers, an especially important feature for slower,

The USS Yorktown *shows the open hangars that became a standard American feature.*

smaller CVE but also significant for fleet units as planes increased in weight. *Saratoga*'s 1942 refit gave her two catapults; even *Ranger* got one before her transfer to night fighter training.

In service, the *Yorktown*s proved extremely tough. *Enterprise* remained in action after three bomb hits in the Solomons. (She had to remain in action, being the only Allied carrier in that ocean at the time.) *Yorktown*, hastily patched after Coral Sea, hustled off to Midway where she took three bombs and two torpedoes. Her skipper ordered her abandoned, doubting the watertight integrity of her patchwork. But she wouldn't go down; she waited, poised on a 25° list, until repair crews went back aboard. They would have saved her, but a Japanese sub found her and finished her with two more torpedoes. *Hornet* gave an amazing performance. Struck by eight bombs, three torpedoes, and two crashing aircraft, she lost power and began to list. With Japanese surface units nearby, the Americans decided to scuttle her. Destroyers hit her with nine torpedoes. She didn't sink. They then showered her with more than four hundred 5-inch shells. That didn't work either. In the end, they had to leave her behind. The Japanese found her burning and beyond repair and delivered four hits with Long Lance torpedoes. *Hornet* finally sank after her sixteenth torpedo hit.

Hornet's loss revealed a weakness in her design, the lack of machinery dispersal that left her propulsion system vulnerable. It was a loss of power that doomed the *Hornet,* rather than flooding or fire. As a late addition to the class, *Hornet* differed a bit from her older sisters and displaced 100 extra tons; the fleet had hoped for machinery dispersal and more subdivision, but time constraints limited the number of changes.

Enterprise survived the war, accumulating top-weight all the while; the navy had her bulged in 1943 to restore some stability and buoyancy. *Wasp*'s loss inspired an updating of her fuel stores to reduce fire risks.

WASP (CV7: 14,700 tons, eight 5-inch DP guns, AC 84, 29.5 knots, 1940): a treaty-induced reversion to smaller size. *Wasp*, in all ways superior to *Ranger*, still remained inferior to the larger designs the navy liked. Under construction as data became available from earlier units, *Wasp* grew. She commissioned at 15,400 tons and later neared 15,800 tons. Fortunately, her engines produced more power than expected, taking her up near 31 knots under favorable conditions.

The design included several noteworthy features, such as an asymmetrical hull that offset the weight of her island. More importantly, she had the first deck-edge lift. Unlike elevators centered in the flight deck (forming a gap in the deck structure or armor), units at the edge suffer little from hangar explosions and perform more reliably in general. They also have no elevator well to be drained, while their smaller size saves weight. *Wasp*'s lift, a tiny thing, evolved as a weightsaving measure.

The *Wasp* had two flight deck catapults and *Yorktown*-like range. Her hull included much more armor and subdivision than *Ranger*'s. The machinery showed a degree of dispersal with her boilers between separate engine rooms. Later, the *Essex*es would alternate their engine and boiler room positions, a full dispersal layout for increased safeguard against power loss.

Designers made special provision to add belt armor to *Wasp*'s sides in time of war. This never took place, and it would have done little to save the ship in 1942 when two torpedoes struck during flight operations. *Wasp* would have survived the flooding, but the gasoline lines servicing her aircraft ruptured, pouring fuel on her fires and spreading the flames between deck levels. Based on this experience, the navy developed new equipment and procedures, and no more large carriers succumbed to fire.

ESSEX, YORKTOWN, INTREPID, HORNET, FRANKLIN, TICONDEROGA, RANDOLPH, LEXINGTON, BUNKER HILL, WASP, HAN-

COCK, BENNINGTON, BOXER, BON HOMME RICHARD, ANTIETAM, SHANGRI-LA, LAKE CHAMPLAIN, plus seven others completed postwar and eight not completed (CV9–21, 31, 36, 38, 39: 27,200 tons, twelve 5-inch DP guns, AC 100, 33 knots, 1942–45): improved and enlarged *Yorktown*s able to carry up to 108 of the new, larger aircraft. The design expanded on their predecessors' toughness with the added dimension of machinery dispersal, plus an armored hangar deck. No *Essex*-class ship sank during the war, though some suffered horrendous damage. Two bombs and two kamikazes slammed into *Bunker Hill* and ignited her aircraft; experienced damage control saved the ship despite the deaths of 400 crewmen. *Franklin* took a pair of bombs among her aircraft; fire swept through the ship, killing more than 700 men, but once again the carrier survived. American damage control, always a strength, had learned many wartime lessons.

The *Franklin*'s experience demonstrated another American forté—reliable machinery. Her hot boilers, flooded with cold seawater, suffered only slight damage and returned immediately to action despite high salt levels.

For American carriers, the air group created a hazard beyond flammability; new aircraft types greatly increased a ship's load above its center of gravity. While the old Wildcat weighed 5,342 lbs, the Hellcat weighed over 9,000 lbs. A Dauntless weighed 6,533 lbs; a Helldiver, over 10,000 lbs. The cumulative effect of 100 increasing weights aggravated the customary American top-heaviness. New planes, new radars, new AA guns—the *Essex*es lost so much stability that some planners doubted their ability to survive three torpedo hits. Whether or not this was simple alarmism, the ships had the good fortune to avoid the sort of damage that made stability a factor in their survival.

The design mounted four of its DP guns on platforms beside the flight deck and the remaining eight in twin turrets around the island. The turrets had wide arcs of fire, but their blast effects could damage planes on the deck. The later *Midway* class mounted all its guns on sponsons at hangar deck level.

Air operations benefited from a deck-edge elevator and two powerful catapults. Ship's endurance exceeded 15,000 miles at 15 knots. Despite their want of stability, the *Essex*-class ships had the overall ruggedness, the ability to deliver unsurpassed aerial firepower, the self-defense capacity, and the operational efficiency to mark them as the war's best carriers.

INDEPENDENCE, PRINCETON, BELLEAU WOOD, COWPENS, MONTEREY, LANGLEY, CABOT, BATAAN, SAN JACINTO (CVL22–30: 10,600 tons, light guns, AC 31, 31.5 knots, 1943): an emergency measure, nine converted *Cleveland*-class CL hulls intended as a supplement for the big CV. The navy, running out of carriers, needed a stopgap until the *Essex* program got rolling. *Essex* entered service on the last day of 1942; *Independence* commissioned the next day, with the other eight following before year's end.

These were not attractive ships. They had no deck-edge elevator, just one catapult, and a small air group (usually 33 planes). Though meant to carry one or two 5-inch DP guns, they never received them. The armor layout provided modest protection, though the first two ships scrambled into service so hurriedly, they never got their side armor. In spite of all this, the design was a success. Not a war-winner, it augmented the fleet's main strength, having sufficient size and speed to bring modern aircraft into battle.

Princeton became the only war loss. A single bomb struck among her aircraft. Her crew struggled long, but in this case the fire won, detonating her inadequately protected torpedo stores. *Independence*, *Cabot*, and *Belleau Wood* endured significant damage without complications.

UNITED STATES

MIDWAY, FRANKLIN D. ROOSEVELT, CORAL SEA (CVB41–43: 47,000 tons, eighteen 5-inch DP guns, AC 137, 33 knots): these ships marked the transition of the aircraft carrier to the status of capital ship. The ships barely missed the war—*Midway* was commissioned on September 10, 1945.

These monstrous warships resulted from a decision to combine an American-type armored hangar deck with an armored flight deck. But unlike British layouts, here the hangar had no armored box; it retained its open sides, with a partial shield of sorts formed by the lines of 5-inch turrets on each side. The overall armor scheme was sufficient to defeat 8-inch gunfire. Torpedo defenses approximated those of a *Montana*-class BB, and the hull boasted extensive subdivision. This elaborate protection didn't prevent a large air group. In fact, the *Midway*s carried more airplanes than the Americans could coordinate.

The new 54cal DP had a slower rate of fire than the old 38cal gun, but its larger shell and increased performance convinced the navy that it had twice the value for AA duty. Even so, it never gained its predecessor's popularity.

Designers provided lavish facilities for radar and command functions, and they anticipated the operational needs of the latest aircraft. The ships came out a bit overweight, and crews found them wet and crowded; but as combatants they lacked little, greatly superior even to the *Essex* class.

Late in the war, the navy began a project for a 35,000-ton design with protection like *Midway*'s, equipped with the latest aircraft and weaponry. Planners wanted a ship drier than *Essex,* with more stability and habitability. By the time of its cancellation in 1946, the design had grown past 40,000 tons with a DP battery of twenty-six 3-inch guns, an air complement of 53 aircraft, and about 33 knots.

SAIPAN, WRIGHT (CVL48, 49: 14,500 tons, light guns, AC 50, 33 knots): an inconsequen-tial mistake. As the *Independence* program drew to a close, the navy pondered a suitable follow-up and decided that, since the *Independence* had converted from a light cruiser, the time had come to convert a heavy cruiser. In fact, CVL production stemmed from the shortage of big CV, so the truly logical next step was to discontinue the small ships and focus on building the large ones. But the *Saipan*s proceeded, beginning as a *Baltimore* conversion, then developing into something distinct. The result resembled a larger *Independence*, improved in general, especially in protection. The design surpassed all like-sized carriers, including their British contemporaries, but to no real purpose. Their careers ended in planeless secondary duties.

Meanwhile, someone suggested escalating to an *Alaska*-class cruiser conversion, but the specifications made a poor comparison with the *Essex* class—a similar displacement, but less range, less underwater protection, and 10% fewer planes.

Between the wars, the United States harbored an interest in hybrids; even *Yorktown*'s plan toyed with 8-inch guns. But large designs, such as one at 15,200 tons (four 8-inch, eight 5-inch DP guns; AC 45, 31 knots) and one at 27,000 tons (ten 8-inch, eight 5-inch DP guns; AC 68, 32.5 knots), conflicted with treaty limits. On the other hand, 10,000-ton aviation vessels had no restrictions. To the navy, this offered a way to spread its air power and cruiser guns across the Pacific. A flurry of 6-inch and 8-inch designs swirled through the 1930s, settling into the most adequate hybrid layout of its time (10,000 tons; nine 6-inch, eight 5-inch DP guns; AC 24, 32 knots). But the fleet, fortunately, gave up trying to balance carrier and cruiser qualities, despite later studies of up to 14,600 tons—beyond the treaty limit. It was this limit that gave the hybrid its allure; thus when the treaty lapsed, so did the allure.

Hybrid battleship-carriers never sparked much interest, though Project 10581 (designed for the Soviets) caught some attention. If any such monstrosity had begun construction, the United States would have seized it as war approached.

Like Britain and Japan, America planned the wartime conversion of liners into aircraft carriers. None of the ships nominated for this duty had the speed expected of a fleet carrier, averaging around 20 knots; but some plans involved 25-knot liners in a class with the Japanese *Junyos*—not a class meriting much respect. The large number of *Essex*-class orders obviated this dubious program, but the design work that emerged from it had an important future as the United States went on to convert dozens of merchant vessels for duty as escort carriers.

LONG ISLAND (CVE1: 11,300 tons; one 5-inch, two 3-inch DP guns; AC 21, 16.5 knots, 1941): the navy's first escort carrier, converted from a cargo ship, half-sister to the British *Archer* (former American hull number BAVG1). *Long Island* represented the most humble conversion possible. Her old superstructure remained visible beneath the added flight deck, and she never gained an island to help with her flight operations. (This made her the only flush-decked American carrier besides old *Langley*.) Her erratic machinery failed to produce the expected 18 knots. At least she had a catapult.

American CVE gave their most important service as AS units, but they performed other duties as well. In 1944, a refitted *Long Island* provided aircraft transport, her displacement rising to 13,324 tons.

The Americans began arming their glamourless CVE with surplus weapons. Early units had to make do with 5-inch, 51cal guns until the 38cal type became available. However, the 38cal guns lacked their usual AA value, being mounted beneath the overhang of the flight deck. The United States generally had little regard for low-angle 5-inchers; their only foreseeable use aboard an escort carrier would have

been to engage a surfaced U-boat or a solitary raider. But then the unforeseeable occurred at Leyte Gulf, when the escort carriers slugged it out with the Japanese battle fleet, and low-angle guns suddenly seemed very useful.

CHARGER (CVE30, ex-BAVG4: 11,800 tons; one 5-inch, two 3-inch DP guns; AC 36, 16.5 knots, 1942): sister to *Avenger*, *Biter*, and *Dasher* (BAVG2, 3, 5), intended for transfer to the Royal Navy. Similar in background to the *Long Island*, *Charger* underwent a more thoughtful conversion, though speed remained poor.

American yards provided most of Britain's escort carriers. The *Attacker* class originally had American names and the hull numbers CVE6–8, 10, 14, 15, 17, 19, 22, 24. *Tracker* had the hull number BAVG6. Some of the *Ameer*-class units started with American names; all had numbers (CVE32–54).

BOGUE, CARD, COPAHEE, CORE, NASSAU, ALTAMAHA, BARNES, BLOCK ISLAND, BRETON, CROATAN (CVE9, 11–13, 16, 18, 20, 21, 23, 25: 9,800 tons, two 5-inch guns, AC 28, 16.5 knots, 1942–43): from the same program as the *Attacker*s; a further improvement of the *Long Island*-type conversion, but given better machinery as in *Tracker*.

These early units barely had speed enough for aviation duty, but the navy saw their great potential. They displayed notable seaworthiness and habitability with good, sometimes startling range (more than 26,000 miles at 15 knots for the *Bogues*). And they maneuvered well, though having only one screw.

SANGAMON, SUWANNEE, CHENANGO, SANTEE (CVE26–29: 10,494 tons, two 5-inch guns, AC 34, 18 knots, 1942): converted from oilers, greatly superior to cargo-type CVE. They had two screws and longer flight decks, with hangars more spacious than those in an *Independence*. The *Sangamon*s actually served with the main fleet for a time in 1943. They and the subsequent *Commencement Bay*s were the only escort carriers capable of operating F6F Hellcats.

As a vestige of their oiler ancestry, the *Sangamon*s carried extra stores of fuel oil. They had *Bogue*-like range but much stronger hulls, providing considerable resistance beneath the waterline. All four ships suffered battle damage, but none sank.

PRINCE WILLIAM (CVE31: 11,000 tons, two 5-inch guns, AC 28, 17 knots, 1943): sister of the British *Ameer*, similar to the *Bogues*.

CASABLANCA, LISCOME BAY, ANZIO, CORREGIDOR, MISSION BAY, GUADALCANAL, MANILA BAY, NATOMA BAY, ST. LO, TRIPOLI, WAKE ISLAND, WHITE PLAINS, SOLOMONS, KALININ BAY, KASAAN BAY, FANSHAW BAY, KITKUN BAY, TULAGI, GAMBIER BAY, NEHENTA BAY, HOGGATT BAY, KADASHAN BAY, MARCUS ISLAND, SAVO ISLAND, OMMANEY BAY, PETROF BAY, RUDYERD BAY, SAGINAW BAY, SARGENT BAY, SHAMROCK BAY, SHIPLEY BAY, SITKOH BAY, STEAMER BAY, CAPE ESPERANCE, TAKANIS BAY, THETIS BAY, MAKASSAR STRAIT, WINDHAM BAY, MAKIN ISLAND, LUNGA POINT, BISMARCK SEA, SALAMAUA, HOLLANDIA, KWAJALEIN, ADMIRALTY ISLANDS, BOUGAINVILLE, MATANIKAU, ATTU, ROI, MUNDA (CVE55–104: 7,848 tons, one 5-inch gun, AC 28, 19 knots, 1943–44): perhaps the supreme example of industrial predominance: 50 mass-produced aircraft carriers with the last ship reaching completion exactly one year after the first. The navy intended some of them for transfer to Britain but later opted to substitute some *Bogue*s (the *Ameer* class).

These purpose-built carriers featured twin screws and a measure of machinery dispersal. Their speed and economy of design made them superior to the conversions, even the *Sangamon*s. The extra knots became vital when a Japanese battleship task force surprised a group of *Casablanca*s meandering off Samar. American escort carriers never earned a reputation for toughness, as several units blew up after submarine or air attack. But the scrambling refugees off Samar showed some heart. *Kalinin Bay* took thirteen 8-inch shells, plus one hit from a battleship (14-inch or 16.1-inch), yet she kept her place in formation. Only *Gambier Bay* fell victim to the gunfire, while *St. Lo* became the first kamikaze victim later that day. These losses led to advances in protection. Typhoon Viper ruptured *Windham Bay*'s hull; other CVE suffered lesser damage in the Third Fleet's typhoon encounters, but none sank. The *Casablanca*s ranged to just above 10,000 miles at 15 knots.

COMMENCEMENT BAY, BLOCK ISLAND, GILBERT ISLANDS, KULA GULF, CAPE GLOUCESTER, SALERNO BAY, VELLA GULF, SIBONEY, PUGET SOUND, BAIROKO, plus nine completed postwar and 16 canceled (CVE105–113, 115: 10,975 tons, two 5-inch guns, AC 34, 19 knots, 1944–45): the best CVE, developed from the *Sangamon*s but built as carriers from the keel up. They retained the ability to carry extra fuel, but less than *Sangamon* did, and they had less range as well. However, they had stronger hulls, thorough subdivision, and a complete layout of machinery dispersal.

Plans for an improved *Commencement Bay* class (CVE128–139) ended with the war.

The Great Lakes gave the United States an invaluable resource that the Japanese never had: an expansive body of water secure from enemy attack, perfect for training naval aviators. In 1942, the navy converted two paddle steamers for carrier training, *Sable* (8,000 tons, 18 knots, 1923) and *Wolverine* (7,200 tons, 16 knots, 1912). These ships had no hangars or maintenance facilities; they served merely as floating flight decks.

LANGLEY (11,050 tons, four 5-inch guns, 15 knots, 1913): seaplane tender. Built as a fleet collier, she had the navy's first turbo-electric power plant. She began conversion in 1920, becoming CV1, the navy's first aircraft carrier. As a carrier, she had only crude operational facilities, but since she exceeded 10,000 tons, treaties would count her as part of America's tonnage allotment. The navy thus cut back her flight deck and re-rated her for seaplane duty.

WRIGHT (8,400 tons; two 5-inch, two 3-inch DP guns; 15 knots, 1921): seaplane tender converted from a cargo ship.

Before the numerous wartime CV orders, the navy placed great importance on seaplanes. Nine *Lapwing*-class minesweepers were converted in 1936 to act as seaplane tenders, and 14 flush-deck destroyers became tenders in 1938–40. (Several of them were reconverted later for other duties.)

CURTISS, ALBEMARLE (9,090 tons, four 5-inch DP guns, 18.7 knots, 1940): purpose-built tenders, protection limited to a torpedo defense scheme. Each could handle 24 seaplanes.

TANGIER, POCOMOKE, CHANDELEUR (8,560 tons; one 5-inch DP, four 3-inch DP guns; 17 knots, 1941–42): tenders converted from cargo ships. They originally carried four 5-inch guns. *Chandeleur* displaced about 500 tons more than the others.

BARNEGAT, BISCAYNE, MACKINAC, HUMBOLDT, MATAGORDA, ABSECON, COOS BAY, CHINCOTEAGUE, HALF MOON, BARATARIA, BERING STRAIT, CASTLE ROCK, COOK INLET, CORSON, DUXBURY BAY, GARDINERS BAY, FLOYDS BAY, GREENWICH BAY, ONSLOW, ORCA, REHOBOTH, SAN CARLOS, SHELIKOF, SUISUN, ROCKAWAY, SAN PABLO, UNIMAK, YAKUTAT, CASCO, plus four completed as MTB tenders

(1,766 tons, two 5-inch DP guns, 20 knots, 1941–45): innovative design intended for operations in contested waters with little support. The navy completed two more units postwar, canceled six others, and dropped plans for as many as 10 more.

The ships could tend one squadron each (12 planes), though their versatility saw them perform a variety of duties. They matched their destroyer-like appearance with a battery of up to four 5/38 guns and a respectable AS outfit. They ranged to 6,000 miles at 12 knots with good habitability. Displacement rose above 2,000 tons.

CURRITUCK, NORTON SOUND, PINE ISLAND, plus one completed postwar (9,106 tons, four 5-inch DP guns, 19.2 knots, 1944–45): similar to *Curtiss* class.

KENNETH WHITING, CUMBERLAND SOUND, ST. GEORGE, HAMLIN (8,510 tons, two 5-inch DP guns, 16 knots, 1944): similar to *Tangier* class, three others canceled.

The Americans began an unusual seaplane project, an oversized aircraft to operate from a catapult lighter (hull number AVC1, 5,800 tons). The navy launched ACV1 in 1940 but, having already lost interest in the project, never installed her engines. She served in trials from 1941 on, but the catapult equipment performed poorly.

Battleships and Battlecruisers

The United States played an important role in dreadnought evolution. The *South Carolina* design actually preceded Britain's *Dreadnought* in mounting an all-big-gun armament, then compounded that efficiency by adopting an all-centerline main battery. No American battleships had wing turrets. Midships turrets disappeared as soon as triple mounts went to sea aboard *Nevada*, the ship that pioneered the all-

or-nothing armor scheme. Amid this air of innovation, designers established a tradition of heavy protection and limited speed. Reconstruction in the wake of Pearl Harbor put the veterans at the vanguard of anti-aircraft and electronics development, two hallmarks of modern BB. But their speed remained outdated, so instead of operating with the fast carriers, they worked mostly in amphibious fire support.

The new battleships did have speed, and they became powerful guardians for the fleet carriers. Their high-angle fire control and weaponry made them the best AA escorts of the war, and they spent most of their time in that role. Ironically, the airplane—the enemy against whom they excelled—made them obsolete. Only the *Iowa*s with their splendid blend of big guns, protection, and speed proved valuable enough to serve through the end of the twentieth century.

A few antiques loitered their way into the war years. *Oregon* (10,288 nt; four 13-inch, eight 8-inch, four 6-inch guns; 15.5 knots, 1896), extant as a memorial, returned to duty as an ammunition hulk. The former *Kearsarge* (11,540 nt, 1900) acted as a floating crane, and *Prairie State* (ex-*Illinois*: 11,565 nt, 17 knots, 1901), as a training hulk. *Utah* (19,800 tons, 18 knots, 1911) was a target and an AA trainer with varying batteries (as many as four 5/38 and four 5/25 guns, four 3-inch guns, and lighter weapons).

WYOMING, ARKANSAS (BB32, 33: 27,900 tons; twelve 12-inch, sixteen 5-inch, eight 3-inch DP guns; AC 3, 21 knots, 1911–12): well advanced in senility, saved from scrapping by the war. *Wyoming* had already diverted to training duty (AG17: 19,700 tons; six 12-inch, sixteen 5-inch, eight 3-inch DP guns; 18 knots). A prewar proposal would have converted her to a specialized amphibious support ship providing escort, transport, and bombardment service. Instead, her training duties continued with the focus shifting to AA gunnery as her former

weaponry gave place to fourteen 5-inch DP and four 3-inch DP.

Prewar refits added a modern thickness of deck armor, but no one mistook *Arkansas* for a vital asset. She puttered through the war in Atlantic convoys and fire support duties. Her 5-inch battery shrank to six guns while the 3-inch battery grew to 12.

NEW YORK, TEXAS (BB34, 35: 28,700 tons; ten 14-inch, sixteen 5-inch, eight 3-inch DP guns; AC 3, 21 knots, 1914): last BB of their generation in the American fleet. Early plans mounted five triple 12-inch mounts; the design evolved with a 14-inch battery in twin mounts, one amidships.

The *New York*s, the last American design before the all-or-nothing revolution, entered service with an armor scheme like that of foreign dreadnoughts, totaling just 30% of their tonnage; refits raised the figure near 40% with adequate deck protection.

These were wet ships with unreliable machinery, and their refits added to their problems, making them roll badly. At 10 knots, they ranged to 15,400 miles; at 18 knots, just 6,500 miles. Nevertheless, they led active careers, performing shore bombardment in Europe and later in the Pacific. *Texas* withstood several 11.1-inch hits from a German shore battery, and *New York* took slight damage from a kamikaze, but they did well to avoid heavy attack. By 1945, they retained six 5-inch with ten 3-inch guns, plus the customary crowds of light AA.

NEVADA, OKLAHOMA (BB36, 37: 29,067 tons; ten 14-inch, twelve 5-inch, eight 5-inch DP guns; AC 3, 20.5 knots, 1916): completely revolutionary, as radical as *Dreadnought* in her day. The protection tonnage jumped to 40% of displacement in an entirely new "all-or-nothing" layout; rather than spreading the armor to cover the entire ship, designers concentrated it between the ship's vitals and the most likely trajectories of incoming fire—especially the shells plunging in from long range. The Battle of Jutland would vindicate this regard for long-range gunfire, and the resulting shift in armor layouts stamped a "post-Jutland" label on subsequent designs, though *Nevada* and *Oklahoma* both preceded that battle. Britain didn't get a "post-Jutland" ship into service until the *Nelson* class.

By fitting two triple turrets, the *Nevada*s shipped the same main battery as the *New York*s without needing a midships mount. The triples had the disadvantage of holding their guns within a single cradle, which could increase the chance of a single hit disabling all three guns. The British held the American 14/45 mounts in low regard, but the Americans seemed quite happy with them. Their light weight helped avoid the problems the British experienced with their jump to triple turrets in the *Nelson* class.

The *Nevada*s handled poorly at low speeds but gave no trouble when cruising. Both ships, like the other Pearl Harbor victims, lay moored and unready at the time of the raid. *Oklahoma* took a bomb and nine torpedoes, the first three of which caused such an abrupt list that she capsized. The navy righted her in 1943 but declined to repair her. *Nevada* ran aground after hits from one torpedo and five bombs, plus numerous near misses. The navy already considered her a secondary unit due to her age; even so, she received a complete rebuild. This included the replacement of her old 5-inch batteries by sixteen 38cal DP in twin mounts, a change the navy intended for even its oldest battleships, though not all received it before the war drew to a close.

PENNSYLVANIA, ARIZONA (BB38, 39: 33,125 tons; twelve 14-inch, ten 5-inch, twelve 5-inch DP guns; AC 4, 21 knots, 1916): at their completion, the world's finest battleships. An enlargement of the *Nevada* layout allowed superb protection with an improved anti-torpedo system. Excellent seaboats, the *Pennsyl-*

The USS Arizona *as modernized prewar with 5/25 and 5/51 batteries.*

*vania*s provided steady gun platforms; in peacetime, their habitability and economic steaming made them instantly popular.

Amid prewar delays in deploying the 1.1-inch gun, 3-inch guns appeared as "light" AA in several old battleships, a few of which, including *Pennsylvania*, may have kept them through the end of 1941.

Arizona's loss at Pearl Harbor has evolved into mythology. In reality, she fell victim to high-level bombing, 10 planes dropping 1,757-lb bombs from a height of 10,480 feet. Two near misses gave a false impression of torpedo explosions, but two bombs scored direct hits. One of them glanced off Y turret and caused minor damage; the other plunged into a powder room beside B barbette, igniting a flash that burst into adjacent powder rooms and continued forward and upward. The blast vented through the forecastle deck, but not before involving the entire ammunition store—582 tons of 14-inch ordnance. Crew readiness had no relevance to this chain of events; *Arizona* was a sitting duck, and this made her vulnerable to horizontal bombers.

Meanwhile, one bomb gave the *Pennsylvania* a slight wound. In time, she mounted the new standard of sixteen 5/38 DP. While anchored off Okinawa in 1945, she suffered damage from an aerial torpedo that struck among her screws, aft of her protection system. The results showed some parallel with the *Prince of Wales* sinking as *Pennsylvania*'s displaced shafts provided entry for additional flooding, but since she lay at anchor, her propeller shaft didn't chew into the hull. Her aged compartmentation prevented a widespread onslaught of seawater but allowed progressive seepage which built up to 3,400 tons in her aft section—a serious situation, but she survived.

NEW MEXICO, MISSISSIPPI, IDAHO (BB40–42: 33,420 tons; twelve 14-inch, twelve 5-inch, eight 5-inch DP guns; AC 3, 22 knots, 1917–19): improved *Pennsylvania*s with clipper bows to reduce wetness. They featured a new and better turret for their 14/50 guns, plus an increase in subdivision; but none of them met with the need to display their toughness.

Reconstruction in the early 1930s added a tower bridge, an imposing structure not unlike the one later seen on France's *Richelieu*. Endurance approached 12,500 miles at 18 knots. Absent from the Pearl Harbor attack, the *New Mexico*s endured only minor wartime changes. *Idaho* traded her 5-inch batteries for a unique set of ten 5/38 single mounts. Her sisters also landed their low-angle secondaries, with *Mississippi* enlarging her 25cal battery to 16 guns and *New Mexico* gaining additional light AA.

TENNESSEE, CALIFORNIA (BB43, 44: 32,300 tons; twelve 14-inch, twelve 5-inch, eight 5-inch DP guns; AC 3, 21 knots, 1920–21): similar to *New Mexico* with further advances in underwater protection. The *Tennessee*s had turbo-electric machinery, which became a standard American feature until the 1930s when weight considerations sent designers back to more conventional power plants.

Unlike previous types, the *Tennessee*s entered the war with their original armor lay-out, lacking a *Nelson*-like concentration of deck protection (5-inch, but divided into 3.5-inch and 1.5-inch layers). *Tennessee* suffered little from two bombs at Pearl Harbor, so she waited until 1943 for a major refit, derived from the *Nevada* pattern. It gave her modern deck thickness and a modern look (a silhouette similar to the new *South Dakota*'s) with sixteen 5-inch DP and 34,858 tons. *California* had less luck; as the Japanese struck, she lay ready for inspection with her access ways and hatches open. Two bombs and two torpedoes caused her to flood and settle on the harbor bottom. She didn't return to service until 1944, rebuilt to resemble her sister. The *Tennessee*s (and *West Virginia*) became the most modern of America's old BB, almost equal to the new types. *California* carried four aircraft.

COLORADO, MARYLAND, WEST VIRGINIA (BB45, 46, 48: 32,000 tons; eight 16-inch, twelve 5-inch, eight 5-inch DP guns; AC 3, 21

The brawny USS Tennessee *had a full modernization after Pearl Harbor, gaining the standard sixteen 5/38 guns.*

knots, 1921–23): plus *Washington* (BB47) canceled after the Washington Treaty. Except in the main battery, the design virtually copied *Tennessee*'s, including the machinery. Turbo-electric drive provided excellent subdivision and great flexibility in dealing with battle damage. None of the *Tennessee*s or *Colorado*s suffered any shock-induced short circuits, and *Saratoga*'s experience remained an isolated one.

No prewar rebuilds increased the *Colorado*s' horizontal protection. At Pearl Harbor, Japanese planes battered *West Virginia* with four bombs and nine torpedoes, but she sank upright instead of capsizing. Her rebuild resembled *California*'s, complete with thickened deck. *Maryland* suffered only two bomb hits; by 1945, she too mounted sixteen 5-inch DP. *Colorado* avoided the Japanese attack and so went relatively unchanged, just landing two secondary guns. Like *Maryland*, she finished her career with the original deck armor.

A wartime proposal to rearm the *Colorado*s with *North Carolina*-type guns came to nothing.

SOUTH DAKOTA, INDIANA, MONTANA, NORTH CAROLINA, IOWA, MASSACHU-SETTS (BB49–54: 41,000 tons; twelve 16-inch, sixteen 6-inch, four 3-inch DP guns, two 21-inch TT; 23 knots): victims of the Washington Treaty, an enlarged *Colorado* design, the ultimate development of the *Nevada* standard. The design had an ugly silhouette dominated by its

While rather compact, the USS **Indiana** *combined good protection with tremendous firepower.*

oversized trunked funnel. It also had tremendous firepower. The 16-inch guns, a new 50cal mark, would fire a 2,240-lb shell near 40,000 yards. The 6-inch guns entered service aboard the *Omaha* class CL. The Americans had an 18-inch gun under development at the time (shell weight near 2,900 lbs) but probably would not have considered it for the *South Dakota*s.

LEXINGTON, CONSTELLATION, SARATOGA, RANGER, CONSTITUTION, UNITED STATES (CC1–6: 41,000 tons; eight 16-inch, sixteen 6-inch, six 3-inch DP guns, eight 21-inch TT; 33.25 knots): America's first and only battlecruiser design, and not a good one, severely lacking in protection. Early versions included a clutter of funnels (as many of seven stacks) with a preliminary armament of ten 14-inch guns. Despite their vulnerability, the *Lexington*s could have excelled as escorts for fast carriers. But of course, *Lexington* and *Saratoga* actually became fast carriers.

If the treaty hadn't ended the *South Dakota* and *Lexington* projects, the fleet would have updated them with increased AA firepower and the removal of torpedoes.

NORTH CAROLINA, WASHINGTON (BB55, 56: 36,600 tons; nine 16-inch, 20 5-inch DP guns; AC 3, 28 knots, 1941): America's first BB after the 15-year "holiday." The treaty ban on battleships extended to 1936, and thereafter the limits stood at 35,000 tons and 14-inch guns. In 1931, American designers began a string of proposals; some displaced as little as 23,500 tons with 12-inch guns, some had 5.3-inch secondary guns, and most had speeds below 25 knots. In the end, the Americans settled on the same basic plan as the British: 35,000 tons, twelve 14-inch guns in quad mounts, 27.5 knots. But everything changed when Japan's renunciation effectively killed the treaties. The Americans, anticipating Japan's decision, had designed a 16-inch triple turret they could substitute for the 14-inch quad. This easy upgrade

spared the *North Carolina* from the shame of *King George V*—an up-to-date warship with outdated guns.

Emerging from a 15-year stagnation to face an arbitrary tonnage limit, the designers inevitably fell short in some areas. Severe vibration problems, never fully remedied, helped place the *North Carolina*s among the slowest of modern battleships. The American protection layout, near 40% of displacement, no longer surpassed foreign types but achieved merely adequate protection, including underwater. When a submarine torpedo hit *North Carolina* abreast the forward turret (where the tapering hull limited the extent of side protection), the ship performed well as regards flooding; 970 tons of seawater created a minor list (5.5°) which the crew corrected in just six minutes. However, structural damage was more serious, effectively disabling the foremost turret, yet repair work took less than three months.

In its weaponry, the design excelled. The DP secondary battery, a concept faithfully embraced in subsequent classes, capitalized on the 5/38's handiness and AA ability. The 16-inch guns derived from the *Colorado* type, but with higher elevation—45° versus 30° in the older mount—for longer range. (The *North Carolina*s could fire the same 2,240-lb ammunition used by the *Colorado*s to a maximum range of 40,200 yards, but they did so only in practice, if at all.) Designers chose to provide the gun with sluggish ballistic performance; while this limited its range, it gave the barrels a long life: 395 rounds, or twice as long as in *Richelieu*. It even outlasted Britain's 15-inch gun. While low velocity can decrease gunfire effectiveness, the Americans compensated with a super-heavy 2,700-lb shell, placing the *North Carolina*s among the most destructive of battleships. *Richelieu*, with her inferior disposition of quad mounts, fired a broadside of 15,591 lbs; *North Carolina* had a 24,300-lb broadside with slightly more penetration.

American gunnery had the advantage of

technology. In a short-range night duel, *Washington's* radar-ranged gunfire scored nine 16-inch hits and forty 5-inch hits on *Kirishima*, crippling her in less than 10 minutes.

Ever conscious of the Pacific expanse, designers gave the *North Carolina* the habitability, reliability, and range that came to typify American designs. Twin rudders provided above-average maneuverability.

An analysis of 35,000-ton BB classes establishes the American design as imperfect but battle-worthy. *Richelieu* edged out *North Carolina* in all-around quality, with a high level of protection and better speed, but an inferior main battery and inadequate AA weaponry. *King George V* bettered *North Carolina's* speed and armor but lagged behind in firepower, maneuverability, radius of action, and AA defense.

SOUTH DAKOTA, INDIANA, MASSACHU-SETTS, ALABAMA (BB57–60: 37,970 tons; nine 16-inch, 20 5-inch DP guns; AC 3, 27.8 knots, 1942): a quick follow-up to the *North Carolina*, attempting to improve protection while retaining other qualities within the same tonnage. The designers knew they could thicken the armor only by reducing the protected area—that is, by shortening the hull. The reduction in length (from 713 feet to 666 feet at the waterline) created complications. Shorter hulls make for less speed while simultaneously providing less room for machinery. But the *South Dakotas*, fitted with a compact and efficient power plant, suffered no significant loss of speed. Vibrations caused fewer problems.

The short-hulled design proved a bit wet; it also compressed the crew accommodations, though the *South Dakotas* still exceeded foreign standards of habitability. A cramping of the upper works restricted some AA arcs of fire, a disadvantage offset by the raising of the DP battery by one deck level, especially helpful in rough weather. The new hull provided a bonus in maneuvering and stability behavior.

From an operational viewpoint, the *South Dakota* regressed from the *North Carolina's* standards; but from a tactical viewpoint, the increased protection created a superior combatant. Though American belt armor fell well below modern British standards, *South Dakota* capitalized on an ingenious layout and internal plates that isolated the magazines from damage that managed to penetrate the citadel. In ship-to-ship combat, *South Dakota* surpassed all other treaty-type designs and could have challenged even *Yamato* with some hope for success.

A wrinkle in the design's protective scheme resulted from an ill-informed effort to guard against shells striking below the waterline—a well-layered system, yet overly rigid, though not to *Yamato's* extreme. The miscalculation carried over into the *Iowa* class as well. The consequences in case of torpedo damage remain uncertain since the *Iowas* and *South Dakotas* led torpedo-free careers. The only instance of underwater damage resulted from a collision; *Washington* smashed her bow into *Indiana* adjacent to the aft turret. The 85,000-ton collision had the potential for catastrophe since flooding of the aft section would have compromised the ship's stability. But the hull resisted flooding beyond the immediate area of impact, and *Indiana* withdrew for repairs without further incident.

Nominally a 35,000-ton design, the *South Dakotas* rose toward 38,000 tons before commissioning, and by 1945 they neared 40,000 tons. Their armament copied the *North Carolina's*, though *South Dakota* herself had only 16 DP guns to make room for command personnel. *Massachusetts* had the opportunity to flex her big-gun muscles during the attack on Casablanca. She sank *Le Malin* and contributed to the sinking of seven other vessels; she also put *Jean Bart* out of action and displayed the quality of American armor-piercing shells by piercing her target's thick deck protection. (For details, see the section on the French navy.) Meanwhile, her armor shrugged off a pair of minor shells (5.1-inch and 7.6-inch), and her maneuverability allowed her to avoid four torpedoes from a French sub.

On the same occasion, the blast from *Massachusetts*'s own guns caused a short-out in her electrical system. This gave her little trouble, and later adjustments corrected the problem—but not soon enough to spare *South Dakota*.

An unlucky ship, *South Dakota* got more than her fair share of enemy attention. In October 1942, a bomb landed square atop her forward turret. The turret suffered no damage, but shrapnel deformed two guns of the second turret. She remained in action for several weeks with her diminished battery, joining forces with *Washington* to confront the Japanese off Guadalcanal. At the enemy's approach, *South Dakota* opened fire, but her guns initiated a series of short circuits that, due to crew error, left entire sections of the ship without power. Most seriously, the radar went out. To add to the confusion, the blast from the aft turret ignited both scout planes on her fantail. (Fortunately, the next salvo blew the planes overboard.) The crew became completely disoriented and blundered toward the Japanese force, which included *Kirishima* and two heavy cruisers. The blinded ship closed to a range of 5,800 yards, and the enemy responded by delivering 27 hits. Japanese gunnery failed to take advantage of the close quarters; only one hit came from a 14-inch gun, and it may not have been a 1,485-lb armor-piercing round but a 1,378-lb high-explosive shell intended for shore bombardment. It scored a direct hit on the aft barbette but caused only minor damage. Most of the remaining hits came from the cruisers' 8-inch guns. They inflicted widespread damage in the upper works, playing havoc with the sensitive electronics. Thirty-eight men died, and *South Dakota* ceased to be an effective night-fighting unit. The damage in no way threatened the ship's survival; her essential structure and watertight integrity remained untouched. But she had lost her communications and fire control. World War II established the vulnerability of such systems and almost everything else in the superstructure, since no design could cover it with thick armor. Unlike the British, the Americans did employ well armored conning towers in their designs, and *South Dakota*'s conning tower admitted no damage off Guadalcanal. The ship withdrew for two months of repair, which included gun replacement and a general overhaul.

Japanese planes continued to plague *South Dakota*, hitting her with another bomb in 1944. But she had the last word; by war's end, the navy credited her with 64 aircraft destroyed, including a one-day record of 26.

IOWA, NEW JERSEY, MISSOURI, WISCONSIN (BB61–64: 48,110 tons; nine 16-inch, 20 5-inch DP guns; AC 3, 33 knots, 1943–44): plus *Illinois* and *Kentucky* (BB65, 66), not completed. Japan's renunciation of the treaty triggered an escalator clause allowing 45,000 tons and 16-inch guns, so the Americans began to ponder the best use of this extra tonnage. Some suggestions merely enlarged the *South Dakota* with a fourth turret. As war approached, designers studied the possibility of nine 18-inch guns firing 3,850-lb shells (a 34,650-lb broadside) to 43,000 yards—an impressive notion, but the weight of the turrets made it impractical. Weight considerations also precluded a secondary battery of twelve 6-inch DP guns.

But *South Dakota* hadn't lacked firepower; a true improvement had to consider her most serious foible: her marginal speed. Some design teams began work on high-speed, ill-armored craft properly termed battlecruisers. Ultimately, however, the project balanced out to a longer, faster *South Dakota*. The *Iowa*s resulted, the world's best battleships.

The design included two subtle but significant advances in armament. The 16-inch guns grew to 50cal, reducing barrel life (290 rounds, still a reasonable total) but raising the destructive potential to near *Yamato* standards; and the lengthened hull created vast stretches of deck space for light AA mounts. The *Iowa*s surpassed all wartime rivals in AA firepower.

They were also the fastest dreadnoughts. Their machinery, the most powerful of World War II, proved extremely efficient and reliable. The long bow and fine hull, additional factors in their speed, would normally inhibit maneuverability, but twin rudders made the ships relatively nimble. Endurance at 12 knots was 18,000 miles, twice *Yamato*'s performance; the *Iowa*s often donated fuel to escorts with shorter "legs."

The long bow had its drawbacks, such as wetness. In postwar exercises, the British *Vanguard* stood dry atop heavy seas that deluged the *Iowa*s. More seriously, the bow presented a large area of relative vulnerability—extremely narrow and thus lacking depth of protection. American designers addressed this problem directly by giving the bow an extensive plan of watertight subdivision. (Reviewing *Yamato*'s response to underwater damage, the Japanese considered reconstructing her with similar subdivision, but technicians warned of serious consequences of the added weight.)

In other regards, the *Iowa*s copied *South Dakota*'s protection, including the anti-torpedo system. A slight adjustment of the side plates gave greater resistance to the largest of shells. This level of protection, along with the 50cal guns and American fire control, made *Iowa* the approximate equal of *Yamato* in a gun fight.

The two incomplete sisterships would have differed in detail: refinements below the waterline for increased torpedo resistance, and weight-saving that might have shaved off as much as 2,000 tons for a half-knot increase in speed.

World War II gave the Americans no opportunity to showcase the *Iowa*s. But if the ships never proved themselves by gun duel, they have proved themselves by longevity. Decades after the retirement of the last foreign dreadnoughts (*Yavuz* and *Jean Bart*, scrapped in the early 1970s), technological upgrades maintained the *Iowa*s as significant wartime assets.

MONTANA, OHIO, MAINE, NEW HAMPSHIRE, LOUISIANA (BB67–71: 60,500 tons; twelve 16-inch, twenty 5-inch DP guns; AC 3, 28 knots): ordered but never laid down. The design continued to evolve until its cancellation, edging nearer *Yamato*'s displacement. Designers gave little thought to an 18-inch battery but selected the new 5-inch, 54cal DP.

Planners allowed the reversion from *Iowa*'s speed in order to gain new degree of protection. While *Yamato* exceeded *Montana* in armor thickness, American refinements in design and armor quality made this layout superior to the bulkier Japanese system. The torpedo defense scheme, a completely new type, showed great depth while eliminating the flaws seen in previous classes. As a classic ship-of-the-line, *Montana* would have surpassed all others, combining unequaled firepower with unmatched protection.

The United States made two unsuccessful moves to supplement its battleship force in the early days of the war: a tentative offer to exchange cruisers for Britain's *Duke of York*, and a more serious attempt to buy *Almirante Latorre* and some destroyers from Chile.

Cruisers

The United States came out of World War I with a large but imbalanced fleet. The absence of modern cruisers leaped to the leaders' attention as they sketched out all the roles they wanted cruisers to perform: scouting (requiring a well-armed vessel equipped with scout planes), screening (requiring ships with rapid-fire guns to defeat enemy torpedo boats), commerce raiding and protection (requiring speed and range), and flag-showing (requiring habitability).

This barrage of requirements and a want of modern prototypes stunted the cruiser program, already withered by the Washington Treaty. Design teams, hypnotized by treaty limits and lacking the sensibilities born of experience, chanted an 8-inch, 10,000-ton mantra while producing a series of imbalanced 8-inch gunships.

The treaty secured the 8-inch gun a place in navies around the world, though it lacked the speed of a 6-inch gun and the size of a heavy armor-piercing weapon. The chaotic night fights in the Solomons revealed the 6-inch gun's superiority against targets scurrying through conditions of poor visibility. Yet it's hard to imagine the American cruisers repelling Japanese battleships off Guadalcanal with a spray of 6-inch shells.

The United States, with all its eggs in one 8-inch basket, tried to maximize the gun's potential. Super-heavy 335-lb shells gave added punch. (Unfortunately for *San Francisco*, it seems she didn't have the heavy rounds for her one-on-one with *Hiei*.) But the slow rate of fire had no remedy until the postwar *Des Moines* class. With the *Des Moines* design, the 8-inch cruiser finally came into its own—just when it was becoming obsolete.

Only once before the war did the navy revert to 6-inch guns, but even here the obsession with firepower crammed 15 guns onto the *Brooklyn* class. The reduction to 12 guns in the wartime *Cleveland*s helped blend a more balanced warship.

Protection received secondary status in most of the world's prewar CA; but unlike European "tinclads," American ships prioritized firepower rather than speed. Survivability increased with each new class up to the *New Orleans*, a fairly balanced design. However, no country produced a 10,000-ton, 8-inch cruiser well rounded for Pacific duty.

America's rampant top-heaviness caused serious problems among the cruisers. Wartime AA and technology added almost 2,000 tons to the *Brooklyn*s; even the post-treaty designs gained up to 500 tons. One of the early efforts to reduce cruiser loads (before the war) landed all CA torpedo tubes to compensate for enlarged DP batteries. Though American torpedoes impressed no one, this suppression of cruiser tubes may itself have fostered the navy's negligence in torpedo development. On the other hand, the enlarged 5-inch DP batteries had indisputable value; American cruisers managed well with air attack, and only one, *Chicago*, fell victim to enemy planes.

By American standards, the cruisers as a group lagged in habitability, though they bettered most foreign counterparts. In endurance and reliability, they excelled. The most surprising quality in this ill-armored lineage was its ruggedness, even with regard to torpedo damage. Cruisers suffered torpedo hits on 31 occasions, but only seven of the ships sank, and none sank from a single hit. By comparison, of 24 torpedoed Japanese cruisers, 20 sank, three of them after single hits. The Americans had the advantage of their expert damage control, especially after the merciless lessons of Savo Island.

Cruiser employment in wartime bore no resemblance to the lengthy list created prewar. The ships acted as AA escorts, shore bombardment vessels, and miniature ships-of-the-line. Though the navy never deployed a wartime cruiser as spectacular as the *Iowa*-class BB or the *Fletcher*-class DD, it did produce a fleet of capable ships equal to the difficult tasks they faced.

Several former cruisers survived as hulks: *Olympia* (5,865 nt, ten 5-inch guns, 19 knots, 1895), *Despatch* (3,000 tons, 1887), the ex-Spanish *Reina Mercedes* (2,835 tons, 1888), *Rochester* (8,150 tons, 1893), *Seattle* (12,500 tons, 1906), and the former cruiser-minelayer *Baltimore* (4,400 tons, 1890).

OMAHA, MILWAUKEE, CINCINNATI, RA-
LEIGH, DETROIT, RICHMOND, CONCORD,
TRENTON, MARBLEHEAD, MEMPHIS (CL4–
13: 7,100 tons; twelve 6-inch, eight 3-inch DP
guns, six 21-inch TT; AC 2, 34 knots, 1923–
25): intended as scouts; initially fitted to lay
224 mines and mounting 10 torpedo tubes.
The layout evolved amid a muddle—the first
cruisers designed since 1905—and early plans
refer to them as destroyers. They represent the
transitional phase in cruiser development,
combining the casemate mounts and four
stacks of World War I with the centerline twin
turrets and high speed of World War II.

When first completed, the *Omaha*s had
impressive specifications, but the first impression soon wore off. The ships were vulnerable
and truly wet; not only did they ship water over
their decks, but their flimsy hulls actually
leaked. On one occasion, *Richmond* went dead
in the water, her fuel lines fouled with brine.
With such frailty, the *Omaha*s seemed almost
eager to sink. *Raleigh* and *Marblehead*, after
modest aerial attacks, survived only because of
extraordinary damage control. Accumulating
top-weight created additional danger. The navy
did its best to keep the ships from frontline
duties, but wherever they went, their crews disliked them—cramped ships, and miserably
hot, except on northern patrols where they
proved too cold.

The main battery that at first glance made
the *Omaha*s seem worthwhile consisted of a 6-
inch mediocrity. The two twin turrets had more
range but a slower rate of fire. The navy
reduced CL6–9, 12 to six casemate mounts—
thus a main battery of just 10 guns. The number of DP guns also varied; some units had
seven, or as few as six to make room for light
AA. All this mattered little since the ships had
no effective high-angle fire control.

The fleet sought a way to turn the *Omaha*s
into something valuable. Proposals included a
conversion into cruiser-carrier hybrids or a
complete reconstruction as aircraft carriers. A

more realistic plan would have specialized the
ships as AA escorts, retaining their twin mounts
with a new DP battery of seven 5-inch guns,
but the navy didn't bother.

America waited five more years before
undertaking another cruiser program, and the
*Omaha*s had no direct descendants—fortunately. They did establish the practice of machinery
dispersal which appeared in almost all subsequent designs.

Milwaukee was transferred to the Soviet
navy as *Murmansk.*

PENSACOLA, SALT LAKE CITY (CA24, 25:
9,100 tons; ten 8-inch, eight 5-inch DP guns;
AC 4, 32.5 knots, 1929–30): well underweight
due to American zeal to observe the 10,000-ton
rule—rather a contrast with the attitudes in
Axis navies.

Full use of the tonnage allowance would
have strengthened the hull—during *Salt Lake
City*'s desperate action off the Komandorski
Islands, the shock of her own gunfire hampered
operation of the steering gear—and thickened
the armor. The *Pensacola*s earned the "tinclad"
label with a tonnage of protection equaling just
5.7% of their displacement. Yet in combat they
seemed robust. A Long Lance slammed into
Pensacola's side during the Solomons campaign,
sparking a fire that touched off 150 8-inch
shells, but damage control saved the ship.

(Each navy calculates its percentages differ-
ently. The American system, used in this section, lists armored decks as part of the hull
structure. Including her horizontal protection,
Pensacola actually equaled 11% armor.)

Designers didn't skimp on firepower. But
the 8-inch guns, sited in twin and triple
mounts, lacked adequate spacing between their
muzzles. The navy responded to the resulting
dispersion problems by testing new shell forms,
reducing muzzle velocity, and adding a slight
delay to the fire of adjacent guns.

Hindered by their imbalance, the *Pensacola*s
nevertheless served well in a variety of tasks.

They had great significance as the starting point for America's modern cruiser lineage, and they established the standard for cruiser range (10,000 miles at 15 knots, though wartime weight gain shrank it to 7,000–7,500 miles by 1945).

NORTHAMPTON, CHESTER, LOUISVILLE, CHICAGO, HOUSTON, AUGUSTA (CA26–31: 9,400 tons; nine 8-inch, eight 5-inch DP guns; AC 4, 32.5 knots, 1930–31): an attempt to utilize *Pensacola's* missing 900 tons, yet cautious designers again overestimated the weights involved; some calculations show a displacement of 9,050 tons. The new layout incorporated modest gains in protection, strength, habitability, and sea-keeping. The 8-inch disposition in three triple mounts recurred in all subsequent CA classes.

While awaiting additional light AA guns, some units shipped four 3-inch DP. This lasted no later than 1942.

Three units became war losses. *Houston* survived a bomb hit but not the 30 shells and four 24-inch torpedoes that came a few days later. Two aerial torpedoes crippled *Chicago*; she would have survived if not for the ensuing attacks that scored four more hits. *Northampton* suffered two simultaneous hits from Long Lances, and after three hours of progressive flooding, she went under.

The *Northamptons*, like the *Pensacolas*, required alterations to tame their violent roll behavior. Presumably, these were the two cruiser classes involved when the United States hinted at a trade with Britain for the *Duke of York*.

PORTLAND, INDIANAPOLIS (CA33, 35: 9,900 tons; nine 8-inch, eight 5-inch DP guns; AC 4, 32.5 knots, 1932–33): nearing 10,000 tons and further improved, especially in protection. However, with the navy scrambling to complete its cruiser forces, these ships were rushed to completion without the refinements seen in the subsequent *New Orleans*. In 1945, *Indianapolis*

succumbed to three submarine torpedoes and her own overweight condition.

NEW ORLEANS, ASTORIA, MINNEAPOLIS, TUSCALOOSA, SAN FRANCISCO, QUINCY, VINCENNES (CA32, 34, 36–39, 44: 10,050 tons; nine 8-inch, eight 5-inch DP guns; AC 4, 32.7 knots, 1934–37): initially rated between 9,375 and 9,950 tons, and much heavier by the end of their service. The individual ships showed more than the usual variation as planners made adjustments while tip-toeing on the brink of 10,000 tons. The new layout placed its greatest emphasis on protection, especially against gunfire. Magazines received more suitable placement, and for the first time, the 8-inch guns sat in thickly-armored turrets; 15% of displacement went to protection.

For these advances, the ships paid with a slight reduction in seaworthiness, habitability, and range (though still rated officially at 10,000 miles at 15 knots). They also forfeited the benefits of machinery dispersal, making them more vulnerable to a loss of power. Curiously, no sinkings resulted from lost power; but three of these ships, designed to resist gunfire, sank under the impact of Japanese cruiser shells at Savo Island. Analyses have shown that no design flaws figured in the losses; rather, blame lay with errors in shipboard readiness, with regard both to the crew's response and to the wealth of flammables eagerly awaiting ignition. Fire destroyed *Astoria*, detonating a 5-inch magazine after she had suffered 34 hits—a significant assault (unofficial estimates go as high as 63 hits) but one the fleet expected her to survive. *Quincy* and *Vincennes* took a heavier pounding, and each suffered torpedo hits as well.

The navy immediately put this humiliation to work, stripping the fleet of extraneous combustibles and installing more emergency power units and firefighting equipment. Fire claimed no more American cruisers. *Minneapolis* demonstrated her survivability after two devastating

Long Lance hits; a fire flared, but the crew quickly quenched it, and the ship limped off under her own power. *New Orleans* survived a torpedo that blew off 150 feet of her bow, everything ahead of the second turret.

San Francisco endured an epic ordeal in November 1942. Having already suffered the impact of a crashing bomber, she encountered a Japanese surface force and found herself exchanging short-range gunfire with the battleship *Hiei*. The cruiser took at least 45 hits, most from 6-inch rounds, but 15 came from *Hiei*'s 14-inchers. Fatalities included the task force commander and his staff, and the ship's captain and executive officer. The brutalized ship remained in action with two turrets still functioning.

By that time, cruisers usually carried just two scout planes to reduce the risk of fire. Some units shipped one or two 3-inch DP while awaiting the availability of light AA. *Minneapolis*, *New Orleans*, and *Astoria* entered service with the older mark of 8-inch gun firing only the 260-lb shell. The others (and eventually *Minneapolis*) mounted the newer model capable of firing 335-lb shells, though they may never have received them. Possibly only the *Baltimore* class cruisers used the super-heavy rounds in wartime.

The appearance of the German pocket battle-ships inspired a proposal to rearm some heavy cruisers with six 10-inch guns (660-lb shells). No conversions began, but the navy maintained an interest in "cruiser-killers" despite treaty restrictions. A variety of plans circulated, most near 24,000 tons with six 12-inch guns or twelve 8-inch guns. A more restrained 18,000-ton design mounted six 10-inch guns. Eventually the 12-inch layouts gained support, and one of them evolved into the *Alaska*.

BROOKLYN, PHILADELPHIA, SAVANNAH, NASHVILLE, PHOENIX, BOISE, HONOLULU, ST. LOUIS, HELENA (CL40–43, 46–50: 10,000 tons; fifteen 6-inch, eight 5-inch DP guns; AC 8, 32.5 knots, 1938–39): developed from *New Orleans* and forming, in turn, the basis for dozens of subsequent cruisers, all of which included armor schemes equal to 12–15% of displacement.

The London Conference returned America's focus to light cruisers but failed to alter American preference for large designs. Reports about Japan's *Mogami* dictated a powerful main battery. The new 6-inch gun, in contrast to previous models, had a heavy shell and a high rate of fire in its 60° triple mounts. The *Brooklyn*s, with 15 barrels discharging up to 10 rpm or more, boasted the strongest gun armament

The USS Helena *(above) differed somewhat from the* USS Brooklyn *but retained the firepower of 15 fast-firing guns.*

among all treaty cruisers. They also provided a steady platform for their gunnery, riding well even in gale conditions.

Most *Brooklyn*s carried 5/25 DP guns, the last cruisers to do so. *St. Louis* and *Helena*, however, had 38cal twin mounts. They also differed from the rest of the class in their internal layout; by a marginal increase in tonnage, they gained a partial dispersal of machinery.

With its lavish weaponry and reasonable armor, the design had to lack something— structural strength. Though the hull itself showed a healthy girth, its slender framework left it susceptible to accidental damage. *Savannah* suffered hull damage in a prewar storm and later tore herself open on her anchor chain. Concerned that the design may have passed a structural deficiency on to subsequent classes, the navy scrutinized *Helena*'s 1943 loss to three Long Lances. Investigators determined that the first hit, which snapped off much of her bow, severely stressed the hull but not sufficiently to prove fatal by itself. The second torpedo struck precisely where it could knock out all her machinery, combining with the nearby third hit to inflict maximum trauma on the ship's structure. Rather than citing hull weakness, the official report expressed surprise that the hull lasted 20 minutes before failing, surprise which would have increased had the navy understood the power of the Long Lance. The navy concluded that no ship short of *Baltimore* size had much chance of surviving such hits.

The other *Brooklyn*s survived the war, and it sometimes seemed their flimsiness was a blessing. When a German guided bomb hit *Savannah*, the explosion vented through the ship's bottom; flooding then drenched her magazine before it could detonate. *Boise* ran afoul of cruiser gunfire off Guadalcanal. The Japanese scored several hits, most of them insignificant, though one jammed a turret. Then an 8-inch round, landing short, plowed into *Boise*'s hull beneath the waterline. Piercing the magazine, it ignited a store of powder totaling 3,000 lbs. A flash engulfed the forward part of the ship, killing a hundred men, but the crew's successful firefighting ended *Boise*'s danger. She had suffered little structural damage, though 1,200 tons of flooding put her down by the bow. Things could have gone much worse; seawater, which followed the shell's path into the magazine, helped suppress the flames. In fact, most of *Boise*'s powder went untouched, and no 6-inch rounds cooked off. (American ammunition had a good safety record in World War II.)

Savannah's repairs became a reconstruction complete with bulges and a new 5-inch battery (like the one in *St. Louis*). The navy wanted similar changes for the whole class, but circumstances permitted only the fitting of 38cal guns on *Honolulu*. Early in the war, some units carried 3-inch DP guns in lieu of light AA.

The design's large hangars could house six planes, and two more could rest on the catapults, but in service the *Brooklyn*s carried four planes each. Though the hangars aggravated some vibration problems, most of the class remained active and well regarded in various navies for decades after the war. *General Belgrano* (ex-*Phoenix*) became a victim of the Falklands War in 1982.

WICHITA (CA45: 10,565 tons; nine 8-inch, eight 5-inch DP guns; AC 4, 33 knots, 1939): basically a *Brooklyn* with 8-inch guns and even thicker armor. *Wichita* surpassed all foreign cruisers with her 6-inch belt (*Hipper*, 3.1-inch; *Algérie*, 4.3-inch; *Zara*, 5.9-inch; *Myoko*, 4-inch*) and 8-inch turret face (*Hipper*, 6.3-inch; *Algérie*, 3.9-inch; *Zara*, 5.9-inch; *Myoko*, 1-inch). The design improved on *Brooklyn*'s subdivision and structure but did not include machinery dispersal. A new 8-inch mount provided more space for the guns (and their muzzles). The DP battery of 38cal guns sat in single mounts, some with enclosed gunhouses.

(*Japanese and German cruisers had additional factors beside armor thickness contributing to their belt protection.)

Wichita certainly rates among the finest treaty cruisers. Yet zealous planners had overloaded her and left her without adequate stability; the navy would have to wait four more years for a balanced CA design.

ATLANTA, JUNEAU, SAN DIEGO, SAN JUAN, OAKLAND, RENO, FLINT, TUCSON (CL51–54, 95–98: 6,593 tons, sixteen 5-inch DP guns, eight 21-inch TT, 32.5 knots, 1942–45): a detour from the typical cruiser lineage, fostered by the Second London Conference's proposal for smaller cruiser displacements. Intended as general-purpose escorts or destroyer leaders, they carried a full AS outfit long after the navy had deleted depth charges from all other cruisers. The crowding of depth charges, light AA, and other gear on the fantail sacrificed some of the *Atlanta*s' already meager maneuverability, making them useless as submarine trackers. They specialized as AA vessels rather than destroyer leaders, and as the war wore on, their depth charges (and later, torpedoes) gave way to light guns.

The DP main battery distinguished the *Atlanta* class. Six twin turrets sat on the centerline with two more in wing positions. The lesser value of the wing turrets led to their omission from CL95–98, leaving twelve 5-inch DP. This decreased the top-weight—a problem critical for the *Atlanta*s—and opened more space for light AA. The navy completed three slightly modified units postwar with 12 guns and no depth charges.

The designed protection equaled only 9% of displacement, but the ships showed great survivability, helped by their machinery dispersal. *Atlanta* took a 24-inch torpedo and 49 shell hits (19 of them from *San Francisco*'s 8-inchers, including seven hits from one salvo—some unfortunately accurate short-range shooting). The deluge knocked out six of her eight gun

mounts (only one still had power) and sparked a magazine fire. One boiler room flooded, but the ship maintained power for 20 minutes before progressive flooding claimed the other boilers. Crewmen continued their damage control efforts for 12 hours before having to scuttle her. A Long Lance hit *Juneau* during the same battle; she continued at 13 knots until a submarine torpedo struck exactly where the Long Lance had and blew the ship to pieces. No other *Atlanta*s sank, though *Reno* almost did when a submarine torpedo struck her stern. She almost capsized because added top-weight had reduced her stability.

Excellent seaboats, the *Atlanta*s nevertheless had many critics who called them cramped and spoke of annoying vibrations. In fact, the cold reception originated from contemporary naval doctrine that pegged the cruiser as an anti-ship platform rather than a swatter of aircraft and submarines. If the navy hadn't rated them as cruisers, the *Atlanta*s might have enjoyed more popularity. They were, in a way, ahead of their time, antedating an appropriate doctrine for their employment and the appropriate weaponry to qualify them as an AS threat.

The need for long range discouraged the development of other small cruisers. The navy rejected a 1940 plan (4,050 tons, eight 6-inch DP or eight 5-inch DP, twelve 21-inch TT, AC 2, 35 knots) despite a desire to introduce the new 5/54 and 6/47 DP guns. And when the time came for a new AA cruiser, the *Worcester* class more than doubled *Atlanta*'s tonnage. The British criticized this insistence on large designs, claiming that American cruisers lacked the vital quality of expendability. The Royal Navy prized its expendable cruisers, and proceeded to expend them in large numbers.

CLEVELAND, COLUMBIA, MONTPELIER, DENVER, SANTA FE, BIRMINGHAM, MOBILE, VINCENNES, PASADENA, SPRINGFIELD, TOPEKA, BILOXI, HOUSTON, PROV-

IDENCE, VICKSBURG, DULUTH, MIAMI, ASTORIA, OKLAHOMA CITY, LITTLE ROCK, AMSTERDAM, PORTSMOUTH, WILKES BARRE, ATLANTA, DAYTON (CL55–58, 60, 62–67, 80–82, 86, 87, 89–92, 101–105: 11,130 tons; twelve 6-inch, twelve 5-inch DP guns; AC 4, 32.5 knots, 1942-45): plus nine other units converted to *Independence*-class carriers, two CL completed postwar, three canceled, two completed postwar with slight modifications (*Fargo* class), and 11 modified units canceled. The design began as an update of the *Helena*, mounting only four main turrets in favor of an enlarged DP battery. The hull received additional strength. Yet doubts arose about the structure of wartime cruisers after Typhoon Cobra wrenched *Miami's* bow out of line and the CA *Pittsburgh* lost her bows completely in Typhoon Viper. But *Houston* showed tremendous strength after two aerial torpedo hits. Though flooding swelled her displacement to 20,900 tons, her hull withstood the pressure.

The *Cleveland*s became inactive soon after the war; a peacetime fleet had no need for such cramped, top-heavy ships. Their instability inspired extreme remedies such as the removal of one or both catapults. But their firepower and toughness rate the *Cleveland*s among the best light cruisers. While not at all fast, they proved almost as nimble as destroyers. Machinery dispersal enhanced their survivability, as it did in all subsequent American cruisers. No other cruiser design entered service in such large numbers, yet not one *Cleveland* fell victim to the war.

BALTIMORE, BOSTON, CANBERRA, QUINCY, PITTSBURGH, ST. PAUL, COLUMBUS, BREMERTON, FALL RIVER, MACON, LOS ANGELES, CHICAGO (CA68–74, 130–132, 135, 136: 13,881 tons; nine 8-inch, twelve 5-inch DP guns; AC 4, 33 knots, 1943–45): plus two completed postwar, six canceled, three completed postwar with slight modifications (*Oregon City* class), and one completed postwar specially adapted as a flagship. The design evolved

from the *Wichita*, a ship lacking stability; the *Baltimore*s boasted a wealth of stability, managing well with wartime weight gain. They also had enough habitability for wartime complements.

At the time the class began entering service, the situation no longer afforded cruisers much opportunity for distinction. The *Baltimore*s spent most of their time herding the fast carriers, drudgery that obscured their potential. They had armor thicker than any other rival cruiser's. Their heavy 8-inch shells gave them an unsurpassed broadside, while no foreign design mounted a secondary battery better than the American standard of twelve 5-inch DP. Superior in firepower and protection, the *Baltimore*s had no equal among wartime CA.

After stormy seas tore off *Pittsburgh*'s bows, her watertight doors held up under the sea's pounding with only minor flooding. She lost none of her crew. Even the severed bows remained watertight, and the navy recovered the "suburb of Pittsburgh."

Though *Cleveland* and *Baltimore* each exceeded 10,000 tons, their designs germinated in the context of treaty limits, and the navy hoped to leap free of these restraints. The urgency of war production precluded an interruption of the *Cleveland* and *Baltimore* programs. Instead, designers performed some minor tinkering (such as giving the *Fargo* and *Oregon City* subclasses a single funnel to increase AA arcs of fire) while awaiting an opportunity for real change. They started two new studies. The CL project generally resembled *Cleveland* but exceeded 13,000 tons; the most dramatic changes included greater protection, 34-plus knots, and a new 141-lb shell. The CA proposals (from 15,400 to 20,000 tons) likewise paralleled *Baltimore*'s layout, though some plans featured 12 main guns. None of this work resulted in any construction, and before the Americans got around to another cruiser program, they settled on something entirely new.

Meanwhile the "cruiser killer" concept had finally borne misshapen fruit.

ALASKA, GUAM (CB1, 2: 27,500 tons; nine 12-inch, twelve 5-inch DP guns; AC 4, 33 knots, 1944): plus four others not completed; planned in response to Japan's powerful CA force and rumors of "super-cruisers." (*Jane's* theorized a 30-knot *Chichibu* class of up to 15,000 tons, armed with six 12-inch guns.) Though designers worked for the first time without displacement limits, they produced one of the few failures of American warship design. At various points during its tortuous path to acceptance, the layout showed distinct balance: sometimes as a mini-battleship, well protected like the *Dunkerque*, other times in more cruiserly form like an overgrown CA. But so many departments and individuals had a hand in the final product, it emerged with the size of a battleship but the capabilities of a cruiser.

The *Alaska*s had a short list of virtues. Their dispersed power plants provided adequate speed. Their hull form made them good seaboats. The 12-inch model performed well.

These were the least maneuverable ships in the fleets except for old *Saratoga*. Their AA firepower barely bettered that of a heavy cruiser half their size. And while their survivability far exceeded that of conventional cruisers, it made for shameful contrast with ships like *Scharnhorst* and *Dunkerque*. The *Alaska*s did carry a credible tonnage of armor, similar in proportion to that of a British battleship; but their cruiser lineage failed to give them a dreadnought's defense against underwater damage. They had poor subdivision and no anti-torpedo scheme.

The *Alaska*s, officially classed as "large cruisers," reached almost 30,000 tons by war's end. Their intended mission as carrier escorts and their nonexistent protection below the waterline distinguish them from true battlecruisers.

WORCESTER, ROANOKE (CL144, 145: 14,800 tons; twelve 6-inch DP, twenty-four 3-inch DP guns; AC 4, 33 knots): new AA design with no thought given to AS ability. In a fleet with a cruiser tradition of anti-ship firepower, the *Atlanta*s seemed alarmingly harmless. Early drafts for their successors stood around 8,000 tons with ten 6-inch DP or a dozen 5/54 DP; this earned a collective yawn from the leadership. The need for more AA punch prompted a new line of development, a large design suited equally to killing ships or planes.

The *Worcester*s became the most powerful "light" cruisers in history. They featured a tough protective layout and the new model 3-inch gun to replace the 40mm Bofors. Navy tests rated the 3-incher as effective as eight Bofors against aircraft and as effective as 20 against *Ohka* rockets. Unfortunately, while the 6-inch guns delivered heavy firepower with a new rapid-fire system (5-second firing cycle), the mounts proved less than successful. Their potential, however, remained obvious. The navy began designing a 6-inch triple mount with each gun firing 20 rounds per minute, but postwar developments rendered the concept obsolete.

After the cancellation of two sisterships, *Worcester* and *Roanoke* joined the peacetime fleet, an impressive pair but not one that the navy really needed. They proved wet in service.

DES MOINES, SALEM, NEWPORT NEWS (CA134, 139, 148: 17,273 tons; nine 8-inch, twelve 5-inch DP, 24 3-inch DP guns; AC 4, 33 knots): without peer, far superior to any other CA ever designed. Encounters with the Japanese in the Solomons brought to light an uncomfortable situation for the Americans; their 8-inch guns fired too slowly while their 6-inch guns had less range than the enemy's torpedoes. So the navy applied the *Worcester*'s rapid-fire principle to the standard 41° 8-inch mount, this time with complete success at a firing cycle of six seconds. In one minute, *Des*

Moines could hurl more than 30,000 lbs of metal at the enemy; this rates her in the same category with the *Richelieu*-class battleships. The initial armor plan gained progressive reinforcement in response to German guided bombs. An extensive plan of subdivision included widely dispersed machinery. No other 8-inch cruiser approached this level of survivability.

Des Moines and her sisters (a fourth unit never reached completion) joined the fleet in 1948–49. If such ships had patrolled the Solomons six years earlier, the enemy could hardly have formed a response.

The high-angle weaponry and fire control in the *Des Moines* and *Worcester* classes made them equal to battleships, perhaps superior, as destroyers of aircraft.

Destroyers

World War I ended amid America's mass production of 279 "flush-deckers." Despite their obsolescence, their vast numbers discouraged further construction for more than ten years. In the mid–1930s, designers began spewing out new plans, a parallel to the frenzied succession of cruiser projects. Like the cruisers, the destroyers used the full tonnage allowed by treaty; this gave them great range (all designed for 6,500 miles at 12 knots). And like the cruisers, they lacked balance.

Their hulls proved weak, though none broke apart in storms and the ships showed some resistance to punishment. Underwater damage posed the greatest threat, but 44% of American destroyers struck by mines or torpedoes survived. Twenty modern units suffered heavy damage below the waterline amidships, where it's most potentially lethal; 11 of them survived, and others would have if circumstances hadn't necessitated their scuttling.

Wartime additions—including huge loads of ammunition—completely altered design performance and overwhelmed the ships' tiny

reserves of stability; hurricanes capsized four destroyers in 1944. The navy finally had to institute rules defining the permissible levels of tonnage bloat.

The interwar designs scrambled into service too quickly for the fleet to assess their individual flaws, but they all mounted the peerless 5-inch, 38cal gun. This standardization streamlined American production, allowing the navy, after it had completed its assessments, to shift mid-stride into *Fletcher*-type construction.

And World War II ended amid America's DD mass production.

ALLEN (DD66: 1,078 tons, four 4-inch guns, twelve 21-inch TT, 29.5 knots, 1917): last of the *Sampson* class (DD63–68), used for training only. A 1940 rearmament plan (3 4-inch, three 3-inch DP guns, six 21-inch TT) apparently simplified into a replacement of six TT by light guns.

After the *Sampson*s, the Navy opted for a new hull form, a flush-deck layout that provided greater strength, though sacrificing the dryness of a raised forecastle. Three classes followed. This flush-decker program, with 273 ships completed, gave America the world's largest destroyer force, a distinction it retained into the Cold War. Individual units showed design variations with displacements ranging from 1020 to 1,220 tons. Two ships mounted a battery of four 4-inch twin mounts, while five had four 5-inch, 51cal guns. The *Clemson*s suffered from inferior workmanship; they required enlarged fuel stores to achieve the *Wickes*'s range.

CONWAY, CONNER, STOCKTON, MANLEY (DD70,72–74: 1,125 tons; four 4-inch, one 3-inch DP gun, twelve 21-inch TT; 32 knots, 1917–20): last of the *Caldwell* class (DD69–74), a transitional design from the *Sampson*s into the flush-deck layout. *Manley* initiated trials as a transport in 1939.

WICKES, PHILIP, EVANS, LITTLE, SIGOUR-NEY, GREGORY, STRINGHAM, COLHOUN, ROBINSON, RINGGOLD, McKEAN, FAIRFAX, SCHLEY, CHEW, WILLIAMS, CRANE, RATH-BURNE, TALBOT, WATERS, DENT, DORSEY, LEA, LAMBERTON, MONTGOMERY, BREESE, GAMBLE, RAMSAY, TATTNALL, BADGER, TWIGGS, BABBITT, JACOB JONES, BU-CHANAN, AARON WARD, HALE, CROWN-INSHIELD, TILLMAN, BOGGS, KILTY, KEN-NISON, WARD, CLAXTON, HAMILTON, TARBELL, YARNALL, UPSHUR, GREER, ELLIOT, ROPER, BRECKINRIDGE, BARNEY, BLAKELEY, BIDDLE, DU PONT, BERNADOU, ELLIS, COLE, J. FRED TALBOTT, DICKER-SON, LEARY, SCHENCK, HERBERT, PALMER, THATCHER, CROSBY, COWELL, MADDOX,

FOOTE, KALK, MACKENZIE, HOGAN, HOWARD, STANSBURY, HOPEWELL, THOMAS, HARADEN, ABBOT, DORAN (DD75, 76, 78, 79, 81–83, 85, 88–90, 93, 103, 106, 108, 109, 113–119, 121–128, 130–162, 164, 167–170, 175, 178–185: 1,100 tons; four 4-inch, one 3-inch DP gun, twelve 21-inch TT; 35 knots, 1918–20): the second flush-deck series, originally included DD75–185. An inactive unit, *Walker* (ex-DD163), served as a hulk until her wartime scrapping. Another hulk (ex-*Taylor*, DD94) returned to active duty, at least in part; the navy removed her bow and used it to repair the war-damaged *Blakeley*.

CLEMSON, DAHLGREN, GOLDSBOROUGH, SEMMES, SATTERLEE, MASON, ABEL P.

Flush-deckers transferred in 1940

70	*Conway—Lewes*	181	*Hopewell—Bath* (N)
72	*Conner—Leeds*	182	*Thomas—St. Albans* (N)—*Dostoinyi*
73	*Stockton—Ludlow*	183	*Haraden—Columbia*
75	*Wickes—Montgomery*	184	*Abbot—Charleston*
76	*Philip—Lancaster*	185	*Doran—St. Mary's*
78	*Evans—Mansfield* (N)	190	*Satterlee—Belmont*
81	*Sigourney—Newport* (N)	191	*Mason—Broadwater*
88	*Robinson—Newmarket*	193	*Abel P. Upshur—Clare*
89	*Ringgold—Newark*	194	*Hunt—Broadway*
93	*Fairfax—Richmond—Zhivuchiy*	195	*Welborn C. Wood—Chesterfield*
108	*Williams—St. Clair*	197	*Branch—Beverley*
127	*Twiggs—Leamington—Zhguchiy*	198	*Herndon—Churchill—Deyatelnyi*
131	*Buchanan—Campbeltown*	252	*McCook—St. Croix*
132	*Aaron Ward—Castleton*	253	*McCalla—Stanley*
133	*Hale—Caldwell*	254	*Rodgers—Sherwood*
134	*Crowninshield—Chelsea—Derzkiy*	256	*Bancroft—St. Francis*
135	*Tillman—Wells*	257	*Welles—Cameron*
140	*Claxton—Salisbury*	258	*Aulick—Burnham*
143	*Yarnall—Lincoln* (N)—*Druzhnyi*	263	*Laub—Burwell*
162	*Thatcher—Niagara*	264	*McLanahan—Bradford*
167	*Cowell—Brighton—Zharkiy*	265	*Edwards—Buxton*
168	*Maddox—Georgetown—Zhostkiy*	268	*Shubrick—Ripley*
169	*Foote—Roxborough—Doblestnyi*	269	*Bailey—Reading*
170	*Kalk—Hamilton*	273	*Swasey—Rockingham*
175	*Mackenzie—Annapolis*	274	*Meade—Ramsey*

UPSHUR, HUNT, WELBORN C. WOOD, GEORGE E. BADGER, BRANCH, HERNDON, DALLAS, CHANDLER, SOUTHARD, HOVEY, LONG, BROOME, ALDEN, BARKER, TRACY, BORIE, JOHN D. EDWARDS, WHIPPLE, PARROTT, EDSALL, MacLEISH, SIMPSON, BULMER, McCORMICK, STEWART, POPE, PEARY, PILLSBURY, JOHN D. FORD, TRUXTON, PAUL JONES, HATFIELD, BROOKS, GILMER, FOX, KANE, HUMPHREYS, McFARLAND, OVERTON, STURTEVANT, CHILDS, KING, SANDS, WILLIAMSON, REUBEN JAMES, BAINBRIDGE, GOFF, BARRY, HOPKINS, LAWRENCE, BELKNAP, McCOOK, McCALLA, RODGERS, OSMOND INGRAM, BANCROFT, WELLES, AULICK, GILLIS, LAUB, McLANAHAN, EDWARDS, GREENE, BALLARD, SHUBRICK, BAILEY, THORNTON, SWASEY, MEADE, LITCHFIELD, ZANE, WASMUTH, TREVER, PERRY, DECATUR, HULBERT, NOA, WILLIAM B. PRESTON, PREBLE, SICARD, PRUITT (DD186–191, 193–199, 206–211, 213–237, 239–258, 260, 263–270, 273, 274, 336–347: 1,100 tons; four 4-inch, one 3-inch DP gun, twelve 21-inch TT; 35 knots, 1918–21): the last flush-decker class, originally included DD186–347. A pair of U-boat torpedoes sank *Reuben James* on October 31, 1941. *Stewart*, damaged and captured in Java in 1942, spent most of the war as the Japanese patrol boat *P102*. *Dallas* became *Alexander Dallas* in 1945 to free the city name for cruiser construction. Private owners bought several flush-deckers prewar; one ship (ex-*Thompson*, DD305) served as a floating restaurant until reacquired by the wartime navy for target duty. The naval hulk *Moosehead* (ex-*Turner*, DD259) survived the war as a water barge.

At the time of their design, the flush-deckers ranked among the most powerful destroyers in the world; by the time their production ended, they had become distantly outdated. The navy let their numbers dwindle prewar, and in 1940 transferred fifty to British and Canadian forces (the "Town" class; new names listed above). Five of them served with their British names and Norwegian crews (N) during 1940–42. Nine later went to the Soviets under Russian names

Adapted as escorts, the "Towns" retained three or six torpedoes and one or more 4-inch guns; yet they remained far from ideal as AS vessels, with disturbing roll behavior (to which the Yanks had apparently grown accustomed)

The Broome *and* Pruitt. *The flush-deckers gave the Americans a numerous but outdated destroyer fleet.*

and a turning radius larger than a battleship's. The Americans also undertook converting their flush-deckers, a policy validated when fighting in the Far East revealed the inadequacy of ships still operating as fleet destroyers. Escort modification involved an increase in range, a decrease to 25 knots, the removal of a boiler and six torpedoes, and a new gun armament (six 3-inch DP, for example). More dramatic changes had already begun. In 1930–37, eight units became minelayers with DM-numbers (*Montgomery, Breese, Gamble, Ramsay, Tracy, Preble, Sicard, Pruitt*: 1,090 tons, three 3-inch DP guns, 70–80 mines, 30 knots). Eighteen others became minesweepers with DMS-numbers in 1940–41 (*Dorsey, Lamberton, Boggs, Hamilton, Elliot, Palmer, Hogan, Howard, Stansbury, Chandler, Southard, Hovey, Long, Hopkins, Zane, Wasmuth, Trever, Perry*: 1,090 tons, three 3-inch DP guns, 32.5 knots). Fourteen spent time with AVP-numbers, later AVD-numbers, as seaplane tenders starting in 1938–40 (*Clemson, Goldsborough, George E. Badger, McFarland, Childs, Williamson, Belknap, Osmond Ingram, Gillis, Greene, Ballard, Thornton, Hulbert, William B. Preston*, each capable of tending one squadron: 1,090 tons, two 3-inch DP guns, 27.5 knots). Reconversion awaited many of these vessels, especially the AVD ships; replaced as tenders by the *Barnegat*s, some regained their DD classification for escort work, while others became transports. From 1940 to 1944, a total of thirty-two vessels took on APD-numbers as fast transports (*Manley, Little, Gregory, Stringham, Colhoun, McKean, Schley, Rathburne, Talbot, Waters, Dent, Tattnall, Kilty, Ward, Roper, Dickerson, Herbert, Crosby, Clemson, Goldsborough, George E. Badger, Brooks, Gilmer, Kane, Humphreys, Overton, Sands, Barry, Belknap, Osmond Ingram, Greene, Noa*: 1,315 tons, three 3-inch DP guns, 27 knots). With all these changes, few flush-deckers retained their full armament and traditional four-stack silhouette by 1943, and variation remained the rule. *Semmes*, used as a test vessel, landed all her torpedoes and 4-inch guns. Before becoming a transport, *Noa* operated with a floatplane replacing half of her TT.

FARRAGUT, DEWEY, HULL, MacDONOUGH, WORDEN, DALE, MONAGHAN, AYLWIN (DD348–355: 1,395 tons, five 5-inch DP guns, eight 21-inch TT, 36.5 knots, 1934–35): a good effort by designers after their long break from DD production. The navy decided to go again with a raised forecastle to correct the flush-deckers' wetness. The *Farragut*'s boilers began a trend toward higher pressure and, as a result, more economical steaming. American boilers never attained the extreme conditions used by the Germans, but they performed with great reliability.

Probably the most important development in the *Farragut*s was their main battery. The navy, aware of the 4-incher's waning value, sought something more powerful. The 5-inch, 51cal gun had a reputation for accuracy from its service as a BB secondary gun; however, its weight made it impractical for destroyers. The fleet's new 5-inch, 25cal DP gun had many vocal supporters touting its handy mount and relatively heavy shell. Some equally ardent critics noted the low muzzle velocity which promised more misses against speedy surface targets like torpedo boats and destroyers. The leadership made its decision in favor of the 25cal gun, on the condition that it be refined for surface engagements. Tests began with a 51cal gun cut back to 38cal, and the results pleased almost everyone. The 5/38 DP gun, basically an enlargement of the 25cal gun and mount, became the main battery of all subsequent destroyers through the end of World War II

Happy about its new weapon, the navy fitted the *Farragut*s with an effective fire-control system. The guns lacked enclosed mounts, though the forward mounts had shields. A lightly built hull detracted from the design's overall value, as did the modest reserve of stability. The *Farragut*s initially displaced 1,345 to

1,410 tons (about 2,064 full load), but incessant wartime additions led the navy to establish a limiting displacement of 2,335 tons, at which the *Farragut*s could make only 31.7 knots. They sacrificed one 5-inch gun to gain light AA during the war.

Stability factored in the loss of *Hull* and *Monaghan*; Typhoon Cobra (December 1944) killed 780 sailors, sank three destroyers, damaged 28 other ships, and destroyed 146 planes. The storm's crushing violence disabled even the 38,000-ton *Indiana*, knocking out her steering control and one engine. At the time, both *Hull* and *Monaghan* had at least 70% of their fuel loads, but they took on no additional ballast. The heavy seas crippled *Dewey;* despite rolls as extreme as 75°, she continued to right herself, her survival a matter of good luck and her captain's skillful ballasting.

The ensuing investigation barely mentioned the fleet's prevalent lack of stability. Rather, blame settled on failures in fleet readiness and mistaken operational priorities, by which skippers labored to maintain formation instead of focusing fully on survival. Just seven months later, the Pacific put this analysis to the test; Typhoon Viper had lesser duration than Cobra but greater ferocity. Several units reported rolls of 75°. The storm wrecked 76 planes, and 33 ships suffered damage, but none sank. By restoring the emphasis on seamanship, the fleet preserved even its least stable ships amid the most savage of storms.

PORTER, SELFRIDGE, McDOUGAL, WINSLOW, PHELPS, CLARK, MOFFET, BALCH (DD356–363: 1,834 tons, eight 5-inch guns, eight 21-inch TT, 37 knots, 1936–37): first of two flotilla leader types.

The leader concept raised sporadic interest among the Americans. They toyed with a 2,200-ton design (five 5/51 guns, 12 TT) during World War I. In the late 1920s, planners again considered designs up to 2,900 tons (four 6-inch guns, four 5/25 DP, 12 TT). The London Conference barred such large ships, but lurking among the DD restrictions, one clause allowed leaders up to 1,850 tons. The Americans, ever eager to use the full allowance, began to plan.

The *Porter* and the later *Somers* classes mounted the heaviest gun armament among American destroyers, with four twin turrets. But these enclosed mounts had only 35° elevation; the tonnage limit precluded heavier DP mounts. This greatly reduced the ships' AA value and forced the navy to perform extensive wartime alterations. Most units landed one or two twin mounts and some torpedoes (or all, late in the war when surface actions became unlikely). In some cases, the main battery changed to five DP guns in two twins and one single mount. This made the ships more battle-worthy but spoiled their powerful, cruiser-like mien.

The *Porter*s had more survivability than the ships built to the 1,500-ton limit, and they carried more fire-control gear. Upon completion, they ranged from 1,805 to 1,850 tons, but the navy eventually set a limiting displacement of 2,840 tons—about 250 tons above the original full load—for a speed of 34.5 knots.

MAHAN, CUMMINGS, DRAYTON, LAMSON, FLUSSER, REID, CASE, CONYNGHAM, CASSIN, SHAW, TUCKER, DOWNES, CUSHING, PERKINS, SMITH, PRESTON, DUNLAP, FANNING (DD364–379, 384, 385: 1,500 tons, five 5-inch DP guns, twelve 21-inch TT, 36.5 knots, 1936–37): built between 1,450 and 1,500 tons, wartime limit at 2,345 tons with 35 knots— typical for the 1,500-ton types. And like many other designs, the *Mahan*s reached or neared 40 knots on trials, though gunnery proved best at 30 knots. The propulsion plant coupled an improved engine design with higher-pressure boilers. This caused some cramping of the machinery spaces. Other features carried over from the *Farragut*s: shielded forward guns, a raised forecastle, and a weak hull. *Dunlap* and *Fanning* had a few differences, including enclosed mounts forward.

Wartime modifications included the removal of one or two guns and some torpedoes. The Pearl Harbor raid smashed *Cassin* and *Downes*, destroying everything but their machinery, weapons, and names. Nevertheless, the navy rebuilt them and returned them to service.

The United States helped Brazil build three modified *Mahan*s.

GRIDLEY, CRAVEN, McCALL, MAURY (DD380, 382, 400, 401: 1,500 tons, four 5-inch DP guns, sixteen 21-inch TT, 38.5 knots, 1937–38): actually 1,590 tons prior to wartime growth (about 200 more tons). The forward 5-inch guns had enclosed mounts.

A portion of the naval leadership, with visions of torpedo attacks dancing in their heads, managed to force the prodigal TT specification into several designs. The failure of American torpedo warfare struck a baleful irony onto this decision, with some unforeseen consequences trailing along; the *Gridley*s became the least stable units in a destroyer force famous for its instability. Even after removing half their tubes, the navy considered the ships so precarious, it declined to fit them with 40mm guns—the only modern destroyers so excluded.

BAGLEY, BLUE, HELM, MUGFORD, RALPH TALBOT, HENLEY, PATTERSON, JARVIS (DD386–393: 1,500 tons, four 5-inch DP guns, sixteen 21-inch TT, 37 knots, 1937): ordered with the *Gridley*s and similar to them. Though designed at 1,500 tons, they actually displaced around 1,625 tons. Compared to the previous class, the *Bagley*s had less powerful machinery but stronger hulls and a touch more stability. They retained all their guns and torpedoes throughout the war.

SOMERS, WARRINGTON, SAMPSON, DAVIS, JOUETT (DD381, 383, 394–396: 1,850 tons, eight 5-inch guns, twelve 21-inch TT, 37.5 knots, 1938–39): the second and final leader class, actual displacement exceeding 2,000 tons. Improved machinery gave more speed and range than in the *Porter*s, but the earlier class proved superior. The extra torpedo tubes had a cost in stability; *Warrington* foundered in a hurricane. The design included only one gun director, and the ships even looked more blandly DD-like than the *Porter*s. Wartime modifications approximated those in the *Porter* class.

BENHAM, ELLET, LANG, MAYRANT, TRIPPE, RHIND, ROWAN, STACK, STERETT, WILSON (DD397–399, 402–408: 1,500 tons, four 5-inch DP guns, sixteen 21-inch TT, 36.5 knots, 1939–40): a *Bagley* descendant and *Sims* ancestor, service displacement about 1,650 tons. The hull had greater strength, while the aft guns gained roofless mounts. The *Benham*s underwent the usual changes. By 1945, kamikazes eclipsed the threat of surface attack, and many destroyers landed some torpedo tubes.

SIMS, HUGHES, ANDERSON, HAMMANN, MUSTIN, RUSSELL, O'BRIEN, WALKE, MORRIS, ROE, WAINWRIGHT, BUCK (DD409–420: 1,570 tons, four 5-inch DP guns, eight 21-inch TT, 36.5 knots, 1939–40): stronger and more seaworthy than the *Benham*s. The original layout attempted five guns and 12 tubes; by reducing this, the designers made them less top-heavy, but some problems remained. The ships suffered the usual wartime alterations.

Though for the first time the navy allowed itself a tonnage figure over 1,500, the ships still overstepped their official displacement (1,760 tons as built, 2,313 tons fully loaded). They reached 1,850 tons by war's end, and at a limiting displacement of 2,530 tons, their speed fell to 34.5 knots.

BENSON, MAYO, MADISON, LANSDALE, HILARY P. JONES, CHARLES F. HUGHES, LAFFEY, WOODWORTH, FARENHOLT, BAILEY, BANCROFT, BARTON, BOYLE,

The USS Sims *represented a major step toward the hull strength and stability of the wartime classes.*

CHAMPLIN, MEADE, MURPHY, PARKER, CALDWELL, COGHLAN, FRAZIER, GANSEVOORT, GILLESPIE, HOBBY, KALK, KENDRICK, LAUB, MACKENZIE, McLANAHAN, NIELDS, ORDRONAUX (DD421, 422, 425–428, 459, 460, 491, 492, 598–617: 1,620 tons, four–five 5-inch DP guns, five–ten 21-inch TT, 35 knots, 1940–43): from the same program as the *Gleaves* class.

GLEAVES, NIBLACK, LIVERMORE, EBERLE, PLUNKETT, KEARNY, GWIN, MEREDITH, GRAYSON, MONSSEN, WOOLSEY, LUDLOW, EDISON, ERICSSON, WILKES, NICHOLSON, SWANSON, INGRAHAM, BRISTOL, ELLYSON*, HAMBLETON*, RODMAN*, EMMONS*, MACOMB*, FORREST*, FITCH*,

CORRY, HOBSON*, AARON WARD, BUCHANAN, DUNCAN, LANSDOWNE, LARDNER, McCALLA, MERVINE*, QUICK*, CARMICK*, DOYLE*, ENDICOTT*, McCOOK*, FRANKFORD, DAVISON*, EDWARDS, GLENNON, JEFFERS*, MADDOX, NELSON, BALDWIN, HARDING*, SATTERLEE, THOMPSON*, WELLES, COWIE*, KNIGHT*, DORAN*, EARLE*, BUTLER*, GHERARDI*, HERNDON, SHUBRICK, BEATTY, TILLMAN, STEVENSON, STOCKTON, THORN, TURNER (DD423, 424, 429–444, 453–458, 461–464, 483–490, 493–497, 618–628, 632–641, 645–648: 1,630 tons, four–five 5-inch DP guns, five–ten 21-inch TT, 35 knots, 1940–43): same as the *Benson*s. The nominal 10-ton increase was irrelevant; both groups exceeded 1,800 tons. At their limiting displacement (2,590 tons), their best speed fell into the low 30s. The two classes began as a single design, then diverged as builders installed differing machinery. Later, the navy ordered a repeat type to keep the fleet stocked with destroyers until the *Fletcher*s could appear in large numbers. Consequently, some accounts refer to *Livermore* and *Bristol* classes when in fact the ships all had the same basic layout. Only the initial order of 24 ships (DD421–444) included a five-gun battery. Some *Benson*s had enclosed turrets for just three of their guns. In addition to more mundane changes, the 24 marked units (*) underwent conversion to minesweepers with DMS-numbers; these ships typically mounted three guns and no TT.

The *Farragut* design had represented a promising prototype for the subsequent classes, despite its twin specters of weakness and instability. The *Sims* project brought a renewed concern for stability, and the *Benson*s managed their wartime growth with almost no trouble. They also introduced machinery dispersal and a well-structured hull, features that provided a new level of survivability. *Kearny* had the misfortune to demonstrate this toughness prior to America's entry into the war; in October 1941, a U-boat struck her with a torpedo near the forecastle break, a point of great stress in the hull. Yet the hull held together. This raised eyebrows among the British, who doubted their own destroyers could survive a hit in such a vulnerable spot. And not only did *Kearny* survive, but her machinery dispersal kept her from losing power and she steamed back to base on her own. After the war, a United States Navy assessment of destroyer experience concluded that the first criterion of DD survivability lay in the details of machinery arrangement.

Duncan exemplified the ruggedness that had grown into American DD design. At Cape Esperance, a torrent of shell hits tore her hull and ignited a series of widespread fires. After

two hours of damage control, the crew abandoned ship, driven off by the flames and a total loss of power. Several hours later, the flames sputtered. Sailors reboarded, but without help from other ships, the absence of power left them with no means to pump the hull dry. *Duncan*'s bulkheads held for 12 hours after the battle before finally collapsing and forcing the sailors overboard once more.

FLETCHER, RADFORD, JENKINS, LA VAL-LETTE, NICHOLAS, O'BANNON, CHEVA-LIER, SAUFLEY, WALKER, STRONG, TAY-LOR, DE HAVEN, BACHE, BEALE, GUEST, BENNETT, FULLAM, HUDSON, HUTCHINS, PRINGLE, STANLY, STEVENS, HALFORD, LEUTZE, PHILIP, RENSHAW, RINGGOLD, SCHROEDER, SIGSBEE, CONWAY, CONY, CONVERSE, EATON, FOOTE, SPENCE, TERRY, THATCHER, ANTHONY, WADS-WORTH, WALKER, BROWNSON, DALY, ISH-ERWOOD, KIMBERLY, LUCE, ABNER READ, AMMEN, MULLANY, BUSH, TRATHEN, HAZELWOOD, HEERMANN, HOEL, McCORD, MILLER, OWEN, THE SULLIVANS, STEPHEN POTTER, TINGEY, TWINING, YARNALL, BOYD, BRADFORD, BROWN, COWELL, CAPPS, DAVID W. TAYLOR, EVANS, JOHN D. HENLEY, FRANKS, HAG-GARD, HAILEY, JOHNSTON, LAWS, LONG-SHAW, MORRISON, PRICHETT, ROBINSON, ROSS, ROWE, SMALLEY, STODDARD, WATTS, WREN, AULICK, CHARLES AUS-BURNE, CLAXTON, DYSON, HARRISON, JOHN RODGERS, McKEE, MURRAY, SPROS-TON, WICKES, WILLIAM D. PORTER, YOUNG, CHARRETTE, CONNER, HALL, HALLIGAN, HARADEN, NEWCOMBE, BELL, BURNS, IZARD, PAUL HAMILTON, TWIGGS, HOWORTH, KILLEN, HART, METCALF, SHIELDS, WILEY, ABBOT, BRAINE, ERBEN, HALE, SIGOURNEY, STEMBEL, ALBERT W. GRANT, CAPERTON, COGSWELL, INGER-SOLL, KNAPP, BEARSS, JOHN HOOD, VAN VALKENBURGH, CHARLES J. BADGER,

UNITED STATES

COLAHAN, DASHIEL, BULLARD, KIDD, BENNION, HEYWOOD L. EDWARDS, RICHARD P. LEARY, BRYANT, BLACK, CHAUNCEY, CLARENCE K. BRONSON, COTTEN, DORTCH, GATLING, HEALY, HICKOX, HUNT, LEWIS HANCOCK, MARSHALL, McDERMUT, McGOWEN, McNAIR, MELVIN, HOPEWELL, PORTERFIELD, STOCKHAM, WEDDERBURN, PICKING, HALSEY POWELL, UHLMANN, REMEY, WADLEIGH, NORMAN SCOTT, MERTZ, CALLAGHAN, CASSIN YOUNG, IRWIN, PRESTON, BENHAM, CUSHING, MONSSEN, JARVIS, PORTER, CALHOUN, GREGORY, LITTLE, ROOKS (DD445–451, 465–481, 498–502, 507–522, 526–541, 544–547, 550–597, 629–631, 642–644, 649–691, 792–804: 2,100 tons, five 5-inch DP guns, ten 21-inch TT, 38 knots, 1942–45): plus nine units canceled (two of them with experimental power plants). The navy rated the *Fletchers* at 2,050–2,100 tons, though they actually neared 2,300 tons, exceeding 2,400 by 1945. The ships had sufficient reserves of stability, though the navy pushed them to their limit, never reluctant to dump more electronics, guns, and ammunition on board. (*Spence* capsized in Typhoon Cobra, but at the time she carried only 15% of her fuel load; her captain hesitated to add extra ballast, concerned it would interfere with later refueling operations.) The original full load of 2,924 tons swelled to a limiting displacement of 3,035 tons, at which they struggled to reach 32.3 knots. Late in the war, some units landed their TT to make room for light AA, but it never became necessary to remove a gun (all of which had enclosed mounts).

As it had once before, the navy decided to go with a flush-decked design which provided hull strength and a dry midships, but also made for wet bows. Since the ships entered service more than 200 tons above their nominal displacement, they at once showed a lack of speed, less than 36 knots on trials. They also had a large turning radius, though not as bad as the WWI flush-deckers.

What the *Fletchers* did well, they did extremely well. They had a strong armament, long range, reliability, and irrepressible toughness. Some of their success came by inheritance; most units joined the fleet after the early, unpleasant lessons of night combat against the Japanese. But the *Fletchers* presented the perfect vehicle for exploiting those lessons, achieving utter triumph at Cape St. George and Surigao Strait.

Most of the losses among the *Fletcher* and *Sumner* classes resulted from kamikaze attacks. In many cases, the ships survived, but the navy at that stage in the war didn't bother to repair them. *Hoel* succumbed to a more traditional fate beneath an avalanche of Japanese gunfire: 40 shells, ranging from 5-inch to 16.1-inch, stopped her dead in the water, and subsequent hits finished her off. *Johnston* received 4,700 lbs of incoming ordnance within the space of one minute. It wrecked half of her machinery, yet she continued at 17 knots and later repelled the charge of an entire DD flotilla. After accumulating damage for two and a half hours, she wallowed so helplessly that her crew couldn't even properly scuttle her; they simply opened her watertight doors and let her flood.

The *Fletchers*' well-rounded capabilities place them among the finest destroyers of the war. None of them endured conversion for mine warfare, but three experimented with a scout plane and catapult replacing a 5-inch gun. The experiment proved a failure, and all three ships returned to the original design.

The navy canceled two projects during the war. The British "Hunt"-class escort destroyers inspired a design between 705 and 900 tons which would have become DD503, 504. The leadership considered another small layout (DD505, 506: about 1150 tons) in an effort to gain ultra-rapid mass production.

ALLEN M. SUMNER, MOALE, INGRAHAM, COOPER, ENGLISH, CHARLES S. SPERRY, AULT, WALDRON, HAYNSWORTH, JOHN W.

WEEKS, HANK, WALLACE L. LIND, BORIE, COMPTON, GAINARD, SOLEY, HARLAN R. DICKSON, HUGH PURVIS, BARTON, WALKE, LAFFEY, O'BRIEN, MEREDITH, DE HAVEN, MANSFIELD, LYMAN K. SWENSON, COLLETT, MADDOX, HYMAN, MANNERT L. ABELE, PURDY, ROBERT H. SMITH*, THOMAS E. FRASER*, SHANNON*, HARRY F. BAUER*, ADAMS*, TOLMAN*, DREXLER, BLUE, BRUSH, TAUSSIG, SAMUEL N. MOORE, HARRY E. HUBBARD, HENRY A. WILEY*, SHEA*, J. WILLIAM DITTER*, ALFRED A. CUNNINGHAM, JOHN R. PIERCE, FRANK E. EVANS, JOHN A. BOLE, BEATTY, PUTNAM, STRONG, LOFBERG, LOWRY, LINDSEY*, GWIN*, AARON WARD*, HUGH W. HADLEY, WILLARD KEITH, JAMES C. OWENS, ZELLARS, MASSEY, DOUGLAS H. FOX, STORMES, ROBERT K. HUNTINGTON, BRISTOL (DD692–709, 722–741, 744–759, 770–781, 857: 2,200 tons, six 5-inch DP guns, ten 21-inch TT, 36.5 knots, 1943–45): plus three units completed postwar. Their actual displacement exceeded 2,500 tons, 2,600 tons by war's end. The 12 marked units (*) became minelayers with DM-numbers, 120 mines, and no torpedoes.

The design emerged from the *Fletcher*s with an attempted increase of firepower supplied by three twin turrets. But *Fletcher*'s singles could fire 10% faster and train 36% faster than the twins. This reduced the *Sumner*'s ability to engage aircraft, but experience also showed the benefit of a twin mount's focused AA firepower. Unfortunately, the concentration of two turrets forward—DP mounts, weighing one-third more than a *Porter* twin—tended to drive the bows down into waves.

The cramped hull design, with its restricted fuel load, also earned criticism. While matching *Fletcher*'s design figure of 6,500 miles at 15 knots, in service the *Sumner*s showed a slight dropoff in range. Speed and acceleration decreased slightly as well.

The list of drawbacks has received more attention than the design advances, which included new operational features such as internal radar accommodations. Twin rudders appeared for the first time in the destroyer fleet, providing more maneuverability. In fact, when the first units reached completion, their sharp turns contributed to a cracking of propeller struts, a problem soon corrected.

The *Sumner*s mounted powerful batteries of light AA, and they retained *Fletcher*-like durability; these two qualities paid vital dividends in the environment of Japanese fanaticism. Twenty-two kamikazes attacked *Laffey* off Okinawa; six scored hits along with four bombs, yet the ship survived. Seven kamikazes and three bombs struck *Aaron Ward* and completely wrecked her; her hull took on 1,650 tons of flooding, settling almost low enough to submerge her deck. She too survived.

GEARING, EUGENE A. GREENE, GYATT, KENNETH D. BAILEY, FRANK KNOX, SOUTHERLAND, ROWAN, GURKE, McKEAN, HENDERSON, CHEVALIER, HIGBEE, BENNER, DENNIS J. BUCKLEY, MYLES C. FOX, EVERETT F. LARSON, GOODRICH, HANSON, HERBERT J. THOMAS, TURNER, CHARLES P. CECIL, GEORGE K. MACKENZIE, SARSFIELD, ERNEST G. SMALL, FRED T. BERRY, NORRIS, McCAFFERY, VOGELGESANG, STEINAKER, HAROLD J. ELLISON, CHARLES R. WARE, CONE, HAWKINS, DUNCAN, HENRY W. TUCKER, ROGERS, PERKINS, VESOLE, LEARY, DYESS, BORDELON, FURSE, NEWMAN K. PERRY, FLOYD B. PARKS, JOHN R. CRAIG (DD710–713, 742, 743, 782–785, 805-808, 829–838, 858–860, 862–866, 873–885: 2,425 tons, six 5-inch DP guns, ten 21-inch TT, 36.8 knots, 1944–45): plus 53 postwar completions (some to a modified design) and 54 others never completed.

By adding 14 feet to the *Sumner*'s length, designers corrected most of the flaws. Seakeeping improved, and range surpassed the

UNITED STATES

Fletcher standard by more than one fourth. The design's actual displacement exceeded 2,600 tons, and when loaded to their limiting displacement of 3,340 tons, the ships reached only 31.3 knots. By this time, the leadership had begun to focus on DD speed; the performance of Free French super-destroyers made high speed seem a realistic goal. However, the French speed came at a cost in endurance that the Americans could never accept.

Planners began studies late in the war for a 3,200-ton design mounting six 5/54 DP and eight 3-inch DP guns with 10 torpedo tubes and a service speed of 34 knots. An envious individual suggested upgrading to 24-inch torpedoes. Only after a complete re-thinking of the project did it evolve into the postwar *Mitscher* class.

The salvaged Japanese *Kikuzuki* provided information but no active service.

Submarines

The American submarine force deprived Japan of more than a thousand large merchant ships and 200 warships. The boats that achieved these results had long range, good speed, heavy armament, and agreeable surface performance. But they were plump and unhurried in the dive with unimpressive underwater handling. Such shortcomings, hugely hazardous in a setting like the Mediterranean, seemed a mere drop in the Pacific where radar kept surprises to a minimum and the enemy refused to emerge from World War I. In fact, the Americans offset much of their vulnerability through operational improvements; dive times shrank, and noise levels reduced by 99%. Meanwhile, decoy and noisemaking systems entered service, and detection devices in 1945 could pinpoint not only enemy ships, but their weaponry.

The greatest challenge facing American subs came from their own torpedoes. The inexcusable parade of flaws—running too deep, failure

of the magnetic detonator, failure of the contact detonator, arming too late, exploding prematurely—eventually met with correction, and by 1945 the largest challenge became the rarity of worthy targets.

America's prewar doctrine resembled Japan's, casting the submarine as an agent of attrition against the enemy battle fleet. But immediately after Pearl Harbor, the mission changed to unrestricted commerce warfare. By accepting this remorseless offensive, the leadership reaped an immense harvest at little cost; of the major powers, the United States enjoyed the lowest loss rate for submarines and the best loss-to-kill ratio.

O2–4, 6–10 (SS63–65, 67–71: 521/629 tons, four 17.7-inch TT, 14/10.5 knots, 1918): plus O1, 5 out of service prewar. The navy sold the similar O11–16 in 1930 and decommissioned the remaining O-boats the following year. These remained inactive until recommissioned for training duty at the approach of war. O9 foundered in June 1941.

The "O's" received good reviews when new, but 20 years later they sufficed only for training. Original weaponry included a 3-inch gun, which proved impractical to operate.

R1–7, 9–20 (SS78–84, 86–97: 569/680 tons, one 3-inch gun, four 21-inch TT, 13.5/10.5 knots, 1918–19): plus R8 lost and the similar but inferior R21–27 sold prewar. An improvement over the "H" and "O" classes (especially in regard to habitability and engine reliability), the "R's" nevertheless served only in training, trials, and target duty. They had a 50-second dive time. R3, 17, 19 transferred to the Royal Navy.

America generally showed good sense in the naming of its ships. But for a time, a madness spurred the fleet to a fevered flinging of submarine letters, beginning early in the century with the assignment of SS-numbers to the "A" class boats. The SS-contagion continued into the "B" class and the "C" class and onward, right through to *AA3* (also known as SS61, SF3, and *T3*). The alphabetic insanity reached its peak when the navy gave its S-boats SS-numbers.

The "S" classes represented variations on the navy's theme for a longer-ranged sub, but this requirement failed to anticipate the emerging rivalry with Japan. The S-boats thus proved ill-suited for offensive patrols in the Pacific, which prompted discussion of a tanker-type boat (2,920 tons?, one 4-inch gun, two 21-inch? TT, 12/6 knots). The idea never had much support, yet the S-boats found themselves in the offensive role during the early days of the war, at which time their old torpedoes actually gave them an advantage over more modern boats. The "S's" soon withdrew for duty in training and local patrol. Their various subtypes originally included *S1–65* (and perhaps six more), but only 51 reached completion. Of these, 13 left service prewar.

S1, 18, 20–41 (SS105, 123, 125–146: 854/ 1,062 tons, one 4-inch gun, four 21-inch TT, 14.5/11 knots, 1920–24): the Electric Boat type. Prewar, they had a dive time of 75 seconds. *S1, 21, 22, 24, 25, 29* transferred to the British, who then turned one over to the Poles as *Jastrząb*.

S11–17 (SS116–122: 876/1,092 tons, one 4-inch gun, four 21-inch TT, 15/11 knots, 1920–23): the navy version, which proved a bit crowded and not very maneuverable. *S11–13* had a fifth TT—the navy's first stern tubes.

S42–47 (SS153–158: 906/1,126 tons, one 4-inch gun, four 21-inch TT, 14.5/11 knots, 1924–25): a modified Electric Boat type. Considered the best of the S-boats, none retired prewar.

S48 (SS159: 903/1,230 tons, one 4-inch gun, five 21-inch TT, 14.5/11 knots, 1922): a modified navy version, not well liked. *S48* avoided

scrapping only due to improvements during a post-accident rebuild. Her sister *S49* lasted at least to 1940 as a public exhibit.

BARRACUDA, BASS, BONITA (SS163–165: 2,000/2,620 tons, one 3-inch gun, six 21-inch TT, 18/8 knots, 1924–26): the "B" class, formerly named *V1–3* and designated at other times as B1–3 and SF4–6. Inspired by a fad for long-range, high-speed boats to operation with the fleet, they proved even less practical than their foreseen role, plagued by poor sea-keeping, cranky machinery, slow diving (about two minutes), and excess weight. Replacement of the original heavy deck gun (5-inch) accomplished little, and the navy tired of them, decommissioning the class in 1937. They emerged from retirement three years later, having endured removal of their main engines and 3-inch guns. An unsuccessful stint as cargo subs followed a humdrum tour as trainers, and the navy dropped plans to use them as transports (which would have afflicted them with yet another designation, APS2–4). Their careers ended at last in early 1945.

ARGONAUT (SS166: 2,710/4,164 tons, two 6-inch guns, four 21-inch TT, 60 mines, 15/8 knots, 1928): also caught up in the nomenclature maelstrom and known variously as V4, A4, and SM1. She derived from the "B" class with high standards of habitability and influence from German design. The introduction of tube-laid mines made specialized minelayers unnecessary, so the plodding and unmaneuverable *Argonaut* became subject to various conversion proposals. In the end, she sacrificed her mine gear to act as a transport (APS1).

NARWHAL, NAUTILUS (SS167, 168: 2,915/ 4,050 tons, two 6-inch guns, six 21-inch TT, 17/8 knots, 1930): formerly *V5, 6* and N1, 2. Bearing a resemblance to the *Argonaut* design, they overcame their own mediocrity to become the war's most successful cruiser-subs. In fact, they won their greatest notoriety as transports for raiding parties. Each boat gained four external tubes early in the war, though the Americans soon acquired a distaste for external torpedoes.

DOLPHIN (SS169: 1,560/2,240 tons, one 4-inch gun, six 21-inch TT, 17/8 knots, 1932): ex-V7, ex-D1. *Dolphin* represented a switch toward smaller designs, and she might have had two or more sisterships if the London Treaty hadn't necessitated further cuts in tonnage. Uninspired and aging, she operated mostly as a training boat.

CACHALOT, CUTTLEFISH (SS170, 171: 1,170/ 1,650 tons, one 3-inch DP gun, six 21-inch TT, 17/8 knots, 1933–34): ex-V8, 9, ex-C1, 2. The final development of the unsuccessful "V" pedigree, the "C's" proved overly compact. Though they tested the submarine fleet's first torpedo data computer, they performed only a few war patrols before becoming trainers.

PORPOISE, PIKE (SS172, 173: 1,310/1,960 tons, one 3-inch DP gun, six 21-inch TT, 19/8 knots, 1935): often grouped with the next two types as the "P" class. The lineage that began with *Porpoise* continued into the major wartime classes, carrying with it the virtues of strong hulls, good sea-keeping, and pleasant habitability (by submarine standards). But the "P's" lacked handiness underwater, and they required over a minute of dive time. *Pike* and *Porpoise* gained two external tubes during the war.

The navy saw high surface speed as a safeguard for Pacific operations; boats could retain mobility despite damage to part of their machinery. The progression from the *Porpoise* to *Gato* shows an increase in armament but, more importantly, development in machinery as the power plants became increasingly compact and practical.

SHARK, TARPON (SS174, 175: 1,315/1,968 tons, one 3-inch DP gun, six 21-inch TT, 19.5/8 knots, 1936): closely related to the *Porpoise*s, but strangely named for a sub-group of the "P" class. *Tarpon* received two additional external tubes, but *Shark* sank before she could get hers.

PERCH, PICKEREL, PERMIT, PLUNGER, POLLACK, POMPANO (SS176–181: 1,330/1,997 tons, one 3-inch DP gun, six 21-inch TT, 19.25/8 knots, 1936–37): last of the P-boats, and suitably named. Only *Permit* and *Pickerel* were selected to mount two external tubes.

SALMON, SEAL, SKIPJACK, SNAPPER, STINGRAY, STURGEON (SS182–187: 1,449/2,198 tons, one 3-inch DP gun, eight 21-inch TT, 21/9 knots, 1937–38): the first new "S" class, based on the "P's." None of them received external tubes except *Stingray* (temporarily). *Salmon* mounted a 4-inch gun instead of the 3-inch DP. Each boat could carry 32 mines instead of torpedoes.

SARGO, SAURY, SPEARFISH, SCULPIN, SQUALUS, SWORDFISH, SEADRAGON, SEALION, SEARAVEN, SEAWOLF (SS188–197: 1,450/2,350 tons, one 3-inch DP gun, eight 21-inch TT, 20/8.75 knots, 1939): a follow-up to the previous "S's." *Seadragon* had a 4-inch gun. *Squalus*, after salvage from a 1939 accident, became *Sailfish*. The Japanese found *Sealion* scuttled in the Philippines but paid her little attention.

TAMBOR, TAUTOG, THRESHER, TRITON, TROUT, TUNA, GAR, GRAMPUS, GRAYBACK, GRAYLING, GRENADIER, GUDGEON (SS198–203, 206–211: 1,475/2,370 tons, one 3-inch DP gun, ten 21-inch TT, 20/8.75 knots, 1940–41): an improved *Sargo*. By reducing their torpedo load to four, they could carry 40 mines. *Tambor*, *Tautog*, *Thresher*, *Tuna*, *Gar*, and *Grayling* mounted 5-inch, 51cal guns by 1942.

MACKEREL, MARLIN (SS204, 205: 940/1,190 tons, one 3-inch DP gun, six 21-inch TT, 16/11 knots, 1941): built to the same specifications, but not identical. The navy saw these smaller boats as "S" and "R" class replacements that could also undertake offensive operations. The design far exceeded the old standards of habitability and range, and it seemed suitable for wartime mass production. In fact, the war curtailed further development; standardization won out over size considerations, and *Gatos* entered service by the dozen.

GATO, GREENLING, GROUPER, GROWLER, GRUNION, GUARD, ALBACORE, AMBERJACK, BARB, BLACKFISH, BLUEFISH, BONEFISH, COD, CERO, CORVINA, DARTER, DRUM, FLYING FISH, FINBACK, HADDOCK, HALIBUT, HERRING, KINGFISH, SHAD, SILVERSIDES, TRIGGER, WAHOO, WHALE, ANGLER, BASHAW, BLUEGILL, BREAM, CAVALLA, COBIA, CROAKER, DACE, DORADO, FLASHER, FLIER, FLOUNDER, GABILAN, GUNNEL, GURNARD, HADDO, HAKE, HARDER, HOE, JACK, LAPON, MINGO, MUSKALLUNGE, PADDLE, PARGO, PETO, POGY, POMPON, PUFFER, RASHER, RATON, RAY, REDFIN, ROBALO, ROCK, RUNNER, SAWFISH, SCAMP, SCORPION, SNOOK, STEELHEAD, SUNFISH, TUNNY, TINOSA, TULLIBEE (SS212–284: 1,825/2,424 tons, one 3-inch DP gun, ten 21-inch TT, 20.25/8.75 knots, 1941–43): based on the *Tambor*s, with a similar minelaying capacity.

BALAO, BILLFISH, BOWFIN, CABRILLA, CAPELIN, CISCO, CREVALLE, DEVILFISH, DRAGONET, ESCOLAR, HACKLEBACK, LANCETFISH, LING, LIONFISH, MANTA, MORAY, RONCADOR, SABALO, SEAHORSE, SKATE, TANG, TILEFISH, APOGON, ASPIRO, BATFISH, ARCHERFISH, BURRFISH, PERCH, SHARK, SEALION, BARBEL, BARBERO, BAYA, BECUNA, BERGALL, BESUGO, BLACKFIN, CAIMAN, BLENNY, BLOWER, BLUEBACK, BOARFISH, CHARR, CHUB, BRILL, BUGARA, BULLHEAD, BUMPER, CABEZON, DENTUDA, CAPITAINE, CARBONERO, CARP, CATFISH, ENTEMEDOR, CHIVO, CHOPPER, CLAMAGORE, COBBLER, COCHINO, GOLET, GUAVINA, GUITARRO, HAMMERHEAD, HARDHEAD, HAWKBILL, ICEFISH, JALLAO, KETE, KRAKEN, LAGARTO, LAMPREY, LIZARDFISH, LOGGERHEAD, MACABI, MAPIRO, MENHADEN, MERO, SAND LANCE, PICUDA, PAMPANITO, PARCHE, BANG, PILOTFISH, PINTADO, PIPEFISH, PIRANHA, PLAICE, POMFRET, STERLET, QUEENFISH, RAZORBACK, REDFISH, RONQUIL, SCABBARDFISH, SEGUNDO, SEA CAT, SEA DEVIL, SEA DOG, SEA FOX, ATULE, SPIKEFISH, SEA OWL, SEA POACHER, SEA ROBIN, SENNET, PIPER, THREADFIN, SPADEFISH, TREPANG, SPOT, SPRINGER, STICKLEBACK (SS285–302, 304–345, 361–378, 381–415: 1,826/2,414 tons, one 3-inch DP gun, ten 21-inch TT, 20.25/8.75 knots, 1943–45): plus nine completed postwar and 10 canceled.

These nearly identical classes (the *Balao*s being *Gato*s with strengthened hulls) added a high level of technology to the assets inherited from earlier designs. Their faults lay in their substandard maneuverability and lengthy dive time (50–60 seconds, reduced in wartime to as short as 30 seconds). They also severely overtaxed the navy's supply of fish names.

The *Gato/Balao* boats formed the bulk of America's wartime submarine fleet. Their unparalleled success derived from their balance of design: long range, habitability, modern electronics, strength, powerful weaponry. The gun armament evolved as the war progressed. When large merchant targets became scarce, submarine skippers had to content themselves with smaller prey, some too small to warrant the cost of a torpedo. At that point, a gun more potent than the 3-inch DP became preferable. *Hake* mounted a 5-inch, 51 cal gun. At least nine boats had 4-inchers. A low-angle version of the 5-inch, 25cal gun served aboard more than a hundred boats, many of which carried two. The success of these heavy gun batteries prompted the fleet to devise elaborate fire-control layouts, which entered service just as the war was ending. Batteries of 5-inch rockets also saw late-war service.

TENCH, THORNBACK, TIGRONE, TIRANTE, TRUTTA, TORO, TORSK, QUILLBACK, ARGONAUT, RUNNER, CONGER, CUTLASS, DIABLO, MEDREGAL, REQUIN, IREX, SEA LEOPARD, ODAX, SIRAGO (SS417–424, 475–485: 1,860/2,414 tons, one 5-inch gun, ten 21-inch TT, 20.25/8.75 knots, 1944–45): plus 14 boats completed postwar and 101 canceled. Similar to the *Gato* types, *Tench* included a stronger hull and other improvements. Apparently all wartime boats entered service with one or two 5-inch, 25cal guns.

Wartime submarine proposals involved various machinery layouts, snorkels, and 24-inch torpedoes. A 1945 study showed a boat of 1,960/2,990 tons with a speed near 22.5/9 knots, a 5-inch deck gun, and a mixed torpedo battery: twelve 21-inch TT plus six external tubes for Mark 27 homing torpedoes.

Wartime reports of European assault craft generated a slight interest in America. The leadership rejected a Chariot-type weapon and mini-sub study (1–3 TT, 10 surface knots), but a proposed one-man semi-submersible motor boat (25 knots maximum) spawned two prototypes (2 TT, 1943). Nevertheless, not even the recovery of some Japanese midget subs sufficed to spur the project into production.

The German *U505*, captured in 1944, became *Nemo* in American service.

Escorts and Gunboats

DUBUQUE, PADUCAH (990 tons; one 5-inch, two 4-inch, one 3-inch DP gun; 12 knots, 1905): old GB used for training, later armed with three 5-inch guns.

Two other elderly combatants continued in training: *Dover* (1,280 tons, one 5-inch gun, 1897) and *Wheeling* (870 tons, 1897).

SACRAMENTO (1,025 tons; two 4-inch, one 3-inch DP gun; 12 knots, 1914): GB. The navy at that time saw gunboats as a cheap alternative to cruisers—similar to the theory underlying the later *Eries*.

SC1 class (75 tons, one 3-inch gun, 17 knots, 1917–19): 13 submarine-chasers. The original program included *SC1–448*, and all but seven reached completion. A hundred transferred to the French, some lasting into World War II. Fourteen American units remained in navy and coast guard service into 1942; 12 of them retired by 1945. The design managed well with most sea conditions despite its size, but provided little in the way of crew comforts.

PE19, 27, 32, 38, 48, 55–57 (430 tons, two 4-inch guns, 18 knots, 1919): last of the 60 famous "eagle boats," a larger design to supplement the SC-craft and provide better open-sea performance. Adequate as AS escorts when built, they had limited value in World War II, and their true significance lay in the lessons they taught concerning mass production.

ASHEVILLE, TULSA (1,200 tons; three 4-inch, one 3-inch DP gun; 12 knots, 1920–23): GB, elderly despite an overhaul in the 1930s. *Tulsa* became *Tacloban* in 1944.

WAKE, TUTUILA (370 tons, two 3-inch guns, 14.5 knots, 1927–28): the first of three river GB classes ordered for service in China. The Japanese captured *Wake* and renamed her *Tatara*. *Tutuila* transferred to China as *Mei Yuan*.

PANAY, OAHU (450 tons, two 3-inch guns, 15 knots, 1928): river gunboats. Japanese aircraft sank *Panay* in 1937.

LUZON, MINDANAO (560 tons, two 3-inch guns, 16 knots, 1928): river gunboats. *Luzon* became *Karatsu* in Japanese service.

ERIE, CHARLESTON (2,000 tons, four 6-inch guns, mines, AC 1, 20 knots, 1936): gunboats. The London Treaty placed no restrictions on 2000-ton, 20-knot gunboats with weapons no larger than 6.1-inch; the Americans tailored their design to fit this loophole. They wanted a ship to "show the flag" in peacetime, placing an emphasis on habitability. Wartime possibilities included escort and AA duty; planners favoring this second choice requested a battery of 5/38 DP guns. Such a vessel, they claimed, could help protect Pearl Harbor from air attack.

The final layout showed versatility but excelled at nothing. Depending on the situation, the stern could accommodate rails for depth charges or mines. The scout plane had no catapult. The ships' structure allowed for the addition of side armor, as in the carrier *Wasp*, and the *Eries* actually received their belts at some point. Armor protection represented a strong suit of the design, with thicknesses matching that of some cruisers. However, the *Eries* never found their niche in fleet doctrine. More intriguing than valuable, they made their greatest contribution by influencing the "Treasury"-class cutter design.

SC449 (96 tons, one 3-inch DP gun, 17 knots, 1940): prototype wood-hulled AS escort.

SC450 (86 tons, one 3-inch DP gun, 16.9 knots, 1940): another prototype, based on the old *SC1* design.

PC451 (270 tons, one 3-inch DP gun, 21.8 knots, 1940): prototype steel-hulled AS escort. She and *PC452* developed into the *PC461*.

PC452 (284 tons, one 3-inch DP gun, 22 knots, 1944): prototype, delivered in 1941 but with-

out engines until 1943. She served in experiments only, renamed *Castine* in 1945.

SC453 (86 tons, one 3-inch DP gun, 22 knots, 1941): improvement over *SC449, 450* using a new diesel design. The supply of engines became a bottleneck in SC mass production.

PC461 class (293 tons, one 3-inch DP gun, 18 knots, 1940–45): 317 vessels, plus 35 more built as landing craft control boats, 24 built as gunboats equipped with a hefty load of automatic weapons (*PGM9–32*), and 43 others canceled. Many units transferred: 32 to France, eight to Brazil, and one each to Norway, Greece, Uruguay, and the Netherlands.

The design called for a well-armed coastal AS vessel capable of 22 knots. The navy then loaded them with weaponry, including a heavy complement of depth charges. (They had to make do with Mousetrap instead of Hedgehog.) All this weight—displacement sometimes topped 400 tons—made the target speed impossible, but most units could sustain 18+ knots. Their range (3,450 miles at 12 knots) put them in a class with the British "Flowers,"

Though terribly overloaded, the PC-crafts served well.

though their design showed the high standards derived from warship stock; they handled with the nimbleness of destroyers, and their slim hull gave an edge in speed. However, their squat British cousins fared better in the open sea. Wet forward and generally uncomfortable in heavy seas, the PC-craft nevertheless proved seaworthy enough, and the navy viewed them as a success.

As with most small combatants, the armament varied with the availability of guns and mounts. Some units carried two 3-inch DP. Eighteen vessels gave temporary, unsatisfactory service as minesweepers.

TEMPTRESS class (898 tons; one 4-inch, one 3-inch DP gun; 16 knots, 1940): 10 corvettes from the British "Flower" class. Upon their transfer to the United States, they were rearmed

with American weapons, two 3-inch DP whenever possible, but many received two 4-inchers. The navy assigned them PG-numbers as patrol gunboats.

ACTION class (976 tons, two 3-inch DP guns, 16 knots, 1942–43): 15 more units from the second series of "Flowers." In fact, only eight entered American service, the others going to the British.

SC497 class (98 tons, one 3-inch DP gun, 20 knots 1942–44): 435 vessels based on *SC453*, plus 37 canceled. A sluggish supply of diesel engines meant only half the craft received the intended model, and speeds varied (15.6–21 knots). America sent eight units to Brazil, 50 to France, three to Norway, and 78 to the Soviet Union.

The SC escort design lacked the capabilities of its larger PC cousin.

Like the larger PC-craft, these vessels handled well; but, unsteady and uncomfortable, they offered no pretense of operating beyond coastal waters. The navy's only postwar plans for its SC-craft was retirement.

The initial armament of one 3/23 gun increased to a 3/50, but experience proved 40mm guns more suitable. Eight units underwent modification as gunboats PGM1–8 (similar to the PC conversions), and 70 became control boats. A few units served as minecraft.

SC1466–1473 (75 tons, light guns, 15 knots, 1942): Fairmile "B" launches transferred from Britain. The United States then sent three of them on to Mexico. Some units carried a 3-inch DP.

PCE827–860, 867–886, 891–904 (640 tons, one 3-inch DP gun, 15.5 knots, 1942–45): SC converted from the Admirable-class MS, begun as a British order. The Royal Navy eventually received 15 vessels (the "Kil" class). The Americans completed 53 more for themselves, including those converted for other duties (rescue vessels, control boats, weather service, etc.). Though slower than the PC-craft, these vessels gained better sea-keeping with their beamier layout; the installation of Hedgehog then made them valuable ocean-going escorts. The initial British and American plans included PCE827– 976 and as many as 123 more.

PCS1376 class (251 tons, one 3-inch DP gun, 14 knots, 1942–45): 59 submarine-chasers converted from YMS1-class MS hulls, with 31 others canceled. Not as successful as the PCE-craft, they couldn't carry Hedgehog. As with other SC classes, many units converted to control boats, radar trainers, and the like.

ASHEVILLE, NATCHEZ (1,400 tons, three 3-inch DP guns, 20 knots, 1942): frigates of the British "River" class. Canada built 10 for the United States, but eight were transferred to the Royal Navy.

TACOMA class (1,500 tons, three 3-inch DP guns, 20 knots, 1943–44): 96 frigates based on the British "Rivers," with 21 going to the British and 28 to the Soviets. This American variant included strengthened bows for ramming, added beam for stability, and new machinery which proved less reliable. Habitability saw a major advance, but not enough to prevent crews from sweltering in tropical duty. Though longer-ranged than the destroyer escorts, the frigates had less power and weaker hulls. The United States, capable of mass-producing warship-type escorts like the DE and PC-craft, had less interest in building merchant-types.

EVARTS class (1,140 tons, three 3-inch DP guns, 21 knots, 1943–44): 97 DE, plus eight canceled. Thirty-two went to Britain, while China received two others. They had average range for destroyer escorts, 6,000 miles at 12 knots.

American planners feared the DE program might conflict with the DD program. (In fact, the DE's main rival turned out to be landing craft.) Only in the 5-inch battery did a problem arise. The navy wanted two 5/38 DP for all units, but a shortage forced the substitution of three 3-inch DP—an anemic battery but sufficient to outgun a surfaced U-boat.

Destroyer escorts existed to fight subs, and while they excelled at it, they had their flaws. The Evarts class ranked among the less successful. British captains, accustomed to their own steady vessels, denounced the type's lurid roll that sent the most seasoned seamen whoozily to the rail. (The Americans made less complaint; apparently they didn't know any better.)

EDSALL class (1,200 tons, three 3-inch DP guns, three 21-inch TT, 21 knots, 1943–44): 85 DE. The lack of torpedoes in the Evarts class instigated criticism, and all subsequent designs had triple mounts. However, some DE landed their tubes in favor of light AA guns.

UNITED STATES

BUCKLEY class (1,400 tons, three 3-inch DP guns, three 21-inch TT, 24 knots, 1943–44): 154 DE, including 46 built for the British. The navy meant the 3-inch battery as a temporary measure, but only a few lucky *Buckley*s were rearmed with 5-inch DP.

CANNON class (1,240 tons, three 3-inch DP guns, three 21-inch TT, 21 knots, 1943–44): 72 DE completed, 148 canceled. Six units went to the French, and eight to Brazil. The *Cannon*s had long range (11,500 miles at 11 knots), but they rolled as badly as the *Evarts* type, which they closely resembled. The navy considered them the least successful DE.

JOHN C. BUTLER class (1,350 tons, two 5-inch DP guns, three 21-inch TT, 24 knots,

1943–45): 80 DE completed in wartime, three postwar, with 106 canceled. The 5-inch battery, torpedoes, and relatively high speed became especially important to the ships surprised by the Japanese off Samar. One of them, *Samuel B. Roberts*, sustained more than 20 hits (including 14-inch high-explosive rounds) before sinking. The destroyer escorts had little opportunity to show ruggedness, but they included machinery dispersal to help them cope with torpedo damage. Only 11 American DE sank during the war.

RUDDEROW class (1,450 tons, two 5-inch DP guns, three 21-inch TT, 24 knots, 1943–45): 72 DE similar to the previous class, plus 180 canceled.

The USS Harmon *of the* Buckley *class. The destroyer escorts excelled at submarine-hunting but never mounted Britain's Squid system.*

The success of flush-decker destroyers modified as fast transports led to similar work with destroyer escorts (43 *Buckleys* and 51 *Rudderows*: one 5-inch DP gun and 23.6 knots). Delays kept at least two units awaiting commission at war's end.

A number of yachts entered naval service. Eleven became auxiliary gunboats (1,420–3,060 tons, about 16 knots), most with two 3-inch DP. Eleven others received PC-numbers and 3-inch guns (35–140 tons, 10–17 knots). Twenty-one yachts with PY-numbers (499–1,130 tons) and 46 with PYc-numbers (75–640 tons) served as coastal escorts with 12–14 knots and, typically, one or two 3-inch guns. Three of them transferred to Ecuador.

The British supplied three of their MFV-craft. The Japanese captured a pair of small craft, the tug *Genesee* and the mercantile *Arayat*.

Motor Boats

America's MTB program sprang full blown within a fleet that never knew it needed such things. The nearly instantaneous appearance of balanced designs resulted from the input of British experience, thoughtful development of domestic design, well-managed trials, and a wealth of powerful engines. The Packard V-12 engine, without doubt the best MTB gasoline engine, became a legend of reliability, capable of full power even when half submerged in seawater.

Domestic designers had some experience that allowed an easy transition into the MTB business; the rescue boats they prepared for the army and navy had many of the same requirements as fast attack craft. The number of rescue boats in wartime service exceeded 2,200, operating with the army, navy, and coast guard, while some were transferred to Allied navies. Typically, such vessels rate as noncombatant, but the Americans used many of them as picket boats, armed but with reduced speed. The

most important pickets include the 37-foot type (about 460 picket boats), the 38-foot type (about 550 picket boats: seven tons, 26.5 knots, 1931–43), and the 45-foot type (about 470 picket boats: 22.6 knots). In addition to these units built as pickets, others underwent conversion for that duty when replaced as rescue boats by the new 63-footers. Thus almost three-quarters of the rescue boats spent time as pickets.

The 63-foot type (26 tons, 33.5–37.3 knots, 1942–45) began with a British order and became America's wartime standard (about 600 completed by 1945). Though never designated as picket boats, the 63-footers often carried significant weaponry, including depth charges. The United States modified 80 craft, *RPC1–80* (including *ex-PTC37–66*), as SC for the Soviets (29 tons, light guns, 28 knots, 1943–44) and delivered at least 62 of them. Other units served with the South Africans, the New Zealanders, the Australians, the Dutch, the Belgians, and the Uruguayans.

If the noncombatants seemed well-armed, the combatants overflowed with weaponry. American PT-boats carried a heavy torpedo armament, but they wound up relying more on their guns. The manic drive for increased firepower mutated the standard provision of .50cal and 20mm guns as crewmen littered the decks with mortars, anti-tank guns, bazookas, recoilless rifles, and a crafty device derived from the 37mm nose cannon of a P-39 fighter. The navy adapted a Bofors for PT-boats and began experiments with a 3-inch gun mount. Launchers for 4.5-inch and 5-inch rockets appeared late in the war.

Such advances belie the MTB program's humble start. In 1936, with preparations underway on the *North Carolina*-class BB, planners suggested equipping each dreadnought with one or two small MTB (20 tons, two 22.4-inch TT, 34.8 knots). More important, the issue of Philippines defense gave rise to a torpedo-armed PB layout, design work that provided a basis for subsequent MTB development. The Filipino plan itself, however, fell victim to American pricing, which sent the leaders of the Philippine Commonwealth venturing elsewhere as they sought to develop an Offshore Patrol of 50 MTB. Thornycroft in Britain presented an affordable option; plans included thirty 55-foot CMB in service by 1946. However, the war's start limited deliveries to one 65-foot MTB in 1939 (*Luzon*: 40 tons, two 17.7-inch TT, 41.2 knots) along with a single CMB (*Abra*: two 17.7-inch TT, 46.5 knots) while the British retained the five other units they had started. Local builders produced another CMB (*Agusan*) while eight incomplete units suffered scuttling during the Japanese invasion. Some confusion has resulted from the three completed boats' alternate designations (*Q111–113*: Arabic, not Roman, numerals), a situation further complicated when *Q111* became a Japanese capture, renamed *114*. Two other minor craft, *Baler* and *Danday*, gave Filipino service as *Q114, 115*.

PT1, 2 (27 tons, two 17.7-inch TT, 40 knots, 1939): experimental boats based on British CMB with torpedoes in stern troughs. They showed little promise, and the navy relegated them to secondary duties.

PT3, 4 (25 tons, two 17.7-inch TT, 40 knots, 1939): experimental.

PT5, 6 (42 tons, two 21-inch TT, 40 knots, 1941): experimental, with torpedoes still in stern troughs. Higgins Industries built the boats to official specifications, and they proved inadequate. Higgins then built a boat of its own design (34 tons, two 21-inch TT) that proved faster, drier, sturdier, and more maneuverable. The navy named it *PT6* as well and sold the previous *PT6* to Finland. Prior to delivery, however, all three boats went to Canada.

PT7, 8 (34 tons, two 21-inch TT, 40 knots, 1941): experimental, one wooden and one alu-

minum. They introduced side-mounted TT, but both boats turned out overweight and underpowered. Engine problems recurred. Though intended for transfer, *PT8* stayed behind and became an unexpected blessing for the Americans. The boat's metal hull remained in fine condition after years of disuse, convincing postwar designers to adopt aluminum construction.

PT9 (32 tons, four 17.7-inch TT, 43.5 knots, 1938): the most important vessel of this period; built by British Power Boat but rejected by the British. The American firm Elco then bought it as a prototype, and *PT9* influenced all subsequent PT-boat design.

Lend-Lease sent *PT3–9* to Canada as rescue boats. The navy received three other prototypes but declined to give them PT-numbers, using them instead in secondary duties.

PT10–19 (32 tons, four 17.7-inch TT, about 40 knots, 1940): Elco boats based on *PT9*, too lightly built. All went to the British.

PTC1–12 (45 tons, light guns, 40 knots, 1940): an AS variant of the *PT9* type, sent to England. The PT-family never displayed great aptitude as submarine-chasers. Many PT-boats with depth charges used them, not against submarines, but as a sort of time-fused mine to discourage pursuit by enemy vessels.

PT20–68 (35 tons, four 21-inch TT, 40 knots, 1941–42): a further Elco development; some units ordered under hull numbers *PTC13–36*. The navy earmarked *PT49–68* for transfer to Britain but delivered only the first 10. The British removed two TT.

The navy preferred to standardize its more powerful 21-inch torpedoes, so it enlarged the *PT20* (originally sister to *PT10–19*) as a 21-inch prototype. Thus the Americans, in typically American fashion, chose firepower over stealth, the MTB's traditional virtue—not a bad choice, allowing America's large boats to embark impressive batteries for their primary duty as gunboats. Many units temporarily landed two or four TT to compensate for the added weight of guns. Further weight-savings came from the replacement of tubes by simpler, lighter brackets; and stubby 22.4-inch aerial torpedoes often replaced the 21-inch weapons.

PT69 (Huckins, 34 tons) and *PT70* (Higgins, 35 tons) performed in trials before assuming secondary duties. The navy carried out an intense competition in 1941 which established the value of the Higgins and Elco designs, and demonstrated how each could be improved.

PT71–94, 197–254, 265–313, 450–485, 625–660, plus *PT791–796* postwar and *PT797–808* canceled (35 tons, four 21-inch TT, 41 knots, 1942–45): built by Higgins, more robust and maneuverable than the Elco boats. Some units, built for transfer, previously bore hull numbers *RPT1–12*, but not all of them went to Russia. The Soviets did eventually receive 55 boats. The British got 23, eight of which served with Yugoslavian crews.

PT95–102, 255–264 (34 tons, four 21-inch TT, 40 knots, 1942–43): built by Huckins based on *PT69*, used for training only.

PT103–196, 314–367, 372–383, 486–563, 565–614, 731–760, plus PT615–622 completed postwar and PT623, 624, 761–790 canceled (38 tons, four 21-inch TT, 40 knots, 1942–45): Elco boats. Sixty transferred to Soviet forces.

The Elco type came out on top of the 1941 trials, and in combat it had the greatest success. More seaworthy than the Higgins type, it also had better speed (42 knots at 45 tons). Its attitude while underway allowed superior forward visibility and, therefore, superior gunnery.

PT368–371, 384–449, 661–730, BPT21–68 (33 tons, two 21-inch TT, 40 knots, 1943–45):

British Vosper design, same as British-built units except for the American engines. Their smaller tonnage and battery shows Britain's greater regard for stealth. *PT368–371*, ordered by the Dutch as *TM32, 35–37*, never got to Dutch forces. *BPT21–68* and 16 others went to the British, and 90 to the Soviets.

PT564 (35 tons, four 21-inch TT, 46 knots, 1943): the Higgins "Hellcat," an experiment in high performance. Smaller, faster, and longer-ranged than other types, it also showed tremendous maneuverability. However, it had less habitability and—most importantly—a smaller gun armament. Rather than tamper with its mass-production program, the navy dropped the Hellcat.

A later experiment with Elco's *PT487* produced a service speed of 53.6 knots. At high speed, it outmaneuvered even the Hellcat, but at low speeds it did poorly.

In 1945, the navy began studies for new MTB, much larger than the wartime types (91 tons full load versus 54 tons for the Elco and Higgins boats). With a service speed near 43.5 knots, the boats would have carried four or six of the new Mark 16 torpedoes, but the war's end brought the project to a close.

The following list shows all transfers, including 115 PT-boats sent to Britain. The official Lend-Lease figure of 105 perhaps reflects the diverting of two boats to target duty and eight boats to the Soviets.

To the Soviets:
Vosper *PT400–449, 661–692* and *BPT53–60* (via Britain) : A1 type
Higgins *PT85–87, 89, 197, 265–276, 289–294, 625–656* : A2 type
Elco *PT498–504, 506–508, 510–521, 552–554, 556, 560–563, 731–760* : A3 type

To the British (renumberings not necessarily respective):

UNITED STATES

The **Auk-*class minesweeper* Staff.**

Vosper *BPT21–68* and *PT384–399 : MTB275–306, 363–378, 396–411 (MTB363–370* then went to the Soviets)

Higgins *PT88, 90–94, 198, 201, 203–217 : MTB419–423, MGB177–192* (eight then transferred to Yugoslavia), and two target-towing boats

Elco *PT49–58 : MTB307–316*

PT3–19, PT6, PTC1–12 : MTB258–274, MGB68, 82–93

The exploits of Italian assault craft inspired an American dalliance with explosive motor boat design (about three tons, at least 500–600 lbs of explosive, 27 knots).

The United States Navy used a YP-designation for vessels employed in local patrol. A catch-all category, it included everything from motor launches to fishing boats to PC-sized yachts. About 580 vessels received YP-numbers, plus others previously rated as coastal minecraft etc. America sent a number of small craft overseas: five launches to France, two YP-craft to Panama, and 54 unrated yachts and motor boats to Britain. American yards also supplied 70 of Britain's HDML's.

Minecraft

LAPWING class (950 tons, two 3-inch DP guns, 14 knots, 1918–20): the "Bird" class MS, capable of taking on ML gear. Of 49 vessels built, 44 survived to 1941, nine of them as seaplane tenders (still with two 3-inch guns). Others served as noncombatants, and only 22 remained on MS duty; most of them converted to tugs by 1942. The Japanese captured one unit—*Finch* became *P103*.

RAVEN, OSPREY (810 tons, one 3-inch DP gun, 80 mines, 18.1 knots, 1940): MS also intended for anti-submarine escort.

AUK class (890 tons, one 3-inch DP gun, 80 mines, 18.1 knots, 1942–45): 90 MS, plus four postwar, the *Raven* design with different machinery to facilitate magnetic sweeping. Unlike British MS, these units carried Hedgehog for AS duty.

America selected 34 of the *Auks* for transfer to Britain (*Catherine* class) but retained 12 of them, while also ordering 15 *Algerine* class MS from Canadian yards for transfer to Britain. At least 56 *Auk* and *Algerine* orders were canceled.

The navy had 151 vessels rated as coastal or harbor minesweepers, including the *Accentor* class (70 vessels: 185–205 tons, light guns, 10 knots, 1941–42). Eleven landing craft underwent modification to assist in mine duties.

The *Adroit* class consisted of 18 PC-craft converted to MS (mentioned above). Their engines provided only 16 knots.

The navy procured 15 trawlers built in 1940 to act as MS (400–585 tons, one 3-inch gun, 9.3–13 knots) and assigned them bird names. The British supplied a pair of auxiliary minesweepers and about 22 other trawler-type vessels.

EAGLE, HAWK, IBIS, MERGANSER (530 tons, light guns, 11.5 knots, 1942): MS also converted from trawlers. *Eagle* differed from the others, a bit smaller, a bit faster, she mounted a 4-inch gun and served variously as a patrol boat, a minesweeper, and a decoy vessel.

Five other vessels operated as decoy vessels, useless things armed with 3-inch or 4-inch guns.

YMS1 class (260 tons, one 3-inch DP gun, 14 knots, 1942–45): 502 vessels, a simple and reliable minesweeping design, nevertheless more naval in nature than Britain's mercantile MMS. Thirty-one units went to the French, four to the Norwegians, and 152 to the British. Though intended for local work, they also traveled the trans-Atlantic route to serve in Europe. An additional 59 units commissioned as PCS-craft.

ADMIRABLE class (650 tons, one 3-inch gun, 14.8 knots, 1943–45): at least 178 MS planned with 125 completed in wartime, 10 others afterward. They had a simpler design than the *Auk*s to facilitate mass production. While they couldn't lay mines, they did carry Hedgehog, and their excellent sea-keeping prompted the construction of the *PCE827* class.

OGLALA (4,200 tons; one 5-inch, two 3-inch DP guns, mines; 20 knots, 1907): minelayer later converted to other roles, gaining two more 3-inch guns. A sistership, *Aroostook*, had become inactive prewar.

The YMS479 *at war's end.*

KEOKUK (5,799 tons, three 3-inch guns, mines, 12 knots, 1914): passenger vessel converted into a minelayer, then converted for cargo work.

SALEM, WEEHAWKEN (6,525 tons, three 3-inch guns, mines, 12 knots, 1916): passenger vessels converted into minelayers. *Salem* became *Shawmut* in the last days of the war.

WASSUC (1,830 tons full load, two 3-inch guns, mines, 13 knots, 1924): passenger vessel converted to a coastal minelayer.

Two converted yachts also served as coastal minelayers.

MONADNOCK, MIANTONOMAH (4,070 tons, two 3-inch guns, mines, 17.5 knots, 1938): passenger vessels converted into minelayers.

TERROR (8,840 tons, four 5-inch DP guns, 875 mines, 20.3 knots, 1942): the navy's only purpose-built ML. She proved extremely useful in a variety of roles. At times, she carried as many as 1,200 small mines.

The navy completed two similar vessels as landing ships.

As noted previously, a number of destroyers converted into minecraft; eight flush-deckers (*Tracy* and *Stribling* classes, though *Stribling* herself left service prewar) and 12 *Sumners* (*Robert M. Smith* class) gave war service as ML; 18 flush-deckers (*Dorsey* and *Chandler* classes) and 24 *Benson*-types (*Ellyson* class) became MS.

The United States Army—responsible for the controlled minefields in Hawaii, the Philippines, the Canal Zone, and along the mainland coastline—had nine "mineplanters" (590–840 grt) in service when the war began. One of them, *Colonel George F. E. Harrison*, fell into Japanese hands and became *Harushima*. The Army added 16 *General Henry Knox*-class vessels (880–1,315 tons, light guns, mines, 10 knots, 1942–43), eight of which shifted to naval command in 1944–45 as the *Chimo* class. Other

minecraft include three "junior mineplanters" (270 grt, 1943) and a miscellany of small craft (among them, 269 tiny "mine yawls" and 77 distribution box boats with L-numbers). In fact, the Army had a significant navy of its own, which included not only the rescue and picket boats noted previously, but more than 2,600 motor craft with J- and P-numbers, four SJ-boat AS launches, 10 patrol launches with AC-numbers, and numerous transfers from the Navy and Coast Guard.

Coast Guard

In addition to its army and navy, the United States has another water-borne force; in times of strategic crisis, the United States Coast Guard transfers from the Treasury Department to the Navy. This took place on November 1, 1941.

GRESHAM (1,090 tons, two 3-inch guns, 16 knots, 1897): GB barely capable of eight knots; gave about one year of war service before retiring.

UNALGA (1,181 tons, two 3-inch guns, 13 knots, 1912): gunboat nearing retirement.

OSSIPEE, TALLAPOOSA (964 tons, two 3-inch guns, 12 knots, 1915): related to *Unalga*. *Ossipee* served as a river gunboat with light guns.

MARITA (1,450 tons, two 3-inch guns, seven knots, 1918): ex-British patrol boat, acquired as a yacht in 1943.

SHAWNEE (900 tons, light guns, 13 knots, 1922): elderly unit serving as tug, gunboat, and AS escort.

TAMPA, HAIDA, MODOC, MOJAVE (1,780 tons; two 5-inch, two 3-inch DP guns; 16 knots, 1921–22): old gunboats, sold soon after the war. Their hull form suited them ill to heavy seas.

ACTIVE class (220 tons, one 3-inch DP gun, 10.2–13 knots, 1927): 33 submarine chasers, designed as "Prohibition" cutters. They had good sea-keeping and strong hulls—one ship served on Ice Patrol. They mounted 3-inch, 23cal guns.

NORTHLAND (1,785 tons, two 3-inch guns, AC 1, 11 knots, 1927): GB for Alaskan service, the best American icebreaker at the war's start despite a lack of power. She had good range (12,000 miles at 10 knots).

"Lake" class (1,546 tons; one 5-inch, two 3-inch DP guns; 16 knots, 1928–32): 10 cutters designed to improve on *Tampa's* sea-keeping. They featured an efficient and innovative power plant. All 10 transferred to England as the *Banff* class.

ARGO class (337 tons, two 3-inch DP guns, 16 knots, 1931–34): 17 submarine-chasers, plus one unit (*Potomac*) serving as the presidential yacht.

For the coast guard, the choice between 23cal and 50cal 3-inch guns depended on availability and the size of the vessel. A similar situation governed the choice of mounts, though DP mounts predominated. The *Argos* began their careers with one 23cal gun; most switched to two 50cal guns.

ALGONQUIN class (1,005 tons, two 3-inch DP guns, 13 knots, 1932–35): six cutters. The coast guard intended them for operations in the harshest conditions; their flush-decked design had plenty of freeboard with a strong hull for light icebreaking. However, they rolled badly.

BIBB, CAMPBELL, DUANE, INGHAM, SPENCER, TANEY, ALEXANDER HAMILTON (2,216 tons, two 5-inch DP guns, AC 1, 20 knots, 1936–37): the highly successful "Treasury" class, adapted from the *Erie* hull structure. They were good seaboats with long range (7,000 miles at 13 knots). The layout specifically allowed for changes in armament. The ships began with two 5-inch, 51cal guns, but this could expand to as many as four 5-inch, 38cal DP and four 3-inch DP.

The USS Taney *mounted two 5/51 and three 3-inch DP guns.*

JUNIPER (790 tons full load, one 3-inch gun, 12.5 knots, 1940): all-purpose design; prototype for the *Balsams*.

BALSAM class (935 tons full load, one 3-inch gun, 14 knots, 1942–44): 38 lighthouse tenders built in three series. Lighthouse tenders typically lie outside the scope of this book, but the versatility demanded by the coast guard made the *Balsams* useful as escorts. They could also provide navigational aid, icebreaking, and search and rescue. (In the Atlantic convoys, coast guard vessels often served in the hazardous function of rescue vessels.) For their AS role, the *Balsams* received sonar, radar, and the long 3-inch gun. They ranged to 12,000 miles at 12 knots.

Other lighthouse tenders fitted with AS weaponry include eight of the *Manzanita* class (1,057 tons full load, one 3-inch gun, 13.5 knots, 1908), six former army mineplanters (1,130 tons full load, one 3-inch gun, 12 knots, 1918–20), and a dozen or so miscellaneous vessels, most with botanical names. A few others plus 12 of the coast guard's 43 lightships (LS-craft) mounted weapons to assist in local security.

STORIS (1,715 tons, two 3-inch guns, AC 1, 13 knots, 1942): the usual coast guard versatility as icebreaker, buoy tender, escort, etc. with endurance of 11,300 miles at 12.5 knots.

NORTHWIND, NORTHWIND, SOUTHWIND, EASTWIND, WESTWIND (3,500 tons, four 5-inch DP guns, AC 1, 16 knots, 1943–45): America's first true icebreakers, with two more completed postwar. They served as escorts on northern convoys. Their design showed good stability. The first *Northwind* transferred to the Soviets, along with *Southwind* and *Westwind*.

A related but unarmed vessel, *Mackinaw*, served on the Great Lakes where she provided training for Soviet crews about to man the transferred *Northwind*s.

OWASCO class (1,563 tons, four 5-inch DP guns, 18 knots, 1945): five gunboats, plus eight completed postwar, a powerful design that never matched the success of the "Treasury" class. The designers attempted too much on the displacement—they originally included an airplane—and the result proved overly compact. Though the ships had good endurance (12,200 miles at 12 knots), they lacked stability.

The Coast Guard converted several auxiliary warships, including the former presidential yacht *Mayflower* (one 5-inch and two 3-inch guns, 1896). *Cobb* (2,522 grt, two 5-inch DP guns, 1906) mounted an experimental helicopter deck; the Coast Guard oversaw all British and American helicopter training during the war. *Sea Cloud* (3,077 tons full load, two 3-inch guns, 1931) also experimented, having a racially mixed crew. Thirteen other yachts, most with light guns, some with sails, provided coastal patrol. The *North Star* (1,780 tons full load, two 3-inch guns, AC 1, 13 knots, 1932) was a wooden-hulled icebreaker. Forty-five former fishing vessels, trawlers, etc. served as patrol craft. Among the more modest vessels were hundreds of "coast guard craft" (both armed and unarmed) and approximately 2,100 vessels in the Coast Guard Reserve for local patrol.

The Coast Guard standardized many motor launch designs; the four largest types proved suitable for coastal patrol and AS escort: the 74-foot type (103 boats: 37 tons, 13.5 knots, 1924–25), the 78-foot type (six boats: 43 tons, 21.7 knots, 1929–31), the 80-foot type (nine boats: 52 tons, 25 knots, 1937), and the 83-foot type (242 boats: 50 tons, 25 knots, 1941–45). None carried a gun larger than 20mm. The United States transferred many 83-footers—12 to Cuba, six to Peru, three to Mexico, two to Colombia, three to the Dominican Republic, one to Haiti, four to Venezuela.

URUGUAY

Uruguay finally declared war in 1945. Its navy, intended only for local patrol, centered around the torpedo-gunboat *Uruguay* (1,400 tons; two 4.7-inch, four 3-inch guns, two 17.7-inch TT; 23 knots, 1910), three patrol craft (*Paysandú*, *Río Negro*, and *Salto*: 180 tons, light guns, 17 knots, 1935), and the presidential yacht *18 de Julio* (678 tons). The United States supplied one PC-craft.

VENEZUELA

In 1945, Venezuela announced that a "state of belligerency" existed between itself and the Axis. The navy centered on a pair of ex-Italian *Ostia*-class ML, *General Soublette* and *General Urdaneta* (615 tons; two 4-inch, one 3-inch DP gun, 80 mines; 15 knots, purchased 1938), serving as gunboats. Leftovers from the previous century included the gunboat *Miranda* (200 tons, light guns, 12 knots, 1895) and the yacht *General Salom* (750 tons, one 3-inch gun,

12 knots, 1884); the gunboat *Mariscal Sucre* (1030 tons, two 4-inch guns?, 1897) lasted only to 1941. The United States provided four 83-foot type cutters.

YUGOSLAVIA

After World War I, the new Yugoslav state hoped to inherit the naval might of Austria-Hungary. Battleships figured prominently in those hopes. The three *Radetzky*-class ships (15,851 nt; four 12-inch, eight 9.4-inch, twenty 3.9-inch guns, three 17.7-inch TT; 20.5 knots, 1910–11), among the last predreadnoughts to enter service, packed a powerful armament onto a light structure. Three *Tegetthoff*-class ships (20,000 nt; twelve 12-inch, twelve 5.9-inch guns, four 21-inch TT; 20 knots, 1912–14) exaggerated the *Radetzy*'s excess of weight; they had low stability, gaps in their armor scheme, and a poor turret layout. Four improved units (24,000 nt; ten 13.8-inch, eighteen 5.9-inch, eight 3.5-inch, twelve 3.5-inch DP guns, six 21-inch TT; 21 knots) never began construction. The table shows the characteristics of the various guns.

*Shown here as she was built in Britain, the **Mariscal Sucre** originally served with the Spanish until sunk by the Americans, who then raised her and sold her to Venezuela.*

YUGOSLAVIA

GUN	SHELL WEIGHT	RATE OF FIRE
13.8/45	1,400 lbs	?
12/45	992 lbs	2 rpm
9.4/45	474 lbs	2.5 rpm
5.9/50	100 lbs	10 rpm
3.9/50	30 lbs	15–20 rpm
3.5/45	22 lbs	?

The Italians had no intention of spectating while another rival emerged in the Adriatic. They used various means, not all of them diplomatic, to disperse the Austro-Hungarian fleet. They even blew up the *Tegetthoff*-class BB *Viribus Unitis* after she came under the control of the Yugoslav government. Ultimately, the Yugoslavs had to settle for a few old and small vessels, and domestic conditions prevented the development of an effective, modern navy.

As war broke out across Europe, Italy ignored Yugoslavia and channeled its waning ardor into a duel with Greece. It was German expansion that cowed Yugoslavia's leaders and prodded them toward an Axis alliance, which spurred the outraged Slavic populace into violent protest. Faced with the Yugoslav tangle of feuding ethnicities and a Balkan situation already muddied by Mussolini's blunders, Hitler abandoned diplomacy. His forces attacked on April 6, 1941, and the fighting lasted less than two weeks. The Yugoslav government fled while the country endured division into zones of Bulgarian, Hungarian, German, and Italian occupation. The Croats received a degree of self-rule under scrutinizing German eyes, and undertook operations against Tito's partisans. However, with the rising of the Allied tide, Croatia slipped away from German puppetry.

MORAVA (390 tons, two 4.7-inch guns, nine knots, 1892): ex-Austrian river monitor; entered Croatian service as *Bosna*. The 4.7-inch shells for Yugoslav monitor guns weighed 52 lbs.

DALMACIJA (2,370 tons, six 3.3-inch DP guns, two 19.7-inch TT, 21 knots, 1900): ex-German cruiser *Niobe;* used as a training ship with DP guns ranging to 18,000 yards. The Italians captured her and renamed her *Cattaro;* then the Germans took her, restoring her original name; the Croatians finally got her as *Zniam.*

SAVA (380 tons, two 4.7-inch guns, one 4.7-inch howitzer, nine knots, 1904): ex-Austrian river monitor; went to Croatian forces.

DRAVA (450 tons, two 4.7-inch guns, three 4.7-inch howitzers, 13 knots, 1914): ex-Austrian river monitor; sister ship of the Romanian *Besarabia.*

T1, 3 (262 tons, four 17.7-inch TT, 28 knots, 1914): ex-Austrian TB, with two sisters deleted prewar. The Italians captured *T1, 3;* the former returned to Yugoslav command as *Golesnica*, but the latter became the German *TA48*. A sister served with the Romanians.

Another ex-Austrian TB, the ancient *D2* (78 tons, 17 knots, 1888), may have endured in minesweeping duty.

VARDAR (530 tons, two 4.7-inch guns, two 4.7-inch howitzers, 13 knots, 1915): ex-Austrian river monitor; sister ship of the Romanian *Bucovina.*

T5–8 (266 tons, four 17.7-inch TT, 28 knots, 1915–16): ex-Austrian TB. The Italians captured all four; the Yugoslavs recovered *T5* as *Cer*, but the Germans gave *T7* to the Croatians. Sister ships operated with the Portuguese, Greeks, and Romanians.

GALEB class (330 tons, two 3.3-inch DP guns, mines, 15 knots, 1918–19): six ex-German Type 1915 MS used as ML. Italy captured all six, but one returned to Yugoslav control after the Italian surrender. The displacement figure seems low.

CETNIK, USKOK (15 tons, two 17.7-inch TT, 37 knots, 1927): 55-foot Thornycrofts, less successful than the *Orjen*s. They became the Italian *MAS1D, 2D*.

HRABRI, NEBOJSA (975/1,164 tons, two 4-inch DP guns, six 21-inch TT, 15.7/10 knots, 1928): British-built submarines. *Hrabri* became the Italian *N3* but never entered Italian service.

ZMAJ (1,870 tons, two 3.3-inch DP guns, 100 mines, 15 knots, 1928): ML and training ship, originally a tender for ten seaplanes. She entered German service as *Drache*.

SMELI, OSVETNIK (630/809 tons, one 3.9-inch gun, six 21.7-inch TT, 14.5/9.2 knots, 1929): French-built submarines. They served with the Italians as *Antonio Bajamonti* and *Francesco Rismondo*.

In the last days of the war, Yugoslav forces captured an ex-Italian midget submarine of the CB-type.

MALINSKA class (130 tons, light guns, nine knots, 1931): five mining tenders of a World War I Austrian design, sisters to the Italian *Albona* class. The Italians captured all five; three returned to the Yugoslavs, and two went to the Germans, who gave one to the Croatians.

DUBROVNIK (1,880 tons; four 5.5-inch, two 3.3-inch DP guns, six 21-inch TT, 40 mines; 37 knots, 1932): a powerful, British-built destroyer captured by the Italians as *Premuda* and the

Germans as *TA32*. The 5.5-inch shells weighed 88 lbs and ranged to 25,600 yards at 45°.

ORJEN class (49 tons, two 21.7-inch TT, 31 knots, 1936–39): eight German-built MTB. Their actual displacement with Yugoslav weapons neared 55 tons. The Italians captured six of them, naming them *MAS3D–8D*, later *MS41–46*. Four of them subsequently fell under German control as *S2–5*.

BELI ORAO (567 tons, light guns, 18 knots, 1939): gunboat and royal yacht. She became the Italian *Alba* until returned to Yugoslav control as *Zagabria*.

BEOGRAD, LJUBLJANA, ZAGREB (1,210 tons, four 4.7-inch guns, six 21.7-inch TT, 30 mines, 38 knots, 1939): destroyers built with French help, based on the *Simoun* class. The 4.7-inch shells weighed 53 lbs. *Beograd* became the Italian *Sebenico* and the German *TA43*. *Ljubljana* became the Italian *Lubiano*.

Prior to Yugoslavia's involvement in the war, discussions with Germany involved an improved *Beograd* class and a pair of subs based on the Type II to be built in German yards. The plans came to nothing. Instead, the Yugoslavs prepared their own DD design and laid down the *Split* (1,875 tons, five 5.5-inch guns, six 21-inch TT, 34 knots); the Italians seized her incomplete and renamed her *Spalato*. Yugoslavia completed her postwar to a modified design.

During the war, the British supplied Yugoslavia with a "Flower" class escort (renamed *Nada*) and *MGB181–188* (renamed *MT1–8*).

SELECT BIBLIOGRAPHY

Bagnasco, Erminio. *Submarines of World War Two* (Naval Institute Press, 1977).

Bekker, Cajus. *The German Navy 1939–1945* (Dial Press, 1974).

Blundell, W. D. *German Navy Warships 1939–45* (Almark Publishing, 1972).

Breyer, Siegfried. *Battleships and Battle Cruisers, 1905–1970* (Doubleday, 1973); *Soviet Warship Development: Vol. I, 1917–1937* (Conway Maritime Press, 1992).

Brown, David. *Warships Losses of World War Two* (Arms and Armour Press, 1990).

Brown, D. K. (Ed.) *The Design and Construction of British Warships 1939–45: Vol. I, Major Surface Warships; Vol. II, Submarines, Escorts, and Coastal Forces; Vol. III, Landing Ships and Auxiliaries* (Naval Institute Press, 1995).

Brown, Eric M. *Duels in the Sky* (Naval Institute Press, 1988).

Buxton, I. L. *Big Gun Monitors* (World Ship Society and Trident Books, 1978).

Campbell, N. J. M. *Naval Weapons of World War Two* (Conway Maritime Press, 1985); *Queen Elizabeth Class* (Conway Maritime Press, 1972).

Chesneau, Roger. *Aircraft Carriers of the World* (Naval Institute Press, 1984).

Cocker, Maurice. *Destroyers of the Royal Navy 1893–1981* (Ian Allan, 1981).

Colledge, J. J. *Ships of the Royal Navy, Vol. 1–2* (Naval Institute Press, 1987).

Couhat, Jean Labayle. *French Warships of World War II* (Ian Allan, 1971).

Du Cane, Peter. *High Speed Small Craft* (Temple Press Books, 1964).

Dull, Paul S. *A Battle History of the Imperial Japanese Navy (1941–1945)* (Naval Institute Press, 1978).

Eliott, Peter. *Allied Escort Ships of World War II* (Naval Institute Press, 1977).

Fock, Harald. *Fast Fighting Boats, 1870–1945* (Nautical Publishing, 1978).

Fraccaroli, Aldo. *Italian Warships of World War Two* (Ian Allan, 1968).

Francillon, René J. *Japanese Aircraft of the Pacific War* (Naval Institute Press, 1987).

Friedman, Norman. *Battleship Design and Development 1905–1945* (Mayflower Books, 1978); *British Carrier Aviation* (Naval Institute Press, 1988); *U.S. Aircraft Carriers* (Naval Institute Press, 1983); *U.S. Battleships* (Naval Institute Press, 1985); *U.S. Cruisers* (Naval Institute Press, 1984); *U.S. Destroyers* (Naval Institute Press, 1982); *U.S. Small Combatants* (Naval Institute Press, 1987); *U.S. Submarines through 1945* (Naval Institute Press, 1995).

Fukui, Shizuo. *Japanese Naval Vessels at the End of World War II* (Naval Institute Press, 1991).

Gardiner, Robert (Ed.) *Conway's All the World's Fighting Ships 1906–1921* (Conway Maritime Press, 1985); *Conway's All the World's Fighting Ships 1922–1946* (Naval Institute Press, 1980).

Garzke, William H.; Dulin, Jr., Robert O. *Battleships: Allied Battleships* (Naval Institute Press, 1980), *Battleships: Axis and Neutral Battleships* (Naval Institute Press, 1985); *Battleships: United States Battleships* (Naval Institute Press, 1976).

Gay, Franco; Gay, Valerio. *The Cruiser Bartolomeo Colleoni* (Conway Maritime Press, 1987).

Green, William. *Famous Fighters of the Second World War* (Doubleday, 1975).

Greene, Jack; Massignani, Alessandro. *The Naval War in the Mediterranean, 1940–1943* (Sarpedon, 2000).

Greger, René. *Battleships of the World* (Naval Institute Press, 1997).

Gröner, Erich. *German Warships 1815–1945: Vol. I, Major Surface Vessels; Vol. II, U-boats and*

Mine Warfare Vessels (Naval Institute Press, 1990–92).

Grover, David. *U.S. Army Ships and Watercraft of World War Two* (Naval Institute Press, 1987).

Hobbs, David. *Aircraft Carriers of the Royal and Commonwealth Navies* (Naval Institute Press, 1996).

Hodges, Peter. *The Big Gun: Battleship Main Armament, 1860–1945* (Naval Institute Press, 1981).

Hodges, Peter; Friedman, Norman. *Destroyer Weapons of World War Two* (Naval Institute Press, 1980).

Hone, Thomas C.; Friedman, Norman; Mandeles, Mark David. *American and British Aircraft Carrier Development, 1919–1941* (Naval Institute Press, 1999).

Jentschura, Hansgeorg; Jung, Dieter; Mickel, Peter. *Warships of the Imperial Japanese Navy, 1869–1945* (Naval Institute Press, 1970).

Johnson, Frank D. *U.S. PT Boats of World War Two* (Blandford Press, 1980).

Kafka, Roger; Pepperburg, Roy L. (Eds.) *Warships of the World* (Cornell Maritime Press, 1944).

Kemp, Paul. *Midget Submarines of the Second World War* (Naval Institute Press, 1999).

Koop, Gerhard; Schmolke, Klaus-Peter. *Battleships of the* Bismarck *Class* (Naval Institute Press, 1998); *Battleships of the* Scharnhorst *Class* (Naval Institute Press, 1999).

Korotkin, I. M. *Battle Damage to Surface Ships during World War II* (Sudpromgiz, 1960).

Lacroix, Eric; Wells II, Linton. *Japanese Cruisers of the Pacific War* (Naval Institute Press, 1997).

Lambert, John; Ross, Al. *Allied Coastal Forces of World War II: Vol. 1, Fairmile Designs, Motor Launches, and Submarine Chasers; Vol. 2, Vosper MTBs and U.S. Elcos* (Naval Institute Press, 1994).

Layman, R. D.; McLaughlin, Stephen. *The Hybrid Warship* (Naval Institute Press, 1991).

Le Masson, Henri. *The French Navy* (Doubleday, 1969).

Lenton, H. T. *American Battleships, Carriers, and Cruisers* (Macdonald and Co., 1968); *American Gunboats and Minesweepers* (Arco Publishing, 1974); *British and Empire Warships of the Second World War* (Naval Institute Press, 1998); *British Escort Ships* (Arco Publishing, 1974); *German Warships of the Second World War* (Macdonald and Jane's, 1975); *Royal Netherlands Navy* (Doubleday, 1968).

Lenton, H. T.; Colledge, J. J. *British Warship Losses of World War II* (Ian Allan, 1964); *Warships of World War Two* (Ian Allan, London, 1963).

Meister, Jurg. *Soviet Warships of the Second World War* (Arco Publishing, 1977).

Morison, S. L. (Ed.) *United States Naval Vessels* (Schiffer Publishing, 1996).

Mooney, James L. (Ed.) *Dictionary of American Naval Fighting Ships* (Naval Historical Center, 1981).

Munson, Kenneth. *Aircraft of World War II* (Doubleday, 1972).

North, A. J. D. *Royal Naval Coastal Forces, 1939–1945* (Almark Publishing, 1972).

Parkes, Oscar. *British Battleships:* Warrior *1860 to* Vanguard *1950* (Naval Institute Press, 1990).

Parkin, Robert S. *Blood on the Sea: American Destroyers Lost in World War II* (Sarpedon, 1996).

Phelan, Keiren; Brice, Martin H. *Fast Attack Craft* (Macdonald and Jane's, 1977).

Polmar, Norman; Noot, Jurrien. *Submarines of the Russian and Soviet Navies, 1718–1990* (Naval Institute Press, 1991).

Reilly, Jr., John C. *United States Navy Destroyers of World War II* (Blandford Press, 1983).

Roberts, John; Raven, Alan. *British Battleships of World War Two* (Naval Institute Press, 1976); *British Cruisers of World War Two* (Naval Institute Press, 1980); *County Class Cruisers* (RSV Publications, 1978); *Town Class Cruisers* (Arms and Armour Press, 1980).

Ross, Jr., Tweed Wallis. *The Best Way to Destroy a Ship* (MA/AH Publishing, 1980).

Rowland, Buford; Boyd, William. *U.S. Navy*

Bureau of Ordnance in World War II (Bureau of Ordnance, Department of the Navy).

Sadkovich, James J. *Re-Evaluating Major Naval Combatants of World War II* (Greenwood Press, 1990).

Scheina, Robert L. *U.S. Coast Guard Cutters and Craft of World War Two* (Naval Institute Press, 1982).

Showell, Jak. *The German Navy in World War II* (Naval Institute Press, 1979); *U-boats under the Swastika* (Ian Allan, 1973).

Silverstone, Paul H. *U.S. Warships of World War 2* (Naval Institute Press, 1965).

Skulski, Janusz. *The Battleship* Fuso (Naval Institute Press, 1999); *The Heavy Cruiser* Takao (Naval Institute Press, 1994).

Stern, Robert C. *The* Lexington *Class Carriers* (Arms and Armour Press, 1993).

Sumrall, Robert F.; Walkowiak, Tom. *The* Iowa *Class Battleships* (Naval Institute Press, 1996).

Tarrant, V. E. King George V *Class Battleships* (Arms and Armour Press, 1995).

Taylor, J. C. *German Warships of World War II* (Doubleday, 1966).

Taylor, John W. P. (Ed.) *Combat Aircraft of the World* (G. P. Putnam's Sons, 1969).

Terzibaschitsch, Stefan. *Battleships of the U.S. Navy in World War II* (Bonanza Books, 1977).

Thetford, Owen. *British Naval Aircraft since 1912* (Putnam, 1978).

Wagner, Ray. *American Combat Planes* (Doubleday, 1982).

Watton, Ross. *Battleship* Warspite (Naval Institute Press, 1986).

Watts, Anthony J. *Allied Submarines* (Arco Publishing Co., 1977); *Axis Submarines* (Macdonald And Jane's, 1977); *Japanese Warships of World War Two* (Ian Allan, London, 1966).

Watts, Anthony J.; Gordon, Brian G. *The Imperial Japanese Navy* (Doubleday, 1971).

Weal, Elke C.; Weal, John A.; Barker, Richard F. *Combat Aircraft of World War Two* (Macmillan Publishing, 1977).

Whitley, M. J. *Battleships of World War Two* (Naval Institute Press, 1999); *Cruisers of World War Two* (Naval Institute Press, 1996); *Destroyers of World War Two* (Naval Institute Press, 1988); *German Capital Ships of World War Two* (Arms and Armour, 1989); *German Cruisers of World War Two* (Naval Institute Press, 1985); *German Coastal Forces in World War Two* (Arms and Armour Press, 1992).

INDEX ABBREVIATIONS

INDEX OF SHIPS

Lung Huan Ch (ex **Falcon** Br) 11, 134
Lung Tuan Ch 9
Luronne Fr 37
Lützow Ger (ex **Deutschland** Ger) 52
Lützow Ger 53
Luzon US (later **Karatsu** Jap) 213, 321, 326
Lyman K. Swenson US 315
Lyn Nor 227
Lynx Fr 31
Lyon Fr 25
Lyon class Fr 25

M1,2 Sw 269
M3-14 Sw 269
M15-26 Sw 269
Ma101 Jap (ex **Barlight** Br) **208**
Maagen Den 15
Macabi US 319
Macalle It 155
Macau Por (later **Maiko** Jap) 213, 233
MacDonough US 309
Machanu Tha 270
MacKay Br 108
MacKenzie US 307
MacKenzie US 312
Mackerel US 319
Mackinac US 289
Mackinaw US 332
MacLeish US 308
Macoma Br 89, 216
Macomb US 312
Macon US 304
Maddox US 307
Maddox US 312
Maddox US 315
Madeira Bz (later **Mersey** Br) 5
Madison US 311
Maestrale It 151
Maggiore Baracca It 156
Magne Sw 266
Magne Sw 266
Mahan US 310
Mahan class US 5, 111, 310, 311
Mahratta Br 113
Mahroussa Egp 16
Maikaze Jap 197

Maiko Jap (ex **Macao** Por) 213, 233
Maillé Brézé Fr 32
Maine US 297
Majestic Br 86
Makassar Strait US 288
Maki Jap 206
Makigumo Jap 197
Makinami Jap 197
Makin Island US 288
Makrelen Den 13
Malachite It 155
Malaya Br 90
Malcolm Br 108
Malinska class Yug (later **Arbe class** It) 159, 335
Mallard Br 125
Malmö Sw 266
Malta class Br 86-87
Mamari Br 127
Mameluck Fr 33
Manazuru Jap 205
Manchester Br 104
Mandovi Por 233
Manila Bay US 288
Manley US 306, 309
Manligheten Sw 265
Mannert L. Abele US 315
Mansfield US 315
Manta US 319
Manxman Br 121
Manzanita class US 332
Maori Br 111
Mapiro US 319
Maranhão Bz 5
Mărăşeşti Rom (later **Logkiy** Sov) 234, 250, 261
Mărăşti Rom (later **Lovkiy** Sov) 234, 250, 261
Marat Sov (ex **Petropavlovsk** Sov) 240
Marblehead US 299
Marcantonio Bragadin It 154
Marcantonio Colonna It 143
Marcantonio Colonna It 153
Marcello It 155
Marcílio Dias Bz 5
Marcus Island US 288
Marder type Ger 73
Mardus Est 16
Marea It 156

Margaree Br (ex **Diana** Br) 110
Mariscal Sucre Col 11
Mariscal Sucre Ven 333
Marita US 330
Mariupol Sov (ex **Ion C. Bratianu** Rom) 235, 257
Mariz e Barros Bz 5
Markin Sov 247
Marlin US 319
Marne Br 113
Marne Fr 37
Marseillaise Fr 30
Marshall US 314
Marshal Ney Br (later **Drake** Br) 97
Marshal Soult Br 97
Marsouin Fr 33
Marsuinul Rom (later **S4** Sov) 235
Marte Sp 263
Marti Sov 255
Marti Tur 272
Martin Br 113
Martinov Sov 247
Maryland US 292, 293
MASB series Br 130
Ma series Jap 208
Mashona Br 111
Mason US 307
Massachusetts US 31-32, 293, 295, 296
MAS series It 161-163, 335
Massey US 315
Matabele Br 111
Matagorda US 289
Matai Br 121
Matchless Br 113
Matinikau US 288
Mato Grosso class Bz 5
Matrozos Gr (ex **P712** Br; ex **Perla** It) 120, 136, 155
MAT series It 163
Matsu Jap 206
Matsukaze Jap 194
Matti Kurki Fin 17
Matwa Pol (later **Pina** Sov) 232, 255
Mauritius Br 106
Maury US 311
Mauvenet Tur 111
Maxim Gorkiy Sov 246
Max Schultz Ger 55
Maya Jap 189

Santee US 287
Santiago del Esterio Arg 3
Santorre Santarosa It153
São Paulo Bz 4
Saphir Fr 34
Saphir Sov 256
Saracen Br 119
Sarasindhu Tha 270
Saratoga US ix, 281, 282, 284, 293
Saratoga US 294
Sardonyx Br 107
Sargent Bay US 288
Sargo US 318
Sarsfield US 315
Sarunda Alb 1
Sarushima Jap 207
Saskatchewan Br (ex **Fortune** Br) 110
Satsuki Jap 195
Satterlee US 307
Satterlee US 312
Satyr Br 119
Saufley US 313
Saukko Fin 19, 68
Saumarez Br 114
Saury US 318
Sava Yug 334
Savage Br 114
Savannah US 301, 302
Savoia It 160
Savo Island US 288
Savorgnan de Brazza Fr 38
Sawakaze Jap 194
Sawarabi Jap 194
Sawfish US 319
Sazanami Jap 195
S-boats Ger 61-62
Sborul Rom (later **Musson** Sov) 235, 257
Scabbardfish US 319
Scamp US 319
Scarborough Br 124
Sceptre Br 119
Scharnhorst Ger 45, 46, 47, 48, 49, 50, 52, 55, 96, 145, 218, 244, 305
Scharnhorst class Ger 46
Schenck US 307
Schlange Ger (ex **Ørn** Nor) 227
Schlesien Ger 45

Schleswig-Holstein Ger 45
Schley US 307, 309
Schroeder US 313
Scimitar Br 107
Scipione Africano It 149
Scire It 155
Scirocco It 151
S class Br 107
Scorcher Br 119
Scorpion Br 114
Scorpion Br 134
Scorpion US 319
Scotsman Br 119
Scott Br 2
Scott class Br 108
Scourge Br 114
Scout Br 107
SC series US 320, 321, 322-323
Sculpin US 318
Scylla Br 105
Scythian Br 119
Sea Cat US 319
Sea Cloud US 332
Sea Devil Br 119
Sea Devil US 319
Seadog Br 119
Sea Dog US 319
Seadragon US 318
Sea Fox US 319
Seahorse Br 117
Seahorse US 319
Seal Br (later **UB** Ger) 71, 117
Seal US 318
Sea Leopard US 320
Sealion Br 117
Sealion US 204
Sealion US 318
Sealion US 319
Seamew Br 134
Sea Nymph Br 119
Sea Owl US 319
Sea Poacher US 319
Searaven US 318
Searcher Br 87
Sea Robin US 319
Sea Rover Br 119
Sea Scout Br 119
Seattle US 298
Seawolf Br 117
Seawolf US 318
Sebastiano Caboto It 160

Sebenico It (ex **Beograd** Yug; later **TA43** Ger) 152, 335
Seeadler Ger 58
Seehund type Ger 74
Seeteufel type Ger 74
Segundo US 319
Selene Br 119
Selfridge US 310
Selve class It (ex **Galeb class** Yug) 159, 334
Semmes US 307
Sendai Jap 186
Sendai class Jap 185
Seneschal Br 119
Senja Nor (later Ger) 228
Sennet US 319
Sentinel Br 119
Sep Pol 231
Seraph Br 119
Serapis Br 114
Serdang Net 223
Serdityi Sov 250
Serpente It 154
Serrano Chl 8
Seta Jap 211
Settsu Jap 177, 194
Sevastopol Sov 244
Severn Br (ex **Solimões** Bz) 5
Severn Br 116
Severni Polius Sov 240
Severni Veter Sov 240
Seydlitz Ger 53
Sfax Fr 34
SGB type Br 133
SH4 series Sov 259
Shad US 319
Shah Br 88
Shahin Irn 138
Shakespeare Br 119
Shakespeare class Br 108
Shakespearian class Br 128, 129
Shalimar Br 119
Shamrock Bay US 288
Shangri-La US 285
Shannon US 315
Shark Br (later **Svenner** Nor) 114, 228
Shark Br 117
Shark US 318
Shark US 319
Shaumyan Sov 248